THE GAZETTEER
OF ENGLAND

Volume 1   A – K

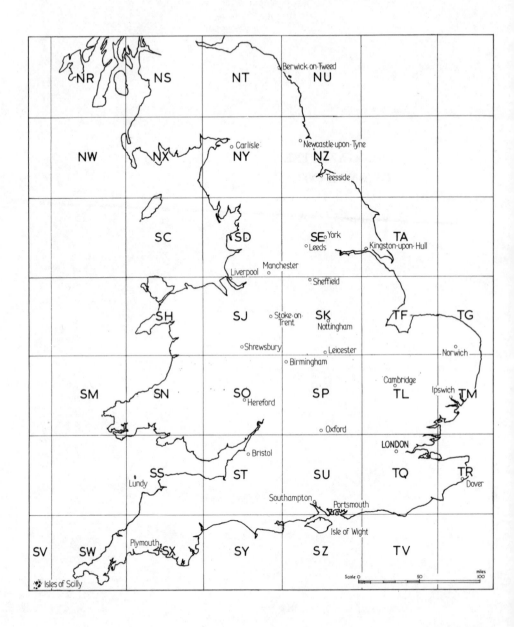

Plan showing incidence of the 100-kilometre squares of the Ordnance Survey National Grid

(Crown copyright reserved)

The GAZETTEER of England

England's Cities, Towns, Villages and Hamlets:
a comprehensive list with basic details on each

Volume 1 A~K

OLIVER MASON

ROWMAN AND LITTLEFIELD

The grid references in this gazetteer are taken from the Ordnance Survey National Grid, Crown copyright reserved.

The map is extracted from the index to the quarter-inch series, with permission.

Population data, which is Crown copyright, is used with the permission of the Controller of HM Stationery Office.

ISBN 0–87471–139–8

Rowman and Littlefield
81 Adams Drive
Totowa: NJ 07512
Printed in Great Britain

CONTENTS

Explanatory notes   vii

Abbreviations   xi

Abbreviations used for counties   xii

GAZETTEER   Volume 1 A – K

                Volume 2 L – Z

Index of buildings mentioned under
  places of a different name   end of each volume

Acknowledgements

A map showing the Ordnance Survey National
  Grid is printed opposite the title page

v

EXPLANATORY NOTES

GENERAL

The aim of this gazetteer is to provide a comprehensive list of English places, from the largest cities down to all but the smallest hamlets, with certain essential information about each. (Administrative areas whose names correspond to no one place on the ground are, however, not listed, eg Aireborough, Yorks; Lakes UD, Westm; Tower Hamlets, London; Hawerby cum Beesby, Lincs; St Thomas the Apostle Rural, Cornwall. Nor are localities which are within boroughs or urban districts and which have become submerged in the larger place).

The main districts in Greater London are listed.

INFORMATION GIVEN

1 **Location** The name of each place is followed by that of the county in which it is situated. Then follows the number(s) of the one-inch Ordnance Survey (O.S.) map(s) (seventh series) on which it appears; its four-figure map reference (O.S. National Grid System); and its distance and direction from another place, the distance being given to the nearest mile measured in a straight line.

Example 1

> SHELFORD Notts
> 112, 121, 122 SK 6642 6m E of Nottingham.

Shelford appears on the three overlapping sheets 112, 121 and 122.

Example 2

> TIXOVER Rutland
> 123/134 SK 9700 5m SW of Stamford.

Tixover appears partly on sheet 123 and partly on sheet 134.

2 **Administrative status and population** according to the latest available information. If the official administrative name of a place differs from the name under which it is listed, the official name is shown in brackets, eg

> SALISBURY Wilts
> 167 SU 1430 21m NW of Southampton.
> MB(New Sarum),35,271.

The official administrative name of the municipal borough of Salisbury is New Sarum.

3 **In the case of a civil parish, the rural district in which it is situated** is given, eg

> PIXLEY Herefs
> 142, 143 SO 6638 3m W of Ledbury.
> CP, 214. Ldbry RD.

The civil parish of Pixley is in the rural district of Ledbury.

In the case of a locality, the administrative area in which it is situated is given.

Example 1

> COTON CLANFORD Staffs
> 119 SJ 8723 3m W of Stafford.
> Loc, Seighford CP.

Reference to Seighford will show that it is in the rural district of Stafford.

Example 2

> TREVISCOE Cornwall
> 185 SW 9455 5m WNW of St Austell.
> Loc, St Stephen-in-Brannel CP. St Astll RD.

The civil parish of St Stephen-in-Brannel is not itself listed as there is no actual place of that name; therefore the rural district (St Austell) is given under the locality.

Example 3

> KEAL COTES Lincs (L)
> 114 TF 3661 8m SE of Horncastle.
> Loc, Spilsby RD.

Keal Cotes is not wholly included in any one civil parish, but is within the rural district of Spilsby.

For all boroughs and urban districts (and for Greater London and the Isles of Scilly), the populations shown are those given in the Census 1971 Preliminary Report. The populations of civil parishes are compiled from the 1961 census, since the 1971 census figures for these areas were not available at the time of going to press; where no population is given, this denotes a boundary change since 1961.

'Localities' have no population figures, since they have no defined boundaries.

4 Post Offices. If there is a post office named after the place listed, this is denoted by the letter P.

If the letter P only is shown, then the postal address is simply the name of the place followed by its county (see *Example 1* below).

If the letter P is followed by the name of another place, then that place is the post town and is included in the postal address (see *Example 2* below).

If the letter P is followed by the name of another place in capital letters, then that place is the post town and does not require the name of the county to be included in the postal address (see *Example 3* below).

If the letter P is followed by the name of the place listed, in capital letters, then the place listed is itself the post town and does not require the name of the county to be included in the postal address (see *Example 4* below).

If the name of a different county appears after the letter P, then that name, and not the name of the county in which the place listed is situated, is included in the postal address (see *Example 5* below).

If the name of the post office is different from the name of the place listed, this is indicated as in *Example 6* below.

EXAMPLES

No.	Place	Indication	Postal address
1	Buckfastleigh, Devon	P.	Buckfastleigh, Devon
2	Yedingham, Yorks(E)	P Malton.	Yedingham, Malton, Yorkshire
3	Guiseley, Yorks(W)	P LEEDS.	Guiseley, Leeds
4	York, Yorks	P(YK).	York
5	Soulbury, Bucks	P Leighton Buzzard, Beds.	Soulbury, Leighton Buzzard, Beds.
6	East Barming, Kent	P(Bmng), Maidstone.	Barming, Maidstone, Kent

Postal addresses of places in Greater London are not given unless the address contains the name of a county other than London, eg Croydon, Surrey; Enfield, Middx.

5 Places of worship and schools. These are denoted respectively by the letters Ch followed by the letter(s) for the denomination(s) concerned, and by the letters Sch followed by the letter(s) for the type(s) of school. (See list of abbreviations.) Private schools are not listed.

Places of worship and schools are listed for all civil parishes and localities therein, but not for boroughs or urban districts, from considerations of space.

6 Parliamentary constituencies. After the 1970 general election, a number of boundary changes, recommended by the Boundary Commission, were approved by Parliament. The constituency of each place for the next general election after that held in 1970 is shown. If this is different from the 1970 constituency, then the latter is shown in brackets.

Example 1

> ALNWICK Nthmb
> 71 NU 1813 17m N of Morpeth.
> UD 7,113. P. Berwick-upon-Tweed CC.

Alnwick is to be in the county constituency of Berwick-upon-Tweed; it was in the same constituency in 1970.

Example 2

> WROXHAM Norfolk
> 126 TG 2917 7m NE of Norwich.
> CP, 1,101. St Faith's and Aylsham RD. P Nrwch.
> Ch e. Sch p. N Nflk CC (Central Nflk).

Wroxham is to be in the county constituency of North Norfolk, although for the 1970 general election it was in the county constituency of Central Norfolk.

Example 3

> GROOMBRIDGE Kent and Sussex(E)
> 171, 183 TQ 5337 4m WSW of Tunbridge Wells.
> Loc, Tonbridge RD, Uckfield RD. P TNBRDGE WLLS.
> Ch e, m. Sch pe. Royal Tunbridge Wells CC (Tonbridge),
> E Grinstead CC.

Groombridge is partly in Kent and partly in East Sussex. The part in Kent is to be in the county constituency of Royal Tunbridge Wells, although for the 1970 general election it was in that of Tonbridge; the part in East Sussex remains in the county constituency of East Grinstead.

If the parliamentary constituency of a locality is not given in its own entry, it may be found by reference to the larger place in which it is situated.

7 In the case of county and municipal boroughs, London boroughs, urban districts, and civil parishes, the names of the localities within them which have their own entries are shown; eg under East Woodhay, Hants, will be found:

> See also Ball Hill, Broad Laying, E End,
> N End, Woolton Hill.

These five localities, all within the civil parish of East Woodhay, have their own separate entries in the gazetteer.

8   Descriptive matter. Brief descriptive notes are given in some cases. Properties open to the public are marked with an asterisk (*). Those open seldom, sporadically, or only by written application, are not so marked. Properties followed by the letters (A.M.) are in the care of the Department of the Environment and are open to the public. The public is usually given free access at all times to open spaces owned by the National Trust (NT) and these are not marked with an asterisk.

ABBREVIATIONS

airpt	airport	j	junior (school)
A.M.	ancient monument (in care of Department of the Environment)	Jcbn	Jacobean
		km	kilometres
		LB	London borough
b	Baptist	Ld	Lord
b	born	Lit	Little
b	boys (school)	loc	locality
BC	borough constituency	Lr	Lower
bldng	building	m	Methodist
blt	built	m	mile(s)
br	bridge	MB	municipal borough
bthplce	birthplace	mdvl	medieval
c	century (eg: 20c)	mkt	market
c	*circa*	mnfg	manufacturing
c	Congregational	mnftre	manufacture
CB	county borough	mnr	manor
CC	county constituency	monmt	monument
CC	cricket club	MP	Member of Parliament
ch	church, place of worship	mt	mount, mountain
chpl	chapel	Nmn	Norman
cmmn	common	NT	National Trust
CP	civil parish	orig	original, originally
cstle	castle	O.S.	Ordnance Survey
Ct	Court	P	post office
d	died	p	primary (school)
Dec	Decorated	par	parish
distr	district	Perp	Perpendicular
e	Church of England	pk	park
eccl	ecclesiastical	plpt	pulpit
EE	Early English	pop.	population
Elizn	Elizabethan	prob	probably
esp	especially	R	River
est	estimated	r	Roman Catholic (place of worship)
f	Society of Friends		
FC	football club	RAF	Royal Air Force
ft	feet	RC	Roman Catholic
g	girls (school)	rd	road
GC	golf club	RD	rural district
gdn	garden	rems	remains
Ggn	Georgian	Revd	Reverend
GLC	Greater London Council	Rgncy	Regency
Govt	Government	rly	railway
grn	green	rsdntl	residential
grnds	grounds	s	secondary (school)
Gt	Great	sch	school
hmlt	hamlet	scrn	screen
HQ	headquarters	St	Saint
hse	house	st	street
hsptl	hospital	stn	station
hth	heath	Tdr	Tudor
i	infants (school)	tn	town
incl	including, inclusive	Trans	Transitional
indstrl	industrial	TV	television
intntl	international	twr	tower

u	undenominational	vllge	village
UD	urban district	w	with (in place names)
Upr	Upper	wd	wood
v	religious denomination other than b, c, e, f, m, r	wks	works
		YWCA	Young Women's Christian Association
Vctrn	Victorian		

ABBREVIATIONS USED FOR COUNTIES
AND THE ISLE OF WIGHT

*Beds	Bedfordshire	Lincs(K)	Lincolnshire (parts of Kesteven)
*Berks	Berkshire		
*Bucks	Buckinghamshire	Lincs(L)	Lincolnshire (parts of Lindsey)
*Cambs	Cambridgeshire		
Ches	Cheshire	*Middx	Middlesex (for postal purposes only)
*Co Durham	County Durham		
Cumb	Cumberland	*Northants	Northamptonshire
Derbys	Derbyshire	*Notts	Nottinghamshire
*Glos	Gloucestershire	Nthmb	Northumberland
*Hants	Hampshire	*Oxon	Oxfordshire
Herefs	Herefordshire	Shrops	Shropshire
*Herts	Hertfordshire	Som	Somerset
Hunts	Huntingdon and Peterborough (administrative county)	*Staffs	Staffordshire
		Warwicks	Warwickshire
		Westm	Westmorland
Hunts	Huntingdonshire (parliamentary constituency)	*Wilts	Wiltshire
		*Worcs	Worcestershire
IOW	Isle of Wight	Yorks(E)	Yorkshire (East Riding)
*Lancs	Lancashire	Yorks(N)	Yorkshire (North Riding)
*Leics	Leicestershire		
Lincs(H)	Lincolnshire (parts of Holland)	Yorks(W)	Yorkshire (West Riding)

*In the case of these counties the abbreviations approved by the post office are as shown. The post office abbreviation for Shropshire is Salop; for Lincolnshire it is Lincs, irrespective of the administrative division of the county. Other counties should be spelt out in full in postal addresses, although the administrative divisions of Suffolk, Sussex and Yorkshire are omitted.

Gazetteer

A - K

ABBAS COMBE Som
166 ST 7022 4m S of Wincanton.CP(Abbas and Templecombe), 910. Wncntn RD. P(Tmplcmbe). Ch e, v. Wells CC.

ABBERLEY Worcs
130 SO 7567 4m SW of Stourport,CP, 526. Martley RD. P WORCESTER. Ch e. Sch pe. Kidderminster CC. Rems of Nmn ch in vllge. On hill, tall Vctrn Gothic clock twr; 20 bells can play 42 tunes.

ABBERTON Essex
149, 162 TM 0019 4m S of Colchester.CP, 177. Lexden and Winstree RD. P Clchstr. Ch e. Clchstr CC. Reservoir to W has wildfowl-ringing stn. On marshes to E, Red Hills, rems of prehistoric salt wks.

ABBERTON Worcs
143, 144 SO 9953 9m E of Worcester. CP, 67. Pershore RD. Ch e. S Worcs CC.

ABBERWICK Nthmb
71 NU 1313 4m W of Alnwick. Loc, Edlingham CP.

ABBESS RODING Essex
148, 161 TL 5711 7m SW of Dunmow. CP(Abbss Beauchamp and Berners Rdng), Epping and Ongar RD. Ch e. Brentwood and Ongr CC (Chigwell). One of eight Rodings, pronounced 'roothing'.

ABBEY Devon
164, 176 ST 1410 6m S of Wellington.Loc, Dunkeswell CP. Ruined gatehouse and portions of wall survive from 13c Cistercian abbey.

ABBEY DORE Herefs
142 SO 3830 10 SW of Hereford. CP, 315. Dore and Bredwardine RD. P HRFD. Ch e. Hrfd CC. See also Kerry's Gate. Ch is sole rems of 12c−13c Cistercian abbey.

ABBEYSTEAD Lancs
94 SD 5654 7m SE of Lancaster. Loc, Over Wyresdale CP. Lncstr RD. P LNCSTR. Sch pe. Lncstr CC. The hse is late 19c Elizn.

ABBEY TOWN Cumb
75 NY 1750 4m ESE of Silloth.Loc, Holme Abbey CP. Wigton RD. P Carlisle. Ch e, m, r. Sch pe. Penrith and the Border CC. Ch is nave of Hlme Cultram Abbey founded mid−12c.

ABBEY VILLAGE Lancs
94, 95 SD 6422 4m SW of Blackburn. Loc, Withnell UD. P Chorley.

ABBOTS BICKINGTON Devon
174 SS 3813 7m NNE of Holsworthy. CP, 22. Hlswthy RD. Ch e. W Dvn CC (Tavistock).

ABBOTS BROMLEY Staffs
120 SK 0824 5m NNE of Rugeley. CP, 1,071. Uttoxeter RD. P Rgly. Ch e, r, v. Sch p. Burton CC. Half-timbered hses. Butter cross. Annual horn dance.

ABBOTSBURY Dorset
177, 178 SY 5785 8m WNW of Weymouth. CP, 470. Dorchester RD. P Wmth. Ch e, c, m. Sch p. W Dst CC. See also Rodden. Ruined abbey (A.M.). Huge 15c tithe barn. Swannery*. Sub-tropical gdns*. Access to Chesil Beach.

ABBOTSHAM Devon
163 SS 4226 2m W of Bideford. CP, 287. Bdfd RD. P Bdfd. Ch e, b. Sch pe. N Dvn CC (Torrington). Cliff walks, 1m. Ch: Nmn font, carved bench-ends.

ABBOTSKERSWELL Devon
188 SX 8568 2m S of Newton Abbot.Loc, Kerswells CP. Ntn Abbt RD. Ch e. Sch p. Totnes CC. Ch: scrn; 13c statue of Virgin, found 1884. Ch hse, 16c.

ABBOTS LANGLEY Herts
160 TL 0901 3m N of Watford.CP, 18,157. Wtfd RD. P Wtfd. Ch e, be, m2, r. Sch i, j, p2, pe2, pr, s. SW Herts CC. See also Bedmond, Hunton Br, Primrosehill.

ABBOTS LEIGH Som
155, 156, 165 ST 5473 3m W of Bristol.CP, 819. Long Ashton RD. P BRSTL. Ch e. Sch p. N Som CC. To E, Leigh Wds (NT), bordering Avon gorge NW of Clifton Suspension Br. Stokeleigh Camp, Iron Age promontory fort.

ABBOTSLEY Hunts
134 TL 2256 4m SE of St Neots.CP, 263. St Nts RD. P HUNTINGDON. Ch e. Hunts CC.

ABBOTS MORTON Worcs
131/144 SP 0255 4m WSW of Alcester. CP, 149. Evesham RD. P WORCESTER. Ch e. S Worcs CC. Many half-timbered hses.

ABBOTS RIPTON Hunts
134 TL 2378 4m N of Huntingdon.CP, 370.
Hntngdn RD. P HNTNGDN. Ch e. Sch pe.
Hunts CC. See also Wennington.

ABBOT'S SALFORD Warwicks
144 SP 0650 4m NNE of Evesham. Loc,
Salford Priors CP. Ch r. Close to Worcs
border. Slfd Hall is partly Elizn.

ABBOTSWOOD Hants
168 SU 3723 2m NE of Romsey. Loc, Rmsy
Extra CP. Rmsy and Stockbridge RD.
Eastleigh CC (Winchester).

ABBOTTS ANN Hants
168 SU 3243 3m SW of Andover. CP, 1,090.
Andvr RD. P Andvr. Ch e, v. Sch pe.
Winchester CC (Basingstoke). 'Maidens'
garlands' in ch.

ABDON Shrops
129 SO 5786 8m NNE of Ludlow. CP, 89.
Ldlw RD. Ch e. Ldlw CC. Three Iron Age
hill forts on Brown Clee to E.

ABERFORD Yorks (W)
97 SE 4337 5m SW of Tadcaster. CP, 836.
Tdcstr RD. P LEEDS. Ch e, m, r. Sch pe.
Barkston Ash CC. Elaborate Vctrn
almshouses. 1m SE, Lotherton Hall*,
18c—19c mansion now country museum.

ABINGDON Berks
158 SU 4997 6m SSW of Oxford. MB,
18,596. P. Abngdn CC. Busy tn beside
R Thames. Scant 13c and 15c rems of abbey
(A.M.) founded in 675. The 17c County
Hall houses a museum.

ABINGER Surrey
170 TQ 1145 4m SW of Dorking. CP, 1,926.
Dkng and Horley RD. P(Abngr Cmmn),
Dkng. Ch e. Sch p. Dkng CC. See also
Oakwoodhill, Walliswood. Stocks and
whipping post on grn.

ABINGER HAMMER Surrey
170 TQ 0947 5m W of Dorking. Loc, Abngr
CP. P Dkng. Sch p. Site of former forge
(hence 'Hammer'). Well known clock on
main st. To E, Crossways Farm, setting
of Meredith's *Diana of the Crossways*.

ABINGTON, GREAT Cambs
148 TL 5348 6m N of Saffron Walden. See
Gt Abngtn.

ABINGTON PIGOTTS Cambs
147 TL 3044 4m NW of Royston. CP,
137. S Cambs RD, Ch e. Cambs CC.

AB KETTLEBY Leics
122 SK 7223 3m NW of Melton Mowbray.
CP, 543. Mltn and Belvoir RD. P Mltn Mbry.
Ch e, m. Sch p. Mltn CC. See also Holwell,
Wartnaby.

ABLINGTON Glos
157 SP 1007 6m NE of Cirencester. Loc,
Bibury CP.

ABNEY Derbys
111 SK 1979 7m N of Bakewell. CP(Abney
and Abney Grange), 48. Bkwll RD. W
Derbys CC.

ABRAM Lancs
101 SD 6001 3m SSE of Wigan. UD, 6,472.
P Platt Br, Wgn. Ince BC.

ABRIDGE Essex
161 TQ 4696 3m S of Epping. Loc,
Lambourne CP. Epping and Ongar RD.
P Romford. Ch e, v. Brentwood and Ongr CC
(Chigwell).

ABSON Glos
156 ST 7074 7m NNW of Bath. CP(Wick and
Absn), 1,524. Sodbury RD. Ch e.
S Glos CC.

ABTHORPE Northants
145, 146 SP 6546 3m WSW of Towcester.
CP, 217. Tcstr RD. P Tcstr. Ch e, m.
Daventry CC (S Nthnts).

ABY Lincs (L)
105 TF 4178 3m NW of Alford. CP(Aby w
Greenfield), 213. Louth RD. P Alfd.
Ch e, m. Sch pe. Lth CC. Water mill in
working order.

ACASTER MALBIS Yorks (W)
97 SE 5845 4m S of York. CP, 271.
Tadcaster RD. P YK. Ch e, m. Barkston Ash
CC.

ACASTER SELBY Yorks (W)
97 SE 5741 6m ESE of Tadcaster. CP, 55.
Tdcstr RD. Ch e. Barkston Ash CC.

ACCRINGTON Lancs
95 SD 7528 5m E of Blackburn. MB,
36,838. P. Accrngtn BC. See also Baxenden,
Huncoat. Textiles, brick mnfg, engineering
(incl spinning machinery). Tn itself mostly
of stone.

ACHURCH Northants
134 TL 0283 3m SSW of Oundle.Loc, Thorpe
Achch CP. Oundle and Thrapston RD.
Ch e. Wellingborough CC (Peterborough).

ACKLAM Yorks (E)
92 SE 7861 6m S of Malton. CP, 145.
Norton RD. P Mltn. Ch e, m. Howden CC.
In the Wolds. Many prehistoric earthworks
E and N.

ACKLETON Shrops
130 SO 7798 5m NE of Bridgnorth. Loc,
Worfield CP. P Wolverhampton, Staffs.

ACKLINGTON Nthmb
71 NU 2201 3m SW of Amble. CP, 406.
Alnwick RD. P Morpeth. Ch e. Sch pe.
Berwick-upon-Tweed CC. See also
Guyzance.

ACKTON Yorks (W)
97 SE 4122 3m SSW of Castleford. Loc,
Featherstone UD.

ACKWORTH MOOR TOP Yorks (W)
103 SE 4316 4m SSW of Pontefract. Loc,
Ackwth CP. Hemsworth RD. P Ackwth,
Pntfrct. Ch e, f, m2, r. Sch p, s. Hmswth CC.

ACLE Norfolk
126 TG 4010 8m WNW of Yarmouth. CP,
1,195. Blofield and Flegg RD. P NORWICH,
NOR 6OZ. Ch e, m, r. Sch pe, s. Ymth CC.
See also Damgate. Ch has 13c round twr
with octagonal belfry.

ACOL Kent
173 TR 3067 4m WSW of Margate.CP, 200.
Eastry RD. P Birchington. Ch e, m. Thanet
W BC (Isle of Thnt CC).

ACOMB Nthmb
77 NY 9366 2m N of Hexham.CP, 1,123.
Hxhm RD. P Hxhm. Ch m. Hxhm CC.

ACONBURY Herefs
142 SO 5133 4m S of Hereford. CP, 82.
Hrfd RD. Ch e. Hrfd CC.

ACRE STREET Sussex (W)
181 SZ 7999 5m SW of Chichester. Loc, W
Wittering CP.

ACTON Ches
109 SJ 5975 4m WNW of Northwich.Loc,
Actn Br CP. Nthwch RD. Ch m. Nthwch CC.

ACTON Ches
110 SJ 6353 1m WNW of Nantwich. CP,
293. Nntwch RD. Ch e, m. Sch pe.
Nntwch CC. Dorfold Hall*, early 17c,
gabled: panelling, furniture.

ACTON London
160 TQ 2080 2m NW of Hammersmith.
Loc, Ealing LB. Actn BC.

ACTON Shrops
129 SO. 3184 3m S of Bishop's Cstle. Loc,
Lydbury N CP.

ACTON Staffs
110, 119 SJ 8241 3m SSW of
Newcastle-under-Lyme. Loc, Whitmore CP.

ACTON Suffolk (W)
149 TL 8944 2m E of Long Melford. CP,
603. Mlfd RD. P Sudbury. Ch e. Sch pe.
Sdbry and Woodbridge CC. Ch contains
famous brass of Sir Robert de Bures, 1302.

ACTON BEAUCHAMP Herefs
142, 143 SO 6750 3m SSE of Bromyard.CP,
146. Brmyd RD. P WORCESTER. Ch e.
Leominster CC. See also Actn Grn.

ACTON BURNELL Shrops
118 SJ 5302 6m WNW of Much Wenlock.
CP, 300. Atcham RD. P Shrewsbury.
Ch e, r. Sch pe. Shrsbry CC. Rems of A.B.
Cstle (A.M.), 13c fortified mnr hse. First
English parliament said to have met there,
1283. EE ch has brass of 1382.

ACTON GREEN Herefs
143 SO 6950 4m SE of Bromyard. Loc,
Actn Beauchamp CP.

ACTON ROUND Shrops
129, 130 SO 6395 3m SSE of Much
Wenlock. CP, 126. Bridgnorth RD. Ch e.
Ludlow CC. A.R. Hall*, 1695, orig blt as
dower hse for Aldenham Pk; panelling,
staircase. Ch: Acton monmts.

ACTON SCOTT Shrops
129 SO 4589 3m S of Ch Stretton.CP, 147.
Ludlow RD. Ch e. Ldlw CC. See also
Alcaston.

ACTON TRUSSELL Staffs
119 SJ 9317 3m S of Stafford. CP(Actn
Trssll and Bednall), 410. Cannock RD.
P STFFD. Ch e. SW Staffs CC (Cnnck).

ACTON TURVILLE Glos
156 ST 8080 8m NW of Chippenham. CP,
278. Sodbury RD. P Badminton. Ch e.
Sch ie. S Glos CC.

ADBASTON Staffs
119 SJ 7627 6m N of Newport. CP, 634.
Stafford RD. P STFFD. Ch e, m. Sch p.
Stffd and Stone CC. See also Bishop's
Offley, Knighton.

ADBER Dorset
166, 177 ST 5920 4m NE of Yeovil. Loc,
Trent CP.

ADDERLEY Shrops
110, 118, 119 SJ 6639 4m NNW of Mkt
Drayton. CP, 248. Mkt Drtn RD. P Mkt
Drtn. Ch e. Sch pe. Oswestry CC.

ADDERSTONE Nthmb
64, 71 NU 1330 3m SE of Belford.
CP(Addrstne w Lucker), 303. Blfd RD.
Berwick-upon-Tweed CC. See also Bellshill,
Newstead, Warenford.

ADDINGHAM Yorks (W)
96 SE 0749 3m WNW of Ilkley. CP, 1,763.
Skipton RD. P Ilkley. Ch e, m2, r, v. Sch p.
Skptn CC.

ADDINGTON Bucks
146 SP 7428 4m SE of Buckingham. CP,
118. Bcknghm RD. Ch e. Bcknghm CC.

ADDINGTON Kent
171 TQ 6559 7m WNW of Maidstone. CP,
600. Malling RD. P Mdstne. Ch e. Tonbridge
and Mllng CC (Sevenoaks). To NW, the
Chestnuts, prehistoric burial chambers.

ADDINGTON London
171 TQ 3764 3m ESE of Croydon. Loc,
Crdn LB. Crdn Central BC (Crdn S).

ADDINGTON, GREAT Northants
134 SO 9575 3m SW of Thrapston. See Gt
Addngtn.

ADDISCOMBE London
170 TQ 3466 1m E of Croydon. Loc, Crdn
LB. P Crdn, Surrey. Crdn NE BC.

ADDLESTONE Surrey
170 TQ 0464 1m S of Chertsey. Loc, Chtsy
UD. P Weybridge.

ADDLETHORPE Lincs (L)
114 TF 5468 4m NNW of Skegness. CP, 282.
Spilsby RD. Ch e, m. Horncastle CC.

ADENEY Shrops
119 SJ 7018 3m W of Newport. Loc,
Edgmond CP.

ADFORTON Herefs
129 SO 4071 7m WSW of Ludlow. CP, 160.
Leominster and Wigmore RD. Ch e, m.
Lmnstr CC.

ADISHAM Kent
173 TR 2253 6m SE of Canterbury. CP,
369. Bridge-Blean RD. P Cntrbry. Ch e, b.
Sch pe. Cntrbry CC.

ADLESTROP Glos
144 SP 2427 3m ENE of Stow-on-the-Wold.
CP, 206. N Cotswold RD. Ch e. Cirencester
and Tewkesbury CC. See also Daylesford.

ADLINGFLEET Yorks (W)
98 SE 8420 6m ESE of Goole. CP, 137.
Gle RD. P Gle. Ch e. Gle CC.

ADLINGTON Ches
101 SJ 9180 4m N of Macclesfield. CP,
1,022. Mcclsfld RD. P Mcclsfld. Ch m2.
Sch p. Mcclsfld CC. Hall*, Tdr—18c. Gdns*:
yew walk, lime avenue.

ADLINGTON Lancs
100 SD 5912 3m S of Chorley. UD, 4,991.
P Chly. Chly CC. Textiles.

ADMASTON Shrops
118, 119 SJ 6313 2m NW of Wellington.
Loc, Wrockwardine CP. P Telford. Ch m.
Two wells brought short-lived fame as Vctrn
spa.

ADMASTON Staffs
120 SK 0523 3m N of Rugeley. Loc, Blith-
field CP. Uttoxeter RD. P Rgly. Burton CC.
Near W bank of Blthfld Reservoir. To
NW, Blthfld Hall*, home of Bagot family
since 1086; Stuart relics, carved oak
staircase, gt hall.

ADMINGTON Warwicks
144 SP 2046 6m S of Stratford. CP, 103.
Strtfd-on-Avon RD. Strtfd-on-Avon CC
(Strtfd). A. Hall to SSW is 17c.

ADSBOROUGH Som
177 ST 2729 4m NE of Taunton.
Loc, Bridgwater RD, Tntn RD. Ch c.
Brdgwtr CC, Tntn CC.

ADSTOCK Bucks
146 SP 7330 4m SE of Buckingham. CP,
261. Bcknghm RD. P Bletchley. Ch e, m.
Sch p. Bcknghm CC.

ADSTONE Northants
145, 146 SP 5951 7m SSE of Daventry.
CP, 80. Towcester RD. Ch e. Dvntry CC
(S Nthnts).

ADWELL Oxon
159 SU 6999 4m S of Thame. CP, 41.
Bullingdon RD. Ch e. Henley CC.

ADWICK LE STREET Yorks (W)
103 SE 5308 4m NNW of Doncaster. UD,
18,000. P Dncstr. Don Valley CC. See also
Carcroft, Skellow, Woodlands.

ADWICK UPON DEARNE Yorks (W)
103 SE 4701 7m W of Doncaster. CP, 134.
Dncstr RD. Ch e. Don Valley CC.

AFFPUDDLE Dorset
178 SY 8093 7m ENE of Dorchester. CP,
425. Wareham and Purbeck RD. Ch e.
S Dst CC. See also Briantspuddle. Ch: bench-
ends, plpt. On hth to S, conical depressions
called Swallow Holes, esp Cull-peppers Dish.

AGGLETHORPE Yorks (N)
90 SE 0886 3m SW of Leyburn.
CP(Coverham w Agglthpe), 127. Lbn RD.
Richmond CC.

AIKE Yorks (E)
99 TA 0445 4m NNE of Beverley. Loc,
Lockington CP.

AIKETGATE Cumb
83 NY 4846 8m SE of Carlisle. Loc,
Hesket CP. Penrith RD. Pnrth and the
Border CC.

AIKTON Cumb
75 NY 2753 3m NNE of Wigton. CP, 481.
Wgtn RD. P Wgtn. Ch e. Penrith and the
Border CC. See also Biglands, Gamelsby,
Wiggonby.

AILEY Herefs
142 SO 3448 8m NE of Hay-on-Wye. Loc,
Kinnersley CP.

AILSWORTH Hunts
134 TL 1199 5m W of Peterborough. CP,
315. Ptrbrgh RD. P PTRBRGH. Ch m.

Ptrbrgh BC (CC). Site of Roman camp to W;
traces of Ermine St leading across R Nene
to Rmn tn of *Durobrivae* to S.

AINDERBY QUERNHOW Yorks (N)
91 SE 3480 5m W of Thirsk. CP, 81.
Thsk RD. Thsk and Malton CC.

AINDERBY STEEPLE Yorks (N)
91 SE 3392 3m WSW of Northallerton. CP,
249. Nthlltn RD. P Nthlltn. Ch e. Sch pe.
Richmond CC.

AINGERS GREEN Essex
150 TM 1120 5m NW of Clacton. Loc, Gt
Bentley CP. Ch m.

AINSDALE Lancs
100 SD 3112 S distr of Southport. Loc,
Sthpt CB. P Sthpt. Wide sandy beach. Large
grn.

AINSTABLE Cumb
83 NY 5346 10m SE of Carlisle. CP, 463.
Penrith RD. P Clsle. Ch e, m. Sch p. Pnrth
and the Border CC. See also Croglin,
Newbiggin.

AINSWORTH Lancs
101 SD 7610 2m W of Bury. Loc,
Radcliffe MB. P Bolton.

AINTHORPE Yorks (N)
86 NZ 7007 6m SSW of Loftus. Loc, Danby
CP.

AINTREE Lancs
100 SJ 3798 5m NNE of Liverpool. CP,
7,050. W Lancs RD. P LVPL 9. Ch e2, m, r.
Sch i, j, pr. Ormskirk CC. Famous Grand
National racecourse. Motor racing circuit.
Electrical components factory etc.

AIRMYN Yorks (W)
97, 98 SE 7225 1m NW of Goole. CP, 582.
Gle RD. P Gle. Ch e. Sch p. Gle CC.

AIRTON Yorks (W)
95 SD 9059 6m SE of Settle. CP, 140.
Sttle RD. P Skipton. Ch f, m. Sch p.
Skptn CC. Stone-blt hses and vllge grn
beside R Aire.

AISBY Lincs (K)
113, 123 TF 0138 6m SW of Sleaford. Loc,
Haydor CP. W Kesteven RD. Grantham CC.

AISBY Lincs (L)
104 SK 8792 4m ENE of Gainsborough.
Loc, Corringham CP.

AISH Devon
187, 188 SX 6960 4m SW of Buckfastleigh.
Loc, S Brent CP.

AISKEW Yorks (N)
91 SE 2788 just NE of Bedale. CP, 881.
Bdle RD. Ch m, r. Thirsk and Malton CC.
See also Leeming Bar.

AISLABY Co Durham
85 NZ 4012 5m SSW of Teesside (Stockton).
CP, 94. Stocktn RD. Easington CC
(Sedgefield).

AISLABY Yorks (N)
86 NZ 8608 3m WSW of Whitby. CP, 215.
Whtby RD. P Whtby. Ch e. Sch pe.
Cleveland and Whtby CC(Scarborough and
Whtby). On edge of moors.

AISLABY Yorks (N)
86, 92 SE 7785 2m NW of Pickering.CP, 66.
Pckrng RD. Scarborough CC (Thirsk and
Malton).

AISTHORPE Lincs (L)
104 SK 9480 6m NNW of Lincoln.CP, 94.
Welton RD. Ch e. Gainsborough CC.

AKELD Nthmb
71 NT 9529 2m WNW of Wooler. CP, 149.
Glendale RD. Berwick-upon-Tweed CC. See
also Humbleton. A. Bastle, old fort with 4ft
thick walls, now a farm.

AKELEY Bucks
146 SP 7037 3m N of Buckingham.CP, 339.
Bcknghm RD. P Bcknghm. Ch e, m. Sch pe.
Bcknghm CC.

AKENHAM Suffolk (E)
150 TM 1448 3m N of Ipswich. CP, 62.
Gipping RD. Ch e. Eye CC.

ALBASTON Cornwall
175, 187 SX 4270 4m E of Callington.Loc,
Calstock CP. P Gunnislake. Ch m.

ALBERBURY Shrops
118 SJ 3614 8m W of Shrewsbury. CP
(Albrbry w Cardeston), 724. Atcham RD,
P Shrsbry. Ch e. Shrsbry CC. Nmn to Perp
ch with massive twr.

ALBOURNE Sussex (E)
182 TQ 2616 4m SW of Burgess Hill. CP,
523. Cuckfield RD. P Hassocks. Ch e.
Sch pe. Mid-Sx CC(Lewes). A. Place, 17c
brick hse to W.

ALBRIGHTON Shrops
118 SJ 4918 4m N of Shrewsbury. Loc,
Pimhill CP. Atcham RD. Ch e. Shrsbry CC.
Black-and-white hses. To SE, Albright
Hussey, part of 16c–17c mnr hse, once
moated.

ALBRIGHTON Shrops
119 SJ 8104 5m ESE of Shifnal. CP, 3,762.
Shfnl RD. P Wolverhampton, Staffs.
Ch e, m. Sch i, j, pe. The Wrekin CC.

ALBURGH Norfolk
137 TM 2687 5m WSW of Bungay.CP, 328.
Depwade RD. P Harleston. Ch e. Sch pe.
S Nflk CC.

ALBURY Herts
148 TL 4324 4m NW of Bishop's Stortford.
CP, 484. Braughing RD. P Much Hadham.
Ch e. Sch pe. E Herts CC.

ALBURY Oxon
158, 159 SP 6505 3m W of Thame. CP
(Tiddington-w-Albury), 382. Bullingdon RD.
Ch e. Mid-Oxon CC (Henley).

ALBURY Surrey
170 TQ 0447 4m ESE of Guildford. CP,
1,239. Gldfd RD. P Gldfd. Ch e. Sch pe.
Dorking CC. See also Farley Grn. Some old
hses. To E, A. Pk, with grnds by John
Evelyn, 17c diarist.

ALBY HILL Norfolk
126 TG 1934 5m SSW of Cromer. Loc,
Alby w Thwaite CP. Erpingham RD. Ch e.
N Nflk CC.

ALCASTON Shrops
129 SO 4587 3m NNE of Craven Arms.
Loc, Acton Scott CP. Black-and-white mnr
hse.

ALCESTER Warwicks
131 SP 0857 7m WNW of Stratford. CP,
3,424. Alcstr RD. P. Ch e, b, r.
Sch i, je, pr, s2, sr. Strtfd-on-Avon CC
(Strtfd). See also King's Coughton. On site
of Roman tn at confluence of R Arrow and
R Alne. Some old hses. 17c tn hall.

ALCISTON Sussex (E)
183 TQ 5005 4m NNE of Seaford. CP, 147.
Hailsham RD. Ch e. Lewes CC (Eastbourne).

ALCONBURY Hunts
134 TL 1875 4m NW of Huntingdon. CP,
629. Hntngdn RD. P HNTNGDN. Ch e, m.
Hunts CC. Vllge beside re-aligned A1. Ch
has broach spire. To E beyond A14, large
U.S. air base.

ALCONBURY WESTON Hunts
134 TL 1776 5m NW of Huntingdon. CP,
297. Hntngdn RD. P HNTNGDN. Sch pe.
Hunts CC.

ALDBOROUGH Norfolk
126 TG 1834 5m SSW of Cromer. CP, 437.
Erpingham RD. P NORWICH, NOR 4OY.
Ch e, m, v. Sch p. N Nflk CC. See also
Thurgarton. Ch: several 15c brasses.

ALDBOROUGH Yorks (W)
91 SE 4066 just E of Boroughbridge. Loc,
Brghbrdge CP. P Brghbrdge, YORK, Ch e.
Maypole on vllge grn. Rems of Roman tn
(A.M.).

ALDBOURNE Wilts
157 SU 2675 6m NE of Marlborough. CP,
1,161. Mlbrgh and Ramsbury RD. P Mlbrgh.
Ch e, m. Sch pe. Devizes CC. See also Upr
Upham, Woodsend.

ALDBROUGH Yorks (E)
99 TA 2438 6m SSE of Hornsea. CP, 835.
Holderness RD. P Hull. Ch e, m. Sch p.
Bridlington CC.

ALDBROUGH Yorks (N)
85 NZ 2011 6m WSW of Darlington. CP,
286. Richmond RD. Ch e, m. Sch pe.
Rchmnd CC. Two vllge grns divided by A.
Beck.

ALDBURY Herts
147, 159, 160 SP 9612 3m ENE of Tring.
CP, 798. Berkhamsted RD. P Trng. Ch e.
Sch pe. Hemel Hempstead CC. Vllge with
pond, stocks, whipping post; some old hses.
To N on W edge of Moneybury Hill (NT),
monmt to Duke of Bridgewater, 1832.

ALDEBURGH Suffolk (E)
150 TM 4656 6m SE of Saxmundham. MB,
2,793. P. Eye CC. Seaside tn. Sea

encroachment; Moot Hall* now on beach.
Sailing at (and from) Slaughden Quay to S.
Music festival — see Snape St.

ALDEBY Norfolk
137 TM 4493 3m NE of Beccles. CP, 478.
Loddon RD. P Bccls, Suffolk. Ch e. Sch pe.
S Nflk CC.

ALDENHAM Herts
160 TQ 1398 2m ENE of Watford. CP.
Wtfd RD. Ch e. S Herts CC (SW Herts). See
also Letchmore Hth, Radlett.

ALDERBURY Wilts
167 SU 1827 3m SE of Salisbury. CP, 1,038.
Slsbry and Wilton RD. P Slsbry. Ch e, m2.
Sch p. Slsbry CC. See also Whaddon. To W,
Longford Cstle*, triangular Tdr hse in large
grnds laid out by Capability Brown.

ALDERFORD Norfolk
125 TG 1218 7m SW of Aylsham. CP, 38.
St Faith's and Aylshm RD. Ch e. N Nflk CC
(Central Nflk).

ALDERHOLT Dorset
179 SU 1212 2m SW of Fordingbridge.
CP, 736. Wimborne and Cranborne RD.
P Fdngbrdge, Hants. Ch e, c, v. Sch pe.
N Dst CC. See also Cripplestyle.

ALDERLEY Glos
156 ST 7690 8m W of Tetbury. CP, 65.
Sodbury RD. Ch e. S Glos CC.

ALDERLEY EDGE Ches
101 SJ 8478 2m S of Wilmslow. UD, 4,458.
P. Macclesfield CC (Knutsford). Rsdntl distr
below hill (NT) of same name to E. See also
Nether Aldrly.

ALDERMASTON Berks
158 SU 5965 8m E of Newbury. CP, 2,816.
Bradfield RD. P Reading. Ch e. Sch pe.
Nbry CC. Vllge of warm brick. Atomic
energy research establishment in grnds of A.
Ct.

ALDERMASTON WHARF Berks
158 SU 6067 8m E of Newbury. Loc,
Bradfield RD. Nbry CC.

ALDERMINSTER Warwicks
144 SP 2348 4m SSE of Stratford. CP, 498.
Strtfd-on-Avon RD. P Strtfd-upon-Avn.
Ch e. Sch pe. Strtfd-on-Avn CC (Strtfd).

ALDERSEY GREEN Ches
109 SJ 4656 7m SSE of Chester. Loc, Aldrsy
CP. Tarvin RD. Nantwich CC.

ALDERSHOT Hants
169 SU 8650 8m W of Guildford. MB,
33,311. P. Aldrsht CC. Garrison tn; both
military and civilian parts being
redeveloped.

ALDERTON Glos
144 SP 0033 3m NNW of Winchcombe. CP,
474. Cheltenham RD. P Tewkesbury.
Ch e, m. Sch pe. Cirencester and Tksbry CC.
See also Dixton.

ALDERTON Northants
146 SP 7446 3m ESE of Towcester. Loc,
Grafton Regis CP. Ch e, m.

ALDERTON Suffolk (E)
150 TM 3441 6m SE of Woodbridge. CP,
449. Deben RD. P Wdbrdge. Ch e. Sch pe.
Sudbury and Wdbrdge CC. Ch with ruined
twr.

ALDERTON Wilts
156 ST 8382 6m WSW of Malmesbury. Loc,
Luckington CP. P Chippenham. Ch e.

ALDERWASLEY Derbys
111 SK 3153 4m NNW of Belper. CP, 358.
Blpr RD. P DERBY. Ch e. Sch pe. Blpr CC.

ALDFIELD Yorks (W)
91 SE 2669 3m WSW of Ripon. CP, 73.
Rpn and Pateley Br RD. Ch e, m. Sch pe.
Rpn CC.

ALDFORD Ches
109 SJ 4159 5m S of Chester. CP, 280.
Chstr RD. P CHSTR. Ch e, m. Sch pe. City
of Chstr CC.

ALDHAM Essex
149 TL 9125 5m W of Colchester. CP, 359.
Lexden and Winstree RD. P Clchstr. Ch e.
Clchstr CC.

ALDHAM Suffolk (W)
149 TM 0444 1m NE of Hadleigh. CP, 126.
Cosford RD. P Colchester, Essex. Ch e, v.
Sudbury and Woodbridge CC.

ALDINGBOURNE Sussex (W)
181 SU 9205 4m E of Chichester. CP,
2,074. Chchstr RD. P Chchstr. Ch e. Sch p.

Arundel CC (Chchstr). See also Norton,
Nyton, Westergate, Woodgate. At E end of
Tangmere Airfield.

ALDINGHAM Lancs
88 SD 2871 4m S of Ulverston. CP, 892.
N Lonsdale RD. Ch e. Sch pe2. Morecambe
and Lnsdel CC. See also Baycliff, Gleaston,
Leece, Newbiggin, Scales.

ALDINGTON Kent
172, 173, 184 TR 0736 6m SE of Ashford.
CP, 725. E Ashfd RD. P Ashfd. Ch e, v.
Sch p. Ashfd CC.

ALDINGTON Worcs
144 SP 0644 2m E of Evesham. CP, 167.
Eveshm RD. S Worcs CC.

ALDRETH Cambs
135 TL 4473 7m SW of Ely. Loc,
Haddenham CP. Ch b.

ALDRIDGE Staffs
120 SK 0500 3m ENE of Walsall.
UD(Aldrdge-Brownhills), 88,475. P Wlsll.
A-B BC(Wlsll S). See also Clayhanger,
Pelsall, Rushall, Shelfield, Shire Oak, Wlsll
Wd.

ALDRINGHAM Suffolk(E)
137 TM 4461 3m NNW of Aldeburgh.
CP(Aldrnghm cum Thorpe), 954. Blyth RD.
P Leiston. Ch e, b. Sch p. Eye CC. See also
Thorpeness.

ALDSWORTH Glos
144 SP 1510 4m SE of Northleach. CP, 238.
Nthlch RD. P Cheltenham. Ch e, m. Sch pe.
Cirencester and Tewkesbury CC.

ALDWARK Derbys
111 SK 2257 5m WSW of Matlock. CP, 62.
Bakewell RD. W Derbys.

ALDWARK Yorks (N)
91, 97 SE 4663 5m ESE of Boroughbridge.
CP, 227. Easingwold RD. P Alne, YORK.
Ch e. Thirsk and Malton CC.

ALDWICK Sussex (W)
181 SZ 9098 2m W of Bognor. Loc, Bgnr
Regis UD. P Bgnr Rgs. Much new bldng.

ALDWINCLE Northants
134 TL 0081 2m N of Thrapston. CP, 296.
Oundle and Thrpstn RD. P Kettering.
Ch e, b. Sch pe. Wellingborough CC

(Peterborough). Two mdvl chs, one now disused. John Dryden b at parsonage 1631.

ALDWORTH Berks
158 SU 5579 5m WNW of Pangbourne. CP, 191. Wantage RD. P Reading. Ch e, m. Abingdon CC. Ch: several monmts to the de la Beche family.

ALFARDISWORTHY Devon
174 SS 2911 6m NE of Bude. Loc, Bradworthy CP.

ALFINGTON Devon
176 SY 1197 4m WSW of Honiton. Loc, Ottery St Mary UD.

ALFOLD Surrey
182 TQ 0334 8m WNW of Horsham. CP, 998. Hambledon RD. P Cranleigh. Ch e, b. Sch p. Guildford CC. A. Hse, 16c, half-timbered. Stocks and whipping post in vllge. Former centre of iron industry.

ALFORD Lincs (L)
105 TF 4575 11m NW of Skegness. UD, 2,278. P. Horncastle CC. Windmill in working order.

ALFORD Som
166 ST 6032 5m WSW of Bruton. CP, 84. Wincanton RD. Ch e. Wells CC.

ALFRETON Derbys
112 SK 4155 9m WSW of Mansfield. UD, 21,670. P DERBY. Ilkeston CC. See also Ironville, Somercotes, Swanwick. Ancient tn among coalfields. Ch: monmts. Double lock-up.

ALFRICK Worcs
143 SO 7453 6m W of Worcester. CP, 457. Martley RD. P WCSTR. Ch e. Sch p. Kidderminster CC.

ALFRISTON Sussex (E)
183 TQ 5203 4m NE of Seaford. CP, 588. Hailsham RD. P Polegate. Ch e, v. Sch p. Lewes CC (Eastbourne). Well known S Downs vllge. A. Clergy Hse (NT)*, 14c; first property acquired by the trust, 1896.

ALGARKIRK Lincs (H)
114, 123 TF 2935 6m SSW of Boston. CP, 534. Bstn RD. Ch e. Sch pe. Holland w Bstn CC.

ALHAMPTON Som
166 ST 6234 3m W of Bruton. Loc, Ditcheat CP.

ALKBOROUGH Lincs (L)
98 SE 8821 7m N of Scunthorpe. CP, 470. Glanford Brigg RD. P Scnthpe. Ch e, m. Sch p. Brgg and Scnthpe CC(Brgg). Ch has Saxon twr. Inside, photographs of floods of 1953; in floor, iron copy of maze called Julian's Bower, just E of vllge.

ALKERTON Oxon
145 SP 3742 5m WNW of Banbury. CP, 82. Bnbry RD. Ch e. Bnbry CC.

ALKHAM Kent
173 TR 2542 4m NE of Folkestone. CP, 558. Dover RD. P Dvr. Ch e. Sch pe. Dvr and Deal CC (Dvr). See also Ewell Minis. Downland vllge. 13c ch. Rems of St Radegund's abbey 1½m E.

ALKMONTON Derbys
120 SK 1838 5m S of Ashbourne. CP, 93. Ashbne RD. Ch e. W Derbys CC.

ALLALEIGH Devon
188 SX 8053 4m S of Totnes. Loc, Cornworthy CP.

ALL CANNINGS Wilts
167 SU 0761 4m E of Devizes. CP(Allcannings), 459. Dvzs RD. P Dvzs. Ch e, m. Sch pe. Dvzs CC. See also Allington. On hills to N, many prehistoric earthworks. A.C. Cross, Iron Age settlement; many finds of pottery, tools, ornaments.

ALLENDALE TOWN Nthmb
77 NY 8355 5m S of Haydon Br. Loc, Allndle CP. Hexham RD. P(Allndle), Hxhm. Ch e, m2. Sch s. Hxhm CC. On E Allen River on side of picturesque valley. Bonfire festival held on New Year's Eve.

ALLENHEADS Nthmb
84 NY 8645 12m SSW of Hexham. Loc, Allendale CP. Hxhm RD. P Hxhm. Ch m. Hxhm CC. Hmlt at top of E Allen valley.

ALLENSMORE Herefs
142 SO 4636 4m SW of Hereford. CP, 403. Hrfd RD. P HRFD. Ch e, r. Hrfd CC.

ALLER Som
166 ST 3929 9m NNE of Ilminster.ÇP, 339.
Langport RD. P Lngpt. Ch e, c. Yeovil CC.
Guthrum the Dane baptized here at King
Alfred's behest after Battle of Ethandune,
879.

ALLERBY Cumb
81, 82 NY 0839 4m ENE of Maryport.
CP(Oughterside and Allrby), 604.
Cockermouth RD. Workington CC.

ALLERFORD Som
164 SS 9046 4m W of Minehead. Loc,
Selworthy CP. P Mnhd. NT vllge. Packhorse
br.

ALLERSTON Yorks (N)
92, 93 SE 8782 5m ESE of Pickering. CP,
244. Pckrng RD. P Pckrng. Ch e, m.
Scarborough CC(Scbrgh and Whitby). On
edge of large state forests to N.

ALLERTHORPE Yorks (E)
97, 98 SE 7847 2m SW of Pocklington.CP,
164. Pcklngtn RD. Ch e, m. Howden CC.

ALLERTON BYWATER Yorks (W)
97 SE 4127 1m NNW of Castleford. Loc,
Garforth UD. P Cstlfd.

ALLERTON MAULEVERER Yorks (W)
97 SE 4158 4m E of Knaresborough.
CP(Allrtn Mlvrr w Hopperton), 102.
Nidderdale RD. Ch e, r. Harrogate CC.
Allrtn Pk, 19c Tdr/Gothic mansion with pk
and lakes.

ALLESLEY Warwicks
132 SP 2980 3m WNW of Coventry. Loc,
Cvntry CB; CP, Meriden RD. P Cvntry.
Cvntry SW BC, Mrdn CC. (Cvntry S BC,
Mrdn CC.)

ALLEXTON Leics
122 SK 8100 3m W of Uppingham.CP, 43.
Billesdon RD. Ch e. Harborough CC
(Melton).

ALLGREAVE Ches
110 SJ 9767 5m SSE of Macclesfield.Loc,
Wincle CP. Ch m. 1m ESE in Dane valley on
Staffs border: cave called Lud's Church,
possibly used as secret ch by Lollards.

ALLHALLOWS Kent
172 TQ 8377 8m NE of Rochester. CP.
Strood RD. P Rchstr. Ch e. Gravesend CC.

ALLIMORE GREEN Staffs
119 SJ 8519 5m WSW of Stafford. Loc,
Haughton CP.

ALLINGTON Lincs (K)
113, 122 SK 8540 5m WNW of Grantham.
CP, 411. W Kesteven RD. P Grnthm. Ch e.
Sch pe. Grnthm CC.

ALLINGTON Wilts
167 SU 0663 4m ENE of Devizes. Loc,
Allcannings CP. Ch b.

ALLINGTON Wilts
156, 157 ST 8975 2m NW of Chippenham.
Loc, Chppnhm Without CP. Calne and
Chppnhm RD. Chppnhm CC.

ALLINGTON Wilts
167 SU 2039 7m NE of Salisbury. CP, 338.
Amesbury RD. Ch e, m. Sch pe. Slsbry CC.
See also Boscombe.

ALLITHWAITE Lancs
88, 89 SD 3876 2m SW of Grange-over-Sands.
Loc, Lr Allthwte CP. N Lonsdale RD.
P Grnge-over-Snds. Ch e, c, f, r. Sch pe.
Morecambe and Lnsdle CC.

ALLONBY Cumb
81, 82 NY 0843 5m NE of Maryport.CP,
493. Wigton RD. P Mrpt. Ch e, c, f, v. Sch p.
Penrith and the Border CC. Small resort
with sand and shingle beach; cobbled main
street.

ALL SAINTS SOUTH ELMHAM Suffolk
(E)
137 TM 3482 4m S of Bungay. CP(All
Snts and St Nicholas, S Elmhm), 154.
Wainford RD. Ch e. Lowestoft CC. All Snts
ch early Nmn. St Nchls sunk under vegetation.

ALL STRETTON Shrops
129 SO 4695 1m NNE of Ch Stretton. Loc,
Ch Strttn CP. P Ch Strttn. Ch e.

ALLWESTON Dorset
178 ST 6614 3m SE of Sherborne. Loc,
Folke CP. Ch m.

ALMELEY Herefs
142 SO 3351 4m SSE of Kington.CP, 534.
Weobley RD. P HEREFORD. Ch e, f, m.
Sch p. Leominster CC. See also Upcott,
Woonton.

ALMER Dorset
178, 179 SY 9198 5m SSE of Blandford.
Loc, Sturminster Marshall CP. P Blndfd
Forum. Ch e.

ALMINGTON Staffs
110, 119 SJ 7034 2m E of Mkt Drayton.
Loc, Tyrley CP. Newcastle-under-Lyme RD.
N-u-L BC.

ALMINSTONE CROSS Devon
174 SS 3420 8m WSW of Bideford. Loc,
Woolfardisworthy CP. Ch m.

ALMONDSBURY Glos
155, 156 ST 6084 4m SE of Severn Rd Br.
CP, 4,144. Thornbury RD. P BRISTOL.
Ch e. Sch pe. S Glos CC. See also Catbrain,
Easter Compton, Hallen, Over. 1m E, A.
Interchange, linking M4 and M5: first
four-level intrchnge in Britain, 1966.

ALNE Yorks (N)
91 SE 4965 6m E of Boroughbridge. CP,
427. Easingwold RD. P YORK. Ch e, m.
Sch p. Thirsk and Malton CC. Former
junction for Easngwld rly.

ALNE, GREAT Warwicks
131 SP 1159 2m NE of Alcester. See Gt
Alne.

ALNHAM Nthmb
71 NT 9910 7m NNW of Rothbury. CP,
155. Rthbry RD. Ch e. Berwick-upon-
Tweed CC. See also Gt Ryle, Lit Rle,
Prendwick, Scrainwood. Scattered hmlt.
Vestigial rems of cstle. 13c ch restored
from ruins in 19c.

ALNMOUTH Nthmb
71 NU 2410 4m ESE of Alnwick. CP, 652.
Alnwick RD. P Alnwick. Ch e, m2.
Berwick-upon-Tweed CC. See also High
Buston. Small resort. Wide sands.

ALNWICK Nthmb
71 NU 1813 17m N of Morpeth. UD, 7,113
P. Berwick-upon-Tweed CC. Busy small mkt
tn of sturdy hses, Nmn cstle*, stronghold of
the Percys, much enlarged, restored and
rebuilt.

ALPERTON London
160 TQ 1883 2m N of Ealing. Loc, Brent
LB. Brnt S BC (Wembley S).

ALPHAMSTONE Essex
149 TL 8735 4m S of Sudbury. CP, 149.
Halstead RD. P Bures, Suffolk. Ch e.
Saffron Walden CC.

ALPHETON Suffolk (W)
149 TL 8850 2m WNW of Lavenham.CP,
203. Melford RD. P Sudbury. Ch e. Sdbry
and Woodbridge CC.

ALPHINGTON Devon
176 SX 9190 S distr of Exeter. Loc, Extr
CB, and CP, 2,085. St. Thomas RD.
Ch e, m. Extr BC, Tiverton CC. (Tvtn CC.)
Vllge swallowed up by Extr. Ch has Nmn
font, copied in Temple Ch, London.

ALPINGTON Norfolk
137 TG 2901 6m SE of Norwich. CP, 161.
Loddon RD. Sch p. S Nflk CC.

ALPORT Derbys
111 SK 2264 2m S of Bakewell. Loc,
Bkwll RD. W Derbys CC. Early 18c br over
R Lathkill.

ALPRAHAM Ches
109 SJ 5859 6m NW of Nantwich. CP,
389. Nntwch RD. P Tarporley. Ch m.
Nntwch CC.

ALRESFORD Essex
149, 162 TM 0621 5m ESE of Colchester.
CP, 926. Tendring RD. P Clchstr. Ch e.
Sch p. Harwich CC. Pronounced 'arlsfd'. In
pk of hall is 'Quarters Hse', painted by
Constable. Gravel wks above creek.

ALRESFORD Hants
168 SU 5832 7m ENE of Winchester. See
New Alresford.

ALREWAS Staffs
120 SK 1715 5m NE of Lichfield.CP, 2,472.
Lchfld RD. P Burton-on-Trent. Ch e, m.
Sch pe. Lchfld and Tamworth CC. See also
Fradley, Hilliard's Cross, Orgreave. Locks on
Trent and Mersey Canal. Basket-making.

ALSAGER Ches
110 SJ 7955 8m NW of Stoke-on-Trent.UD,
10,202. P Stke-on-Trnt, Staffs. Crewe CC.

ALSAGERS BANK Staffs
110 SJ 8048 3m WNW of
Newcastle-under-Lyme. Loc, Audley Rural
CP. P Stoke-on-Trent. Ch e. Sch p.

ALSOP EN LE DALE Derbys
111 SK 1655 6m N of Ashbourne. CP(Eaton and Alsp), 95. Ashbne RD. Ch e. W Derbys CC. Ch: Nmn S doorway.

ALSTON Cumb
83 NY 7146 16m NE of Penrith. CP(Alstn w Garrigill), 2,105. Alstn w Grrgll RD. P. Ch e, f, m3, r, v. Sch p, s. Pnrth and the Border CC. See also Leadgate, Nenthead. Claims to be highest mkt tn in England. Covered mkt cross.

ALSTONE Glos
143, 144 SO 9832 6m E of Tewkesbury. Loc, Teddington CP.

ALSTONEFIELD Staffs
111 SK 1355 6m NNW of Ashbourne. CP, 333. Leek RD. P Ashbne, Derbyshire. Ch e, m2. Sch pe. Lk CC. Nearly 900 ft up between valleys of R Dove and R Manifold.

ALSWEAR Devon
163 SS 7222 3m S of S Molton. Loc, S Mltn RD. P: S Mltn. Ch m. N Dvn CC.

ALTARNUN Cornwall
186 SX 2281 7m WSW of Launceston. CP, 680. Lncstn RD. P Lncstn. Ch e, m3. Sch p. N Cnwll CC. See also Bolventor. Large par on Bodmin Moor. Granite-towered ch known as 'cathedral of the moors'.

ALTCAR, GREAT Lancs
100 SD 3206 1m ESE of Formby. See Gt Altcr.

ALTHAM Lancs
95 SD 7732 4m W of Burnley. CP, 643. Bnly RD. P Accrington. Ch e. Sch pe. Clitheroe CC.

ALTHORNE Essex
162 TQ 9198 3m NW of Burnham-on-Crouch. CP, 483. Maldon RD. P Chelmsford. Ch e, m. Mldn CC. Caravan colony to S.

ALTHORPE Lincs (L)
104 SE 8309 4m W of Scunthorpe. CP(Keadby w Althpe), 2,001. Isle of Axholme RD. P Scnthpe. Ch e, m. Gainsborough CC. Ch has brass of 1360.

ALTOFTS Yorks (W)
96, 102 SE 3723 3m ENE of Wakefield. Loc, Normanton UD. P Nmntn.

ALTON Derbys
111 SK 3664 5m SSW of Chesterfield. Loc, Ashover CP. P Chstrfld.

ALTON Hants
169 SU 7139 9m WSW of Farnham. UD, 12,686. P. Petersfield CC. See also Beech, Holybourne. Old mkt tn with breweries. Large hsptl and sch for disabled. Curtis Museum — agricultural and domestic.

ALTON Staffs
120 SK 0742 4m E of Cheadle. CP, 1,182. Chdle RD. P Stoke-on-Trent. Ch e, m, r. Sch pe, pr. Leek CC. See also Bradley-in-the-Moors. Rems of Nmn cstle beside R Churnet. To N across river, A. Twrs, ruined Pugin hse; grnds*. Circular lock-up in vllge.

ALTON BARNES Wilts
167 SU 1061 4m WNW of Pewsey. Loc, Alton CP. Psy RD. P Marlborough. Ch e. Sch pe. Devizes CC. On hill N, many prehistoric earthworks, esp Adam's Grave, chambered long barrow, and section of Wansdyke (see Stanton Prior).

ALTON PANCRAS Dorset
178 ST 6902 8m N of Dorchester. CP, 122. Dchstr RD. P Dchstr. Ch e. W Dst CC.

ALTON PRIORS Wilts
167 SU 1162 4m WNW of Pewsey. Loc, Alton CP. Psy RD. Ch e. Devizes CC. See A. Barnes.

ALTRINCHAM Ches
101 SJ 7687 8m SW of Manchester. MB, 40,752. P. Altrnchm and Sale CC. See also Broadheath, Timperley. Indstrl, rsdntl. Mnchstr Airpt 4m ESE.

ALVANLEY Ches
109 SJ 4974 5m S of Runcorn. CP, 332. Rncn RD. P WARRINGTON. Ch e. Sch p. Rncn CC.

ALVECHURCH Worcs
131 SP 0272 3m NNW of Redditch. CP. Bromsgrove RD. P BIRMINGHAM. Ch e, b, m. Sch i, je. Brmsgrve and Rddtch CC (Brmsgrve). See also Barnt Grn, Hopwood, Rowney Grn.

ALVECOTE Warwicks
120 SK 2404 3m E of Tamworth. Loc, Shuttington CP. P Tmwth, Staffs.

ALVEDISTON Wilts
167 ST 9723 7m E of Shaftesbury. CP, 98.
Mere and Tisbury RD. Ch e. Westbury CC.

ALVELEY Shrops
130 SO 7684 6m SSE of Bridgnorth. CP,
1,076. Brdgnth RD. P Brdgnth. Ch e, m.
Sch p. Ludlow CC.

ALVERDISCOTT Devon
163 SS 5225 4m E of Bideford. CP, 231.
Torrington RD. Ch e, m. W Dvn CC
(Trrngtn).

ALVERSTOKE Hants
180 SZ 6098 S distr of Gosport. Loc, Gspt
MB. P Gspt. Bathing beach and boats.
Rgncy crescent.

ALVERSTONE IOW
180 SZ 5785 2m NW of Sandown. Loc,
Brading CP.

ALVERTON Notts
112, 122 SK 7942 7m S of Newark. CP, 29.
Nwk RD. Nwk CC.

ALVESCOT Oxon
157 SP 2704 5m NE of Lechlade. CP, 309.
Witney RD. P OXFORD. Ch e, b. Sch pe.
Mid-Oxon CC (Banbury).

ALVESTON Glos
155, 156 ST 6388 4m E of Severn Rd Br.
CP, 1,820. Thornbury RD. P BRISTOL.
Ch e, m2. Sch pe. S Glos CC. See also
Earthcott Grn, Rudgeway.

ALVESTON Warwicks
131 SP 2356 2m ENE of Stratford. Loc,
Strtfd-upon-Avon MB. P Strtfd-upn-Avn.

ALVINGHAM Lincs (L)
105 TF 3691 3m NE of Louth. CP, 215.
Lth RD. P Lth. Ch e, m. Lth CC. Ch shares
churchyard with ch of N Cockerington (cf
Swaffham Prior). Water mill in working
order.

ALVINGTON Glos
155, 156 SO 6000 2m SW of Lydney. CP,
407. Ldny RD. P Ldny. Ch e. W Glos CC.

ALWALTON Hunts
134 TL 1395 4m WSW of Peterborough. CP,
210. Norman Cross RD. P PTRBRGH. Ch e.
Sch pe. Hunts CC.

ALWINGTON Devon
163 SS 4023 4m SW of Bideford. CP, 319.
Bdfd RD. Ch e, m. N Dvn CC (Torrington).
See also Fairy Cross, Ford. Place itself
consists of ch and one house; ch contains
Portledge family pew.

ALWINTON Nthmb
71 NT 9206 9m WNW of Rothbury.
CP, 154. Rthbry RD. Ch e.
Berwick-upon-Tweed CC. Small vllge in upr
Coquetdale.

AMBASTON Derbys
112, 121 SK 4232 5m ESE of Derby. Loc,
Elvaston CP. Ch e.

AMBERGATE Derbys
111 SK 3451 3m N of Belper. Loc,
Ripley UD. P DERBY.

AMBER HILL Lincs (H)
114 TF 2346 6m WNW of Boston. CP, 430.
Bstn RD. P Bstn. Ch e, m. Sch p. Holland w
Bstn CC.

AMBERLEY Glos
156 SO 8501 3m S of Stroud. Loc,
Minchinhampton CP. P Strd. Ch e. Sch pe.

AMBERLEY Sussex (W)
182 TQ 0213 4m N of Arundel. CP, 599.
Chanctonbury RD. P Arndl. Ch, e, c.
Sch pe. Shoreham CC (Arndl and Shrhm).
See also N Stoke. On R Arun, finely
situated. Mdvl cstle. Nmn and later ch just
outside cstle walls.

AMBLE Nthmb
71 NU 2604 7m SE of Anwick. UD, 4,745.
P Morpeth. Berwick-upon-Tweed CC. Small
port and resort at mouth of R Coquet.
Many caravans. Sands. Offshore, Coquet
Island.

AMBLECOTE Worcs
130, 131 SO 8985 1m N of Stourbridge.
Loc, Stbrdge MB. Halesowen and
Stbrdge BC (Brierley Hill CC).

AMBLER THORN Yorks (W)
96, 102 SE 0929 3m N of Halifax. Loc,
Queensbury and Shelf UD. P Qunsbry,
Bradford.

AMBLESIDE Westm
88, 89 NY 3704 4m NNW of Windermere.
Loc, Lakes UD. P. Westm CC. Lake Distr
holiday centre near shores of Lake
Windermere.

AMBROSDEN Oxon
145, 146 SP 6019 2m SE of Bicester. CP,
2,265. Ploughley RD. P Bcstr. Ch e, c.
Sch p. Mid-Oxon CC (Henley).

AMCOTTS Lincs (L)
104 SE 8514 5m E of Crowle. CP, 225. Isle
of Axholme RD. P Scunthorpe. Ch e, m.
Gainsborough CC.

AMERSHAM Bucks
159, 160 SU 9597 3m S of Chesham. CP,
14,612. Amrshm RD. P. Ch e3, b, f, m2, v2.
Sch j, p, pe2, s2, sb, sg. Chshm and
Amrshm CC (S Bucks). See also Lit
Chalfont. Mkt tn, with 17c mkt hall. To
W, Shardeloes Pk, by Robert Adam.

AMESBURY Wilts
167 SU 1541 7m N of Salisbury. CP, 5,611.
Amesbury RD. P Slsbry. Ch e, m, r.
Sch i, je, pr, s. Slsbry CC. Dominated by
Army (two large camps and training area to
N). Ch, Nmn and EE. 2m NW, Stonehenge
(A.M.), famous Neolithic-Bronze Age
earthwork and stone circle.

AMINGTON Staffs
120 SK 2304 2m E of Tamworth. Loc,
Tmwth MB. P Tmwth. Lichfield and
Tmwth CC (Meriden).

AMOTHERBY Yorks (N)
92 SE 7473 2m WNW of Malton. CP, 322.
Mltn RD. P Mltn. Ch e. Sch p. Thirsk and
Mltn CC.

AMPFIELD Hants
168 SU 4023 3m ENE of Romsey. CP, 917.
Rmsy and Stockbridge RD. P Rmsy. Ch e.
Eastleigh CC.

AMPLEFORTH Yorks (N)
92 SE 5878 4m SSW of Helmsley. CP, 745.
Hlmsly RD. P YORK. Ch e, m2, r2.
Sch pe, pr. Thirsk and Malton CC. Large RC
monastery and boys' public sch.

AMPNEY CRUCIS Glos
157 SP 0601 3m E of Cirencester. CP, 402.
Crncstr RD. P Crncstr. Ch e, m. Sch pe.
Crncstr and Tewkesbury CC. 15c cross in
churchyard, restored 19c.

AMPNEY ST MARY Glos
157 SP 0802 4m E of Cirencester. CP, 120.
Crncstr RD. Crncstr and Tewkesbury CC.
Ch has mdvl wall-paintings.

AMPNEY ST PETER Glos
157 SP 0801 4m E of Cirencester. CP, 117.
Crncstr RD. Ch e. Crncstr and
Tewkesbury CC.

AMPORT Hants
168 SU 2944 4m W of Andover. CP, 1,215.
Andvr RD. P. Andvr. Ch e, m. Sch pe.
Winchester CC (Basingstoke).

AMPTHILL Beds
147 TL 0338 7m S of Bedford. UD, 5,575.
P BDFD. Mid-Beds CC. Mkt tn. Houghton
Hse (A.M.), ruined 16c hse, 1m N.

AMPTON Suffolk (W)
136 TL 8671 4m N of Bury St Edmunds.
CP, 89. Thingoe RD. P Bury St Eds. Ch e.
Bury St Eds CC. Late 17c almshouses.
Former bluecoat sch of 1705.

AMWELL, GREAT Herts
148, 161 TL 3712 1m SE of Ware. See Gt
Amwll.

ANCASTER Lincs (K)
113, 123 SK 9843 5m WSW of Sleaford. CP,
722. W Kesteven RD. P Grantham.
Ch e, m2. Sch pe. Grnthm CC. Site of
Roman stn; many Roman rems unearthed.
Famous for production of building stone.

ANCROFT Nthmb
64 NU 0045 5m S of Berkwick-upon-
Tweed. CP, 1,012. Norham and Island-
shires RD. P BRWCK-UPN-TWD. Ch e, v.
Brwck-upn-Twd CC. See also Cheswick,
Goswick, Haggerston, Scremerston.

ANCTON Sussex (W)
181, 182 SU 9800 3m E of Bognor. Loc,
Middleton-on-Sea CP.

ANDERBY Lincs (L)
105 TF 5275 4m E of Alford. CP, 195.
Spilsby RD. P Skegness. Ch e. Horncastle CC.

ANDERSON Dorset
178 SY 8797 6m S of Blandford. CP, 67.
Blndfd RD. Ch e. N Dst CC. See also
Winterborne Tomson.

ANDERTON Ches
101 SJ 6475 1m NW of Northwich. CP, 459.
Nthwch RD. P Nthwch. Ch b, m.
Nthwch CC.

ANDOVER Hants
168 SU 3645 13m NW of Winchester. MB,
25,538. P. Winchester CC (Basingstoke). See
also Enham Alamein, Picket Piece. New tn
being developed by GLC.

ANDOVER DOWN Hants
168 SU 3945 2m E of Andover. Loc,
Andvr MB. 1m SE in Harewood Forest,
'Deadman's Plack', memorial of murder of
King Athelwold.

ANDOVERSFORD Glos
144 SP 0219 5m ESE of Cheltenham. CP,
352. Northleach RD. P Chltnhm. Ch m.
Sch p. Cirencester and Tewkesbury CC.

ANGARRACK Cornwall
189 SW 5838 4m W of Camborne. Loc,
Hayle CP. P Hayle. Ch m.

ANGERSLEIGH Som
164 ST 1918 4m ESE of Wellington. Loc,
Pitminster CP. Ch e.

ANGMERING Sussex (W)
182 TQ 0604 3m NE of Littlehampton. CP,
2,850. Worthing RD. P Lttlhmptn.
Ch e, b, r. Sch pe, pr. Arundel CC (Arndl
and Shoreham). Rapid modern expansion.
Pigeon Hse, mdvl yeoman's hse.

ANGMERING-ON-SEA Sussex (W)
182 TQ 0701 3m E of Littlehampton. Loc,
E Preston CP. P: E Prstn, Lttlhmptn.
Resort; shingle beach. Mostly private
estates.

ANGRAM Yorks (W)
97 SE 5248 4m NNE of Tadcaster. CP, 47.
Wetherby RD. Barkston Ash CC.

ANLABY Yorks (E)
99 TA 0328 4m W of Hull. Loc, Haltemprice UD. P Hll, Hltmprce CC.

ANMER Norfolk
124 TF 7429 10m NE of King's Lynn. CP,
98. Docking RD. P K's Lnn. Ch e, m.
NW Nflk CC (K's Lnn).

ANNA VALLEY Hants
168 SU 3443 1m SW of Andover. Loc,
Andvr RD. P Andvr. Ch v. Winchester CC
(Basingstoke).

ANNESLEY WOODHOUSE Notts
112 SK 5053 5m SSW of Mansfield. Loc,
Kirkby in Ashfield UD, Basford RD.
P Kby-in-Ashfld, NOTTINGHAM.
Ashfld CC. Colliery vllge.

ANNFIELD PLAIN Co Durham
78 NZ 1751 4m E of Consett. Loc,
Stanley UD. P Stnly. Ball-bearing plant.

ANNITSFORD Nthmb
78 NZ 2674 6m NNE of Newcastle. Loc,
Longbenton UD. P Dudley.

ANNSCROFT Shrops
118 SJ 4507 4m SW of Shrewsbury. Loc,
Bayston Hill CP. P Shrsbry. Ch e.

ANSFORD Som
166 ST 6333 3m WSW of Bruton. CP, 494.
Wincanton RD. Ch e. Wells CC.

ANSLEY Warwicks
132 SP 2991 4m W of Nuneaton. CP, 2,462.
Atherstone RD. P Nntn. Ch e, c. Sch p, pe.
Meriden CC.

ANSLOW Staffs
120 SK 2125 2m NW of Burton-on-Trent.
CP, 503. Tutbury RD. Ch e. Sch p. Btn CC.
See also Anslw Gate.

ANSLOW GATE Staffs
120 SK 1924 3m WNW of Burton-on-Trent.
Loc, Anslw CP.

ANSTEY Herts
148 TL 4032 6m SSE of Royston. CP, 284.
Braughing RD. P Buntingford. Ch e, v.
Sch p. E Herts CC. Partly Nmn ch; Nmn
font portrays four mermen.

ANSTEY Leics
121 SK 5508 4m NW of Leicester. CP.
Barrow upon Soar RD. P LCSTR.
Ch e, c, m. Sch p, s. Melton CC.

ANSTON Yorks (W)
103 SK 5284 5m NW of Workshop. CP (N
and S Anstn), 3,487. Kiveton Pk RD.
P SHEFFIELD. Ch e, c, m2. Sch i, j, p.
Rother Valley CC.

ANSTY Dorset
178 ST 7603 8m W of Blandford. Hr A., Lit
A., Lr A., and A. Cross. Loc, Hilton CP.
Ch m.

ANSTY Sussex (E)
182 TQ 2923 3m W of Haywards Hth. Loc,
Cuckfield Rural CP. Cckfld RD. Mid-Sx CC
(E Grinstead).

ANSTY Warwicks
132 SP 3983 5m NE of Coventry. CP, 234.
Rugby RD. Ch e. Rgby CC.

ANSTY Wilts
167 ST 9526 6m ENE of Shaftesbury. CP,
144. Mere and Tisbury RD. Ch e.
Westbury CC.

ANTHILL COMMON Hants
180, 181 SU 6412 6m NW of Havant. Loc,
Denmead CP.

ANTHORN Cumb
75 NY 1958 3m WNW of Kirkbride. Loc,
Bowness CP. Wigton RD. P Carlisle. Penrith
and the Border CC.

ANTINGHAM Norfolk
126 TG 2532 2m NW of N Walsham. CP,
239. Erpingham RD. Ch e. N Nflk CC. In
churchyard, ruins of second ch.

ANTONY Cornwall
186/187 SX 3954 3m W of Torpoint. CP,
445. St Germans RD. P Tpnt. Ch e, m.
Sch pe. Bodmin CC. 1½m NE, A. Hse
(NT)*, early 18c Gibbs-style hse.

ANWICK Lincs (K)
113 TF 1150 4m NE of Sleaford. CP, 218.
E Kesteven RD. P Slfd. Ch e, m. Sch pe.
Grantham CC. Post office is 19c cottage
orné.

APETHORPE Northants
134 TL 0295 5m N of Oundle. CP,
276. Oundle and Thrapston RD. P PETER-
BOROUGH. Ch e. Sch pe. Wellingborough CC (Ptrbrgh). Old stone vllge. A.
Hall (now a sch), of all periods 15c–20c,
was seat of Mildmay family whose monmts
fill ch.

APLEY Lincs (L)
104/113 TF 1075 9m S of Mkt Rasen. CP,
105. Welton RD. Ch e. Gainsborough CC.

APPERKNOWLE Derbys
103,111 SK 3878 4m N of Chesterfield. Loc,
Unstone CP. P SHEFFIELD. Ch m. Sch i.

APPERLEY Glos
143 SO 8628 3m SW of Tewkesbury. Loc,
Deerhurst CP. P GLOUCESTER. Ch e, m.

APPERSETT Yorks (N)
90 SD 8590 1m NW of Hawes. Loc, Hws CP.

APPLEBY Lincs (L)
104 SE 9514 4m NE of Scunthorpe. CP,
731. Glanford Brigg RD. P Scnthpe.
Ch e, m. Sch p. Brgg and Scnthpe CC (Brgg).
Estate vllge.

APPLEBY Westm
83 NY 6820 12m ESE of Penrith. MB,
1,946. P. Westm CC. Small tn on R Eden
mostly blt of dark red stone. Handsome
main st parallel to main rd; ch at bottom
(Clifford monmts) and cstle (private) at top.

APPLEBY MAGNA Leics
120, 121 SK 3109 5m SSW of Ashby de la
Zouch. CP, 691. Ashby de la Zouch RD.
P Burton-on-Trent, Staffs. Ch e. Sch pe.
Loughborough CC. See also Appleby Parva.

APPLEBY PARVA Leics
120, 121 SK 3008 6m SSW of Ashby de la
Zouch. Loc, Appleby Magna CP. Grammar
sch* blt 1693-7 by E India merchant Sir
John Moore.

APPLEBY STREET Herts
160 TL 3304 2m NW of Cheshunt. Loc,
Chshnt UD.

APPLEDORE Devon
163 SS 4630 3m N of Bideford. Loc,
Northam UD. P Bdfd. Narrow streets.
Boat-building, yachting, fishing. 1m W,
Royal N Devon GC.

APPLEDORE Devon
164, 176 ST 0614 7m E of Tiverton. Loc,
Burlescombe CP. Ch v. Sch p.

APPLEDORE Kent
184 TQ 9529 6m NNE of Rye. CP, 667.
Tenterden RD. P Ashford. Ch e, m. Sch pe.
Ashfd CC. See also Appldre Hth. On Rother
Levels, beside old Royal Military Canal.
Once a seaport.

APPLEDORE HEATH Kent
184 TQ 9530 5m ESE of Tenterden. Loc,
Appldre CP. To N, Horne's Place, mdvl
farmhouse with 14c domestic chpl.

APPLEFORD Berks
158 SU 5293 2m N of Didcot. CP, 263.
Abingdon RD. P Abngdn. Ch e. Abngdn CC.

APPLESHAW Hants
168 SU 3048 4m NW of Andover. CP, 559.
Andvr RD. P Andvr. Ch e, m. Sch pe.
Winchester CC (Basingstoke).

APPLETON Berks
158 SP 4401 4m NW of Abingdon. CP
(Appltn w Eaton), 756. Abngdn RD.
P Abngdn. Ch e, v. Sch pe. Abngdn CC.
Partly 12c mnr hse is oldest in county.

APPLETON Ches
101 SJ 6383 3m SE of Warrington. CP,
4,636. Runcorn RD. P WRRNGTN.
Ch e, b, r. Sch pe. Rncn CC.

APPLETON-LE-MOORS Yorks (N)
86, 92 SE 7387 5m WNW of Pickering. CP,
194. Kirkbymoorside RD. P YORK.
Ch e, m. Sch p. Thirsk and Malton CC.

APPLETON-LE-STREET Yorks (N)
92 SE 7373 3m WNW of Malton.
CP(Appltn-le-Strt w Easthorpe), 114.
Mltn RD. P Mltn. Ch e. Thirsk and Mltn CC.

APPLETON ROEBUCK Yorks (W)
97 SE 5542 4m E of Tadcaster. CP, 345.
Tdcstr RD. P YORK. Ch e, m. Sch p.
Barkston Ash CC.

APPLETON WISKE Yorks (N)
91 NZ 3904 7m NNE of Northallerton.CP,
318. Nthlltn RD. P Nthlltn. Ch e, m2.
Sch p. Richmond CC.

APPLETREEWICK Yorks (W)
90 SE 0560 7m NE of Skipton. CP, 169.
Skptn RD. P Skptn. Ch e, m. Skptn CC.
Stone vllge above R Wharfe. 1m NE,
Percival Hall*, Elizn hse with hillside gdn; to
N of it, Troller's Ghyll, limestone gorge.

APPLEY Som
164 ST 0721 4m of Wellington. Loc,
Stawley CP.

APPLEY BRIDGE Lancs
100 SD 5209 4m NW of Wigan. Loc,
Wrightington CP. Wgn RD. P Wgn. Ch m.
Sch ie. Westhoughton CC.

APSE HEATH IOW
180 SZ 5683 2m NW of Shanklin. Loc,
Newchurch CP. P Sandown. Ch m.

APSLEY END Beds
147 TL 1233 4m NW of Hitchin. Loc,
Shillington CP.

APULDRAM Sussex (W)
181 SU 8403 2m SW of Chichester.
CP(Appledram), 199. Chchstr RD. Ch e.
Chchstr CC. Ch and a hse or two by Chchstr
harbour. To SE of ch, Rymans, small 15c
mnr hse.

ARBORFIELD Berks
169 SU 7567 4m W of Wokingham. CP
(Arbrfld and Newland), 2,999. Wknghm
RD. Ch e. Sch pe. Reading S CC (Wknghm).
The 'Aberleigh' of Mary Mitford's *Our
Village.*

ARBORFIELD CROSS Berks
169 SU 7667 3m WSW of Wokingham.Loc,
Abrfld and Newland CP. P Reading. Ch c.

ARCHDEACON NEWTON Co Durham
85 NZ 2517 3m NW of Darlington.CP, 65.
Dlngtn RD. Bishop Auckland CC
(Sedgefield).

ARCLID GREEN Ches
110 SJ 7861 2m ENE of Sandbach. Loc,
Arcld CP. Congleton RD. Ch m. Knutsford CC.

ARDELEY Herts
147 TL 3027 5m ENE of Stevenage. CP,
373. Braughing RD. P Stvnge. Ch e. Sch pe.
E Herts CC. See also Cromer, Wood End.

ARDENS GRAFTON Warwicks
144 SP 1154 5m W of Stratford. Loc,
Alcester RD, Strtfd-on-Avon RD. P Alcstr.
Ch v. Strtfd-on-Avn CC (Strtfd). An old
cider mill here with original machinery.

ARDINGLY Sussex (E)
182 TO 3429 3m N of Haywards Hth. CP,
1,300. Cuckfield RD. P Hwds Hth. Ch e, c.
Sch pe. Mid-Sx CC (E Grinstead). A.
College, a (Woodard) boys' boarding sch to
SW. 1m NNW, Wakehurst Place, Elizn hse
with gdns* administered by Royal Botanical
Gdns, Kew.

ARDINGTON Berks
158 SU 4388 2m E of Wantage. CP, 340.
Wntge RD. P Wntge. Ch e. Sch pe.
Abingdon CC. See also W Ginge. Ch
contains sculpture of 1830 by E.H. Baily,
sculptor of figure of Nelson in Trafalgar
Square, London.

ARDLEIGH Essex
149 TM 0529 5m NE of Colchester. CP,
1,860. Tendring RD. P Clchstr. Ch e, m.
Sch pe. Harwich CC. See also Crockleford
Hth. A. Reservoir to S.

ARDLEY Oxon
145 SP 5427 4m NW of Bicester.CP, 311.
Ploughley RD. P Bcstr. Ch e. Banbury CC
(Henley). Site of Nmn cstle; mound now
only rems.

ARDSLEY EAST Yorks (W)
96, 102 SE 3025 3m NW of Wakefield.Loc,
Morley MB.

ARELEY KINGS Worcs
130 SO 8070 1m SW of Stourport. Loc,
Stpt-on-Severn UD. P Stpt-on-Svn.

ARKENDALE Yorks (W)
91 SE 3860 4m NE of Knaresborough.CP,
123. Nidderdale RD. P Knsbrgh. Ch e.
Harrogate CC.

ARKESDEN Essex
148 TL 4834 4m SW of Saffron Walden.CP,
282. Sffrn Wldn RD. P Sffrn Wldn. Ch e, m.
Sffrn Wldn CC. Attractive vllge. Ch: 15c
brasses.

ARKHOLME Lancs
89 SD 5872 4m SSW of Kirkby Lonsdale. CP(Arkhlme-w-Cawood), 257. Lunesdale RD. P Carnforth. Ch e, m. Sch pe.
Lancaster CC.

ARKLEBY Cumb
82 NY 1439 7m ENE of Maryport. Loc,
Plumbland CP. P Carlisle.

ARKLEY London
160 TQ 2295 2m W of Barnet. Loc, Bnt LB.
P Bnt, Herts. Chipping Bnt BC (Bnt CC). A.
Mnr Gdns*, Rowley Lane; weedless gdns.

ARKSEY Yorks (W)
103 SE 5806 2m N of Doncaster.
UD(Bentley w Arksey), 22,888. P Dncstr.
Don Valley CC.

ARKWRIGHT TOWN Derbys
112 SK 4270 3m E of Chesterfield. Loc,
Sutton cum Duckmanton CP. Chstrfld RD.
P Chstrfld. Sch p. NE Derbys CC.

ARLECDON Cumb
82 NY 0419 5m E of Whitehaven.
CP(Arlcdn and Frizington), 4,094.
Ennerdale RD. P Frzngtn. Ch e. Sch p.
Whthvn CC. See also Asby, Rowrah. Mining
vllge.

ARLESEY Beds
147 TL 1936 4m N of Hitchin.CP, 3,282.
Biggleswade RD. P. Ch e, m2. Sch p.
Mid-Beds CC. See also Church End.

ARLESTON Shrops
118, 119 SJ 6610 just SE of Wellington.
Loc, Wllngtn UD; Wllgntn Rural CP,
Wllngtn RD. The Wrekin CC. Suburb of
Wllngtn. Early 17c black-and-white hse, A.
Hse.

ARLEY Ches
101 SJ 6780 5m WNW of Knutsford. Loc,
Bucklow RD, Runcorn RD. P Northwich.
Sch p. Kntsfd CC, Rncn CC. Gdns* of A.
Hall.

ARLEY Warwicks
131 SP 2890 5m W of Nuneaton.CP, 3,319.
Meriden RD. P Coventry. Ch e,.m, r.
Sch p, pe, s. Mrdn CC. Colliery distr; A.
Mine to SE.

ARLINGHAM Glos
143 SO 7010 9m WNW of Stroud.CP, 343.
Gloucester RD. P GLCSTR. Ch e, v. Sch pe.
Strd CC. On huge tidal loop of R Severn.

ARLINGTON Devon
163 SS 6140 6m NNE of Barnstaple. CP,
121. Bnstple RD. P Bnstple. Ch e.
N Dvn CC. Estate of A. Ct (NT)*, home
of Chichesters 1384−1949. Present hse early
19c; hse and gdns open.

ARLINGTON Glos
157 SP 1106 6m NE of Cirencester. Loc,
Bibury CP. Ch b. Part of Bbry vllge. A. Row
(NT), 17c Cotswold hses. A. Mill*, 17c−18c
Ctswld hse now museum with working
machinery.

ARLINGTON Sussex (E)
183 TQ 5407 3m WSW of Hailsham. CP,
532. Hlshm RD. Ch e. Sch p. Lewes CC
(Eastbourne).

ARMATHWAITE Cumb
83 NY 5046 9m SE of Carlisle. Loc,
Penrith RD. P Clsle. Ch e, m. Sch p. Pnrth
and the Border CC. Cstle: pele twr with Ggn
facade.

ARMINGHALL Norfolk
126 TG 2504 3m SSE of Norwich. Loc,
Bixley CP. Forehoe and Henstead RD. Ch e.
S Nflk CC (Central Nflk).

ARMITAGE Staffs
120 SK 0716 3m SE of Rugeley. CP(Armitge
w Handsacre), 2,302. Lichfield RD. P Rgly.
Ch e, c. Sch p. Lchfld and Tamworth CC.

ARMSCOTE Warwicks
144 SP 2444 7m SSE of Stratford. Loc,
Tredington CP. 17c Cotswold-style mnr hse.

ARMSTON Northants
134 TL 0685 2m SE of Oundle. Loc,
Polebrook CP.

ARMTHORPE Yorks (W)
103 SE 6204 3m ENE of Doncaster. CP,
7,631. Dncstr RD. P Dncstr. Ch e, m, r, v.
Sch i, ie, j, p, s. Don Valley CC.

ARNCLIFFE Yorks (W)
90 SD 9371 9m NE of Settle. CP, 78.
Sttle RD. P Skipton. Ch e. Sch pe.
Skptn CC. Several becks here join R Skirfare.
Celtic field systems clearly evident.

ARNE Dorset
179 SY 9788 3m E of Wareham. CP, 1,066.
Wrhm and Purbeck RD. Ch e. S Dst CC. See
also Ridge, Stoborough, Stbrgh Grn.

ARNESBY Leics
132, 133 SP 6192 8m WNW of Mkt
Harborough. CP, 278. Lutterworth RD. P
LEICESTER. Ch e, b. Sch pe. Blaby CC
(Hbrgh).

ARNOLD Notts
112 SK 5845 3m NNE of Nottingham. UD,
33,254. P NTTNGHM. Carlton CC. Mainly
rsdntl suburb of Nttnghm.

ARNOLD Yorks (E)
99 TA 1241 6m E of Beverley. Loc,
Riston CP. Holderness RD. Bridlington CC.

ARNSIDE Westm
89 SD 4578 6m NNW of Carnforth. CP,
1,561. S Westm RD. P Cnfth, Lancs.
Ch e, m, r. Sch pe. Westm CC. Small resort
just N of Morecambe Bay. Rems of pele
twrs 1m S and 1m E.

ARRAD FOOT Lancs
88, 89 SD 3080. 2m NE of Ulverston. Loc,

Egton w Newland CP. N Lonsdale RD.
Morecambe and Lnsdle CC.

ARRAM Yorks (E)
99 TA 0344 3m N of Beverley. Loc,
Leconfield CP.

ARRATHORNE Yorks (N)
91 SE 2093 5m NW of Bedale. CP, 77.
Leyburn RD. Richmond CC.

ARRETON IOW
180 SZ 5486 3m SE of Newport. Loc, S
Arrtn CP. Isle of Wight RD and CC. P Npt.
Ch e, m. Sch pe. A. Mnr*, 17c hse, toy and
doll museum.

ARRINGTON Cambs
147 TL 3250 6m NNW of Royston. CP, 360.
S Cambs RD. P Rstn, Herts. Ch e.
Cambs CC. Imposing entrance gates to
Wimpole Hall, enormous 17c—18c red brick
hse in pk to E; more impressive approach
from S along two-mile avenue of elms.

ARROW Warwicks
131 SP 0856 just SW of Alcester. CP, 160.
Alcstr RD. Ch e. Stratford-on-Avon CC
(Strtfd). To E, Ragley Hall*, 17c home of
the Seymours; gdns, pk, lake.

ARTHINGTON Yorks (W)
96 SE 2644 4m E of Otley. CP, 450.
Wharfedale RD. P Otley. Ch e, m. Sch pe.
Ripon CC. To W, well known long rly
tunnel, and viaduct over R Wharfe.

ARTHINGWORTH Northants
133 SP 7581 4m SSE of Mkt Harborough.
CP, 189. Brixworth RD. P Mkt Hbrgh,
Leics. Ch e. Daventry CC (Kettering).

ARUNDEL Sussex (W)
181, 182 TQ 0107 10m E of Chichester.
MB, 2,382. P. Arndl CC (Arndl and
Shoreham). Well sited above R Arun. Cstle*,
orig Nmn but more of 19c; grnds open but
cars not allowed. 19c RC ch in prominent
position gives tn foreign appearance.

ASBY Cumb
82 NY 0620 6m ENE of Whitehaven. Loc,
Arlecdon and Frizington CP.

ASBY, GREAT Westm
83 NY 6813 5m S of Appleby. See Gt Asby.

ASCOT Berks
169 SU 9268 6m SSW of Windsor. Loc,
Sunninghill CP. P. Ch e2, b. Famous
racecourse.

ASCOTT-UNDER-WYCHWOOD Oxon
145 SP 3018 4m W of Charlbury. CP, 404.
Chipping Norton RD. P OXFORD. Ch e, b.
Sch pe. Banbury CC. Nmn ch in stone vllge.

ASENBY Yorks (N)
91 SE 3975 5m SSW of Thirsk. CP, 161.
Wath RD. Thsk and Malton CC.

ASFORDBY Leics
122 SK 7019 3m W of Melton Mowbray. CP,
2,582. Mltn and Belvoir RD. P Mltn Mbry.
Ch e, m2. Sch pe. Mltn CC.

ASFORDBY HILL Leics
122 SK 7219 2m W of Melton Mowbray.
Loc, Asfdby CP. P Mltn Mbry. Ch m. Sch p.
Ironworks.

ASGARBY Lincs (K)
113 TF 1145 3m E of Sleaford. CP(Asgby
and Howell), 114. E Kesteven RD. Ch e.
Grantham CC.

ASGARBY Lincs (L)
114 TF 3366 5m ESE of Horncastle. CP, 22.
Hncstle RD. Ch e. Hncstle CC.

ASH Kent
171 TQ 6064 7m SSW of Gravesend. Loc,
Ash-cum-Ridley CP. Dartford RD.
P Sevenoaks. Ch e, b. Sch pe. Svnks CC
(Dtfd).

ASH Kent
173 TR 2858 3m W of Sandwich. CP,
2,341. Eastry RD. P Canterbury. Ch e, c, m.
Sch pe. Dover and Deal CC (Dvr). See also
Hoaden. 2½m NE, rems of Richborough
Cstle* (Roman). 13c–15c ch: brasses.

ASH Som
177 ST 4720 3m WSW of Ilchester. CP, 395.
Yeovil RD. P Martock. Ch e. Sch pe.
Yvl CC.

ASH Surrey
169 SU 8950 1m E of Aldershot. CP,
10,794. Guildford RD. P Aldrsht, Hants.
Ch e, m, r2. Sch p, pe, s. Woking CC. See
also Ash Vale.

ASHAMPSTEAD Berks
158 SU 5676 5m W of Pangbourne. CP, 331.
Bradfield RD. P Reading. Ch e, b, m.
Sch pe. Newbury CC. Ch has 13c
wall-paintings.

ASHBOCKING Suffolk (E)
150 TM 1754 6m N of Ipswich. CP, 255.
Gipping RD. P Ipswch. Ch e. Eye CC.
Scattered hses among flat fields. Aircraft
noise. View across fields to weird Swilland
ch.

ASHBOURNE Derbys
111 SK1746 13m NW of Derby. UD, 5,577
P. W Derbys CC. Mkt tn and centre for
Dales. Large spired ch mainly 13c–14c;
'Penelope' monmt. Former grammar sch
16c.

ASHBRITTLE Som
164 ST 0521 5m W of Wellington. CP,
185. Wllngton RD. P Wllngton. Ch e.
Taunton CC.

ASHBURNHAM Sussex (E)
183 TQ 6814 4m W of Battle. CP, 312.
Bttle RD. P Bttle. Ch e, c2. Rye CC.
Former centre of Sussex iron industry. Ch
isolated. A. Place largely demolished; rems
being adapted by present owners.

ASHBURTON Devon
187,188 SX 7569 7m W of Newton Abbot.
UD, 3,495. P Ntn Abbt. Totnes CC. Mkt tn
since 12c or earlier; former stannary tn. Ch
has twr with stair turret.

ASHBURY Berks
157 SU 2685 7m E of Swindon. CP, 624.
Faringdon RD. P Swndn, Wilts. Ch e, m, v.
Sch pe. Abingdon CC. See also Idstone.
Downland vllge largely made of chalk, incl
ch and 15c mnr hse. 1m W, Wayland's
Smithy (A.M.) prehistoric barrow. 3m SE,
Ashdown Hse (NT)*, 17c.

ASHBURY Devon
175 SX 5097 5m WNW of Okehampton. CP,
51. Okhmptn RD. Ch e. W Dvn CC
(Torrington).

ASHBY BY PARTNEY Lincs (L)
114 TF 4266 6m SSW of Alford. CP, 64.
Spilsby RD. P(Ashby), Splsby. Ch e, m.
Horncastle CC.

ASHBY CUM FENBY Lincs (L)
105 TA 2500 5m S of Grimsby. CP, 125.
Grmsby RD. P Grmsby. Ch e. Louth CC.

ASHBY DE LA LAUNDE Lincs (K)
113 TF 0555 6m N of Sleaford. CP(Ashby de la Lnde and Bloxholm), 609. E Kesteven RD. Ch e. Sch pe. Grantham CC. 1m N, radio stn.

ASHBY DE LA ZOUCH Leics
120,121 SK 3516 8m SE of Burton-on-Trent. UD, 8,291. P. Loughborough CC. See also Blackfordby. Old mkt and spa tn. Rems of cstle (A.M.). Fine 15c ch has monmts, incl one to Countess of Huntingdon, founder of 18c nonconformist 'Connexion'.

ASHBY FOLVILLE Leics
122 SK 7012 5m SW of Melton Mowbray. Loc, Gaddesby CP. Ch e. To NE, A. Pastures, famous fox-cover.

ASHBY MAGNA Leics
132, 133 SP 5690 4m NNE of Lutterworth. CP, 234. Lttrwth RD. P Rugby, Warwickshire. Ch e. Blaby CC (Harborough).

ASHBY PARVA Leics
132 SP 5288 3m NNW of Lutterworth.CP, 114. Lttrwth RD. P Rugby, Warwickshire. Ch e. Blaby CC (Harborough).

ASHBY PUERORUM Lincs (L)
114 TF 3271 4m ENE of Horncastle. Loc, Somersby CP. P Hncstle. Ch e.

ASHBY ST LEDGERS Northants
132, 133 SP 5768 4m N of Daventry.CP, 142. Dvntry RD. P Rugby, Warwickshire. Ch e. Dvntry CC (S Nthnts). Mnr hse was seat of Catesby family; Gunpowder Plot of 1605 allegedly planned in the timbered gatehouse. Alterations and gdns by Lutyens in 1930s.

ASHBY ST MARY Norfolk
126 TG 3202 7m SE of Norwich. CP, 172. Loddon RD. Ch e. S Nflk CC.

ASHCHURCH Glos
143, 144 SO 9233 2m E of Tewkesbury. CP, 2,049. Cheltenham RD. Ch e, v. Sch p2. Cirencester and Tksbry CC. See also Aston Cross, Fiddington.

ASHCOMBE Devon
176, 188 SX 9179 6m NE of Newton Abbot. CP, 126. St Thomas RD. Ch e. Tiverton CC.

ASHCOTT Som
165 ST 4337 4m WSW of Glastonbury. CP, 942. Bridgwater RD. P Brdgwtr. Ch e, m, v. Sch p. Brdgwtr CC. See also Pedwell.

ASHDON Essex
148 TL 5842 4m NE of Saffron Walden. CP, 686. Sffrn Wldn RD. P Sffrn Wldn. Ch e, b. Sch p. Sffrn Wldn CC. See also Ch End. Rose and Crown Inn has 17c wall-paintings.

ASHELDHAM Essex
162 TL 9701 8m ESE of Maldon. CP, 180. Mldn RD. Ch e. Mldn CC. 14c ch. To W, rems of prehistoric camp.

ASHEN Essex
148, 149 TL 7442 2m SW of Clare. CP, 160. Halstead RD. Ch e. Saffron Walden CC. Ch largely 14c, with Tdr turrets.

ASHENDON Bucks
146, 159 SP 7014 5m N of Thame. CP, 204. Aylesbury RD. P Aylesbury. Ch e. Aylesbury CC.

ASHFIELD Suffolk (E)
137 TM 2162 5m W of Framlingham. CP (Ashfld cum Thorpe), 172. Gipping RD. P Stowmarket. Ch e. Sch pe. Eye CC.

ASHFIELD, GREAT Suffolk (W)
136 TM 0068 6m NNW of Stowmarket. See Gt Ashfld.

ASHFIELD GREEN Suffolk (E)
137 TM 2673 7m N of Framlingham. Loc, Stradbroke CP.

ASHFORD Derbys
111 SK 1969 2m NW of Bakewell. CP (Ashfd in the Water), 709. Bkwll RD. P(Ashfd in the Wtr), Bkwll. Ch e, m. W Derbys CC. Sheepwash Br, old packhorse br with sheepfold. Well-dressing on Trinity Sunday.

ASHFORD Devon
163 SS 5335 2m NW of Barnstaple. CP, 192. Bnstple RD. P Bnstple. Ch e, v. N Dvn CC.

ASHFORD Kent
172, 184 TR 0042 13m SW of Canterbury. UD, 35,560. P Ashfd CC. See also Kennington, Willesborough. Mkt, indstrl, and dormitory tn. On NW outskirts. Jcbn Godington Pk*, with formal 18c gdns.

ASHFORD Surrey
160, 170 TQ 0671 2m E of Staines. Loc,
Stns UD. P(Ashfd, Middx).

ASHFORD BOWDLER Shrops
129 SO 5170 3m S of Ludlow. CP, 60.
Ldlw RD. Ch e. Ldlw CC.

ASHFORD CARBONEL Shrops
129 SO 5270 3m S of Ludlow. CP, 223.
Ldlw RD. P Ldlw. Ch e, m. Sch pe.
Ldlw CC.

ASHFORD HILL Hants
168 SU 5561 6m ESE of Newbury. Loc,
Kingsclere CP. P Nbry, Berks. Ch m. Sch p.

ASHILL Devon
164, 176 ST 0811 7m SW of Wellington. Loc,
Uffculme CP. P Cullompton. Ch b.

ASHILL Norfolk
125 TF 8804 3m NW of Watton. CP,
498. Swaffham RD. P Thetford. Ch e, m.
Sch pe. SW Nflk CC.

ASHILL Som
177 ST 3217 3m NW of Ilminster. CP,
405. Chard RD. P Ilmnstr. Ch e. Sch p.
Yeovil CC. See also Windmill Hill.

ASHINGDON Essex
162 TQ 8693 5m N of Southend. CP,
2,220. Rochford RD. P Rchfd. Ch e, v.
Sch p. Maldon CC (SE Essex). See also
S Fambridge. Site of Canute's victory over
Edmund Ironside, 1016.

ASHINGTON Nthmb
78 NZ 2787 5m E of Morpeth. UD, 25,645.
P. Mpth CC. See also Bothal, Hirst,
Woodhorn. Mining tn.

ASHINGTON Som
166, 177 ST 5621 3m ESE of Ilchester.
Loc, Chilton Cantelo CP. Ch e.

ASHINGTON Sussex (W)
182 TQ 1316 8m N of Worthing. CP, 1,160.
Chanctonbury RD. P Pulborough. Ch e, m.
Sch p. Shoreham CC (Arundel and Shrhm).

ASHLEWORTH Glos
143 SO 8125 5m N of Gloucester. CP, 323.
Glcstr RD. P GLCSTR. Ch e. Sch pe.
W Glos CC. 15c tithe barn (NT)*, 120ft
long.

ASHLEY Cambs
135 TL 6961 4m ESE of Newmarket. CP,
465. Nmkt RD. P Nmkt, Suffolk. Ch e, m.
Sch p. Cambs CC.

ASHLEY Ches
101 SJ 7784 2m S of Altrincham. CP, 421.
Bucklow RD. P Altrnchm. Ch e. Sch pe.
Kntsfd CC.

ASHLEY Devon
163, 175 SS 6411 10m SSW of S Molton. Loc,
Winkleigh CP.

ASHLEY Glos
157 ST 9394 3m ENE of Tetbury. CP, 117.
Ttbry RD. Ch e. Stroud CC. See also
Culkerton.

ASHLEY Hants
168 SU 3831 6m NNE of Romsey. CP, 74.
Rmsy and Stockbridge RD. Ch e. Sch p.
Winchester CC.

ASHLEY Northants
133 SP 7990 5m ENE of Mkt Harborough.
CP, 195. Kettering RD. P Mkt Hbrgh, Leics.
Ch e. Kttrng CC. Vllge and ch largely rebuilt
mid-19c by Sir Giles Gilbert Scott.

ASHLEY Staffs
110, 119 SJ 7636 6m ENE of Mkt Drayton
CP, 1,237. Newcastle-under-Lyme RD.
P Mkt Drtn, Salop. Ch e, c, m, r. Sch pe, s.
N-u-L BC. See also Hookgate.

ASHLEY GREEN Bucks
159, 160 SP 9705 2m SW of Berkhamsted.
CP, 897. Amersham RD. P Chesham. Ch e.
Sch pe. Chshm and Amrshm CC
(Aylesbury). See also Whelpeyhill.

ASHLEY HEATH Hants
179 SU 1104 2m W of Ringwood. Loc, St
Leonards and St Ives CP. P Rngwd.

ASH MAGNA Shrops
118 SJ 5739 2m ESE of Whitchurch. Loc,
Whtchch Rural CP. N Shrops RD. Ch e.
Oswestry CC.

ASHMANHAUGH Norfolk
126 TG 3121 3m NNE of Wroxham. CP, 151.
Smallburgh RD. Ch e. N Nflk CC.

ASHMANSWORTH Hants
168 SU 4157 7m SSW of Newbury. CP, 208.
Kingsclere and Whitchurch RD. P Nbry,
Berks. Ch e. Basingstoke CC. See also Crux
Easton. Ch has 12c and 15c wall-paintings.

ASHMANSWORTHY Devon
174 SS 3318 9m N of Holsworthy. Loc,
Woolfardisworthy CP.

ASH MILL Devon
163 SS 7823 5m ESE of S Molton. Loc,
S Mltn RD. Ch m. N Dvn CC.

ASHMORE Dorset
178, 179 ST 9117 5m SE of Shaftesbury.
CP, 156. Shftsbry RD. P Salisbury, Wilts.
Ch e, m. Sch p. N Dst CC.

ASHORNE Warwicks
132 SP 3057 5m S of Leamington. Loc,
Newbold Pacey CP. P WARWICK. Sch pe.

ASHOVER Derbys
111 SK 3463 6m SSW of Chesterfield. CP,
1,839. Chstrfld RD. P Chstrfld. Ch e, m4, v.
Sch p. NE Derbys CC. See also Alton,
Milltown. Ch: rare Nmn lead font. Mdvl
Crispin Inn.

ASHOW Warwicks
132 SP 3170 2m SE of Kenilworth. CP, 152.
Warwick RD. P Knlwth. Ch e. Wrwck and
Leamington CC.

ASH PARVA Shrops
118 SJ 5739 2m ESE of Whitchurch. Loc,
Whtchch Rural CP. N Shrops RD.
Oswest.y CC.

ASHPERTON Herefs
142, 143 SO 6441 5m NW of Ledbury. CP,
285. Ldbry RD. Ch e. Sch p. Leominster
CC.

ASHPRINGTON Devon
188 SX 8157 2m SSE of Totnes. CP, 327.
Ttns RD. P Ttns. Ch e. Ttns CC. See also
Bow, Tuckenhay. Views of Dart estuary. 1m
NE, Sharpham Hse, late 18c; grnds laid out
by Capability Brown.

ASH PRIORS Som
164 ST 1529 5m NW of Taunton. CP, 96.
Tntn RD. Ch e. Tntn CC.

ASHREIGNEY Devon
163, 175 SS 6213 9m ESE of Torrington. CP,
421. Trrngtn RD. P Chulmleigh. Ch e, m, v.
Sch pe. W Dvn CC (Trrngtn). See also
Riddlecombe.

ASHTEAD Surrey
170 TQ 1858 2m NE of Leatherhead. Loc,
Lthrhd UD. P.

ASH THOMAS Devon
164, 176 ST 0010 3m ESE of Tiverton. Loc,
Halberton CP.

ASHTON Ches
109 SJ 5069 7m ENE of Chester. CP, 474.
Tarvin RD. P CHSTR. Ch e, m. Sch p.
Northwich CC.

ASHTON Cornwall
189 SW 6028 4m W of Helston. Loc, Breage
CP. P Helston. Ch m.

ASHTON Herefs
129 SP 5164 4m NNE of Leominster.
CP(Eye, Moreton and Ashtn), 192. Lmnstr
and Wigmore RD. Lmnstr CC.

ASHTON Northants
134 TL 0588 1m E of Oundle. CP, 142.
Oundle and Thrapston RD. Ch e.
Wellingborough CC (Peterborough). Largely
rebuilt early 20c.

ASHTON Northants
146 SP 7649 5m E of Towcester. CP, 398.
Northampton RD. P NTHMPTN. Ch e, m.
Sch pe. Daventry CC (S Nthnts).

ASHTON COMMON Wilts
166, 167 ST 8958 3m E of Trowbridge. Loc,
Steeple Ashton CP.

ASHTON-IN-MAKERFIELD Lancs
100 SJ 5799 4m S of Wigan. UD, 26,271. P.
Wgn. Ince CC. See also Bryn, Brn Gates,
Garswood, Leyland Grn, N Ashtn.
Coal-mining, engineering (locks, hinges).

ASHTON KEYNES Wilts
157 SU 0494 5m SSE of Cirencester. CP,
944. Cricklade and Wootton Bassett RD. P
Swindon. Ch e, c. Sch pe. Chippenham CC.
Vllge threaded by streams, tributaries of
R Thames.

ASHTON UNDER HILL Worcs
143, 144 SO 9938 4m SSW of Evesham. CP,
427. Eveshm RD. P Eveshm. Ch e, v.
Sch p, s. S Worcs CC.

ASHTON-UNDER-LYNE Lancs
101 SJ 9399 6m E of Manchester. MB,
48,865. P. Ashtn-undr-Lne BC. See also
Hurst. Textiles, engineering, rubber,
tobacco. Large mdvl parish ch.

ASHTON UPON MERSEY Ches
101 SJ 7792 5m SW of Manchester.Loc,
Sale MB. P Sle.

ASHURST Hants
180 SU 3310 3m NE of Lyndhurst. Loc,
Eling CP. P SOUTHAMPTON. Sch i, j.

ASHURST Kent
171 TQ 5038 5m W of Tunbridge Wells. Loc,
Speldhurst CP. P Tnbrdge Wlls. Ch e.

ASHURST Sussex (W)
182 TQ 1716 3m N of Steyning. CP, 297.
Chanctonbury RD. P Stnng. Ch e. Sch pe.
Shoreham CC (Arundel and Shrhm). View
to Downs.

ASHURSTWOOD Sussex (E)
171, 183 TQ 4236 2m SE of E Grinstead. Loc
E Grnstd UD. P: E Grnstd.

ASH VALE Surrey
169 SU 8952 2m NE of Aldershot.Loc, Ash
CP. P Aldrsht, Hants. Ch e, m. Sch p.

ASHWATER Devon
174 SX 3895 6m SSE of Holsworthy. CP,
569. Hlswthy RD. P Beaworthy. Ch e, m2.
Sch p. W Dvn CC (Tavistock).Ch: Nmn font;
unusual pillars to S aisle; royal arms of
Charles I; effigy.

ASHWELL Herts
147 TL 2639 4m NNE of Baldock. CP,
1,336. Hitchin RD. P Bldck. Ch e, b, m, v.
Sch p. Htchn CC. Large vllge well known for
its many good hses and EE and later ch with
impressive twr. Vllge museum.

ASHWELL Rutland
122 SK 8613 3m N of Oakham. CP, 306.
Oakhm RD. P Oakhm. Ch e, m. Rtlnd and
Stamford CC. 1¼m S, Cottesmore Hunt
Kennels. Also HM prison.

ASHWELLTHORPE Norfolk
136 TM 1497 3m SE of Wymondham.
CP, 494. Depwade RD. P NORWICH, NOR
89W. Ch e. S Nflk CC.

ASHWICK Som
166 ST 6348 3m NNE of Shepton Mallet.
CP, 929. Shptn Mllt RD. Ch e.
Shptn Mllt CC. See also Oakhill.

ASHWICKEN Norfolk
124 TF 7019 5m E of King's Lynn. Loc,
Leziate CP. Freebridge Lynn RD. Ch e.
Sch pe. NW Nflk CC (K's Lnn).

ASKAM IN FURNESS Lancs
88 SD 2177 5m N of Barrow. Loc,
Dalton-in-Fnss UD. P.

ASKERN Yorks (W)
103 SE 5613 7m N of Doncaster.CP, 5,710.
Dncstr RD. P Dncstr. Ch e, b, m2, r, v2.
Sch i, j, p, s. Don Valley CC.

ASKERSWELL Dorset
177 SY 5292 4m E of Bridport.CP, 137.
Brdpt RD. P Dorchester. Ch e. W Dst CC.

ASKETT Bucks
159 SP 8105 1m N of Princes Risborough.
Loc, Prncs Rsbrgh CP. Ch b.

ASKHAM Notts
112 SK 7474 5m SSE of Retford. CP, 171.
E Rtfd RD. Ch e, m. Bassetlaw CC.

ASKHAM Westm
83 NY 5123 4m S of Penrith. CP, 363.
N Westm RD. P Pnrth, Cumberland. Ch e.
Sch pe. Westm CC. See also Helton. To E,
Lowther Cstle − see Lowther.

ASKHAM BRYAN Yorks (W)
97 SE 5548 4m WSW of York.CP, 432.
Tadcaster RD. P YK.Ch e. Barkston Ash CC.

ASKHAM RICHARD Yorks (W)
97 SE 5347 5m WSW of York.CP, 227.
Tadcaster RD. P YK. Ch e, m. Sch pe.
Barkston Ash CC.

ASKRIGG Yorks (N)
90 SD 9491 5m E of Hawes. CP, 370.
Aysgarth RD. P Leyburn. Ch e, m2.
Sch pe, s2. Richmond CC. See also
Newbiggin, Askrigg. Stone vllge on moor's
edge above R Ure.

ASKWITH Yorks (W)
96 SE 1648 3m NW of Otley. CP, 177.
Wharfedale RD. P Otley. Ch m. Sch p.
Ripon CC. Whfdle vllge of stone and
timbered cottages; moors to N.

ASLACKBY Lincs (K)
113, 123 TF 0830 7m N of Bourne.
CP (Aslckby and Laughton), 221.
S Kesteven RD. P Sleaford. Ch e, m.
Rutland and Stamford CC.

ASLACTON Norfolk
137 TM 1591 7m NNE of Diss. CP, 210.
Depwade RD. Ch e. Sch p. S Nflk CC.

ASLOCKTON Notts
112,122 SK 7440 11m E of Nottingham. CP,
398. Bingham RD. P NTTNGHM. Ch e.
Sch pe. Rushcliffe CC (Carlton). Bthplce of
Thomas Cranmer, 1489.

ASPATRIA Cumb
82 NY 1441 7m ENE of Maryport. CP,
2,924. Wigton RD. P Carlisle. Ch e, m2.
Sch i, j, s. Penrith and the Border CC.

ASPENDEN Herts
148 TL 3528 8m S of Royston. CP, 207.
Braughing RD. Ch e. E Herts CC.

ASPLEY GUISE Beds
146 SP 9436 4m ENE of Bletchley.
CP, 1,921. Ampthill RD. P Bltchly, Bucks.
Ch e, m, r, v. Sch p, s. Mid-Beds CC. Pines
and heaths to S, M1 to N. Aspley Hse, late
17c, perhaps designed by Wren.

ASPLEY HEATH Beds
146 SP 9235 3m E of Bletchley. CP, 490.
Ampthill RD. Sch p. Mid-Beds CC.

ASPULL Lancs
101 SD 6108 3m NE of Wigan. UD, 7,510.
P(Aspll Moor), Wgn. Westhoughton CC.
Large grn at centre.

ASSELBY Yorks (E)
97, 98 SE 7128 3m NNW of Goole. CP, 207.
Howden RD. P Gle. Ch m. Hdn CC. See also
Knedlington.

ASSINGTON Suffolk (W)
149 TL 9338 4m SE of Sudbury. CP, 406.
Melford RD. P Colchester, Essex. Ch e.
Sch p. Sdbry and Woodbridge CC. The hall,
home of Gurdons from 16c, burnt down in
1957.

ASTBURY Ches
110 SJ 8461 1m SW of Congleton. Loc,
Newbold Astbury CP. Cngltn RD. P Cngltn.
Ch e. Sch pe. Knutsford CC. The 14c–15c
ch has two twrs.

ASTCOTE Northants
145, 146 SP 6753 3m NNW of Towcester.
Loc, Pattishall CP. Ch m.

ASTERLEIGH Oxon
145 SP 4022 4m NW of Woodstock.

CP(Kiddington w Astrlgh), 159. Chipping
Norton RD. Banbury CC.

ASTERLEY Shrops
118 SJ 3707 8m WSW of Shrewsbury. Loc,
Pontesbury CP. Ch m.

ASTERTON Shrops
129 SO 3991 4m SW of Ch Stretton. Loc,
Myndtown CP.

ASTHALL Oxon
145 SP 2811 2m ESE of Burford.
CP(Asthal), 242. Witney RD. Ch e.
Mid-Oxon CC (Banbury). See also Asthll
Leigh. Nmn to Perp ch. Elizn mnr hse,
beside R Windrush.

ASTHALL LEIGH Oxon
145 SP 3012 4m WNW of Witney. Loc,
Asthal CP. Ch e.

ASTLEY Shrops
118 SJ 5218 5m NNE of Shrewsbury. CP.
Atcham RD. Ch e. Shrsbry CC.

ASTLEY Warwicks
132 SP 3189 4m WSW of Nuneaton.
CP, 210. Meriden RD. Ch e. Sch pe.
Mrdn CC. A. Cstle, 13c–17c, belonged to
Lady Jane Grey's family. To E, Arbury*,
part Elizn, part 18c Gothic, in pk with lake;
bthplce of George Eliot.

ASTLEY Worcs
130 SO 7867 3m SW of Stourport. CP, 806.
Martley RD. P Stpt-on-Severn. Ch e. Sch pe.
Kidderminster CC. See also Dunley. A. Hall
was home of Baldwin, prime minister in
1920s and 30s.

ASTLEY ABBOTTS Shrops
130 SO 7096 2m NNW of Bridgnorth.
CP, 387. Brdgnth RD. Ch e. Ludlow CC. See
also Nordley.

ASTLEY CROSS Worcs
130 SO 8069 1m S of Stourport. Loc,
Stpt UD, Martley RD. Kidderminster CC.

ASTLEY GREEN Lancs
101 SJ 7099 6m S of Bolton. Loc, Tyldesley
UD.

ASTON Berks
159 SU 7884 2m NE of Henley. Loc,
Remenham CP. P Hnly-on-Thames, Oxon.

ASTON Ches
100, 109 SJ 5578 4m SE of Runcorn.CP.
Rncn RD. Ch e. Sch p. Rncn CC.

ASTON Ches
110 SJ 6146 4m SW of Nantwich. Loc,
Newhall CP. P Nntwch. Ch m.

ASTON Derbys
111 SK 1883 10 NNW of Bakewell.CP, 76.
Chapel en le Frith RD. High Peak CC.

ASTON Herefs
129 SO 4671 4m WSW of Ludlow. CP(Pipe
Astn), 28. Leominster and Wigmore RD.
Ch e. Lmnstr CC.

ASTON Herts
147 TL 2722 3m SE of Stevenage. CP, 578.
Hertford RD. P Stvnge. Ch e. Sch pe. Htfd
and Stvnge CC (Htfd). See also Astn End.
To S, A. Bury*, 16c mnr hse; large gdns.

ASTON Oxon
158 SP 3403 4m S of Witney. CP(Astn
Bampton and Shifford), 646. Wtny RD. P
OXFORD. Ch e. Sch pe. Mid-Oxon CC
(Banbury). See also Chimney, Cote.

ASTON Shrops
118 SJ 5328 1m E of Wem.Loc, Wm Rural
CP. N Shrops RD. Oswestry CC.

ASTON Shrops
118, 119 SJ 6109 3m WSW of Wellington.
Loc, Lit Wenlock CP. The Wrekin CC.

ASTON Shrops
130 SO 8093 6m E of Bridgnorth. Loc,
Claverley CP.

ASTON Staffs
110,119 SJ 7541 7m WSW of
Newcastle-under-Lyme.Loc, Maer CP. P Mkt
Drayton, Salop. Sch p.

ASTON Staffs
110, 119 SJ 9131 2m SSE of Stone. Loc,
Stne Rural CP. Stne RD. P Stne. Ch e, r.
Sch pe. Stafford and Stne CC.

ASTON Yorks (W)
103 SK 4685 5m SSE of Rotherham.
CP(Astn cum Aughton). Rthrhm RD.
P Sheffield. Ch e, m2. Sch p2. Rother Valley
CC. See also Swallownest.

ASTON ABBOTTS Bucks
146 SP 8420 4m NNE of Aylesbury. CP,

270. Wing RD. P Aylesbury. Ch e, m.
Sch pe. Buckingham CC.

ASTON BLANK Glos
144 SP 1219 3m NNE of Northleach.CP,
250. Nthlch RD. P(Cold Astn), Cheltenham.
Ch b. Sch pe. Cirencester and Tewkesbury
CC. Noble sycamore on grn.

ASTON BOTTERELL Shrops
129, 130 SO 6384 8m SW of Bridgnorth.CP,
92. Brdgnth RD. Ch e. Ludlow CC.

ASTON CANTLOW Warwicks
131 SP 1359 5m NW of Stratford.CP, 1,231.
Alcester RD. P Solihull. Ch e.
Strtfd-on-Avon CC (Strtfd). See also Lit
Alne, Wilmcote. Former guildhall is Tdr.
Shakespeare's parents reputedly married in
the ch.

ASTON CLINTON Bucks
146, 159, SP 8712 4m ESE of Aylesbury.
CP, 2,393. Aylesbury RD. P Aylesbury.
Ch e, b. Sch p. Aylesbury CC.

ASTON CREWS Herefs
142, 143 SO 6723 5m E of Ross-on-Wye.
Loc, Rss and Whitchurch RD. Hereford CC.

ASTON CROSS Glos
143, 144 SO 9433 3m E of Tewkesbury.
Loc, Ashchurch CP. P Tksbry. Ch m.

ASTON END Herts
147 TL 2624 3m SE of Stevenage.Loc, Astn
CP.

ASTON EYRE Shrops
129, 130 SO 6594 4m W of Bridgnorth. CP,
71. Brdgnth RD. Ch e. Ludlow CC. Ch:
tympanum over S door has remarkable Nmn
carving depicting Christ's Entry into
Jerusalem.

ASTON FIELDS Worcs
130, 131 SO 9669 1m S of Bromsgrove.
Loc, Brmsgrve UD.

ASTON FLAMVILLE
132 SP 4692 2m ESE of Hinckley. CP, 137.
Blaby RD. Ch e. Blby CC (Harborough).

ASTON INGHAM Herefs
143 SO 6823 5m E of Ross-on-Wye.
CP, 529. Rss and Whitchurch RD. Ch e.
Hereford CC.

ASTON JUXTA MONDRUM Ches
110 SJ 6556 3m N of Nantwich. CP, 140.
Nntwch RD. Ch m. Sch pe. Nntwch CC.

ASTON LE WALLS Northants
145 SP 4950 7m NNE of Banbury. CP, 180.
Brackley RD. P Rugby, Warwickshire.
Ch e, r. Sch pr. Daventry CC (S Nthnts).

ASTON MAGNA Glos
144 SP 1935 2m N of Moreton-in-Marsh.
Loc, Blockley CP. P Mtn-in-Msh. Ch e, b. Lr
part of mdvl cross on grn.

ASTON ON CLUN Shrops
129 SO 3981 3m W of Craven Arms. Loc,
Hopesay CP. P Crvn Arms. Ch b. Stone hmlt
with two round hses and an inn called The
Kangaroo.

ASTON PIGOTT Shrops
118 SJ 3305 7m E of Welshpool. Loc,
Worthen CP.

ASTON ROGERS Shrops
118 SJ 3406 7m E of Welshpool. Loc,
Worthen CP. Ch m.

ASTON ROWANT Oxon
159 SU 7299 4m SSE of Thame. CP, 477.
Bullingdon RD. Ch e, c. Sch pe. Henley CC.
See also Kingston Blount.   Ch: brasses,
glass.

ASTON SANDFORD Bucks
159 SP 7507 3m ENE of Thame. CP, 55.
Aylesbury RD. Ch e. Aylesbury CC.

ASTON SOMERVILLE Worcs
144 SP 0438 3m S of Evesham. CP, 178.
Eveshm RD. P Broadway. Ch e. Sch pe.
S Worcs CC.

ASTON SUBEDGE Glos
144 SP 1341 2m NNW of Chipping
Campden. CP, 101. N Cotsld RD. Ch e.
Cirencester and Tewkesbury CC.

ASTON TIRROLD Berks
158 SU 5585 3m SE of Didcot. CP, 267.
Wallingford RD. P Ddct. Ch e, v. Sch pe.
Abingdon CC.

ASTON UPON TRENT Derbys
121 SK 4129 6m SE of Derby. CP.
SE Derbys RD. P DBY. Ch e, m. Sch p.
SE Derbys CC.

ASTON UPTHORPE Berks
158 SU 5586 3m SE of Didcot. CP, 144.
Wallingford RD. Ch e. Abingdon CC.

ASTROP Northants
145 SP 5036 4m SE of Banbury. Loc, King's
Sutton CP. Popular spa in 18c. A. Pk has
grnds by Capability Brown.

ASTWICK Beds
147 TL 2138 3m NNW of Baldock. CP, 35.
Biggleswade Rd. Ch e. Mid-Beds CC.

ASTWITH Derbys
112 SK 4464 6m SE of Chesterfield. Loc,
Ault Hucknall CP.

ASTWOOD Bucks
147 SP 9547 5m ENE of Newport Pagnell.
CP, 176. Npt Pgnll RD. P Npt Pgnll. Ch e, v.
Buckingham CC.

ASTWOOD BANK Worcs
131 SP 0462 3m S of Redditch. Loc,
Rddtch UD. P Rddtch.

ASWARBY Lincs (K)
113, 123 TF 0639 4m S of Sleaford.
CP(Aswby and Swarby), 163. E Kesteven RD.
Ch e. Rutland and Stamford CC.

ASWARDBY Lincs (L)
114 TF 3770 6m SW of Alford. CP, 48.
Spilsby RD. P Splsby. Ch e, m. Horncastle
CC.

ATCHAM Shrops
118 SJ 5409 4m ESE of Shrewsbury. CP.
Atchm RD. P Shrsbry. Ch e. Sch pe.
Shrsbry CC. Ggn br over R Severn, blt by
Gwynne, builder of Magdalen Br, Oxford.
Red brick Ggn hotel hard by. To NE,
Attingham (NT)*, 18c mansion in large pk.
Part used as Adult Education Centre.

ATCH LENCH Worcs
144 SP 0350 4m N of Evesham. Loc, Ch
Lnch CP. Ch b.

ATHELHAMPTON Dorset
178 SY 7794 5m ENE of Dorchester. CP,
48. Dchstr RD. Ch e. W Dst CC. Hall*,
mdvl; extensive gdns.

ATHELINGTON Suffolk(E)
137 TM 2171 5m ESE of Eye. CP, 47.
Hartismere RD. Ch e. Eye CC.

ATHELNEY Som
177 ST 3428 8m ENE of Taunton. Loc,
Bridgwater RD, Tntn RD. Brdgwtr CC, Tntn
CC. Osier beds; basket-making. King Alfred
hid here in 878; commemorative obelisk
erected 1801.

ATHERINGTON Devon
163 SS 5923 7m ENE of Torrington.CP,
360. Barnstaple RD. P Umberleigh.
Ch e, b, m, v. N Dvn CC. Ch: rood scrn with
orig rood loft; cf Compton, Surrey.

ATHERSTONE Warwicks
132 SP 3097 5m NW of Nuneaton. CP,
5,453. Athrstne RD. P. Ch e, m, r2, s, v2.
Sch i2, j2, pr, s. Meriden CC.

ATHERSTONE ON STOUR Warwicks
144 SP 2051 3m S of Stratford.CP, 66.
Strtfd-on-Avon RD. Ch e. Strtfd-on-Avn CC
(Strtfd).

ATHERTON Lancs
101 SD 6703 2m NE of Leigh.UD, 21,758.
P MANCHESTER. Lgh BC. Textiles and
coal. Mining sharply declined in recent
years.

ATLOW Derbys
111 SK 2348 4m ENE of Ashbourne. CP,
84. Ashbne RD. Ch e. W Derbys CC.

ATTENBOROUGH Notts
112, 121 SK 5134 5m SW of Nottingham.
Loc, Beeston and Stapleford UD. P Bstn,
NTTNGHM. Gravel wks by R Trent. Ch:
nave capitals.

ATTLEBOROUGH Norfolk
136 TM 0495 6m SW of Wymondham.CP,
3,027. Wayland RD. P. Ch e, b, m, s, v.
Sch p, s. S Nflk CC. Cider-making. Turkey
farms. Ch has notable early 16c scrn.

ATTLEBRIDGE Norfolk
125 TG 1316 8m NW of Norwich.CP, 126.
St. Faith's and Aylsham RD. P NRWCH,
NOR 57X. Ch e. N Nflk CC (Central Nflk).

ATWICK Yorks (E)
99 TA 1950 2m NNW of Hornsea.CP, 311.
Holderness RD. P Driffield. Ch e, m.
Bridlington CC. Lonely place; sandy beach.

ATWORTH Wilts
156 ST 8665 6m SW of Chippenham.
CP, 817. Bradford and Melksham RD.

P Mlkshm. Ch e, b, c. Sch p. Westbury CC.
See also Gt Chalfield.

AUBOURN Lincs (K)
113 SK 9262 6m SSW of Lincoln. CP(Aubn
Haddington and S Hykeham), 755.
N Kesteven RD. P LNCLN. Ch e, m. Sch p.
Grantham CC. A. Hall*, 16c brick hse.

AUCKLEY Yorks (W)
103 SE 6501 5m ESE of Doncaster. CP,
2,121. Dncstr RD. Ch m. Don Valley CC.

AUDENSHAW Lancs
101 SJ 9296 5m E of Manchester.
UD, 11,887. P MNCHSTR. Mnchstr,
Gorton BC.

AUDLEM Ches
110, 118, 119 SJ 6643 5m S of Nantwich.
CP, 1,172. Nntwch RD. P Crewe.
Ch e, b, m2. Sch pe. Nntwch CC. See also
Coxbank. Old mkt tn, with mkt cross and
Perp ch.

AUDLEY Staffs
110 SJ 7950 6m NW of Stoke-on-Trent.
CP(Audley Rural), 8,018.
Newcastle-under-Lyme RD. P Stke-on-Trnt.
Ch e, b, m9. Sch i, p. N-u-L BC. See also
Alsagers Bank, Halmer End, Miles Grn. Ch:
14c brass.

AUGHTON Lancs
89 SD 5567 4m ESE of Carnforth.
CP(Halton-w-Aughton), 1,486. Lunesdale RD.
Ch e. Lancaster CC.

AUGHTON Lancs
100 SD 3905 2m SW of Ormskirk. CP, 5,055.
W Lancs RD. P Ormskk. Ch e2, b, r. Sch p,
pe2, pr. Ormskk CC. See also Aghtn Pk, Tn
Grn.

AUGHTON Yorks (E)
97, 98 SE 7038 7m NE of Selby. Loc,
Ellerton CP. Ch e.

AUGHTON Yorks (W)
103 SK 4586 4m SSE of Rotherham.
CP(Aston cum Aughtn). Rthrhm RD. P
SHEFFIELD. Ch e. Sch p. Rother Valley
CC.

AUGHTON PARK Lancs
100 SD 4106 1m SSW of Ormskirk. Loc,
Aughtn CP.

AULDEN Herefs
142 SO 4654 3m SW of Leominster. Loc,
Lmnstr MB.

AULT HUCKNALL Derbys
112 SK 4665 5m NW of Mansfield. CP,
1,746. Blackwell RD. Ch e. Bolsover CC. See
also Astwith, Bramley Vale, Doe Lea,
Hardstoft. 1m S, Hardwick Hall (NT)*, Elizn.

AUNSBY Lincs (K)
113, 123 TF 0438 5m SSW of Sleaford.
CP(Aunsby and Dembleby), 160. E Kesteven
RD. P Slfd. Ch e. Rutland and Stamford CC.

AUST Glos
155, 156 ST 5789 10m N of Bristol.
CP, 380. Thornbury RD. P BRSTL. Ch e, m.
S Glos CC. See also Elberton,
Littleton-upon-Severn. Site of car ferry
across R Severn replaced in 1966 by
Svn Rd Br, suspension br with main span of
3,240ft.

AUSTERFIELD Yorks (W)
103 SK 6694 8m SE of Doncaster.CP, 525.
Dncstr RD. P Dncstr. Ch e. Sch p. Don
Valley CC.

AUSTREY Warwicks
120, 121 SK 2906 6m ENE of Tamworth.
CP, 299. Atherstone RD. P Athrstne.
Ch e, b. Sch pe. Meriden CC.

AUSTWICK Yorks (W)
90 SD 7668 5m NW of Settle.CP, 470. Sttle
RD. P LANCASTER. Ch e, m. Sch pe.
Skipton CC. See also Wharfe. Limestone
hills. Stone cottages, some with carved
lintels.

AUTHORPE Lincs (L)
105 TF 4080 5m NW of Alford. CP, 130.
Louth RD. P Lth. Ch e, m. Lth CC.

AVEBURY Wilts
157 SU 1069 6m W of Marlborough. CP,
631. Mlbrgh and Ramsbury RD. P Mlbrgh.
Ch e, c. Sch pe. Devizes CC. See also
Beckhampton, W Kennett. Vllge A.M. and
NT, within prehistoric earthwork; stone
circle and avenue, prob c1800 BC. Museum
of finds. A. Mnr*, 16c hse in formal gdns. 1m
S, Silbury Hill, man-made conical hill 130ft
high, date and purpose unknown.

AVELEY Essex
161 TQ 5680 2m NE of Purfleet. Loc,
Thurrock UD. P: S Ockendon. Thrrck BC

(CC). Gravel wks and vast areas of new
bldng. Ch, largely Nmn, contains 14c Flemish
brass. To N, Belhus Pk, grnds by Capability
Brown of now vanished B. Hse.

AVENING Glos
156, 157 ST 8897 3m N of Tetbury. CP,
790. Ttbry RD. P Ttbry. Ch e, b. Sch p.
Stroud CC. Partly Nmn ch; good setting.

AVERHAM Notts
112 SK 7654 2m W of Newark. CP, 184.
Southwell RD. Ch e, m. Sch p. Nwk CC. Ch
stands close to R Trent.

AVETON GIFFORD Devon
187, 188 SX 6947 3m NW of Kingsbridge.
CP, 599. Kngsbrdge RD. P Kngsbrdge.
Ch e, m. Sch pe. Totnes CC. 13c ch almost
totally destroyed in World War II air raid.
Direct route to Bigbury impassable at high
tide.

AVINGTON Berks
158 SU 3768 2m E of Hungerford. Loc,
Kintbury CP. Ch e. Pure Nmn ch.

AVINGTON Hants
168 SU 5332 4m ENE of Winchester. Loc,
Itchen Valley CP. Wnchstr RD. Ch e.
Wnchstr CC. A. Pk*, 17c hse in wooded pk.
Ch Ggn.

AVON Hants
179 SZ 1498 4m N of Christchurch. Loc,
Sopley CP.

AVON DASSETT Warwicks
145 SO 4150 7m NNW of Banbury.
CP, 224. Southam RD. P Leamington Spa.
Ch e, m, r. Stratford-on-Avon CC (Strtfd).

AVONMOUTH Glos
155 ST 5178 NW distr of Bristol. Loc, Brstl
CB. P BRSTL. Brstl NW BC. Port of Brstl.
Large docks.

AVONWICK Devon
187, 188 SX 7158 6m WSW of Totnes. Loc,
N Huish CP. P: S Brent. Ch e.

AWBRIDGE Hants
168 SU 3323 2m NW of Romsey. Loc,
Sherfield English CP. P Rmsy. Ch e. Sch p.

AWKLEY Glos
155, 156 ST 5885 8m N of Bristol. Loc,
Olveston CP.

AWLISCOMBE Devon
176 ST 1301 2m WNW of Honiton. CP,
429. Hntn RD. P Hntn. Ch e, b. Sch pe.
Hntn CC.

AWRE Glos
156 SO 7008 6m NE of Lydney. CP, 1,805.
E Dean RD. P Newnham. Ch e. W Glos CC.
See also Blakeney. Situated on last big loop
of R Severn.

AWSWORTH Notts
112, 121 SK 4844 2m NE of Ilkeston. CP,
1,529. Basford RD. P NOTTINGHAM.
Ch e, m2. Sch p. Beeston CC (Rushcliffe).

AXBRIDGE Som
165 ST 4354 2m WNW of Cheddar. CP,
1,087. Axbrdge RD. P. Ch e, m. Sch pe.
Weston-super-Mare CC. Tn hall has
exhibition of civic documents and apparatus
of punishments and sports. To SE, large
round reservoir.

AXFORD Hants
168 SU 6143 6m SSW of Basingstoke. Loc,
Bsngstke RD. Bsngstke CC.

AXFORD Wilts
157 SU 2370 3m E of Marlborough. Loc,
Ramsbury CP. P Mlbrgh. Ch e, m.

AXMINSTER Devon
177 SY 2998 5m NNW of Lyme Regis.
CP, 2,656. Axmnstr RD. P. Ch e, c, m, r, v2.
Sch p, pr, s. Honiton CC. See also
Raymond's Hill. Ancient tn at junction of
Roman rds. Carpets made here 1755–1835
and again from 1937.

AXMOUTH Devon
177 ST 2591 1m NE of Seaton. CP, 489.
Axminster RD. P Seaton. Ch e, v.
Honiton CC. See also Hr Bruckland. Former
port; now small resort.

AYCLIFFE Co Durham
85 NZ 2822 5m N of Darlington. Loc,
Gt Aycliffe CP. Dlngtn RD. P Dlngtn.
Ch e, m. Sch p. Bishop Auckland CC
(Sedgefield). A. Indstrl Estate to N. New tn
pop. 20,190.

AYDON Nthmb
77 NZ 0066 2m NE of Corbridge. Loc,
Cbrdge CP. A. Cstle*, 14c fortified mnr hse
above ravine.

AYLBURTON Glos
155, 156 SO 6101 1m SW of Lydney.
CP, 812. Ldny RD. P Ldny. Ch e, m. Sch p.
W Glos CC. In vllge centre, base of 14c cross
mounted on steps.

AYLESBEARE Devon
176 SY 0392 7m E of Exeter. CP, 392. St
Thomas RD. P Extr. Ch e, c. Sch p. Honiton
CC.

AYLESBURY Bucks
146, 159 SP 8113 36m NW of London.
MB, 41,288. P. Aylesbury CC. Busy tn with
many old bldngs and streets. The King's
Head (NT), still an inn, is partly l5c.

AYLESBY Lincs (L)
105 TA 2007 4m W of Grimsby. CP, 122.
Grmsby RD. Ch e. Lth CC.

AYLESFORD Kent
171, 172 TQ 7258 3m NW of Maidstone.
CP, 5,278. Malling RD. P Mdstne.
Ch e, m, r. Sch p, pe2, s. Tonbridge and
Mllng CC (Sevenoaks). See also British
Legion Vllge, Eccles. Old tn on R Medway,
with 14c br. The Friars*, l3c Carmelite hse,
restored 1950s.

AYLESHAM Kent
173 TR 2352 7m SE of Canterbury. CP,
4,142. Eastry RD. P Cntrbry. Ch e, b, r, v2.
Sch i, j, pr, s. Dover and Deal CC (Dvr).
Mining vllge.

AYLMERTON Norfolk
126 TG 1839 3m SW of Cromer. CP, 342.
Erpingham RD. P NORWICH, NOR 25Y.
Ch e, m. Sch p. N Nflk CC.

AYLSHAM Norfolk
126 TG 1926 12m N of Norwich.
CP, 2,635. St Faith's and Aylshm RD.
P NRWCH, NOR 07Y. Ch e, b, m, r, s, v2.
Sch pe, s. N Nflk CC (Central Nflk). 18c
hses in mkt square. Ch: monmts, incl
cadaver brasses of 1499.

AYLTON Herefs
142, 143 SO 6537 3m W of Ledbury. CP,
102. Ldby RD. Ch e. Leominster CC.

AYMESTREY Herefs
129 SO 4265 6m NW of Leominster. CP,
380. Lmnstr and Wigmore RD. P Lmnstr.
Ch e, m. Lmnstr CC. See also Leinthall
Earls, Lr Lye, Yatton. Ch: l6c screen. 1½m
NE, Iron Age hill fort, where bronze work
was found.

AYNHO Northants
145 SP 5133 5m WSW of Brackley. CP, 465. Brckly RD. P Banbury, Oxon. Ch e. Sch pe. Daventry CC (S Nthnts). Stone vllge. A. Pk*, late 17c hse with later alterations. Ch in domestic style of 1720.

AYOT ST LAWRENCE Herts
147 TL 1916 4m NW of Welwyn Gdn City. CP, 124. Wlwn RD. P Wlwn. Ch e. Wlwn and Hatfield CC (Hertford). 18c ch in classical style replaced former ch whose ruins still stand. Bernard Shaw's hse(NT)*. Lullingstone Silk Farm* at Ayot Hse.

AYOT ST PETER Herts
147 TL 2115 2m NW of Welwyn Gdn City. CP, 199. Wlwn RD. P Wlwn. Ch e. Wlwn and Hatfield CC (Hertford).

AYSGARTH Yorks (N)
90 SE 0088 7m WSW of Leyburn. CP, 196. Aysgth RD. P Lbn. Ch e, m. Richmond CC. On R Ure, with famous falls. Museum of horse-drawn transport in old corn mill.

AYSHFORD Devon
164 ST 0415 ENE of Tiverton. Loc, Burlescombe CP.

AYSIDE Lancs
88, 89 SD 3983 4m NNW of Grange-over-Sands. Loc, Staveley CP.

AYSTON Rutland
122 SK 8601 1m N of Uppingham. CP, 58. Uppnghm RD. Ch e. Rtlnd and Stamford CC. Ironstone vllge.

AYTHORPE RODING Essex
148 TL 5815 SW of Dunmow. CP, 169. Dnmw RD. Ch e. Saffron Walden CC. One of eight Rodings, pronounced 'roothing'.

AYTON, GREAT Yorks (N)
86 NZ 5510 5m SW of Guisborough. See Gt Aytn.

AZERLEY Yorks (W)
91 SE 2674 4m WNW of Ripon. CP, 273. Rpn and Pateley Br RD. Rpn CC. See also Galphay, Mickley.

B

BABBINSWOOD Shrops
118 SJ 3330 3m E of Oswestry. Loc, Whittington CP.

BABCARY Som
166, 177 ST 5628 5m NE of Ilchester. CP, 214. Langport RD. P Somerton. Ch e, m. Yeovil CC. Parson Woodforde, 18c diarist, was vicar here.

BABINGTON Som
166 ST 7051 3m SSE of Radstock. Loc, Kilmersdon CP. Ch e.

BABRAHAM Cambs
148 TL 5150 6m SE of Cambridge. CP, 344. S Cambs RD. P CMBRDGE. Ch e. Sch pe. Cambs CC. Ch stands apart from vllge: Piper E window of St Peter; dolorous monmt to Bennet brothers in S aisle.

BABWORTH Notts
103 SK 6880 1m W of Retford. CP, 985. E Rtfd RD. P Rtfd. Ch e. Bassetlaw CC. See also Ranby. Ch stands in grnds (laid out by Repton) of Ggn B. Hall.

BACKBARROW Lancs
88, 89 SD 3584 6m NE of Ulverston. Loc, Haverthwaite CP. P Ulvstn. Ch m, v. Ironworks set up here in 18c by Isaac Wilkinson, pioneer of cast iron.

BACKFORD Ches
109 SJ 3971 3m N of Chester. CP, 174. Chstr RD. P CHSTR. Ch e. Sch pe. City of Chstr CC.

BACKWELL Som
155, 165 ST 4968 7m WSW of Bristol. CP, 3,185. Long Ashton RD. P BRSTL. Ch e. Sch p, pe, s. N Som CC. See also Farleigh, W Tn.

BACKWORTH Nthmb
78 NZ 3072 3m W of Whitley Bay. Loc, Seaton Valley UD. P Shiremoor. Blyth BC.

BACON END Essex
148 TL 6018 3m SW of Dunmow. Loc, Gt Canfield CP.

BACONSTHORPE Norfolk
125 TG 1237 3m ESE of Holt. CP, 243. Erpingham RD. P Hlt. Ch e, m. Sch pe. N Nflk CC. To N, B. Cstle (A.M.), rems of moated 15c fortified hse.

BACTON Herefs
142 SO 3732 10m WSW of Hereford. CP, 77. Dore and Bredwardine RD. P HRFD. Ch e. Hrfd CC.

BACTON Norfolk
126 TG 3433 4m ENE of N Walsham.
C P , 8 1 1 . S m a l l b u r g h R D .
P NORWICH, NOR 22Z. Ch e, b. Sch p.
N Nflk CC. See also Edingthorpe, Keswick.
Shore terminal for N Sea gas. Rems of
Broomholme Priory to S.

BACTON Suffolk (E)
136 TM 0567 5m N of Stowmarket.
CP, 428. Hartismere RD. P Stwmkt. Ch e.
Sch p, s. Eye CC. 18c mnr hse. Ch: roof;
doom (picture of Last Judgement) over
chancel arch.

BACUP Lancs
95 SD 8623 6m SSE of Burnley. MB,
15,102.. P. Rossendale BC. See also
Britannia, Stacksteads, Weir. Predominantly
textile tn. Pop. declined by c 12% from
1961 to 1971.

BADBURY Wilts
157 SU 1980 4m SE of Swindon. Loc,
Chiseldon CP.

BADBY Northants
132, 133 SP 5559 2m SSW of Daventry. CP,
483. Dvntry RD. P Dvntry. Ch e, c. Sch p.
Dvntry CC (S Nthnts).

BADDESLEY CLINTON Warwicks
131 SP 2072 7m NW of Warwick. CP, 186.
Wrwck RD. Ch e, r. Sch pr. Wrwck and
Leamington CC. To SSW, B.C. Hall, moated
mdvl mnr hse. Ch nearby.

BADDESLEY ENSOR Warwicks
131 SO 2798 2m W of Atherstone. CP,
1,824. Athrstne RD. P Athrstne. Ch e, m, v.
Sch p. Meriden CC.

BADDOW, GREAT Essex
161, 162 TL 7204 2m SE of Chelmsford.
See Gt Bddw.

BADGER Shrops
130 SO 7699 5m NE of Bridgnorth. CP,
101. Shifnal RD. Ch e. The Wrekin CC.

BADGERS MOUNT Kent,
171 TQ 4962 4m SSE of Orpington. Loc,
Shoreham CP. P Sevenoaks.

BADGEWORTH Glos
143, 144 SO 9019 3m WSW of Cheltenham.
CP, 1,755. Chltnhm RD. Ch e. Cirencester
and Tewkesbury CC. See also Bentham, Lit
Witcombe.

BADGWORTH Som
165 ST 3952 4m W of Cheddar. CP, 347.
A x b r i d g e R d . Ch e. Sch pe.
Weston-super-Mare CC. See also Biddisham.

BADINGHAM Suffolk(E)
137 TM 3068 3m NNE of Framlingham. CP,
369. Blyth RD. P Woodbridge. Ch e. Eye CC.
Ch has sloping floor and seven-sacrament
font.

BADLESMERE Kent
172 TR 0054 4m S of Faversham. CP, 148.
Swale RD. Ch e. Fvrshm CC.

BADMINTON Glos
156 ST 8082 8m WSW of Malmesbury. CP,
347. Sodbury RD. P. Ch e. Sch pe. S Glos
CC. B. Hse*, 17c and later, in large pk where
well known three-day horse trials are held
annually. Seat of Duke of Beaufort.

BADSEY Worcs
144 SP 0743 2m E of Evesham. CP, 1,668.
Eveshm RD. P Eveshm. Ch e, f. Sch p.
S Worcs CC.

BADSWORTH Yorks (W)
103 SE 4614 4m S of Pontefract CP, 192.
Hemsworth RD. P Pntfrct. Ch e, m. Sch pe.
Hmswth CC.

BADWELL ASH Suffolk (W)
136 TL 9969 7m NNW of Stowmarket. CP,
331. Thedwastre RD. P Bury St Edmunds.
Ch e. Sch pe. Bury St Eds CC.

BAGBY Yorks (N)
91 SE 4680 2m ESE of Thirsk. CP, 235.
Thsk RD. P Thsk. Ch e, m. Thsk and Malton
CC.

BAG ENDERBY Lincs (L)
114 TF 3472 6m ENE of Horncastle. Loc,
Somersby CP. Ch e. Ch: carved font.
Tennyson's father was vicar (see Somersby).

BAGENDON Glos
157 SP 0106 3m N of Cirencester. CP, 243.
Crncstr RD. Ch e. Crncstr and Tewkesbury
CC. To E, B. Dykes, large system of Iron
Age ditches, above valley of R Churn.

BAGE, THE Herefs
142 SO 2943 5m E of Hay-on-Wye. Loc,
Dorstone CP.

BAGINTON Warwicks
132 SP 3474 3m SSE of Coventry. CP.
Warwick RD. P Cvntry. Ch e. Sch pe. Wrwck
and Leamington CC. Ch: 15c brasses. Faint
rems of B. Cstle, prob 14c, E of ch. Roman
fort discovered and reconstructed in 1960s.

BAGLEY Shrops
118 SJ 4027 5m S of Ellesmere. Loc,
Hordley CP. Ch m.

BAGNALL Staffs
110 SJ 9250 5m NE of Stoke-on-Trent. CP.
Leek RD. P Stke-on-Trnt. Ch e, v. Sch p.
Lk CC.

BAGSHOT Surrey
169 SU 9163 3m NE of Camberley. Loc,
Windlesham CP. P. Ch e, m, r, v. Sch p.
Rsndtl and military. B. Hth to S formerly
haunt of highwaymen.

BAGSHOT Wilts
158 SU 3165 3m SSW of Hungerford. Loc,
Shalbourne CP. Ch e.

BAGTHORPE Norfolk
125 TF 7932 8m WNW of Fakenham.
CP(Bgthpe w Barmer), 107. Docking RD.
Ch e. NW Nflk CC (King's Lynn).

BAGTHORPE Notts
112 SK 4751 5m SE of Alfreton. Loc,
Selston CP. P NOTTINGHAM. Ch b. Sch p.

BAGWORTH Leics
121 SK 4408 4m SSE of Coalville. CP,
1,869. Mkt Bosworth RD. P LEICESTER.
Ch e, m. Sch p. Bswth CC. See also
Thornton. Coal-mining.

BAGWY LLYDIART Herefs
142 SO 4426 9m SSW of Hereford. Loc,
Orcop CP.

BAILDON Yorks (W)
96 SE 1529 4m N of Bradford. UD, 14,690.
P Shipley. Shply CC. Indstrl and rsdntl on
steep hill, with stretch of open moor to N.

BAILIFF BRIDGE Yorks (W)
96, 102 SE 1425 3m E of Halifax. Loc,
Brighouse MB. P Brghse.

BAILRIGG Lancs
94 SD 4858 2m S of Lancaster. Loc,
Scotforth CP. University of Lncstr is here.

BAINBRIDGE Yorks (N)
90 SD 9390 4m E of Hawes. CP, 439.
Aysgarth RD. P Leyburn. Ch c, f, m. Sch pe.
Richmond CC. See also Countersett,
Marsett, Stalling Busk. Stone hses round
large grn; river (Ure) cascades down wide
flat 'steps'. 1½m SW, Semerwater, small
natural lake.

BAINTON Hunts
123 TF 0906 4m E of Stamford. CP, 201.
Barnack RD. P Stmfd, Lincs. Ch e.
Peterborough BC (CC). Limestone cottages.
Ch Nmn and later; broach spire.

BAINTON Yorks (E)
98 SE 9652 5m SW of Driffield. CP, 304.
Drffld RD. P Drffld. Ch e, m. Howden CC.

BAKER STREET Essex
161 TQ 6381 4m N of Tilbury. Loc,
Thurrock UD. Thrrck BC (CC).

BAKEWELL Derbys
111 SK 2168 7m NW of Matlock.
UD, 4,240. P W Derbys CC. Ancient mkt tn
and centre for Dales. Sxn cross in
churchyard. 15c br spans R Wye.

BALCOMBE Sussex (E)
182 TQ 3030 4m NNW of Haywards Hth.
CP, 1,507. Cuckfield RD. P Hwds Hth.
Ch e, b, c. Sch pe. Mid-Sx CC (E Grinstead).
1½m SSE, B. Viaduct, 1,475ft, 37 brick
arches, carries London–Brighton rly over
R Ouse.

BALDERSBY Yorks (N)
91 SE 3578 5m WSW of Thirsk. CP, 224.
Wath RD. P Thsk. Ch e. Sch pe. Thsk and
Malton CC. Ch and most of vllge designed
by Vctrn architect Butterfield.

BALDERSTONE Lancs
94, 95 SD 6332 4m NW of Blackburn.
CP, 368. Blckbn RD. Ch e. Sch pe.
Darwen CC.

BALDERTON Notts
113 SK 8151 2m SE of Newark. CP, 5,605.
Nwk RD. P Nwk. Ch e, m2. Sch p2, s.
Nwk CC. Suburb of Nwk on former A1. Ch:
spire, glass, bench-ends, Nmn doorway.

BALDHU Cornwall
190 SW 7742 4m WSW of Truro. Loc,
Kea CP. Ch e, m. Sch p. Old tin-workings.

BALDOCK Herts
147 TL 2433 5m N of Stevenage.
UD, 6,270. P. Hitchin CC. Ggn hses in High
St. Hosiery factory. Formerly on A1, now
bypassed by A1(M).

BALDWIN'S GATE Staffs
110, 119 SJ 7940 5m SW of
Newcastle-under-Lyme. Loc,
Ncstle-undr-Lme RD. P Ncstle. Ch m. N-u-L
BC.

BALE Norfolk
125 TG 0136 4m WSW of Holt. Loc,
Gunthorpe CP. P Fakenham. Ch e, m.

BALHAM London
160, 170 TQ 2873 2m ESE of Wandsworth.
Loc, Wndswth LB. Battersea S BC
(Clapham).

BALKHOLME Yorks (E)
97, 98 SE 7828 4m NE of Goole. Loc,
Kilpin CP.

BALL Shrops
118 SJ 3026 2m SSE of Oswestry. Loc,
Oswstry Rural CP. Oswstry RD.
Oswstry CC.

BALL HILL Hants
168 SU 4163 4m SW of Newbury. Loc, E
Woodhay CP.

BALLIDON Derbys
111 SK 2054 5m NNE of Ashbourne. CP,
110. Ashbne RD. Ch e. W Derbys CC.

BALLINGHAM Herefs
142 SO 5731 7m SE of Hereford. CP, 97.
Ross and Whitchurch RD. Ch e. Hrfd CC.

BALLS CROSS Sussex (W)
181, 182 SU 9826 3m N of Petworth. Loc,
Kirdford CP. P Ptwth.

BALL'S GREEN Sussex (E)
171, 183 TQ 4936 6m WSW of Tunbridge
Wells. Loc, Withyham CP.

BALMERLAWN Hants
180 SU 3003 just NE of Brockenhurst. Loc,
Brcknhst CP.

BALSALL COMMON Warwicks
131 SP 2377 6m W of Coventry. Loc, Blsll
CP. Meriden RD. P Cvntry. Ch e, m, v.
Sch p, s. Mrdn CC.

BALSCOTT Oxon
145 SP 3941 4m W of Banbury. Loc,
Wroxton CP. P Bnbry. Ch e.

BALSHAM Cambs
148 TL 5850 6m NW of Haverhill. CP, 712.
S Cambs RD. P CAMBRIDGE. Ch e. Sch p.
Cambs CC. Large long vllge with large long
ch: clerestory, scrn, S door.

BALTERLEY Staffs
110 SJ 7650 5m SE of Crewe. CP, 183.
Newcastle-under-Lyme RD. P Crwe,
Cheshire. N-u-L BC.

BALTONSBOROUGH Som
165, 166 ST 5434 4m SE of Glastonbury.
CP, 591. Wells RD. P Glstnsbry. Ch e, m.
Sch pe. Wlls CC. See also Ham St,
Southwood.

BAMBER BRIDGE Lancs
94 SD 5625 3m SE of Preston. Loc,
Walton-le-Dale UD. P Prstn. Textiles.

BAMBURGH Nthmb
71 NU 1835 14m N of Alnwick. CP, 558.
Belford RD. P. Ch e. Sch pe.
Berwick-upon-Tweed CC. See also Budle,
Burton. Ancient settlement; now vllge
dominated by huge cstle*, Nmn but much
restored. St Aidan d here, 651. 13c ch. Grace
Darling buried in churchyard. Grace Darling
Museum. Out to sea, Farne Islands (NT).

BAMFORD Derbys
111 SK 2083 9m N of Bakewell. CP, 1,097.
Chapel en le Frith RD. P SHEFFIELD.
Ch e, m, r. Sch p. High Peak CC.

BAMPTON Devon
164 SS 9522 6m N of Tiverton. CP, 1,517.
Tvtn RD. P Tvtn. Ch e, b, m. Sch pe, s.
Tvtn CC. See also Petton, Shillingford. Mkt
tn. Pony fair held in October. Limestone
quarries to S.

BAMPTON Oxon
158 SP 3103 5m SW of Witney. CP, 1,427.
Wtny RD. P OXFORD. Ch e, b, m. Sch pe.
Mid-Oxon CC (Banbury). Famous for Morris
dancers. Dancing in st on Whit Monday.

BAMPTON Westm
83 NY 5118 8m S of Penrith. CP, 382.
N Westm RD. P Pnrth, Cumberland. Ch e.
Sch pe. Westm CC. See also Bmptn Grange,
Burnbanks.

BAMPTON GRANGE Westm
83 NY 5218 8m S of Penrith. Loc,
Bmptn CP.

BANBURY Oxon
145 SP 4540 22m N of Oxford. MB, 29,216.
P. Bnbry CC. Mkt tn, largely Midland in
character. Orig famous cross dismantled late
16c; present one 19c.

BANGORS Cornwall
174 SX 2099 4m S of Bude. Loc,
Poundstock CP. Ch m.

BANHAM Norfolk
136 TM 0688 5m S of Attleborough. CP,
942. Wayland RD. P NORWICH, NOR 05X.
Ch e, m. Sch p. S Nflk CC. B. Zoo* to NE.

BANK Hants
180 SU 2807 1m SW of Lyndhurst. Loc,
Lndhst CP.

BANK NEWTON Yorks (W)
95 SD 9153 5m WNW of Skipton. CP, 76.
Skptn RD. Skptn CC.

BANKS Cumb
76 NY 5664 3m NE of Brampton. Loc,
Burtholme CP. Border RD. P Brmptn. Ch m.
Penrith and the Bdr CC.

BANKS Lancs
94 SD 3920 4m NE of Southport. Loc, N
Meols CP. W Lancs RD. P Sthpt. Ch e, m.
Sch pe, pm. Ormskirk CC.

BANK STREET Worcs
129, 130 SO 6362 4m SE of Tenbury Wells.
Loc, Stoke Bliss CP.

BANNINGHAM Norfolk
126 TG 2129 2m NE of Aylsham. Loc, Colby
CP. P NORWICH, NOR 49Y. Ch e.

BANNISTER GREEN Essex
148 TL 6920 4m E of Dunmow. Loc,
Felsted CP. Ch v.

BANSTEAD Surrey
170 TQ 2559 3m E of Epsom. UD, 44,986.
P. Reigate BC (Carshalton CC). See also
Burgh Hth, Chipstead, Kingswood, Lr
Kngswd, Tadworth, Walton-on-the-Hill,
Woodmansterne. Rsdntl distr.

BANTHAM Devon
187, 188 SX 6643 4m W of Kingsbridge.
Loc, Thurlestone CP. P Kngsbrdge.

BANWELL Som
165 ST 3959 5m ESE of Weston. CP, 2,824.
Axbridge RD. P Wstn-super-Mare.
Ch e, b, m. Sch p. W-s-M CC. Iron Age fort;
cruciform earthwork; bones of many
prehistoric animals (now in Taunton
Museum) found in cave. B. Cstle a Vctrn
Gothic folly.

BAPCHILD Kent
172 TQ 9263 2m ESE of Sittingbourne. CP,
358. Swale RD. P Sttngbne. Ch e, Sch pe.
Faversham CC.

BARBER BOOTH Derbys
102, 111 SK 1184 8m NNE of Buxton. Loc,
Edale CP. Ch m.

BARBON Westm
89 SD 6282 3m NNE of Kirkby Lonsdale.
CP, 237. S Westm RD. P Carnforth, Lancs.
Ch e, m. Sch pe. Westm CC.

BARBRIDGE Ches
110 SJ 6156 4m NW of Nantwich. Loc,
Stoke CP. Nntwch RD. Ch m. Nntwch CC.

BARBROOK Devon
163 SS 7147 SSW of Lynton. Loc,
Lntn UD. P Lntn.

BARBY Northants
132 SP 5470 4m SE of Rugby. CP, 427.
Daventry RD. P Rgby, Warwickshire. Ch e.
Sch pe. Dvntry CC (S Nthnts).

BARCHESTON Warwicks
144 SP 2639 just SE of Shipston on Stour.
CP, 124. Shpstn on Stour RD. Ch e.
Stratford-on-Avon CC (Strtfd). See also
Willington.

BARCOMBE Sussex (E)
183 TQ 4214 3m N of Lewes. CP, 1,269.
Chailey RD. P Lws. Ch e, b, v. Sch pe. Lws
CC. See also Bcmbe Cross, Spithurst.

BARCOMBE CROSS Sussex (E)
183 TQ 4215 4m N of Lewes. Loc, Bcmbe
CP.

BARDEN Yorks (N)
91 SE 1493 3m NE of Leyburn. CP, 63.
Lbn RD. Ch m. Richmond CC.

BARDFIELD, GREAT Essex
148 TL 6730 4m E of Thaxted. See Gt Bdfld.

BARDFIELD SALING Essex
148 TL 6826 5m NE of Dunmow. CP, 176. Braintree RD. Ch e. Brntree CC (Saffron Walden). Ch has round twr, rare in Essex.

BARDNEY Lincs (L)
113 TF 1169 6m NW of Woodhall Spa. CP, 1,570. Welton RD. P LINCOLN. Ch e, m2, r, s. Sch pv. Gainsborough CC. See also Southrey. Faint traces of important Saxon abbey. Large sugar beet factory.

BARDON Leics
121 SK 4412 1m E of Coalville. CP. Ashby de la Zouch RD. P(Bdn Hill), LEICESTER. Ch e, v. Loughborough CC. To NE, B. Hill, 912ft, highest point in Charnwood Forest and in Leics.

BARDON MILL Nthmb
77 NY 7864 4m W of Haydon Br. CP, 388. Haltwhistle RD. P Hexham. Ch m. Hxhm CC. Beside S Tyne and Newcastle—Carlisle rly. 1m N at Chesterholme, rems of Roman stn. 2½m NNE, at Housesteads, Roman Wall stn (A.M.).

BARDSEA Lancs
88, 89 SD 3074 3m SSE of Ulverston. Loc, Urswick CP. N Lonsdale RD. P Ulvstn. Ch e. Morecambe and Lnsdle CC. Overlooks Mcmbe Bay.

BARDSEY Yorks (W)
96 SE 3643 4m SW of Wetherby. CP(Bdsy cum Rigton), 1,556. Wthrby RD. P LEEDS. Ch e, r. Sch p. Barkston Ash CC. See also E Rgtn. Ch largely Nmn; Saxon twr.

BARDWELL Suffolk(W)
136 TL 9473 7m SE of Thetford. CP, 592. Thingoe RD. P Bury St Edmunds. Ch e, b, m. Sch pe. Bury St Eds CC. Fine 15c ch.

BAREWOOD Herefs
129 SO 3856 5m E of Kington. Loc, Dilwyn CP. Ch m.

BARFORD Norfolk
125 TG 1107 4m N of Wymondham. CP, 297 Forehoe and Henstead RD. P NORWICH, NOR 38X. Ch e, m. Sch p. S Nflk CC (Central Nflk).

BARFORD Warwicks
131 SP 2760 3m SSW of Warwick. CP, 838. Wrwck RD. P WRWCK. Ch e, m. Sch pe. Wrwck and Leamington CC.

BARFORD, GREAT Beds
147 TL 1252 3m NW of Sandy. See Gt Bfd.

BARFORD ST JOHN Oxon
145 SP 4333 5m SSW of Banbury. CP (Bfd St Jn and St Michael), 277. Bnbry RD. Ch e. Bnbry CC.

BARFORD ST MARTIN Wilts
167 SU 0531 6m W of Salisbury. CP, 545. Slsbry and Wilton RD. P Slsbry. Ch e, m. Sch pe. Slsbry CC.

BARFORD ST MICHAEL Oxon
145 SP 4332 5m SSW of Banbury. CP(Bfd St John and St Mchl), 277. Bnbry RD. P OXFORD. Ch e, v. Bnbry CC.

BARFRESTON Kent
173 TR 2650 6m NW of Dover. Loc, Eythorne CP. Ch e. Nmn ch: carvings.

BARHAM Hunts
134 TL 1375 7m WNW of Huntingdon. CP(Brhm and Woolley), 78. Hntngdn RD. Ch e. Hunts CC.

BARHAM Kent
173 TR 2050 6m SE of Canterbury. CP, 1,108. Bridge-Blean RD. P Cntrbry. Ch e, m. Sch pe. Cntrbry CC. See also Derringstone.

BARHAM Suffolk (E)
150 TM 1451 4m NNW of Ipswich. CP, 592. Gipping RD. Ch e. Eye CC.

BAR HILL Cambs
125 TL 3863 5m NW of Cambridge. CP. Chesterton RD. P CMBRDGE. Sch p. Cambs CC. Late 1960s village.

BARHOLM Lincs (K)
123 TF 0810 5m NE of Stamford. CP(Brhlm and Stowe), 117. S Kesteven RD. Ch e. Rutland and Stmfd CC.

BARKBY Leics
121, 122 SK 6309 5m NE of Leicester. CP, 363. Barrow upon Soar RD. P LCSTR. Ch e, m. Sch pe. Melton CC.

BARKBY THORPE Leics
121, 122 SK 6309 4m NE of Leicester. CP,
67. Barrow upon Soar RD. Melton CC.

BARKESTONE Leics
112, 122 SK 7734 8m W of Grantham. Loc,
Redmile CP. P NOTTINGHAM. Ch e.
Sch pe.

BARKHAM Berks
169 SU 7866 2m SW of Wokingham. CP,
1,977. Wknghm RD. P Wknghm. Ch e.
Sch pe. Reading S CC (Wknghm).

BARKING London
161 TQ 4584 10m ENE of Charing Cross.
LB, 160,499. P Essex. BCs: Bkng;
Dagenham. See also Dgnhm. Thames-side
(N) borough bounded by Bkng Creek to W
and Beam River to E. Eastbury Mnr Hse
(NT)*, 16c, off Ripple Rd.

BARKING Suffolk (E)
149 TM 0753 4m SSE of Stowmarket.
CP, 397. Gipping RD. Ch e. Eye CC. See
also Bkng Tye. Ch: scrns, charcoal braziers,
serpent.

BARKING TYE Suffolk (E)
149 TM 0652 4m SSE of Stowmarket. Loc,
Bkng CP. P Ipswich.

BARKISLAND Yorks (W)
96, 102 SE 0520 4m SW of Halifax. Loc,
Ripponden UD. P Hlfx.

BARKSTON Lincs (K)
113, 122 SK 9341 4m NNE of Grantham.
CP, 393. W Kesteven RD. P Grnthm.
Ch e, m. Sch pe. Grnthm CC.

BARKSTON Yorks (W)
97 SE 4936 5m S of Tadcaster. CP, 249.
Tdcstr RD. P(Bkstn Ash), Tdcstr. Sch pr.
Bkstn Ash CC.

BARKWAY Herts
148 TL 3835 4m SE of Royston. CP, 554.
Hitchin RD. P Rstn. Ch e, v. Sch pe. Htchn
CC. Handsome vllge. To N, Newsells Pk; hse
burnt down 1940s.

BARLASTON Staffs
110, 119 SJ 8938 4m S of Stoke-on-Trent.
CP. Stone RD. P Stke-on-Trnt. Ch e, m.
Sch pe. Stafford and Stne CC. To NW,
Wedgwood Pottery wks* and museum.

BARLAVINGTON Sussex (W)
181, 182 SU 9716 4m S of Petworth. CP,
147. Ptwth RD. Ch e. Chichester CC
(Horsham). 13c ch. Fine view of wooded
downs.

BARLBOROUGH Derbys
103 SK 4777 7m W of Worksop. CP, 2,083.
Clowne RD. P Chesterfield. Ch e, m.
Bolsover CC. B. Hall*, Elizn (now a sch).

BARLBY Yorks (E)
97, 98 SE 6334 2m NE of Selby. CP, 3,206.
Derwent RD. P Slby. Ch e, m. Sch p, s.
Howden CC. See also Osgodby.

BARLESTONE Leics
121 SK 4205 5m S of Coalville. CP, 1,205.
Mkt Bosworth RD. P Nuneaton,
Warwickshire. Ch e, b, m. Sch pe. Bswth CC.

BARLEY Herts
148 TL 3938 3m ESE of Royston. CP, 515.
Hitchin RD. P. Rstn. Ch e, c. Sch pe. Htchn
CC. Sign of Fox and Hounds Inn spans road.

BARLEY Lancs
95 SD 8240 3m NW of Nelson.
CP (Bly-w-Wheatley Booth), 281.
Burnley RD. P Bnly. Ch e, m. Clitheroe CC.

BARLEYTHORPE Rutland
122 SK 8409 1m NW of Oakham. CP, 187.
Oakhm RD. Rtlnd and Stamford CC.

BARLING Essex
162 TQ 9389 4m NE of Southend. CP(Blng
Magna), 1,075. Rochford RD.
P Sthnd-on-Sea. Ch e, v. Sch p. Maldon CC
(SE Essex). See also Lit Wakering.

BARLOW Co Durham
78 NZ 1561 6m WSW of Newcastle. Loc,
Blaydon UD.

BARLOW Derbys
111 SK 3474 3m NW of Chesterfield.
CP, 956. Chstrfld RD. Ch e. Sch pe.
NE Derbys CC. See also Common Side,
Moorhall.

BARLOW Yorks (W)
97, 98 SE 6428 3m SE of Selby. CP, 324.
Slby Rd. P Slby. Ch e, m. Sch pe. Barkston
Ash CC. Wks to E; Drax power stn beyond.

BARMBY MOOR Yorks (E)
97, 98 SE 7749 2m W of Pocklington. CP,
502. Pcklngtn RD. P YORK. Ch e, m.
Sch pe. Howden CC. Old mkt tn; disused
airfield SE.

BARMBY ON THE MARSH Yorks (E)
97, 98 SE 6928 4m NW of Goole. CP, 289.
Howden RD. P Gle. Ch e, m. Sch p. Hdn
CC. Where rivers Ouse and Derwent meet.
Drax power stn 1½m S.

BARMER Norfolk
125 TF 8133 7m WNW of Fakenham.
CP(Bagthorpe w Bmr), 107. Docking RD.
Ch e. NW Nflk CC (King's Lynn).

BARMPTON Co Durham
85 NZ 3118 3m NE of Darlington. CP, 82.
Dlngtn RD. Bishop Auckland CC
(Sedgefield).

BARMSTON Yorks (E)
99 TA 1659 5m SSW of Bridlington. CP,
297. Brdlngtn RD. P Driffield. Ch e, m.
Brdlngtn CC. See also Fraisthorpe. Lonely;
flat sandy beach. Old Hall moated.

BARNACK Hunts
123 TF 0705 3m ESE of Stamford.
CP, 703. Bnck RD. P Stmfd, Lincs. Ch e, m.
Sch pe. Peterborough BC (CC). Ch: Saxon
twr topped by very early spire (13c). 'Hills
and Holes': rems of Bnck limestone quarries
famous for centuries up to 18c.

BARNACLE Warwicks
132 SP 3884 5m NE of Coventry. Loc,
Shilton CP. Ch m.

BARNARD CASTLE Co Durham
84 NZ 0516 15m W of Darlington.
UD, 5,228. P. Bishop Auckland CC. Stone
tn with 12c cstle (A.M.) on banks of Tees.
Bowes Museum has large collection of art
treasures. To SE, rems of 12c Egglestone
Abbey (A.M.).

BARNARD GATE Oxon
145 SP 4010 3m E of Witney. Loc,
Eynsham CP. Ch m.

BARNARDISTON Suffolk (W)
148, 149 TL 7148 3m NE of Haverhill.
CP, 115. Clare RD. P Hvrhll. Ch e, m.
Bury St Edmunds CC.

BARNBURGH Yorks (W)
103 SE 4803 6m W of Doncaster. CP, 959.
Dncstr RD. P Dncstr. Ch e, m. Sch p. Don
Valley CC.

BARNBY Suffolk (E)
137 TM 4789 3m E of Beccles. CP, 278.
Lothingland RD. Ch e, m. Sch p.
Lowestoft CC. Small Broad. Thatched ch.

BARNBY DUN Yorks (W)
103 SE 6109 5m NNE of Doncaster.
CP(Bnby Dn w Kirk Sandall), 3,141.
Dncstr RD. P Dncstr. Ch e, m. Sch p. Don
Valley CC.

BARNBY IN THE WILLOWS Notts
113 SK 8652 4m E of Newark. CP, 216.
Nwk RD. P(Bnby), Nwk. Ch e, m. Nwk CC.
Solid dovecote 63ft in circumference.

BARNBY MOOR Notts
103 SK 6684 3m NW of Retford. CP, 262.
E Rtfd RD. P Rtfd. Ch e. Bassetlaw CC. The
Bell is famous old coaching inn on former
Gt N Rd.

BARNES London
160, 170 TQ 2276 2m NW of Wandsworth.
Loc, Richmond upon Thames LB. Rchmnd
BC. On S bank of Thms in loop of river.
(Loop forms most of Oxford v Cambridge
Universities annual boat race course.)
Hammersmith Br to N; Bns (rly) Br to W.

BARNES STREET Kent
171 TQ 6448 4m ENE of Tonbridge. Loc,
Hadlow CP.

BARNET London
160 TQ 2496 11m NNW of Charing Cross.
LB, 303,578. P Herts. BCs: Chipping Bnt,
Finchley, Hendon N, Hndn S. (Bnt CC;
Fnchly BC, Hndn N, Hndn S.) See also
Arkley, Burnt Oak, Colindale, E Bnt,
Edgware, Fnchly, Friern Bnt, Golders Grn,
Hndn, Mill Hill, Monken Hadley, Totteridge.

BARNETBY LE WOLD Lincs (L)
104 TA 0509 4m ENE of Brigg. CP, 1,279.
Glanford Brgg RD. P(Bntby). Ch e, m.
Sch p. Brgg and Scunthorpe CC (Brgg).
Abandoned but still impressive 10c–12c ch
on hillside E of vllge.

BARNEY Norfolk
125 TF 9932 5m ENE of Fakenham. Loc,
Fulmodeston CP. P Fknhm. Ch e, m.

BARNHAM Suffolk (W)
136 TL 8679 3m S of Thetford. CP, 921.
Thingoe RD. P Thtfd, Norfolk. Ch e, m.
Sch pe. Bury St Edmunds CC.

BARNHAM Sussex (W)
181, 182 SU 9604 6m E of Chichester. CP,
459. Chchstr RD. P Bognor Regis. Ch e, m.
Sch p, sr. Arundel CC (Chchstr). Mostly by
the rly, but Nmn and later ch and 17c mnr
hse are to SW.

BARNHAM BROOM Norfolk
125 TG 0807 4m NNW of Wymondham.
CP, 331. Forehoe and Henstead RD.
P NORWICH, NOR 35X. Ch e, m. Sch pe.
S Nflk CC (Central Nflk).

BARNINGHAM Suffolk (W)
136 TL 9676 7m SE of Thetford. CP, 534.
Thingoe RD. P Bury St Edmunds. Ch e, m.
Sch pe. Bury St Eds CC. Ch: bench-ends.

BARNINGHAM Yorks (N)
84 NZ 0810 4m SSE of Barnard Cstle. CP,
188. Startforth RD. P Richmond. Ch e, m.
Rchmnd CC. Moorside vllge with stone hses
round grn.

BARNOLDBY LE BECK Lincs (L)
105 TA 2303 4m SSE of Grimsby. CP, 317.
Grmsby RD. Ch e, m. Louth CC.

BARNOLDSWICK Yorks (W)
95 SD 8746 4m N of Colne. UD, 9,937.
P Clne, Lancs. Skipton CC.

BARNS GREEN Sussex (W)
182 TQ 1226 3m ENE of Billingshurst. Loc,
Itchingfield CP. P Horsham. Ch c.

BARNSLEY Glos
157 SP 0705 4m NE of Cirencester. CP,
168. Crncstr and Tewkesbury CC. Cotswold
vllge. B. Pk, 18c mansion; Sir Isaac Newton's
library discovered in the hse, 1927. In pk,
rems of Roman villa.

BARNSLEY Yorks (W)
102 SE 3406 12m N of Sheffield. CB,
75,330. P. Bnsly BC. Coal-mining centre;
engineering wks. Monk Bretton Priory
(A.M.), rems of Benedictine monastery.

BARNSTAPLE Devon
163 SS 5533 34m NW of Exeter. MB,
17,342. P. N Dvn CC. See also Newport. Mkt
tn and chief tn of N Devon. Claims to be
oldest borough in England. Restored 13c br
over R Taw.

BARNSTON Ches
100, 109 SJ 2883 4m SW of Birkenhead.
Loc, Wirral UD. P Heswall, Wrrl. Wrrl CC.

BARNSTON Essex
148 TL 6419 2m SE of Dunmow. CP, 293.
Dnmw RD. P Dnmw. Ch e. Saffron
Walden CC.

BARNSTONE Notts
112, 122 SK 7335 10m ESE of Nottingham.
CP(Langar cum Bnstne), 520. Bingham RD.
Ch e, m. Rushcliffe CC (Carlton).

BARNT GREEN Worcs
131 SP 0073 4m NE of Bromsgrove. Loc,
Alvechurch CP. P BIRMINGHAM.
Ch e, b, f. Sch pe. Dormitory for Bmnghm.

BARNTON Ches
101/110 SJ 6375 2m WNW of Northwich.
CP, 4,485. Nthwch RD. P Nthwch.
Ch e, m4, r. Sch i, j. Nthwch CC.

BARNWELL Northants
134 TL 0584 2m S of Oundle. CP, 452.
Oundle and Thrapston RD.
P PETERBOROUGH. Ch e. Sch pe.
Wellingborough CC (Ptrbrgh). Orig two
vllges, hence second (disused) ch. B. Cstle,
home of Duke of Gloucester, Elizn hse with
20c alterations. Rems of old cstle in grnds.

BARRASFORD Nthmb
77 NY 9173 6m NNW of Hexham. Loc,
Chollerton CP. P Hxhm. Ch m.

BARRINGTON Cambs
148 TL 3949 6m NNE of Royston. CP, 531.
S Cambs RD. P CAMBRIDGE. Ch e, v.
Sch pe. Cambs CC. Very large grn. Cement
wks.

BARRINGTON Som
177 ST 3818 3m NE of Ilminster. CP, 403.
Langport RD. P Ilmnstr. Ch e, m. Sch pe.
Yeovil CC. Vllge of stone and thatch. B.Ct
(NT)*, Tdr mansion blt of Ham stone.

BARRINGTON COLLIERY Nthmb
78 NZ 2683 4m ESE of Morpeth. Loc,
Bedlingtonshire UD. Blyth BC.

BARRINGTON, GREAT Glos
144 SP 2013 3m WNW of Burford. See Gt Brrngtn.

BARRIPPER Cornwall
189 SW 6338 2m SW of Camborne. Loc, Cmbne—Redruth UD, W Penwith RD. P Cmbne. Falmouth and Cmbne CC.

BARROW Glos
143, 144 SO 8824 4m WNW of Cheltenham. Loc, Boddington CP.

BARROW Lancs
95 SD 7338 2m S of Clitheroe. Loc, Wiswell CP. P Blackburn. Ch v. Sch pc.

BARROW Rutland
122 SK 8915 4m NNE of Oakham. CP, 75. Oakhm RD. Ch e. Rtlnd and Stamford CC.

BARROW Shrops
118, 119 SJ 6500 2m E of Much Wenlock. CP. Bridgnorth RD. Ch e. Ludlow CC. See also Benthall, Linley, Willey.

BARROW Som
166 ST 7231 2m NNE of Wincanton. Loc, Charlton Musgrove CP.

BARROW Suffolk (W)
136 TL 7663 6m W of Bury St Edmunds. CP, 856. Thingoe RD. P Bury St Eds. Ch e,. c. Sch pe. Bury St Eds CC.

BARROWAY DROVE Norfolk
124 TF 5703 2m W of Downham Mkt. Loc, Stow Bardolph CP. P Dnhm Mkt. Sch p.

BARROWBY Lincs (K)
113, 122 SK 8836 2m W of Grantham. CP, 784. W Kesteven RD. P Grnthm. Ch e. Sch pe. Grnthm CC.

BARROWDEN Rutland
122/123/133 SK 9400 5m E of Uppingham. CP, 327. Uppnghm RD. Ch e, b. Rtlnd and Stamford CC. Straggling limestone vllge in valley of R Welland, here crossed by mdvl br. Ch has broach spire.

BARROWFORD Lancs
95 SD 8539 1m N of Nelson. UD, 5,130. P Nlsn. Nlsn and Colne BC. See also Higherford, Wheatley Lane.

BARROW, GREAT Ches
109 SJ 4768 4m ENE of Chester. See Gt Brrw.

BARROW GURNEY Som
155, 156, 165 ST 5367 5m SW of Bristol. CP, 769. Long Ashton RD. P BRSTL. Ch e. N Som CC.

BARROW HAVEN Lincs (L)
99 TA 0622 2m E of Barton-upon-Humber. Loc, Brrw upn Hmbr CP. P Brrw-on-Hmbr.

BARROW-IN-FURNESS Lancs
88 SD 1969 19m W of Carnforth across Morecambe Bay. CB, 63,998. P. Brrw-in-Fnss BC. See also Biggar, N Scale, Rampside, Roa Island, S End, Vickerstown. Shipbuilding employs nearly half the working pop. Some diversification in recent years.

BARROW UPON HUMBER Lincs (L)
99 TA 0721 2m E of Barton-upon-Humber. CP, 2,475. Glanford Brigg RD. P. Ch e, m2, s, v. Sch pe. Brgg and Scunthorpe CC (Brgg). See also Brrw Haven, New Holland.

BARROW UPON SOAR Leics
121, 122 SK 5717 3m ESE of Loughborough. CP, 3,194. Brrw upn Sr RD. P Lghbrgh. Ch e, b, m2, r. Sch i, je, s. Melton CC. Almshouses of 1644.

BARROW UPON TRENT Derbys
120, 121 SK 3528 5m S of Derby. CP. SE Derbys RD. P DBY. Ch e, m. Sch pe. SE Derbys CC.

BARSBY Leics
122 SK 6911 6m SW of Melton Mowbray. Loc, Gaddesby CP. Ch m.

BARSHAM Suffolk (E)
137 TM 3989 2m W of Beccles. CP, 213. Wainford RD. Ch e. Lowestoft CC. Ch has round Nmn twr and thatched roof; approach over cattle grid and past football pitch. Nelson's mother born in rectory alongside.

BARSTON Warwicks
131 SP 2078 3m ESE of Solihull. CP. Meriden RD. P Slhll. Ch e. Mrdn CC. See also Eastcote.

BARTESTREE Herefs
142 SO 5640 4m E of Hereford. CP, 139. Hrfd RD. P HRFD. Ch e. Leominster CC.

BARTHOMLEY Ches
110 SJ 7652 4m ESE of Crewe. CP, 285.
Nantwich RD. P Crwe. Ch e. Crwe CC. See
also Radway Grn. Score of villagers hid in
ch from marauding Royalists in Civil War;
smoked out and killed one by one.

BARTLEY Hants
180 SU 3013 6m SSW of Romsey. Loc,
Copythorne CP. P SOUTHAMPTON. Sch s.

BARTLOW Cambs
148 TL 5845 5m NE of Saffron Walden.
CP, 68. S Cambs RD. P CAMBRIDGE. Ch e.
On Essex border. Ch: round twr;
wall-painting of large fierce dragon. At B.
Hills, rems of Romano-British settlement
where finds of glass, bronze, enamel made in
19c excavations.

BARTON Cambs
135 TL 4055 3m SW of Cambridge. CP,
788. Chesterton RD. P CMBRDGE. Ch e, b.
Sch pe. Cambs CC. Ch: wall-paintings, font,
scrn, plpt.

BARTON Ches
109 SJ 4454 8m ENE of Wrexham. CP, 72.
Tarvin RD. Ch c. Nantwich CC.

BARTON Glos
144 SP 1025 5m ESE of Winchcombe. Loc,
Temple Guiting CP.

BARTON Lancs
94 SD 5137 5m N of Preston. CP, 1,487.
Prstn RD. Ch e2. Sch pe. S Fylde CC. See
also Newsham.

BARTON Lancs
100 SD 3509 3m E of Formby. Loc, Downholland CP. W Lancs RD. Ormskirk CC.

BARTON Warwicks
144 SP 1051 6m WSW of Stratford. Loc,
Bidford-on-Avon CP. 17c mnr hse.

BARTON Westm
83 NY 4826 3m SW of Penrith. CP, 281.
N Westm RD. Ch e. Westm CC. See also
Pooley Br. Ch has curious Nmn central twr
and Nmn doorway.

BARTON Yorks (N)
85 NZ 2308 5m SW of Darlington. CP, 505.
Croft RD. P Richmond. Ch e, m. Sch pe.
Rchmnd CC.

BARTON BENDISH Norfolk
124 TF 7105 7m ENE of Downham Mkt.
CP, 261. Dnhm RD. P King's Lynn. Ch e2.
Sch pe. SW Nflk CC.

BARTON COMMON Norfolk
126 TG 3522 5m NE of Wroxham. Loc, Btn
Turf CP.

BARTON, GREAT Suffolk (W)
136 TL 8967 3m NE of Bury St Edmunds.
See Gt Btn.

BARTON HARTSHORN Bucks
145, 146 SP 6430 4m WSW of Buckingham.
CP, 64. Bcknghm RD. Ch e. Bcknghm CC.

BARTON IN FABIS Notts
112, 121 SK 5232 6m SW of Nottingham.
CP, 197. Basford RD. P(Btn), NTTNGHAM
Ch e. Rushcliffe CC. Known also as Btn in
the Beans. Octagonal brick dovecote with
1,200 nesting places.

BARTON IN THE BEANS Leics
120, 121 SK 3906 5m SSW of Coalville.
Loc, Shackerstone CP. P Nuneaton,
Warwickshire. Ch b. Sch p.

BARTON IN THE CLAY Beds
147 TL 0830 6m N of Luton.
CP(Btn-le-Clay), 2,755. Ltn RD.
P(Btn-le-Clay), BEDFORD. Ch e, b, m.
Sch je, p, s. S Beds CC. Under N edge of
Chilterns.

BARTON-LE-STREET Yorks (N)
92 SE 7274 4m WNW of Malton. CP, 159.
Mltn RD. P Mltn. Ch e. Thirsk and Mltn CC.

BARTON-LE-WILLOWS Yorks (N)
92, 97, 98 SE 7163 7m SW of Malton.
CP, 157. Mltn RD. P YORK. Ch m. Thirsk
and Mltn CC.

BARTON MILLS Suffolk (W)
135 TL 7173 8m NE of Newmarket.
CP, 666. Mildenhall RD.
P Bury St Edmunds. Ch e, b.
Bury St Eds CC. Large corn mill beside
R Lark and A11 rd.

BARTON-ON-SEA Hants
179 SZ 2393 5m E of Christchurch. Loc,
Lymington MB. P New Milton.

BARTON-ON-THE HEATH Warwicks
144 SP 2532 3m E of Moreton-in-Marsh.
CP, 103. Shipston on Stour RD.
P Mtn-in-Msh, Glos. Ch e.
Stratford-on-Avon CC (Strtfd).

BARTON ST DAVID Som
165, 166 ST 5432 5m SSE of Glastonbury.
CP, 267. Langport RD. P Somerton. Ch e.
Yeovil CC.

BARTON SEAGRAVE Northants
133 SP 8877 1m SE of Kettering. Loc,
Kttrng MB. P Kttrng.

BARTON STACEY Hants
168 SU 4341 5m ESE of Andover. CP,
1,479. Andvr RD. P Winchester. Ch e.
Sch pe. Wnchstr CC(Basingstoke). See also
Newton Stcy. Ch mainly 12c; 14c twr.

BARTON TOWN Devon
163 SS 6840 6m SSW of Lynton. Loc,
Challacombe CP. Ch e.

BARTON TURF Norfolk
126 TG 3421 4m NE of Wroxham. CP, 375.
Snallburgh RD. P NORWICH, NOR 36Z.
Ch e, m. N Nflk CC. See also Btn Cmmn,
Irstead. Ch: 15c painted scrn. Btn Broad
to E.

BARTON-UNDER-NEEDWOOD Staffs
120 SK 1818 4m SW of Burton-on-Trent.
CP, 2,468. Tutbury RD. Ch e, m, r.
Sch i, j, s. Btn CC.

BARTON-UPON-HUMBER Lincs (L)
99 TA 0321 11m NE of Scunthorpe. UD,
7,496. P. Brigg and Scnthpe CC (Brgg).
Formerly important port. Two 12c-13c chs,
one partly Saxon. Many Ggn hses.

BARUGH Yorks (W)
102 SE 3108 3m NW of Barnsley. Loc,
Darton UD. P (Brgh Grn), Bnsly.

BARUGH, GREAT Yorks (N)
92 SE 7479 4m SW of Pickering. See Gt
Brgh.

BARWAY Cambs
135 TL 5475 3m S of Ely. Loc, Soham CP.
Ch e.

BARWELL Leics
132 SP 4496 2m NNE of Hinckley. Loc,
Hnckly UD. P LEICESTER.

BARWICK Som
177, 178 ST 5613 2m S of Yeovil. CP, 800.
Yvl RD. Ch e. Sch p. Yvl CC. See also
Stoford. In grnds of B. Hse, early 19c Gothic
follies.

BARWICK IN ELMET Yorks (W)
96/97 SE 4037 7m ENE of Leeds. CP,
3,087. Tadcaster RD. P LDS. Ch e, m2.
Sch pe. Barkston Ash CC. See also Scoles.

BASCHURCH Shrops
118 SJ 4222 7m NW of Shrewsbury. CP,
1,508. N Shrops RD. P Shrsbry. Ch e, m.
Sch pe, s. Oswestry CC. See also Prescott,
Stanwardine in the Fields, Stnwdne in the
Wd, Walford, Weston Lullingfields, Yeaton.

BASFORD GREEN Staffs
110 SJ 9951 3m S of Leek. Loc,
Cheddleton CP.

BASHALL EAVES Yorks (W)
94, 95 SD 6943 3m WNW of Clitheroe. CP,
174. Bowland RD. P Clthroe, Lancs. Sch pe.
Skipton CC. 1m N, Browsholme Hall*, Tdr
mnr hse in landscaped grnds.

BASHLEY Hants
179 SZ 2497 6m ENE of Christchurch. Loc,
Lymington MB. P New Milton.

BASILDON Berks
158 SU 6178 2m NW of Pangbourne. CP,
1,102. Bradfield RD. Ch e. Newbury CC. See
also Upr Bsldn. Child-Beale Wildlife Trust:
lakes and riverside walks; peacocks, wildfowl.
Summer regattas on Thames.

BASILDON Essex
161, 162 TQ 7288 10m W of Southend.
UD, 129,073. P. Bsldn BC (Billericay CC).
See also Bllrcy, Bowers Gifford, Crays Hill,
Dunton Wayletts, Gt Burstead, Laindon,
Langdon Hills, Lit Bstd, Nevendon,
N Benfleet, Pitsea, Ramsden Bellhouse,
Shotgate, S Grn, Vange, Wickford. Indstrl
and rsdntl tn almost entirely blt since 1950s.
Pedestrian precinct in centre. New tn pop.
77,154

BASING Hants
168, 169 SU 6652 2m E of Basingstoke. CP,
2,964. Bsngstke RD. Ch e, m. Sch pe.
Bsngstke CC. See also Chineham, Hatch. B.
Hse Ruins*, 16c gatehouse and dovecote,
rems of mansion destroyed in Civil War.
Museum, secret passage.

BASINGSTOKE Hants
168, 169 SU 6351 15m SSW of Reading. MB, 52,502. P. Bsngstke CC. Engineering wks. Large new development planned. Willis museum of local history. 1½m NW, Winklebury Camp, prehistoric earthwork of 4c–1c BC.

BASLOW Derbys
111 SK 2572 3m NE of Bakewell. CP (Bslw and Bubnell), 1,007. Bkwll RD. P Bkwll. Ch e, m. Sch pe. W Derbys CC. Two brs over R Derwent; older has tiny toll hse or guard hse.

BASON BRIDGE Som
165 ST 3445 4m ST of Burnham. Loc, E Huntspill CP. P Highbridge.

BASSENTHWAITE Cumb
82 NY 2332 7m E of Cockermouth. CP, 477. Cckrmth RD. P Keswick. Ch e, m. Sch p. Workington CC. Lake over 1m SW. Skiddaw, 3053ft, 2¾m SE; most easily approached from S.

BASSINGBOURN Cambs
147 TL 3343 3m NW of Royston. CP(Bssngbn cum Kneesworth), 2,653. S Cambs RD. P Rstn, Herts. Ch e, c, m. Sch p, s. Cambs CC. The secondary sch is one of the vllge colleges which are a speciality of the county. Airfield to N.

BASSINGFIELD Notts
112, 121, 122 SK 6137 4m ESE of Nottingham. Loc, Holme Pierrepont CP.

BASSINGHAM Lincs (K)
113 SK 9059 8m SSW of Lincoln. CP, 667. N Kesteven RD. P LNCLN. Ch e, m. Sch p. Grantham CC.

BASSINGTHORPE Lincs (K)
123 SK 9628 5m SSE of Grantham. CP(Bitchfield and Bssngthpe), 160. W Kesteven RD. Ch e. Rutland and Stamford CC.

BASTON Lincs (K)
123 TF 1113 4m S of Bourne. CP, 540. S Kesteven RD. P PETERBOROUGH. Ch e. Sch pe. Rutland and Stamford CC.

BASTWICK Norfolk
126 TG 4217 8m E of Wroxham. CP(Repps w Bstwck), 347. Blofield and Flegg RD. Sch p. Yarmouth CC.

BASWICH Staffs
119 SJ 9422 2m SE of Stafford. Loc, Stffd MB; CP, 1,505. Stffd RD. Stffd and Stone CC. See also Milford, Walton-on-the-Hill. In loop of Staffs and Worcs Canal.

BATCOMBE Dorset
178 ST 6104 8m S of Sherborne. CP, 116. Shbne RD. Ch e. W Dst CC. Ch Perp twr. 1m E, Cross and (or in) Hand, stone pillar, purpose and origin unknown.

BATCOMBE Som
166 ST 6939 3m N of Bruton. CP, 387. Shepton Mallet RD. P Shptn Mllt. Ch e, m. Wells CC. See also Westcombe. Ch: outstanding 14c–15c twr.

BATH Som
156/166 ST 7564 11m ESE of Bristol. CB, 84,545. P. Bth BC. See also Combe Down, Twerton. Roman spa tn of *Aquae Sulis*; hot springs unique in Britain. Abbey ch, rebuilt 1501. 18c hses, shops, crescents; spa bldngs both Roman and 18c.

BATHAMPTON Som
156 ST 7766 2m ENE of Bath. CP, 1,244. Bathavon RD. P Bth. Ch e, m. Sch p. N Som CC.

BATHEALTON Som
164 ST 0724 4m NW of Wellington. CP, 203. Wllngtn RD. P Taunton. Ch e. Tntn CC.

BATHEASTON Som
156 ST 7767 3m NE of Bath. CP, 3,307. Bathavon RD. P Bth. Ch e, c, m, r2. Sch pe. N Som CC.

BATHFORD Som
156 ST 7866 3m ENE of Bath. CP, 1,281. Bathavon RD. P Bth. Ch e, b. Sch pe. N Som CC.

BATHLEY Notts
112 SK 7759 4m NNW of Newark. CP, 151. Southwell RD. Ch m. Nwk CC.

BATHPOOL Cornwall
186 SX 2874 6m NW of Callington. Loc, N Hill CP. P Launceston. Ch m.

BATHPOOL Som
177 ST 2526 2m ENE of Taunton. Loc, W Monkton CP. P Tntn.

BATLEY Yorks (W)
96, 102 SE 2424 2m N of Dewsbury. MB,
42,004. P. Btly and Morley BC. See also
Birstall Smithies. Wool tn; processing of
rags, shoddy, mungo, etc.

BATSFORD Glos
144 SP 1833 2m NW of Moreton-in-Marsh.
CP, 259. N Cotswold RD. Ch e. Cirencester
and Tewkesbury CC. See also Lr Lemington.
Buddhas and Chinese temples in gdns of B.
Pk.

BATTERSBY Yorks (N)
86 NZ 5907 4m E of Stokesley. Loc,
Ingleby Greenhow CP.

BATTERSEA London
160, 170 TQ 2775 3m SSW of Charing
Cross. Loc,Wandsworth LB. Bttrsea N BC,
Bttrsea S BC. On S bank of Thames; Bttrsea,
Albert, Chelsea Brs. Power stn to E of
Grosvenor (rly) Br. Bttrsea Pk (fun fair in
summer).

BATTISBOROUGH CROSS Devon
187 SX 5948 6m SSW of Ivybridge. Loc,
Holbeton CP. P Plymouth. Ch m.

BATTISFORD Suffolk (E)
149 TM 0554 3m S of Stowmarket. CP,
392. Gipping RD. Ch e, c, v. Eye CC. See
also Bttsfd Tye.

BATTISFORD TYE Suffolk(E)
149 TM 0254 3m SW of Stowmarket. Loc,
Bttsfd CP. P Stwmkt.

BATTLE Sussex (E)
183, 184 TQ 7416 6m NW of Hastings.
CP, 4,517. Bttle RD. P. Ch e, b, c, m, r.
Sch pe, s. Rye CC. See also Netherfield.
Rems of abbey* founded by William I after
Battle of Hastings (fought here), incl 14c
gatehouse giving on to tn square.

BATTLEFIELD Shrops
118 SJ 5116 3m NNE of Shrewsbury. Loc,
Shrwsbry MB. P Shrsbry. Ch blt by Henry
IV to commemorate victory at Battle of
Shrsbry in 1403.

BATTLESBRIDGE Essex
162 TQ 7894 6m NE of Basildon. Loc,
Rayleigh UD. P Wickford.

BATTLESDEN Beds
147 SP 9628 4m NE of Leighton Buzzard.
CP, 54. Ampthill RD. Ch e. Mid-Beds CC.

BATTLETON Som
164 SS 9127 just S of Dulverton. Loc, Dlvtn
CP.

BATTRAMSLEY Hants
180 SZ 3099 2m S of Brockenhurst. Loc,
Boldre CP.

BATT'S CORNER Surrey
169 SU 8240 4m SSW of Farnham. Loc,
Dockenfield CP. Hambledon RD.
P(Dcknfld), Fnhm. Ch m. Fnhm CC.

BAUGHURST Hants
168 SU 5860 6m NNW of Basingstoke. CP,
2,268. Kingsclere and Whitchurch RD.
P Bsngstke. Ch e, m2. Sch s. Bsngstke CC.
See also Wolverton.

BAULKING Berks
158 SU 3190 4m SSE of Faringdon. CP,
122. Frngdn RD. Ch e. Abingdon CC.

BAUMBER Lincs (L)
114 TF 2274 4m NW of Horncastle. CP,
224. Hncstle RD. P Hncstle. Ch e. Sch p.
Hncstle CC. Ggn ch, standing in field.

BAUNTON Glos
157 SP 0204 2m N of Cirencester. CP, 164.
Crncstr RD. Ch e. Crncstr and Tewkesbury
CC.

BAVERSTOCK Wilts
167 SU 0232 8m W of Salisbury. Loc,
Dinton CP. Ch e.

BAVINGTON, GREAT Nthmb
77 NY 9880 10m N of Corbridge. See Gt
Bvngtn.

BAWBURGH Norfolk
126 TG 1508 5m W of Norwich. CP
Forehoe and Henstead RD. P NRWCH,
NOR 46X. Ch e, m. Sch p. S Nflk CC
(Central Nflk).

BAWDESWELL Norfolk
125 TG 0420 6m NE of E Dereham. CP,
364. Mitford and Launditch RD. P Drhm.
Ch e, b, m. Sch p. SW Nflk CC. Neo-Ggn ch
of 1950 replaces Vctrn ch destroyed by air
crash.

BAWDRIP Som
165 ST 3439 3m NE of Bridgwater. CP,
510. Brdgwtr RD. P Brdgwtr. Ch e, v. Sch p.
Brdgwtr CC.

BAWDSEY Suffolk (E)
150 TM 3440 7m SE of Woodbridge.
CP, 549. Deben RD. P Wdbrdge. Ch e, m.
Sch pe. Sudbury and Wdbrdge CC. 1¾m SW
at B. Quay, motorboat ferry for pedestrians
across R Deben.

BAWTRY Yorks (W)
103 SK 6593 8m SE of Doncaster. CP,
1,439. Dncstr RD. P Dncstr. Ch e, m.
Sch i, j. Don Valley CC. Old Gt N Rd tn;
coaching inns and wide cobbled verges. Now
bypassed.

BAXENDEN Lancs
95 SD 7726 2m SSE of Accrington. Loc
Accrngtn MB.

BAXTERLEY Warwicks
131 SO 2797 2m W of Atherstone. CP, 422.
Athrstne RD. P Athrstne. Ch e. Meriden CC.

BAYCLIFF Lancs
88 SD 2872 4m S of Ulverston. Loc,
Aldingham CP. P Ulvstn.

BAYDON Wilts
158 SU 2878 8m NE of Marlborough. CP,
286. Mlbrgh and Ramsbury RD. P Mlbrgh.
Ch e, m. Sch pe. Devizes CC. Highest vllge in
county, 750ft.

BAYFORD Herts
160 TL 3108 3m SSW of Hertford. CP, 493.
Htfd RD. P HTFD. Ch e. Sch pe. Htfd and
Stevenage CC (Htfd).

BAYFORD Som
166 ST 7229 1m ENE of Wincanton. Loc,
Stoke Trister CP. P Wncntn.

BAYLHAM Suffolk (E)
150 TM 1051 6m NW of Ipswich. CP, 247.
Gipping RD. Ch e. Eye CC.

BAYSTONHILL Shrops
118 SJ 4808 2m S of Shrewsbury. CP (Bstn
Hill). Atcham RD. P Shrsbry. Ch e, m.
Sch je, p. Shrsbry CC. See also Annscroft.

BAYSWATER London
160 TQ 2680 3m W of Charing Cross. Loc,
City of Westminster LB. Paddington BC

(Pddngtn S). Rsdntl distr. Orig 'Baynard's
Water', name given to stretch of Westbourne
Brook. Many small hotels and lodgings.

BAYTHORN END Essex
148, 149 TL 7242 3m WSW of Clare. Loc,
Birdbrook CP. P Halstead.

BAYTON Worcs
130 SO 6973 6m W of Bewdley. CP, 416.
Tenbury RD. P Kidderminster. Ch e. Sch pe.
Kddrmnstr CC.

BEACHAMPTON Bucks
146 SP 7737 2m SSW of Stony Stratford.
CP, 117. Buckingham RD. P Wolverton. Ch e.
Bcknghm CC.

BEACHAMWELL Norfolk
124/125 TF 7505 5m WSW of Swaffham.
CP, 322. Swffhm RD. P King's Lynn.
Ch e, m. Sch p. SW Nflk CC.

BEACHLEY Glos
155, 156 ST 5591 2m SSE of Chepstow.
Loc, Tidenham CP. P Chpstw. Ch e. Sch j.
At W end of Severn Rd Br (see Aust).

BEACON Devon
176 ST 1805 3m NNE of Honiton. Loc,
Luppitt CP.

BEACON END Essex
149, 162 TL 9524 2m W of Colchester. Loc,
Stanway CP.

BEACON'S BOTTOM Bucks
159 SU 7895 5m WNW of High Wycombe.
Loc, Stokenchurch CP. Sch p.

BEACONSFIELD Bucks
159 SU 9490 5m ESE of High Wycombe.
UD, 11,861. P. Bcnsfld CC (S Bucks). In
gently sloping wooded area. Ggn hses. Burial
place of Edmund Burke and Edmund
Waller; sometime home of G.K. Chesterton.
Bekonscot Gdns*, with model vllge and rly.

BEADLAM Yorks (N)
92 SE 6584 3m ENE of Helmsley. CP, 336.
Hlmsly RD. Ch e. Thirsk and Malton CC.

BEADNELL Nthmb
71 NU 2329 5m SE of Bamburgh. CP, 586.
Belford RD. P Chathill. Ch e. Sch pe.
Berwick-upon-Tweed CC. See also Benthall,
Fleetham, Swinhoe, Tughall. Fishing vllge ;
18c lime kilns (NT) by harbour. Sands and
shacks.

BEAFORD Devon
163 SS 5514 5m SE of Torrington. CP, 303. Trrngtn RD. P Winkleigh. Ch e, m. Sch p. W Dvn CC (Trrngtn).

BEAL Nthmb
64 NU 0642 8m SSE of Berwick-upon-Tweed. Loc, Kyloe CP. Norham and Islandshires RD. P BRWCK-UPN-TWD. Brwck-upn-Twd CC. 1m E, causeway (passable at low tide) to Holy Island (qv).

BEAL Yorks (W)
97 SE 5325 6m E of Castleford. CP, 513. Osgoldcross RD. Sch p. Goole CC.

BEALINGS, GREAT Suffolk (E)
150 TM 2348 2m W of Woodbridge. See Gt Blngs.

BEAMINSTER Dorset
177 ST 4801 5m N of Bridport. CP, 2,000. Bmnstr RD. P. Ch e, m, v. Sch pe, s. W Dst CC. Ch: Tdr twr of Ham stone.

BEAMISH Co Durham
78 NZ 2253 3m WNW of Chester-le-Street. Loc, Urpeth CP. Chstr-le-Strt RD. P Stanley. Ch e, m. Chstr-le-Strt CC. To NW at B. Hall, Drhm Indstrl Museum (open air).

BEAMSLEY Yorks (W)
96 SE 0752 4m NW of Ilkley. CP, 167. Skipton RD. Ch m. Sch pe. Skptn CC. Between R Wharfe and moors. B. Beacon, landmark, to E.

BEAN Kent
161, 171 TQ 5872 3m ESE of Dartford. Loc, Stone CP. P Dtfd. Sch p.

BEANACRE Wilts
156, 157 ST 9066 5m S of Chippenham. Loc, Melksham Without CP. Bradford and Melksham RD. P Mlkshm. Ch e. Westbury CC.

BEANLEY Nthmb
71 NU 0818 7m WNW of Alnwick. Loc, Hedgeley CP. Alnwck RD. Berwick-upon-Tweed CC.

BEARE GREEN Surrey
170, 182 TQ 1743 4m S of Dorking. Loc, Capel CP. P Dkng. Sch s. Hmlt blt round grn containing cricket grnd.

BEARLEY Warwicks
131 SP 1760 4m NNW of Stratford. CP, 853. Strtfd-on-Avon RD. P Strtfd-upon-Avn. Ch e, m. Sch p. Strtfd-on-Avn CC (Strtfd).

BEARPARK Co Durham
85 NZ 2343 2m WNW of Durham. CP, 2,229. Drhm RD. P DRHM. Ch e, m. Sch p. Drhm CC.

BEARSBRIDGE Nthmb
77 NY 7857 6m SW of Haydon Br. Loc, Plenmeller and Whitfield CP.

BEARSTED Kent
172 TQ 7955 2m E of Maidstone. CP, 3,267. Mdstne RD. P Mdstne. Ch e. Sch p, pe. Mdstne CC. Blt round grn where Wat Tyler assembled men of Peasants' Revolt, 1381.

BEARSTONE Shrops
110, 119 SJ 7239 5m NE of Mkt Drayton. Loc, Woore CP.

BEARWOOD Dorset
179 SZ 0596 4m NNW of Bournemouth. Loc, Poole MB. P Bnmth.

BEAUCHAMP RODING Essex
161 TL 5809 5m NNE of Ongar. CP(Abbess Bchmp and Berners Rdng), 516. Epping and Ongar RD. Ch e. Brentwood and Ongr CC (Chigwell). One of eight Rodings, pronounced 'roothing'.

BEAUDESERT Warwicks
131 SP 1565 7m NNW of Stratford. CP, 782. Strtfd-on-Avon RD. Ch e. Sch pr. Strtfd-on-Avn CC (Strtfd). Motte and bailey cstle to N.

BEAULIEU Hants
180 SU 3802 6m E of Brockenhurst. CP, 1,165. New Forest RD. P Brcknhst. Ch e. Sch p. Nw Frst CC. See also Buckler's Hard. Beside reedy Beaulieu River. Boats. Ch is refectory of 13c abbey, Palace Hse* its gatehouse. Motor museum.

BEAUMONT Cumb
76 NY 3459 4m NW of Carlisle. CP, 404. Border RD. Ch e, m. Penrith and the Border CC. See also Grinsdale, Kirkandrews upon Eden. Course of Hadrian's Wall runs through vllge.

BEAUMONT Essex
150 TM 1725 6m N of Clacton.
CP(Bmnt-cum-Moze), 352. Tendring RD.
P Clctn-on-Sea. Ch e, m. Harwich CC.

BEAUSALE Warwicks
131 SP 2470 5m NNW of Warwick. CP, 268.
Warwick RD. Wrwck and Leamington CC.
To SE, Iron Age fort.

BEAUWORTH Hants
168 SU 5726 6m ESE of Winchester. CP,
149. Wnchstr RD. Ch e. Wnchstr CC.

BEAWORTHY Devon
175 SX 4699 8m ESE of Holsworthy.
CP, 240. Okehampton RD. P. Ch e, m.
W Dvn CC (Torrington).

BEAZLEY END Essex
148, 149 TL 7428 4m NNW of Braintree.
Loc, Wethersfield CP.

BEBINGTON Ches
100, 109 SJ 3384 3m S of Birkenhead.
MB, 61,488. P Wirral. Bbngtn and Ellesmere
Port BC (Bbngtn). See also Bromborough,
Eastham, Port Sunlight, Raby, Storeton,
Thornton Hough. Rapid indstrl growth;
soaps, detergents, edible oils and fats, etc.

BEBSIDE Nthmb
78 NZ 2881 2m W of Blyth. Loc, Blth MB.

BECCLES Suffolk (E)
137 TM 4290 8m WSW of Lowestoft.
MB, 8,015. P. Lwstft CC. R Waveney and
Broads resort. Mkt tn of agricultural distr.
Engineering and printing wks. Perp ch with
detached twr. To W, Roos Hall, Elizn.

BECCONSALL Lancs
94 SD 4423 7m SW of Preston.
CP(Hesketh-w-Bccnsll), 1,820. W Lancs RD.
Ch e2, m. Ormskirk CC.

BECKBURY Shrops
119 SJ 7601 4m SSE of Shifnal. CP, 391.
Shfnl RD. P Shfnl. Ch e, m. Sch pe. The
Wrekin CC.

BECKENHAM London
171 TQ 3769 2m W of Bromley. Loc, Brmly
LB. P Kent. Bcknhm BC. Largely rsdntl
suburb.

BECKERING Lincs (L)
104 TF 1280 5m S of Mkt Rasen.
CP(Holton cum Bckrng), 115. Welton RD.
Gainsborough CC.

BECKFOOT Cumb
81, 82 NY 0949 3m SSW of Silloth. Loc,
Holme St Cuthbert CP. Ch f.

BECK FOOT Westm
89 SD 6196 4m NW of Sedbergh. Loc,
Dillicar CP. S Westm RD. Ch m. Westm CC.

BECKFORD Worcs
143, 144 SO 9735 5m ENE of Tewkesbury.
CP, 521. Evesham RD. P Tksbry, Glos.
Ch e, r. S Worcs CC. See also Grafton.

BECKHAMPTON Wilts
157 SU 0868 6m W of Marlborough. Loc,
Avebury CP.

BECK HOLE Yorks (N)
86, 92 NZ 8202 7m SW of Whitby. Loc,
Goathland CP.

BECKINGHAM Lincs (K)
113 SK 8753 5m E of Newark. CP, 240. N
Kesteven RD. P LINCOLN. Ch e, m.
Grantham CC.

BECKINGHAM Notts
104 SK 7890 2m W of Gainsborough. CP
706. E Retford RD. P Doncaster, Yorkshire.
Ch e, m2. Sch p. Bassetlaw CC.

BECKINGTON Som
166 ST 8051 3m NE of Frome. CP, 784.
Frme RD. P Bath. Ch e, b. Sch pe. Wells CC.
See also Rudge. Many stone 16c–17c hses.

BECKLEY Oxon
145, 146 SP 5611 4m NE of Oxford.
CP(Bckly and Stowood), 475.
Bullingdon RD. P OXFD. Ch e. Sch pe.
Mid-Oxon CC (Henley).

BECKLEY Sussex (E)
184 TQ 8524 5m WNW of Rye. CP, 931.
Battle RD. P Rye. Ch e, m, v. Sch pe.
Rye CC. See also Four Oaks.

BECK ROW Suffolk (W)
135 TL 6977 9m NNE of Newmarket. Loc,
Mildenhall CP. P Bury St Edmunds. Ch m.
Sch p.

BECK SIDE Lancs
88 SD 2382 4m NW of Ulverston. Loc,
Kirkby Ireleth CP. N Lonsdale RD. Ch e.
Morecambe and Lnsdle CC.

BECKWITHSHAW Yorks (W)
96 SE 2653 3m WSW of Harrogate. Loc,
Pannal CP. P Hrrgte. Ch e, m. Sch p.

BEDALE Yorks (N)
91 SE 2688 7m WSW of Northallerton. CP,
8,215. Bdle Rd. P. Ch e, m. Sch pe, s. Thirsk
and Malton CC. Old mkt tn in Lr
Wensleydale with wide main street. B. Hall*,
Ggn hse with small museum.

BEDBURN Co Durham
84 NZ 1031 7m WNW of Bishop Auckland.
Loc, S Bdbn CP. Barnard Cstle RD. Bshp
Aucklnd CC.

BEDCHESTER Dorset
178 ST 8517 4m S of Shaftesbury. Loc,
Fontmell Magna CP. P Shftsbry. Ch m.

BEDDALL'S END Essex
148, 149, 162 TL 7421 1m SSW of
Braintree. Loc, Brntree and Bocking UD.

BEDDINGHAM Sussex (E)
183 TQ 4407 2m SE of Lewes. CP, 354.
Chailey RD. Ch e. Lws CC.

BEDDINGTON London
170 TQ 2964 2m W of Croydon. Loc,
Sutton LB. Carshalton BC (Mitcham).

BEDFIELD Suffolk (E)
137 TM 2266 4m WNW of Framlingham.
CP, 254. Hartismere RD. P Woodbridge.
Ch e, v. Sch pe. Eye CC.

BEDFORD Beds
147 TL 0449 46m NNW of London.
MB, 73,064. P(BDFD). Bdfd CC. On
R Ouse; br blt by Wing in 1813. John
Bunyan imprisoned here 1660—72.

BEDHAMPTON Hants
181 SU 6906 1m W of Havant. Loc, Hvnt
and Waterloo UD. P Hvnt.

BEDINGFIELD Suffolk (E)
137 TM 1868 4m SE of Eye. CP, 231.
Hartismere RD. P Eye. Ch e. Eye CC. Ch:
double-hammerbeam roof; bench-ends. 1m
SE, Flemings Hall, 16c hse on site of earlier
one; moated.

BEDLINGTON Nthmb
78 NZ 2582 4m W of Blyth. Loc,
Bedlingtonshire UD. P. Blth BC.
Coal-mining; manufacture of electrical
equipment.

BEDLINGTON STATION Nthmb
78 NZ 2783 3m WNW of Blyth. Loc,
Bedlingtonshire UD. Blth CC.

BEDMOND Herts
160 TL 0903 4m SE of Hemel Hempstead.
Loc, Abbots Langley CP. P Abbts Lngly,
Watford.

BEDNALL Staffs
119 SJ 9517 4m SSE of Stafford. CP(Acton
Trussell and Bdnll), 410. Cannock RD. Ch e.
Sch pe. SW Staffs CC (Cnnck).

BEDSTONE Shrops
129 SO 3675 6m ENE of Knighton. CP, 75.
Clun and Bishop's Cstle RD. P Bucknell.
Ch e. Ludlow CC.

BEDWORTH Warwicks
132 SP 3687 5m NNE of Coventry.
UD, 40,535. P Nuneaton. Nntn BC (CC).
See also Bulkington. Coal-mining distr.

BEDWYN, GREAT Wilts
167 SU 2764 5m SW of Hungerford. See
Gt Bdwn.

BEEBY Leics
121, 122 SK 6608 5m ENE of Leicester.
CP, 104. Barrow upon Soar Rd. Ch e.
Melton CC.

BEECH Hants
169 SU 6938 2m W of Alton. Loc, Alton
UD. P Altn.

BEECH Staffs
110, 119 SJ 8538 5m SSW of
Stoke-on-Trent. Loc, Swynnerton CP.

BEECH HILL Berks
169 SU 6964 6m S of Reading. CP, 336.
Bradfield RD. P Rdng. Ch e, b. Newbury
CC.

BEECHINGSTOKE Wilts
167 SU 0859 5m W of Pewsey. CP, 235.
Devizes RD. Ch e. Dvzs CC.

BEEDON Berks
158 SU 4878 7m N of Newbury. CP, 377.
Wantage RD. P (Bdn Hill), Nbry. Ch e.
Sch pe. Abingdon CC. See also Stanmore,
World's End.

BEEFORD Yorks (E)
99 TA 1354 6m NW of Hornsea. CP, 543.
Driffield RD. P Drffld. Ch e, m. Sch pe.
Howden CC.

BEELEY Derbys
111 SK 2667 3m E of Bakewell. CP, 214.
Bkwll RD. P Matlock. Ch e, m. Sch pe.
W Derbys CC.

BEELSBY Lincs (L)
105 TA 2001 6m SW of Grimsby. CP, 113.
Grmsby RD. Ch e. Louth CC.

BEENHAM Berks
158 SU 5868 7m E of Newbury. CP, 783.
Bradfield RD. P(Bnhm Vllge), Reading.
Ch e, m. Sch p. Newbury CC.

BEER Devon
177 SY 2289 1m WSW of Seaton.
CP, 1,453. Axminster RD. P Stn. Ch e, v2.
Sch pe. Honiton CC. Small resort at foot of
high chalk cliffs. Formerly fishing vllge and
smugglers' haunt.

BEERCROCOMBE Som
177 ST 3220 4m NNW of Ilminster.
CP, 101. Langport RD. Ch e. Yeovil CC.

BEER HACKETT Dorset
177, 178 ST 5911 4m SE of Yeovil. CP, 74.
Sherborne RD. Ch e. W Dst CC.

BEESANDS Devon
188 SX 8140 6m ESE of Kingsbridge. Loc,
Stokenham CP. P Kngsbrdge. Fishing vllge.

BEESBY Lincs (L)
105 TF 4680 3m NNE of Alford. CP(Bsby
in the Marsh), 100. Louth RD. P Alfd. Lth
CC.

BEESON Devon
188 SX 8140 5m ESE of Kingsbridge. Loc,
Stokenham CP. P Kngsbrdge.

BEESTON Beds
147 TL 1748 just S of Sandy. Loc, Sndy
UD. P Sndy.

BEESTON Ches
109 SJ 5458 8m NW of Nantwich. CP, 259.
Tarvin RD. Ch m. Nntwch CC. On hill
to NW is B. Cstle (A.M.), 13c ruin and well
known landmark.

BEESTON Norfolk
125 TF 9015 5m WNW of E Dereham.
CP (Bstn w Bittering), 394, Mitford and
Launditch RD. P King's Lynn. Ch e, m.
Sch p. SW Nflk CC.

BEESTON Notts
112, 121 SK 5236 3m SW of Nottingham.
UD (Bstn and Stapleford), 63,498.
P NTTNGHM. Bstn CC (Rushcliffe). See
also Attenborough. Factory of Boots, mnfg
chemists. To NE just within Nttngham CB
boundary, Nttnghm University.

BEESTON REGIS Norfolk
126 TG 1742 1m ESE of Sheringham.
CP, 472. Erpingham RD. P Shrnghm. Ch e.
N Nflk CC. Acres of caravans. Rems of 13c
priory to N.

BEETHAM Westm
89 SD 4979 6m N of Carnforth. CP, 1,293.
S Westm RD. P Milnthorpe. Ch e. Sch pe.
Westm CC. See also Farleton Storth.

BEETLEY Norfolk
125 TF 9718 4m NNW of E Dereham.
CP, 491. Mitford and Launditch RD.
P Drhm. Ch e, m. Sch p. SW Nflk CC. See
also E Bilney.

BEGBROKE Oxon
145 SP 4613 2m SE of Woodstock. CP, 565.
Ploughley RD. P OXFORD. Ch e, r.
Mid-Oxon CC (Banbury).

BEIGHTON Norfolk
126 TG 3808 9m W of Yarmouth. CP, 368.
Blofield and Flegg RD.
P NORWICH, NOR 62Z. Ch e, m. Ymth CC.
See also Moulton St Mary.

BEKESBOURNE Kent
173 TR 1955 3m ESE of Canterbury. CP,
538. Bridge-Blean RD. Ch e. Sch pe.
Cntrbry CC.

BELAUGH Norfolk
126 TG 2818 1m NW of Wroxham. CP, 108.
St Faith's and Aylsham RD. Ch e. N Nflk
CC (Central Nflk).

BELBROUGHTON Worcs
130, 131 SO 9277 5m S of Stourbridge.
CP, 2,579. Bromsgrove RD. P Stbrdge.
Ch e, m2. Sch p. Brmsgrve and
Redditch CC (Brmsgrve). See also Fairfield,
Wildmoor.

BELCHALWELL Dorset
178 ST 7909 6m WNW of Blandford. Loc,
Okeford Fitzpaine CP. Ch e.

BELCHAMP OTTEN Essex
149 TL 8041 4m W of Sudbury. CP, 133.
Halstead RD. Ch e. Saffron Walden CC.

BELCHAMP ST PAUL Essex
149 TL 7942 2m SE of Clare. CP, 359.
Halstead RD. P Sudbury, Suffolk. Ch e.
Sch pe. Saffron Walden CC. 15c ch has
misericord seats, rare in Essex.

BELCHAMP WALTER Essex
149 TL 8140 4m W of Sudbury. CP, 228.
Halstead RD. P Sdbry, Suffolk. Ch e.
Saffron Walden CC. B. Hall*, early 18c;
period furniture, portraits.

BELCHFORD Lincs (L)
105 TF 2975 4m NNE of Horncastle. CP
265. Hncstle RD. P Hncstle. Ch e. Sch p.
Hncstle CC.

BELFORD Nthmb
64, 71 NU 1033 14m SSE of
Berwick-upon-Tweed. CP, 1,070. Blfd RD.
P. Ch e, m2, v. Sch p, s. Brwck -upn -Twd
CC. See also Warenton. Gt N Rd vllge.

BELGRAVIA London
160, 170 TQ 2879 1m SW of Charing Cross.
Loc, City of Westminster LB. The City of
Lndn and Wstmnstr S BC (The Cities of
Lndn and Wstmnstr). High-class area blt on
former swamp W of Buckingham Palace. St
George's Hsptl at NE corner.

BELL BUSK Yorks (W)
95 SD 9056 6m NW of Skipton. Loc,
Coniston Cold CP. P Skptn.

BELLEAU Lincs (L)
105 TF 4078 4m NW of Alford. CP, 36.
Louth RD. Ch e. Lth CC.

BELLERBY Yorks (N)
91 SE 1192 2m N of Leyburn. CP, 318.
Lbn RD. P Lbn. Ch e, m. Sch pe.
Richmond CC.

BELLINGDON Bucks
159 SP 9405 3m NNW of Chesham. Loc,
Chartridge CP.

BELLINGHAM Nthmb
77 NY 8383 13m NNW of Hexham. CP,
1,224. Bllnghm RD. P Hxhm. Ch e, m2, r, v.
Sch s. Hxhm CC. Mkt tn on N Tyne,
surrounded by hills.

BELLSHILL Nthmb
64, 71 NU 1230 2m SSE of Belford. Loc,
Adderstone w Lucker CP.

BELLS YEW GREEN Sussex (E)
171, 183 TQ 6036 3m SE of Tunbridge
Wells. Loc, Frant CP. P TNBRDGE WLLS.
Ch v. To E, Bayham Wds; beyond, Bayham
Abbey (A.M.), 13c monastic ruin in grnds of
present Tdr mansion.

BELMESTHORPE Rutland
123 TF 0410 2m NNE of Stamford. Loc,
Ryhall CP.

BELMONT Lancs
95, 101 SD 6716 5m NW of Bolton. Loc
Turton UD. P Bltn. Darwen CC. To N,
Blmnt Reservoir. To SW, TV masts on
Winter Hill, 1,498ft.

BELOWDA Cornwall
185 SW 9661 7m NNW of St Austell. Loc,
Roche CP. Ch m.

BELPER Derbys
111 SK 3447 7m N of Derby. UD, 16,665.
P DBY. Blpr CC. See also Blackbrook,
Milford, Openwoodgate. Indstrl tn; iron
foundry, cotton mills.

BELSAY Nthmb
77, 78 NZ 1078 5m NW of Ponteland. CP,
524. Cstle Ward RD. P NEWCASTLE UPON
TYNE. Ch m. Hexham CC. See also Bolam.
Early 19c Hall; nearby in pk, 14c cstle.

BELSFORD Devon
187, 188 SX 7659 2m WSW of Totnes. Loc,
Harberton CP.

BELSTEAD Suffolk (E)
150 TM 1341 3m SW of Ipswich. CP, 205.
Samford RD. P Ipswch. Ch e. Sudbury and
Woodbridge CC.

BELSTONE Devon
175 SX 6193 2m ESE of Okehampton. CP,
316. Okhmptn RD. P Okhmptn. Ch e, m.
W Dvn CC (Torrington). Small vllge; some
new hses. Stocks and whipping-post on grn.
Starting point for moorland walks.

BELTHORN Lancs
95 SD 7124 3m SE of Blackburn. Loc,
Oswaldtwistle UD. P Blckbn.

BELTOFT Lincs (L)
104 SE 8106 3m NE of Epworth. Loc,
Belton CP. Ch m.

BELTON Leics
121 SK 4420 6m W of Loughborough. CP.
Cstle Donington RD. P Lghbrgh. Ch e, b, m.
Sch pe. Lghbrgh CC.

BELTON Lincs (K)
113, 122 SK 9339 3m NNE of Grantham.
CP(Bltn and Manthorpe), 214. W Kesteven
RD. P Grnthm. Ch e. Grnthm CC. B. Pk*,
Seat of Brownlow family since it was blt,
1685. Brownlow monmts fill ch.

BELTON Lincs (L)
104 SE 7806 2m N of Epworth. CP. Isle of
Axholme RD. P Doncaster, Yorkshire.
Ch e, m. Sch pe. Gainsborough CC. See also
Beltoft, Westgate.

BELTON Rutland
122 SK 8101 3m WNW of Uppingham. CP,
262. Uppnghm RD. P Uppnghm. Ch e, b.
Rtlnd and Stamford CC. Hilltop vllge
grouped round ch.

BELTON Suffolk (E)
126 TG 4802 4m SW of Yarmouth.
CP, 805. Lothingland RD. P Gt Ymth,
Norfolk. Ch e, m. Lowestoft CC. To W, B.
Marshes, R Waveney, Norfolk Broads.

BELVOIR Leics
113, 122 SK 8233 6m W of Grantham.
CP, 425. Melton and Belvoir RD. Sch s.
Mltn CC. See also Harston, Knipton.
Pronounced 'beever'. B. Cstle*, seat of
Dukes of Rutland, early 19c 'mdvl' cstle by
James Wyatt. Family mausoleum. Museum
of 17/21 Lancers. HQ of famous hunt.

BEMBRIDGE IOW
180 SZ 6488 4m NE of Sandown. CP,
2,429. Isle of Wight RD and CC. P.
Ch e, b, m, r, v. Sch pe. Yachting centre.
Airpt. 17c twr windmill (NT)*. SW on B.
Down, obelisk of 1849 commemorating
founder of Royal Yacht Squadron.

BEMPTON Yorks (E)
93 TA 1972 3m NNE of Bridlington. CP,
670. Brdlngtn RD. P Brdlngtn. Ch e, m.
Sch p. Brdlngtn CC. Inland from
Flamborough Head. High cliffs; colonies of
sea birds.

BENACRE Suffolk (E)
137 TM 5184 5m N of Southwold. CP, 134.
Lothingland RD. Ch e. Lowestoft CC. Seat
of Gooch family since mid-18c. 1½m SE, B.
Broad and desolate coast.

BENEFIELD Northants
134 SP 9988 3m W of Oundle. CP, 357.
Oundle and Thrapston RD. P
PETERBOROUGH. Ch e. Wellingborough
CC (Ptrbrgh). See also Upr Bnfld.

BENENDEN Kent
184 TQ 8132 5m W of Tenterden. CP,
1,718. Cranbrook RD. P Crnbrk. Ch e, r.
Sch pe. Royal Tunbridge Wells CC (Ashford).
See alse E End, Iden Grn. Blt round grn
famous for cricket. On outskirts, well
known girls' boarding sch.

BENHALL GREEN Suffolk (E)
137 TM 3861 1m S of Saxmundham. Loc,
Bnhll CP. Blyth RD. P Sxmndhm. Sch pe.
Eye CC. Bnhall ch (no vllge) is ¾m WNW at
371619; Nmn doorway.

BENINGBROUGH Yorks (N)
97 SE 5357 6m NW of York. CP, 46.
Easingwold RD. Thirsk and Malton CC. On
R. Ouse. To NW, B. Hall (NT)*,
Vanburgh-style mansion.

BENINGTON Herts
147 TL 3023 4m ESE of Stevenage. CP,
692. Hertford RD. P Stvnge. Ch e, m.
Sch pe. Htfd and Stvnge CC (Htfd). Vllge
has handsome grn. The Lordship, Ggn hse
with pseudo-Nmn gatehouse to match rems
of adjoining B. Cstle.

BENINGTON Lincs (H)
114 TF 3946 5m ENE of Boston. CP, 555.
Bstn RD. P Bstn. Ch e, m. Sch pe. Holland
W Bstn CC.

BENNACOTT Cornwall
174 SX 2992 5m NNW of Launceston. Loc,
Boyton CP. Ch m.

BENNIWORTH Lincs (L)
105 TF 2181 8m WSW of Louth. CP, 172.
Horncastle RD. P LINCOLN. Ch e. Hncstle
CC.

BENOVER Kent
171, 172, 184 TQ 7048 6m SSW of
Maidstone. Loc, Yalding CP.

BEN RHYDDING Yorks (W)
96 SE 1347 1m E of Ilkley. Loc, Ilkley UD.
P Ilkley. Rsdntl; former health resort on
edge of Ilkley Moor.

BENSON Oxon
158 SU 6191 2m NNE of Wallingford. CP,
2,624. Bullingdon RD. P OXFORD. Ch e, v.
Sch p, pe. Henley CC. Large RAF stn.

BENTHALL Nthmb
71 NU 2328 5m SE of Bamburgh. Loc,
Beadnell CP.

BENTHALL Shrops
118, 119 SJ 6602 3m ENE of Much
Wenlock. Loc, Barrow CP. Ch e. 16c hall of
grey stone (NT)*.

BENTHAM Glos
143, 144 SO 9116 4m SW of Cheltenham.
Loc, Badgeworth CP. Ch e.

BENTLEY Hants
169 SU 7844 4m WSW of Farnham. CP,
847. Alton RD. P Fnhm. Ch e. Sch pe.
Petersfield CC. On edge of vllge, stone book
given by Ld Baden-Powell. Jenkyn Place
gdns*.

BENTLEY Suffolk (E)
150 TM 1138 5m SW of Ipswich. CP, 468.
Samford RD. P Ipswch. Ch e. Sch pe.
Sudbury and Woodbridge CC.

BENTLEY Warwicks
132 SP 2895 2m SW of Atherstone. CP,
159. Athrstne RD. Ch e. Sch pe. Meriden
CC.

BENTLEY Yorks (E)
99 TA 0235 3m SSW of Beverley. Loc,
Rowley CP.

BENTLEY Yorks (W)
103 SE 5605 2m NNW of Doncaster.
UD(Bntly w Arksey), 22,888. P Dncstr. Don
Valley CC. See also Toll Bar. Coal-mining
and general industry.

BENTLEY, GREAT Essex
150 TM 1121 6m NW of Clacton. See Gt
Bntly.

BENTON Devon
163 SS 6536 7m ENE of Barnstaple. Loc,
Bnstple RD. N Dvn CC.

BENTWORTH Hants
168, 169 SU 6640 3m WNW of Alton. CP,
596. Altn RD. P Altn. Ch e. Sch pe.
Petersfield CC.

BENWICK Cambs
134 TL 3490 5m NE of Ramsey. CP, 657.
N Witchford RD. P March. Ch·e, m. Sch p.
Isle of Ely CC.

BEOLEY Worcs
131 SP 0669 2m NE of Redditch. CP.
Bromsgrove RD. P Rddtch. Ch e, m. Sch p.
Brmsgrve and Rddtch CC (Brmsgrve). See
also Holt End. Ch: 15c-16c tombs of
Sheldon family.

BEPTON Sussex (W)
181 SU 8518 3m SW of Midhurst. CP.
Mdhst RD. Ch e. Chichester CC (Horsham).

BERDEN Essex
148 TL 4629 5m NNW of Bishop's
Stortford. CP, 263. Saffron Walden RD. P
Bshp's Sttfd, Herts. Ch e. Sffrn Wldn CC.

BERE ALSTON Devon
187 SX 4466 5m SSW of Tavistock. Loc,
Bere Ferrers CP. P Yelverton.
Ch e, c, m, v. Sch p. In mkt-gdning area.
Centre of a silver-mining industry in Middle
Ages.

BERE FERRERS Devon
187 SX 4563 7m SSW of Tavistock. CP,
1,976. Tvstck RD. P Bere Alston, Yelverton.
Ch e, m. W Dvn CC (Tvstck). See also Bere
Alstn, Cotts. On tongue of land between
two rivers. Abandoned quays and silver
mines on Tamar side. Early 14c ch.

BEREPPER Cornwall
189 SW 6522 3m S of Helston. Loc, Kerrier
RD. Ch m. St Ives CC.

BERE REGIS Dorset
178 SY 8494 7m NW of Wareham. CP, 1,157.
Wrhm and Purbeck RD. P Wrhm. Ch e, c, m.
Sch p. S Dst CC. Ch: nave roof; Turberville
monmts.

BERGH APTON Norfolk
137 TG 3001 7m NNW of Bungay. CP, 430.
Loddon RD. P NORWICH, NOR 38W. Ch e.
Sch pe. S Nflk CC.

BERKELEY Glos
156 ST 6899 9m NE of Severn Rd Br.
CP, 1,583. Thornbury RD. P. Ch e, v2.
Sch j, s. S Glos CC. Ch has detached twr.
Mdvl B. Cstle*, scene of Edward II's
murder, 1327. To W beside R Severn, B.
Nuclear Power Stn.

BERKHAMSTED Herts
159, 160 SP 9907 4m WNW of Hemel
Hempstead. UD, 15,439. P. Hml
Hmpstd CC. Rsdntl. Boys' public sch
founded 16c. Rems of cstle (A.M.). To N, B.
Cmmn (NT).

BERKLEY Som
166 ST 8149 3m ENE of Frome. CP, 293.
Frme RD. Ch e. Sch pe. Wells CC.

BERKSWELL Warwicks
131 SP 2479 6m W of Coventry. CP, 2,044.
Meriden RD. P Cvntry. Ch e, r. Sch pe.
Mrdn CC. See also Four Oaks. Nmn ch:
crypt. Stocks on grn.

BERMONDSEY London
160, 170 TQ 3379 1m SE of Lndn Br. Loc,
Southwark LB. Bmndsy BC. On S bank of
Thames below Twr Br. Formerly marshland.

BERNERS RODING
161 TL 6009 5m NE of Ongar. CP(Abbess
Beauchamp and Bnrs Rdng), 516. Epping
and Ongr RD. Ch e. Brentwood and Ongr
CC (Chigwell). One of eight Rodings,
pronounced 'roothing'.

BERRICK SALOME Oxon
158 SU 6093 3m NNE of Wallingford. CP,
113. Bullingdon RD. P OXFORD. Ch e.
Henley CC.

BERRINGTON Nthmb
64 NU 0043 6m S of Berwick-upon-Tweed.
Loc, Kyloe CP. Norham and
Islandshires RD. Brwck-upn-Twd CC.

BERRINGTON Shrops
118 SJ 5206 4m SSE of Shrewsbury. CP.
Atcham RD. P Shrsbry. Ch e. Sch pe.
Shrsbry CC. See also Cross Hses.

BERRINGTON Worcs
129 SO 5767 1m W of Tenbury Wells. Loc,
Tnbry CP.

BERROW Som
165 ST 3051 1m N of Burnham. Loc,
Bnhm-on-Sea UD; CP, 456, Axbridge RD. P
Bnhm-on-Sea. Ch e. Bridgwater CC,
Weston-super-Mare CC. Shacks, caravans,
chalets.

BERROW Worcs
143 SO 7934 6m ESE of Ledbury. CP, 285.
Upton upon Severn RD.-Ch e. S Worcs CC.

BERRY DOWN CROSS Devon
163 SS 5743 4m ESE of Ilfracombe. Loc,
Berrynarbor CP. Ch v.

BERRY HILL Glos
142 SP 5712 4m E of Monmouth. Loc, W
Dean CP. W Dn RD. P Coleford. Ch m, v.
Sch p, s2. W Glos CC.

BERRYNARBOR Devon
163 SS 5646 3m E of Ilfracombe. CP, 626.
Barnstaple RD. P Ilfrcmbe. Ch e, c. Sch pe.
N Dvn CC. See also Berry Down Cross. Ch
has tall twr of late 15c.

BERRY POMEROY Devon
188 SX 8261 2m E of Totnes. CP, 366. Ttns
RD. Ch e. Sch pe. Ttns CC. Ch scrn. 1m NE,
ruins of mdvl cstle (A.M.).

BERSTED Sussex (W)
181 SU 9201 1m NW of Bognor. CP, 1,857.
Chichester RD. Ch e. Sch p. Arundel CC
(Chchstr). See also Shripney.

BERWICK Sussex (E)
183 TQ 5105 4m NNE of Seaford. CP, 302.
Hailsham RD. P Polegate. Ch e. Lewes CC
(Eastbourne). Vllge under S Downs. Ch has
wall-paintings of 1942–3.

BERWICK BASSETT Wilts
157 SU 0973 6m WNW of Marlborough. CP,
69. Mlbrgh and Ramsbury RD. Ch e.
Devizes CC.

BERWICK HILL Nthmb
78 NZ 1775 2m NNE of Ponteland. Loc,
Pntlnd CP.

BERWICK ST JAMES Wilts
167 SU 0739 8m NW of Salisbury. CP, 168.
Slsbry and Wilton RD. P Slsbry. Ch e. Sch p.
Slsbry CC.

BERWICK ST JOHN Wilts
167 ST 9422 5m E of Shaftesbury. CP, 268.
Mere and Tisbury RD. P Shftsbry, Dorset.
Ch e. Westbury CC. To SE, Winklebury
Camp. Iron Age fort and Saxon cemetery.
1m W, Ferne Hse, animal sancturary.

BERWICK ST LEONARD Wilts
166, 167 ST 9233 8m NNE of Shaftesbury.
CP, 39. Mere and Tisbury RD. Ch e.
Westbury CC.

BERWICK-UPON-TWEED Nthmb
64 NT 9953 47m ESE of Edinburgh.
MB, 11,644. P(BRWCK-UPN-TWD).
Brwck-upn-Twd CC. See also Marshall
Meadows, Spittal, Tweedmouth. Border tn
with stormy history. Mdvl tn walls*, rems of
Nmn cstle*. Early 18c barracks*. 18c tn
hall*. Three fine brs cross R Tweed. Busy
mkt; small fishing industry.

BESCAR Lancs
100 SD 3913 4m SE of Southport. Loc,
Scarisbrick CP. Ch r.

BESCAR LANE Lancs
100 SD 3914 4m ESE of Southport. Loc,
Scarisbrick CP. P Ormskirk. Ch m, r.

BESFORD Worcs
143, 144 SO 9144 2m W of Pershore.
CP, 270. Pshre RD. Ch e, r. S Worcs CC. Ch:
carved 15c rood scrn; 16c—17c monmts. B.
Ct, Tdr hse now sch.

BESSELS GREEN Kent
171 TQ 5055 2m W of Sevenoaks. Loc,
Chevening CP. P Svnks. Ch b, v.

BESSELS LEIGH Berks
158 SP 4501 4m SW of Oxford. CP, 64.
Abingdon RD. Ch e. Abngdn CC.
Unrestored 15c ch in pk.

BESSINGHAM Norfolk
126 TG 1636 4m S of Sheringham. Loc,
Sustead CP. Ch e.

BESTHORPE Norfolk
136 TM 0595 1m ENE of Attleborough.
CP, 469. Wayland RD. P Attlbrgh. Ch e, m.
S Nflk CC.

BESTHORPE Notts
113 SK 8264 7m NNE of Newark. CP, 146.
Nwk RD. P Nwk. Ch e, m. Sch p. Nwk CC.

BESWICK Yorks (E)
99 TA 0148 6m NNW of Beverley. CP, 310.
Bvrly RD. P Driffield. Ch e, m. Sch pe.
Haltemprice CC. See also Kilnwick.

BETCHWORTH Surrey
170 TQ 2149 3m E of Dorking. CP, 1,657.
Dkng and Horley RD. P. Ch e, b, v. Sch p.
Dkng CC. See also Strood Grn.

BETHERSDEN Kent
172, 184 TQ 9240 5m WSW of Ashford. CP,
1,096. W Ashfd RD. P Ashfd. Ch e, b, m.
Sch p. Ashfd CC. Formerly famous for
marble quarries.

BETHNAL GREEN London
161 TQ 3583 4m ENE of Charing Cross.
Loc, Twr Hmlts LB. Bthnl Grn and Bow BC
(Bthnl Grn). In heart of Lndn's 'East End'.
Victoria Pk to N. B. Grn Museum, extension
of Vctria and Albert Msm.

BETLEY Staffs
110 SJ 7548 5m SE of Crewe. CP, 636.
Newcastle-under-Lyme RD. P. Crwe,
Cheshire. Ch e, m. Sch pe. N-u-L BC. See
also Wrinehill. Half-timbered hses. To SW,
B. Mere, small lake on Cheshire border.

BETSHAM Kent
161, 171 TQ 6071 3m WSW of Gravesend.
Loc, Southfleet CP. P Grvsnd.

BETTESHANGER Kent
173 TR 3252 4m W of Deal. Loc,
Northbourne CP. Ch e.

BETTISCOMBE Dorset
177 SY 3999 6m NE of Lyme Regis.
CP, 78. Beaminster RD. Ch e. W Dst CC.

BETTON Shrops
110, 119 SJ 6936 2m NNE of Mkt Drayton.
Loc, Norton in Hales CP.

BETTON Shrops
118 SJ 3102 7m ESE of Welshpool. Loc,
Worthen CP.

BETTWS-Y-CRWYN Shrops
128 SO 2081 6m W of Clun. CP, 247. Cln
and Bishop's Cstle RD. Ch e, b, m.
Ludlow CC.

BEVERCOTES Notts
112 SK 6972 4m NE of Ollerton. CP, 30.
E Retford RD. Ch e. Bassetlaw CC.

BEVERLEY Yorks (E)
99 TA 0339 8m NNW of Hull. MB, 17,124.
P. Haltemprice CC. Mkt tn. Two
outstanding 14c chs (one B. Minster), and
many mdvl hses. Racecourse.

BEVERSTONE Glos
156 ST 8693 2m WNW of Tetbury. CP, 211.
Ttbry RD. Ch e. Stroud CC. Rems of mdvl
B. Cstle. To NE, Chavenage Hse, Elizn and
later.

BEVINGTON Glos
155, 156 ST 6596 7m NE of Severn Rd Br.
Loc, Ham and Stone CP.

BEWALDETH Cumb
82 NY 2134 6m ENE of Cockermouth.
CP(Bwldth and Snittlegarth), 40. Cckrmth
RD. Workington CC.

BEWCASTLE Cumb
76 NY 5674 9m NNE of Brampton. CP,
456. Border RD. P Carlisle. Ch e, v. Sch p.
Penrith and the Bdr CC. 7c cross in
churchyard. Rems of mdvl cstle within site
of Roman fort.

BEWDLEY Worcs
130 SO 7875 3m W of Kidderminster.
MB, 7,212. P. Kddrmnstr CC. See also
Wribbenhall. Mainly 17c and 18c tn on
R Severn. Br by Telford.

BEWERLEY Yorks (W)
91 SE 1565 just SW of Pateley Br. CP, 594.
Ripon and Ptly Br RD. Sch je. Rpn CC. See
also Greenhow Hill.

BEWHOLME Yorks (E)
99 TA 1650 3m WNW of Hornsea. CP, 241.
Holderness RD. P Driffield. Ch e. Sch p.
Bridlington CC. See also Dunnington.

BEXHILL Sussex (E)
183, 184 TQ 7407 5m WSW of Hastings.
MB, 32,849. P (Bxhll-on-Sea). Rye CC. See
also Cooden, Lit Cmmn, Sidley. Seaside
rsdntl tn and resort.

BEXLEY London
161, 171 TQ 4875 ESE of Greenwich.
LB, 216,172. P Kent. BCs: Bexleyheath,
Erith and Crayford, Sidcup.
(Chislehurst CC; Bxly BC, Erith and
Crfd BC). See also Crfd, Erith, Sdcp.

Thames-side borough; most easterly Lndn
borough on S side of river.

BEXWELL Norfolk
124 TF 6303 1m E of Downham Mkt. Loc,
Ryston CP. Dnhm RD. Ch e. SW Nflk CC.

BEYTON Suffolk (W)
136 TL 9363 5m E of Bury St Edmunds.
CP, 447. Thedwastre RD. P Bury St Eds.
Ch e. Sch p, s. Bury St Eds CC.

BIBURY Glos
157 SP 1106 7m NE of Cirencester.
CP, 720. Northleach RD. P Crncstr. Ch e.
Sch pe. Crncstr and Tewkesbury CC. See
also Ablington, Arlington. Cotswold-stone
vllge on R Coln. Ch of many periods from
Saxon onwards.

BICESTER Oxon
145, 146 SP 5822 11m NNE of Oxford.
UD, 12,340. P. Banbury CC (Henley). Mkt
tn in flat hunting country.

BICKENHALL Som
177 ST 2717 5m SE of Taunton. CP, 138.
Tntn RD. Ch e. Tntn CC.

BICKENHILL Warwicks
131 SP 1882 3m NE of Solihull. CP, 2,922.
Meriden RD. P Slhll. Ch e. Mrdn CC. See
also Marston Grn.

BICKER Lincs (H)
114, 123 TF 2237 8m WSW of Boston. CP,
721. Bstn RD. P Bstn. Ch e, m. Sch pe.
Holland w Bstn CC.

BICKERSTAFFE Lancs
100 SD 4404 3m SE of Ormskirk. CP,
1,302. W Lancs RD. P Ormskk. Ch e.
Sch pe. Ormskk CC.

BICKERTON Ches
109 SJ 5052 7m NNW of Whitchurch. CP,
205. Nantwich RD. P Malpas. Ch e. Sch pe.
Nntwch CC. On far side of B. Hill stands
Maiden Cstle, British hill fort.

BICKERTON Yorks (W)
97 SE 4550 3m ENE of Wetherby. Loc,
Bilton in Ainsty CP. P Wthrby. Ch m.

BICKINGTON Devon
163 SS 5332 2m WSW of Barnstaple. Loc,
Fremington CP. P Bnstple. Ch v.

BICKINGTON Devon
175, 187, 188 SX 7972 3m ENE of
Ashburton. CP, 250. Newton Abbot RD. P
Ntn Abbt. Ch e, m. Totnes CC.

BICKLEIGH Devon
176 SS 9407 4m S of Tiverton. CP, 217.
Tvtn RD. P Tvtn. Ch e. Sch pe. Tvtn CC.
Beauty spot. Thatched cottages.-

BICKLEIGH Devon
187 SX 5262 6m NNE of Plymouth.
CP, 957. Plympton St Mary RD. Ch e.
Sch pe. W Dvn CC (Tavistock). See also
Maristow, Roborough.

BICKLETON Devon
163 SS 5031 4m WSW of Barnstaple. Loc,
Instow CP.

BICKLEY MOSS Ches
109 SJ 5449 5m N of Whitchurch. Loc,
Bckly CP. Tarvin RD. P Whtchch, Salop.
Ch e. Nantwich CC.

BICKNACRE Essex
162 TL 7802 6m ESE of Chelmsford. Loc,
Woodham Ferrers CP. P Chlmsfd. Scanty
rems of priory ch.

BICKNOLLER Som
164 ST 1139 3m SE of Watchet. CP, 323.
Williton RD. P Taunton. Ch e.
Bridgwater CC.

BICKNOR Kent
172 TQ 8658 4m SW of Sittingbourne. CP,
57. Hollingbourn RD. Ch e. Maidstone CC.

BICKTON Hants
179 SU 1412 lm S of Fordingbridge. Loc,
Fdngbrdge CP.

BICTON Devon
176 SY 0785 5m NE of Exmouth. CP, 191.
St Thomas RD. Ch e. Honiton CC. See also
Yettington. B. Hse, 18c mansion with 20c
additions, now agricultural institute. Gdns*
laid out in 18c; 19c pinetum*; 20c
narrow-gauge rly*.

BICTON Shrops
118 SJ 4414 3m WNW of Shrewsbury. CP.
Atcham RD. Ch e. Shrsbry CC. The old
(18c) ch is a ruin.

BICTON Shrops
129 SO 2882 1m NNW of Clun. Loc,
Cln CP. Sch pe.

BIDBOROUGH Kent
171 TQ 5643 3m NNW of Tunbridge Wells.
CP, 801. Tonbridge_ RD. P Tnbrdge Wlls CC
Ch e. Sch p. Royal Tnbrdge Wlls CC
(Tnbrdge).

BIDDENDEN Kent
172, 184 TQ 8538 4m NW of Tenterden.
CP, 1,674. Tntdn RD. P Ashford. Ch e, b.
Sch pe. Ashfd CC. See also Standen. Home
of Siamese twin sisters depicted in vllge sign.
Ch 15c twr, brasses.

BIDDENHAM Beds
147 TL 0249 2m W of Bedford. CP, 693.
Bdfd RD. P BDFD. Ch e. Sch pe. Bdfd CC.

BIDDESTONE Wilts
156 ST 8673 4m W of Chippenham. CP,
462. Calne and Chppnhm RD. P Chppnhm.
Ch e, b, m. Sch pe. Chppnhm CC. See also
Slaughterford.

BIDDISHAM Som
165 ST 3853 5m W of Cheddar. Loc,
Badgworth CP. Ch e.

BIDDLESDEN Bucks
145, 146 SP 6340 4m NE of Brackley. CP,
119. Buckingham RD. Ch e. Bcknghm CC.

BIDDLESTONE Nthmb
71 NT 9608 8m NW of Rothbury. CP, 103.
Rthbry RD. Ch r. Berwick-upon-Tweed CC.

BIDDULPH Staffs
110 SJ 8857 4m SSE of Congleton.
UD, 17,372. P Stoke-on-Trent. Leek CC.
See also Gillow Hth, Marsh Grn, Poolfold.

BIDDULPH MOOR Staffs
110 SJ 9058 4m SE of Congleton. Loc,
Bddlph UD. P Stoke-on-Trent.

BIDEFORD Devon
163 SS 4526 36m NW of Exeter.
MB, 11,766. P. N Dvn CC (Torrington).
Minor port with quay on R Torridge. 15c
stone br with 24 unequal arches; widened
1925. Part of tn E of river is known as
East-the-Water.

BIDFORD-ON-AVON Warwicks
144 SP 1051 7m WSW of Stratford.
CP, 2,436. Alcester RD. P Alcstr. Ch e, m, r.
Sch pe, s. Strtfd-on-Avon CC (Strtfd). See
also Barton, Broom. 15c br.

BIELBY Yorks (E)
97, 98 SE 7943 3m SSW of Pocklington.
CP, 141. Pcklngtn RD. P YORK. Ch e, m.
Howden CC.

BIERLEY IOW
180 SZ 5178 3m W of Ventnor. Loc, Niton
CP.

BIERTON Bucks
146, 159 SP 8315 lm NE of Aylesbury.
CP(Btn w Broughton), 1,249. Aylesbury
RD. P Aylesbury. Ch e, b, m. Sch pe.
Aylesbury CC.

BIGBURY Devon
187, 188 SX 6646 4m WNW of Kingsbridge.
CP, 458. Kngsbrdge RD. P Kngsbrdge. Ch e.
Totnes CC.

BIGBURY-ON-SEA Devon
187, 188 SX 6544 7m S of Ivybridge. Loc,
Bigbury CP. P Kngsbrdge. Resort with
extensive sands. Many bungalows and
caravans.

BIGBY Lincs (L)
104 TA 0507 4m E of Brigg. CP, 283.
Caistor RD. P Barnetby. Ch e.
Gainsborough CC. In ch, monmt of 1581 to
Sir John Tyrwhitt with his 22 children. 14c
and later brasses.

BIGGAR Lancs
88 SD 1966 2m S of Barrow, on Walney Is.
Loc, Brrw-in-Furness CB.

BIGGIN Derbys
111 SK 1559 7m SW of Bakewell. Loc,
Hartington Nether Quarter CP.
Ashbourne RD. P Buxton. Ch e, m2. Sch pe.
W Derbys CC.

BIGGIN Derbys
111 SK 2648 5m E of Ashbourne. CP, 100.
Ashbne RD. W Derbys CC.

BIGGIN Yorks (W)
97 SE 5434 5m WNW of Selby. CP, 83.
Tadcaster RD. P LEEDS. Ch m. Sch p.
Barkston Ash CC.

BIGGIN HILL London
171 TQ 4158 7m S of Bromley. Loc,
Brmly LB. P Westerham, Kent.
Orpington BC (CC). Airfield — famous in
Battle of Britain in World War II. Ch,

completed 1959 from materials of All
Saints, Peckham, known as 'The Moving
Church'.

BIGGLESWADE Beds
147 TL 1944 9m ESE of Bedford.
UD, 9,598. P. Mid-Beds CC.

BIGHTON Hants   ,
168 SU 6134 7m WSW of Alton. CP, 179.
Winchester RD. P Alresford. Ch e. Wnchstr
CC.

BIGLANDS Cumb
75 NY 2553 3m N of Wigton. Loc, Aikton
CP.

BIGNOR Sussex (W)
181, 182 SU 9814 5m SW of Pulborough.
CP, 123. Petworth RD. Ch e. Chichester CC
(Horsham). Rems of Roman villa*.

BILBERRY Cornwall
185, 186 SX 0260 5m N of St Austell. Loc,
Roche CP.

BILBROUGH Yorks (W)
97 SE 5346 4m ENE of Tadcaster. CP, 198.
Tdcstr RD. P YORK. Ch e. Sch p. Barkston
Ash CC.

BILDESTON Suffolk (W)
149 TL 9949 5m E of Lavenham. CP, 800.
Cosford RD. P Ipswch. Ch e, b, s. Sch p.
Sudbury and Woodbridge CC. Large vllge;
old half-timbered hses in centre, modern
accretions at edges. Aircraft noise.
Rewarding ch up dead end lane to E.

BILLERICAY Essex
161 TQ 6794 5m E of Brentwood. Loc,
Basildon UD. P. Extensive indstrl and rsdntl
development round old mkt tn, partly mdvl
but largely Ggn.

BILLESDON Leics
122 SK 7202 8m E of Leicester. CP, 727.
Bllsdn RD. P LCSTR. Ch e, b. Sch pe.
Harborough CC (Melton). lm NW, B.
Coplow, 700ft, famous fox-cover.

BILLESLEY Warwicks
131 SP 1456 4m WNW of Stratford. CP, 45.
Strtfd-on-Avon RD. Ch e. Strtfd-on-Avn CC
(Strtfd).

BILLINGBOROUGH Lincs (K)
113, 123 TF 1134 8m SSE of Sleaford. CP, 1,008. S Kesteven RD. P Slfd. Ch e, m2. Sch p, s. Rutland and Stamford CC.

BILLINGE Lancs
100 SD 5200 3m NNW of St Helens. UD (Bllnge-and-Winstanley), 11,379. P Wigan. Ince BC. See also Gt Moss, Longshaw Cmmn.

BILLINGFORD Norfolk
125 TG 0120 5m NNE of E Dereham. CP, 243. Mitford and Launditch RD. P Drhm. Ch e, m. SW Nflk CC.

BILLINGFORD Norfolk
137 TM 1678 3m E of Diss. Loc, Scole CP. P Dss. Ch e.

BILLING, GREAT Northants
133 SP 8162 4m ENE of Northampton. See Gt Bllng.

BILLINGHAM Yorks (N)
85 NZ 4522 3m NNE of Teesside (Stockton). Loc, Tssde CB. P(BLLNGHM, Tssde). Tssde, Stcktn BC. Chemical wks. Part of Tssde indstrl complex. Modern tn centre

BILLINGHAY Lincs (K)
113 TF 1554 6m SSW of Woodhall Spa. CP, 1,634. E Kesteven RD. P LINCOLN. Ch e, b, m2. Sch pe, s. Grantham CC.

BILLINGLEY Yorks (W)
103 SE 4304 6m ESE of Barnsley. CP, 136. Hemsworth RD. Ch m. Hmswth CC.

BILLINGSHURST Sussex (W)
182 TQ 0825 6m WSW of Horsham. CP, 3,098. Hshm RD. P. Ch e, c, r, v. Sch i, j, s. Hshm and Crawley CC (Hshm). See also Five Oaks. Large vllge or small tn of pleasant aspect.

BILLINGSLEY Shrops
130 SO 7085 5m SSW of Bridgnorth. CP, 88. Brdgnth RD. P Brdgnth. Ch e. Ludlow CC.

BILLINGTON Beds
146 SP 9422 2m SE of Leighton Buzzard. CP, 633. Luton RD. P(Gt Bllngtn), Lghtn Bzzd. Ch e, m. S Beds CC.

BILLINGTON Lancs
95 SD 7235 4m SSW of Clitheroe. CP, 4,510. Blackburn RD. P Blckbn. Ch e2, b. Sch pr, sr. Darwen CC. See also Langho.

BILLOCKBY Norfolk
126 TG 4213 7m NW of Yarmouth. Loc, Fleggburgh CP. Blofield and Flegg RD. Ch e. Ymth CC.

BILLY ROW Co Durham
85 NZ 1637 lm N of Crook. Loc, Crk and Willington UD. P Crk.

BILSBORROW Lancs
94 SD 5139 7m N of Preston. CP, 314. Garstang RD. P Prstn. Ch e, m. Sch pe. N Fylde CC.

BILSBY Lincs (L)
105 TF 4776 lm ENE of Alford. CP, 251. Spilsby RD. P Alfd. Ch e, m. Horncastle CC. See also Thurlby.

BILSINGTON Kent
173, 184 TR 0434 6m SSE of Ashford. CP, 278. E Ashfd RD. P Ashfd. Ch e. Sch pe. Ashfd CC.

BILSTHORPE Notts
112 SK 6460 4m S of Ollerton. CP, 2,744. Southwell RD. P Newark. Ch e, m. Sch p. Nwk CC.

BILSTON Staffs
130, 131 SO 9596 3m SE of Wolverhampton. Loc, Wlvrhmptn CB. P. Wlvrhmptn SE BC (Blstn).

BILSTONE Leics
120, 121 SK 3605 6m NE of Atherstone. Loc, Shackerstone CP.

BILTING Kent
172, 173, 184 TR 0549 5m NE of Ashford. Loc, E Ashfd RD. Ashfd CC.

BILTON Nthmb
71 NU 2210 3m SE of Alnwick. Loc, Lesbury CP.

BILTON Yorks (E)
99 TA 1633 5m ENE of Hull. CP. Holderness RD. P Hll. Ch e. Sch p. Bridlington CC. See also Ganstead, Wyton.

BILTON Yorks (W)
97 SE 4750 5m ENE of Wetherby. CP(Bltn in Ainsty), 346. Wthrby RD. P(Bltn in Ainsty), YORK. Ch e, m. Barkston Ash CC. See also Bickerton.

BINBROOK Lincs (L)
105 TF 2193 7m ENE of Mkt Rasen. CP, 732. Louth RD. P LINCOLN. Ch e, m. Sch pe. Lth CC. Large mkt square and Vctrn ch by Fowler 1869. To N, RAF stn.

BINCHESTER BLOCKS Co Durham
85 NZ 2332 2m SW of Spennymoor. Loc, Bishop Auckland UD. P Bshp Aucklnd.

BINCOMBE Dorset
178 SY 6884 4m S of Dorchester. CP, 100. Dchstr RD. Ch e. S Dst CC.

BINEGAR Som
166 ST 6149 4m N of Shepton Mallet. CP, 288. Shptn Mllt RD. Ch e. Sch pe. Wells CC. See also Gurney Slade.

BINFIELD Berks
169 SU 8471 2m NW of Bracknell. CP, 2,583. Easthampstead RD. P Brcknll. Ch e, v. Sch pe2. Wokingham CC. See also Popeswood. Rsdntl vllge. Ch has tablet to Catherine Macaulay, who was subject of unflattering quip by Dr Johnson.

BINFIELD HEATH Oxon
159 SU 7478 3m SSW of Henley. Loc, Shiplake CP. P Hnly-on-Thames. Ch c.

BINGFIELD Nthmb
77 NY 9772 5m N of Corbridge. Loc, Whittington CP. Hexham RD. Ch e. Sch pe. Hxhm CC.

BINGHAM Notts
112, 122 SK 7039 8m E of Nottingham. CP, 2,457. Bnghm RD. P NTTNGHM. Ch e, m, v. Sch j, p, s. Rushcliffe CC (Carlton). Ch 14c twr and spire.

BINGHAM'S MELCOMBE Dorset
178 ST 7702 8m WSW of Blandford. Loc, Mlcmbe Horsey CP. Dorchester RD. Ch e. W Dst CC. Mdvl mnr hse.

BINGLEY Yorks (W)
96 SE 1039 5m NW of Bradford. UD, 26,540. P. Shipley CC. See also Cullingworth, Eldwick, Harden, Wilsden. Rsdntl and cloth-mnfg tn on R Aire. Leeds—Liverpool canal rises steeply here in series of locks.

BINHAM Norfolk
125 TF 9839 5m SE of Wells. CP, 346. Walsingham RD. P Fakenham. Ch e, m.

NW Nflk CC (N Nflk). See also Cockthorpe, Westgate. Rems of 13c priory (A.M.).

BINLEY Hants
168 SU 4253 6m NE of Andover. Loc, St Mary Bourne CP.

BINLEY COMMON Warwicks
132 SP 3977 4m ESE of Coventry. Loc, Bnly Wds CP. Rugby RD. P(Bnly Wds), Coventry. Sch p. Rgby CC.

BINSOE Yorks (N)
91 SE 2579 2m ESE of Masham. Loc, W Tanfield CP.

BINSTEAD IOW
180 SZ 5792 1m W of Ryde. Loc, Rde MB. P Rde. To NW, Quarr Abbey, enclosed monastery blt early 20c.

BINSTED Hants
169 SU 7741 4m ENE of Alton. CP, 1,604. Altn RD. P Altn Ch e. Sch pe. Petersfield CC. See also Blacknest, Wheatley, Wyck.

BINTON Warwicks
144 SP 1454 4m W of Stratford. CP, 222. Strtfd-on-Avon RD. P Strtfd-upon-Avn. Ch e. Strtfd-on-Avn CC (Strtfd).

BINTREE Norfolk
125 TG 0123 7m NNE of E Dereham. CP, 285. Mitford and Launditch RD. P Drhm. Ch e, m. SW Nflk CC.

BIRCH Essex
149, 162 TL 9419 5m SW of Colchester. CP, 636. Lexden and Winstree RD. P Clchstr. Ch e. Sch pe. Clchstr CC. See also Bch Grn.

BIRCH Lancs
101 SD 8507 4m SE of Bury. Loc, Middleton MB. P Heywood.

BIRCHAM GREAT Norfolk
125 TF 7632 8m SE of Hunstanton. See Gt Bchm.

BIRCHAM NEWTON Norfolk
125 TF 7633 7m SE of Hunstanton. Loc, Bchm CP. Docking RD. Ch e. NW Nflk CC (King's Lynn). Large airfield to E.

BIRCHAM TOFTS Norfolk
125 TF 7732 8m SE of Hunstanton. Loc, Bchm CP. Docking RD. NW Nflk CC (King's Lynn).

BIRCHANGER Essex
148 TL 5122 2m NE of Bishop's Stortford.
CP, 808. Saffron Walden RD. P Bshp's
Sttfd, Herts. Ch e. Sch pe. Sffrn Wldn CC.

BIRCHER Herefs
129 SO 4765 4m N of Leominster. Loc,
Yarpole CP. Ch m.

BIRCH GREEN Essex
149, 162 TL 9418 3m NE of Tiptree. Loc,
Bch CP.

BIRCHINGTON Kent
173 TR 3069 4m W of Margate. Loc, Mgte
MB. P. Seaside rsdntl tn. 1m SE, Quex Pk*,
museum of native arts and zoology; steel
lattice Waterloo twr in grnds.

BIRCHOVER Derbys
111 SK 2362 4m WNW of Matlock. CP,
297. Bakewell RD. P Mtlck. Ch e, m, v.
Sch ie. W Derbys CC.

BIRCH VALE Derbys
102, 111 SK 0286 5m S of Glossop. Loc,
Hayfield CP. P Stockport, Cheshire. Ch m.

BIRCOTES Notts
103 SK 6391 8m NNW of Retford. Loc,
Harworth CP. P Doncaster, Yorkshire.
Ch m. Sch p, s. Coal-mining locality.
Impressive slag heap.

BIRDBROOK Essex
148, 149 TL 7041 4m SE of Haverhill.
CP, 340. Halstead RD. Ch e. Saffron
Walden CC. See also Baythorn End. To W,
Moyns Pk, moated Elizn hse.

BIRDHAM Sussex
181 SU 8200 4m SW of Chichester. CP,
1,198. Chchstr RD. P Chchstr. Ch e, v.
Sch pe. Chchstr CC. Has own harbour off
Chchstr Channel.

BIRDINGBURY Warwicks
132 SP 4368 4m N of Southam. CP, 223.
Rugby RD. P Rgby. Ch e. Rgby CC.

BIRDLIP Glos
143, 144 SO 9214 5m SSW of Cheltenham.
Loc, Cowley CP. P GLOUCESTER. Sch p.
At top of steep hill on edge of Cotswold
escarpment.

BIRDSALL Yorks (E)
92 SE 8165 4m SSE of Malton. CP, 318.

Norton RD. P Mltn. Ch e. Howden CC. See
also N Grimston. On edge of Wolds. To SE,
many prehistoric burial mounds.

BIRDS EDGE Yorks (W)
102 SE 2007 4m NW of Penistone. Loc,
Denby Dale UD. P Huddersfield.

BIRDSGREEN Shrops
130 SO 7685 6m SSE of Bridgnorth. Loc,
Brdgnth RD. Ludlow CC.

BIRDWELL Yorks (W)
102 SE 3401 3m S of Barnsley. Loc,
Worsbrough UD. P Bnsly.

BIRDWOOD Glos
143 SO 7418 6m W of Gloucester. Loc,
Churcham CP. Ch m.

BIRKBY Cumb
81, 82 NY 0637 2m ENE of Maryport. Loc,
Crosscanonby CP.

BIRKBY Yorks (N)
91 NZ 3302 6m NNW of Northallerton. CP,
56. Nthlltn RD. Ch e. Richmond CC.

BIRKDALE Lancs
100 SD 3214 S distr of Southport. Loc,
Sthpt CB. P Sthpt. Famous golf course.

BIRKENHEAD Ches
100, 109 SJ 3288 1m SW of Liverpool.
CB, 137,738. P. Bknhd BC, Wirral CC.
(Bknhd BC, Bebington BC.) Ship-building;
shipping. Connected to Lvrpl by two rd
tunnels and one rly tunnel under R Mersey.

BIRKENSHAW Yorks (W)
96, 102 SE 2028 4m SE of Bradford. Loc,
Spenborough MB. P Brdfd. Brighouse and
Spnbrgh BC.

BIRKIN Yorks (W)
97 SE 5326 6m E of Castleford. CP, 110.
Osgoldcross RD. P Knottingley. Ch e.
Goole CC. Nmn ch.

BIRLEY Herefs
142 SO 4553 5m SW of Leominster. CP,
127. Weobley RD. Ch e. Lmnstr CC.

BIRLING Kent
171 TQ 6860 6m SW of Rochester. CP,
1,366. Malling RD. P Maidstone. Ch e.
Tonbridge and Mllng CC (Sevenoaks).

BIRLINGHAM Worcs
143, 144 SO 9343 2m SSW of Pershore. CP,
269. Pshre RD. P Pshre. Ch e. S Worcs CC.

BIRMINGHAM Warwicks
131 SP 0686 100m NW of London.
CB, 1,013,366. P(BMNGHM). BCs:
Edgbaston, Erdington, Hall Grn,
Handsworth, Ladywood, Northfield, Perry
Barr, Selly Oak, Small Hth, Sparkbrook,
Stechford, Yardley (same plus All Saints,
Aston, part of Sutton Coldfield; minus
Erdington). See also Bournville, Edgbstn,
Rubery. Mnfg, commercial, and
communications centre. Cathedral, former
par ch, in Baroque style. University. Modern
city centre development. Intntl airpt:
Elmdon, 6m SE.

BIRSTALL Leics
121, 122 SK 5909 3m N of Leicester. CP.
Barrow upon Soar RD. P LCSTR.
Ch e, m2, r. Sch i, j, p, s2. Melton CC (Mltn
CC, Lcstr NE BC).

BIRSTALL SMITHIES Yorks (W)
96, 102 SE 2226 3m NNW of Dewsbury.
Loc, Batley MB. To N, Oakwell Hall*, Elizn
moated mnr hse, now museum.

BIRSTWITH Yorks (W)
96 SE 2359 5m NW of Harrogate. CP, 412.
Ripon and Pateley Br RD. P Hrrgte.
Ch e, m2. Sch pe. Rpn CC.

BIRTLEY Co Durham
78 NZ 2755 3m N of Chester-le-Street. CP,
10,880. Chstr-le-Strt RD. P.
Ch e, m2, r, s, v. Sch p4, s3. Chstr-le-Strt
CC.

BIRTLEY Herefs
129 SO 3669 5m ESE of Knighton. Loc,
Lingen CP. P Bucknell, Salop. Ch m.

BIRTLEY Nthmb
77 NY 8778 4m SE of Bellingham. CP, 190.
Bllnghm RD. P Wark, Hexham. Ch e.
Sch pe. Hxhm CC.

BIRTSMORTON Worcs
143 SO 8035 6m W of Tewkesbury.
CP, 241. Upton upon Severn RD. Ch e, m.
S Worcs CC. See also Birts St. B. Ct, moated
hse of all periods 13c–20c. Cardinal Wolsey
was family chaplain here in his youth.

BIRTS STREET Worcs
143 SO 7836 5m E of Ledbury. Loc,
Birtsmorton CP.

BISBROOKE Rutland
133 SP 8899 1m E of Uppingham. CP, 166.
Uppnghm RD. Ch e. Rtlnd and
Stamford CC.

BISCATHORPE Lincs (L)
105 TF 2284 7m WSW of Louth. Loc,
Gayton le Wold CP. Lth RD. Ch e. Lth CC.
Large gravel wks nearby.

BISHAM Berks
159 SU 8585 just S of Marlow. CP, 1,034.
Cookham RD. P Mlw, Bucks. Ch e. Sch pe.
Windsor and Maidenhead CC (Wndsr.) B.
Abbey, physical recreation training centre,
is Elizn.

BISHAMPTON Worcs
143, 144 SO 9851 9m ESE of Worcester.
CP, 276. Pershore RD. P Pshre. Ch e.
S Worcs CC.

BISH MILL Devon
163 SS 7425 2m E of S Molton. Loc,
Bishop's Nympton CP. P: S Mltn.

BISHOP AUCKLAND Co Durham
85 NZ 2029 10m NNW of Darlington.
UD, 33,292. P. Bshp Aucklnd CC. See also
Binchester Blocks, Coundon, Cndn Grange,
Escomb, Etherley Dene, Leasingthorne,
Middlestone, Newfield, St Helen Aucklnd,
S Ch, Tindale Crescent, Toronto,
W Aucklnd, Westerton, Witton Pk. Wearside
tn with cstle residence of Bishops of Drhm.

BISHOP BURTON Yorks (E)
98 SE 9839 3m W of Beverley. CP, 425.
Bvrly RD. P Bvrly. Ch e, m. Sch pe.
Haltemprice CC. Whitewashed cottages
grouped round grn and large duck pond.
Archbishops of York had palace here, hence
name.

BISHOP MIDDLEHAM Co Durham
85 NZ 3231 2m NW of Sedgefield. CP,
1,078. Sdgfld RD. P Ferryhill. Ch e, m.
Sch pe. Drhm CC (Sdgfld). Site of mdvl
cstle belonging to Bishops of Drhm.

BISHOP MONKTON Yorks (W)
91 SE 3366 3m SSE of Ripon. CP, 420.
Rpn and Pateley Br RD. P Harrogate.
Ch e, m. Sch pe. Rpn CC.

BISHOP NORTON Lincs (L)
104 SK 9892 8m WNW of Mkt Rascn. CP, 282. Caistor RD. P LINCOLN. Ch e, m2. Gainsborough CC. 1½m SW, Ntn Place, Ggn mansion by Carr of York, 1776.

BISHOPSBOURNE Kent
173 TR 1852 4m SE of Canterbury. CP, 255. Bridge-Blean RD. P Cntrbry. Ch e. Cntrbry CC. Home of Joseph Conrad, novelist.

BISHOPS CANNINGS Wilts
167 SU 0364 3m NE of Devizes. CP, 1,067. Dvzs RD. Ch e. Sch pe. Dvzs CC. See also Coate, Horton. EE ch. On downs to N, many prehistoric earthworks and section of Wansdyke (see Stanton Prior). Vllge of (legendary?) 'moonrakers'.

BISHOP'S CASTLE Shrops
129 SO 3288 8m WNW of Craven Arms. CP, 1,228. Clun and Bp's Cstle RD. P. Ch e, c, m. Sch p, s. Ludlow CC. Scanty rems of cstle at top of hilly little tn set in Welsh border hills. Small brewery and clothing factory.

BISHOP'S CAUNDLE Dorset
178 ST 6913 4m SE of Sherborne. CP, 322. Shbne RD. P Shbne. Ch e, m. Sch pe. W Dst CC.

BISHOP'S CLEEVE Glos
143, 144 SO 9527 3m N of Cheltenham. CP, 4,244. Chltnhm RD. P Chltnhm. Ch e, m. Sch i, j, s. Cirencester and Tewkesbury CC. Mdvl ch with Jcbn carved oak gallery. 15c tithe barn now vllge hall.

BISHOP'S FONTHILL Wilts
167 ST 9333 8m NE of Shaftesbury. CP(Fnthll Bshp), 134. Mere and Tisbury RD. P Salisbury. Ch e. Sch pe. Westbury CC. Stone vllge on edge of F. Pk, with large ornamental lake. Orig hse blt for William Beckford, 18c-19c eccentric, collapsed 1825; present hse Vctrn Scottish baronial.

BISHOP'S FROME Herefs
142, 143 SO 6648 4m S of Bromyard. CP, 673. Brmyd RD. P WORCESTER. Ch e, m. Sch pe. Leominster CC. See also Fromes Hill.

BISHOP'S HULL Som
177 ST 2024 2m W of Taunton. CP(Bshp's Hll Without), 1,815. Tntn RD. P Tntn. Ch e, v. Sch p. Tntn CC.

BISHOP'S ITCHINGTON Warwicks
132 SP 3857 3m SSW of Southam. CP, 1,184. Sthm RD. P Leamington Spa. Ch e, c, m. Sch p. Stratford-on-Avon CC (Strtfd).

BISHOP'S LYDEARD Som
164 ST 1629 4m NW of Taunton. CP, 3,099. Tntn RD. P Tntn. Ch e, v. Sch pe. Tntn CC. See also E Combe. Ch: Perp twr.

BISHOP'S NYMPTON Devon
163 SS 7523 3m ESE of S Molton. CP, 708. S Mltn RD. P: S Mltn. Ch e, m. Sch p. N Dvn CC. See also Bish Mill, Newtown. Thatched cottages; ch with large Perp twr.

BISHOP'S OFFLEY Staffs
119 SJ 7829 7m NNE of Newport. Loc, Adbaston CP. P STAFFORD.

BISHOP'S STORTFORD Herts
148 TL 4821 7m NNE of Harlow. UD, 22,084. P. E Herts CC. Perp ch has prominent spire. Bthplce of Cecil Rhodes. Rhodes Memorial Museum. 3m ENE, Stansted Airpt.

BISHOPS SUTTON Hants
168 SU 6031 8m SW of Alton. CP, 538. Winchester RD. P Alresford. Ch e. Wnchstr CC. See also Gundleton.

BISHOP'S TACHBROOK Warwicks
132 SP 3161 3m S of Leamington. CP, 801. Warwick RD. P Lmngtn Spa. Ch e. Sch pe. Wrwck and Lmngtn CC.

BISHOP'S TAWTON Devon
163 SS 5630 2m S of Barnstaple. CP, 1,056. Bnstple RD. P Bnstple. Ch e, m, v. Sch p. N Dvn CC. Almost suburb of Bnstple. Ch has crocketed octagonal spire.

BISHOPSTEIGNTON Devon
176, 188 SX 9073 3m ENE of Newton Abbot. CP, 1,451. Ntn Abbt RD. P Teignmouth. Ch e, b, m, r. Sch p. Totnes CC. See also Luton. Bishops of Exeter once had palace here (½m NE); slight rems thereof. Ch has richly carved Nmn W door, and tympanum in S wall at W end.

BISHOPSTOKE Hants
180 SU 4619 just E of Eastleigh. Loc,
Eastlgh MB. P Eastlgh.

BISHOPSTONE Bucks
146, 159 SP 8010 2m SSW of Aylesbury.
Loc, Stone CP. P Aylesbury. Ch m.

BISHOPSTONE Herefs
142 SO 4143 6m WNW of Hereford. CP,
153. Weobley RD. P HRFD. Ch e.
Leominster CC.

BISHOPSTONE Sussex (E)
183 TQ 4701 1m NW of Seaford. Loc,
Sfd UD. P Sfd. Interesting ch, Saxon to E.

BISHOPSTONE Wilts
157 SU 2483 6m E of Swindon. CP, 591.
Highworth RD. P Swndn. Ch e, m. Sch pe.
Devizes CC. See also Hinton Parva.

BISHOPSTONE Wilts
167 SU 0625 6m WSW of Salisbury. CP,
473. Slsbry and Wilton RD. P Slsbry.
Ch e, m. Sch pe. Slsbry CC. Cruciform
14c-15c ch. Streams and watercress beds.

BISHOPSTROW Wilts
166, 167 ST 8943 2m SE of Warminster.
CP, 184. Wmnstr and Westbury RD. Ch e.
Wstbry CC.

BISHOP SUTTON Som
165, 166 ST 5859 8m S of Bristol. Loc,
Stowey-Sutton CP. Clutton RD. P BRSTL.
Ch e, m2. Sch p. N Som CC.

BISHOP'S WALTHAM Hants
180 SU 5517 7m N of Fareham. CP, 3,171.
Droxford RD. P SOUTHAMPTON.
Ch e, c, m, r, v2. Sch j, p. Petersfield CC.
See also Dean. Rems of 13c Bishop's Palace
(A.M.).

BISHOP'S WOOD Som
177 ST 2512 5m NW of Chard. Loc,
Otterford CP. P Chd. Ch v.

BISHOP'S WOOD Staffs
119 SJ 8309 6m E of Shifnal. Loc, Brewood
CP. P STAFFORD. Ch e. Sch pe.

BISHOP THORNTON Yorks (W)
91 SE 2663 6m NNW of Harrogate. CP,
398. Ripon and Pateley Br RD. Ch e, r.
Sch pe, pr. Rpn CC. See also Shaw Mills.

BISHOPTHORPE Yorks (W)
97 SE 5947 3m SSW of York. CP, 1,263.
Tadcaster RD. P YK. Ch e, m. Sch pe.
Barkston Ash CC. Palace of Archbishops of
Yk, beside R Ouse.

BISHOPTON Co Durham
85 NZ 3621 5m WNW of
Teesside(Stockton). CP, 253. Darlington
RD. P STCKTN-ON-TEES, Tssde. Ch e, m.
Bishop Auckland CC (Sedgefield).

BISHOPTON Yorks (W)
91 SE 2971 just W of Ripon. Loc, Rpn MB.

BISHOP WILTON Yorks (E)
97, 98 SE 7955 4m N of Pocklington. CP,
477. Pcklngtn RD. P YORK. Ch e m.
Sch pe. Howden CC. See also Youlthorpe.
Site of former palace of Archbishops of Yk,
on edge of Wolds, with B.W. Beck flowing
through vllge. Many prehistoric burial
mounds.

BISLEY Glos
156, 157 SO 9006 3m E of Stroud. CP
(Bsly-w-Lypiatt), 1,639. Strd RD. P Strd.
Ch e, b. Sch pe. Strd CC. See also Bournes
Grn, Eastcombe, Oakridge Lynch. Various
round barrows in vicinity, incl Money
Tump to S of vllge. In churchyard, Poor
Souls' Light, 13c, prob unique out of doors
in England. Well-dressing on Ascension Day.

BISLEY Surrey
169 SU 9459 4m W of Woking. CP, 1,165.
Bagshot RD. P Wkng. Ch e. Sch je. NW Srry
CC (Chertsey). To SW, B. Camp, with
famous rifle ranges.

BISPHAM GREEN Lancs
100 SD 4813 6m NE of Ormskirk. Loc,
Bsphm CP. W, Lancs RD. Sch pe.
Ormskk CC. B. Hall, 16c.

BISSOE Cornwall
190 SW 7741 4m WSW of Truro. Loc, Kea
CP. P Truro. Old tin-miners' settlement.

BISTERNE CLOSE Hants
179 SU 2203 5m ESE of Ringwood. Loc,
Burley CP.

BITCHFIELD Lincs (K)
123 SK 9828 6m SE of Grantham.
CP(Btchfld and Bassingthorpe), 160.
W, Kesteven RD. P Grnthm. Ch e. Sch p.
Rutland and Stamford CC.

BITTADON Devon
163 SS 5441 4m SSE of Ilfracombe. CP, 45.
Barnstaple RD. Ch e. N Dvn CC.

BITTAFORD Devon
187, 188 SX 6657 2m ENE of Ivybridge.
Loc, Ugborough CP. P Ivybrdge. Ch m.

BITTERING Norfolk
125 TF 9317 4m NW of E Dereham.
CP(Beeston w Bttrng), 394. Mitford and
Launditch RD. Ch e. SW Nflk CC.

BITTERLEY Shrops
129 SO 5677 4m ENE of Ludlow. CP, 729.
Ldlw RD. Ch e. Sch pe. Ldlw CC. See also
Cleeton St Mary, Middleton.

BITTESWELL Leics
132 SP 5385 1m NNW of Lutterworth.
CP, 320. Lttrwth RD. P RUGBY. Ch e.
Sch pe. Blaby CC (Harborough).

BITTON Glos
156 ST 6869 5m NW of Bath. CP, 3,632
Warmley RD. P BRISTOL. Ch e, m2.
Sch p2. Kingswood CC (S Glos). See also
Upton Cheyney. Ch: outstanding Perp twr.

BIX Oxon
159 SU 7285 3m NW of Henley. CP, 529.
Hnly RD. P Hnly-on-Thames. Ch e. Hnly
CC. See also Lr Assendon.

BLABY Leics
132, 133 SP 5697 4m S of Leicester.
CP, 4,242. Blby RD. P LCSTR.
Ch e, b, c, m, v. Sch je. Blby CC
(Harborough).

BLACKAWTON Devon
188 SX 8050 5m W of Dartmouth. CP, 489.
Kingsbridge RD. P Totnes. Ch e, m. Sch p.
Ttns CC.

BLACKBOROUGH Devon
176 ST 0909 7m NW of Honiton. Loc,
Kentisbeare CP. Ch e.

BLACKBOROUGH END Norfolk
124 TF 6614 4m SE of King's Lynn. Loc,
Middleton CP. P K's Lnn. Ch m.

BLACK BOURTON Oxon
158 SP 2804 6m SW of Witney. CP, 3,640.
Wtny RD. P OXFORD. Ch e, m. Mid-Oxon
CC (Banbury). See also Carterton. Ch has
13c wall-paintings.

BLACKBOYS Sussex
183 TQ 5220 4m E of Uckfield. Loc,
Framfield CP. P Uckfld. Ch m2,v. Sch pe.
To E along A265, Holy Cross Priory*, 19c
mansion now used partly as old people's
home, in large grnds.

BLACKBROOK Derbys
111 SK 3347 1m W of Belper. Loc, Blpr UD,
Blpr RD. P Blpr, DERBY. Blpr CC.

BLACKBROOK Staffs
110, 119 SJ 7639 6m ENE of Mkt Drayton.
Loc, Maer CP. Ch m.

BLACKBURN Lancs
94, 95 SD 6828 21m NNW of Manchester.
CB, 101,672. P. Darwen CC. Blckbn BC. See
also Guide, Lr Darwen. Textiles, textile
machinery, general engineering. Parish ch
was made a cathedral 1926.

BLACK CALLERTON Nthmb
78 NZ 1769 2m SSE of Ponteland. Loc,
Woolsington CP. Cstle Ward RD. Ch v.
Hexham CC.

BLACK DOG Devon
176 SS 8009 6m NNW of Crediton. Loc,
Crdtn RD. P Crdtn. Ch m. Tiverton CC
(Torrington).

BLACKDOWN Dorset
177 ST 3903 5m SW of Crewkerne. Loc,
Broadwindsor CP. Ch e.

BLACKER HILL Yorks (W)
102, 103 SE 3602 3m SSE of Barnsley. Loc,
Worsbrough UD. P Bnsly.

BLACKFIELD Hants
180 SU 4402 1m SW of Fawley. Loc, Fwly
CP. P SOUTHAMPTON. Ch b. Sch i, j.

BLACKFORD Cumb
76 NY 3962 4m N of Carlisle. Loc,
Westlinton CP. P Clsle. Ch e. Sch pe.

BLACKFORD Som
165 ST 4147 5m SW of Cheddar. Loc,
Wedmore CP. P Wdmre. Ch e. Sch p, s.

BLACKFORD Som
166 ST 6526 4m WSW of Wincanton. Loc,
Compton Pauncefoot CP. Ch e.

BLACKFORDBY Leics
120, 121 SK 3217 2m NW of Ashby de la
Zouch. Loc, Ashby de la Zch UD. P
Burton-on-Trent, Staffs.

BLACKGANG IOW
180 SZ 4876 5m W of Ventnor. Loc,
Chale CP. B. Chine, tourist amusement pk.
Museum of shipwrecks.

BLACKHALL COLLIERY Co Durham
85 NZ 4539 2m SE of Peterlee. Loc, Monk
Hesleden CP. P Hartlepool. Ch e, m, r, s, v.
Sch p, pr, s.

BLACKHALL MILL Co Durham
77, 78 NZ 1256 4m N of Consett. Loc,
Blaydon UD. P NEWCASTLE UPON TYNE.

BLACKHAM Sussex (E)
171 TQ 4940 6m W of Tunbridge Wells.
Loc, Withyham CP. P TNBRDGE WLLS.
Ch e.

BLACKHEATH Essex
149, 162 TM 0021 2m S of Colchester. Loc,
Clchstr MB, Lexden and Winstree RD. P
Clchstr. Clchstr CC.

BLACKHEATH London
161, 171 TQ 4076 1m SE of Greenwich.
Loc, Grnwch LB, Lewisham LB. Grnwch
BC, Lwshm E BC. (Grnwch BC, Lwshm N
BC.) The hth is breezy open space lined
with some handsome hses; former haunt of
robbers.

BLACKHEATH Surrey
170 TQ 0346 3m SE of Guildford. Loc,
Wonersh CP. P Gldfd. Ch e. 1m W,
Gt Tangley Mnr, 16c moated hse.

BLACKLAND Wilts
157 SU 0168 2m SSE of Calne. Loc Clne
Without CP. Clne and Chippenham RD.
Ch e. Chppnhm CC.

BLACK LANE Lancs
101 SD 7708 2m SW of Bury. Loc,
Radcliffe MB.

BLACK MARSH Shrops
129 SO 3299 7m N of Bishop's Cstle. Loc,
Shelve CP.

BLACKMOOR Hants
169, 181 SU 7833 5m SE of Alton. Loc,
Selborne CP. P Liss. Ch e. Sch pe.

BLACKMOOR GATE Devon
163 SS 6443 6m SW of Lynton. Loc,
Barnstaple RD. N Dvn CC. Marks edge of
Exmoor National Pk.

BLACKMORE Essex
161 TL 6001 3m ESE of Ongar. CP, 1,507.
Epping and Ongr RD. P Ingatestone.
Ch e, b. Sch p. Brentwood and Ongr CC
(Chigwell). 12c–15c ch has splendid
timbered twr, and incorporates parts of 12c
Austin canons' priory.

BLACKMORE END Essex
148, 149 TL 7430 5m N of Braintree. Loc,
Wethersfield CP. P Brntree.

BLACKNEST Hants
169 SU 7941 4m SW of Farnham. Loc,
Binsted CP.

BLACK NOTLEY Essex
149, 162 TL 7620 2m S of Braintree. CP,
1,388. Brntree RD. P Brntree. Ch e, c, v.
Brntree CC (Maldon).

BLACKO Lancs
95 SD 8641 2m N of Nelson. CP, 453.
Burnley RD. P Nlsn. Ch v. Sch p. Clitheroe
CC. Beacon Twr to N, origin uncertain.

BLACKPOOL Devon
188 SX 8547 3m SW of Dartmouth. Loc,
Kingsbridge RD. Sch pe. Totnes CC.

BLACKPOOL Lancs
94 SD 3036 15m WNW of Preston.
CB, 151,311. P. BCs: Blckpl N, Blckpl S.
Resort. Well known twr, over 500ft. Annual
illuminations along sea front.

BLACKROD Lancs
101 SD 6110 4m NNE of Wigan. UD, 4,801.
P Bolton. Westhoughton CC. See also Scot
Lane End.

BLACKSHAW HEAD Yorks (W)
95 SD 9527 2m W of Hebden Br. Loc,
Blckshw CP. Hepton RD. P Hbdn Br. Ch m.
Sowerby CC.

BLACKSMITH'S CORNER Essex
149 TM 0131 4m NNE of Colchester. Loc,
Langham CP.

BLACKSTONE Sussex (W)
182 TQ 2416 2m E of Henfield. Loc,
Woodmancote CP. Chanctonbury RD.

P Hnfld. Shoreham CC (Arundel and Shrhm).

BLACKTHORN Oxon
145, 146 SP 6219 3m SE of Bicester. CP, 563. Ploughley RD. P Bcstr. Ch c. Mid-Oxon CC (Henley).

BLACKTHORPE Suffolk (W)
136 TL 9063 3m E of Bury St Edmunds. Loc, Rougham CP. Thingoe RD. Bury St Eds CC.

BLACKTOFT Yorks (E)
98 SE 8424 6m E of Goole. CP, 395. Howden RD. P Gle. Ch e, m. Hdn CC. See also Faxfleet, Yokefleet. Rivers Trent and Ouse meet here and become Humber.

BLACK TORRINGTON Devon
175 SS 4605 8m E of Holsworthy. CP, 429. Hlswthy RD. P Beaworthy. Ch e, m2. Sch pe. W Dvn CC (Tavistock).

BLACKWALL London
161 TQ 3880 5m E of Charing Cross. Loc, Twr Hmlts LB. Stepney and Poplar BC (Pplr). Docks on N bank of Thames. Road tunnels under river.

BLACKWATER Cornwall
190 SW 7346 4m NE of Redruth. Loc, Truro RD. P Truro. Ch m. Sch p. Truro CC.

BLACKWATER Hants
169 SU 8559 1m W of Camberley. Loc, Hawley CP. P Cmbrly, Surrey. Ch e.

BLACKWATER IOW
180 SZ 5086 2m S of Newport. Loc, S Arreton CP. Isle of Wight RD and CC. P Npt.

BLACKWATER Suffolk (E)
137 TM 5077 just N of Southwold. Loc, Reydon CP.

BLACKWELL Co Durham
85 NZ 2712 1m SW of Darlington, Loc, Dlngtn CB, Dlngtn RD. Dlngtn BC, Bishop Auckland CC. (Sedgefield CC.)

BLACKWELL Derbys
111 SK 1272 4m E of Buxton. CP, 25. Bakewell RD. W Derbys CC. See also Upr Langwith.

BLACKWELL Derbys
112 SK 4458 3m NE of Alfreton. CP, 4,084. Blckwll RD. P DERBY. Ch e, m3. Sch i, j. Bolsover CC. See also Newton, Westhouses.

BLACKWELL Warwicks
144 SP 2443 2m NNW of Shipston on Stour. Loc, Tredington CP. P Shpstn on Str.

BLACKWELL Worcs
130, 131 SO 9972 2m ENE of Bromsgrove. Loc, Brmsgrve UD. P Brmsgrve.

BLACKWOOD HILL Staffs
110 SJ 9255 4m W of Leek. Loc, Horton CP.

BLADON Oxon
145 SP 4414 1m S of Woodstock. CP, 680. Witney RD. P OXFORD. Ch e, m. Sch pe. Mid-Oxon CC (Banbury). On S edge of Blenheim Pk (see Wdstck). Burial place of Sir Winston Churchill and of his parents.

BLAGDON Som
165 ST 5058 5m NE of Cheddar. CP, 1,025. Axbridge RD. P BRISTOL. Ch e, b, m. Weston-super-Mare CC. See also Charterhouse, Rickford. Ch: 116ft Perp twr. Large reservoir to NE.

BLAGDON Som
177 ST 2118 4m S of Taunton. Loc, Pitminster CP. P (Blgdn Hill), Tntn. Ch c. Sch p.

BLAISDON Glos
143 SO 7016 3m NE of Cinderford. CP, 341. E Dean RD. P Longhope. Ch e, r. W Glos CC. See also Flaxley.

BLAKEDOWN Worcs
130 SO 8878 3m ENE of Kidderminster. CP(Churchill and Blkdn), 1,273. Kddrmnstr RD. P Kddrmnstr. Ch e. Sch pe. Kddrmnstr CC.

BLAKEMERE Herefs
142 SO 3641 9m W of Hereford. CP, 101. Weobley RD. P HRFD. Ch e. Leominster CC.

BLAKENEY Glos
155, 156 SO 6707 3m NE of Lydney. Loc, Awre CP. P. Ch e, b, c. Sch p.

BLAKENEY Norfolk
125 TG 0243 4m NW of Holt. CP, 705. Walsingham RD. P Hlt. Ch e, m, r, s. Sch pe. NW Nflk CC (N Nflk). Former port, now holiday camp and yachting centre. Rems of 15c guildhall (A.M.). B. Point (NT), nature reserve, bird sanctuary.

BLAKENHALL Ches
110 SJ 7247 5m SSE of Crewe. CP, 141.
Nantwich RD. Ch m. Nntwch CC.

BLAKENHAM, GREAT Suffolk (E)
150 TM 1150 5m NW of Ipswich. See Gt
Blknhm.

BLAKESHALL Worcs
130 SO 8381 3m N of Kidderminster. Loc,
Wolverley CP.

BLAKESLEY Northants
145, 146 SP 6250 4m W of Towcester. CP,
338. Tcstr RD. P Tcstr. Ch e. Sch pe.
Daventry CC (S Nthnts).

BLANCHLAND Nthmb
77 NY 9650 8m W of Consett. CP, 190.
Hexham RD. P Cnstt, Co Durham. Ch e.
Sch pe. Hxhm CC. See also Newbiggin.
Noble vllge square surrounded by stone
hses, set in steep valley.

BLANDFORD FORUM
178, 179 ST 8806 16m NW of
Bournemouth. MB, 3,643. P. N Dst CC.
Centre burnt down 1731, hence present
consistency of Ggn style. Cf Honiton.

BLANDFORD ST MARY Dorset
178, 179 ST 8905 just S of Blandford.
CP, 307. Blndfd RD. Ch e. N Dst CC.

BLANKNEY Lincs (K)
113 TF 0660 9m SE of Lincoln. CP, 424.
E Kesteven RD. P LNCLN. Ch e. Sch pe.
Grantham CC. 19c 'Tdr' estate vllge. Fine
Vctrn ch.

BLASHFORD Hants
179 SU 1507 1m N of Ringwood. Loc,
Ellingham CP.

BLASTON Leics
133 SP 8095 5m SW of Uppingham. CP, 55.
Mkt Harborough RD. Ch e. Hbrgh CC.

BLATHERWYCKE Northants
134 SP 9795 6m NE of Corby. CP, 64.
Oundle and Thrapston RD.
P PETERBOROUGH. Ch e.
Wellingborough CC (Ptrbrgh).

BLAWITH Lancs
88 SD 2888 6m N of Ulverston. CP, 118.
N Lonsdale RD. P Ulvstn. Ch e. Morecambe
and Lnsdle CC. See also Water Yeat.

BLAXHALL Suffolk (E)
137 TM 3657 4m SSW of Saxmundham.
CP, 336. Deben RD. P Woodbridge. Ch e.
Eye CC.

BLAXTON Yorks (W)
103 SE 6700 6m ESE of Doncaster.
CP, 476. Doncstr RD. Ch m. Don
Valley CC.

BLAYDON Co Durham
78 NZ 1863 4m W of Newcastle. UD,
32,018. P(Bldn-on-Tyne). Bldn BC (CC).
See also Barlow, Blackhall Mill, Chopwell,
Highfield, High Spen, Rowland's Gill,
Winlaton, Wnltn Mill. Indstrl Tyneside tn
featured in famous song.

BLEADON Som
165 ST 3456 3m SSE of Weston. CP, 707.
Axbridge RD. P Wstn-super-Mare. Ch e, m.
W-s-M CC.

BLEAN Kent
173 TR 1260 2m NW of Canterbury. Loc,
St Cosmus and St Damian in the Bln CP.
Bridge-Blean RD. P Cntrbry. Ch e, m.
Sch p. Cntrbry CC.

BLEASBY Notts
112 SK 7149 6m WSW of Newark. CP, 434.
Southwell RD. P NOTTINGHAM. Ch e.
Sch pe. Nwk CC.

BLEASDALE Lancs
94 SD 5745 10m NNE of Preston. CP, 176.
Garstang RD. P Prstn. Ch e. Sch pe. N Fylde
CC.

BLEDINGTON Glos
144 SP 2422 4m SE of Stow-on-the-Wold.
CP, 344. N Cotswold RD. P OXFORD.
Ch e, m. Sch p. Cirencester and Tewkesbury
CC. Maypole. Ch: 15c glass.

BLEDLOW Bucks
159 SP 7702 2m WSW of Princes
Risborough. CP(Bldlw-cum-Saunderton),
1,871. Wycombe RD. P Aylesbury. Ch e, m.
Sch pe. Aylesbury CC (Wcmbe). See also
Pitch Grn.

BLEDLOW RIDGE Bucks
159 SU 7997 5m NW of High Wycombe.
Loc, Bldlw-cum-Saunderton CP. P Hgh
Wcmbe. Ch e, m. Sch p. Extensive views
from N escarpment of Chilterns.

BLENCARN Cumb
83 NY 6331 8m E of Penrith. Loc, Culgaith
CP. P Pnrth. Ch m. To NE on slopes of
Pennines, ancient terraces known as Hanging
Walls of Mark Anthony.

BLENCOGO Cumb
82 NY 1948 4m W of Wigton. Loc,
Bromfield CP. Sch pe.

BLENCOW, GREAT Cumb
83 NY 4532 4m WNW of Penrith. Loc,
Dacre CP. P(Blncw), Pnrth.

BLENDWORTH Hants
181 SU 7113 4m N of Havant. Loc,
Horndean CP. Ch e. Sch pe.

BLENNERHASSET Cumb
82 NY 1741 7m SW of Wigton.
CP(Blnnrhsst and Torpenhow), 509. Wgtn
RD. P Carlisle. Ch m, v. Sch p. Penrith and
the Border CC.

BLETCHINGDON Oxon
145 SP 5017 4m E of Woodstock. CP, 602.
Ploughley RD. P OXFORD. Ch e. Sch pe.
Mid-Oxon CC (Henley).

BLETCHINGLEY Surrey
170 TQ 3250 5m E of Reigate. CP, 3,395.
Godstone RD. P Redhill. Ch e, c, m2, r.
Sch p. E Srry CC (Rgte). Ch: brasses,
monmt. To N, Brewer St Farm,
half-timbered 15c hse.

BLETCHLEY Bucks
146 SP 8733 16m NW of Luton.
UD, 30,608. P. Buckingham CC. See also
Fenny Stratford, Simpson.

BLETCHLEY Shrops
110, 118, 119 SJ 6233 3m W of Mkt
Drayton. Loc, Moreton Say CP.

BLETSOE Beds
134 TL 0258 6m NNW of Bedford. CP, 235.
Bdfd RD. P BDFD. Ch e. Bdfd CC. Bthplce
of Margaret Beaufort, grandmother of
Henry VIII and founder of St John's
College, Cambridge.

BLEWBURY Berks
158 SU 5385 3m S of Didcot. CP, 1,126.
Wantage RD. P Ddct. Ch e, m. Sch pe.
Abingdon CC.

BLICKLING Norfolk
126 TG 1728 1m NW of Aylsham. CP, 215.
St Faith's and Aylshm RD. Ch e. Sch pe.
N Nflk CC (Central Nflk). B. Hall (NT)*,
mainly 17c hse in fine grnds with classical
temple, lake, 18c mausoleum. Ch: many 14c
and 15c brasses.

BLIDWORTH Notts
112 SK 5956 5m SE of Mansfield. CP,
7,308. Southwell RD. P Mnsfld.
Ch e2, m2 v2. Sch p, pe. Newark CC. See
also Fishpool. Colliery vllge in Sherwood
Forest. Traditional home of Friar Tuck.

BLINDCRAKE Cumb
82 NY 1434 3m NE of Cockermouth. CP,
297. Cckrmth RD. P Cckrmth. Ch m.
Workington CC. See also Sunderland.

BLINDLEY HEATH Surrey
171 TQ 3645 5m NNW of E Grinstead.
Loc, Godstone CP. P Lingfield. Ch e, c.
Sch pe.

BLISLAND Cornwall
186 SX 1073 4m NNE of Bodmin. CP, 529.
Wadebridge and Padstow RD. P Bdmn. Ch e.
Sch p. Bdmn CC. See also Temple. Blt
round large grn — unusual in Cornwall. Ch of
much interest. Stone circles, china clay
workings to E.

BLISSFORD Hants
179 SU 1713 2m ESE of
Fordingbridge. Loc, Frngbrdge CP.

BLISS GATE Worcs
130 SO 7472 3m SW of Bewdley. Loc,
Rock CP. P Kidderminster.

BLISWORTH Northants
146 SP 7253 4m NE of Towcester. CP,
1,192. Tcstr RD. P NORTHAMPTON.
Ch e, b. Sch p. Daventry CC (S Nthnts). On
Grand Union Canal, which to S enters
tunnel 1¾m long.

BLOCKLEY Glos
144 SP 1634 3m NW of Moreton-in-Marsh.
CP, 2,395. N Cotswold RD. P Mtn-in-Msh.
Ch e, b. Sch ie, je. Cirencester and
Tewkesbury CC. See also Aston Magna,
Draycott, Paxford. Late Nmn ch with 18c
Gothic twr.

BLOFIELD Norfolk
126 TG 3309 7m E of Norwich. CP, 1,479.
Blfld and Flegg RD. P NRWCH, NOR 84Z.
Ch e, m, v. Sch p. Yarmouth CC.

BLO NORTON Norfolk
136 TM 0179 6m W of Diss. CP, 245.
Wayland RD. P Dss. Ch e, m. S Nflk CC.

BLOOMSBURY London
160 TQ 3082 1m N of Charing Cross. Loc,
Camden LB. Holborn and St Pancras S BC.
Contains British Museum and Lndn
University.

BLORE Staffs
111 SK 1349 3m NW of Ashbourne.
CP(Blre w Swinscoe), 131. Cheadle RD.
Ch e. Leek CC. 800ft up at S end of
Dovedale and Peak Distr National Pk.

BLOXHAM Oxon
145 SP 4235 3m SSW of Banbury. CP,
1,359. Bnbry RD. P Bnbry. Ch e, b, m.
Sch pe. Bnbry CC. Mainly 13c ch has lofty
spire; was restored 19c by G. E. Street, who
also blt boys' sch 1860.

BLOXHOLM Lincs (K)
113 TF 0653 5m N of Sleaford. CP(Ashby
de la Launde and Blxhlm), 609.
E Kesteven RD. Ch e. Grantham CC. B.
Hall, 17c hse with later additions, now
romantic ruin.

BLOXWORTH Dorset
178, 179 SY 8894 5m NNW of Wareham.
CP, 184. Wrhm and Purbeck RD. P Wrhm.
Ch e. S Dst CC.

BLUBBERHOUSES Yorks (W)
96 SE 1655 6m NE of Ilkley. CP, 29.
Wharfedale RD. P Otley. Ch e. Ripon CC.
On moors; many reservoirs in Washburn
valley NW and SE.

BLUE ANCHOR Som
164 ST 0343 3m W of Watchet. Loc, Old
Cleeve CP. Small resort.

BLUEBELL HILL Kent
171,172 TQ 7462 4m S of Rochester. Loc,
Burham CP. P Rchstr. Ch b.

BLUNDESTON Suffolk (E)
137 TM 5197 3m NNW of Lowestoft. CP,
638. Lothingland RD. P Lwstft. Ch e, m.
Sch pe. Lwstft CC.

BLUNHAM Beds
147 TL 1551 2m NW of Sandy. CP, 612.
Biggleswade RD. P BEDFORD. Ch e, b2.
Sch pe. Mid-Beds CC.

BLUNSDON ST ANDREW Wilts
157 SU 1389 4m N of Swindon. CP, 1,444.
Highworth RD. P(Blnsdn), Swndn. Ch e, m.
Sch pe. Devizes CC. See also Broad Blnsdn.

BLUNTINGTON Worcs
130, 131 SO 8974 4m E of Kidderminster.
Loc, Chaddesley Corbett CP. Ch m.

BLUNTISHAM Hunts
135 TL 3674 4m NE of St Ives. CP, 617. St
Ives RD. P HUNTINGDON. Ch e, b. Sch p.
Hunts CC.

BLYBOROUGH Lincs (L)
104 SK 9394 8m ENE of Gainsborough. CP,
180. Gnsbrgh RD. Ch e. Gnsbrgh CC.

BLYFORD Suffolk (E)
137 TM 4276 2m E of Halesworth. CP, 145.
Wainford RD. Ch e. Lowestoft CC.

BLYMHILL Staffs
119 SJ 8012 5m NE of Shifnal. CP, 459.
Cannock RD. P Shfnl, Salop. Ch e. Sch pe.
SW Staffs CC (Cnnck). See also Brineton,
Gt Chatwell, Orslow.

BLYTH Notts
103 SK 6287 6m NW of Retford. CP, 856.
Worksop RD. P Wksp. Ch e, m. Sch pe.
Bassetlaw CC. Vllge situated in curve of
R Ryton. Ch, rems of former priory, has
Perp twr but is mainly Nmn.

BLYTH Nthmb
78 NZ 3181 6m NNW of Whitley Bay.
MB, 34,617. P. Blth BC. See also Bebside,
Cowpen, New Delaval, Newsham. Port;
mining tn. Power stn.

BLYTHBURGH Suffolk (E)
137 TM 4575 4m W of Southwold. CP, 551.
Blyth RD. P Halesworth. Ch e, m. Eye CC.
Once a seaport, now 4m inland. Noble 15c
ch stands sentinel over marshes.

BLYTHE BRIDGE Staffs
110, 119 SJ 9541 5m ESE of
Stoke-on-Trent. Loc, Fulford CP. P
Stke-on-Trnt. Sch j, s.

BLYTHE MARSH Staffs
110, 119 SJ 9641 6m ESE of
Stoke-on-Trent. Loc, Forsbrook CP. Ch m.
Sch p.

BLYTON Lincs (L)
104 SK 8594 4m NE of Gainsborough. CP,
878. Gnsbrgh RD. P Gnsbrgh. Ch e, m2.
Sch pe. Gnsbrgh CC. Ch contains flags of all
Allies of World War II.

BOARHUNT Hants
180 SU 6008 2m NE of Fareham. CP, 462.
Droxford RD. Ch e. Petersfield CC. See also
N Brhnt. Ch largely Saxon.

BOAR'S HEAD Lancs
100 SD 5708 2m N of Wigan. Loc,
Standish-w-Langtree UD.

BOARSHEAD Sussex (E)
183 TQ 5332 2m NE of Crowborough. Loc,
Rotherfield CP. Ch m.

BOARS HILL Berks
158 SP 4802 3m N of Abingdon. Loc,
Wootton CP. P OXFORD. Ch r. Extensive
views from Jarn Mound.

BOARSTALL Bucks
145, 146 SP 6214 6m SSE of Bicester. CP,
123. Aylesbury RD. Ch e. Aylesbury CC. B.
Tower, stone gatehse of long-demolished
fortified hse (NT).

BOASLEY CROSS Devon
175 SX 5093 6m W of Okehampton. Loc,
Okhmptn RD. P Okhmptn. Sch p. W Dvn
CC (Torrington).

BOBBING Kent
172 TQ 8865 1m NW of Sittingbourne. CP,
758. Swale RD. Ch e. Sch p. Faversham CC.

BOBBINGTON Staffs
130 SO 8090 6m ESE of Bridgnorth. CP,
478. Seisdon RD. P Stourbridge, Worcs.
Ch e, m. Sch pe. SW Staffs CC (Brierley
Hill). See also Halfpenny Grn. On Shrops
border.

BOBBINGWORTH Essex
161 TL 5305 2m NW of Ongar. CP, 397.
Epping and Ongr RD. Ch e. Brentwood and
Ongr CC (Chigwell). To SE, Blake Hall, 18c
hse with 19c additions, used as RAF
Operations Centre in World War II. To SW,
large radio stn.

BOCKING Essex
149, 162 TL 7524 just N of Braintree.
UD(Brntree and Bckng), 24,839. P.
Brntree CC(Maldon). Well preserved
post-mill.

BOCKING CHURCHSTREET Essex
149 TL 7525 2m N of Braintree. Loc,
Brntree and Bckng UD. P Brntree.

BOCKLETON Worcs
129 SO 5962 4m S of Tenbury Wells. CP,
200. Tnbry RD. P Tnbry Wlls. Ch e.
Kidderminster CC. See also Grafton.

BOCONNOC Cornwall
186 SX 1460 3m E of Lostwithiel. CP, 159.
Liskeard RD. Ch e. Bodmin CC. No vllge,
but hse, ch, deer pk and lake; a few farms.
Hse 18c classical.

BODDINGTON Glos
143, 144 SO 8925 4m NW of Cheltenham.
CP, 263. Chltnhm RD. Ch e. Cirencester and
Tewkesbury CC. See also Barrow.

BODENHAM Herefs
142 SO 5351 6m SSE of Leominster.
CP, 671. Lmnstr and Wigmore RD.
P HEREFORD. Ch e, m. Sch pe.
Lmnstr CC. See also Bowley, Maund Bryan.
14c ch. Gravel wks.

BODENHAM Wilts
167 SU 1626 3m SSE of Salisbury. Loc,
Odstock CP. P Slsbry. Ch e, b. On edge of
Longford Pk (see Alderbury).

BODHAM STREET Norfolk
125 TG 1240 3m SW of Sheringham. Loc,
Bdhm CP. Erpingham RD. P(Bdhm), Holt.
Ch e, m. Sch p. N Nflk CC.

BODIAM Sussex (E)
184 TQ 7825 3m SSE of Hawkhurst. CP,
404. Battle RD. P Robertsbridge. Ch e.
Sch pe. Rye CC. Late 14c moated cstle
(NT)*, overlooking Rother valley. Annual
pancake race against N Somercotes, Lincs.

BODICOTE Oxon
145 SP 4637 2m S of Banbury. CP. Bnbry
RD. P Bnbry. Ch e, m. Bnbry CC.

BODIEVE Cornwall
185 SW 9973 just N of Wadebridge. Loc,
Wdbrdge CP.

BODINNICK Cornwall
186 SX 1352 across river from Fowey. Loc,
Lanteglos CP. Liskeard RD. Bodmin CC.
Colour-washed hses; car ferry; china clay
ships.

BODLE STREET GREEN Sussex (E)
183 TQ 6514 6m W of Battle. Loc,
Warbleton CP. P(Bdle St), Hailsham. Ch v.

BODMIN Cornwall
185, 186 SX 0767 26m WNW of Plymouth.
MB, 9,204. P. Bdmn CC. See also
St Lawrence. Old county tn at W edge of
Bdmn Moor. Cathedral-like ch. 2½m S,
Lanhydrock Pk (NT)*, restored 17c hse;
open (N wing only).

BODNEY Norfolk
136 TL 8398 7m S of Swaffham. Loc,
Hilborough CP. Ch e, m.

BODSHAM GREEN Kent
173 TR 1045 6m ENE of Ashford. Loc,
Elmsted CP. Elham RD. Sch pe. Folkestone
and Hythe CC.

BODYMOOR HEATH Warwicks
131 SP 1996 4m N of Coleshill. Loc,
Kingsbury CP. P Sutton Coldfield. Ch m.

BOGNOR REGIS Sussex (W)
181 SZ 9399 6m SE of Chichester.
UD, 34,389. P. Arundel CC (Chchstr). See
also Aldwick, Felpham. Seaside resort.
'Regis' conferred after convalescence of
George V in 1929.

BOG, THE Shrops
129 SO 3597 6m NNE of Bishop's Cstle.
Loc, Worthen CP.

BOHORTHA Cornwall
190 SW 8632 1m SE of St Mawes across
river. Loc, Gerrans CP.

BOJEWYAN Cornwall
189 SW 3934 6m WNW of Penzance. Loc,
St Just UD. P Pnznce.

BOLAM Co Durham
85 NZ 1922 4m S of Bishop Auckland. CP,
102. Barnard Cstle RD. P Darlington. Ch e.
Bshp Aucklnd CC.

BOLAM Nthmb
77, 78 NZ 0982 7m WSW of Morpeth. Loc,
Belsay CP. Ch e. Ch Saxon twr; Nmn nave.

BOLAS, GREAT Shrops
118, 119 SJ 6421 6m N of Wellington. See
Gt Bls.

BOLD HEATH Lancs
100, 109 SJ 5389 3m NNE of Widnes. Loc,
Bld CP. Whiston RD. P Wdns. Wdns CC. To
NW, Bld Colliery. (Bld Hth is on edge of
colliery disʰʳ.)

BOLDON Co Durham
78 NZ 3561 4m SSW of S Shields.
UD, 23,904. Jarrow BC. See also
Bldn Colliery, Cleadon, Marsden, Whitburn,
Whtbn Cllry.

BOLDON COLLIERY Co Durham
78 NZ 3462 3m SSW of S Shields. Loc,
Bldn UD. P.

BOLDRE Hants
180 SZ 3298 2m N of Lymington. CP,
2,235. New Forest RD. P Lmngtn.
Ch e, b, c. Sch pe. Nw Frst CC. See also
Battramsley, Norleywood, Portmore, S
Baddesley.

BOLDRON Yorks (N)
84 NZ 0314 2m SW of Barnard Cstle. CP,
99. Startforth RD. P Bnd Cstle, Co Durham.
Ch m. Richmond CC.

BOLE Notts
104 SK 7987 2m SW of Gainsborough. CP,
93. E Retford RD. Ch e, m. Bassetlaw CC.

BOLEHILL Derbys
111 SK 2955 3m S of Matlock. Loc,
Wirksworth UD. P DERBY.

BOLHAM Devon
164, 176 SS 9514 1m N of Tiverton. Loc,
Tvtn MB. P Tvtn.

BOLHAM WATER Devon
164, 176 ST 1612 6m SSE of Wellington.
Loc, Clayhidon CP.

BOLINGEY Cornwall
185, 190 SW 7653 6m SSW of Newquay.
Loc, Perranzabuloe CP. P Perranporth.
Ch m.

BOLLINGTON Ches
101 SJ 7286 3m WSW of Altrincham. CP,
231. Bucklow RD. P Altrnchm. Ch e.
Sch pe. Knutsford CC.

BOLLINGTON Ches
101 SJ 9377 3m NNE of Macclesfield.
UD, 6,610. P Mcclsfld. Mcclsfld CC. See also
Kerridge. Cotton tn. On hill to S is White
Nancy, 19c Waterloo memorial in
white-painted stone.

BOLNEY Sussex (E)
182 TQ 2622 4m W of Haywards Hth.
CP, 1,112. Cuckfield RD. P Hwds Hth.
Ch e, v2. Sch pe. Mid-Sx CC (E Grinstead).

BOLNHURST Beds
134 TL 0859 6m NNE of Bedford.
CP(Blnhst and Keysoe), 583. Bdfd RD.
P BDFD. Ch e. Bdfd CC. See also Keysoe
Row.

BOLSOVER Derbys
112 SK 4770 6m E of Chesterfield.
UD, 10,956. P Chstrfld. Blsvr CC. See also
Carr Vale, Hills Tn, Shuttlewood, Stanfree,
Whaley. B. Cstle (A.M.), Nmn, rebuilt and
enlarged early 17c.

BOLSTERSTONE Yorks (W)
102 SK 2796 8m NW of Sheffield. Loc,
Stocksbridge UD. P SHFFLD.

BOLSTONE Herefs
142 SO 5532 5m SSE of Hereford. CP, 45.
Hrfd RD. Ch e. Hrfd CC.

BOLTBY Yorks (N)
91 SE 4986 5m NE of Thirsk. CP, 146.
Thsk RD. P Thsk. Ch e, m. Thsk and Malton
CC. 1m SE, pre-Roman cliff camp.

BOLTON Lancs
101 SD 7109 10m NW of Manchester.
CB, 153,977. P. BCs: Bltn E, Bltn W. See
also Lostock Junction. Textiles, esp
spinning. Aero-engineering. To NW,
Smithills Hall*, 14c and later, half-timbered.
To N, Hall i' th' Wd, 16c hse now museum,
childhood home of Crompton, inventor of
spinning mule.

BOLTON Nthmb
71 NU 1013 5m W of Alnwick. Loc,
Hedgeley CP. Alnwck RD. Ch e.
Berwick-upon-Tweed CC.

BOLTON Westm
83 NY 6323 3m NW of Appleby. CP, 321.
N Westm RD. P Appleby. Ch e, m. Sch p.
Westm CC.

BOLTON Yorks (E)
97, 98 SE 7752 3m NW of Pocklington.
Loc, Fangfoss CP. Ch m.

BOLTON ABBEY Yorks (W)
96 SE 0753 5m NW of Ilkley. CP, 135.
Skipton RD. P Skptn. Ch e. Skptn CC.
Beside R Wharfe. Rems of 12c priory. 1½m
N, the Strid, rocky canyon formed by river.

BOLTON BY BOWLAND Yorks (W)
95 SD 7849 5m NNE of Clitheroe. CP, 471.
Blnd RD. P Clthroe, Lancs. Ch e, v. Sch pe.
Skipton CC. See also Holden.

BOLTONFELLEND Cumb
76 NY 4768 6m NW of Brampton. Loc,
Hethersgill CP.

BOLTONGATE Cumb
82 NY 2240 5m SSW of Wigton. Loc,
Boltons CP. Wgtn RD. P Carlisle. Ch e.
Penrith and the Border CC.

BOLTON-LE-SANDS Lancs
89 SD 4868 2m SW of Carnforth. CP,
2,883. Lancaster RD. P Cnfth. Ch e, c, r.
Sch pe. Morecambe and Lonsdale CC. See
also Bltn Tn End.

BOLTON LOW HOUSES Cumb
82 NY 2344 3m SSW of Wigton. Loc, Bltns
CP. Wgtn RD. P Wgtn. Ch m. Sch pe.
Penrith and the Border CC.

BOLTON-ON-SWALE Yorks (N)
91 SE 2599 5m ESE of Richmond. CP, 46.
Rchmnd RD. Ch e. Sch pe. Rchmnd CC.
1½m SE, Kiplin Hall*, blt early 17c by Ld
Baltimore, founder of State of Maryland,
U.S.A; naval museum, boating lake, gdn.

BOLTON PERCY Yorks (W)
97 SE 5341 3m ESE of Tadcaster. CP, 218.
Tdcstr RD. P YORK. Ch e. Sch pe. Barkston
Ash CC.

BOLTON TOWN END Lancs
89 SD 4867 2m SW of Carnforth. Loc,
Bltn-le-Sands CP.

BOLTON UPON DEARNE Yorks (W)
103 SE 4502 7m ESE of Barnsley. Loc,
Dne UD. P Rotherham. Hemsworth CC.

BOLVENTOR Cornwall
186 SX 1876 7m SE of Camelford. Loc,
Altarnun CP. P Launceston. Ch e. Sch p.

Jamaica Inn is here, beside main rd. 1½m SSE, Dozmary Pool, large natural lake, subject of dubious legends.

BOMARSUND Nthmb
78 NZ 2784 5m ESE of Morpeth. Loc, Bedlingtonshire UD. Blyth BC.

BOMERE HEATH Shrops
118 SJ 4715 5m N of Shrewsbury. Loc, Pimhill CP. Atcham RD. P Shrsbry. Ch m2, v. Shrsbry CC.

BONBY Lincs (L)
104 TA 0015 5m N of Brigg. CP, 298. Glanford Brgg RD. P Brgg. Ch e, m2. Sch pe. Brgg and Scunthorpe CC (Brgg).

BONDLEIGH Devon
175 SS 6504 7m NE of Okehampton. CP, 102. Okhmptn RD. P: N Tawton. Ch e, v. W Dvn CC (Torrington).

BONDS Lancs
94 SD 4944 10m NNW of Preston. CP(Barnacre-w-Bnds), 1,222. Garstang RD. Ch e, r. Sch pr. N Flyde CC.

BONEHILL Staffs
120 SK 1902 1m SW of Tamworth. Loc, Fazeley CP.

BONINGALE Shrops
119 SJ 8102 5m ESE of Shifnal. CP, 311. Shfnl RD. Ch e. The Wrekin CC.

BONNINGTON Kent
172, 173 184 TR 0535 5m SSE of Ashford. CP, 90. E Ashfd RD. P Ashfd. Ch e. Ashfd CC.

BONSALL Derbys
111 SK 2758 2m SW of Matlock. Loc, Mtlck UD. P Mtlck. King's Head Inn, 1677. Ball-topped cross in mkt place. 13c–14c ch with banded spire.

BOOKHAM, GREAT Surrey
170 TQ 1354 2m WSW of Leatherhead. See Gt Bkhm.

BOOLEY Shrops
118 SJ 5725 4m SE of Wem. Loc, Stanton upon Hine Hth CP.

BOOSBECK Yorks (N)
86 NZ 6617 3m S of Saltburn. Loc, Skelton and Brotton UD. P Sltbn-by-the-Sea.

BOOT Cumb
88 NY 1701 9m E of Seascale. Loc, Eskdale CP. Millom RD. P Holmrook. Ch e. Whitehaven CC. Principal vllge of Eskdle, near terminus of Ravenglass and Eskdle Rly (narrow gauge).

BOOTHBY GRAFFOE Lincs (K)
113 SK 9858 8m S of Lincoln. CP, 181. N Kesteven RD. Ch e. Sch pe. Grantham CC.

BOOTHBY PAGNELL Lincs (K)
113, 123 SK 9730 5m SE of Grantham. CP, 124. W Kesteven RD. P(Bthby), Grnthm. Ch e. Rutland and Stamford CC. Moated Nmn mnr hse* in grnds of Ggn B.P. Hall.

BOOTHSTOWN Lancs
101 SD 7200 4m E of Leigh. Loc, Worsley UD. P Wsly, MANCHESTER.

BOOTLE Cumb
88 SD 1088 7m NW of Millom. CP, 1,007. Mllm RD. P Btle Station. Ch e, c. Sch pe2. Whitehaven CC. See also Hycemoor.

BOOTLE Lancs
100 SJ 3494 3m N of Liverpool. CB, 74,208. P. Btle BC. Docks and general industry. Largest tin plant in Britain.

BOOTON Norfolk
125 TG 1222 5m WSW of Aylsham. CP, 133. St Faith's and Aylshm RD. Ch e. N Nflk CC (Central Nflk).

BORASTON Shrops
129, 130 SO 6170 2m NE of Tenbury Wells. CP, 171. Ludlow RD. Ch e. Ldlw CC.

BORDEN Kent
172 TQ 8862 1m SW of Sittingbourne. CP, 1,330. Swale RD. P Sttngbne. Ch e, m. Sch pe. Faversham CC. See also Oad St.

BORDLEY Yorks (W)
90 SD 9464 9m NNW of Skipton. CP, 21. Skptn RD. Skptn CC.

BORDON Hants
169 SU 7935 6m ESE of Alton. Loc, Whitehill CP. P. Ch r. Sch i, j, p, s. Large Army camp.

BOREHAM Essex
162 TL 7509 4m NE of Chelmsford. CP, 1,496. Chlmsfd RD. P Chlmsfd. Ch e.

Sch p. Braintree CC (Chlmsfd). B. Hall, by Gibbs, now Ford's tractor and equipment training centre. New Hall, orig blt for Henry VIII, had eulogy to Elizabeth I over doorway; convent since 1798.

BOREHAM Wilts
166, 167 ST 8844 1m ESE of Warminster. Loc, Wmnstr UD. P Wmnstr.

BOREHAM STREET Sussex (E)
183 TQ 6611 5m NW of Bexhill. Loc, Wartling CP. P Hailsham.

BOREHAMWOOD Herts
160 TQ 1996 6m E of Watford. Loc, Elstree CP. P. Ch e2, b, cv, m, r2, v3. Sch i, ie, , j3, p4, pr, s4.

BORLEY Essex
149 TL 8443 2m NW of Sudbury. CP, 130. Halstead RD. Ch e. Saffron Walden CC. The famous haunted rectory now demolished.

BOROUGHBRIDGE Yorks (W)
91 SE 3966 6m SE of Ripon. CP, 1,819. Nidderdale RD. P YORK. Ch e, m. Sch p, s. Harrogate CC. See also Aldborough, Minskip. Old coaching tn on R Ure and Gt N Rd. On E side, Devil's Arrows, three monoliths, prob neolithic. To SE, Aldborough Roman tn (A.M.).

BOROUGH GREEN Kent
171 TQ 6057 5m E of Sevenoaks. CP, 2,826. Malling RD. P Svnks. Ch b. Sch p. Tonbridge and Mllng CC (Svnks).

BORROWASH Derbys
112, 121 SK 4134 4m ESE of Derby. Loc, Ockbrook CP. P DBY. Ch e, m, r2. Sch i, j.

BORROWBY Yorks (N)
86 NZ 7715 4m SE of Loftus. CP, 49. Whitby RD. Cleveland and Whtby CC (Scarborough and Whtby).

BORROWBY Yorks (N)
91 SE 4289 5m N of Thirsk. CP, 290. Northallerton RD. P Thsk. Ch m. Richmond CC.

BORROWDALE Cumb
82 NY 2514 6m S of Keswick. CP, 736. Cockermouth RD. Ch e. Sch pe. Workington CC. See also Grange, Rosthwaite, Seathwaite, Seatoller. Tiny hmlt on R Derwent running into Derwentwater. Dale and environs largely NT.

BORWICK Lancs
89 SD 5273 2m NE of Carnforth. CP, 141. Lunesdale RD. Lancaster CC. B. Hall*, Elizn hse incorporating 14c pele twr.

BOSBURY Herefs
143 SO 6943 4m N of Ledbury. CP, 711. Ldbry RD. P Ldbry. Ch e. Sch pe. Leominster CC. Ch: detached twr; 16c monmts. Many oast hses.

BOSCASTLE Cornwall
174, 185 SX 0990 4m N of Camelford. Loc, Forrabury and Minster CP. Cmlfd RD. P. Ch m. Sch p. N Cnwll CC. Rugged coastal scenery. Harbour, difficult of access from open sea, and adjoining cliffs are property of NT.

BOSCOMBE Wilts
167 SU 2038 7m NE of Salisbury. Loc, Allington CP. P Slsbry. Ch e. Sch pe.

BOSCOPPA Cornwall
185, 186, 190 SX 0353 1m ENE of St Austell. Loc, St Astll w Fowey MB. Truro CC.

BOSHAM Sussex (W)
181 SU 8004 3m W of Chichester. CP, 3,147. Chchstr RD. P Chchstr. Ch e, v. Sch p. Chchstr CC. See also Broadbridge, Old Fishbourne. Yachting centre on arm of Chchstr harbour. B. ch appears on Bayeux Tapestry.

BOSLEY Ches
110 SJ 9165 4m ENE of Congleton. CP, 413. Macclesfield RD. P Mcclsfld. Ch e, m. Sch pe. Mcclsfld CC. To NE is B. Reservoir, large stretch of water backed by hills.

BOSSALL Yorks (N)
92, 97, 98 SE 7160 8m SW of Malton. CP (Buttercrambe w Bssll), 124. Flaxton RD. Ch e. Thirsk and Mltn CC.

BOSSINEY Cornwall
174, 185, 186 SX 0688 4m NW of Camelford. Loc, Tintagel CP. Ch m. Vllge blt round a cstle, only the mound of which survives.

BOSSINGHAM Kent
173 TR 1549 6m S of Canterbury. Loc, Upr Hardres CP. Bridge-Blean RD. P(Bssnghm St), Cntrbry. Cntrbry CC.

BOSSINGTON Som
164 SS 8947 5m W of Minehead. Loc Selworthy CP. Ch m. NT vllge (Holnicote estate).

BOSTOCK GREEN Ches
110 SJ 6769 3m SSE of Northwich. Loc Bstck CP. Nthwch RD. Nthwch CC.

BOSTON Lincs (H)
114, 123 TF 3244 28m SE of Lincoln. MB, 25,995. P. Holland w Bstn CC. Ancient seaport, still busy. Pilgrim Fathers sailed hence, 1620. Links still retained with Boston, USA. Many old bldngs; magnificent mdvl ch with twr called The Stump, 272ft.

BOSTON SPA Yorks (W)
97 SE 4345 2m SE of Wetherby. CP, 2,426. Wthrby RD. P. Ch e, m. Sch p, pe. Barkston Ash CC. Rsdntl. Ggn stone-blt hses.

BOSWINGER Cornwall
190 SW 9941 7m S of St Austell. Loc, St Goran CP. St Astll RD. Ch m. Truro CC.

BOTALLACK Cornwall
189 SW 3632 7m WNW of Penzance. Loc, St Just UD. Ruined engine hse on rocks above site of worked out submarine tin mine.

BOTANY BAY London
160 TQ 2999 2m NW of Enfield. Loc, Enfld LB. Enfld N BC (Enfld W).

BOTCHESTON Leics
121 SK 4804 7m W of Leicester. Loc, Desford CP.

BOTESDALE Suffolk (E)
136 TM 0475 5m WSW of Diss. CP, 487. Hartismere RD. P Dss, Norfolk. Ch e, m, v. Eye CC. Runs into Rickinghall Superior and Inferior to make one of longest vllges in England.

BOTHAL Nthmb
78 NZ 2386 3m E of Morpeth. Loc, Ashington UD. P Mpth. In valley of R Wansbeck. 13c ch. Small 14c cstle.

BOTHAMSALL Notts
112 SK 6773 4m NNE of Ollerton. CP, 226. E Retford RD. P Rtfd. Ch e. Bassetlaw CC. Earthwork to W is sole rems of B. Cstle, prob Nmn.

BOTHEL Cumb
82 NY 1838 6m NE of Cockermouth. CP(Bthl and Threapland), 297. Cckrmth RD. P Carlisle. Ch m. Sch pe. Workington CC.

BOTHENHAMPTON Dorset
177 SY 4691 1m S of Bridport. CP, 943. Brdpt RD. P Brdpt. Ch e. W Dst CC. See also Walditch.

BOTLEY Berks
158 SP 4806 2m W of Oxford. Loc, N Hinksey CP. P OXFD. Ch b, r, v. Sch p.

BOTLEY Bucks
159,160 SP 9802 1m E of Chesham. Loc, Chshm UD. P Chshm.

BOTLEY Hants
180 SU 5113 4m SW of Bishop's Waltham. CP, 1,423. Winchester RD. P SOUTHAMPTON. Ch e, c. Sch pe. Eastleigh CC. See also Long Cmmn. Area famous for strawberries and nursery gdns. Home of William Cobbett from 1806 to 1826.

BOTOLPH CLAYDON Bucks
146 SP 7324 6m SSE of Buckingham. Loc, E Claydon CP. P Bletchley. Ch m.

BOTOLPHS Sussex (W)
182 TQ 1909 3m NW of Shoreham-by-Sea. Loc, Bramber CP. Ch e.

BOTTESFORD Leics
113 122 SK 8038 7m WNW of Grantham. CP, 1,551. Melton and Belvoir RD. P NOTTINGHAM. Ch e, m. Sch pe. Mltn CC. See also Muston, Normanton. 14c-15c ch: monmts to Rutland family of Blvr, qv. Brass of 1404 to rector.

BOTTESFORD Lincs (L)
104 SE 8907 2m S of Scunthorpe. CP, 3,120. Glanford Brigg RD. P Scnthpe. Ch e. Sch j, p, s. Brgg and Scnthpe CC (Brgg). See also Yaddlethorpe.

BOTTISHAM Cambs
135 TL 5460 6m E of Cambridge. CP, 975.
Newmarket RD. P CMBRDGE. Ch e, v.
Sch p, s. Cambs CC. Has vllge college — a
Cambs speciality; also outstanding ch.

BOTTOM O' TH' MOOR Lancs
101 SD 6511 4m WNW of Bolton. Loc,
Horwich UD.

BOTTOMS Yorks (W)
95 SD 9321 2m S of Todmorden. Loc,
Tdmdn MB.

BOTUS FLEMING Cornwall
187 SX 4061 2m NW of Saltash. CP, 276. St
Germans RD. Ch e, m. Bodmin CC. See also
Hatt.

BOUGH BEECH Kent
171 TQ 4846 3m E of Edenbridge. Loc,
Chiddingstone CP. P Ednbridge. Reservoir
to NE.

BOUGHSPRING Glos
155, 156 ST 5597 3m NNE of Chepstow.
Loc, Tidenham CP.

BOUGHTON Norfolk
124 TF 7002 6m E of Downham Mkt.
CP, 182. Dnhm RD. P King's Lynn. Ch e, m.
Sch p. SW Nflk CC.

BOUGHTON Northants
133 SP 7565 3m N of Northampton. CP.
Brixworth RD. P NTHMPTN. Ch e, m.
Sch p. Daventry CC (Kettering). 18c Gothic
lodges and follies around B. Hall, itself 19c
Tdr.

BOUGHTON Notts
112 SK 6768 2m ENE of Ollerton.
CP, 1,374. Southwell RD. P Newark. Ch e.
Sch pr. Nwk CC.

BOUGHTON ALUPH Kent
172, 173, 184 TR 0348 4m NNE of
Ashford. CP, 664. E Ashfd RD. Ch e, b.
Ashfd CC.

BOUGHTON GREEN Kent
172 TQ 7651 3m S of Maidstone. Loc, Btn
Monchelsea CP. Mdstne RD. P(Btn
Mnchlsea), Mdstne. Sch p. Mdstne CC.
Modern rsdntl centre of Btn Mnchlsea
parish. Mdvl ch lm S, on edge of hillside,
with spectacular views. Btn Mnchlsea

Place*, Tdr and Rgncy mnr hse in 18c deer
pk.

BOUGHTON LEES Kent
172, 173, 174 TR 0247 3m NNE of
Ashford. Loc, E Ashfd RD. P Ashfd. Ashfd
CC.

BOUGHTON MALHERBE Kent
172, 184 TQ 8849 4m W of Charing. CP,
337. Hollingbourn RD. Ch e. Maidstone CC.

BOUGHTON STREET Kent
172, 173 TR 0559 3m ESE of Faversham.
Loc, Btn under Blean CP. Swale RD. P(Btn),
Fvrshm. Ch e, m. Sch pm. Fvrshm CC.

BOULBY Yorks (N)
86 NZ 7619 3m E of Loftus. Loc, Lfts UD.
Cliffs nearly 700ft, some of highest in
England.

BOULDON Shrops
129 SO 5485 7m NNE of Ludlow. Loc,
Diddlebury CP. Ch e.

BOULGE Suffolk (E)
150 TM 2552 2m NNW of Woodbridge. CP,
44. Deben RD. Ch e. Eye CC. Once home of
Edward Fitzgerald, who is buried in
churchyard.

BOULMER Nthmb
71 NU 2614 5m E of Alnwick. Loc,
Longhoughton CP. P Alnwck. Ch m.

BOUNDARY Staffs
110, 119 SJ 9842 7m ESE of
Stoke-on-Trent. Loc, Forsbrook CP. Ch m.

BOURN Cambs
134 TL 3256 8m W of Cambridge. CP, 832.
Chesterton RD. P CMBRDGE. Ch e, m.
Sch pe. Cambs CC. See also Caxton End. Ch
has crooked spire. Ancient post-mill* to
NW.

BOURNE Lincs (K)
123 TF 0920 9m W of Spalding. UD, 6,461.
P. Rutland and Stamford CC. See also Dyke,
Twenty Motor wks (racing cars).

BOURNEBRIDGE Essex
161 TQ 5094 6m W of Brentwood. Loc,
Stapleford Abbotts CP.

BOURNE END Bucks
159 SU 8986 3m E of Marlow. Loc,
Wooburn CP. P. Ch m, r. Sch i, j, s.
Thames-side resort.

BOURNE END Herts
159, 160 TL 0206 2m ESE of Berkhamsted.
Loc, Hemel Hempstead MB. P Hml Hmpstd.

BOURNEMOUTH Hants
179 SZ 0891 93m SW of London.
CB, 153,425. P. BCs: Bnmth E, Bnmth W.
Health and holiday resort with
exceptionally mild climate, largely
developed mid-19c. Wooded ravines running
down to sea; gdns, pine trees.

BOURNES GREEN Glos
156, 157 SO 9104 4m E of Stroud. Loc,
Bisley-w-Lypiatt CP.

BOURNHEATH Worcs
130, 131 SO 9474 2m N of Bromsgrove.
Loc, Brmsgrve UD.

BOURNMOOR Co Durham
78 NZ 3151 2m E of Chester-le-Street. CP,
1,818. Chstr-le-Strt RD. Chstr-le-Strt CC.
See also New Lambton.

BOURNVILLE Warwicks
131 SP 0481 4m SSW of Birmingham. Loc,
bmnghm CB. P BRMGHM 30. Bmnghm,
Selly Oak BC. Originated as estate
developed late 19c by George Cadbury for
workers in chocolate factory.

BOURTON Berks
157 SU 2387 5m E of Swindon. CP, 271.
Faringdon RD. P Swndn, Wilts. Ch e, b.
Sch pe. Abingdon CC.

BOURTON Dorset
166 ST 7630 4m ENE of Wincanton. CP,
579. Shaftesbury RD. P Gillingham.
Ch e, b, m. N Dst. See also Queen Oak.

BOURTON Shrops
129 SO 5996 3m SW of Much Wenlock.
Loc, Mch Wnlck CP. P Mch Wnlck. Ch e.

BOURTON, GREAT Oxon
145 SP 4545 3m N of Banbury. See Gt Btn.

BOURTON ON DUNSMORE Warwicks
132 SP 4370 5m SW of Rugby CP(Btn and
Draycote), 281. Rgby RD. P Rgby. Ch e.
Sch pe. Rgby CC.

BOURTON-ON-THE-HILL Glos
144 SP 1732 2m W of Moreton-in-Marsh.
CP, 307. N Cotswold RD. P Mtn-in-Msh.
Ch e. Cirencester and Tewkesbury CC.
Ctswld vllge with Nmn − Perp ch containing
'Winchester bushel' for weights and
measures. To S, Sezincote, early 19c hse in
Indian style.

BOURTON-ON-THE-WATER Glos
144 SP 1620 4m SSW of Stow-on-the-Wold.
CP, 1,895. N Cotswold RD. P Cheltenham.
Ch e, b, r. Sch p, s. Cirencester and
Tewkesbury CC. Beautiful and much visited.
R Windrush crossed by many brs.

BOUTH Lancs
88, 89 SD 3285 5m NE of Ulverston. Loc,
Colton CP. P Ulvstn.

BOUTHWAITE Yorks (W)
91 SE 1271 4m NNW of Pateley Br. Loc,
Fountains Earth CP. Ripon and Ptly Br RD.
Ch m. Rpn CC.

BOVENEY Bucks
159 SU 9377 3m WSW of Slough. Loc,
Dorney CP. Ch e. The Old Place*, 15c hse.

BOVERIDGE Dorset
179 SU 0615 5m W of Fordingbridge. Loc,
Cranborne CP. Ch e.

BOVEY TRACEY Devon
176, 188 SX 8178 5m NNW of Newton
Abbot. CP, 3,357. Ntn Abbt, RD. ˋ P Ntn
Abbt. Ch e, b, c, m, r, v. Sch p. Totnes CC.
See also Heathfield. On R Bovey; former ch
blt by Sir William de Tracey, one of the
knights concerned in murder of Becket. S of
river, pottery and brick wks.

BOVINGDON Herts
159, 160 TL 0103 4m SW of Hemel
Hempstead. CP, 2,934. Hml Hmpstd RD.
P Hml Hmpstd. Ch e, b. Sch p. Hml
Hmpstd CC.

BOW Devon
175 SS 7201 7m W of Crediton. CP, 608.
Crdtn RD. P Crdtn. Ch e, c, v. Sch p.
Tiverton CC (Torrington). See also Nymet
Tracey.

BOW Devon
188 SX 8156 3m SSE of Totnes. Loc,
Ashprington CP.

BOW London
161 TQ 3683 4m ENE of Charing Cross. Loc
Twr Hmlts LB. Bethnal Grn and Bow BC
(Poplar).

BOWBANK Yorks (N)
84 NY 9423 lm S of Middleton-in-Teesdale.
Loc, Lunedale CP. Startforth RD.
Richmond CC.

BOW BRICKHILL Bucks
146 SP 9034 2m E of Bletchley. CP, 512.
Newport Pagnell RD. P Bltchly. Ch e. Sch p.
Buckingham CC.

BOWBURN Co Durham
85 NZ 3038 4m SE of Durham. Loc,
Cassop-cum-Quarrington CP. Drhm RD. P
DRHM. Ch m. Sch p, s. Drhm CC.

BOWCOMBE IOW
180 SZ 4686 2m SW of Newport. Loc, Npt
MB.

BOWD Devon
176 SY 1089 2m NNW of Sidmouth. Loc,
Sdmth UD.

BOWDEN Devon
188 SX 8449 3m SW of Dartmouth. Loc,
Stoke Fleming CP.

BOWDEN, GREAT Leics
133 SP 7488 lm NE of Mkt Harborough.
Loc Mkt Hbrgh UD. P Mkt Hbrgh.

BOWDEN HILL Wilts
157 ST 9367 4m SSE of Chippenham. Loc,
Lacock CP. P Chppnhm. Ch e, r.

BOWDON Ches
101 SJ 7586 lm SW of Altrincham.
UD, 4,825. P Altrnchm. Knutsford CC.
Mainly rsdntl.

BOWERCHALKE Wilts
167 SU 0123 9m WSW of Salisbury. CP,
392. Slsbry and Wilton RD. P Slsbry.
Ch e, b. Sch pe. Slsbry CC. Watercress beds.

BOWERS Staffs
110, 119 SJ 8135 5m WNW of Stone. Loc,
Standon CP.

BOWERS GIFFORD Essex
162 TQ 7588 2m E of Basildon. Loc, Bsldn
UD. P Bsldn. Ch e. Sch pe.

BOWES Yorks (N)
84 NY 9913 4m WSW of Barnard Cstle. CP,
478. Startforth RD. P Bnd Cstle, Co
Durham. Ch e, m2. Sch pe. Richmond CC.
One of Yorkshire schs exposed by Dickens
in Nicholas Nickleby was here; churchyard
contains graves of many pupils. Site of
Roman fort *Lavatrae*. Nmn Keep (A.M.).

BOWGREAVE Lancs
94 SD 4944 10m NNW of Preston. Loc,
Barnacre-w-Bonds CP. Garstang RD. P Prstn.
N Fylde CC.

BOWLAND BRIDGE Westm
89 SD 4189 6m S of Windermere. Loc,
Crosthwaite and Lyth CP. S Westm RD. P
Grange-over-Sands, Lancs. Westm CC.

BOWLEY Herefs
142 SO 5352 5m SSE of Leominster. Loc,
Bodenham CP.

BOWLHEAD GREEN Surrey
169 SU 9138 4m N of Haslemere. Loc,
Thursley CP. Ch v.

BOWLING GREEN Worcs
143 SO 8151 3m SW of Worcester. Loc,
Powick CP.

BOWMANSTEAD Lancs
88 SD 2996 just S of Coniston. Loc, Cnstn
CP.

BOWNESS-ON-SOLWAY Cumb
75 NY 2262 4m N of Kirkbride. CP(Bnss),
1,218. Wigton RD. P(Bnss), Carlisle.
Ch e, m, r. Sch p. Penrith and the Border
CC. Western end of Hadrian's Wall.

BOWNESS-ON-WINDERMERE Westm
89 SD 4096 lm SSW of Windermere. Loc,
Wndrmre UD. P Wndrmre. Holiday centre;
boating, fishing. Boat-building. Offshore,
Belle Isle, with circular domed hse of 1774.

BOWSDEN Nthmb
64 NT 9941 7m S of Berwick-upon-Tweed.
CP, 153. Glendale RD.
P BRWCK-UPN-TWD. Brwck-upn-Twd CC.

BOX Glos
156 SO 8500 3m S of Stroud. Loc,
Minchinhampton CP. P Strd. Ch v.

BOX Wilts
156 ST 8268 5m ENE of Bath. CP, 4,209.
Calne and Chippenham RD. P Chppnhm.
Ch e, m2, v. Sch p, pe. Chppnhm CC. See
also Ditteridge, Hawthorn, Kingsdown,
Wadswick. Nearby quarries produce Bth
stone. To E, Brunel's famous rly tunnel.

BOXBUSH Glos
143 SO 7412 6m E of Cinderford. Loc,
Westbury-on-Severn CP.

BOXFORD Berks
158 SU 4271 4m NW of Newbury. CP, 288.
Nbry RD. P Nbry. Ch e, m. Sch pe.
Nbry CC.

BOXFORD Suffolk (W)
149 TL 9640 4m WSW of Hadleigh. CP,
755. Cosford RD. P Colchester, Essex. Ch e.
Sch pe. Sudbury and Woodbridge CC. Pretty
vllge in a hollow, draped in wires.

BOXGROVE Sussex (W)
181 SU 9007 3m NE of Chichester. CP,
1,018. Chchstr RD. P Chchstr. Ch e. Sch p.
Chchstr CC. See also Halnaker. Fine ch, part
of former priory.

BOXLEY Kent
172 TQ 7758 2m NNE of Maidstone.
CP, 1,752. Hollingbourn RD. P Mdstne.
Ch e. Mdstne CC. See also Sandling. On edge
of N Downs, in conservation area.

BOXTED Essex
149 TL 9933 5m N of Colchester.
CP, 1,192. Lexden and Winstree RD.
P Clchstr. Ch e, m. Sch pe. Clchstr CC.

BOXTED Suffolk (W)
149 TL 8251 4m NNW of Long Melford.
CP, 144. Mlfd RD. Ch e. Sudbury and
Woodbridge CC. Ch has monmts to Poley
family whose 16c moated hse stands in
valley below.

BOXWELL Glos
156 ST 8192 5m W of Tetbury. CP(Bxwll
w Leighterton), 179. Ttbry RD. Ch e.
Stroud CC. Ch: 13c bellcote.

BOXWORTH Cambs
134 TL 3464 5m SSE of St Ives. CP, 194.
Chesterton RD. P CAMBRIDGE. Ch e.
Cambs CC.

BOYDEN GATE Kent
173 TR 2265 3m ESE of Herne Bay. Loc,
Chislet CP.

BOYLESTONE Derbys
120 SK 1835 6m E of Uttoxeter. CP, 160.
Ashbourne RD. P DERBY. Ch e, m2.
W Derbys RD.

BOYNTON Yorks (E)
93 TA 1368 3m WNW of Bridlington.
CP, 155. Brdlngtn RD. Ch e. Sch p.
Brdlngtn CC. B. Hall*, Tdr and 18c hse,
former seat of Strickland family.

BOYTON Cornwall
174 SX 3292 5m N of Launceston. CP, 265.
Lncstn RD. P Lncstn. Ch e, m. Sch p.
N Cnwll CC. See also Bennacott.

BOYTON Suffolk (E)
150 TM 3747 7m E of Woodbridge.
CP, 169. Deben RD. P Wdbrdge. Ch e, v.
Sudbury and Wdbrdge CC. Heath and marsh
vllge near coast.

BOYTON Wilts
167 ST 9539 6m SE of Warminster. CP,
189. Wmnstr and Westbury RD. Ch e.
Wstbry CC. See also Corton.

BOZEAT Northants
133 SP 9059 5m N of Olney. CP, 1,082.
Wellingborough RD. P Wllngbrgh.
Ch e, b, m, v. Sch p. Wllngbrgh CC.

BRABOURNE Kent
173 TR 1041 6m E of Ashford. CP, 717.
E Ashfd RD. Ch e. Sch pe. Ashfd CC. Ch:
Nmn glass; brasses.

BRABOURNE LEES Kent
172, 173, 184 TR 0740 5m ESE of
Ashford. Loc, E Ashfd RD. P Ashfd. Ch b.
Ashfd CC.

BRABLING GREEN Suffolk (E)
137 TM 2964 1m NE of Framlingham. Loc,
Frmlnghm CP.

BRACEBOROUGH Lincs (K)
123 TF 0813 4m S of Bourne. CP(Brcbrgh
and Wilsthorpe), 169. S Kesteven RD.
P Stamford. Ch e. Rutland and Stmfd CC.

BRACEBRIDGE HEATH Lincs (K)
113 SK 9867 3m S of Lincoln. CP, 2,825.
N Kesteven RD. P LNCLN. Ch e, m. Sch p.
Grantham CC.

BRACEBY Lincs (K)
113, 123 TF 0135 6m E of Grantham.
CP(Brcby and Sapperton), 91. W Kesteven RD.
Ch e. Rutland and Stamford CC.

BRACEWELL Yorks (W)
95 SD 8648 6m NNW of Colne. CP, 97.
Skipton RD. P Skptn. Ch e. Skptn CC.

BRACKENFIELD Derbys
111 SK 3759 3m NW of Alfreton. CP, 238.
Chesterfield RD. Ch e, m2. NE Derbys CC.

BRACKLEY Northants
145, 146 SP 5837 8m ESE of Banbury. MB,
4,615. P. Daventry CC (S Nthnts). Magdalen
College Sch incorporates rems of 13c hsptl,
with orig chpl.

BRACKNELL Berks
169 SU 8769 4m E of Wokingham. CP.
Easthampstead RD. P. Ch e, b, c, m2, r, v3.
Sch i5, j5, p3, pr, s3. Wknghm CC. See also
Bullbrook, Easthmpstd. New tn, pop.
33,953. Home of Meteorological Office.
Many modern bldngs, incl Point Royal,
17-storey hexagonal block of flats.

BRACON ASH Norfolk
137 TM 1899 5m ESE of Wymondham. CP,
332. Forehoe and Henstead RD. Ch e.
Sch p. S Nflk CC (Central Nflk).

BRADBOURNE Derbys
111 SK 2152 4m NNE of Ashbourne. CP,
125. Ashbne RD. P Ashbne. Ch e. W Derbys
CC. Ch: Nmn S doorway.

BRADBURY Co Durham
85 NZ 3128 7m E of Bishop Auckland.
CP(Brdbry and The Isle), 172. Sedgefield
RD. Ch m. Sch pe. Drhm CC (Sdgfld).

BRADDEN Northants
145, 146 SP 6448 3m W of Towcester. CP,
102. Tcstr RD. P Tcstr. Ch e. Daventry CC
(S Nthnts).

BRADENHAM Bucks
159 SU 8297 4m NW of High Wycombe.
CP, 724. Wcmbe RD. P Hgh Wcmbe. Ch e.

Aylesbury CC (Wcmbe). Vllge almost
entirely NT, incl Mnr Hse, once home of
Disraeli's father.

BRADENSTOKE Wilts
157 SU 0079 5m N of Calne. Loc, Lyneham
CP. P Chippenham. Ch e. On edge of
Lyneham RAF stn.

BRADFIELD Berks
158 SU 6072 3m SW of Pangbourne. CP,
1,493. Brdfld RD. P Reading. Ch e, m.
Sch pe. Newbury CC. See also S End, Tutts
Clump. Dominated by well known public
sch.

BRADFIELD Essex
150 TM 1430 2m ESE of Manningtree. CP,
811. Tendring RD. P Mnnngtree. Ch e, m.
Sch p. Harwich CC. See also Brdfld Hth.

BRADFIELD Norfolk
126 TG 2733 2m NNW of N Walsham. Loc,
Swafield CP. P: N Wlshm. Ch e, c.

BRADFIELD Yorks (W)
102 SK 2692 6m NW of Sheffield. CP,
13,014. Wortley RD. P SHFFLD. Ch e, m2.
Sch s. Penistone CC. See also Low Brdfld,
Loxley, Midhopestones, Oughtibridge,
Stannington, Wharncliffe Side, Wigtwizzle,
Worrall.

BRADFIELD COMBUST Suffolk (W)
136 TL 8957 5m SSE of Bury St Edmunds.
CP, 108. Thingoe RD. Ch e, m. Bury St Eds
CC. Name recalls burning of hall during 14c
riots.

BRADFIELD GREEN Ches
110 SJ 6859 3m NW of Crewe. Loc,
Minshull Vernon CP. Nantwich RD.
Nntwch CC.

BRADFIELD HEATH Essex
150 TM 1329 2m ESE of Manningtree. Loc,
Brdfld CP. Ch m.

BRADFIELD ST CLARE Suffolk (W)
136 TL 9057 5m SE of Bury St Edmunds.
CP, 140. Thingoe RD. Ch e. Bury St Eds
CC.

BRADFIELD ST GEORGE Suffolk (W)
136 TL 9160 4m SE of Bury St Edmunds.
CP, 337. Thingoe RD. P Bury St Eds.
Ch e, v. Sch p. Bury St Eds CC.

BRADFORD Devon
175 SS 4207 5m ENE of Holsworthy. CP,
296. Hlswthy RD. Ch e, m. Sch p. W Dvn
CC (Tavistock). See also Brandis Corner.

BRADFORD Yorks (W)
96 SE 1633 8m W of Leeds. CB,293,756. P.
BCs: Brdfd N, S, W. (E,N,S,W.) See also
Esholt. Centre of wool industry. Old parish
ch is cathedral. City is largely Vctrn, but
much modern rebuilding in centre.
University.

BRADFORD ABBAS Dorset
177, 178 ST 5814 2m SE of Yeovil. CP,
632. Sherborne RD. P Shbne. Ch e. Sch pe.
W Dst CC. Ch: W front, bench-ends, scrn. lm
E, at Wyke Farm, a 268ft long tithe barn.

BRADFORD LEIGH Wilts
166 ST 8362 3m NNW of Trowbridge. Loc,
S Wraxall CP.

BRADFORD-ON-AVON Wilts
166 ST 8260 3m NW of Trowbridge. UD,
8,001 P. Westbury CC. Hillside tn of Bath
stone; centre of cloth trade in 18c. Saxon ch
of St Laurence; 14c tithe barn (A.M.); mdvl
br with chpl subsequently used as lock-up
(cf Rotherham; St Ives, Hunts; Wakefield).
Elizn hall.

BRADFORD-ON-TONE Som
164 ST 1722 3m WSW of Taunton. CP, 575.
Wellington RD. P Tntn. Ch e. Sch p.
Tntn CC.

BRADFORD PEVERELL Dorset
178 SY 6593 3m NW of Dorchester. CP,
301. Dchstr RD. P Dchstr. Ch e. W Dst CC.

BRADING IOW
180 SZ 6087 4m S of Ryde. CP, 1,613. Isle
of Wight RD and CC. P Sandown.
Ch e, c, m2. Sch pe. See also Alverstone. To
SW, Roman villa*. Ch: monmts.

BRADLEY Derbys
111 SK 2245 3m E of Ashbourne. CP, 226.
Ashbne RD. P Ashbne. Ch e. Sch pe.
W Derbys CC.

BRADLEY Hants
168, 169 SU 6341 6m S of Basingstoke. CP,
73. Bsngstke RD. Ch e. Bsngstke CC.

BRADLEY Lincs (L)
105 TA 2406 2m SW of Grimsby. CP, 196.
Grmsby RD. Ch e. Louth CC.

BRADLEY Staffs
119 SJ 8817 4m SW of Stafford. CP, 280.
Stffd RD. P STFFD. Ch e. Sch pe. Stffd and
Stone CC.

BRADLEY Worcs
130, 131 SO 9860 6m ESE of Droitwich.
Loc, Redditch UD; CP(Stock and Brdly),
270, Drtwch RD. Ch e. Bromsgrove and
Rddtch CC, Worcester BC.

BRADLEY, GREAT Suffolk (W)
148 TL 6653 5m N of Haverhill. See Gt
Brdly.

BRADLEY GREEN Worcs
130, 131 SO 9862 5m E of Droitwich. Loc,
Stock and Brdly CP. Drtwch RD.
P Redditch. Worcester BC.

BRADLEY IN THE MOORS Staffs
120 SK 0641 3m ESE of Cheadle. Loc,
Alton CP. Ch e.

BRADMORE Notts
112, 121, 122 SK 5831 6m S of
Nottingham. CP, 224. Basford RD.
P NTTNGHM. Ch m. Rushcliffe CC.

BRADNINCH Devon
176 SS 9903 6m SSE of Tiverton. CP,
1,663. Tvtn RD. P Exeter. Ch e, b, s. Sch p.
Tvtn CC. Formerly, for 600 years, a
borough whose mayor claimed precedence
over that of Extr.

BRADNOP Staffs
111 SK 0155 2m SE of Leek. CP, 183.
Lk RD. Ch m2. Sch pe. Lk CC.

BRADPOLE Dorset
177 SY 4894 lm NE of Bridport. CP, 1,230.
Brdpt RD. P Brdpt. Ch e, r. W Dst CC.

BRADSHAW Lancs
101 SD 7312 2m NNE of Bolton. Loc,
Turton UD. P Bltn. Darwen CC. New
shopping centre.

BRADSTONE Devon
186 SX 3880 4m SE of Launceston. CP, 57.
Tavistock RD. Ch e. W Dvn CC (Tvstck).

BRADWALL GREEN Ches
110 SJ 7563 2m N of Sandbach. Loc,
Brdwll CP. Congleton RD. Ch m. Knutsford
CC.

BRADWELL Bucks
146 SP 8339 1m SE of Wolverton. CP, 387.
Newport Pagnell RD. P Wlvtn. Ch e, m.
Buckingham CC.

BRADWELL Derbys
111 SK 1781 8m NNW of Bakewell. CP,
1,368. Bkwll RD. P SHEFFIELD. Ch e, m3.
Sch ie, j. W Derbys CC. Bagshaw Cavern,
with chrystalline formations. Large cement
works to NW; see Hope.

BRADWELL Essex
149, 162 TL 8023 3m E of Braintree. CP,
478. Brntree RD. P Brntree. Ch e, c2.
Brntree CC (Maldon). Ch: 14c
wall-paintings; 15c scrn; monmts to Maxey
family serve as reredos.

BRADWELL Suffolk (E)
126 TG 5003 3m SSW of Yarmouth. CP,
2,194. Lothingland RD. P Gt Ymth,
Norfolk. Ch e, m. Sch ie, j. Lowestoft CC.

BRADWELL-ON-SEA Essex
162 TM 0006 10m E of Maldon. CP, 1,116.
Mldn RD. P Southminster. Ch e. Sch pe.
Mldn CC. See also Brdwll Waterside.
Enormous nuclear power stn to N. 2m
NE, rems of Roman Fort of the Saxon
Shore, and 7c St Peter's Chpl blt from
Roman bricks. B. Lodge*, 16c−18c hse with
Adam decorations.

BRADWELL WATERSIDE Essex
162 TL 9907 9m E of Maldon. Loc,
Brdwll-on-Sea CP. Marina for 250 yachts.

BRADWORTHY Devon
174 SS 3214 7m N of Holsworthy. CP, 697.
Hlswthy RD. P Hlswthy. Ch e, m3. Sch p.
W Dvn CC. (Tavistock). See also
Alfardisworthy, E Youlstone, Kimworthy.
Vllge blt round large square.

BRAFFERTON Co Durham
85 NZ 2921 4m N of Darlington. CP, 160.
Dlngtn RD. P Dlngtn. Ch m. Bishop
Auckland CC (Sedgefield).

BRAFFERTON Yorks (N)
91 SE 4370 3m NE of Boroughbridge. CP,
207. Easingwold RD. Ch e. Sch pe. Thirsk
and Malton CC.

BRAFIELD-ON-THE-GREEN Northants
133 SP 8258 4m ESE of Northampton. CP,
611. Nthmptn RD. P(Brfld), NTHMPTN.
Ch e, b. Sch pe. Daventry CC (S Nthnts).

BRAGBURY END Herts
147 TL 2621 3m SE of Stevenage. Loc,
Datchworth CP.

BRAILSFORD Derbys
120 SK 2541 7m NW of Derby. CP, 668.
Ashbourne RD. P DBY. Ch e, m2. Sch pe.
W Derbys CC. See also Ednaston.

BRAINTREE Essex
149, 162 TL 7523 11m NNE of
Chelmsford. UD(Brntree and Bocking),
24,839. P. Brntree CC (Maldon). See also
Beddall's End, Bckng Churchstreet, High
Garrett. Much modern industry, incl mnfg
of prefabricated bldngs. Orig a mdvl mkt tn,
with cloth industry in 16c and 17c. Samuel
Courtauld blt silk mills in 19c.

BRAISEWORTH Suffolk (E)
136 TM 1371 2m SSW of Eye. CP, 66.
Hartismere RD. Ch e. Eye CC.

BRAISHFIELD Hants
168 SU 3725 3m NNE of Romsey. CP, 512.
Rmsy and Stockbridge RD. P Rmsy. Ch e, c.
Sch p. Eastleigh CC (Winchester).

BRAITHWAITE Cumb
82 NY 2323 2m W of Keswick. Loc, Above
Derwent CP. Cockermouth RD. P Kswck
Ch e, m. Sch pe. Workington CC.

BRAITHWAITE Yorks (W)
103 SE 6112 4m W of Thorne. Loc, Kirk
Bramwith CP. Ch m.

BRAITHWELL Yorks (W)
103 SK 5394 6m SSW of Doncaster. CP,
848. Dncstr RD. P Rotherham. Ch e. Sch p.
Don Valley CC. See also Micklebring.

BRAMBER Sussex (W)
182 TQ 1810 4m NW of Shoreham-by-Sea.
CP, 585. Chanctonbury RD. Ch e. Shrhm
CC (Arundel and Shrhm). See also Botolphs.
Ruins of Nmn cstle (NT)*. St Mary's*,
timber-framed 15c hse. Potter's Museum.

BRAMCOTE Warwicks
132 SP 4088 3m SE of Nuneaton. Loc,
Wolvey CP. P Nntn.

BRAMDEAN Hants
168 SU 6128 8m E of Winchester. CP, 535.
Wnchstr RD. P Alresford. Ch e. Wnchstr CC.
See also Brockwood, Hinton Ampner.

BRAMERTON Norfolk
126 TG 2904 5m SE of Norwich. CP, 313.
Forehoe and Henstead RD. P NRWCH,
NOR 06W. Ch e. S Nflk CC (Central Nflk).

BRAMFIELD Herts
147 TL 2915 3m NW of Hertford. CP, 237.
Htfd RD. P HTFD. Ch e. Htfd and
Stevenage CC (Htfd).

BRAMFIELD Suffolk(E)
137 TM 3973 3m SSE of Halesworth. CP,
480. Blyth RD. P Hlswth. Ch e, c, m.
Sch pe. Eye CC. Ch: scrn, Coke monmt,
detached 13c twr. Hall, Tdr and Ggn, has
'crinkle-crankle' (wavy brick) gdn wall.

BRAMFORD Suffolk (E)
150 TM 1246 3m WNW of Ipswich. CP,
1,210. Gipping RD. P Ipswch. Ch e, m.
Sch pe. Eye CC.

BRAMHALL Ches
101 SJ 8985 3m S of Stockport. UD(Hazel
Grove and Brmhll), 39,534. P Stckpt. Hzl
Grove BC (Cheadle CC). B. Hall*, 15c half-
timbered hse.

BRAMHAM Yorks (W)
97 SE 4242 4m W of Tadcaster. CP(Brmhm
cum Oglethorpe), 1,230. Wetherby RD.
P Boston Spa. Ch e, m. Sch p. Barkston Ash
CC. Estate vllge. B. Pk* 18c classical
mansion in Versailles-type grnds.

BRAMHOPE Yorks (W)
96 SE 2543 3m ESE of Otley. CP, 3,054.
Wharfedale RD. P LEEDS Ch e, m. Sch p.
Ripon CC. Rsdntl for Leeds. Puritan chpl*
blt 1646-9 almost unique

BRAMLEY Hants
168, 169 SU 6458 4m N of Basingstoke.
CP, 1,856. Bsngstke RD. P Bsngstke. Ch e, m.
Sch pe. Bsngstke CC. Ch has many 13c and
15c wall-paintings, incl one of Becket's
murder.

BRAMLEY Surrey
169, 170 TQ 0044 3m S of Guildford. CP,
2,891. Hambledon RD. P Gldfd. Ch e, r, v.
Sch pe. Gldfd CC. See also Thorncombe St.

BRAMLEY Yorks (W)
103 SK 4892 4m E of Rotherham. CP,
4,536. Rthrhm RD. P Rthrhm. Ch e, m.
Sch i, j, p. Rother Valley CC.

BRAMLEY VALE Derbys
112 SK 4666 6m NW of Mansfield. Loc,
Ault Hucknall CP. Sch p.

BRAMPFORD SPEKE Devon
176 SX 9298 4m N of Exeter. CP, 289. St
Thomas RD. P Extr. Ch e. Sch pe. Tiverton
CC. Cob and thatch vllge by R Exe.

BRAMPTON Cumb
76 NY 5361 9m ENE of Carlisle. CP, 3,521.
Border RD. P. Ch e, m, r, v. Sch i, j, s2.
Penrith and the Bdr CC. See also Milton. 2m
NE, Naworth Cstle, 14c, in pk.

BRAMPTON Hunts
134 TL 2170 2m WSW of Huntingdon. CP,
3,068. Hntngdn RD. P HNTNGDN. Ch e, m.
Sch i, j. Hunts CC. Pepys Hse*, owned by
the diarist from 1664 to 1680.

BRAMPTON Lincs (L)
104 SK 8479 7m SSE of Gainsborough. CP,
65. Gnsbrgh RD. Gnsbrgh CC.

BRAMPTON Norfolk
126 TG 2224 3m SE of Aylsham. CP, 195.
St Faith's and Aylshm RD. P NORWICH,
NOR 53Y. Ch e. N Nflk CC (Central Nflk).
See also Oxnead. Ch has 15c and 16c
brasses.

BRAMPTON Suffolk (E)
137 TM 4381 4m NE of Halesworth. CP,
306. Wainford RD. P Beccles. Ch e. Sch pe.
Lowestoft CC.

BRAMPTON Westm
83 NY 6823 2m N of Appleby. Loc,
Crackenthorpe CP. P Appleby. Ch m.

BRAMPTON Yorks (W)
103 SE 4101 5m SE of Barnsley.
CP(Brmptn Bierlow), 3,593. Rotherham RD.
Ch e, m. Sch i. Rother Valley CC.

BRAMPTON ABBOTTS Herefs
142, 143 SO 6026 2m N of Ross-on-Wye.
CP, 219. Rss and Whitchurch RD. P Rss-on-
Wye. Ch e. Sch pe. Hereford CC.

BRAMPTON ASH Northants
133 SP 7987 4m E of Mkt Harborough. CP,
139. Kettering RD. Ch e. Kttrng CC.

BRAMPTON BRYAN Herefs
129 SO 3772 5m E of Knighton. CP, 176.
Leominster and Wigmore RD. P Bucknell,
Salop. Ch e. Lmnstr CC. Rems of 13c and
later cstle. Ch 17c, rebuilt after destruction
of older ch in Civil War.

BRAMPTON EN LE MORTHEN Yorks (W)
103 SK 4888 5m SE of Rotherham. Loc,
Thurcroft CP.

BRAMSHALL Staffs
120 SK 0633 2m W of Uttoxeter. Loc,
Uttxtr UD. P Uttxtr.

BRAMSHAW Hants
179 SU 2715 7m SW of Romsey. CP, 636.
New Forest RD. P Lyndhurst. Ch e, m, r.
Sch p. Nw Frst CC. See also Brook,
Fritham. Much NT land N and E. 3½m W in
Islands Thorn Enclosure, many Roman
pottery kilns.

BRAMSHILL Hants
169 SU 7461 8m S of Reading. CP, 411.
Hartley Wintney RD. Basingstoke CC
(Aldershot). B. Hse, magnificent Jcbn hse,
now police college.

BRAMSHOTT Hants
169, 181 SU 8433 4m W of Haslemere. CP,
4,876. Petersfield RD. P Liphook. Ch e.
Sch pe. Ptrsfld CC. See also Lphk.

BRANCASTER Norfolk
125 TF 7743 6m ENE of Hunstanton.
CP, 1,063. Docking RD. P King's Lynn.
Ch e, m. Sch pe. NW Nflk CC (K's Lnn).
See also Brncstr Staithe, Burnham Deepdale.
Small resort. Golf course.

BRANCASTER STAITHE Norfolk
125 TF 7944 8m ENE of Hunstanton.Loc,
Brncstr CP. P King's Lynn. Ch m. Yachting.

BRANCEPETH Co Durham
85 NZ 2238 4m SW of Durham. CP, 342.
Drhm RD. P. DRHM. Ch e. NW Drhm CC
(Drhm). Mdvl cstle almost entirely rebuilt
early 19c.

BRANCH END Nthmb
77, 78 NZ 0661 2m WSW of Prudhoe. Loc,
Broomley and Stocksfield CP. Hexham RD.
P Stcksfld. Ch m. Hxhm CC.

BRANDESBURTON Yorks (E)
99 TA 1147 6m W of Hornsea. CP, 1,044.

Holderness RD. P Driffield. Ch e, m. Sch p.
Bridlington CC. See also Burshill.

BRANDESTON Suffolk (E)
137 TM 2460 3m SW of Framlingham. CP,
259. Blyth RD. P Woodbridge. Ch e, c. Eye
CC. Attractive vllge; large trees stand by ch.

BRANDIS CORNER Devon
175 SS 4103 4m E of Holsworthy. Loc,
Bradford CP. P Hlswthy. Ch m.

BRANDISTON Norfolk
125 TG 1321 5m SW of Aylsham. CP, 72.
St Faith's and Aylshm RD. Ch e, v.
N Nflk CC (Central Nflk). On edge of large
disused airfield.

BRANDON Co Durham
85 NZ 2439 3m SW of Durham. UD (Brndn
and Byshottles), 16,849. P DRHM. NW
Drhm CC. See also Broom, Esh Winning,
New Brancepeth, Ushaw Moor,
Waterhouses.

BRANDON Lincs (K)
113 SK 9048 8m N of Grantham. Loc,
Hough-on-the-Hill CP.

BRANDON Nthmb
71 NU 0417 8m SSE of Wooler. Loc,
Ingram CP.

BRANDON Suffolk (W)
136 TL 7886 6m WNW of Thetford.
CP, 3,344. Mildenhall RD. P. Ch e, b, m2, s.
Sch p, s. Bury St Edmunds CC. See also
Tn St. Breckland mkt tn on R Lit Ouse,
famous for once-flourishing flint-knapping
industry.

BRANDON Warwicks
132 SP 4076 5m ESE of Coventry.
CP(Brndn and Bretford). Rugby RD.
Sch pe. Rgby CC. Faint rems of B. Cstle,
13c, to SW beside R Avon.

BRANDON CREEK Norfolk
135 TL 6091 4m NNE of Littleport. Loc,
Southery CP. Ch m.

BRANDON PARVA Norfolk
125 TG 0708 5m NW of Wymondham. Loc,
Runhall CP. Ch e.

BRANDSBY Yorks (N)
92 SE 5872 4m ENE of Easingwold.
CP(Brndsby-cum-Stearsby), 270. Easngwld
RD. P YORK. Ch e. Thirsk and Malton CC.

BRANE Cornwall
189 SW 4028 5m WSW of Penzance. Loc,
Sancreed CP. Ch m.

BRAN END Essex
148 TL 6525 3m NE of Dunmow. Loc,
Stebbing CP. P Stbbng, Dnmw.

BRANKSOME Dorset
179 SZ 0492 3m W of Bournemouth. Loc,
Poole MB. Rsdntl distr famous for pine-clad
chine.

BRANSCOMBE Devon
176 SY 1988 4m E of Sidmouth. CP, 626.
Honiton RD. P Seaton. Ch e, m. Sch pe.
Hntn CC. See also Vicarage. Vllge of
thatched cottages in a combe, with some
new hses, running down to pebble beach.
Caravans to E.

BRANSFORD Worcs
143 SO 7952 4m WSW of Worcester. CP,
267. Martley RD. P WCSTR. Ch e.
Kidderminster CC.

BRANSGORE Hants
179 SZ 1897 4m NE of Christchurch. Loc,
Chrstchch E CP. Ringwood and
Fordingbridge RD. P Chrstchch. Ch e, m.
Sch pe. New Forest CC.

BRANSTON Leics
122 SK 8129 7m NNE of Melton Mowbray.
Loc, Croxton Kerrial CP. P Grantham,
Lincs. Ch e, m.

BRANSTON Lincs (K)
113 TF 0267 4m SE of Lincoln. CP(Brnstn
and Mere), 2,038. N Kesteven RD.
P LNCLN. Ch e, m2. Sch pe, s. Grantham CC.

BRANSTON Staffs
120 SK 2221 2m SW of Burton-on-Trent.
CP, 2,794. Tutbury RD. P Btn-on-Trnt.
Ch e, v. Sch p. Btn CC.

BRANSTONE IOW
180 SZ 5583 2m NW of Shanklin. Loc,
Newchurch CP.

BRANT BROUGHTON Lincs (K)
113 SK 9154 7m E of Newark. CP(Brnt
Brghtn and Stragglethorpe), 618.
N Kesteven RD. P LINCOLN. Ch e, f, m, v.
Sch pe, pm. Grantham CC. 14c ch, tall spire.
Many 18c hses.

BRANTHAM Suffolk (E)
150 TM 1134 2m N of Manningtree. CP,
1,316. Samford RD. P Mnnngtree, Essex.
Ch e, m, r. Sch p. Sudbury and Woodbridge
CC. See also Cattawade.

BRANTHWAITE Cumb
82 NY 0524 4m SE of Workington. Loc,
Dean CP.

BRANTINGHAM Yorks (E)
98 SE 9429 10m W of Hull. CP, 363.
Beverley RD. P Brough. Ch e. Haltemprice CC.
On S tip of Wolds; views N to York Minster,
S to Lincoln Cathedral.

BRANTON Nthmb
71 NU 0416 8m SSE of Wooler. Loc,
Ingram CP. Ch v.

BRANTON GREEN Yorks (W)
91 SE 4462 4m SE of Boroughbridge. Loc,
Gt Ouseburn CP. Ch m.

BRANXTON Nthmb
64, 70 NT 8937 4m ESE of Coldstream. CP,
162. Glendale RD. P Cornhill-on-Tweed.
Ch e. Berwick-upon-Tweed CC. At site of
Battle of Flodden, 1513.

BRASSEY GREEN Ches
109 SJ 5260 9m ESE of Chester. Loc,
Tiverton CP. Ch b.

BRASSINGTON Derbys
111 SK 2354 6m NE of Ashbourne. CP,
529. Ashbne RD. P DERBY. Ch e, c, m.
Sch p. W Derbys CC. See also Longcliffe.
Limestone vllge in rock-climbing area. Nmn
ch.

BRASTED Kent
171 TQ 4755 4m W of Sevenoaks. CP,
1,500. Svnks RD. P Westerham. Ch e, b.
Sch pe. Svnks CC. See also Brstd Chart,
Toy's Hill. B. Place, late 18c Adam mansion.
Napoleon III resided here in 1840. 2m S,
Emmetts(NT); shrub gdn*.

BRASTED CHART Kent
171 TQ 4653 4m WSW of Sevenoaks. Loc,
Brstd CP. P Westerham.

BRATOFT Lincs (L)
114 TF 4764 6m W of Skegness. CP, 144.
Spilsby RD. Ch e. Horncastle CC.

BRATTLEBY Lincs (L)
104 SK 9480 7m NNW of Lincoln. CP, 84. Welton RD. P LNCLN. Ch e. Gainsborough CC.

BRATTON Wilts
166, 167 ST 9152 3m ENE of Westbury. CP, 721. Warminster and Wstbry RD. P Wstbry. Ch e, b. Sch p. Wstbry CC. 1m SW, B. Cstle (A.M.), Iron Age fort; Wstbry White Horse (A.M.), 18c.

BRATTON CLOVELLY Devon
175 SX 4691 8m WSW of Okehampton. CP, 373. Okhmptn RD. P Okhmptn. Ch e, m2. W Dvn CC (Torrington). Views across Dartmoor to E.

BRATTON FLEMING Devon
163 SS 6437 6m NE of Barnstaple. CP, 488. Bnstple RD. P Bnstple. Ch e, b, m. Sch p. N Dvn CC. See also Knightacott, Leworthy, Stowford.

BRATTON SEYMOUR Som
166 ST 6729 2m WNW of Wincanton. CP, 144. Wncntn RD. Ch e. Yeovil CC.

BRAUGHING Herts
148 TL 3925 6m WNW of Bishop's Stortford. CP, 920. Brghng RD. P Ware. Ch e, c, m. Sch p. E Herts CC. Stream runs through large vllge. Rems of Roman tn excavated.

BRAUNSTON Northants
132 SP 5366 3m NW of Daventry. CP, 1,198. Dvntry RD. P RUGBY. Ch e, b, m. Sch pe. Dvntry CC (S Nthnts). On Grand Union Canal, with flight of locks and long tunnel to SE. Wharves, barges, boat-building, yachts.

BRAUNSTON Rutland
122 SK 8306 2m SW of Oakham. CP, 317. Oakhm RD. P Oakhm. Ch e. Rtlnd and Stamford CC. In the hilly country on the Leics border. Many ironstone hses.

BRAUNSTONE Leics
121, 122 SK 5502 2m WSW of Leicester. CP, 13,174. Blaby RD. P LCSTR. Ch e. Sch i, j, p2, s. Blby CC (Harborough). Old vllge developed as rsdntl estate for Lcstr.

BRAUNTON Devon
163 SS 4836 5m WNW of Barnstaple. CP, 4,303. Bnstple RD. P. Ch e, m, r, v3.

Sch p2, s. N Dvn CC. See also Halsinger, Knowle, Pippacott, Saunton. To W, B. Burrows, partly a nature reserve; beyond the Burrows, Sntn Sands.

BRAWBY Yorks (N)
92 SE 7378 5m NW of Malton. CP, 142. Mltn RD. P Mltn. Ch m. Sch p. Thirsk and Malton CC.

BRAXTED, GREAT Essex
149, 162 TL 8614 2m E of Witham. See Gt Brxtd.

BRAY Berks
159 SU 9079 1m SE of Maidenhead. CP, 4,858. Cookham RD. P Mdnhd. Ch e. Sch pe. Windsor and Mdnhd CC (Wndsr). See also Fifield, Holyport, Oakley Grn. Turncoat vicar is celebrated in famous 18c ballad.

BRAYBROOKE Northants
133 SP 7684 3m SE of Mkt Harborough. CP, 239. Kettering RD. P Mkt Hbrgh. Ch e, b. Sch p. Kttrng CC. Ch: monmts; vamping horn, formerly used to summon congregation and accompany singing, one of few surviving in England.

BRAYFORD Devon
163 SS 6834 6m NNW of S Molton. Loc, Charles CP. P Barnstaple. Ch b, m.

BRAY SHOP Cornwall
186 SX 3374 4m NNW of Callington. Loc, Launceston RD, Liskeard RD. Ch m. N Cnwll CC, Bodmin CC.

BRAYTON Yorks (W)
97, 98 SE 6030 1m SW of Selby. CP, 1,061. Slby RD. P Slby. Ch e, m. Sch pe. Barkston Ash CC.

BRAY WICK Berks
159 SU 8979 1m S of Maidenhead. Loc, Bray CP.

BREACHWOOD GREEN Herts
147 TL 1522 4m E of Luton. Loc, King's Walden CP. P Hitchin. Ch b. Sch p.

BREADSALL Derbys
120, 121 SK 3739 2m NNE of Derby. CP. SE Derbys RD. P DBY. Ch e, m2. Sch pe. SE Derbys CC.

BREADSTONE Glos
156 SO 7000 4m WNW of Dursley. Loc,
Hamfallow CP. Thornbury RD. S Glos CC.

BREAGE Cornwall
189 SW 6128 3m W of Helston. CP, 2,230.
Kerrier RD. P Hlstn. Ch e, m3, v. Sch pe. St
Ives CC. See also Ashton, Godolphin Cross,
Praa Sands, Rinsey, Trescowe. 15c granite
ch with wall-paintings.

BREAM Glos
155, 156 SO 6005 2m NW of Lydney. Loc,
W Dean CP. W Dn RD. P Ldny. Ch e, m, v.
Sch i, pe, s. W Glos CC.

BREAMORE Hants
179 SU 1518 3m N of Fordingbridge.
CP, 510. Ringwood and Fdngbrdge RD.
P Fdngbrdge. Ch e, m. Sch pe. New
Forest CC. See also Upr St. Saxon ch.
B. Hse*, Elizn mnr blt 1583.

BREAM'S EAVES Glos
155, 156 SO 6006 3m NW of Lydney. Loc,
W Dean CP. W Dn RD. Ch m. W Glos CC.

BREAN Som
165 ST 2956 4m SSW of Weston. CP, 323.
Axbridge RD. P Burnham-on-Sea. Ch e, m.
Wstn-super-Mare CC. Chalets, shacks. B.
Down (NT) is bird sanctuary.

BREARTON Yorks (W)
91 SE 3261 3m NW of Knaresborough. CP,
100. Nidderdale RD. P Harrogate. Ch e.
Hrrgte CC.

BREASTON Derbys
112, 121 SK 4633 7m ESE of Derby. CP,
3,626. SE Derbys RD. P DBY. Ch e, m.
Sch p, s. SE Derbys CC.

BRECKLES Norfolk
136 TL 9594 6m W of Attleborough. Loc,
Stow Bedon CP. Ch e.

BREDBURY Ches
101 SJ 9391 3m ENE of Stockport. UD
(Brdbry and Romiley), 28,472. P Woodley,
Stckpt. Hazel Grove BC (Cheadle CC). See
also Compstall.

BREDE Sussex (E)
184 TQ 8218 6m N of Hastings. CP, 1,011.
Battle RD. P Rye. Ch e. Sch p. Rye CC. See
also Broad Oak. 1m E, B. Place, Tdr hse.

BREDENBURY Herefs
129, 130 SO 6056 3m WNW of Bromyard.
CP, 63. Brmyd RD. P Brmyd. Ch e. Sch p.
Leominster CC.

BREDFIELD Suffold (E)
150 TM 2653 3m N of Woodbridge. CP,
287. Deben RD. P Wdbrdge. Ch e, v. Sch p.
Eye CC. Bthplce of Edward Fitzgerald.

BREDGAR Kent
172 TQ 8860 3m SSW of Sittingbourne. CP,
574. Swale RD. P Sttngbne. Ch e, m.
Sch pe. Faversham CC.

BREDHURST Kent
172 TQ 7962 3m SSE of Gillingham. CP,
162. Hollingbourn RD. P Gllnghm. Ch e.
Sch pe. Maidstone CC.

BREDICOT Worcs
143, 144 SO 9054 4m E of Worcester. CP,
28. Pershore RD. S Worcs CC.

BREDON Worcs
143, 144 SO 9236 3m NNE of Tewkesbury.
CP, 1,240. Pershore RD. P Tksbry, Glos.
Ch e, b, m. Sch pe. S Worcs CC. See also
Kinsham. Between R Avon and B. Hill,
made famous by A.E. Housman's poem.
Nmn — 14c ch: chpl. 14c tithe barn (NT)*.

BREDON'S NORTON Worcs
143, 144 SO 9339 5m NE of Tewkesbury.
CP, 155. Pershore RD. P Tksbry, Glos. Ch e.
S Worcs CC.

BREDWARDINE Herefs
142 SO 3344 7m E of Hay-on-Wye. CP,
177. Dore and Brdwdne RD. P
HEREFORD. Ch e. Hrfd CC.

BREEDON ON THE HILL Leics
121 SK 4022 5m NE of Ashby de la Zouch.
CP, 793. Cstle Donington RD. P DERBY.
Ch e, m2. Sch pe. Loughborough CC. See
also Tonge, Wilson. Ch is within ramparts of
Iron Age fort. Contains exceptionally fine
Saxon sculpture from 8c ch formerly on
site.

BREIGHTON Yorks (E)
97, 98 SE 7034 6m E of Selby. Loc,
Bubwith CP.

BREINTON Herefs
142 SO 4739 2m W of Hereford. CP, 840.
Hrfd RD. P HRFD. Ch e. See also Upr

Brntn. Leominster CC. To SW, Iron Age hill fort.

BREMHILL Wilts
157 ST 9873 2m NW of Calne. CP, 893. Clne and Chippenham RD. P Clne. Ch e. Chppnhm CC. See also E Tytherton, Foxham, Spirthill.

BRENCHLEY Kent
171 TQ 6741 6m ESE of Tonbridge. CP, 2,599. Tnbrdge RD. P Tnbrdge. Ch e, b, m. Sch pe. Royal Tunbridge Wells CC (Tnbrdge). See also Matfield. Typical Wealden vllge among hop gdns and orchards. lm S, Brattles Grange, Tdr half-timbered hse; gdn*.

BRENDON Devon
163 SS 7648 3m ESE of Lynton. CP, 213. Barnstaple RD. P Lntn. Ch e. N Dvn CC. See also Cheriton. Exmoor holiday centre for walkers and riders.

BRENT ELEIGH Suffolk (W)
149 TL 9447 2m ESE of Lavenham. CP, 134. Cosford RD. P Sudbury. Ch e. Sdbry and Woodbridge CC.

BRENTFORD London
160, 170 TQ 1678 3m W of Hammersmith. Loc, Hounslow LB. P Middx. Brntfd and Isleworth BC (Brntfd and Chiswick). R Brent flows from N into R Thames. M4 motorway flyover. Kew Br spans Thames. Piano Museum in Kew Br Rd. To S in Thames-side grnds, Syon Hse*, 18c hse with Robert Adam interiors.

BRENTINGBY Leics
122 SK 7818 2m E of Melton Mowbray. Loc, Freeby CP.

BRENT KNOLL Som
165 ST 3350 2m NE of Burnham. CP, 759. Axbridge RD. P Highbridge. Ch e, m. Sch pe. Weston-super-Mare CC. Ch: 15c bench-ends. Steep circular hill rises from lowlands; Iron Age fort on summit.

BRENTOR Devon
175 SX 4881 4m N of Tavistock. See N Brentor.

BRENT PELHAM Herts
148 TL 4330 7m NNW of Bishop's Stortford. CP, 154. Braughing RD. P Buntingford. Ch e. E Herts CC.

BRENTWOOD Essex
161 TQ 5993 11m SW of Chelmsford. UD, 57,976. P. Brntwd and Ongar CC (Billericay). See also Brook St, Havering's Grove, Herongate, Hutton, Ingrave, Lit Warley, Pilgrim's Hatch, Shenfield, S Weald, W Horndon. Light industry. Much traffic despite bypass.

BRENZETT Kent
184 TR 0027 7m NE of Rye. CP, 289. Romney Marsh RD. P Rmny Msh. Ch e. Sch pe. Folkestone and Hythe CC. See also Snave.

BRERETON Staffs
120 SK 0516 1m SSE of Rugeley. Loc, Rgly UD. P Rgly.

BRERETON GREEN Ches
110 SJ 7764 5m ESE of Middlewich. Loc, Brtn CP. Congleton RD. P(Brtn), Sandbach. Ch e. Sch pe. Knutsford CC. The Bear's Head is 17c, half-timbered.

BRERETON HEATH Ches
110 SJ 8065 4m WNW of Congleton. Loc, Brtn CP. Cngltn RD. Ch m. Knutsford CC.

BRESSINGHAM Norfolk
136 TM 0780 3m W of Diss. CP, 620. Depwade RD. P Dss. Ch e, m2. Sch p. S Nflk CC. See also Fersfield. B. Gdns* and Steam Engine Museum; miniature rly.

BRETBY Derbys
120, 121 SK 2923 3m E of Burton-on-Trent. CP, 809. Repton RD. P Btn-on-Trnt, Staffs. Ch e, m. Sch p. Belper CC.

BRETFORD Warwicks
132 SP 4377 6m E of Coventry. CP(Brandon and Brtfd). Rugby RD. Rgby CC.

BRETFORTON Worcs
144 SP 0943 3m E of Evesham. CP, 936. Eveshm RD. P Eveshm. Ch e. Sch p. S Worcs CC. Old stone and timbered hses. 13c—15c ch: carved capitals.

BRETHERTON Lancs
94 SD 4720 7m SW of Preston. CP, 597. Chorley RD. P Prstn. Ch e, c, m. Sch pe. Chly CC. At Carr Hse*, Barry Elder's Doll Museum.

BRETTENHAM Norfolk
136 TL 9383 4m E of Thetford. CP, 153.
Wayland RD. Ch e. S Nflk CC. See also
Rushford.

BRETTENHAM Suffolk (W)
149 TL 9654 4m NE of Lavenham. CP, 263.
Cosford RD. P Ipswch. Ch e, v. Sudbury and
Woodbridge CC.

BREWOOD Staffs
119 SJ 8808 6m W of Cannock. CP. Cnnck
RD. P STAFFORD. Ch e. Sch pe, pr, s. SW
Staffs CC (Cnnck). See also Bishop's Wd,
Coven, Horsebrook, Kiddemore Grn,
Standeford. Ch: Giffard tombs. 1¾m SW,
Chillington Hall*, 18c. Grnds by Capability
Brown.

BRIANTSPUDDLE Dorset
178 SY 8193 8m WNW of Wareham. Loc,
Affpuddle CP. P Dorchester. Sch pe. 1½m
SSE, Clouds Hill (NT)*, once the home of
T.E. Lawrence. ½m S, Cull-peppers Dish —
see Affpuddle.

BRICETT, GREAT Suffolk (E)
149 TM 0350 5m N of Hadleigh. See Gt
Brctt.

BRICKET WOOD Herts
160 TL 1302 4m NNE of Watford. Loc, St
Stephen CP. St Albans RD. Ch c, v. Sch j. S
Herts CC (St Albns). Bldng Research Stn.
Picture Hse, with exterior panels bearing
sporting reliefs.

BRICKHILL, GREAT Bucks
146 SP 9030 3m SE of Bletchley. See Gt
Brckhll.

BRICKLEHAMPTON Worcs
143, 144 SO 9842 4m W of Evesham. CP,
163. Pershore RD. Ch e. S Worcs CC.

BRIDEKIRK Cumb
82 NY 1133 2m N of Cockermouth. CP,
792. Cckrmth RD. Ch e. Sch pe.
Workington CC. See also Dovenby,
Tallentire.

BRIDESTOWE Devon
175 SX 5189 6m SW of Okehampton. CP,
505. Okhmptn RD. P Okhmptn. Ch e, m.
Sch p. W Dvn CC (Torrington). Ch stands on
summit of tor, 1,130ft hill, once a volcano.

BRIDFORD Devon
176 SS 8186 4m E of Moretonhampstead.
CP, 436. St Thomas RD. P Exeter. Ch e, v.
Tiverton CC. Ch has famous 16c scrn,
showing Tdr rose (for Henry VIII) and
pomegranate (for Catherine of Aragon).

BRIDGE Kent
173 TR 1854 3m SE of Canterbury. CP,
761. Brdge-Blean RD. P Cntrbry. Ch e, m.
Sch pe. Cntrbry CC.

BRIDGE END Lincs (K)
113, 123 TF 1436 8m SE of Sleaford. Loc,
Horbling CP.

BRIDGEFOOT Cumb
82 NY 0529 3m E of Workington. Loc,
Cockermouth RD. Ch m. Wkngtn CC.

BRIDGEFORD, GREAT Staffs
119 SJ 8827 3m NW of Stafford. Loc,
Seighford CP. P STFFD.

BRIDGE GREEN Essex
148 TL 4637 5m W of Saffron Walden. Loc,
Elmdon CP.

BRIDGEHAMPTON Som
166, 177 ST 5624 3m ENE of Ilchester.
Loc, Yeovilton CP.

BRIDGE HEWICK Yorks (W)
91 SE 3370 2m ESE of Ripon. CP, 72. Rpn
and Pateley Br RD. Rpn CC.

BRIDGEMARY Hants
180 SU 5803 2m S of Fareham. Loc,
Gosport MB. P Gspt.

BRIDGEND Westm
83 NY 4014 7m NNE of Ambleside. Loc,
Lakes UD. Westm CC.

BRIDGERULE Devon
174 SS 2702 4m W of Holsworthy. CP, 366.
Hlswthy RD. P Hlswthy. Ch e, m. Sch pe.
W Dvn CC (Tavistock).

BRIDGES Shrops
129 SO 3996 4m WNW of Ch Stretton. Loc,
Clun and Bishop's Cstle RD. Ludlow CC.

BRIDGE SOLLERS Herefs
142 SO 4142 6m WNW of Hereford. CP, 46.
Weobley RD. Ch e. Leominster CC.

BRIDGE STREET Suffolk (W)
149 TL 8749 2m W of Lavenham. Loc, Long Melford CP. P Sudbury.

BRIDGETOWN Cornwall
174, 186 SX 3489 3m N of Launceston. Loc, Werrington CP. Ch m.

BRIDGETOWN Som
164 SS 9233 3m N of Dulverton. Loc, Dlvtn RD. P Dlvtn. Ch m. Taunton CC.

BRIDGETOWN Staffs
119 SJ 9808 1m S of Cannock. Loc, Cnnck UD. Cnnck CC.

BRIDGE TRAFFORD Ches
109 SJ 4470 4m NE of Chester. CP. Chstr RD. City of Chstr CC.

BRIDGEYATE Glos
155, 156 ST 6873 6m E of Bristol. Loc, Siston CP. Ch m.

BRIDGHAM Norfolk
136 TL 9685 6m ENE of Thetford. CP, 229. Wayland RD. P NORWICH, NOR 16X. Ch e. Sch p. S Nflk CC.

BRIDGNORTH Shrops
130 SO 7192 13m WSW of Wolverhampton. CP, 7,552. Brdgnth RD. P. Ch e, b, cm, r, v2. Sch i, je, pe, pr, s2, sb, sg. Ludlow CC. See also Oldbury, Quatford. On cliff above R Severn. Rly, steepest in England, connects upr and lr tns. Rems of Nmn cstle. Half-timbered tn hall, 17c.

BRIDGWATER Som
165 ST 2937 9m NNE of Taunton. MB, 26,598. P. Brdgwtr CC. Expanding indstrl tn and small port. Bthplce of Admiral Blake, 1599; his hse now museum.

BRIDLINGTON Yorks (E)
93 TA 1766 24m NNE of Hull. MB, 26,729. P. Brdlngtn CC. See also Hilderthorpe, Marton, Sewerby. Old port; fishing fleet; holiday resort. Sewerby Hall*, Ggn hse; small zoo in grnds.

BRIDPORT Dorset
177 SY 4692 14m W of Dorchester. MB, 6,362. P. W Dst CC. See also Pymore, W Bay. Mkt tn and former centre of rope-making industry. Ggn tn hall.

BRIDSTOW Herefs
142 SO 5824 1m W of Ross-on-Wye. CP, 710. Rss and Whitchurch RD. Ch e. Sch pe. Hereford CC.

BRIERFIELD Lancs
95 SD 8436 1m SW of Nelson. UD, 7,572. P Nlsn. Nlsn and Colne BC.

BRIERLEY Glos
142, 143 SO 6215 2m WNW of Cinderford. Loc, Drybrook CP. P Drbrk.

BRIERLEY Herefs
129 SO 4956 2m S of Leominster. Loc, Lmnstr MB.

BRIERLEY Yorks (W)
103 SE 4110 5m NE of Barnsley. CP, 8,259. Hemsworth RD. P Bnsly. Ch e, m, v. Sch pe. Hmswth CC. See also Grimethorpe.

BRIERLEY HILL Staffs
130, 131 SO 9187 3m SW of Dudley. Loc, Ddly CB. P. Ddly W BC (Brly Hll CC). Ironworks. Glass-mnfg. 18c ch in classical style.

BRIERTON Co Durham
85 NZ 4730 3m SW of Hartlepool. CP. Stockton RD. Easington CC. (Sedgefield).

BRIGG Lincs (L)
104 TA 0007 7m ESE of Scunthorpe. UD, 4,793. P. Brgg and Scnthpe CC (Brgg).

BRIGGSWATH Yorks (N)
86 NZ 8608 3m SW of Whitby. Loc, Whtby UD. P Whtby.

BRIGHAM Cumb
81, 82 NY 0830 2m W of Cockermouth. CP, 820. Cckrmth RD. P Cckrmth. Ch e, m2. Sch pe. Workington CC.

BRIGHAM Yorks (E)
99 TA 0753 4m SE of Driffield. Loc, Foston CP.

BRIGHOUSE Yorks (W)
96, 102 SE 1422 4m N of Huddersfield. MB, 34,111. P. Brghse and Spenborough BC. See also Bailiff Br, Hipperholme, Lightcliffe, Norwood Grn, Rastrick, Southowram. Indstrl tn; mostly wool textile mills.

BRIGHSTONE IOW
180 SZ 4282 6m SW of Newport. CP, 838.
Isle of Wight RD and CC. P Npt. Ch e, m.
Sch pe. See also Brook, Moortown,
Mottistone.

BRIGHTGATE Derbys
111 SK 2659 2m W of Matlock. Loc, Mtlck
UD.

BRIGHTHAMPTON Oxon
158 SP 3803 4m SSE of Witney. Loc,
Standlake CP.

BRIGHTLING Sussex (E)
183 TQ 6821 5m NW of Battle. CP, 373.
Bttle RD. P Robertsbridge. Ch e, c. Rye CC.
Obelisk and observatory on B. Down to E,
creations of 'Mad Jack' Fuller, whose
pyramidal mausoleum (blt by him in 1810)
is in churchyard.

BRIGHTLINGSEA Essex
149, 162 TM 0816 8m SE of Colchester.
UD, 6,515. P Clchstr. Harwich CC. Yachting
centre. Oyster fisheries. Once a busy trading
port with boat-bldng industry. Ch: 15c flint
twr; brasses.

BRIGHTON Sussex (E)
182 TQ 3104 48m S of London. CB,
166,081. P. BCs: Brghtn, Kemptown;
Brghtn, Pavilion. See also Kemp Tn,
Rottingdean, Stanmer, Woodingdean.
Resort (two piers); commercial centre.
Rgncy squares. Pavilion* blt in Oriental
style for Prince Regent. University of Sussex
at Falmer, qv.

BRIGHTWALTON Berks
158 SU 4279 8m NNW of Newbury. CP,
304. Wantage RD, P Nbry. Ch e, m. Sch pe.
Abingdon CC.

BRIGHTWELL Berks
158 SU 5790 2m NW of Wallingford.
CP(Brtwll-cum-Sotwell), 1,358. Wllngfd RD.
P(B-cum-S), Wllngfd. Ch e, v. Sch pe.
Abingdon CC.

BRIGHTWELL Suffolk (E)
150 TM 2543 5m E of Ipswich. CP, 73.
Deben RD. Ch e. Sudbury and Woodbridge
CC.

BRIGHTWELL BALDWIN Oxon
158, 159 SU 5m NE of Wallingford. CP,
150. Bullingdon RD. P OXFORD. Ch e.

Henley CC. Watercress grown in area. Ch:
brasses, glass. Ruined mnr hse behind ch.

BRIGNALL Yorks (N)
84 NZ 0712 3m SSE of Barnard Cstle. CP,
98. Startforth RD. Ch e. Richmond CC.

BRIGSLEY Lincs (L)
105 TA 2501 5m S of Grimsby. CP, 303.
Grmsby RD. Ch e, m. Louth CC.

BRIGSTEER Westm
89 SD 4889 3m SW of Kendal. Loc, S
Westm RD. P Kndl. Westm CC.

BRIGSTOCK Northants
133 SP 9485 4m SE of Corby. CP, 1,406.
Oundle and Thrapston RD. P Kettering.
Ch e, c. Sch pe. Wellingborough CC
(Peterborough). Ch has Saxon twr. Kennels
of Woodland Pytchley Hunt.

BRILL Bucks
145, 146, 159 SP 6513 6m NW of Thame.
CP, 905. Aylesbury RD. P Aylesbury.
Ch e, c, m. Sch pe. Aylesbury CC. 17c
windmill. Dorton Hse*, 17c-18c hse now a
school.

BRILLEY Herefs
141 SO 2649 5m NNE of Hay-on-Wye. CP,
257. Kington RD. Ch e, m, v. Sch pe.
Leominster CC.

BRIMFIELD Herefs
129 SO 5267 4m W of Tenbury Wells. CP,
532. Leominster and Wigmore RD. P
Ludlow, Salop. Ch e, m. Sch pe. Lmnstr CC.

BRIMFIELDCROSS Herefs
129 SO 5468 3m W of Tenbury Wells. Loc,
Brimfield CP.

BRIMINGTON Derbys
112 SK 4073 2m NE of Chesterfield. CP,
8,163. Chstrfld RD. P Chstrfld.
Ch e, c, m3, v3. Sch i2, j, sb. Chstrfld BC.

BRIMPSFIELD Glos
143, 144 SO 9312 6m S of Cheltenham. CP,
235. Cirencester RD. P GLOUCESTER.
Ch e. Crncstr and Tewkesbury CC. High
Cotswold vllge. Faint traces of 13c cstle.

BRIMPTON Berks
168 SU 5564 6m ESE of Newbury. CP, 473.
Nbry RD. P Reading. Ch e, b. Sch pe. Nbry
CC.

BRIMSCOMBE Glos
156 SO 8602 2m SE of Stroud. Loc,
Thrupp CP. P Strd. Ch e, m, v. Sch pe.

BRIND Yorks (E)
97, 98 SE 7430 5m N of Goole. Loc,
Wressle CP.

BRINDLE Lancs
94 SD 5924 5m SE of Preston. CP, 818.
Chorley RD. P Chly. Ch e, m, r.
Sch p, pe, pr. Chly CC.

BRINETON Staffs
119 SJ 8013 5m SE of Newport. Loc,
Blymhill CP.

BRINGHURST Leics
133 SP 8492 4m NW of Corby. CP, 45. Mkt
Harborough RD. Ch e. Sch p. Hbrgh CC.

BRINGTON Hunts
134 TL 0875 6m ESE of Thrapston.
CP(Brngtn and Molesworth), 635.
Huntingdon RD. P HNTNGDN. Ch e.
Hunts CC.

BRINGTON, GREAT Northants
132, 133 SP 6665 6m WNW of
Northampton. See Gt Brngtn.

BRININGHAM Norfolk
125 TG 0334 4m SW of Holt. CP, 126.
Walsingham RD. P Melton Constable.
Ch e, v. NW Nflk CC (N Nflk).

BRINKHILL Lincs (L)
114 TF 3773 5m WSW of Alford. CP, 80.
Spilsby RD. P Louth. Ch e, m.
Horncastle CC.

BRINKLEY Cambs
148 TL 6254 6m SSW of Newmarket. CP,
204. Nmkt RD. P Nmkt, Suffolk. Ch e.
Cambs CC.

BRINKLOW Warwicks
132 SP 4379 6m E of Coventry. CP, 1,092.
Rugby RD. P Rgby. Ch e, v. Sch pe.
Rgby CC. Close to the Fosse Way. Motte and
bailey cstle. 2m W, rems of Coombe
Abbey*, 12c, beside 17c hse in grnds laid
out by Capability Brown.

BRINKWORTH Wilts
157 SU 0184 5m ESE of Malmesbury. CP,
1,018. Mlmsbry RD. P Chippenham.
Ch e, m. Sch p. Chppnhm CC. See also
Grittenham.

BRINSCALL Lancs
94, 95 SD 6221 4m NE of Chorley. Loc,
Withnell UD. P Chly.

BRINSLEY Notts
112 SK 4548 4m ESE of Ripley. CP, 1,915.
Basford RD. Ch e, m. Sch p. Beeston CC
(Ashfield). See also New Brnsly.

BRINSOP Herefs
142 SO 4344 5m NW of Hereford. CP, 111.
Weobley RD. Ch e. Leominster CC. Ch
mostly 14c; highly decorated and colourful
interior. B. Hall, well preserved hall-hse.

BRINSWORTH Yorks (W)
103 SK 4190 2m SSW of Rotherham. CP,
5,343. Rthrhm RD. P Rthrhm. Ch e.
Sch i, j, p, s. Rother Valley CC.

BRINTON Norfolk
125 TG 0335 3m SW of Holt. CP, 202.
Walsingham RD. Ch e, m. Sch p. NW Nflk
CC (N Nflk). See also Sharrington.

BRISLEY Norfolk
125 TF 9521 5m SSE of Fakenham. CP,
260. Mitford and Launditch RD. P
Dereham. Ch e, m. Sch pe. SW Nflk CC.

BRISTOL Glos
155, 156, 165 ST 5872 106m W of London.
CB, 425,203. P(BRSTL). BCs: Brstl NE,
NW, S, SE, W. (Central, NE, NW, S, SE, W.)
See also Avonmouth, Chittening Trading
Estate, Clifton, Frenchay, Shirehampton.
Port; commercial and indstrl city. Historical
links with N America. Cathedral. St Mary
Redcliffe, vast 13c-15c ch. University.

BRISTON Norfolk
125 TG 0632 4m SSW of Holt. CP, 1,201.
Walsingham RD. P Melton Constable.
Ch e, c2, m2, s. Sch pe. NW Nflk CC
(N Nflk).

BRITANNIA Lancs
95 SD 8821 1m SE of Bacup. Loc, Bcp MB.
P Bcp.

BRITFORD Wilts
167 SU 1628 2m SE of Salisbury. CP, 705.
Slsbry and Wilton RD. Ch e. Sch pe.
Slsbry CC.

BRITISH LEGION VILLAGE Kent
171, 172 TQ 7257 2m NW of Maidstone.
Loc, Aylesford CP.

BRITWELL Oxon
158, 159 SU 6793 5m ENE of Wallingford.
CP, 139. Bullingdon RD. P(Brtwll Salome),
OXFORD. Ch e. Henley CC. Full name as
post office; Salome, pronounced Saylm,
derived from de Sulham, mdvl lords of the
mnr.

BRIXHAM Devon
188 SX 9256 S distr of Torbay. Loc, Tby CB.
P. Tn with steep streets and a harbour at S
end of Tor Bay where William of Orange
landed in 1688. Chief industries: tourism,
fishing. Limestone quarries at Berry Head.

BRIXTON Devon
187 SX 5552 5m ESE of Plymouth. CP,
1,048. Plympton St Mary RD. P Plmth.
Ch e, m. W Dvn CC (Tavistock).

BRIXTON London
160, 170 TQ 3176 3m SSE of Charing
Cross. Loc, Lambeth LB. Lmbth Central
BC. (Lmbth, Brxtn). B. Prison to S.

BRIXTON DEVERILL Wilts
166 ST 8638 4m S of Warminster. CP, 76.
Wmnstr and Westbury RD. Ch e. Wstbry CC.

BRIXWORTH Northants
133 SP 7470 6m N of Northampton. CP,
1,578. Brxwth RD. P NTHMPTN.
Ch c, m, r. Sch pe. Daventry CC (Kettering).
Impressive mainly Saxon ch, incorporating
Roman bldg materials. Kennels of Pytchley
Hunt. Pitsford Reservoir to SE.

BRIZE NORTON Oxon
158 SP 3007 4m WSW of Witney. CP, 984.
Wtny RD. P OXFORD. Ch e, m. Sch p2.
Mid-Oxon CC (Banbury). Large airfield.

BROAD BLUNSDON Wilts
157 SU 1590 4m N of Swindon. Loc,
Blnsdn St Andrew CP. Ch e.

BROADBOTTOM Ches
101 SJ 9993 3m W of Glossop. Loc,
Longdendale UD. P Hyde. Ch e. Stalybridge
and Hde CC.

BROADBRIDGE Sussex (W)
181 SU 8105 3m W of Chichester. Loc,
Bosham CP.

BROADBRIDGE HEATH Sussex (W)
182 TQ 1531 2m W of Horsham. Loc, Hshm
Rural CP. Hshm RD. P Hshm. Ch b. Sch p.

Hshm and Crawley CC (Hshm). Suburb of
Hshm. To N, Field Place, bthplce of Shelley.

BROAD CAMPDEN Glos
144 SP 1537 1m SSE of Chipping Campden.
Loc, Chppng Cmpdn CP. Ch e, f.

BROAD CHALKE Wilts
167 SU 0325 7m WSW of Salisbury. CP,
556. Slsbry and Wilton RD. P Slsbry.
Ch e, v. Sch pe. Slsbry CC.

BROAD CLYST Devon
176 SX 9897 5m NE of Exeter. CP, 2,043.
St Thomas RD. P Extr. Ch e. Sch p, s.
Tiverton CC. See also Budlake, Dog Vllge,
Westwood. 2m N, Killerton Pk (NT); gdns*.
Estate incl most of B.C. itself.

BROADHEATH Ches
101 SJ 7689 1m N of Altrincham. Loc,
Altrincham MB. P Altrnchm.

BROADHEATH Worcs
129, 130 SO 6665 5m ESE of Tenbury
Wells. Loc, Hanley CP. Tnbry RD. P Tnbry
Wlls. Ch v. Sch pe. Kidderminster CC.
Bthplce of Elgar, 1857; cottage now a
museum.

BROADHEMBURY Devon
176 ST 1004 5m NW of Honiton. CP, 556.
Hntn RD. P Hntn. Ch e. Sch pe. Hntn CC.
See also Dulford, Kerswell. Square of
whitewashed thatched cottages in vllge. 1¼m
SE, Hembury, large Iron Age fort.

BROADHEMPSTON Devon
188 SX 8066 4m N of Totnes. CP, 467.
Newton Abbot RD. P Ttns. Ch e, m, v.
Sch p. Ttns CC.

BROAD HINTON Wilts
157 SU 1076 6m SW of Swindon. CP, 391.
Marlborough and Ramsbury RD. P Swndn.
Ch e, v. Sch pe. Devizes CC.

BROADHOLME Notts
113 SK 8974 5m WNW of Lincoln. CP, 90.
Newark RD. Nwk CC.

BROAD LAYING Hants
168 SU 4362 4m SSW of Newbury. Loc, E
Woodhay CP.

BROADLEY COMMON Essex
161 TL 4207 3m SW of Harlow. Loc,
Roydon CP. P Waltham Abbey. Ch c.

BROAD MARSTON Worcs
144 SP 1446 5m N of Chipping Campden.
Loc, Pebworth CP.

BROADMAYNE Dorset
178 SY 7286 4m SE of Dorchester. CP, 598.
Dchstr RD. P Dchstr. Ch e, m. Sch p. W Dst
CC.

BROADMERE Hants
168 SU 6247 3m SSW of Basingstoke. Loc,
Farleigh Wallop CP.

BROADOAK Cornwall
186 SX 1662 4m ENE of Lostwithiel. CP,
185. Liskeard RD. Ch e, m. Sch pe. Bodmin
CC. See also Middle Taphouse, W Tphse.

BROAD OAK Dorset
177 SY 4396 3m NW of Bridport. Loc,
Symondsbury CP. Ch e.

BROAD OAK Dorset
178 ST 7812 7m NW of Blandford. Loc,
Sturminster Newton CP. P Stmnstr Ntn.
Ch m.

BROAD OAK Herefs
142 SO 4821 6m NNW of Monmouth. Loc,
Ross and Whitchurch RD. P HEREFORD.
Ch m. Hrfd CC.

BROADOAK Kent
173 TR 1661 3m NNE of Canterbury. Loc,
Sturry CP. P Cntrbry. Ch v.

BROADOAK Sussex (E)
183 TQ 6022 2m ENE of Heathfield. Loc,
Hthfld CP. P Hthfld. Ch b. Sch p.

BROAD OAK Sussex (E)
184 TQ 8219 6m W of Rye. Loc, Brede CP.
P Rye. Ch m.

BROADSTAIRS Kent
173 TR 3967 2m NNE of Ramsgate.
UD(Brdsts and St Peter's), 19,996. Thanet E
BC (Isle of Thnt CC). Resort with sandy
beaches and cliff walks. 1½m N, N Foreland
lighthouse. Many schs. Dickens lived at
Bleak Hse* in 1850.

BROADSTONE Dorset
179 SZ 0095 3m S of Wimborne. Loc,
Poole MB. P. Rsdntl suburb.

BROADSTONE Shrops
129 SO 5489 6m ESE of Ch Stretton. Loc,
Munslow CP.

BROAD STREET Kent
172 TQ 8256 4m E of Maidstone. Loc,
Hollingbourne CP.

BROAD TOWN Wilts
157 SU 0977 6m SW of Swindon. CP, 503.
Cricklade and Wootton Bassett RD. P Swndn.
Ch e. Sch pe. Chippenham CC.

BROADWAS Worcs
130 SO 7655 6m W of Worcester. CP, 251.
Martley RD. P WCSTR. Ch e, v. Sch pe.
Kidderminster CC.

BROADWATER Herts
147 TL 2422 2m S of Stevenage. Loc,
Stvnge UD. On B197, formerly A1.

BROADWAY Som
177 ST 3215 3m W of Ilminster. CP, 393.
Chard RD. Ch e, v. Sch pe. Yeovil CC.

BROADWAY Worcs
144 SP 0937 5m SE of Evesham. CP, 2,722.
Eveshm RD. P. Ch e, c, m, r. Sch p, pr. S
Worcs CC. Famous vllge of Cotswold stone.
Hses mostly Ggn. Ch Vctrn. To E, look-out
twr on steep hill.

BROADWELL Glos
144 SP 2027 1m NNE of Stow-on-the-Wold.
CP, 328. N Cotswold RD. P
Moreton-in-Marsh. Ch e. Sch pe. Cirencester
and Tewkesbury CC.

BROADWELL Oxon
157 SP 2504 4m NE of Lechlade. CP, 134.
Witney RD. P Lchlde, Glos. Ch e.
Mid-Oxon CC (Banbury). Splendid Nmn ch;
13c spire.

BROADWELL Warwicks
132 SP 4565 4m NE of Southam. Loc,
Leamington Hastings CP. P Rugby.

BROADWELL LANE END Glos
142 SO 5811 5m E of Monmouth. Loc,
W Dean CP. W Dn RD. P Coleford. Sch p.
W Glos CC.

BROADWEY Dorset
178 SY 6683 3m N of Weymouth. Loc,
Wmth and Melcombe Regis MB. P Wmth.

BROADWINDSOR Dorset
177 ST 4302 4m S of Crewkerne. CP, 919.
Beaminster RD. P Bmnstr. Ch e, b, c, m, v.
Sch pe. W Dst CC. See also Blackdown,
Drimpton, Kittwhistle.

BROADWOOD-KELLY Devon
175 SS 6105 7m NNE of Okehampton.
CP(Broadwoodkelly), 181. Okhmptn RD.
P Winkleigh. Ch e. W Dvn CC (Torrington).
See also Ingleigh Grn, Splatt.

BROADWOODWIDGER Devon
175 SX 4189 6m ENE of Launceston. CP,
589. Holsworthy RD. P Lifton. Ch e, b, m.
Sch p. W Dvn CC (Tavistock). See also
Grinacombe Moor, Rexon.

BROBURY Herefs
142 SO 3444 7m E of Hay-on-Wye. CP, 20.
Weobley RD. Ch e. Leominster CC.

BROCKBRIDGE Hants
180 SU 6118 4m E of Bishop's Waltham.
Loc, Droxford RD. Petersfield CC.

BROCKDISH Norfolk
137 TM 2179 6m E of Diss. CP, 416.
Depwade RD. P Dss. Ch e, m. Sch pe.
S Nflk CC. See also Thorpe Abbotts.

BROCKENHURST Hants
180 SU 3002 15m ENE of Bournemouth.
CP, 2,661. New Forest RD. P.
Ch e2, b, m, r. Sch pe, s. Nw Frst CC. See
also Balmerlawn, Setley.

BROCKFORD STREET Suffolk (E)
136 TM 1166 5m SSW of Eye. Loc,
Wetheringsett-cum-Brckfd CP. Ch v.

BROCKHALL Northants
132, 133 SP 6362 4m E of Daventry. CP,
29. Dvntry RD. Ch e. Dvntry CC (S Nthnts).
M1 motorway runs between vllge and Grand
Union Canal.

BROCKHAM Surrey
170 TQ 1949 2m E of Dorking. Loc, Dkng
UD. P(Brckhm Grn), Betchworth.

BROCKHAMPTON Glos
144 SP 0322 5m E of Cheltenham. Loc,
Sevenhampton CP. P Chltnhm. Ch b.

BROCKHAMPTON Herefs
130 SO 6855 2m E of Bromyard. CP, 111.
Brmyd RD. Ch e. Sch p. Leominster CC. B.
Pk (NT), Ggn hse with early Gothic revival
chpl alongside. In same grnds, Lr B. (NT)*,
14c moated mnr hse and rems of 12c chpl.

BROCKHAMPTON Herefs
142 SO 5831 7m SE of Hereford. CP, 225.

Ross and Whitchurch RD. P HRFD. Ch e.
Sch pe. Hrfd CC. See also Fawley Chpl.

BROCKHOLES Yorks (W)
102 SE 1511 3m S of Huddersfield. Loc,
Holmfirth UD. P Hddsfld.

BROCKLESBY Lincs (L)
104 TA 1411 3m SW of Immingham. CP,
178. Caistor RD. P Habrough. Ch e. Sch p.
Gainsborough CC. Estate vllge at gates of B.
Pk, seat of Pelham family (Earls of
Yarborough) since 1603. Present hse 18c
and 19c. Plhm monmts in ch. Family
mausoleum* by Wyatt in grnds by
Capability Brown. See also Caistor.

BROCKLEY Som
155, 165 ST 4767 3m NE of Congresbury.
CP, 225. Long Ashton RD. Ch e. N Som CC.
See also Chelvey.

BROCKLEY GREEN Suffolk (W)
149 TL 8254 6m NNW of Long Melford.
Loc, Brckly CP. Thingoe RD. P Bury St
Edmunds. Ch b. Bury St Eds CC.

BROCKTON Shrops
118 SJ 3104 6m ESE of Welshpool. Loc,
Worthen CP. Ch b.

BROCKTON Shrops
119 SJ 7203 3m SSW of Shifnal. Loc,
Sutton Maddock CP.

BROCKTON Shrops
129 SO 3285 2m S of Bishop's Cstle. Loc,
Lydbury N CP. Ch m.

BROCKTON Shrops
129 SO 5793 5m SW of Much Wenlock. Loc,
Bridgnorth RD. P Mch Wnlck. Sch pe.
Ludlow CC.

BROCKWEIR Glos
155, 156 SO 5401 5m N of Chepstow. Loc,
Hewelsfield CP. P Chpstw. Ch b, m. Sch p.

BROCKWOOD Hants
168 SU 6226 8m WNW of Petersfield. Loc,
Bramdean CP.

BROCKWORTH Glos
143, 144 SO 8916 4m E of Gloucester. CP,
6,820. Glcstr RD. P GLCSTR. Ch e, c, r.
Sch i, j, p, s. W Glos CC (Glcstr BC). Ch has
Nmn central twr. Textile factory.
Cheese-rolling down Cooper's Hill on Whit
Monday.

BROCTON Staffs
119 SJ 9619 4m SE of Stafford. CP, 778.
Stffd RD. P STFFD. Stffd and Stone CC.
On W edge of Cannock Chase.

BRODSWORTH Yorks (W)
103 SE 5007 5m WNW of Doncaster. CP,
2,816. Dncstr RD. P Dncstr. Ch e. Sch pe.
Don Valley CC.

BROGBOROUGH Beds
147 SP 9638 W of Ampthill. Loc,
Ampthll RD. P BEDFORD. Mid-Beds CC.
Large brickworks beside M1.

BROKENBOROUGH Wilts
156, 157 ST 9189 2m NW of Malmesbury.
CP, 413. Mlmsbry RD. P Mlmsbry. Ch e.
Chippenham CC.

BROKEN CROSS Ches
110 SJ 6873 2m E of Northwich. Loc,
Rudheath CP. Nthwch RD. Ch m.
Nthwch CC.

BROKEN CROSS Ches
110 SJ 8973 2m W of Macclesfield. Loc,
Mcclsfld MB. P Mcclsfld.

BROMBOROUGH Ches
100, 109 SJ 3481 5m SSE of Birkenhead.
Loc, Bebington MB. P Wirral.

BROME Suffolk (E)
136 TM 1376 2m NNW of Eye. CP, 230.
Hartismere RD. Ch e. Eye CC.

BROME STREET Suffolk (E)
137 TL 1576 2m NNE of Eye. Loc,
Hartismere RD. Eye CC.

BROMESWELL Suffolk (E)
150 TM 3050 2m ENE of Woodbridge. CP,
274. Deben RD. Ch e. Sudbury and
Wdbrdge CC. To SE, Wdbrdge Airfield.

BROMFIELD Cumb
82 NY 1746 5m W of Wigton. CP, 545.
Wgtn RD. P Carlisle. Ch e, v. Sch pe.
Penrith and the Border CC. See also
Blencogo, Langrigg.

BROMFIELD Shrops
129 SO 4876 2m NW of Ludlow. CP, 365.
Ldlw RD. P Ldlw. Ch e. Sch pe. Ldlw CC.

BROMHAM Beds
147 TL 0051 3m WNW of Bedford. CP,
2,722. Bdfd RD. P BDFD. Ch e, b. Sch ie, j.
Bdfd CC. Ch: 15c brass.

BROMHAM Wilts
157 ST 9665 4m SSW of Calne. CP, 1,524.
Devizes RD. P Chippenham. Ch e, m.
Sch p, pe. Dvzs CC. See also Chittoe,
Netherstreet, St Edith's Marsh. Ch
Beauchamp chpl, 1492.

BROMLEY London
161 TQ 3782 5m ENE of Charing Cross.
Loc, Twr Hmlts LB. Bethnal Grn and Bow
BC (Poplar). Sometimes called
Bromley-by-Bow.

BROMLEY London
171 TQ 4069 9m SE of Charing Cross. LB,
304,357. P Kent. BCs: Beckenham,
Chislehurst, Orpington, Ravensbourne.
(CCs: Chslhst, Orpngtn; BCs: Bcknhm,
Brmly.) See also Bcknhm, Biggin Hill,
Chelsfield, Chslhst, Crystal Palace, Cudham,
Downe, Elmers End, Farnborough, Grn
Street Grn, Hayes, Keston, Leaves Grn,
Mottingham, Orpngtn, Penge, Petts Wd,
Pratt's Bottom, St Mary Cray, St Paul's
Cray, Shortlands, W Wickham.Rsdntl distr
and shopping centre.

BROMLEY CROSS Lancs
101 SD 7213 3m NNE of Bolton. Loc,
Turton UD. P Bltn. Darwen CC.

BROMLEY, GREAT Essex
149 TM 0826 SSW of Manningtree. See Gt
Brmly.

BROMLEY GREEN Kent
172, 184 TQ 9936 4m SSW of Ashford.
Loc, Ruckinge CP. P Ashfd.

BROMPTON Yorks (N)
91 SE 3796 2m NNE of Northallerton. CP,
1,587. Nthlltn RD. P Nthlltn. Ch e, m2.
Sch p. Richmond CC.

BROMPTON Yorks (N)
93 SE 9482 7m SW of Scarborough. CP,
571. Scbrgh RD. P(Brmptn-by-Sawdon),
Scbrgh. Ch e, m. Sch p. Scbrgh CC (Scbrgh
and Whitby). See also Sawdon.

BROMPTON-ON-SWALE Yorks (N)
91 SE 2199 3m ESE of Richmond. CP, 559.
Rchmnd RD. P Rchmnd. Ch e, m2. Sch pe.
Rchmnd CC. See also Citadilla.

BROMPTON RALPH Som
164 ST 0832 7m S of Watchet. CP, 199.
Williton RD. P Taunton. Ch e, v.

Bridgwater CC. 1m NE, Willett's Twr, folly of 1820 representing ruined ch.

BROMPTON REGIS Som
164 SS 9531 3m NE of Dulverton. CP, 442. Dlvtn RD. P Dlvtn. Ch e, m. Sch pe. Taunton CC. See also Bury, Withiel Florey.

BROMSASH Herefs
142, 143 SO 6424 3m E of Ross-on-Wye. Loc, Rss and Whitchurch RD. P Rss-on-Wye. Hereford CC.

BROMSBERROW Glos
143 SO 7434 3m SE of Ledbury. CP, 239 Newent RD. Ch e. Sch pe. W Glos CC.

BROMSBERROW HEATH Glos
143 SO 7333 3m SSE of Ledbury. Loc, Dymock CP. P Ldbry, Herefordshire.

BROMSGROVE Worcs
130, 131 SO 9670 9m ESE of Kidderminster. UD, 40,669 P. Brmsgrve and Redditch CC (Brmsgrve). See also Aston Fields, Blackwell, Bournheath, Catshill, Lickey, Lcky End, Rubery. Engineering wks. Ch: monmts, incl headstone depicting rly engine.

BROMSTEAD HEATH Staffs
119 SJ 7917 3m ESE of Newport. Loc, Gnosall CP.

BROMYARD Herefs
142, 143 SO 6554 13m NE of Hereford. CP, 1,680. Brmyd RD. P. Ch e, m, r, v. Sch i, j, s2. Leominster CC. Old mkt tn. Nmn ch. Many timbered hses.

BROMYARD DOWNS Herefs
129, 130 SO 6655 just NE of Bromyard. Loc, Norton CP. Brmyd RD. Ch m. Leominster CC. Hth and wds (NT) to E: panoramic view over Brmyd and surrounding country.

BRONDESBURY London
160 TQ 2484 4m NW of Charing Cross. Loc, Brent LB. Brnt E BC (Willesden E).

BROOK Hants
168 SU 3428 5m N of Romsey. Loc, Kings Somborne CP.

BROOK Hants
179 SU 2714 7m SW of Romsey. Loc, Bramshaw CP.

BROOK IOW
180 SZ 3983 4m SE of Yarmouth. Loc, Brighstone CP. P Newport. Ch e, m. To NW at Hanover Point, a submarine forest.

BROOK Kent
172, 173 184 TR 0644 4m ENE of Ashford. CP, 245. E Ashfd RD. P Ashfd. Ch e, b. Sch p. Ashfd CC. Downland vllge. Nmn ch with wall-paintings.

BROOK Surrey
169 SU 9338 4m SW of Godalming. Loc, Witley CP. P Gdlmng.

BROOKE Norfolk
137 TM 2899 7m SSE of Norwich. CP, 695. Loddon RD. P NRWCH, NOR 37W. Ch e, b, m. Sch pe. S Nflk CC.

BROOKE Rutland
122 SK 8405 2m SSW of Oakham. CP, 37. Oakhm RD. Ch e. Rtlnd and Stamford CC. Tiny vllge on a hillside. Ch has four-square 13c twr, 12c interior.

BROOKHOUSE Lancs
89, 94 SD 5464 4m ENE of Lancaster. Loc, Caton-w-Littledale CP. Ch e, m. Ch e is ch of Caton.

BROOKHOUSE Yorks (W)
103 SK 5189 6m ESE of Rotherham. Loc, Thurcroft CP.

BROOKHOUSE GREEN Ches
110 SJ 8161 3m WSW of Congleton. Loc, Smallwood CP. Ch m.

BROOKLAND Kent
184 TQ 9825 6m NE of Rye. CP, 444. Romney Marsh RD. P Rmny Msh. Ch e, m. Sch pe. Folkestone and Hythe CC. Ch has curious detached timber bell twr and Nmn lead font.

BROOKMANS PARK Herts
160 TL 2403 2m NNW of Potters Bar. Loc, N Mymms CP. Hatfield RD. P Htfld. Ch c. Welwyn and Htfld CC (Hertford). Rsdntl.

BROOKSBY Leics
121, 122 SK 6716 5m WSW of Melton Mowbray. Loc, Hoby w Rotherby CP. Ch e. B. Hall, now agricultural college, once seat

of Villiers family, famous in early Stuart times. Later tenants: Ld Cardigan; Admiral Ld Beatty.

BROOK STREET Essex
161 TQ 5792 1m W of Brentwood. Loc, Brntwd UD.

BROOKTHORPE Glos
143 SO 8312 4m S of Gloucester. CP(Brkthpe-w-Whaddon), 302. Glcstr RD. P GLCSTR. Ch e. Stroud CC.

BROOKWOOD Surrey
169 SU 9457 4m W of Woking. Loc, Wkng UD. P Wkng. Largest cemetery in England. To W, staircase of locks on former Basingstoke Canal.

BROOM Beds
147 TL 1742 2m SW of Biggleswade. Loc, Southill CP. P Bgglswde. Ch m.

BROOM Co Durham
85 NZ 2441 2m W of Durham. Loc, Brandon and Byshottles UD.

BROOM Warwicks
144 SP 0953 7m W of Stratford. Loc, Bidford-on-Avon CP. P Alcester.

BROOME Norfolk
137 TM 3591 1m NE of Bungay. CP, 424. Loddon RD. P Bngy, Suffolk. Ch e, m. S Nflk CC.

BROOME Shrops
129 SO 4080 2m WSW of Craven Arms. Loc, Hopesay CP.

BROOME Worcs
130, 131 SO 9078 4m S of Stourbridge. CP, 314. Kidderminster RD. Ch e. Kddrmnstr CC.

BROOMEDGE Ches
101 SJ 7086 4m WSW of Altrincham. Loc, Lymm UD. P Lmm.

BROOMER'S CORNER Sussex (W)
182 TQ 1221 4m SE of Billingshurst. Loc, Shipley CP.

BROOMFIELD Essex
148, 161, 162 TL 7010 2m N of Chelmsford. CP, 2,695. Chlmsfd RD. P Chlmsfd. Ch e, m2. Sch p, s. Braintree CC (Chlmsfd).

BROOMFIELD Kent
172 TQ 8352 5m ESE of Maidstone. CP, 546. Hollingbourn RD. Ch e. Mdstne CC. See also Kingswood.

BROOMFIELD Kent
173 TR 1966 2m SE of Herne Bay. Loc, Hne Bay UD. P Hne Bay.

BROOMFIELD Som
165 ST 2232 6m SW of Bridgwater. CP, 207. Brdgwtr RD. P Brdgwtr. Ch e. Brdgwtr CC.

BROOMFLEET Yorks (E)
98 SE 8827 9m S of Mkt Weighton. CP, 290. Howden RD. P Brough. Ch e, m. Hdn CC.

BROOMHAUGH Nthmb
77 NZ 0161 3m SE of Corbridge. CP(Brmhgh and Riding), 648. Hexham RD. Sch p. Hxhm CC. See also Rdng Mill.

BROOM HILL Dorset
179 SU 0302 2m NE of Wimborne. Loc, Holt CP. Ch m.

BROOMHILL Nthmb
71 NU 2401 2m SSW of Amble. Loc, E Chevington CP. Ch m, r, v. Sch p.

BROOMIELAW Co Durham
84 NZ 0918 3m ENE of Barnard Cstle. Loc, Streatlam and Stainton CP. Bnd Cstle RD. Bishop Auckland CC.

BROSELEY Shrops
118, 119 SJ 6701 3m ENE of Much Wenlock. CP. Bridgnorth RD. P. Ch e, b, c, r. Sch pe. Ludlow CC. Former centre of coal and iron industries and a mnfg tn; importance has dwindled.

BROTHERTOFT Lincs (H)
114 TF 2746 4m WNW of Boston. CP, 407. Bstn RD. Ch e. Sch p2. Holland w Bstn CC.

BROTHERTON Yorks (W)
97 SE 4825 3m E of Castleford. CP, 741. Osgoldcross RD. Ch e, m, v. Sch p. Goole CC.

BROTTON Yorks (N)
86 NZ 6819 2m ESE of Saltburn. UD(Skelton and Brttn), 15,083. P Sltbn-by-the-Sea. Cleveland and Whitby CC (Clvlnd). Iron-mining tn.

BROUGH Derbys
111 SK 1882 9m NNW of Bakewell.
CP(Brgh and Shatton), 150. Chapel en le
Frith RD. High Peak CC. Rems of Roman
fort.

BROUGH Notts
113 SK 8358 4m NE of Newark. Loc, S
Collingham CP. Ch e. Site of Roman
Crocolana on Fosse Way; some Roman rems
found.

BROUGH Westm
84 NY 7914 4m NNE of Kirkby Stephen.
CP, 623. N Westm RD. P Kby Stphn.
Ch e, m. Sch p. Westm CC. Rems of 11c and
later moated cstle (A.M.) on site of Rmn tn;
restored mid-17c by Lady Anne Clifford.

BROUGH Yorks (E)
98 SE 9326 10m W of Hull. Loc,
Elloughton CP. P. Ch m. Sch p. On site of
Roman settlement where ferry across
Humber linked rd from Lincoln to York.
Indstrl.

BROUGHALL Shrops
118 SJ 5641 2m E of Whitchurch. Loc,
Whtchch Rural CP. N Shrops RD.
Oswestry CC.

BROUGH SOWERBY Westm
84 NY 7912 1m S of Brough. CP, 93.
N Westm RD. Ch m. Westm CC.

BROUGHTON Bucks
146 SP 8940 3m SSE of Newport Pagnell.
CP, 91. Npt Pgnll RD. Ch e. Buckingham
CC. Between M1 motorway and Milton
Keynes New Tn. Ch: wall-paintings.

BROUGHTON Bucks
146, 159 SP 8413 2m E of Aylesbury.
CP(Bierton-w-Brtn), 1,249. Aylesbury RD.
Aylesbury CC.

BROUGHTON Cumb
81, 82 NY 0731 3m W of Cockermouth. CP,
1,421. Cckrmth RD. Ch e, b, f, m2. Sch p.
Workington CC.

BROUGHTON Hants
168 SU 3033 8m SSW of Andover. CP, 889.
Romsey and Stockbridge RD. P Stckbrdge.
Ch e, b, m. Sch p. Winchester CC. 17c
dovecote in churchyard.

BROUGHTON Hunts
134 TL 2877 5m NE of Huntingdon. CP,
227, St Ives RD. P HNTNGDN. Ch e, b.
Hunts CC.

BROUGHTON Lancs
94 SD 5235 4m N of Preston. CP, 532.
Prstn RD. P Prstn. Ch e, r2. Sch pe.
S Fylde CC.

BROUGHTON Lincs (L)
104 SE 9608 3m WNW of Brigg. CP, 2,764.
Glanford Brgg RD. P Brgg. Ch e, m. Sch p.
Brgg and Scunthorpe CC (Brgg).

BROUGHTON Northants
133 SP 8375 3m SW of Kettering. CP,
1,570. Kttrng RD. P Kttrng. Ch e, v. Sch p.
Kttrng CC.

BROUGHTON Oxon
145 SP 4238 3m SW of Banbury. CP, 158.
Bnbry RD. P Bnbry. Ch e. Bnbry CC.
Cstle*, 14c-16c.

BROUGHTON Yorks (N)
86 NZ 5406 2m SE of Stokesley. CP(Gt and
Lit Brghtn), 597. Stksly RD. Ch m.
Richmond CC.

BROUGHTON Yorks (N)
92 SE 7673 1m NW of Malton. CP, 127.
Mltn RD. Thirsk and Mltn CC.

BROUGHTON Yorks (W)
95 SD 9451 3m W of Skipton. CP, 107.
Skptn RD. Ch e, r. Skptn CC.

BROUGHTON ASTLEY Leics
132 SP 5292 8m SSW of Leicester. CP,
1,660. Lutterworth RD. P LCSTR. Ch e, b.
Sch pe. Blaby CC (Harborough). See also
Primethorpe.

BROUGHTON GIFFORD Wilts
166 ST 8763 4m NNE of Trowbridge. CP,
656. Bradford and Melksham RD. P
Mlkshm. Ch e, b, m. Sch pe. Westbury CC.
See also Norrington Cmmn.

BROUGHTON HACKETT Worcs
143, 144 SO 9254 5m E of Worcester. CP,
136. Pershore RD. Ch e. S Worcs CC.

BROUGHTON IN FURNESS Lancs
88 SD 2187 5m NNE of Millom. Loc,
Brghtn W CP. N Lonsdale RD. P. Ch e, m.
Sch pe. Morecambe and Lnsdle CC. Mkt tn
overlooking Duddon estuary. Tree-lined mkt
square.

BROUGHTON MILLS Lancs
88 SD 2290 7m SW of Coniston. Loc,
Brghtn W CP. N Lonsdale RD. Morecambe
and Lnsdle CC.

BROUGHTON MOOR Cumb
81, 82 NY 0533 2m SE of Maryport. CP,
976. Cockermouth RD. P Mrpt. Ch e, m2.
Sch p. Workington CC.

BROUGHTON POGGS Oxon
157 SP 2303 3m NNE of Lechlade.
CP(Filkins and Brghtn Pggs), 482. Witney
RD. Ch e. Mid-Oxon CC (Banbury).

BROWN CANDOVER Hants
168 SU 5739 9m NE of Winchester. Loc,
Candovers CP. Basingstoke RD. P Alresford.
Ch e. Bsngstke CC. Ch: 16c brass of
husband and wife.

BROWN EDGE Staffs
110 SJ 9053 6m NNE of Stoke-on-Trent.
CP. Leek RD. P Stke-on-Trnt. Ch e.
Sch p, pe. Lk CC.

BROWNHILLS Staffs
120 SK 0405 5m NE of Walsall.
UD(Aldridge-Brnhlls), 88,475. P Wlsll. A-B
BC (Wlsll N). Mining and general industry.

BROWNSHILL Glos
156, 157 SO 8802 3m SE of Stroud. Loc,
Chalford CP. P Strd.

BROWNSTON Devon
187, 188 SX 6952 5m SE of Ivybridge. Loc,
Modbury CP. Ch e.

BROXA Yorks (N)
93 SE 9491 6m WNW of Scarborough. CP,
19. Scbrgh RD. Scbrgh CC (Scbrgh and
Whitby).

BROXBOURNE Herts
161 TL 3607 3m N of Cheshunt. Loc,
Hoddersdon UD. P.

BROXTED Essex
148 TL 5727 3m SW of Thaxted. CP, 510.
Dunmow RD. P Dnmw. Ch e. Saffron
Walden CC.

BROXTON Ches
109 SJ 4953 8m NNW of Whitchurch. CP,
444. Tarvin RD. P CHESTER. Ch m.
Nantwich CC. See also Fuller's Moor.

BROXWOOD Herefs
142 SO 3654 5m ESE of Kington. Loc,
Pembridge CP. P Leominster. Ch r, v.

BRUERA Ches
109 SJ 4360 4m SSE of Chester. Loc,
Buerton CP. Chstr RD. Ch e. City of Chstr CC.

BRUISYARD Suffolk (E)
137 TM 3266 3m ENE of Framlingham. CP,
102. Blyth RD. P Saxmundham. Ch e. Eye
CC.

BRUISYARD STREET Suffolk (E)
137 TM 3365 3m ENE of Framlingham.
Loc, Brsyd CP.

BRUNDALL Norfolk
126 TG 3208 6m E of Norwich. CP, 1,119.
Blofield and Flegg RD. P NRWCH, NOR
86Z. Ch e. Sch p. Yarmouth CC.

BRUNDISH Suffolk (E)
137 TM 2669 4m NNW of Framlingham.
CP, 228. Hartismere RD. P Woodbridge.
Ch e. Eye CC.

BRUNSWICK VILLAGE Nthmb
78 NZ 2372 5m N of Newcastle.
CP(Brnswck), 909. Cstle Ward RD. P
NCSTLE UPON TYNE. Ch m. Sch p.
Hexham CC.

BRUNTINGTHORPE Leics
132, 133 SP 6089 5m NE of Lutterworth.
CP, 918. Lttrwth RD. P Rugby,
Warwickshire. Ch e, b. Blaby CC
(Harborough).

BRUNTON Nthmb
71 NU 2024 7m N of Alnwick. Loc,
Newton-by-the-Sea CP. Alnwck RD.
Berwick-upon-Tweed CC.

BRUSHFORD Devon
175 SS 6707 9m NE of Okehampton. CP,
53. Crediton RD. Ch e. Tiverton. CC
(Torrington). A ch and a farm.

BRUSHFORD Som
164 SS 9225 2m SSE of Dulverton. CP,
495. Dlvtn RD. P Dlvtn. Ch e, m. Sch pe.
Taunton CC.

BRUTON Som
166 ST 6834 7m SE of Shepton Mallet. CP,
1,700. Wincanton RD. P. Ch e, m. Sch p, s.

Wells CC. See also Redlynch, Wyke Champflower. Blt mainly of Doulting stone. Fine ch. Rems of Augustinian abbey and its dovecote (NT). King's Sch and Sexey's Sch founded in Tdr times. Tdr almshouses.

BRYANSTON Dorset
178 ST 8706 1m W of Blandford. CP, 466. Blndfd RD. P Blndfd Forum. Ch e. N Dst CC. Brnstn Sch, in hse blt by the Portmans in landscaped grnds, 1890.

BRYHER Isles of Scilly
189 SV 8715, CP, 66. Is of S RD. P. Ch e, b. Sch p. St Ives CC. The smallest of the populated islands.

BRYMPTON Som
177 ST 5215 2m W of Yeovil. CP, 1,427. Yvl RD. Ch e. Yvl CC. See also Thorne. B. D'Evercy*, 16c-18c hse of Ham stone, with adjoining ch and chantry.

BRYN Lancs
100 SD 5700 3m SSW of Wigan. Loc, Ashton-in-Makerfield UD. P Ashtn-in-Mkfld, Wgn.

BRYN GATES Lancs
100 SD 5901 3m SSE of Wigan. Loc, Ashton-in-Makerfield UD.

BUBBENHALL Warwicks
132 SP 3672 4m SSE of Coventry. CP, 294. Warwick RD. P Cvntry. Ch e. Sch pe. Wrwck and Leamington CC.

BUBNELL Derbys
111 SK 2472 3m NNE of Bakewell. CP(Baslow and Bubnell), 1,007. Bkwll RD. W Derbys CC.

BUBWITH Yorks (E)
97, 98 SE 7136 7m ENE of Selby. CP, 661. Howden RD. P Slby. Ch e, m. Sch p. Hdn CC. See also Breighton, Willitoft. On R Derwent. Old many-arched br. EE ch.

BUCKABANK Cumb
83 NY 3749 5m SSW of Carlisle. Loc, Dalston CP.

BUCKDEN Hunts
134 TL 1967 4m SW of Huntingdon. CP, 1,158. St Neots RD. P HNTNGDN. Ch e, bc, m. Sch pe. Hunts CC. Rems of B. Palace*, ancient palace of Bishops of Lincoln. Catherine of Aragon virtually a prisoner here.

BUCKDEN Yorks (W)
90 SD 9477 9m SSE of Hawes. CP, 192. Skipton RD. Ch m. Skptn CC. See also Cray, Hubberholme.

BUCKENHAM Norfolk
126 TG 3505 8m ESE of Norwich. Loc, Strumpshaw CP. Ch e.

BUCKERELL Devon
176 ST 1200 3m W of Honiton. CP, 195. Hntn RD. P Hntn. Ch e, v. Hntn CC.

BUCKFAST Devon
187, 188 SX 7467 1m N of Buckfastleigh. Loc, Bckfstlgh UD. P Bckfstlgh. Abbey blt by monks themselves first half 20c. Wool textile factory. Quarry. Caravan site.

BUCKFASTLEIGH Devon
187, 188 SX 7366 5m NW of Totnes. UD, 2,657. P. Ttns CC. See also Buckfast. Mkt and mnfg tn. Dart Valley Rly Museum; trains run between B. and Ttns in summer.

BUCKHORN WESTON Dorset
166 ST 7524 4m SE of Wincanton. CP, 324. Shaftesbury RD. P Gillingham. Ch e. Sch p. N Dst CC.

BUCKHURST HILL Essex
161 TQ 4193 2m W of Chigwell. Loc, Chgwll UD. P. Rsdntl.

BUCKINGHAM Bucks
146 SP 6933 11m W of Bletchley. MB, 5,075. P(BCKNGHM). Bcknghm CC. See also Gawcott. Once the county tn, its importance has declined; charm is retained. Chantry chpl, with Norman doorway (NT). 2½m NNW, Stowe School: see Chackmore.

BUCKLAND Berks
158 SU 3497 4m ENE of Faringdon. CP, 539. Frngdn RD. P Frngdn. Ch e, b, r. Sch pe. Abingdon CC.

BUCKLAND Bucks
146, 159 SP 8812 4m E of Aylesbury. CP, 464. Aylesbury RD. Ch e, m, v. Aylesbury CC.

BUCKLAND Devon
187, 188 SX 6743 4m W of Kingsbridge. Loc, Thurlestone CP. Ch m.

BUCKLAND Glos
144 SP 0836 1m SW of Broadway. CP, 219.

Cheltenham RD. Ch e. Cirencester and Tewkesbury CC. See also Laverton. Interesting ch of many periods. 15c rectory*.

BUCKLAND Herts
148 TL 3533 4m S of Royston. CP, 279. Braughing RD. P Buntingford. Ch e. E Herts CC. See also Chipping.

BUCKLAND Surrey
170 TQ 2250 2m W of Reigate. CP, 650. Dorking and Horley RD. P Betchworth. Ch e. Sch pe. Dkng CC.

BUCKLAND BREWER Devon
163 SS 4120 4m SSW of Bideford. CP, 515. Bdfd RD. P Bdfd. Ch e, b, m3. Sch p. N Dvn CC (Torrington). See also Eckworthy.

BUCKLAND COMMON Bucks
159 SP 9207 3m S of Tring. Loc, Cholesbury and St Leonards CP. Ch b.

BUCKLAND DINHAM Som
166 ST 7551 3m NNW of Frome. CP, 351. Frme RD. P Frme. Ch e, m. Sch pe. Wells CC.

BUCKLAND FILLEIGH Devon
175 SS 4609 8m ENE of Holsworthy. CP, 150. Torrington RD. Ch e. W Dvn CC (Trrngtn). Ch and Bcklnd Hse, in pk with lake.

BUCKLAND IN THE MOOR Devon
175, 187, 188 SX 7273 3m NW of Ashburton. CP, 48. Newton Abbot RD. Ch e. Totnes CC. On edge of Dartmoor; well known beauty spot with thatched cottages.

BUCKLAND MONACHORUM Devon
187 SX 4968 4m S of Tavistock. CP, 2,687. Tvstck RD. P Yelverton. Ch e, b. Sch pe. W Dvn CC (Tvstck). See also Clearbrook, Crapstone, Miltoncombe, Ylvrtn. Vllge of stone cottages round ch, with modern accretions. lm S, Bcklnd Abbey (NT)*, former home of the Drakes.

BUCKLAND NEWTON Dorset
178 ST 6805 8m SSE of Sherborne. CP, 470. Dorchester RD. P Dchstr. Ch e, c. Sch pe. W Dst CC. See also Duntish, Henley.

BUCKLAND ST MARY Som
177 ST 2613 5m NW of Chard. CP, 434. Chd RD. P Chd. Ch e, b. Sch pe. Yeovil CC.

BUCKLAND-TOUT-SAINTS Devon
187, 188 SX 7546 2m NE of Kingsbridge. CP, 155. Kngsbrdge RD. Ch e. Totnes CC. See also Goveton.

BUCKLEBURY Berks
158 SU 5570 6m ENE of Newbury. CP. Bradfield RD. P Reading. Ch e, b, c. Sch pe. Nbry CC. See also Chpl Row, Upr Bcklbry. B. Cmmn to S is well known beauty spot.

BUCKLER'S HARD Hants
180 SU 4000 7m E of Brockenhurst. Loc, Beaulieu CP. Single street of wide grass verges with 18c cottages. In 18c, busy shipyard. Maritime museum.

BUCKLESHAM Suffolk (E)
150 TM 2441 5m ESE of Ipswich. CP, 353. Deben RD. P Ipswch. Ch e, m. Sch p. Sudbury and Woodbridge CC.

BUCKLOW HILL Ches
101 SJ 7383 3m NNW of Knutsford. Loc, Bcklw RD. Ch v. Kntsfd CC.

BUCKMINSTER Leics
122 SK 8822 8m ENE of Melton Mowbray. CP, 441. Mltn and Belvoir RD. P Grantham, Lincs. Ch e, m. Sch p. Mltn CC. See also Sewstern. Largely Vctrn estate vllge.

BUCKNALL Lincs (L)
113 TF 1668 4m NNW of Woodhall Spa. CP, 239. Horncastle RD. P LINCOLN. Ch e. Sch p. Hncstle CC.

BUCKNELL Oxon
145, 146 SP 5525 2m NW of Bicester. CP, 318. Ploughley RD. P Bcstr. Ch e. Banbury CC (Henley).

BUCKNELL Shrops
129 SO 3573 4m E of Knighton. CP, 455. Clun and Bishop's Cstle RD. P. Ch e. Sch pe. Ludlow CC.

BUCKRIDGE Worcs
130 SO 7274 4m W of Bewdley. Loc, Rock CP.

BUCK'S CROSS Devon
174 SS 3422 7m W of Bideford. Loc, Woolfardisworthy CP. P Bdfd.

BUCKS GREEN Sussex (W)
182 TQ 0832 6m WNW of Horsham. Loc, Rudgwick CP. P Hshm.

BUCKS HILL Herts
160 TL 0500 4m NW of Watford. Loc,
Sarratt CP. P King's Langley.

BUCK'S MILLS Devon
174 SS 3523 6m W of Bideford. Loc, Bdfd
RD. Ch e, m. N Dvn CC. Comparatively
quiet cliffside vllge with steep street;
footpath winds down to quay. Old limekiln
at bottom.

BUCKTON Herefs
129 SO 3873 6m E of Knighton. CP(Bcktn
and Coxall), 94. Leominster and Wigmore
RD. Lmnstr CC.

BUCKTON Nthmb
64, 71 NU 0838 3m NNW of Belford. Loc,
Kyloe CP. Norham and Islandshires RD.
Berwick-upon-Tweed CC.

BUCKWORTH Hunts
134 TL 1476 7m NW of Huntingdon. CP,
138. Hntngdn RD. P HNTNGDN. Ch e.
Hunts CC.

BUDBROOKE Warwicks
131 SP 2565 2m W of Warwick. CP, 705.
Wrwck RD. Ch e. Sch p. Wrwck and
Leamington CC. See also Hampton on the
Hill. To N, series of locks on Grand Union
Canal. To E, Wrwck bypass.

BUDBY Notts
112 SK 6170 3m NW of Ollerton.
CP(Perlethorpe cum Bdby), 332. Southwell
RD. Newark CC. Orig early 19c model vllge
in the Dukeries.

BUDD'S TITSON Cornwall
174 SS 2401 3m SE of Bude. Loc,
Marhamchurch CP. Ch m.

BUDE Cornwall
174 SS 2106 15m NNW of Launceston.
UD(Bde-Stratton), 5,629. P. N Cnwll CC.
See also Flexbury, Poughill. Resort.

BUDLAKE Devon
176 SS 9800 6m NE of Exeter. Loc, Broad
Clyst CP. P Extr. Mainly NT.

BUDLE Nthmb
71 NU 1535 2m W of Bamburgh. Loc,
Bmbrgh CP

BUDLEIGH SALTERTON Devon
176 SY 0682 4m E of Exmouth. UD, 4,139.
P. Hntn CC. See also Knowle. Quiet resort.

BUDOCK WATER Cornwall
190 SW 7832 2m W of Falmouth. Loc,
Bdck CP. Kerrier RD. P Flmth. Sch pe.
Flmth and Camborne CC. lm S, Penjerrick
Gdns*(sub-tropical plants, flowering
shrubs).

BUDWORTH, GREAT Ches
101 SJ 6677 2m N of Northwich. See Gt
Bdwth.

BUERTON Ches
110, 119 SJ 6843 6m SSE of Nantwich. CP,
426. Nntwch RD. Ch m2. Sch p. Nntwch
CC.

BUGBROOKE Northants
132, 133 SP 6757 5m WSW of
Northampton. CP, 1,184. Nthmptn RD.
P NTHMPTN. Ch e, b. Sch p, s. Daventry CC
(S Nthnts).

BUGLE Cornwall
185, 186 SX 0158 4m N of St Austell. Loc,
St Astll w Fowey MB. P St Astll. Truro CC.
In the heart of the china clay area.

BUGTHORPE Yorks (E)
97, 98 SE 7757 6m NNW of Pocklington.
CP, 165. Pcklngtn RD. P YORK. Ch e.
Sch pe. Howden CC. Blt round vllge grn.

BUILDWAS Shrops
118, 119 SJ 6304 3m NNE of Much
Wenlock. CP, 329. Atcham RD. P Telford.
Ch e. Sch p. Shrewsbury CC. Rems of 12c
abbey (A.M.) beside R Severn.

BULCOTE Notts
112, 121, 122 SK 6544 6m ENE of
Nottingham. CP, 194. Southwell RD. Ch e.
Newark CC.

BULFORD Wilts
167 SU 1643 2m NE of Amesbury. CP,
4,125. Amesbury RD. P Salisbury. Ch e, s, v.
Sch p2, pe. Slsbry CC. Large Army camp
nearby.

BULKELEY Ches
109 SJ 5354 8m WNW of Nantwich. CP,
214. Nntwch RD. P Malpas. Ch m. Nntwch
CC.

BULKINGTON Warwicks
132 SP 3986 6m NE of Coventry. Loc,
Bedworth UD. P Nuneaton.

BULKINGTON Wilts
167 ST 9458 4m WSW of Devizes. CP, 146.
Warminster and Westbury RD. P Dvzs.
Ch e, m. Wstbry CC. Large dairy wks.

BULKWORTHY Devon
174 SS 3914 7m NNE of Holsworthy. CP,
83. Bideford RD. Ch e, m. N Dvn CC
(Torrington).

BULLBROOK Berks
169 SU 8869 just E of Bracknell. Loc,
Brcknll CP. P Brcknll. Part of Brcknll New
Tn; bldngs incl Castrol Research
Laboratories and several blocks of flats and
shops.

BULLEY Glos
143 SO 7619 4m W of Gloucester. Loc,
Churcham CP. Ch e.

BULLINGTON Hants
168 SU 4541 6m ESE of Andover. CP, 105.
Andvr RD. Ch e. Winchester. CC (Basingstoke).

BULMER Essex
149 TL 8440 2m WSW of Sudbury. CP,
506. Halstead RD. P Sdbry, Suffolk. Ch e, c.
Sch pe. Saffron Walden CC.

BULMER Yorks (N)
92 SE 7067 6m WSW of Malton. CP, 176.
Mltn RD. P YORK. Ch e. Thirsk and Mltn
CC. Estate vllge. Cstle Howard(see
Coneysthorpe)1½m NE.

BULPHAN Essex
161 TQ 6385 6m SSE of Brentwood. Loc,
Thurrock UD. P Upminster. Thrrck BC
(CC).

BULWICK Northants
134 SP 9694 5m NE of Corby. CP, 175.
Oundle and Thrapston RD. P Cby. Ch e.
Sch pe. Wellingborough CC (Peterborough).

BUMBLE'S GREEN Essex
161 TL 4005 4m NW of Epping. Loc,
Nazeing CP.

BUNBURY Ches
109 SJ 5658 7m NW of Nantwich. CP, 833.
Nntwch RD. P Tarporley. Ch e, m2. Sch pe.
Nntwch CC.

BUNCTON Sussex (W)
182 TQ 1413 3m NW of Steyning. Loc,

Wiston CP. Ch e. Lies under S Downs to N of
Chanctonbury Ring, 779ft, well known S
Dns landmark topped by beech wd — see
also Washington.

BUNGAY Suffolk (E)
137 TM 3389 5m W of Beccles. UD, 3,961.
P. Lowestoft CC. Small mkt tn above
Waveney valley. Rems of 12c cstle* of the
Bigods. 17c mkt cross. Ggn hses. Printing
works.

BUNNY Notts
121, 122 SK 5829 7m S of Nottingham. CP,
570. Basford RD. P NTTNGHM. Ch e.
Sch pe. Rushcliffe CC. Large Dec and Perp
ch contains unusual monmt to Sir Thomas
Parkyns, the 'Wrestling Baronet' who also
blt the hall and sch.

BUNTINGFORD Herts
148 TL 3629 7m S of Royston. CP, 1,559.
Braughing RD. P. Ch e, c, r. Sch pe, s.
E Herts CC. Many old bldngs. 17c almshouses.

BUNWELL Norfolk
136 TM 1292 5m S of Wymondham. CP,
709. Depwade RD. P NORWICH,
NOR O1X. Ch e. Sch p. S Nflk CC. See also
Bnwll St.

BUNWELL STREET Norfolk
136 TM 1193 5m S of Wymondham. Loc,
Bnwll CP. Ch m.

BURBAGE Derbys
111 SK 0472 1m W of Buxton. Loc, Bxtn
MB. P Bxt. Ch e.

BURBAGE Leics
132 SP 4492 1m SE of Hickley. Loc, Hnckly
UD. P Hnckly. Hosiery wks.

BURBAGE Wilts
167 SU 2361 5m E of Pewsey. CP, 999. Psy
RD. P Marlborough. Ch e, m. Sch p. Devizes
CC. See also Durley, Stibb Grn.

BURCHETT'S GREEN Berks
159 SU 8381 3m W of Maidenhead. Loc,
Cookham RD. P Mdnhd. Sch pe. Windsor
and Mdnhm CC (Wndsr).

BURCOMBE Wilts
167 SU 0730 5m W of Salisbury. CP(Bcmbe
Without), 170. Slsbry and Wilton RD.
P Slsbry. Ch e. Slsbry CC.

BURCOT Oxon
158 SU 5696 4m E of Abingdon. Loc, Clifton Hampden CP. Ch e. Beside R Thames.

BURDALE Yorks (E)
92, 98 SE 8762 8m SE of Malton. Loc, Wharram CP. Norton RD. Howden CC.

BURDON, GREAT Co Durham
85 NZ 3116 2m NE of Darlington. See Gt Bdn.

BURES Essex and Suffolk
149 TL 9034 5m SSE of Sudbury. CP(Brs Hmlt), 388, Halstead RD; CP(Brs St Mary), 662, Melford RD. P(Brs, Suffolk). Ch e, b. Sch pe. Saffron Walden CC, Sdbry and Woodbridge CC. St Edmund crowned here, 855. To NE, St Stephen's Chpl, with 13c and 14c tombs of de Veres. 2m SE beside R Stour, Smallbridge Hall, visited by Elizabeth I, 1561.

BURFORD Oxon
144 SP 2512 7m W of Witney. CP(Bfd and Upton and Signet), 1,453. Witney RD. P. Ch e, b, f, m, r. Sch p, s. Mid-Oxon CC (Banbury). Handsome Cotswold tn with main st climbing side of Windrush valley. Large 'wool' ch at foot of tn. Tolsey Museum of local relics.

BURFORD Shrops
129 SO 5868 just W of Tenbury Wells. CP, 466. Ludlow RD. Ch e. Sch pe. Ldlw CC. Ch: monmts.

BURGESS HILL Sussex (E)
182 TQ 3119 9m N of Brighton. UD, 19,309. P. Mid-Sx CC (Lewes). Rsdntl area.

BURGH Suffolk (E)
150 TM 2351 3m WNW of Woodbridge. CP, 157. Deben RD. Ch e. Eye CC. Ch is away to NE, within ¼m of Clopton ch.

BURGH BY SANDS Cumb
75 NY 3259 5m WNW of Carlisle. CP, 821. Border RD . P Clsle. Ch e. Sch p. Penrith and the Bdr CC. See also Moorhouse, Thurstonfield. Ch blt with stones from Roman Wall. Edward I died here, 1307. (Monmt 1m N.)

BURGH CASTLE Suffolk (E)
126 TG 4805 3m WSW of Yarmouth. CP, 594. Lothingland RD. P Gt Ymth, Norfolk.

Ch e. Lowestoft CC. Walls of 3c fort of the Saxon Shore (A.M.). guarding former estuary, now marshes.

BURGHCLERE Hants
168 SU 4761 4m S of Newbury. CP, 1,121. Kingsclere and Whitchurch RD. P Nbry, Berks. Ch e, m. Sch p, s. Basingstoke CC. See also Old Bghclre. Sandham Memorial Chpl (NT)*; frescoes by Stanley Spencer.

BURGHFIELD Berks
158, 169 SU 6668 5m SW of Reading. CP, 2,323. Bradfield RD. P Rdng. Ch e, m. Sch ie, j, pe, s. Newbury CC.

BURGHFIELD COMMON Berks
158, 169 SU 6566 6m SW of Reading. Loc, Bghfld CP. P Rdng. Ch m, r.

BURGH HEATH Surrey
170 TQ 2457 3m SE of Epsom. Loc, Banstead UD. P Tadworth.

BURGHILL Herefs
142 SO 4744 4m NNW of Hereford. CP, 1,552. Hrfd RD. P HRFD. Ch e. Sch p. Leominster CC. See also Portway, Tillington, Tllngtn Cmmn.

BURGH LE MARSH Lincs (L)
114 TF 5065 4m WNW of Skegness. CP, 1,190. Spilsby RD. P Skgnss. Ch e, b, m. Sch pe. Horncastle CC. To SE, six-sailed windmill in working order.

BURGH NEXT AYLSHAM Norfolk
126 TG 2125 2m SE of Aylsham. Loc, Tuttington CP. P(Burgh), NORWICH, NOR 52Y. Ch e. Sch p.

BURGH ON BAIN Lincs (L)
105 TF 2286 7m W of Louth. CP, 108. Lth RD. P LINCOLN. Ch e. Lth CC.

BURGH ST MARGARET Norfolk
126 TG 4414 6m NW of Yarmouth. Loc, Fleggburgh CP. Blofield and Flegg RD. Ch e, b, m. Sch pe. Ymth CC. To E, Filby Broad.

BURGH ST PETER Norfolk
137 TM 4693 3m NE of Beccles. CP, 212. Loddon RD. P Bccls, Suffolk. Ch e, m. S Nflk CC.

BURGHWALLIS Yorks (W)
103 SE 5311 6m NNW of Doncaster. CP,

271. Dncstr RD. P Dncstr. Ch e, r. Don Valley CC.

BURHAM Kent
171, 172 TQ 7262 4m S of Rochester. CP, 1,501. Malling RD. P Rchstr. Ch e, m. Sch p, pe. Tonbridge and Mllng CC (Sevenoaks). See also Bluebell Hill.

BURITON Hants
181 SU 7320 2m S of Petersfield. CP, 644. Ptrsfld RD. P Ptrsfld. Ch e, m. Sch p. Ptrsfld CC. See also Nursted, Weston. Mnr hse, childhood home of Gibbon, the historian.

BURLAND Ches
110 SJ 6153 3m WNW of Nantwich. CP, 522. Nntwch RD. Ch m. Nntwch CC. See also Ravensmoor.

BURLAWN Cornwall
185 SW 9970 2m SSE of Wadebridge. Loc, St Breock CP. P Wdbrdge. Ch m.

BURLEIGH Berks
169 SU 9070 2m E of Bracknell. Loc, Winkfield CP.

BURLESCOMBE Devon
164 ST 0716 5m SW of Wellington. CP, 725. Tiverton RD. P Tvtn. Ch e. Sch pe. Tvtn CC. See also Appledore, Ayshford, Westleigh.

BURLESTON Dorset
178 SY 7794 6m ENE of Dorchester. CP, 39. Dchstr RD. Ch e. W Dst CC.

BURLEY Hants
179 SU 2103 4m ESE of Ringwood. CP, 1,613. Rngwd and Fordingbridge RD. P Rngwd. Ch e, c. Sch p. New Forest CC. See also Bisterne Close, Brly St, Picket Post.

BURLEY Rutland
122 SK 8810 2m ENE of Oakham. CP, 554. Oakhm RD. P Oakhm. Ch e. Rtlnd and Stamford CC. Small vllge on the heights; wide views. B.-on-the-Hill, large early 18c hse (exterior only*). S terrace gdn*.

BURLEYDAM Ches
110, 118, 119 SJ 6042 4m E of Whitchurch. Loc, Nantwich RD. P Whtchch, Salop. Ch e. Nntwch CC.

BURLEY GATE Herefs
142 SO 5947 7m NE of Hereford. Loc, Bromyard RD. P HRFD. Leominster CC.

BURLEY-IN-WHARFEDALE Yorks (W)
96 SE 1646 3m ESE of Ilkley. Loc, Ilkley UD. P Ilkley.

BURLEY STREET Hants
179 SU 2004 4m E of Ringwood. Loc, Brly CP. P Brly, Rngwd.

BURLEY WOODHEAD Yorks (W)
96 SE 1544 3m SE of Ilkley. Loc, Ilkley UD.

BURLTON Shrops
118 SJ 4526 4m WSW of Wem. Loc, Loppington CP. P Shrewsbury.

BURMARSH Kent
173 TR 1032 4m WSW of Hythe. CP, 247. Romney Marsh RD. P Rmny Msh. Ch e. Folkestone and Hthe CC.

BURMINGTON Warwicks
144 SP 2637 2m S of Shipston on Stour. CP, 132. Shpstn on Str RD. P Shpstn on Str. Ch e. Stratford-on-Avon CC (Strtfd).

BURN Yorks (W)
97 SE 5928 3m SSW of Selby. CP, 332. Slby RD. P Slby. Ch m. Barkston Ash CC.

BURNASTON Derbys
120, 121 SK 2832 5m WSW of Derby. CP. Repton RD. Belper CC.

BURNBANKS Westm
83 NY 5016 9m S of Penrith. Loc, Bampton CP.

BURNBY Yorks (E)
98 SE 8346 3m SE of Pocklington. Loc, Hayton CP. Ch e. B. Hall gdns* have fine lily ponds. Museum of sporting trophies.

BURNESIDE Westm
89 SD 5095 2m NNW of Kendal. Loc, S Westm RD. P Kndl. Ch e. Sch pe. Westm CC.

BURNESTON Yorks (N)
91 SE 3085 3m SE of Bedale. CP, 237. Bdle RD. P Bdle. Ch e, m. Sch pe. Thirsk and Malton CC.

BURNETT Som
155, 156 ST 6665 5m W of Bath. Loc, Compton Dando CP. Ch e.

BURNHAM Bucks
159 SU 9382 3m WNW of Slough. CP, 16,143. Eton RD. P. Ch e, c, m, r. Sch p, pe, s. Beaconsfield CC (S Bucks). See also Lent Rise. Largely rsdntl. Rems of 13c abbey, restored. To NE, B. Beeches, large wooded area owned by City of London; at W edge thereof, Dorney Wd (NT), at disposal of prime minister as residence of a minister of the crown.

BURNHAM Lincs (L)
104 TA 0517 3m SSE of Barton-upon-Humber. Loc, Thornton Curtis CP.

BURNHAM DEEPDALE Norfolk
125 TF 8044 7m W of Wells. Loc, Brancaster CP. Ch e. Sch pe. Ch has Saxon round twr and Nmn font carved with labours of the seasons.

BURNHAM GREEN Herts
147 TL 2616 3m NE of Welwyn Gdn Cty. Loc, Hertford RD. P Wlwn. Htfd and Stevenage CC (Htfd).

BURNHAM MARKET Norfolk
125 TF 8342 5m W of Wells. CP, 1,211. Docking RD. P King's Lynn. Ch e2, m, r, s, v. Sch p. NW Nflk CC (K's Lnn). Ggn hses flank wide main street. Ruins of Bnhm Sutton ch.

BURNHAM NORTON Norfolk
125 TF 8243 6m W of Wells. CP, 125. Docking RD. Ch e. NW Nflk CC (King's Lynn).

BURNHAM-ON-CROUCH Essex
162 TQ 9496 17m ESE of Chelmsford. UD, 4,546. P. Maldon CC. See also Ostend, Stoneyhills. Yachting and oyster fisheries. Formerly busy commercial port much used by sailing barges.

BURNHAM-ON-SEA Som
165 ST 3049 8m N of Bridgwater. UD, 12,281. P. Brdgwtr CC. See also Berrow, Highbridge. Small resort; indstrl development inland. Ch: altar orig commissioned by James II for Whitehall Palace. Modern RC ch, round, of white stone.

BURNHAM OVERY Norfolk
125 TF 8442 5m W of Wells. CP, 433. Docking RD. Ch e. NW Nflk CC (King's Lynn). See also Overy Staithe.

BURNHAM THORPE Norfolk
125 TF 8541 4m WSW of Wells. CP, 258. Docking RD. P King's Lynn. Ch e, m. NW Nflk CC (K's Lnn). Bthplce of Nelson, 1758. His father was rector.

BURNHILL GREEN Staffs
119 SJ 7800 5m SSE of Shifnal. Loc, Patshull CP. Seisdon RD. P Wolverhampton. SW Staffs CC (Brierley Hill); On Shrops border.

BURNHOPE Co Durham
85 NZ 1948 2m ENE of Lanchester. Loc, Lnchstr RD. P DRHM. Ch m2. Sch p. NW Drhm CC.

BURNISTON Yorks (N)
93 TA 0193 3m NW of Scarborough. CP, 556. Scbrgh RD. P Scbrgh. Ch b, m. Sch p. Scbrgh CC (Scbrgh and Whitby).

BURNLEY Lancs
95 SD 8332 22m N of Manchester. CB, 76,483. P. Bnly BC. Textiles, engineering, tyre mnfg etc. Some shift from txtls to engnrng and general industry. Some coal-mining. Wild Pennine country close at hand.

BURNOPFIELD Co Durham
78 NZ 1756 6m SW of Gateshead. Loc, Stanley UD. P NEWCASTLE UPON TYNE.

BURNSALL Yorks (W)
90 SE 0361 7m NNE of Skipton. CP, 115. Skptn RD. P Skptn. Ch e, m. Sch pe. Skptn CC. Stone vllge with many-arched br over R Wharfe. 3m S, rems of Barden Twr*, 15c fortified twr hse.

BURNT OAK London
160 TQ 2091 2m NW of Hendon. Loc, Barnet LB. Hndn N BC.

BURNTWOOD Staffs
120 SK 0609 3m W of Lichfield. CP, 12,085. Lchfld RD. P Walsall. Ch e, m3, v. Sch p5. Lchfld and Tamworth CC. See also Chase Terrace, Chasetown.

BURNT YATES Yorks (W)
91 SE 2561 5m NW of Harrogate. Loc, Clint CP. P Hrrgte. Ch e. Sch pe.

BURPHAM Sussex (W)
182 TQ 0408 2m NE of Arundel. CP, 223. Worthing RD. P Arndl. Ch e. Arndl CC

(Arndl and Shoreham). Views: N to Arndl, S to Downs. Ch mainly Nmn.

BURRADON Nthmb
71 NT 9806 5m WNW of Rothbury. Loc, Netherton CP.

BURRADON Nthmb
78 NZ 2772 5m NNE of Newcastle. Loc, Longbenton UD. P Dudley.

BURRATON Cornwall
187 SX 4167 4m ESE of Callington. Loc, St Dominick CP. Ch m.

BURRIDGE Hants
180 SU 5110 5m NW of Fareham. Loc, Frhm UD. P SOUTHAMPTON.

BURRILL Yorks (N)
91 SE 2387 2m WSW of Bedale. CP(Brrll w Cowling), 104. Bdle RD. P Bdle. Ch e. Thirsk and Malton CC.

BURRINGHAM Lincs (L)
104 SE 8309 4m W of Scunthorpe. CP, 986. Glanford Brigg RD. P Scnthpe. Ch e, m. Brgg and Scnthpe CC (Brgg).

BURRINGTON Devon
163 SS 6316 7m SW of S Molton. CP, 444. S Mltn RD. P Umberleigh. Ch e, m, v. Sch pe. N Dvn CC.

BURRINGTON Herefs
129 SO 4472 5m WSW of Ludlow. CP, 82. Leominster and Wigmore RD. Ch e. Lmnstr CC. In churchyard, 17c cast-iron tomb slabs, rare in Herefs.

BURRINGTON Som
165 ST 4759 4m NNE of Cheddar. CP, 439. Axbridge RD. P BRISTOL. Ch e. Sch pe. Weston-super-Mare CC. B. Combe: large rocky outcrops, potholes; caves where human and animal Stone Age relics found.

BURROUGH GREEN Cambs
135 TL 6355 5m S of Newmarket. CP, 289. Nmkt RD. P Nmkt, Suffolk. Ch e. Sch pe. Cambs CC. Large grn; early 18c sch of grey stone, still so used though supplemented by new bldng alongside.

BURROUGH ON THE HILL Leics
122 SK 7510 5m S of Melton Mowbray. Loc, Somerby CP. P Mltn Mbry. Ch e. Sch pe. 1m N on rocky escarpment, Iron Age fort.

BURROW Devon
176 SY 0789 3m WNW of Sidmouth. Loc, Harpford CP.

BURROW BRIDGE Som
177 ST 3529 9m ENE of Taunton. Loc, Stoke St Gregory CP. P Bridgwater. Ch e, b. Sch pe. Among withy beds. Brrw Mump (NT), small conical hill topped by unfinished ch, traditionally site of King Alfred's fort.

BURROWHILL Surrey
169, 170 SU 9763 4m NW of Woking. Loc, Chobham CP.

BURSCOUGH Lancs
100 SD 4310 2m NE of Ormskirk. Loc, Ormskk UD. P(Bscgh Town), Ormskk.

BURSCOUGH BRIDGE Lancs
100 SD 4412 3m NE of Ormskirk. Loc, Ormskk UD. P Ormskk.

BURSEA Yorks (E)
98 SE 8033 7m SW of Mkt Weighton. Loc, Holme upon Spalding Moor CP.

BURSHILL Yorks (E)
99 TA 0948 7m NNE of Beverley. Loc, Brandesburton CP.

BURSLEDON Hants
180 SU 4809 5m ESE of Southampton. CP, 3,560. Winchester RD. P STHMPTN. Ch e, c, r, v. Sch pe. Eastleigh CC. Brickworks, boat yards, strawberries.

BURSLEM Staffs
110 SJ 8649 N distr of Stoke-on-Trent. Loc, Stke-on-Trnt CB. P Stke-on-Trnt. S-on-T BC. Pottery and coal-mining distr. Bthplace of Josiah Wedgwood, 1735. One of Arnold Bennett's *Five Towns* ('Bursley'). To S at Cobridge, Arnold Bennett's Hse*.

BURSTALL Suffolk (E)
149 TM 0944 4m W of Ipswich. CP, 237. Samford RD. P Ipswch. Ch e. Sudbury and Woodbridge CC.

BURSTEAD, GREAT Essex
161 TQ 6892 1m S of Billericay. Loc, Basildon UD.

BURSTOCK Dorset
177 ST 4202 4m SSW of Crewkerne. CP, 96. Beaminster RD. Ch e. W Dst CC.

BURSTON Norfolk
136 TM 1383 2m NNE of Diss. CP, 475.
Depwade RD. P Dss. Ch e, m. Sch p, S Nflk
CC. See also Shimpling.

BURSTON Staffs
110, 119 SJ 9330 3m SE of Stone. Loc,
Sandon CP. Ch e.

BURSTOW Surrey
170, 182 TQ 3141 2m SE of Horley. CP,
4,374. Godstone RD. Ch e. E Srry CC
(Reigate). See also Outwood, Smallfield.

BURSTWICK Yorks (E)
99 TA 2227 8m E of Hull. CP, 680.
Holderness RD. P Hll. Ch e, m. Sch p.
Bridlington CC. Once capital of Holderness
distr. Ch has painting on wood of Charles I's
execution.

BURTERSETT Yorks (N)
90 SD 8989 lm ESE of Hawes. Loc, Hws
CP. Ch m, v.

BURTON Ches
109 SJ 3174 7m NW of Chester. Loc,
Neston UD. P Nstn, Wirral. Above the
village, B. Wd (NT), Scots pines; views of
Dee estuary and Welsh hills.

BURTON Ches
109 SJ 5063 7m ESE of Chester. CP, 41.
Tarvin RD. Northwich CC.

BURTON Hants
179 SZ 1694 lm N of Christchurch. Loc,
Chrstchch E CP. Ringwood and
Fordingbridge RD. P Chrstchch. Ch e, c.
Sch pe. New Forest CC.

BURTON Lincs (L)
113 SK 9674 2m NNW of Lincoln. CP, 165.
Welton RD. P LNCLN. Ch e. Gainsborough
CC.

BURTON Nthmb
71 NU 1733 lm S of Bamburgh. Loc,
Bmbrgh CP.

BURTON Som
164 ST 1944 8m E of Watchet. Loc,
Stogursey CP. P Bridgwater. Ch b.

BURTON Westm
89 SD 5376 4m NNE of Carnforth. CP, 646.
S Westm RD. P Cnfth, Lancs. Ch e. Sch pe.
Westm CC.

BURTON Wilts
156 ST 8179 7m NW of Chippenham. Loc,
Nettleton CP. P Chppnhm. Ch e. Ch is par
ch of Nttltn.

BURTON AGNES Yorks (E)
99 TA 1063 5m WSW of Bridlington. CP,
582. Brdlngtn RD. P Driffield. Ch e, m.
Sch pe. Brdlngtn CC. See also Gransmoor,
Thornholme. Large pond and trees in
middle of vllge. B.A. Hall*, large brick Tdr
hse. B.A. Nmn Mnr Hse (A.M.) dates from
1170.

BURTON BRADSTOCK Dorset
177 SY 4889 3m SSE of Bridport. CP, 602.
Brdpt RD. P Brdpt. Ch e, m. Sch pe.
W Dst CC.

BURTON COGGLES Lincs (K)
123 SK 9725 7m SSE of Grantham. CP,
163. W Kesteven RD. P Grnthm. Ch e, m.
Sch pe. Rutland and Stamford CC.

BURTON CONSTABLE Yorks (E)
99 TA 1936 8m NE of Hull. CP, 200.
Holderness RD. Ch m. Bridlington CC.. See
also Marton, New Ellerby, W Newton. B.C.
Hall*, Tdr hse with 18c state rooms, in
landscape gdns by Capability Brown.
Transport museum.

BURTON DASSETT Warwicks
145 SP 3951 8m NNW of Banbury. CP,
1,289. Southam RD. Ch e.
Stratford-on-Avon CC (Strtfd). See also
Knightcote, Northend. Main vllge at
Northend. Ch away to SE on hill, 600ft;
splendid bldng. Holy well nearby. Beacon
on hilltop.

BURTON FLEMING Yorks (E)
93 TA 0872 6m SSW of Filey. CP, 365.
Bridlington RD. P Driffield. Ch e, m2.
Sch p. Brdlngtn CC.

BURTON GREEN Warwicks
131 SP 2675 5m WSW of Coventry. Loc,
Kenilworth UD, Meriden RD. P Knlwth.
Warwick and Leamington CC, Mrdn CC.

BURTON HASTINGS Warwicks
132 SP 4189 3m ESE of Nuneaton. CP,
190. Rugby RD. P Nntn. Ch e. Sch pe. Rgby
CC.

BURTON IN LONSDALE Yorks (W)
89 SD 6572 5m SSE of Kirkby Lonsdale.

CP, 401. Settle RD. P Carnforth, Lancs. Ch e, m. Sch pe. Skipton CC. Mainly 18c vllge, neatly laid out.

BURTON JOYCE Notts
112, 121, 122 SK 6443 5m ENE of Nottingham. CP, 2,447. Basford RD. P NTTNGHM. Ch e, c, m. Sch p. Carlton CC.

BURTON LATIMER Northants
133 SP 9074 4m N of Wellingborough. UD, 5,419. P Kettering. Kttrng CC. Ch has mdvl wall-paintings.

BURTON LAZARS Leics
122 SK 7616 2m SE of Melton Mowbray. Loc, Btn and Dalby CP. Mltn and Belvoir RD. P Mltn Mbry. Ch e. Mltn CC. Takes name from vanished mdvl lepers' hsptl. In churchyard, flamboyant monmt of 1781.

BURTON LEONARD Yorks (W)
91 SE 3263 5m S of Ripon. CP, 463. Nidderdale RD. P Harrogate. Ch e, m. Sch pe. Hrrgte CC.

BURTON ON THE WOLDS Leics
121, 122 SK 5921 4m ENE of Loughborough. CP, 420. Barrow upon Soar RD. P Lghbrgh. Ch m. Sch p. Melton CC.

BURTON-ON-TRENT Staffs
120 SK 2423 25m NNE of Birmingham. Alternative name for Burton upon Trent, qv.

BURTON OVERY Leics
132, 133 SP 6797 7m SE of Leicester. CP, 250. Billesdon RD. P LCSTR. Ch e, v. Harborough CC (Melton).

BURTON PEDWARDINE Lincs (K)
113, 123 TF 1142 4m SE of Sleaford. CP, 127. E Kesteven RD. Ch e. Sch p. Grantham CC.

BURTON PIDSEA Yorks (E)
99 TA 2431 6m WNW of Withernsea. CP, 355. Holderness RD. P Hull. Ch e, m. Sch p. Bridlington CC.

BURTON SALMON Yorks (W)
97 SE 4927 4m ENE of Castleford. CP, 252. Osgoldcross RD. P Leeds. Ch m. Sch p. Goole CC.

BURTON UPON STATHER Lincs (L)
104 SE 8717 5m NNW of Scunthorpe. CP, 1,398. Glanford Brigg RD. P Scnthpe. Ch e, m. Sch p. Brgg and Scnthpe CC (Brgg). See also Normanby, Thealby. Set on N tip of Cliff Ridge; wide views W to Derbys and N to Yorks.

BURTON UPON TRENT Staffs
120 SK 2423 25m NNE of Birmingham. CB, 50,175. P. Btn CC. Breweries.

BURTONWOOD Lancs
100 SJ 5692 4m ESE of St Helens. CP, 2,766. Warrington RD. P Wrrngtn. Ch e, m, r. Sch p, pr. Newton CC. See also Collins Grn. B. Airfield to S.

BURWARDSLEY Ches
109 SJ 5156 9m SE of Chester. CP, 268. Tarvin RD. P CHSTR. Ch e, m. Nntwch CC.

BURWARTON Shrops
129, 130 SO 6185 8m SW of Bridgnorth. CP. 131. Brdgnth RD. Ch e, v. Sch pe. Ludlow CC.

BURWASH Sussex (E)
183 TQ 6724 6m ENE of Heathfield. CP, 1,998. Battle RD. P Etchingham. Ch e, c, r2. Sch pe. Rye CC. See also Witherenden Hill. Picturesque vllge on ridge. To SW, Bateman's (NT)*, 17c hse, former home of Rudyard Kipling.

BURWASH COMMON Sussex (E)
183 TQ 6423 4m ENE of Heathfield. Loc, Bwsh CP. P Etchingham. Ch e.

BURWASH WEALD Sussex (E)
183 TQ 6523 4m ENE of Heathfield. Loc, Bwsh CP. Ch m.

BURWELL Cambs
135 TL 5866 4m NW of Newmarket. CP, 2,734. Nmkt RD. P CAMBRIDGE. Ch e, b, m2, v2. Sch p, pe, s. Cambs CC. Spacious Perp ch.

BURWELL Lincs (L)
105 TF 3579 5m SSE of Louth. CP, 110. Lth RD. P Lth. Ch e. Lth CC.

BURY Hunts
134 TL 2883 just S of Ramsey. CP, 1,700. St Ives RD. P HUNTINGDON. Ch e. Sch pe. Hunts CC. Nmn and later ch: twr, scrn.

BURY Lancs
101 SD 8010 8m NNW of Manchester. CB, 67,776. P. Bury and Radcliffe BC. See also

Summerseat, Walshaw. Textiles and general industry. Paper. Bthplce of Kay, inventor of the flying shuttle; and of Sir Robert Peel.

BURY Som
164 SS 9427 2m E of Dulverton. Loc, Brompton Regis CP. Ch m.

BURY Sussex (W)
181, 182 TQ 0113 4m N of Arundel. CP, 649. Petworth RD. P Pulborough. Ch e. Sch pe. Chichester CC (Horsham). See also W Burton. At N end of Arun Gap. John Galsworthy lived and died here.

BURY GREEN Herts
148 TL 4521 2m W of Bishop's Stortford. Loc, Lit Hadham CP.

BURY ST EDMUNDS Suffolk (W)
136 TL 8564 23m NW of Ipswich. MB, 25,629. P. Bury St Eds CC. County tn of W Sfflk, and mkt tn. Brewing. Many old bldngs esp Ggn. Rems of abbey (A.M.). St James' Ch now cathedral. Moyse's Hall, 12c, E Anglian museum. Angel Corner (NT)*, 18c; collection of clocks and watches.

BURYTHORPE Yorks (E)
92 SE 7964 4m S of Malton. CP, 290. Norton RD. P Mltn. Ch e, m. Howden CC. See also Kennythorpe.

BUSBY, GREAT Yorks (N)
85 NZ 5205 2m S of Stokesley. See Gt Bsby.

BUSCOT Berks
157 SU 2397 9m NE of Swindon. CP, 248. Faringdon RD. P Frngdn. Ch e. Abingdon CC. NT Vllge on R Thames. B. Hse*, late 18c; The Old Parsonage*, early 18c.

BUSH BANK Herefs
142 SO 4551 6m SSW of Leominster. Loc, Weobley RD. Lmnstr CC.

BUSHEY Herts
160 TQ 1395 2m SE of Watford. UD, 23,729. P Wtfd. SW Herts CC. Rsdntl. Royal Masonic Sch, vast red brick bldngs of early 20c.

BUSHEY HEATH Herts
160 TQ 1594 3m SE of Watford. Loc, Bshy UD. P Wtfd. Rsdntl.

BUSHLEY Worcs
143 SO 8734 2m NW of Tewkesbury. CP, 260. Upton upon Severn RD. P Tksbry, Glos. Ch e. S Worcs CC.

BUSHMOOR Shrops
129 SO 4387 3m N of Craven Arms. Loc, Wistanstow CP.

BUSHTON Wilts
157 SU 0677 6m NE of Calne. Loc, Clyffe Pypard CP.

BUSSAGE Glos
156, 157 SO 8803 2m ESE of Stroud. Loc, Chalford CP. Ch e. Sch pe.

BUTCHER'S PASTURE Essex
148 TL 6024 2m NW of Dunmow. Loc, Lit Easton CP.

BUTCOMBE Som
165 ST 5161 8m SW of Bristol. CP, 187. Axbridge RD. P BRSTL. Ch e. Weston-super-Mare CC.

BUTLEIGH Som
165 ST 5233 4m SSE of Glastonbury. CP, 479. Wells RD. P Glstnbry. Ch e. Sch pe. Wlls CC. See also Btlgh Wootton. 1m W of Windmill Hill (NT), monmt to Admiral Hood, d 1814.

BUTLEIGH WOOTTON Som
165 ST 5035 3m S of Glastonbury. Loc, Butleigh CP.

BUTLER'S CROSS Bucks
159 SP 8407 5m SSE of Aylesbury. Loc, Ellesborough CP. P Aylesbury. On the ancient track Icknield Way below Coombe Hill (NT), highest viewpoint on the Chilterns.

BUTLERS MARSTON Warwicks
145 SP 3150 8m ESE of Stratford. CP, 226. Shipston on Stour RD. P WARWICK. Ch e, m. Sch pe. Strtfd-on-Avon CC (Strtfd).

BUTLEY Suffolk (E)
150 TM 3651 6m E of Woodbridge. CP, 268. Deben RD. P Wdbrdge. Ch e, m. Sch pe, s. Sudbury and Wdbrdge CC. Near head of Btly Creek. Priory gatehouse, 14c, rems of large monastic foundation.

BUTTERCRAMBE Yorks (N)
97, 98 SE 7358 7m NW of Pocklington. CP(Bttrcrmbe w Bossall), 124. Flaxton RD. Ch e. Thirsk and Malton CC.

BUTTERKNOWLE Co Durham
84 NZ 1025 7m NNE of Barnard Cstle. Loc,
Lynesack and Softley CP. Bnd Cstle RD. P
Bishop Auckland. Ch m. Sch p. Bshp
Aucklnd CC.

BUTTERLEIGH Devon
176 SS 9708 3m SSE of Tiverton. CP, 79.
Tvtn RD. P Cullompton. Ch e. Tvtn CC.

BUTTERMERE Cumb
82 NY 1717 7m SW of Keswick. CP, 205.
Cockermouth RD. Ch e. Workington CC.

BUTTERMERE Wilts
168 SU 3461 5m S of Hungerford. CP, 42.
Marlborough and Ramsbury RD. Ch e.
Devizes CC.

BUTTERTON Staffs
110, 119 SJ 8342 2m SSW of
Newcastle-under-Lyme. Loc, Whitmore CP.
Ch e. Sch pe.

BUTTERTON Staffs
111 SK 0756 6m E of Leek. CP, 250. Lk
RD. P Lk. Ch e, m. Sch p. Lk CC.

BUTTERWICK Lincs (H)
114 TF 3845 4m E of Boston. CP, 552.
Bstn RD. P Bstn. Ch e, m. Sch pe. Holland
w Bstn CC.

BUTTERWICK Yorks (E)
93 SE 9971 9m NNW of Driffield. Loc,
Foxholes CP. Ch e.

BUTTERWICK Yorks (N)
92 SE 7377 5m NW of Malton. CP(Bttrwck
w Newsham), 41. Mltn RD. Ch e. Thirsk and
Mltn CC.

BUTT GREEN Ches
110 SJ 6651 1m ESE of Nantwich. Loc,
Stapeley CP.

BUTTOCK'S BOOTH Northants
133 SP 7864 3m NE of Northampton. Loc,
Nthmptn CB. Nthmptn N BC (Kettering CC,
S Nthnts CC).

BUTTONOAK Shrops
130 SO 7578 3m NW of Bewdley. Loc,
Kinlet CP.

BUXHALL Suffolk (E)
136 TM 0057 3m W of Stowmarket. CP,
396. Gipping RD. P Stwmkt. Ch e, m. Eye
CC.

BUXTED Sussex (E)
183 TQ 4923 2m NE of Uckfield. CP,
2,503. Uckfld RD. P Uckfld. Ch e2, m, r.
Sch pe. E Grinstead CC. See also High
Hurstwood. One ch (St Margaret's) in grnds
of Ggn B. Pk.

BUXTON Derbys
111 SK 0573 9m E of Macclesfield. MB,
20,316. P. High Peak CC. See also Burbage,
Harpur Hill. Mkt tn and spa. 18c Crescent,
by Carr of York.

BUXTON Norfolk
126 TG 2322 4m SE of Aylsham. CP(Bxtn
w Lammas), 1,041. St Faith's and
Aylshm RD. P NORWICH, NOR 61Y. Ch e.
Sch p. N Nflk CC (Central Nflk). See also
Lit Hautbois.

BUXTON HEATH Norfolk
126 TG 1821 3m S of Aylsham. Loc,
Hevingham CP. Ch v.

BYERMOOR Co Durham
78 NZ 1857 6m SW of Gateshead. Loc,
Whickham UD.

BYERS GREEN Co Durham
85 NZ 2234 2m ESE of Willington. Loc,
Spennymoor UD. P Spnnmr.

BYFIELD Northants
145 SP 5153 7m SSW of Daventry. CP, 838.
Dvntry RD. P Rugby, Warwickshire.
Ch e, m, v. Sch p. Dvntry CC (S Nthnts). 14c
ch has 140ft spire. To W, lake with sailing
boats.

BYFLEET Surrey
170 TQ 0661 5m ENE of Woking. Loc,
Wkg UD. P Weybridge.

BYFORD Herefs
142 SO 3942 7m WNW of Hereford. CP,
118. Weobley RD. Ch e. Leominster CC.

BYGRAVE Herts
147 TL 2636 2m NE of Baldock. CP, 321.
Hitchin RD. Ch e. Htchn CC.

BYLAUGH Norfolk
125 TG 0318 4m NE of E Dereham. CP, 86.
Mitford and Launditch RD. Ch e.
SW Nflk CC.

BYLEY Ches
110 SJ 7269 2m NNE of Middlewich. CP,

177. Northwich RD. P Mddlwch. Ch e. Sch p. Nthwch CC.

BYRNESS Nthmb
70 NT 7602 10m NW of Otterburn. Loc, Rochester CP. P(Bnss Vllge), NEWCASTLE UPON TYNE. Ch e. On the A68 main rd over the Scottish border by Carter Bar; surrounded by Forestry Commission forest.

BYTHORN Hunts
134 TL 0575 4m ESE of Thrapston. CP(Bthn and Keyston), 244. Huntingdon RD. P HNTNGDN. Ch e. Sch pe. Hunts CC.

BYTON Herefs
129 SO 3764 4m E of Presteigne. CP, 95. Kington RD. P PRSTGNE, Radnor. Ch e. Leominster CC. See also Combe Moor.

BYWORTH Sussex (W)
181, 182 SU 9820 just SE of Petworth. Loc, Ptwth CP. P Ptwth.

C

CABOURNE Lincs (L)
104 TA 1401 1m ENE of Caistor. CP, 156. Cstr RD. Ch e. Gainsborough CC.

CADBURY Devon
176 SS 9104 6m NE of Crediton. CP, 134. Tiverton RD. P Crdtn. Ch e. Tvtn CC. Under C. Cstle, Iron Age fort.

CADDINGTON Beds
147 TL 0619 2m SW of Luton. CP, 4,921. Ltn RD. P Ltn. Ch e, b, bv, r. Sch p, s. S Beds CC. See also Slip End.

CADEBY Leics
121 SK 4202 6m N of Hinckley. CP, 170. Mkt Bosworth RD. P Nuneaton, Warwickshire. Ch e. Sch j. Bswth CC.

CADEBY Yorks (W)
103 SE 5100 4m WSW of Doncaster. CP, 115. Dncstr RD. Ch e. Don Valley CC.

CADELEIGH Devon
176 SS 9107 4m SW of Tiverton. CP, 142. Tvtn RD. P Tvtn. Ch e. Tvtn CC. See also Lit Silver.

CADE STREET Sussex (E)
183 TQ 6021 2m E of Heathfield. Loc, Hthfld CP. Ch v.

CADGWITH Cornwall
190 SW 7214 9m SSE of Helston. Loc, Grade-Ruan CP. Kerrier RD. P Ruan Minor, Hlstn. St Ives CC. Fishing village of rock and thatch. On cliffs to S, Devil's Frying Pan, rock ring sea rushes through.

CADISHEAD Lancs
101 SJ 7091 7m ENE of Warrington. Loc, Irlam UD. P MANCHESTER.

CADLEY Wilts
157 SU 2066 2m SSE of Marlborough. Loc, Savernake CP. Mlbrgh and Ramsbury RD.

CADMORE END Bucks
159 SU 7892 5m W of High Wycombe. Loc, Wcmbe RD. P Hgh Wcmbe. Sch pe. Wcmbe CC.

CADNAM Hants
180 SU 2913 6m SW of Romsey. Loc, Copythorne CP. P SOUTHAMPTON. Ch m. Sch ie.

CADNEY Lincs (L)
104 TA 0103 3m SSE of Brigg. CP, 432. Glanford Brgg RD. Ch e, m. Brgg and Scunthorpe CC (Brgg). See also Howsham.

CAENBY Lincs (L)
104 TF 0089 7m W of Mkt Rasen. CP, 86. Welton RD. Ch e. Gainsborough CC.

CAISTER-ON-SEA Norfolk
126 TG 5212 3m N of Yarmouth. CP, 4,104. Blofield and Clegg RD. P Gt Ymth. Ch e, m2. Sch i, j, s. Ymth CC. Resort. Many caravans. Rems of 15c moated cstle*. Partly excavated Roman tn (A.M.).

CAISTOR Lincs (L)
104 TA 1101 11m WSW of Grimsby. CP, 1,778. Cstr RD. P LINCOLN. Ch e, m, r, v. Sch pem, s. Gainsborough CC. Slight rems

of Roman tn. Large mkt square. 2m NE, Pelham's Pillar, 1849, commemorates planting of 12 million trees by lst Ld Yarborough (see Brocklesby).

CAISTOR ST EDMUND Norfolk
126 TG 2303 3m S of Norwich. CP, 282. Forehoe and Henstead RD. Ch e. S Nflk CC (Central Nflk). Site of Roman tn of *Venta Icenorum.*

CALBOURNE IOW
180 SZ 4286 5m WSW of Newport. CP, 818. Isle of Wight RD and CC. P Npt. Ch e, m2. See also Newtown, Porchfield.

CALCOT ROW Berks
158, 169 SU 6672 3m W of Reading. Loc, Tilehurst CP. P(Clct), Rdng. Sch p.

CALDBECK Cumb
82 NY 3239 7m SE of Wigton. CP, 641. Wgtn RD. P Wgtn. Ch e, m. Sch p. Penrith and the Border CC. See also Hesket Newmarket. John Peel, the huntsman, is buried in churchyard.

CALDECOTE Cambs
134 TL 3456 7m W of Cambridge CP, 368. Chesterton RD. P CMBRDGE. Ch e. Sch p. Cambs CC. See also Highfields.

CALDECOTE Herts
147 TL 2338 3m N of Baldock. CP, 30. Hitchin RD. Ch e. Htchn CC.

CALDECOTE Hunts
134 TL 1488 7m SSW of Peterborough. CP(Denton and Cldcte), 89. Norman Cross RD. Hunts CC.

CALDECOTE Northants
146 SP 6851 2m N of Towcester. Loc, Tcstr CP. Ch m.

CALDECOTE Warwicks
132 SP 3594 2m NNW of Nuneaton. CP, 137. Atherstone RD. Ch e. Meriden CC.

CALDECOTT Northants
134 SP 9868 3m NE of Rushden. CP(Chelveston cum Cldctt), 974. Oundle and Rshdn RD. Ch e. Wellingborough CC.

CALDECOTT Rutland
133 SP 8693 4m S of Uppingham. CP, 275. Uppnghm RD. P Mkt Harborough, Leics. Ch e. Rtlnd and Stamford CC. Vllge of golden ironstone.

CALDER Cumb
88 NY 0303 2m N of Seascale. Loc, Ponsonby CP. Ennerdale RD. Whitehaven CC. To W, Cldr Hall, world's first full-scale nuclear power stn, opened 1956.

CALDER BRIDGE Cumb
82 NY 0406 9m SSE of Whitehaven. Loc, St Bridget Beckermet CP. P Seascale. Ch e. Sch pe. To ENE, rems of Cldr Abbey.

CALDERBROOK Lancs
95, 101 SD 9418 4m NE of Rochdale. Loc, Littleborough UD.

CALDER VALE Lancs
94 SD 5345 10m N of Preston. Loc, Barnacre-w-Bonds CP. Garstang RD. P Prstn. Ch e, m. Sch pe. N Fylde CC. Ch e is at Oakenclough, qv.

CALDWELL Yorks (N)
85 NZ 1613 8m W of Darlington. CP, 119. Richmond RD. P Rchmnd. Ch e. Rchmnd CC.

CALDY Ches
100, 109 SJ 2285 6m WSW of Birkenhead. Loc, Hoylake UD.

CALIFORNIA Norfolk
126 TG 5114 5m N of Yarmouth. Loc, Ormesby St Margaret w Scratby CP.

CALKE Derbys
120, 121 SK 3722 4m NNE of Ashby de la Zouche. CP, 26. Repton RD. Ch e. Belper CC. C. Abbey, early 18c hse, stands on site of former priory.

CALLALY Nthmb
71 NU 0509 5m N of Rothbury. CP, 166. Rthbry RD. Berwick-upon-Tweed CC. C. Cstle*, 15c and later.

CALLESTICK Cornwall
185, 190 SW 7750 5m NW of Truro. Loc, Perranzabuloe CP. P Truro. Ch m.

CALLINGTON Cornwall
186 SX 3669 8m ENE of Liskeard. CP, 2,209. St Germans RD. P. Ch e, m3, r. Sch p, s2. Bodmin CC. See also Kelly Bray.

CALLOW Herefs
142 SO 4934 4m S of Hereford. CP, 63. Hrfd RD. P HRFD. Ch e. Hrfd CC.

CALLOW END Worcs
143 SO 8349 4m S of Worcester. Loc,
Powick CP. P WCSTR. Ch r. Sch pe.

CALLOW HILL Wilts
157 SU 0384 7m W of Swindon. Loc,
Malmesbury RD, Cricklade and Wootton
Bassett RD. P Chippenham. Ch m.
Chppnhm CC.

CALLOW HILL Worcs
130 SO 7473 3m W of Bewdley. Loc, Rock
CP. Ch m.

CALLOWS GRAVE Worcs
129 SO 5966 1m S of Tenbury Wells. Loc,
Tnbry CP.

CALMORE Hants
180 SU 3314 5m WNW of Southampton.
Loc, Eling CP. P STHMPTN.

CALMSDEN Glos
157 SP 0408 4m NNE of Cirencester. Loc,
N Cerney CP. 14c wayside cross.

CALNE Wilts
157 ST 9971 5m ESE of Chippenham. MB,
9,685. P. Chppnhm CC. Dominated visually
by famous bacon and pork pie factory. 2m
W, Bowood Pk, Ggn and later hse in grnds*
laid out by Capability Brown and Repton.

CALOW Derbys
112 SK 4070 2m E of Chesterfield. CP,
2,768. Chstrfld RD. P Chstrfld. Ch e, c, m.
NE Derbys CC.

CALSHOT Hants
180 SU 4701 2m SE of Fawley. Loc, Fwly
CP. P SOUTHAMPTON. Cstle blt by Henry
VIII for coastal defence.

CALSTOCK Cornwall
187 SX 4368 5m E of Callington. CP,
3,884. St Germans RD. P. Ch e, b, m.
Sch p2, s. Bodmin CC. See also Albaston,
Chilsworthy, Gunnislake, Harrowbarrow,
Latchley, Metherell, St Ann's Chpl. Once
port for surrounding mines. Immense
disused rly viaduct crosses Tamar. 1m W, 16c
Cotehele Hse and gdns (NT)*.

CALSTONE WELLINGTON Wilts
157 SU 0268 3m SE of Calne. Loc, Clne
Without CP. Clne and Chippenham RD.
Ch e. Chppnhm CC.

CALTHORPE Norfolk
126 TG 1831 3m NNW of Aylsham. Loc,
Erpingham CP. Ch e.

CALTHWAITE Cumb
83 NY 4640 7m NNW of Penrith. Loc,
Hesket CP. Pnrth RD. P Pnrth. Sch pe.
Pnrth and the Border CC.

CALTON Staffs
111 SK 1050 5m WNW of Ashbourne. Loc,
Waterhouses CP. P Stoke-on-Trent. Ch e.
Sch pe.

CALTON Yorks (W)
95 SD 9059 6m SE of Settle. CP, 55.
Skipton RD. Skptn CC.

CALVELEY Ches
109 SJ 5958 6m NW of Nantwich. CP, 217.
Nntwch RD. Sch p. Nntwch CC.

CALVER Derbys
111 SK 2474 4m NNE of Bakewell. CP,
442. Bkwll RD. P SHEFFIELD. Ch m. W
Derbys CC.

CALVERHALL Shrops
110, 118, 119 SJ 6037 5m SE of
Whitchurch. Loc, Ightfield CP. P Whtchch.
Ch e.

CALVER HILL Herefs
142 SO 3748 10m NW of Hereford. Loc,
Norton Canon CP.

CALVERLEIGH Devon
164, 176 SS 9214 3m WNW of Tiverton.
Loc, Loxbeare CP. P Tvtn. Ch e.

CALVERLEY Yorks (W)
96 SE 2036 4m NE of Bradford. Loc,
Pudsey MB. P Pdsy.

CALVERT Bucks
146 SP 6824 6m S of Buckingham. Loc,
Bcknghm RD. Bcknghm CC. Brick wks.

CALVERTON Bucks
146 SP 7938 just S of Stony Stratford. Loc,
Wolverton UD. P Wlvtn. Ch e.

CALVERTON Notts
112 SK 6149 6m NNE of Nottingham. CP,
5,658. Basford RD. P NTTNGHM.
Ch e, b, m2, r. Sch i, j, p, pe2, s. Carlton CC.
Colliery vllge. Bthplce of the Revd William
Lee, inventor of the stocking frame in Elizn
times. Stocking knitters' cottages.

CAM Glos
156 ST 7599 7m WSW of Stroud. CP, 4,874. Dursley RD. P Dsly. Ch e, v2. Sch i, p, pe. Strd CC. See also Lr Cm, Quarry.

CAMBER Sussex (E)
184 TQ 9618 3m ESE of Rye. CP, 432. Battle RD. P Rye. Ch e. Rye CC. Bungalows and caravans. Popular resort.

CAMBERLEY Surrey
169 SU 8660 6m N of Aldershot. UD(Frimley and Cmbrly), 44,784. P. NW Srry CC (Woking). Rsndtl and military distr. Royal Staff College.

CAMBERWELL London
160, 170 TQ 3376 2m NE of Lambeth. Loc, Southwark LB. Dulwich BC.

CAMBLESFORTH Yorks (W)
97, 98 SE 6426 4m SSE of Selby. CP, 364. Slby RD. P Slby. Ch m. Sch p. Barkston Ash CC.

CAMBO Nthmb
77 NZ 0285 11m W of Morpeth. Loc, Wallington Demesne CP. Mpth RD. P Mpth. Ch e. Sch p. Mpth CC. 18c estate vllge. 1m S, Wllgntn Hall (NT)*, 17c–18c hse in large estate.

CAMBOIS Nthmb
78 NZ 3083 1m N of Blyth. Loc, Bedlingtonshire UD. P Blth. Blth CC.

CAMBORNE Cornwall
189 SW 6440 4m WSW of Redruth. UD(Cmbne-Rdrth), 42,029. P. Falmouth and Cmbne CC. See also Barripper, Carharrock, Carnbrea, Four Lanes, Illogan, Kehelland, Lanner, Mt Ambrose, Pool, Portreath, St Day, Scorrier, Troon. Once centre of tin-mining industry. Bthplce in 1771 of Richard Trevithick, steam engine pioneer.

CAMBRIDGE Cambs
135 TL 4458 49m NNE of London. MB, 98,519. P(CMBRDGE). Cmbrdge BC. See also Cherry Hinton, Chesterton, Trumpington. Ancient university city and modern commercial centre. Mecca of tourists.

CAMBRIDGE Glos
156 SO 7403 4m N of Dursley. Loc, Dsly RD. P GLOUCESTER. Ch bc. Stroud CC.

CAMDEN London
160 TQ 2984 3m NNW of Charing Cross. LB, 200,784. BCs: Hampstead, Holborn and St Pancras S, St Pncrs N. See also Bloomsbury, Gospel Oak, Hmpstd, Hlbn, Kentish Tn, St Pncrs.

CAMELEY Som
166 ST 6157 5m WNW of Radstock. CP, 575. Clutton RD. Ch e. Sch pe. N Som CC. See also Temple Cloud.

CAMELFORD Cornwall
186 SX 1083 11m N of Bodmin. CP, 1,220. Cmlfd RD. P. Ch e, m4. Sch p, s. N Cnwll CC. See also Helstone.

CAMELSDALE Sussex (W)
169, 181 SU 8832 1m SW of Haslemere. Loc, Fernhurst CP. P Hslmre, Surrey. Sch p.

CAMERTON Cumb
81, 82 NY 0330 3m NE of Workington. CP, 201. Cockermouth RD. P Wkngtn. Ch e. Sch pe. Wkngtn CC.

CAMERTON Som
166 ST 6857 2m N of Radstock. CP, 620. Bathavon RD. P Bath. Ch e, m. Sch pe. N Som CC. In mining area. Rems of Bronze Age barrows, Roman vllge, Saxon cemetery.

CAMMERINGHAM Lincs (L)
104 SK 9482 7m NNW of Lincoln. CP, 121. Welton RD. Ch e. Gainsborough CC.

CAMPERDOWN Nthmb
78 NZ 2772 5m NNE of Newcastle. Loc, Longbenton UD.

CAMPSALL Yorks (W)
103 SE 5413 7m NNW of Doncaster. Loc, Norton CP. P Dncstr. Ch e, m.

CAMPSEY ASH Suffolk (E)
150 TM 3255 5m NE of Woodbridge. CP, 340. Deben RD. P Wdbrdge. Ch e. Sch pe. Eye CC. Snall, picturesque. Sometimes spelt Campsey Ashe, e.g. on vllge sign. Aircraft noise.

CAMPS GREEN Cambs
148 TL 6343 3m WSW of Haverhill. Loc, Cstle Cmps CP.

CAMP, THE Glos
156, 157 SO 9109 5m ENE of Stroud. Loc, Miserden CP. P Strd. To SW, 335ft Long Barrow.

CAMPTON Beds
147 TL 1338 6m NNW of Hitchin. CP, 358.
Biggleswade RD. P Shefford. Ch e. Sch p.
Mid-Beds CC.

CANADA Hants
180 SU 2818 5m WSW of Romsey. Loc,
Wellow CP. Rmsy and Stockbridge RD.
Ch m. Eastleigh CC.

CANDLESBY Lincs (L)
114 TF 4567 5m S of Alford. CP, 144.
Spilsby RD. P Splsby. Ch e. Horncastle CC.

CANE END Oxon
158, 159 SU 6779 3m NE of Pangbourne.
Loc, Kidmore End CP.

CANEWDON Essex
162 TQ 8994 6m N of Southend. CP, 713.
Rochford RD. P Rchfd. Ch e, v. Sch pe.
Maldon CC (SE Essx). Ch blt on hill above
marshes, with 75ft 15c twr formerly used as
lighthouse. New 'model vllge' bldngs 1960.

CANFIELD, GREAT Essex
148 TL 5918 3m SW of Dunmow. See Gt
Cnfld.

CANFORD BOTTOM Dorset
179 SU 0300 2m E of Wimborne. Loc,
Colehill CP.

CANN Dorset
166 ST 8721 1m SSE of Shaftesbury. CP,
442. Shftsbry RD. Ch e. N Dst CC. See also
Guy's Marsh.

CANN COMMON Dorset
166, 167 ST 8820 2m SE of Shaftesbury.
Loc, Cnn CP.

CANNINGTON Som
165 ST 2539 3m WNW of Bridgwater. CP,
1,333. Brdgwtr RD. P Brdgwtr. Ch e, c.
Sch pe. Brdgwtr CC.

CANNING TOWN London
161 TQ 4081 7m E of Charing Cross. Loc,
Newham LB. Nwhm S BC (W Ham S). To S,
Royal Victoria Dock; to SE, Royal Albert
Dock, King George V Dock.

CANNOCK Staffs
119 SJ 9810 8m NNW of Walsall. UD,
55,873. P. Cnnck CC (Cnnck CC, Wlsll N
BC). See also Bridgetown, Hazelslade, Heath
Hayes, Hednesford, Littleworth, Lit Wyrley,
Norton Canes, Pye Green, Rawnsley.
Coal-mining distr. To N, Cnnck Chase, hths
and wds.

CANNOCK WOOD Staffs
120 SK 0412 4m S of Rugeley. Loc,
Cnnck UD. Cnnck CC.

CANON BRIDGE Herefs
142 SO 4341 5m W of Herefs. Loc, Madley
CP.

CANONBURY London
160 TQ 3284 3m NNE of Charing Cross.
Loc, Islington LB. Islngtn Central BC
(Islngtn E).

CANON FROME Herefs
142, 143 SO 6543 7m S of Bromyard. CP,
85. Ledbury RD. P Ldbry. Ch e. Sch s.
Leominster CC.

CANON PYON Herefs
142 SO 4649 6m NNW of Hereford. CP,
485. Weobley RD. P HRFD. Ch e. Sch pe.
Leominster CC. See also Westhope.

CANONS ASHBY Northants
145, 146 SP 5750 8m S of Daventry. CP,
23. Dvntry RD. Dvntry CC (S Nthnts).
Disused 13c-14c ch contains monmts to
Dryden family who blt grand 16c-17c hse
alongside.

CANON'S TOWN Cornwall
189 SW 5335 3m SSE of St. Ives. Loc,
W Penwith RD. P Hayle. Ch m. St Ives CC.

CANTERBURY Kent
173 TR 1457 54m ESE of London. CB,
33,157. P. Cntrbry CC. See also Thanington.
Premier cathedral city. Roman rems, mdvl
walls, many chs. Modern shopping centre;
indstrl development on outskirts.
University. Tourists.

CANTLEY Norfolk
126 TG 3803 9m WSW of Yarmouth. CP,
522. Blofield and Flegg RD. P NORWICH,
NOR 73Z. Ch e. Sch p. Ymth CC. See also
Limpenhoe, Southwood. Cargo boats,
barges, sugar beet refinery.

CANTLEY Yorks (W)
103 SE 6202 3m E of Doncaster. CP, 1,244.
Dncstr RD. P Dncstr. Ch e. Sch pe. Don
Valley CC.

CANTSFIELD Lancs
89 SD 6272 4m S of Kirkby Lonsdale. CP, 87. Lunesdale RD. Lancaster CC.

CANVEY Essex
162 TQ 7883 5m SE of Basildon. UD(Cnvy Island), 26,642. P (Cnvy Islnd). SE Essx CC. Thames estuary island linked to mainland by br at S Benfleet. Bungalow and indstrl development.

CANWICK Lincs (K)
113 SK 9869 1m SSE. of Lincoln. CP. N Kesteven RD, P LNCLN. Ch e. Grantham CC.

CANWORTHY WATER Cornwall
174 SX 2291 8m NW of Launceston. Loc, Lncstn RD. Stratton RD. P Lncstn. N Cnwll CC.

CAPEL Kent
171 TQ 6344 3m E of Tonbridge. CP, 1,738. Tnbrdge RD. Ch e. Sch p. Royal Tunbridge Wells CC (Tnbrdge). See also Five Oak Grn, Tudeley, Whetsted.

CAPEL Surrey
170, 182 TQ 1740 6m S of Dorking. CP, 2,900. Dkng and Horley RD. P Dkng. Ch e, f, m, v. Sch pe. Dkng CC. See also Beare Grn, Coldharbour. Main rd vllge. Inn is former vicarage.

CAPEL LE FERNE Kent
173 TR 2438 2m NE of Foldestone. CP, 1,284. Dover RD. P Flkstne. Ch e, b. Sch pe. Dvr and Deal CC (Dvr).

CAPEL ST ANDREW Suffolk (E)
150 TM 3748 6m E of Woodbridge. CP, 119. Deben RD. Sudbury and Wdbrdge CC.

CAPEL ST MARY Suffolk (E)
149 TM 0938 5m SE of Hadleigh. CP, 632. Samford RD. Ch e, c, m. Sch pe. Sudbury and Woodbridge CC.

CAPENHURST Ches
109 SJ 3673 3m SW of Ellesmere Port. CP, 338. Chester RD. Ch e. Sch pe. City of Chstr CC.

CAPERNWRAY Lancs
89 SD 5371 2m ENE of Carnforth. Loc, Over Kellet CP.

CAPHEATON Nthmb
77, 78 NZ 0380 11m WSW of Morpeth. CP,

170. Cstle Ward RD. P NEWCASTLE UPON TYNE. Ch m. Hexham CC. See also Kirkheaton. Tiny estate vllge by C. Hall, 17c hse in pk laid out by Capability Brown.

CAPSTONE Kent
172 TQ 7865 1m S of Gillingham. Loc, Chatham MB.

CAPTON Devon
188 SX 8353 3m WNW of Dartmouth. Loc, Dittisham CP.

CARBIS BAY Cornwall
189 SW 5238 1m SSE of St Ives. Loc, St Ives MB. P St Ives. Resort.

CARBROOKE Norfolk
125 TF 9502 2m ENE of Watton. CP, 1,215. Wayland RD. P Thetford. Ch e, m. Sch pe. S Nflk CC.

CARBURTON Notts
112 SK 6173 4m NNW of Ollerton. CP, 101. Worksop RD. Ch e. Sch pe. Bassetlaw CC. To NE, Clumber Pk. Hse demolished, but grnds with lake and lime avenue survive; also ch (NT)* blt orig as private chpl.

CAR COLSTON Notts
112, 122 SK 7242 8m SW of Newark. CP, 191. Bingham RD. P NOTTINGHAM. Ch e, m. Sch p. Rushcliffe CC (Carlton). Large vllge grn.

CARCROFT Yorks (W)
103 SE 5409 5m NNW of Doncaster. Loc, Adwick le Street UD. P Dncstr.

CARDESTON Shrops
118 SJ 3912 W of Shrewsbury. CP(Alberbury w Cdstn), 724. Atcham RD. Ch e. Shrsbry CC.

CARDINGTON Beds
147 TL 0847 3m ESE of Bedford. CP. Bdfd RD. P BDFD. Ch e, c, m. Sch p. Mid-Beds CC. R101 and other airships were blt here. Ch: 16c brass.

CARDINGTON Shrops
129 SO 5095 3m ENE of Ch Stretton. CP, 395. Atcham RD. P Ch Strttn. Ch e. Sch pe. Shrewsbury CC.

CARDINHAM Cornwall
186 SX 1268 4m ENE of Bodmin. CP, 461. Wadebridge and Padstow RD. P Bdmn.

Ch e, m2. Sch p. Bdmn CC. See also Millpool. Carved ancient cross in churchyard; earthwork rems of mdvl cstle.

CARDURNOCK Cumb
75 NY 1758 4m WNW of Kirkbride. Loc, Bowness CP. Wigton RD. Penrith and the Border CC.

CAREBY Lincs (K)
123 TF 0216 6m N of Stamford. CP(Cby Aunby and Holywell), 179. S Kesteven RD. P Stmfd. Ch e. Rutland and Stmfd CC.

CAREY Herefs
142 SO 5631 7m SSE of Hereford. Loc, Hrfd RD, Ross and Whitchurch RD. P HRFD. Hrfd CC.

CARGO Cumb
76 NY 3659 3m NW of Carlisle. Loc, Kingmoor CP. Border RD. P Clsle. Ch m. Sch p. Penrith and the Border CC. Beside Kngmr rly marshalling yard.

CARGREEN Cornwall
187 SX 4362 2m N of Saltash. Loc, Landulph CP. P Sltsh. Ch b.

CARHAM Nthmb
64, 70 NT 7938 3m WSW of Coldstream. CP, 560. Glendale RD. Ch e. Berwick-upon-Tweed CC. See also Downham, E Learmouth, Mindrum, Pressen, Wark, W Lmth. Tiny place with 18c ch beside R Tweed.

CARHAMPTON Som
164 ST 0042 4m W of Watchet. CP, 779. Williton RD. P Minehead. Ch e, m. Sch p. Bridgwater CC..

CARHARRACK Cornwall
190 SW 7341 2m E of Redruth. Loc, Camborne-Rdrth UD. P Rdrth. Former mining vllge.

CARISBROOKE IOW
180 SZ 4888 1m SW of Newport. Loc, Npt MB. P Npt. C. Cstle (A.M.), mainly Tdr. Charles I imprisoned here.

CARK Lancs
88, 89 SD 3676 3m WSW of Grange-over-Sands. Loc, Lr Holker CP. N Lonsdale RD. P(Ck-in-Cartmel), Grnge-over-Snds. Ch m. Morecambe and Lnsdle CC. To N, Holker Hall*, 16c and later, in pk with large herd of fallow deer.

CARLBURY Co Durham
85 NZ 2115 5m W of Darlington. Loc, Dlngtn RD. Bishop Auckland CC (Sedgefield).

CARLBY Lincs (K)
123 TF 0514 5m NNE of Stamford. CP, 143. S Kesteven RD. Ch e. Rutland and Stmfd CC.

CARLECOTES Yorks (W)
102 SE 1703 4m W of Penistone. Loc, Dunford CP. Pnstne RD. Pnstne CC.

CARLETON Cumb
76 NY 4252 3m SE of Carlisle. Loc, St Cuthbert Without CP. Border RD. Sch pe. Penrith and the Bdr CC. To N, Garlands Hsptl (Cumb and Westm Mental Hsptl).

CARLETON Lancs
94 SD 3339 3m NE of Blackpool. Loc, Poulton-le-Fylde UD.

CARLETON Yorks (W)
95 SD 9749 2m SW of Skipton. CP, 944. Skptn RD. P Skptn. Ch e, m. Sch pe. Skptn CC.

CARLETON FOREHOE Norfolk
125 TG 0905 3m NNW of Wymondham. Loc, Kimberley CP. Ch e.

CARLETON RODE Norfolk
136 TM 1192 5m S of Wymondham. CP, 542. Depwade RD. P NORWICH, NOR 03X. Ch e, b. Sch pe. S Nflk CC.

CARLETON ST PETER Norfolk
126 TG 3402 8m ESE of Norwich. CP, 48. Loddon RD. Ch e. S Nflk CC.

CARLINGCOTT Som
166 ST 6958 2m NNE of Radstock. Loc, Peasedown St John CP. Ch m.

CARLIN HOW Yorks (N)
86 NZ 7019 1m NW of Loftus. Loc, Skelton and Brotton UD. P Saltburn-by-the-Sea.

CARLISLE Cumb
76 NY 4056 53m W of Newcastle. CB, 71,497. P. Clsle BC. County capital; cathedral and indstrl city. Cstle(A.M.). M6 motorway passes to E.

CARLTON Beds
134 SP 9555 7m NW of Bedford. CP(Cltn and Chellington), 550. Bdfd RD. P BDFD. Ch e, b. Sch pe. Bdfd CC.

CARLTON Cambs
148 TL 6453 5m NNW of Haverhill. CP,
138. S Cambs RD. Ch e. Cambs CC.

CARLTON Co Durham
85 NZ 3921 4m NW of Teesside (Stockton).
CP. Stcktn RD. Ch m2. Easington CC
(Sedgefield).

CARLTON Leics
120, 121 SK 3905 7m NE of Atherstone.
CP, 179. Mkt Bosworth RD. P Nuneaton,
Warwickshire. Ch e. Bswth CC.

CARLTON Notts
112, 121, 122 SK 6141 3m ENE of
Nottingham. UD, 45,211. P NTTNGHM.
Carlton CC.

CARLTON Suffolk (E)
137 TM 3764 1m NNW of Saxmundham.
CP(Kelsale cum Cltn), 1,076. Blyth RD. P
Sxmndhm. Ch e. Eye CC.

CARLTON Yorks (N)
86, 92 SE 6186 2m N of Helmsley. Loc,
Hlmsly CP. Ch e, m. On moors 2m N,
C. Watercourse, which by an optical illusion
appears to run uphill.

CARLTON Yorks (N)
90 SE 0684 4m SW of Middleham. CP(Cltn
Tn), 136. Leyburn RD. P Lbn. Ch m.
Sch pe. Richmond CC.

CARLTON Yorks (N)
92 NZ 5004 3m SSW of Stokesley. CP, 380.
Stksly RD. P(Cltn-in-Cleveland),
MIDDLESBROUGH, Teesside. Ch e, m.
Sch pe. Richmond CC.

CARLTON Yorks (W)
96, 102 SE 3327 4m N of Wakefield. Loc,
Rothwell UD. P Wkfld.

CARLTON Yorks (W)
97, 98 SE 6424 6m SSE of Selby. CP, 765.
Slby RD. P Goole. Ch e, m, r. Sch p.
Barkston Ash CC.

CARLTON COLVILLE Suffolk (E)
137 TM 5190 3m SW of Lowestoft. CP,
1,466. Lothingland RD. P Lwstft. Ch e, m.
Sch p. Lwstft CC. E Anglia Transport
Museum.

CARLTON CURLIEU Leics
133 SP 6997 7m NNW of Mkt Harborough.

CP, 55. Billesdon RD. Ch e. Hbrgh CC
(Melton).

CARLTON, GREAT Lincs(L)
105 TF 4185 5m ESE of Louth. See Gt
Cltn.

CARLTON HUSTHWAITE Yorks (N)
91/92 SE 4976 6m SE of Thirsk. CP, 127.
Easingwold RD. P Thsk. Ch e, m. Thsk and
Malton CC. Vllge of warm-looking stone
with tiny ch.

CARLTON IN LINDRICK Notts
103 SK 5984 3m N of Worksop. CP, 3,513.
Wksp RD. P Wksp. Ch e, m. Sch p.
Bassetlaw CC. Nmn ch.

CARLTON-LE-MOORLAND Lincs (K)
113 SK 9057 7m ENE of Newark. CP, 250.
N Kesteven RD. P LINCOLN. Ch e, m.
Sch pe. Grantham CC.

CARLTON MINIOTT Yorks (N)
91 SE 3981 2m WSW of Thirsk. CP, 526.
Thsk RD. P Thsk. Ch e, m. Sch p. Thsk and
Malton CC.

CARLTON-ON-TRENT Notts
112 SK 7963 6m N of Newark. CP, 195.
Southwell RD. Ch e. Nwk CC.

CARLTON SCROOP Lincs (K)
113 SK 9545 6m NNE of Grantham. CP,
198. W Kesteven RD. Ch e, m. Sch pe.
Grnthm CC.

CARLYON BAY Cornwall
185, 186, 190 SX 0552 3m E of St Austell.
Loc, St Astll w Fowey MB. P St Astll.
Truro CC.

CARNABY Yorks (E)
93 TA 1465 2m WSW of Bridlington. CP,
380. Brdlngtn RD. P Brdlngtn. Ch e.
Brdlngtn CC. See also Haisthorpe.

CARNBREA Cornwall
189 SW 6841 just SW of Redruth. Loc,
Camborne-Redrth UD. Former mining vllge.
To SW, Carn Brea Hill (A.M.).

CARNFORTH Lancs
89 SD 4970 6m NNE of Lancaster. UD,
4,258. P. Lncstr CC. Iron and rly tn. C.
Lakeside Rly Estates Co Museum houses
steam locomotives.

CARNHELL GREEN Cornwall
189 SW 6137 3m WSW of Camborne. Loc,
Gwinear-Gwithian CP. P Cmbne.

CARNKIE Cornwall
190 SW 7134 5m SSE of Redruth. Loc,
Wendron CP. P Rdrth. Ch m.

CARNON DOWNS Cornwall
190 SW 7940 3m SSW of Truro. Loc, Feock
CP. P Truro. Ch m.

CARNYORTH Cornwall
189 SW 3733 6m WNW of Penzance. Loc,
St Just UD.

CARPERBY Yorks (N)
90 SE 0089 7m W of Leyburn.
CP(Cpby-cum-Thoresby), 192. Aysgarth RD.
P Lbn. Ch f, m. Richmond CC.

CARR CROSS Lancs
101 SD 3713 3m SE of Southport. Loc,
Scarisbrick CP.

CARRINGTON Ches
101 SJ 7492 7m WSW of Manchester. CP,
642. Bucklow RD. P Urmston, MNCHSTR.
Ch e, m. Knutsford CC. Petro-chemical wks.

CARRINGTON Lincs (L)
114 TF 3155 7m N of Boston. CP, 526.
Spilsby RD. Ch e. Sch p. Horncastle CC. See
also New Bolingbroke.

CARR SHIELD Nthmb
84 NY 8047 13m SSW of Hexham. Loc,
W Allen CP. Hxhm RD. P Hxhm. Ch e.
Sch p. Hxhm CC.

CARR VALE Derbys
112 SK 4669 just SW of Bolsover. Loc,
Blsvr UD. P Blsvr, Chesterfield.

CARRVILLE Co Durham
85 NZ 3043 2m ENE of Durham. Loc,
Belmont CP. Drhm RD. P DRHM. Ch m2.
Drhm CC.

CARSHALTON London
170 TQ 2764 3m W of Croydon. Loc,
Sutton LB. P Surrey. Cshltn BC (CC). C.
Hse*, early 18c, now RC convent.

CARSINGTON Derbys
111 SK 2553 5m SW of Matlock. CP, 114.
Ashbourne RD. P DERBY. Ch e. Sch pe.
W Derbys CC.

CARTER'S CLAY Hants
168 SU 3024 4m NW of Romsey. Loc,
Lockerley CP.

CARTERTON Oxon
157/158 SP 2806 5m WSW of Witney. Loc,
Black Bourton CP. P OXFORD. Ch e, m, r.
Sch p, pr.

CARTERWAY HEADS Nthmb
77, 78 NZ 0451 4m W of Consett. Loc,
Shotley Low Quarter CP. Hexham RD.
Hxhm CC.

CARTHEW Cornwall
185, 186 SX 0056 2m N of St Austell. Loc,
St Astll w Fowey MB. P St Astll. Truro CC.
In the china clay distr.

CARTHORPE Yorks (N)
91 SE 3083 4m SE of Bedale. CP, 243.
Bdle RD. P Bdle. Ch m. Thirsk and Malton CC.

CARTINGTON Nthmb
71 NU 0304 2m NW of Rothbury. CP, 143.
Rthbry RD. Berwick-upon-Tweed CC.

CARTMEL Lancs
88, 89 SD 3878 2m WNW of
Grange-over-Sands. Loc, Lr Allithwaite CP.
N Lonsdale RD. P Grnge-over-Snds.
Ch e, f, m. Sch pe, se. Morecambe and
Lnsdle CC. C. Priory Gatehouse (NT)*, 14c.
Priory ch is also parish ch: woodwork,
monmts.

CARTMEL FELL Lancs
89 SD 4188 7m S of Windermere. CP, 328.
N Lonsdale RD. Ch e. Sch pe. Morecambe
and Lnsdle CC.

CASHMOOR Dorset
179 ST 9713 7m NE of Blandford. Loc,
Sixpenny Handley CP.

CASSINGTON Oxon
145 SP 4510 5m NW of Oxford. CP, 532.
Witney RD. P OXFD. Ch e, m. Sch pe.
Mid-Oxon CC (Banbury). Ch has 13c
benches.

CASSOP COLLIERY Co Durham
85 NZ 3438 5m ESE of Durham. Loc,
Cssp-cum-Quarrington CP. Drhm RD.
P(Cssp), DRHM. Ch e, m. Sch p. Drhm CC.

CASTERTON Westm
89 SD 6279 1m NE of Kirkby Lonsdale. CP,

253. S Westm RD. Ch e. Sch pe. Westm CC.
See also High Csttn. Ch full of Vctrn and
early 20c wall-paintings. C. Sch founded
1833 for daughters of clergymen.

CASTERTON, GREAT Rutland
123 TF 0009 2m NW of Stamford. See Gt
Cstrtn.

CASTLE ACRE Norfolk
125 TF 8115 4m N of Swaffham. CP, 872.
Freebridge Lynn RD. P King's Lynn.
Ch e, m. Sch pe. NW Nflk CC (K's Lnn).
Impressive rems of 11c-13c cstle and 12c
priory (both A.M.). 15c ch: scrn, font
cover.

CASTLE ASHBY Northants
133 SP 8659 6m SSW of Wellingborough.
CP, 166. Northampton RD. P NTHMPTN.
Ch e. Daventry CC (S Nthnts). C. A. Hse*,
Elizn hse with later additions, in fine grnds
with lakes; seat of Earl of Nthmptn. 14c
priest's brass in ch.

CASTLE BANK Staffs
119 SJ 9021 1m SW of Stafford. Loc, Cstle
Ch CP. Stffd RD. Stffd and Stone CC. Rems
of motte and bailey cstle beside M6
motorway.

CASTLE BOLTON Yorks (N)
90 SE 0391 5m WNW of Leyburn. CP(Cstle
Bltn w E and W Bltn), 75. Lbn RD. P Lbn.
Ch e. Richmond CC. 14c cstle, well
preserved. Mary Queen of Scots imprisoned
here 1568.

CASTLE BROMWICH Warwicks
131 SP 1489 5m ENE of Birmingham. CP,
9,205. Meriden RD. P BMNGHM 36.
Ch e, m, v. Sch i2, j, pe, s. Mrdn CC.

CASTLE BYTHAM Lincs (K)
123 SK 9818 6m WSW of Bourne. CP, 513.
S Kesteven RD. P Grantham. Ch e, m.
Sch p. Rutland and Stamford CC.
Earthworks are only rems of 11c cstle.

CASTLE CAMPS Cambs
148 TL 6242 3m WSW of Haverhill. CP,
535. S Cambs RD. P CAMBRIDGE. Ch e, v.
Sch p. Cambs CC. See also Cmps Grn. Ch
stands in outer moat of former cstle blt by
1st Earl of Oxford in 12c.

CASTLE CARROCK Cumb
76 NY 5455 4m S of Brampton. CP, 286.

Border RD. P Carlisle. Ch e, m. Sch pe.
Penrith and the Bdr CC.

CASTLE CARY Som
166 ST 6432 3m WSW of Bruton. CP,
1,843. Wincanton RD. P. Ch e, m, r, v2.
Sch p. Wells CC.

CASTLE COMBE Wilts
156 ST 8477 5m WNW of Chippenham. CP,
486. Calne and Chppnhm RD. P Chppnhm.
Ch e, c. Sch p. Chppnhm CC. Show vllge of
golden stone; 15c ch much enriched by
wealthy local clothiers in 16c.

CASTLE DONINGTON Leics
121 SK 4427 5m SW of Long Eaton. CP,
3,563. Cstle Dnngtn RD. P DERBY.
Ch e, b, m, r. Sch pe, s. Loughborough CC.
Ch: 15c brasses. Power stn. To SE, E
Midlands Airpt.

CASTLE EATON Wilts
157 SU 1495 7m N of Swindon. CP, 298.
Highworth RD. P Swndn. Ch e. Sch pe.
Devizes CC.

CASTLE EDEN Co Durham
85 NZ 4238 2m S of Peterlee. CP, 420.
Easington RD. P. Ch e. Easngtn CC. See also
Edn Vale. The cstle is 18c with 19c
additions.

CASTLEFORD Yorks (W)
97 SE 4325 7m ENE of Wakefield. MB,
38,220. P. Pontefract and Cstlefd BC
(Pntfrct). See also Whitwood. Coal-mining
tn.

CASTLE FROME Herefs
142, 143 SO 6645 6m S of Bromyard. CP,
150. Ledbury RD. P Ldbry. Ch e. Sch pe.
Leominster CC.

CASTLE GRESLEY Derbys
120 SK 2718 4m SSE of Burton-on-Trent.
CP, 1,175. Repton RD. P Btn-on-Trnt,
Staffs. Ch b, m. Sch i. Belper CC. See also
High Cross Bank.

CASTLE HEATON Nthmb
64 NT 9041 4m ENE of Coldstream. Loc,
Cornhill-on-Tweed CP.

CASTLE HEDINGHAM Essex
149 TL 7835 4m NNW of Halstead. CP,
936. Hlstd RD. P Hlstd. Ch e, v. Sch p.
Saffron Walden CC. Old mkt tn. Nmn

Castlemorton

Castlemorton
Cstle*. 12c-13c ch has 14c screen, double hammerbeam roof and early 17c brick twr. 12c churchyard cross.

CASTLEMORTON Worcs
143 SO 7937 6m S of Malvern. CP, 551. Upton upon Severn RD. P Mlvn. Ch e. Sch pe. S Worcs CC. See also Hollybush.

CASTLE PULVERBATCH Shrops
118 SJ 4202 8m SSW of Shrewsbury. Loc, Ch Plvrbtch CP. Motte is sole rems of Nmn cstle.

CASTLE RISING Norfolk
124 TF 6624 4m NE of King's Lynn. CP, 185. Freebridge Lynn RD. P K's Lnn. Ch e. NW Nflk CC(K's Lnn). Rems of Nmn cstle (A.M.). Trinity Hsptl*, almshouses of 1616 with orig furnishings still in use.

CASTLESIDE Co Durham
84 NZ 0748 2m SW of Consett. Loc, Healeyfield CP. Lanchester RD. P Cnstt. Ch e, m2. Sch p. NW Drhm CC.

CASTLETHORPE Bucks
146 SP 7944 2m NNW of Wolverton. CP, 492. Newport Pagnell RD. P Wlvtn. Ch e, m. Sch p. Buckingham CC.

CASTLETON Derbys
111 SK 1582 8m NE of Buxton. CP, 671. Chapel en le Frith RD. P SHEFFIELD. Ch e, m. Sch pe. High Peak CC. Peveril Cstle (A.M.), Nmn. Many caverns and potholes, esp Peak Cavern, with electrically lit ½m underground walk.

CASTLETON Yorks (N)
86 NZ 6808 7m SE of Guisborough. Loc, Danby CP. P Whitby. Ch e, m. Sch p.

CASTON Norfolk
136 TL 9597 6m WNW of Attleborough. CP, 347. Wayland RD. P Attlbrgh. Ch e, m. Sch pe. S Nflk CC.

CASTOR Hunts
134 TL 1298 4m W of Peterborough. CP, 627. Ptrbrgh RD. Ch e, c. Sch pe. Ptrbrgh BC (CC). Roman Cstr pottery made here; known throughout Rmn empire. Ch has outstanding Nmn twr. To E, standing stones known as Little John and Robin Hood.

CATBRAIN Glos
155,156 ST 5780 5m N of Bristol. Loc, Almondsbury CP.

CATCHGATE Co Durham
78 NZ 1652 4m E of Consett. Loc, Stanley UD. P Stnly.

CATCLIFFE Yorks (W)
103 SK 4288 3m S of Rotherham. CP, 2,030. Rthrhm RD. P Rthrhm. Ch m. Sch p. Rother Valley CC.

CATCOTT Som
165 ST 3939 6m ENE of Bridgwater. CP, 420. Brdgwtr RD. P Brdgwtr. Ch e, m. Sch p. Brdgwtr CC.

CATERHAM Surrey
170 TQ 3355 6m S of Croydon. UD(Ctrhm and Warlingham), 35,781. P. E Srry CC. See also Chaldon, Hamsey Grn, Whyteleafe, Woldingham. Rsdntl distr on slopes of N Downs.

CATFIELD Norfolk
126 TG 3821 6m ENE of Wroxham. CP, 653. Smallburgh RD. P Gt Yarmouth. Ch e, m. Sch pe. N Nflk CC.

CATFORD London
161, 171 TQ 3773 6m SE of Lndn Br. Loc, Lewisham LB. Lwshm W BC(Lwshm S). Location of tn hall and borough council offices.

CATFORTH Lancs
94 SD 4735 6m NW of Preston. Loc, Woodplumpton CP. P Prstn. Ch m2, r. Sch p.

CATHARINE SLACK Yorks (W)
96, 102 SE 0928 2m N of Halifax. Loc, Queensbury and Shelf UD.

CATHERINGTON Hants
181 SU 6914 5m NNW of Havant. Loc, Horndean CP. P Portsmouth. Ch e, m. Sch pe. Ch has 14c wall-paintings.

CATHERSTON LEWESTON Dorset
177 SY 3794 2m NE of Lyme Regis. CP, 31. Bridport RD. Ch e. W Dst CC.

CATMORE Berks
158 SU 4580 6m SE of Wantage. CP, 47. Wntge RD. Ch e. Abingdon CC.

CATON Lancs
89, 94 SD 5364 4m NE of Lancaster. CP(Ctn-w-Littledale), 2,048. Lunesdale RD. P LNCSTR. Ch e, b, m, r. Sch pe. Lncstr CC. See also Brookhouse, Crossgill. On R Lune

near bend in river painted by Turner. Ch at Brookhouse, qv.

CATSFIELD Sussex (E)
183, 184 TQ 7213 2m SW of Battle. CP, 710. Bttle RD. P Bttle. Ch e, m. Sch pe. Rye CC.

CATSHILL Worcs
130, 131 SO 9573 2m N of Bromsgrove. Loc, Brmsgrve UD. P Brmsgrve.

CATTAL Yorks (W)
97 SE 4454 5m NE of Wetherby. CP, 110. Nidderdale RD. Ch m. Harrogate CC.

CATTAWADE Suffolk (E)
150 TM 1033 1m N of Manningtree. Loc, Brantham CP. P Mnnngtree. Xylonite wks beside rly.

CATTERALL Lancs
94 SD 4942 9m NNW of Preston. CP, 702. Garstang RD. P Prstn. Ch m. N Fylde CC.

CATTERICK Yorks (N)
91 SE 2497 5m ESE of Richmond. CP, 2,011. Rchmnd RD. P Rchmnd. Ch e, m. Sch, pe. Rchmnd CC. Racecourse.

CATTERICK BRIDGE Yorks (N)
91 SE 2299 4m ESE of Richmond. Loc, Rchmnd RD. Rchmnd CC. The br carries the old Gt N Rd over the R Swale.

CATTERICK CAMP Yorks (N)
91 SE 1897 2m SSE of Richmond. Loc, Rchmnd RD. P. Ch e2, bc, m, v. Sch i, p3, s. Rchmnd CC. Large permanent military camp.

CATTERLEN Cumb
83 NY 4833 3m NW of Penrith. CP, 408. Pnrth RD. Pnrth and the Border CC. See also Newton Reigny.

CATTERTON Yorks (W)
97 SE 5146 2m NE of Tadcaster. CP, 39. Tdcstr RD. Barkston Ash CC.

CATTHORPE Leics
132, 133 SP 5578 4m ENE of Rugby. CP, 122. Lutterworth RD. P Rgby, Warwickshire. Ch e. Blaby CC (Harborough). Wedged between M1 motorway and A5 rd.

CATTISTOCK Dorset
177, 178 SY 5999 9m NE of Bridport. CP, 504. Dorchester RD. P Dchstr. Ch e, m. Sch pe. W Dst CC. Ch has carillon of 25 bells cast in Belgium.

CATTON Norfolk
126 TG 2312 2m N of Norwich. CP. St Faith's and Aylsham RD. Ch e. Sch pe. N Nflk CC (Central Nflk).

CATTON Nthmb
77 NY 8257 4m S of Haydon Br. Loc, Allendale CP. Hexham RD. P Allndle, Hxhm. Hxhm CC.

CATTON Yorks
91 SE 3778 4m WSW of Thirsk. CP, 44. Thsk RD. Ch m. Sch p. Thsk CC.

CATWICK Yorks (E)
99 TA 1345 5m WSW of Hornsea. CP, 173. Holderness RD. P Hull. Ch e, m. Bridlington CC.

CATWORTH Hunts
134 TL 0873 7m ESE of Thrapston. CP, 262. St Neots RD. P HUNTINGDON. Ch e, m. Hunts CC.

CAULCOTT Oxon
145 SP 5024 5m WNW of Bicester. Loc, Lr Heyford CP.

CAULDON Staffs
111 SK 0749 6m NE of Cheadle. Loc, Waterhouses CP. Ch e, m. Sch pe. Quarries.

CAULDWELL Derbys
120 SK 2617 4m S of Burton-on-Trent. CP, 71. Repton RD. Belper CC.

CAUNDLE MARSH Dorset
178 ST 6713 3m SE of Sherborne. CP, 86. Shbne RD. Ch e. W Dst CC.

CAUNSALL Worcs
130 SO 8481 3m NNE of Kidderminster. Loc, Wolverley CP.

CAUNTON Notts
112 SK 7460 5m NW of Newark. CP, 334. Southwell RD. P Nwk. Ch e, m. Sch pe. Nwk CC. Picturesque vllge with stream and partly Nmn ch.

CAVENDISH Suffolk (W)
149 TL 8046 2m ENE of Clare. CP, 701.

Clre RD. P Sudbury. Ch e, c. Sch p. Bury St Edmunds CC. Stour valley vllge with Perp ch and thatched cottages beside grn.

CAVENHAM Suffolk (W)
136 TL 7669 7m NW of Bury St Edmunds. CP, 200. Mildenhall RD. P Bury St Eds. Ch e. Bury St Eds CC.

CAVERSFIELD Oxon
145, 146 SP 5825 2m N of Bicester. CP,937. Ploughley RD. Ch e. Banbury CC (Henley). Nmn ch with Saxon twr and oldest inscribed bell (early 13c) in England.

CAVERSHAM Berks
159 SU 7274 N distr of Reading. Loc, Rdng CB. P Rdng. Rdng N BC (Rdng). Rsdntl distr across river from tn centre.

CAVERSWALL Staffs
110, 119 SJ 9542 5m ESE of Stoke-on-Trent. CP. Cheadle RD. P Stke-on-Trnt. Ch e, m, r. Sch pe, pr. Leek CC. See also Cookshill, Hulme, Washerwall, Werrington. The Cstle, Jcbn, on site of former cstle; now a convent.

CAWOOD Yorks (W)
97 SE 5737 4m NW of Selby. CP, 967. Selby RD. P Slby. Ch e, m. Sch pe. Barkston Ash CC. Archbishops of York had palace here, of which 15c gatehouse remains. Swing br over R Ouse.

CAWSAND Cornwall
187 SX 4350 3m S of Torpoint. Loc, Maker-with-Rame CP. St Germans RD. P Plymouth, Devon. Ch e, c. Sch p. Bodmin CC. Vllge at bottom of wooded valley, with sand and shingle beach.

CAWSTON Norfolk
125 TG 1323 4m SW of Aylsham. CP, 944. St Faith's and Aylshm RD. P NORWICH, NOR 75X. Ch e, m, v. Sch pe. N Nflk CC (Central Nflk). Outstanding 14c—15c ch.

CAWTHORNE Yorks (W)
102 SE 2808 4m NE of Penistone. CP, 1,091. Pnstne RD. P Barnsley. Ch e, m. Sch pe. Pnstne CC. Cannon Hall*, 18c hse by Carr of York. Museum of furniture and paintings.

CAWTON Yorks (N)
92 SE 6476 5m SSE of Helmsley. CP, 61. Hlmsly RD. Thirsk and Malton CC.

CAXTON Cambs
134 TL 3058 8m E of St Neots. CP, 368. Chesterton RD. P CAMBRIDGE. Ch e, b. Cambs CC. Vllge on Ermine St (A14); once an important coaching stage.

CAXTON END Cambs
134 TL 3157 9m E of St. Neots. Loc, Bourn CP.

CAYNHAM Shrops
129 SO 5573 3m ESE of Ludlow. CP, 1,063. Ldlw RD. P Ldlw. Ch e, m. Sch pe. Ldlw CC. See also Cleehill. Iron Age fort on Tinker's Hill.

CAYTHORPE Lincs (K)
113 SK 9348 8m N of Grantham. CP, 846. W Kesteven RD. P Grnthm. Ch e, m. Sch p. Grnthm CC. See also Frieston.

CAYTHORPE Notts
112 SK 6845 8m ENE of Nottingham. CP, 215. Southwell RD. P NTTNGHM. Newark CC. Mid-18c water mill.

CAYTON Yorks (N)
93 TA 0583 4m SSE of Scarborough. CP, 892. Scbrgh RD. P Scbrgh. Ch e, m2. Sch p. Scbrgh CC (Scbrgh and Whitby).

CELLARHEAD Staffs
110 SJ 9547 5m ENE of Stoke-on-Trent. Loc, Cheadle RD. Ch m. Sch s. Leek CC.

CERNE ABBAS Dorset
178 ST 6601 7m NNW of Dorchester. CP, 513. Dchstr RD. P Dchstr. Ch e, c. Sch pe. W Dst CC. Slight rems of mdvl abbey. On hillside NE, C. Giant (NT), virile figure cut in the chalk.

CERNEY WICK Glos
157 SU 0796 5m SE of Cirencester. Loc, S Cny CP. Ch e.

CHACELEY Glos
143 SO 8530 3m WSW of Tewkesbury. CP, 162. Gloucester RD. P GLCSTR. Ch e. W Glos CC.

CHACEWATER Cornwall
190 SW 7444 4m ENE of Redruth. CP, 1,270. Truro RD. P Truro. Ch e, m3. Sch p. Truro CC. Former mining vllge.

CHACKMORE Bucks
146 SP 6835 1m NNW of Buckingham.

CP(Radclive-cum-Chckmre), 231. Bcknghm RD. P BCKNGHM. Ch e, m. Sch pe. Bcknghm CC. At S edge of grnds of Stowe Sch; hse is 18c, once home of Duke of Bcknghm. Large grnds, laid out 18c, sometimes open.

CHACOMBE Northants
145 SP 4943 3m NE of Banbury. CP, 310. Brackley RD. P Bnbry, Oxon. Ch e, m. Sch pe. Daventry CC (S Nthnts). C. Priory*, 17c hse on site of Augustinian priory of which 13c chpl survives.

CHADDERTON Lancs
101 SD 9105 1m W of Oldham. UD, 32,406. P Oldhm. Oldhm W BC. Foxdenton Hse*, 17c–18c.

CHADDESLEY CORBETT Worcs
130, 131 SO 8973 4m ESE of Kidderminster. CP, 1,462. Kddrmnstr RD. P Kddrmnstr. Ch e. Sch pe. Kddrmnstr CC. See also Bluntington, Drayton, Harvington. Half-timbered hses. Ch partly Nmn with carved font.

CHADDLEWORTH Berks
158 SU 4177 7m NNW of Newbury. CP, 458. Wantage RD. P Nbry. Ch e. Sch pe. Abingdon CC.

CHADLINGTON Oxon
145 SP 3221 3m SSE of Chipping Norton. CP, 620. Chppng Ntn RD. P OXFORD. Ch e, b, m. Sch pe. Banbury CC.

CHADSHUNT Warwicks
145 SP 3452 7m SW of Southam. CP, 57. Sthm RD. Ch e. Stratford-on-Avon CC (Strtfd).

CHADWELL Leics
122 SK 7824 4m NNE of Melton Mowbray. Loc, Scalford CP. Ch e.

CHADWELL ST MARY Essex
161, 171 TQ 6478 2m N of Tilbury. Loc, Thurrock UD. P Grays. Thrrck BC (CC).

CHADWICK END Warwicks
131 SP 2073 5m SE of Solihull. Loc, Balsall CP. Meriden RD. P Slhll. Ch v2. Mrdn CC.

CHAFFCOMBE Som
177 ST 3510 2m NE of Chard. CP, 176. Chd RD. P Chd. Ch e. Yeovil CC.

CHAGFORD Devon
175 SX 7087 3m WNW of Moretonhampstead. CP, 1,346. Okehampton RD. P Newton Abbot. Ch e, m, r, v. Sch pe, s. W Dvn CC (Torrington). See also Easton, Frenchbeer. Former stannary tn (tax assessment for tin). Centre for Dartmoor visitors.

CHAILEY Sussex (E)
183 TQ 3919 6m N of Lewes. CP, 1,963. Chly RD. Ch e, v. Sch pe, s. Lws CC. See also N Cmmn, S St.

CHAINHURST Kent
171, 172, 184 TQ 7347 5m SSW of Maidstone. Loc, Marden CP.

CHALBURY Dorset
179 SU 0106 4m N of Wimborne. CP, 126. Wmbne and Cranborne RD. Ch e. N Dst CC. Ch: rare Ggn interior.

CHALDON Surrey
170 TQ 3155 6m S of Croydon. Loc, Caterham and Warlingham UD. P Ctrhm. Ch: 12c wall-painting; 13c bell.

CHALDON HERRING Dorset
178 SY 7983 8m SE of Dorchester. CP, 196. Wareham and Purbeck RD. P(E Chldn), Dchstr. Ch e. S Dst CC. See also W Chldn.

CHALE IOW
180 SZ 4877 5m W of Ventnor. CP, 511. Isle of Wght RD and CC. P Vntnr. Ch e, bv, m. Sch pe. See also Blackgang, Chle Grn, Pyle. To SE on St Catherine's Hill, rems of 14c lighthouse and oratory (A.M.) and 18c lighthouse. 1m NE, Hoy's Monmt commemorates visit of Tsar, 1814.

CHALE GREEN IOW
180 SZ 4879 6m S of Newport. Loc, Chle CP. P Ventnor.

CHALFIELD, GREAT Wilts
166 ST 8663 3m N of Trowbridge. See Gt Chlfld.

CHALFONT ST GILES Bucks
159, 160 SU 9893 3m SSE of Amersham. CP, 5,957. Amrshm RD. P. Ch e, c, m, r. Sch i, j, s. Chesham and Amrshm CC (S Bucks). See also Jordans. Milton's Cottage*, where the poet stayed during plague in 1665.

CHALFONT ST PETER Bucks
159, 160 TQ 0090 1m N of Gerrards Cross.
CP, 12,460. Amersham RD. P Grrds Crss.
Ch e, b, r, v. Sch i2, j, je, pr, s. Chesham and
Amrshm CC (S Bucks). See also Horn Hill.

CHALFORD Glos
156, 157 SO 8902 3m ESE of Stroud. CP,
2,556. Strd RD. P Strd. Ch e, b, m, v2.
Sch p, pe. Strd CC. See also Brownshill,
Bussage. Blt on very steep side of the
Golden Valley.

CHALGRAVE Beds
147 TL 0127 3m N of Dunstable. CP, 319.
Luton RD. Ch e. Sch pe. S Beds CC. See
also Tebworth, Wingfield.

CHALGROVE Oxon
158, 159 SU 6396 5m NNE of Wallingford.
CP, 652. Bullingdon RD. P OXFORD.
Ch e, m. Sch p. Henley CC. Monmt
commemorates Civil War skirmish of 1643
in which John Hampden was mortally
wounded.

CHALLACOMBE Devon
163 SS 6941 6m SSW of Lynton. CP, 153.
Barnstaple RD. P Bnstple. Ch e, m. N Dvn CC.
See also Barton Tn.

CHALLOCK LEES Kent
172 TR 0050 4m E of Charing. Loc, Chllck
CP. E/Ashford RD. P(Chllck), Ashfd.
Ch e, m. Sch, p. Ashfd CC.

CHALTON Beds
147 TL 0326 3m NNE of Dunstable. Loc,
Toddington CP. P Luton. Ch m. Sch p.

CHALTON Hants
181 SU 7316 5m S of Petersfield. Loc,
Clanfield CP. P Portsmouth. Ch e.

CHALVINGTON Sussex (E)
183 TQ 5109 4m W of Hailsham. CP, 126.
Hlshm RD. Ch e. Lewes CC (Eastbourne).

CHANDLER'S CROSS Herts
160 TQ 0698 3m WNW of Watford. Loc,
Sarratt CP.

CHANDLER'S FORD Hants
168 SU 4320 2m W of Eastleigh. Loc,
Eastlgh MB. P Eastlgh.

CHANTRY Som
166 ST 7146 4m W of Frome. Loc, Whatley
CP. P Frme. Ch e.

CHAPEL ALLERTON Som
165 ST 4050 4m SW of Cheddar. CP, 268.
Axbridge RD. Ch e. Weston-super-Mare CC.
See also Stone Allerton. To E, Ashton Mill,
restored stone circular windmill.

CHAPEL AMBLE Cornwall
185 SW 9975 2m NNE of Wadebridge. Loc,
St Kew CP. P Wdbrdge.

CHAPEL BRAMPTON Northants
133 SP 7266 4m NNW of Northampton. CP,
230. Brixworth RD. P NTHMPTON. Sch p.
Daventry CC(Kettering).

CHAPEL CHORLTON Staffs
110, 119 SJ 8137 5m SSW of
Newcastle-under-Lyme. CP(Chpl and Hill
Chltn), 455. Ncstle-undr-Lme RD. Ch e.
Sch pe. N-u-L BC.

CHAPELEND WAY Essex
148, 149 TL 7038 5m SSE of Haverhill.
Loc, Stambourne CP.

CHAPEL-EN-LE-FRITH Derbys
111 SK 0680 5m N of Buxton. CP, 6,460.
Chpl en le Frth RD. P Stockport, Cheshire.
Ch e, m4, r. Sch i, ie, j, s. High Peak CC.
Mnfg tn, esp brake linings.

CHAPEL HADDLESEY Yorks (W)
97 SE 5826 4m SSW of Selby. CP, 155.
Slby RD. P Slby. Ch m. Sch pe. Barkston
Ash CC.

CHAPEL HILL Lincs (K)
114 TF 2054 6m S of Woodhall Spa. Loc,
Dogdyke CP. P LNCLN. Ch e, m.

CHAPEL LAWN Shrops
129 SO 3176 3m NE of Knighton. Loc,
Clun CP. Ch e. Sch pe.

CHAPEL LE DALE Yorks (W)
90 SD 7477 10m NNW of Settle. Loc,
Ingleton CP. P Carnforth, Lancs. Ch e.
Sch pe. Among massive limestone scars. To
N, Weathecote Cave and several potholes.
2m NE, Ribblehead rly viaduct on
Settle—Carlisle line; many navvies who died
during its building are buried in C. le D.
churchyard.

CHAPEL ROW Berks
158 SU 5769 7m ENE of Newbury. Loc,
Bucklebury CP. P Reading. At end of
mile-long oak avenue planted in 18c to

commemorate Queen Anne's visit to Bucklebury.

CHAPEL ST LEONARDS Lincs (L)
114 TF 5572 6m N of Skegness. CP, 909. Spilsby RD. P Skgnss. Ch e, m. Sch p. Horncastle CC. Massive sea defences. Caravans.

CHAPEL STILE Westm
82 NY 3205 4m WNW of Ambleside. Loc, Lakes UD. P Amblsde. Westm CC.

CHAPELTON Devon
163 SS 5726 5m SSE of Barnstaple. Loc, Tawstock CP.

CHAPELTOWN Lancs
95, 101 SD 7315 4m NNE of Bolton. Loc, Turton UD. P Ttn, Bltn. Darwen CC. To S, Ttn Twr*, hse of various dates blt on site of 15c pele twr.

CHAPELTOWN Yorks (W)
102, 103 SK 3596 6m N of Sheffield. Loc, Ecclesfield CP. P SHFFLD. Ch e, m4, v3. Sch p.

CHAPMANSLADE Wilts
166 ST 8247 3m E of Frome. CP, 457. Warminster and Westbury RD. P Wstbry. Ch e, b, c. Sch pe. Wstbry CC.

CHAPPEL Essex
149 TL 8928 5m ESE of Halstead. CP, 373. Lexden and Winstree RD. P Colchester. Ch e, c. Sch pe. Clchstr CC.

CHARD Som
177 ST 3208 12m SE of Taunton. MB, 7,905. P. Yeovil CC. Highest' tn in Som (400ft). Light industries, producing lace, twine, shirts, pencils, etc.

CHARDSTOCK Devon
177 ST 3104 3m SSW of Chard. CP, 1,965. Axminster RD. P Axmnstr. Ch e. Sch pe2. Honiton CC. See also Smallridge, Tytherleigh.

CHARFIELD Glos
156 ST 7292 10m W of Tetbury. CP, 730. Thornbury RD. P Wotton-under-Edge. Ch e, v. Sch p. S Glos CC.

CHARING Kent
172, 184 TQ 9549 6m NW of Ashford. CP, 2,322. W Ashfd RD. P Ashfd. Ch e, m.

Sch pe. Ashfd CC. See also Chrng Hth, Westwell Leacon. Small tn on hillside below Pilgrims' Way. Scant rems of former Archbishop's Palace. 4m N, Otterden Pk*, restored Tdr/Ggn mansion.

CHARING HEATH Kent
172, 184 TQ 9249 2m W of Charing. Loc, Chrng CP. P Ashford. Ch e. Sch pe.

CHARINGWORTH Glos
144 SP 2039 3m E of Chipping Campden. Loc, Ebrington CP.

CHARLBURY Oxon
145 SP 3519 6m SSE of Chipping Norton. CP. Chppng Ntn RD. P OXFORD. Ch e, b, m, r. Sch p, s. Banbury CC. Small tn on R Evenlode. To SW in 600-acre pk, Cornbury Pk, mainly 17c hse.

CHARLCOMBE Som
156 ST 7467 2m N of Bath. CP, 486. Bathavon RD. Ch e. N Som CC. See also Langridge, Lansdown, Woolley.

CHARLECOTE Warwicks
131 SP 2656 4m E of Stratford. CP, 177. Strtfd-on-Avon RD. Ch e. Strtfd-on-Avn CC (Strtfd). C. Pk (NT)*, Elizn hse; deer pk, where Shakespeare is said to have poached.

CHARLES Devon
163 SS 6832 5m NNW of S Molton. CP, 203. S Mltn RD. Ch e, m. N Dvn CC. See also Brayford.

CHARLESTOWN Cornwall
185, 186, 190 SX 0351 2m ESE of St Austell. Loc, St Astll w Fowey MB. P St Astll. Truro CC. Port, exporting china clay; named after Charles Rashleigh, who blt harbour late 18c.

CHARLESTOWN Dorset
178 ST 6479 2m W of Weymouth. Loc, Chickerell CP. P Wmth.

CHARLESTOWN Yorks (W)
95 SD 9726 1m WSW of Hebden Br. Loc, Blackshaw CP. Hepton RD. Ch e, b. Sowerby CC.

CHARLES TYE Suffolk (E)
149 TM 0252 4m SSW of Stowmarket. Loc, Ringshall CP.

CHARLESWORTH Derbys
102 SK 0092 2m WSW of Glossop. CP,

Charleton

1,189. Chapel en le Frith RD. P
Broadbottom, Hyde, Cheshire. Ch e, b, c, r.
Sch p, pe. High Peak CC. See also Chunal.

CHARLETON Devon
187, 188 SX 7542 2m SE of Kingsbridge.
CP, 289. Kngsbrdge RD. Ch e. Sch pe.
Totnes CC.

CHARLINCH Som
165 ST 2337 4m W of Bridgwater. CP, 55.
Brdgwtr RD. Ch e. Brdgwtr CC.

CHARLTON London
161, 171 TQ 4177 6m ESE of Lndn Br.
Loc, Greenwich LB. Grnwch BC. A London
'village'. C. Hse*, Jcbn mnr hse, is
community centre and library.

CHARLTON Northants
145 SP 5235 4m W of Brackley. Loc,
Newbottle CP. P Banbury, Oxon. Ch v.
Sch pe.

CHARLTON Sussex (W)
181 SU 8812 5m NNE of Chichester. Loc,
Singleton CP. Flint hses in valley N of
Goodwood Racecourse.

CHARLTON Wilts
157 ST 9688 2m ENE of Malmesbury. CP,
376. Mlmsbry RD. P Mlmsbry. Ch e. Sch pe.
Chippenham CC. C. Pk, turreted 17c
mansion with 18c alterations.

CHARLTON Wilts
166, 167 ST 9021 3m E of Shaftesbury.
Loc, Donhead St Mary CP. Ch e.

CHARLTON Wilts
167 SU 1156 4m SW of Pewsey. CP, 92.
Psy RD. Ch e. Devizes CC.

CHARLTON Wilts
167 SU 1724 4m SSE of Salisbury. Loc,
Downton CP. P(Chltn All Saints), Slsbry.
Ch e.

CHARLTON Worcs
144 SP 0145 2m NW of Evesham. CP, 401.
Pershore RD. P Pshre. Ch e. S Worcs CC.

CHARLTON Yorks (N)
86 NZ 6415 2m E of Guisborough. Loc,
Skelton and Brotton UD. P Saltburn-by-the-
Sea.

CHARLTON ABBOTS Glos
144 SP 0324 3m S of Winchcombe. Loc,

Sudeley CP. Cheltenham RD. Ch e.
Cirencester and Tewkesbury CC. Early 17c
Cotswold mnr hse.

CHARLTON ADAM Som
166, 177 ST 5328 4m NNE of Ilchester.
Loc, Charlton Mackrell CP. P Somerton.
Ch e.

CHARLTON HORETHORNE Som
166 ST 6623 4m SW of Wincanton. CP,
460. Wncntn RD. P Sherborne, Dorset.
Ch e. Sch pe. Wells CC. See also Stowell.

CHARLTON KINGS Glos
143, 144 SO 9620 2m SSE of Cheltenham.
UD, 10,088 P. Chltnhm BC. Rsdntl suburb
of Chltnhm.

CHARLTON MACKRELL Som
177 ST 5228 4m N of Ilchester. CP, 626.
Langport RD. Ch e, m. Sch pe. Yeovil CC.
See also Chltn Adam.

CHARLTON MARSHALL Dorset
178, 179 ST 9003 2m SE of Blandford. CP,
637. Blndfd RD. P Blndfd Forum. Ch e. N
Dst CC.

CHARLTON MUSGROVE Som
166 ST 7229 1m NE of Wincanton. CP,
374. Wncntn RD. P Wncntn. Ch e. Wells CC.
See also Barrow.

CHARLTON-ON-OTMOOR Oxon
145, 146 SP 5615 4m SSW of Bicester. CP,
296. Ploughley RD. P OXFORD. Ch e, b.
Sch pe. Mid-Oxon CC(Henley). Ch: scrn.

CHARLWOOD Surrey
170, 182 TQ 2441 3m WSW of Horley. CP,
2,801. Dorking and Hly RD. P Hly.
Ch e, c, v. Sch p. Dkng CC. See also
Gatwick, Hookwood, Lowfield Hth. Partly
Nmn ch: wall-paintings.

CHARMINSTER Dorset
178 SY 6792 2m NNW of Dorchester. CP,
2,134. Dchstr RD. P Dchstr. Ch e. Sch pe. W
Dst CC. See also Forston.

CHARMOUTH Dorset
177 SY 3693 2m ENE of Lyme Regis. CP,
890. Bridport RD. P Brdpt. Ch e, v. Sch p.
W Dst CC. Small resort of Rgncy hses.
Described by Jane Austen. Scene of Charles
II's attempt to escape to France, 1651.

CHARNDON Bucks
145, 146 SP 6724 5m E of Bicester. CP,
381. Buckingham RD. P Bcstr, Oxon. Ch e.
Sch p. Bcknghm CC.

CHARNEY BASSETT Berks
158 SU 3794 5m NNW of Wantage. CP,
195. Faringdon RD. P Wntge. Ch e. Sch pe.
Abingdon CC. C. Mnr, partly 13c.

CHARNOCK RICHARD Lancs
100 SD 5515 2m WSW of Chorley. CP,
1,307. Chly RD. P Chly. Ch e. Sch pe. Chly
CC.

CHARSFIELD Suffolk (E)
150 TM 2556 5m NNW of Woodbridge. CP,
298. Deben RD. P Wdbrdge. Ch e, b. Sch pe.
Eye CC.

CHART CORNER Kent
172 TQ 7950 4m SE of Maidstone. Loc, Cht
Sutton CP.

CHARTER ALLEY Hants
168 SU 5957 4m NW of Basingstoke. Loc,
Bsngstke RD. Ch m. Bsngstke CC.

CHARTERHOUSE Som
165 ST 4955 3m ENE of Cheddar. Loc,
Blagdon CP. Ch e. Centre of Mendip
lead-mining in Roman times.

CHARTERVILLE ALLOTMENTS Oxon
145 SP 3110 3m W of Witney. Loc, Minster
Lovell CP.

CHART, GREAT Kent
172, 184 TQ 9842 2m W of Ashford. See Gt
Cht.

CHARTHAM Kent
173 TR 1054 3m SW of Canterbury. CP,
3,774. Bridge-Blean RD. P Cntrbry. Ch e.
Sch p, s. Cntrbry CC. See also Chthm Hatch,
Shalmsford St. Dominated by paper mill.
Fine brass in ch.

CHARTHAM HATCH Kent
173 TR 1056 3m W of Canterbury. Loc,
Chthm CP. P Cntrbry. Ch m.

CHARTRIDGE Bucks
159 SP 9303 2m NW of Chesham. CP,
1,578. Amersham RD. Chshm and Amrshm
CC(Aylesbury). See also Bellingdon.

CHART SUTTON Kent
172, 184 TQ 8049 5m SE of Maidstone. CP,

758. Hollingbourn RD. P Mdstne. Ch e.
Mdstne CC. See also Cht Corner.

CHART, THE Surrey
171 TQ 4251 2m E of Oxted. Loc,
Limpsfield CP. P Oxtd. Ch e.

CHARWELTON Northants
132 SP 5355 5m SSW of Daventry. CP, 157.
Dvntry RD. P Rugby, Warwickshire. Ch e.
Dvntry CC (S Nthnts). Ch: brasses. Packhorse
br.

CHASE TERRACE Staffs
120 SK 0409 4m E of Cannock. Loc,
Burntwood CP. P Walsall. Sch s. Coal-mining
distr.

CHASETOWN Staffs
120 SK 0408 4m W of Lichfield. Loc,
Burntwood CP. P Walsall. Ch m2, r. Sch pr.
Mining distr. To W, Chasewater, large lake.

CHASTLETON Oxon
144 SP 2429 3m SE of Moreton-in-Marsh.
CP, 148. Chipping Norton RD. P Mtn-in-Msh,
Glos. Ch e. Banbury CC. C. Hse*, early 17c
Cotswold mnr hse; box gdn. Small Nmn and
later ch alongside.

CHATBURN Lancs
95 SD 7644 2m NE of Clitheroe. CP, 1,047.
Clthroe RD. P Clthroe. Ch e, m. Sch pe.
Clthroe CC.

CHATCULL Staffs
110, 119 SJ 7934 8m SSW of
Newcastle-under-Lyme. Loc, Eccleshall CP.

CHATHAM Kent
172 TQ 7567 28m ESE of London. MB,
56,921. P. Rochester and Chthm BC. See
also Capstone, Walderslade, Wayfield. Naval
base.

CHATHILL Nthmb
71 NU 1827 6m SE of Belford. Loc,
Ellingham CP. P.

CHATTENDEN Kent
172 TQ 7571 2m NNE of Rochester. Loc,
Strood RD. P Rchstr. Sch p. Gravesend CC.
Royal Engineers' barracks.

CHATTERIS Cambs
135 TL 3985 7m S of March. UD, 5,566. P.
Isle of Ely CC. See also Horseway. Has
six-storey windmill.

CHATTERTON Lancs
95, 101 SD 7918 5m N of Bury. Loc, Ramsbottom UD.

CHATTISHAM Suffolk (E)
149 TM 0942 4m E of Hadleigh. CP, 108. Samford RD. Ch e. Sudbury and Woodbridge CC.

CHATTON Nthmb
71 NU 0528 4m E of Wooler. CP, 630. Glendale RD. P Alnwick. Ch e, v. Sch pe. Berwick-upon-Tweed CC. See also Greendykes, Horton, N Hazelrigg, S Hzlrgg.

CHATWELL, GREAT Staffs
119 SJ 7914 4m SE of Newport. See Gt Chtwll.

CHAWLEIGH Devon
163, 175 SS 7112 8m S of S Molton. CP, 488. Crediton RD. P Chulmleigh. Ch e, m. Sch p. Tiverton CC (Torrington). Ch has famous scrn.

CHAWSTON Beds
134 TL 1556 3m SSW of St Neots. Loc, Roxton CP. Formerly known as Chalverstone.

CHAWTON Hants
169 SU 7037 1m S of Alton. CP, 481. Altn RD. P Altn. Ch e. Sch pe. Petersfield CC. Jane Austen lived here; hse now museum.

CHEADLE Ches
101 SJ 8588 3m WSW of Stockport. UD(Chdle and Gatley), 60,648. P. Chdle BC (CC). See also Chdle Hulme, Heald Grn.

CHEADLE Staffs
120 SK 0043 8m E of Stoke-on-Trent. CP, 8,010. Chdle RD. P Stke-on-Trnt. Ch e, c, m3, r, v3. Sch p, pe, pr, s2, sr. Leek CC.

CHEADLE HULME Ches
101 SJ 8786 3m SW of Stockport. Loc, Chdle and Gatley UD. P Chdle.

CHEAM London
170 TQ 2464 5m W of Croydon. Loc, Sutton LB. P Sttn, Surrey. Sttn and Chm BC. On Surrey border (formerly in Surrey). Rsdntl distr.

CHEARSLEY Bucks
146, 159 SP 7110 3m NNE of Thame. CP, 309. Aylesbury RD. P Aylesbury. Ch e. Sch p. Aylesbury CC.

CHEBSEY Staffs
119 SJ 8628 4m SW of Stone. CP, 525. Stne RD. P STFFD. Ch e. Sch pe. Stffd and Stne CC. See also Norton Br.

CHECKENDON Oxon
158, 159 SU 6682 5m NNE of Pangbourne. CP, 855. Henley RD. P Reading, Berks. Ch e. Sch pe. Hnly CC. Chiltern vllge. Nmn ch.

CHECKLEY Ches
110 SJ 7346 6m SSE of Crewe. CP(Chckly cum Wrinehill), 221. Nantwich RD. P Stoke-on-Trent, Staffs. Nntwch CC.

CHECKLEY Staffs
120 SK 0237 4m SSE of Cheadle. CP, 2,534. Chdle RD. P Stoke-on-Trent. Ch e, m. Sch pe. Leek CC. See also Hollington, Lr Tean, Upr Tean. Outstanding mdvl ch. Shafts of Saxon crosses in churchyard.

CHEDBURGH Suffolk (W)
136 TL 7957 6m SW of Bury St Edmunds. CP, 218. Thingoe RD. Ch e. Sch p. Bury St Eds CC.

CHEDDAR Som
165 ST 4553 8m NW of Wells. CP, 2,845. Axbridge RD. P. Ch e, b2, m, r. Sch p, s. Weston-super-Mare CC. At foot of famous gorge with 450ft cliffs and vast caves*. Vllge devoted to tourist industry. Large round reservoir to W.

CHEDDINGTON Bucks
146, 159 SP 9217 4m N of Tring. CP, 655. Wing RD. P Leighton Buzzard, Beds. Ch e, m. Sch p. Buckingham CC.

CHEDDLETON Staffs
110 SJ 9752 3m SSW of Leek. CP, 5,215. Cheadle RD. P Lk. Ch e, m. Sch i, pe. Lk CC. See also Basford Grn. Beside R Churnet, Chddltn Flint Mill*, corn mill converted in 18c to grind flint.

CHEDDON FITZPAINE Som
177 ST 2427 2m NNE of Taunton. CP, 564. Tntn RD. P Tntn. Ch e. Sch pe. Tntn CC. See also Upr Chddn.

CHEDGRAVE Norfolk
137 TM 3699 6m NNE of Bungay. CP, 399.
Loddon RD. Ch e. S Nflk CC.

CHEDINGTON Dorset
177 ST 4805 4m SE of Crewkerne. CP, 97.
Beaminster RD. P Bmnstr. Ch e. W Dst CC.

CHEDISTON Suffolk (E)
137 TM 3577 2m W of Halesworth. CP,
224. Blyth RD. P Hlswth. Ch e. Eye CC.

CHEDWORTH Glos
144 SP 0511 4m WSW of Northleach. CP,
720. Nthlch RD. P Cheltenham. Ch e, c.
Sch pe. Cirencester and Tewkesbury CC. 1m
N, in Chdwth Wd, Roman villa (NT)*.

CHEDZOY Som
165 ST 3437 3m E of Bridgwater. CP, 304.
Brdgwtr RD. P Brdgwtr. Ch e. Sch j.
Brdgwtr CC.

CHEESEMAN'S GREEN Kent
172, 173, 184 TR 0238 3m SSE of Ashford.
Loc, E Ashfd RD, W Ashfd RD. Ashfd CC.

CHELDON Devon
163, 175 SS 7313 8m S of S Molton. CP,
32. S Mltn RD. Ch e. N Dvn CC.

CHELFORD Ches
110 SJ 8174 6m W of Macclesfield. CP, 437.
Mcclsfld RD. P Mcclsfld. Ch e. Sch pe.
Mcclsfld CC.

CHELLINGTON Beds
134 SP 9555 7m NW of Bedford.
CP(Carlton and Chllngtn), 550. Bdfd RD.
Ch e. Bdfd CC.

CHELMARSH Shrops
130 SO 7287 3m S of Bridgnorth. CP, 475.
Brdgnth RD. P Brdgnth. Ch e. Sch pe.
Ludlow CC. See also Hampton, Sutton.

CHELMONDISTON Suffolk (E)
150 TM 2037 5m SE of Ipswich. CP, 784.
Samford RD. P Ipswch. Ch e, b, m. Sudbury
and Woodbridge CC. See also Pin Mill.

CHELMORTON Derbys
111 SK 1170 4m ESE of Buxton. CP, 312.
Bakewell RD. P Bxtn. Ch e, m. Sch p.
W Derbys CC.

CHELMSFORD Essex
161, 162 TL 7006 30m NE of London. MB,
58,125. P. Chlmsfd CC. See also Springfield,
Widford. Cathedral and county tn, with
shire hall of 1791. Centre for electrical and
radio industry.

CHELSEA London
160, 170 TQ 2778 2m SW of Charing Cross.
LB(Kensington and Chlsea), 208,480. BCs:
Knsngtn, Chlsea (Knsngtn N, Knsngtn S,
Chlsea). On N bank of Thames; Battersea,
Albert, Chlsea Brs. Famous sts: C.
Embankment, Cheyne Walk. Royal Hspl (by
Wren) houses pensioners. Barracks.

CHELSFIELD London
171 TQ 4864 2m SE of Orpington. Loc,
Bromley LB. P Oprngtn, Kent. Orpngtn BC
(CC). On Kent border (formerly in Kent).

CHELSHAM Surrey
171 TQ 3759 5m SE of Croydon.
CP(Chlshm and Farleigh). Godstone RD.
Ch e. E Srry CC (Reigate).

CHELSWORTH Suffolk (W)
149 TL 9848 4m E of Lavenham. CP, 151.
Cosford RD. Ch e. Sudbury and Woodbridge
CC. Picturesque; colour-washed thatched
hses — townsmen's country retreats. Ch
approached by drive of private hse; has mdvl
wall-painting over chancel arch.

CHELTENHAM Glos
143, 144 SO 9422 8m ENE of Gloucester.
MB, 69,734. P. Chltnhm BC. Largely rsdntl
and shopping tn; erstwhile spa. Many Rgncy
bldngs; also Vctrn.

CHELVESTON Northants
134 SP 9969 3m NE of Rushden.
CP(Chlvstn cum Caldecott), 974. Oundle
and Thrapston RD. P Wellingborough.
Ch e, b. Wllngbrgh CC.

CHELVEY Som
155, 165 ST 4668 8m WSW of Bristol. Loc,
Brockley CP. Ch e.

CHELWOOD Som
166 ST 6361 6m NNW of Radstock. CP,
150. Clutton RD. P BRISTOL. Ch e. N Som
CC.

CHELWOOD GATE Sussex (E)
183 TQ 4130 5m SSE of E Grinstead. Loc,
Danehill CP. P Haywards Hth.

CHENEY LONGVILLE Shrops
129 SO 4284 2m NNW of Craven Arms.
Loc, Wistanstow CP.

CHENIES Bucks
159, 160 TQ 0198 4m SE of Chesham. CP,
1,068. Amersham RD. P Rickmansworth,
Herts. Ch e, b. Sch p. Chshm and Amrshm
CC (S Bucks). Chpl, monmts, brasses in ch.
16c mnr hse, restored.

CHERHILL Wilts
157 SU 0370 3m E of Calne. CP, 2,620.
Clne and Chippenham RD. P Clne. Ch e.
Sch pe. Chppnhm CC. See also Yatesbury.
White Horse, cut 1780, on hillside to S.

CHERINGTON Glos
156, 157 ST 9098 4m N of Tetbury. CP,
184. Ttbry RD. P Ttbry. Ch e. Stroud CC.

CHERINGTON Warwicks
145 SP 2936 3m SE of Shipston on Stour.
CP, 195. Shpstn on Str RD. P Shpstn on Str.
Ch e. Sch pe. Stratford-on-Avon CC
(Strtfd).

CHERITON Devon
163 SS 7346 2m SSE of Lynton. Loc,
Brendon CP.

CHERITON Hants
168 SU 5828 6m E of Winchester. CP, 563.
Wnchstr RD. P Alresford. Ch e, m. Sch p.
Wnchstr CC.

CHERITON BISHOP Devon
175 SX 7793 5m NNE of
Moretonhampstead. CP, 521. Crediton RD.
P Exeter. Ch e, v. Sch p. Tiverton CC
(Torrington).

CHERITON CROSS Devon
175 SX 7793 5m NNE of
Moretonhampstead. Loc, Crediton RD, St
Thomas RD. Ch m. Tiverton CC (Torrington
CC, Tvtn CC).

CHERITON FITZPAINE Devon
176 SS 8606 4m NNE of Crediton. CP, 545.
Crdtn RD. P Crdtn. Ch e, m. Sch p.
Tiverton CC (Torrington). See also Upham.
Cob and thatch. Almshouses, founded 1594.

CHERRINGTON Shrops
118, 119 SJ 6619 5m W of Newport. CP,
122. Wellington RD. The Wrekin CC.
Half-timbered mnr hse of 1635.

CHERRY BURTON Yorks (E)
98 SE 9842 3m NW of Beverley. CP, 404.
Bvrly RD. P Bvrly. Ch e. Sch pe.
Haltemprice CC.

CHERRY HINTON Cambs
135 TL 4856 3m ESE of Cambridge. Loc,
Cmbrdge MB. P CMBRDGE.

CHERRY WILLINGHAM Lincs (L)
113 TF 0372 3m E of Lincoln. CP, 1,061.
Welton RD. P LNCLN. Ch e, m. Sch p, s.
Gainsborough CC. Ggn ch.

CHERTSEY Surrey
170 TQ 0466 3m S of Staines. UD, 44,886.
P. Chtsy and Walton BC (Chtsy CC). See
also Addlestone, Lyne, Ottershaw,
Woodham. On R Thames; seven-arched 18c
br. Scant rems of C. Abbey, founded in 7c.

CHESELBOURNE Dorset
178 SY 7699 7m NE of Dorchester. CP,
206. Dchstr RD. P Dchstr. Ch e, m. Sch p.
W Dst CC.

CHESHAM Bucks
159, 160 SP 9501 7m WSW of Hemel
Hempstead. UD, 20,416. P. Chshm and
Amersham CC (Aylesbury). See also Botley,
Lye Grn.

CHESHAM BOIS Bucks
159, 160 SU 9699 1m S of Chesham. CP,
2,054. Amersham RD. P Amrshm. Ch e, r2.
Sch pe. Chshm and Amrshm CC (S Bucks).

CHESHUNT Herts
161 TL 3502 14m NNE of London. UD,
44,947. P Waltham Cross. E Herts CC. See
also Appleby St, Goff's Oak, Wlthm Crss.
Large rsdntl area in Lea valley.

CHESLYN HAY Staffs
119 SJ 9707 2m S of Cannock. CP, 2,991.
Cnnck RD. P Walsall. Ch m. Sch p. SW
Staffs CC (Cnnck).

CHESSINGTON London
170 TQ 1863 4m S of Kingston. Loc,
Kngstn upon Thames LB. P Surrey.
Surbiton BC. Zoo on W side of Leatherhead
Rd.

CHESTER Ches
109 SJ 4066 15m SSE of Birkenhead. CB,
62,696. P(CHSTR). City of Chstr CC. The
Roman 'Deva'; walls (A.M.) well preserved.

Cathedral, mainly 14c, has fine cloisters. The Rows, with raised shops, are unique.

CHESTERBLADE Som
166 ST 6641 3m ESE of Shepton Mallet. Loc, Evercreech CP. Ch e.

CHESTERFIELD Derbys
111 SK 3871 10m S of Sheffield. MB, 70,153. P. Chstrfld BC. See also Hasland, Newbold, New Whittington, Whttngtn. Mkt and indstrl tn; coal, iron, engineering. Ch has famous twisted spire.

CHESTERFIELD Staffs
120 SK 1005 3m SSW of Lichfield. Loc, Wall CP.

CHESTERFORD, GREAT Essex
148 TL 5042 4m NNW of Saffron Walden. See Gt Chstrfd.

CHESTER-LE-STREET Co Durham
78 NZ 2751 6m N of Durham. UD, 20,531. P. Chstr-le-Strt CC. See also Chester Moor, Pelton Fell. Colliery tn on site of Roman fort. Chemicals. Ch: effigies. To E, Lumley Cstle, 14c. To NE, Lambton Cstle, 19c.

CHESTER MOOR Co Durham
85 NZ 2649 2m SSW of Chester-le-Street. Loc, Chstr-le-Strt UD. P Chstr-le-Strt.

CHESTERTON Cambs
135 TL 4759 2m ENE of Cambridge. Loc, Cmbrdge MB. P CMBRDGE.

CHESTERTON Hunts
134 TL 1295 5m WSW of Peterborough. CP, 131. Norman Cross RD. Ch e. Hunts CC.

CHESTERTON Oxon
145, 146 SP 5621 2m SW of Bicester. CP, 421. Ploughley RD. P Bcstr. Ch e. Sch pe. Banbury CC (Henley).

CHESTERTON Warwicks
132 SP 3558 5m WSW of Southam. CP(Chstrtn and Kingston), 156. Sthm RD. Ch e. Stratford-on-Avon CC (Strtfd). On hill to NW, windmill of curious construction. Beyond it, rems of Roman stn on Fosse Way.

CHESTERWOOD Nthmb
77 NY 8365 just NW of Haydon Br. Loc, Hdn CP. Hxhm RD. Hxhm CC.

CHESTFIELD Kent
173 TR 1365 2m SE of Whitstable. Loc, Whtstble UD.

CHESWARDINE Shrops
119 SJ 7129 4m SE of Mkt Drayton. CP, 871. Mkt Drtn RD. P Mkt Drtn. Ch e. Sch p. Oswestry CC. See also Chipnall, Gt Soudley.

CHESWICK Nthmb
64 NU 0346 5m SSE of Berwick-upon-Tweed. Loc, Ancroft CP.

CHETNOLE Dorset
178 ST 6008 6m SSW of Sherborne. CP, 221. Shbne RD. P Shbne. Ch e. W Dst CC.

CHETTISHAM Cambs
135 TL 5483 2m NNE of Ely. Loc, Ely UD.

CHETTLE Dorset
179 ST 9513 6m NE of Blandford. CP, 86. Blndfd RD. P Blndfd Forum. Ch e. N Dst CC.

CHETTON Shrops
129, 130 SO 6690 4m WSW of Bridgnorth. CP, 360. Brdgnth RD. P Brdgnth. Ch e. Sch p. Ludlow CC.

CHETWODE Bucks
145, 146 SP 6429 4m SW of Buckingham. CP, 94. Bcknghm RD. Ch e. Bcknghm CC.

CHETWYND ASTON Shrops
119 SJ 7517 1m SSE of Newport. CP, 302. Wellington RD. Ch e. The Wrekin CC.

CHEVELEY Cambs
135 TL 6860 3m SE of Newmarket. CP, 1,624. Nmkt RD. P Nmkt, Suffolk. Ch e, c. Sch pe. Cambs CC.

CHEVENING Kent
171 TQ 4857 3m NW of Sevenoaks. CP, 2113. Svnks RD. Ch e. Sch pe. Svnks CC. See also Bessels Grn, Chipstead, Whitley Row. Estate vllge of 17c–18c mansion in large pk, home of Stanhope family.

CHEVERELL, GREAT Wilts
167 ST 9854 5m SSW of Devizes. See Gt Chvrll.

CHEVINGTON Suffolk (W)
136 TL 7859 5m SW of Bury St Edmunds. CP, 373. Thingoe RD. P Bury St Eds. Ch e. Sch pe. Bury St Eds CC.

CHEVINGTON DRIFT Nthmb
71 NZ 2699 3m S of Amble. Loc, E
Chvngtn CP. P Morpeth. Ch m.

CHEVITHORNE Devon
164 SS 9715 2m NE of Tiverton. Loc, Tvtn
MB. P Tvtn. C. Barton, rebuilt c 1600; gdn*.

CHEW MAGNA Som
165, 166 ST 5763 6m S of Bristol. CP,
1,038. Clutton RD. P BRSTL. Ch e, b, m, r.
Sch p, s. N Som CC. See also N Wick. Ch has
fine twr. Many stone hses. To S, C. Valley
Lake (Brstl Waterworks).

CHEW STOKE Som
165, 166 ST 5561 7m S of Bristol. CP, 819.
Clutton RD. P BRSTL. Ch e, m. Sch pe. N
Som CC. To SE, C. Valley Lake (Brstl
Waterworks). To N on Pagan's Hill, traces of
Roman temple.

CHEWTON KEYNSHAM Som
155, 156 ST 6566 6m SE of Bristol. Loc,
Compton Dando CP.

CHEWTON MENDIP Som
165, 166 ST 5953 6m NE of Wells. CP, 560.
Wlls RD. P Bath. Ch e, m. Sch pe. Wlls CC.
Ch has fine 126ft twr.

CHICHELEY Bucks
146 SP 9045 2m NE of Newport Pagnell.
CP, 145. Npt Pgnll RD. P Npt Pgnll. Ch e.
Buckingham CC.

CHICHESTER Sussex (W)
181 SU 8604 14m ENE of Portsmouth. MB,
20,547. P. Chchstr CC. See also New
Fishbourne. On site of Roman tn. County
tn of W Sussex. Cathedral largely Nmn. 16c
mkt cross at tn centre. Festival theatre,
1962.

CHICKERELL Dorset
178 SY 6480 2m WNW of Weymouth. CP,
2,299. Dorchester RD. P Wmth.
Ch e, b, c, m, v. Sch p. S Dst CC. See also
Charlestown.

CHICKLADE Wilts
166, 167 ST 9134 7m SSE of Warminster.
CP, 50. Mere and Tisbury RD. Ch e.
Westbury CC.

CHICKNEY Essex
148 TL 5728 3m SW of Thaxted. CP, 32.
Dunmow RD. Ch e. Saffron Walden CC. Ch
partly Saxon.

CHIDDEN Hants
180, 181 SU 6517 7m SW of Petersfield.
Loc, Hambledon CP.

CHIDDINGFOLD Surrey
169, 170, 182 SU 9635 4m ENE of
Haslemere. CP, 2,411. Hambledon RD.
P Godalming. Ch e, b, r, v. Sch pe. Farnham
CC. Former centre of glass and iron
industries. Some old hses.

CHIDDINGLY Sussex (E)
183 TQ 5414 4m NW of Hailsham. CP, 814.
Hlshm RD. P Lewes. Ch b, v. Sch p. Lws CC
(Eastbourne). See also Golden Cross.

CHIDDINGSTONE Kent
171 TQ 5045 4m E of Edenbridge. CP, 915.
Sevenoaks RD. P Ednbrdge. Ch e,. Sch pe.
Svnks CC. See also Bough Beech,
Chddngstne Causeway, Chddngstne Hoath.
Vllge st owned by NT. Cstle (17c hse
castellated in 19c Gothic revival) contains
oriental museum*.

CHIDDINGSTONE CAUSEWAY Kent
171 TQ 5246 4m W of Tonbridge. Loc,
Chddngstne CP. P Tnbrdge. Ch e. Sch pe.

CHIDDINGSTONE HOATH Kent
171 TQ 4942 4m SE of Edenbridge. Loc,
Chddngstne CP. P Ednbrdge.

CHIDEOCK Dorset
177 SY 4292 3m W of Bridport. CP, 559.
Brdpt RD. P Brdpt. Ch e, r. W Dst CC. See
also N Chdck. Ch r blt on to mnr hse 1870.
1m SW, Golden Cap, on Wear Cliffs.

CHIDHAM Sussex (W)
181 SU 7903 4m W of Chichester. CP, 936.
Chchstr RD. P Chchstr. Ch e. Sch pe.
Chchstr CC. On arm of Chchstr harbour
opposite Bosham.

CHIEVELEY Berks
158 SU 4773 4m N of Newbury. CP. Nbry
RD. P Nbry. Ch e, b, m. Sch p. Nbry CC.
See also Curridge, Downend.

CHIGNALL ST JAMES Essex
161 TL 6609 3m NW of Chelmsford. Loc,
Chgnll CP. Chlmsfd RD. Ch e, b, c.
Braintree CC (Chlmsfd).

CHIGNALL SMEALY Essex
148, 161 TL 6611 4m NW of Chelmsford.
Loc, Chgnll CP. Chlmsfd RD. P Chlmsfd.
Ch e. Braintree CC (Chlmsfd).

CHIGWELL Essex
161 TQ 4493 6m SSW of Epping. UD,
53,620. P. Eppng Forest CC (Chgwll). See
also Loughton. Ch 17c brass of Archbishop
Harsnett. Ggn hses. Large housing
developments.

CHIGWELL ROW Essex
161 TQ 4693 2m E of Chigwell. Loc,
Chgwll UD.

CHILBOLTON Hants
168 SU 3940 4m SSE of Andover. CP, 688.
Andvr RD. P Stockbridge. Ch e. Winchester
CC (Basingstoke).

CHILCOMB Hants
168 SU 5028 2m ESE of Winchester. CP,
176. Wnchstr RD. Ch e. Wnchstr CC.

CHILCOMBE Dorset
177 SY 5291 4m ESE of Bridport. CP, 14.
Brdpt RD. Ch e. W Dst CC.

CHILCOMPTON Som
166 ST 6451 3m SW of Radstock. CP,
1,436. Clutton RD. P Bath. Ch e, m, r.
Sch ie. N Som CC. See also Downside.

CHILCOTE Leics
120, 121 SK 2811 6m SW of Ashby de la
Zouch. CP, 137. Ashby de la Zch RD.
Loughborough CC.

CHILDER THORNTON Ches
100, 109 SJ 3677 3m W of Ellesmere Port.
Loc, Ellesmre Pt MB. P Little Sutton,
Wirral.

CHILD OKEFORD Dorset
178 ST 8312 5m NW of Blandford. CP, 667.
Sturminster RD. P Blndfd Forum. Ch e.
Sch pe. N Dst CC.

CHILDREN'S HOMES Lancs
95, 101 SD 7418 6m NNE of Bolton. Loc,
Turton UD. Darwen CC.

CHILDREY Berks
158 SU 3687 3m W of Wantage. CP, 450.
Wntge RD. P Wntge. Ch e, m. Sch p.
Abingdon CC. Vast cedar tree, in vicarage
grnds, grown from seed brought from
Aleppo in 17c. Ch contains largest brass in
county.

CHILD'S ERCALL Shrops
118, 119 SJ 6625 6m S of Mkt Drayton.
CP, 653. Mkt Drtn RD. P Mkt Drtn. Ch e.
Sch pe. Oswestry CC.

CHILDSWICKHAM Worcs
144 SP 0738 4m SSE of Evesham. CP, 602.
Eveshm RD. P Broadway. Ch e. Sch p.
S Worcs CC.

CHILFROME Dorset
177, 178 SY 5898 9m NE of Bridport. CP,
60. Dorchester RD. Ch e. W Dst CC.

CHILGROVE Sussex (W)
181 SU 8214 6m NNW of Chichester. Loc,
W Dean CP.

CHILHAM Kent
172, 173 TR 0653 6m SW of Canterbury.
CP, 1,293. E Ashford RD. P Cntrbry.
Ch e. Sch pe. Ashfd CC. See also Old Wives
Lees, Shottenden. Old vllge grouped round
cobbled square. Jcbn hse and rems of mdvl
cstle; gdn* by Capability Brown.

CHILLAND Hants
168 SU 5232 3m NE of Winchester. Loc,
Itchen Valley CP. Wnchstr RD. Wnchstr CC.

CHILLATON Devon
175 SX 4381 6m NW of Tavistock. Loc,
Milton Abbot CP. P Lifton. Ch m.

CHILLENDEN Kent
173 TR 2653 5m SW of Sandwich. Loc,
Goodnestone CP. Ch e. To N, restored
post-mill.

CHILLERTON IOW
180 SZ 4984 3m S of Newport. Loc,
Gatcombe CP. P Npt. Ch m. Sch p.

CHILLESFORD Suffolk (E)
150 TM 3852 7m ENE of Woodbridge. CP,
157. Deben RD. P Wdbrdge. Ch e. Eye CC.
Approached through large Forestry
Commission plantations — or by boat up
Butley Creek.

CHILLINGHAM Nthmb
71 NU 0626 4m ESE of Wooler. CP, 109.
Glendale RD. P Alnwick. Ch e.
Berwick-upon-Tweed CC. See also Hepburn.
12c ch restored in 1966; contains richly
carved 15c table tomb. 14c-19c cstle,
semi-derelict. Famous cattle herd in pk*.

CHILLINGTON Devon
187, 188 SX 7942 4m ESE of Kingsbridge.
Loc, Stokenham CP. P Kngsbrdge. Ch m.

CHILLINGTON Som
177 ST 3811 3m SE of Ilminster. Cp, 82.
Chard RD. Ch e. Sch p. Yeovil CC.

CHILMARK Wilts
167 ST 9732 9m NE of Shaftesbury.
CP, 414. Mere and Tisbury RD. P Salisbury.
Ch e, b. Sch pe. Westbury CC. Local quarries
produced pale stone of which, *inter alia,*
Salisbury Cathedral and Wilton Hse are blt.

CHILSON Oxon
145 SP 3119 2m W of Charlbury. CP, 129.
Chipping Norton RD. Ch m. Banbury CC.

CHILSWORTHY Cornwall
175, 187 SX 4172 4m NE of Callington.
Loc, Calstock CP. P Gunnislake. Ch m.

CHILSWORTHY Devon
174 SS 3206 2m NNW of Holsworthy. Loc,
Hlswthy Hmlts CP. Hlswthy RD. P Hlswthy.
Ch m. W Dvn CC (Tavistock).

CHILTHORNE DOMER Som
177 ST 5219 3m NW of Yeovil. CP, 484.
Yvl RD. P Yvl. Ch e. Sch pe. Yvl CC.

CHILTON Berks
158 SU 4985 3m SW of Didcot. CP, 680.
Wantage RD. P Ddct. Ch e. Sch p. Abingdon
CC.

CHILTON Bucks
146, 159 SP 6811 4m NNW of Thame. CP,
362. Aylesbury RD. P Aylesbury. Ch e.
Sch pe. Aylesbury CC. See also Easington.
Several old bldngs in picturesque setting.

CHILTON Co Durham
85 NZ 3031 4m ESE of Spennymoor. CP,
6,242. Sedgefield RD. P Ferryhill.
Ch e, m2, s. Sch p, s. Drhm CC (Sdgfld). See
also Chltn Bldngs.

CHILTON Suffolk (W)
149 TL 8942 1m ENE of Sudbury. CP, 200.
Melford RD. Ch e. Sdbry and Woodbridge CC.

CHILTON BUILDINGS Co Durham
85 NZ 2829 5m E of Bishop Auckland. Loc,
Chltn CP.

CHILTON CANTELO Som
166, 177 ST 5722 4m N of Yeovil. CP, 93.
Yvl RD. Ch e. Yvl CC. See also Ashington.

CHILTON FOLIAT Wilts
158 SU 3270 2m NW of Hungerford. CP,
346. Marlborough and Ramsbury RD.
P Hngrfd, Berks. Ch e, m. Sch pe. Devizes CC.
Vllge with duck pond on R Kennet. To W,
Littlecote*, Tdr mnr hse; riverside grnds.

CHILTON POLDEN Som
165 ST 3739 5m ENE of Bridgwater. CP,
426. Brdgwtr RD. P Brdgwtr. Ch e. Brdgwtr
CC.

CHILTON STREET Suffolk (W)
149 TL 7547 1m NW of Clare. Loc, Clre CP.

CHILTON TRINITY Som
165 ST 2939 1m N of Bridgwater. CP, 180.
Brdgwtr RD. Ch e. Brdgwtr CC.

CHILWORTH Hants
180 SU 4018 4m N of Southampton. CP,
1,137. Romsey and Stockbridge RD. P
STHMPTN. Ch e. Eastleigh CC. C. Mnr part
of Sthmptn University.

CHILWORTH Surrey
169, 170 TQ 0247 2m SE of Guildford.
Loc, St Martha CP. Gldfd RD. P Gldfd.
Ch e, r, v. Sch pe. Dorking CC.

CHIMNEY Oxon
158 SP 3500 6m S of Witney. Loc, Aston
Bampton and Shifford CP.

CHINEHAM Hants
168, 169 SU 6554 2m NE of Basingstoke.
Loc, Basing CP. P Bsngstke.

CHINGFORD London
161 TQ 3894 7m SW of Epping. Loc,
Waltham Forest LB. Chngfd BC (Epping
CC). To NE, Eppng Forest. To W, Lea
Valley reservoirs. Queen Elizabeth's Hunting
Lodge* now museum (Eppng Frst exhibits).

CHINLEY Derbys
111 SK 0482 6m N of Buxton. CP(Chnly,
Buxworth and Brownside), 2,107. Chapel en
le Frith RD. P Stockport, Cheshire.
Ch e, m2, v. Sch p. High Peak CC.

CHINLEY HEAD Derbys
102, 111 SK 0484 7m N of Buxton. Loc,
Chnly, Buxworth and Brownside CP.

CHINNOR Oxon
159 SP 7500 4m SE of Thame. CP, 1,751.
Bullingdon RD. P OXFORD. Ch e, m, v.
Sch pe. Henley CC. See also Emmington,
Henton. Below Chiltern ridge. Large modern
housing estate. Extensive quarries, cement
wks to S. Dec ch: brasses.

CHIPNALL Shrops
110, 119 SJ 7231 4m ESE of Mkt Drayton.
Loc, Cheswardine CP.

CHIPPENHAM Cambs
135 TL 6669 4m NNE of Newmarket. CP,
366. Nmkt RD. P Ely. Ch e, c. Sch p. Cambs
CC. Model vllge; sch 1714. C. Pk 17c–19c.
C. Fen to W is nature reserve.

CHIPPENHAM Wilts
156, 157 ST 9173 16m WSW of Swindon.
MB, 18,662. P. Chppnhm CC. Busy tn with
modern indstrl development; large brake
factory.

CHIPPERFIELD Herts
160 TL 0401 4m S of Hemel Hempstead.
CP, 1,522. Hml Hmpstd RD. P King's
Langley. Ch e, bv. Sch pe. Hml Hmpstd CC.

CHIPPING Herts
148 TL 3532 5m S of Royston. Loc,
Buckland CP.

CHIPPING Lancs
94, 95 SD 6243 8m W of Clitheroe. CP,
951. Clthroe RD. P Preston. Ch e, r.
Sch pe, pr. Clthroe CC. See also Hesketh
Lane.

CHIPPING CAMPDEN Glos
144 SP 1539 8m ESE of Evesham. CP,
1,951. N Cotswold RD. P. Ch e, b, m, r.
Sch pe, pr, s. Cirencester and Tewkesbury
CC. See also Broad Cmpdn. Handsome
stone-blt Ctswld tn. Wool trade centre in
mdvl times. Large Perp 'wool' ch. Arcaded
mkt hall (NT)*, Jcbn.

CHIPPINGHILL Essex
149, 162 TL 8115 just N of Witham. Loc,
Wthm UD. P Wthm.

CHIPPING NORTON Oxon
145 SP 3127 12m SW of Banbury. MB,
4,763. P. Bnbry CC. Old Cotswold 'wool'
tn, 700ft up. Wide main st and mkt place.
Brewing, wool textiles (19c tweed mill to
W).

CHIPPING ONGAR Essex
161 TL 5502 6m NNW of Brentwood. See
Ongar.

CHIPPING SODBURY Glos
156 ST 7282 11m NE of Bristol. Loc,
Sdbry CP. Sdbry RD. P BRSTL. Ch e, b, r.

Sch pe, s. S Glos CC. Old mkt tn. Ch has
huge W twr.

CHIPPING WARDEN Northants
145 SP 4948 6m NNE of Banbury. CP, 423.
Brackley RD. P Bnbry, Oxon. Ch e, m.
Sch p. Daventry CC (S Nthnts).

CHIPSTABLE Som
164 ST 0427 6m NE of Bampton. CP, 281.
Wellington RD. Ch e. Taunton CC. See also
Waterrow.

CHIPSTEAD Kent
171 TQ 4956 2m WNW of Sevenoaks. Loc,
Chevening CP. P Svnks.

CHIPSTEAD Surrey
170 TQ 2757 5m ESE of Epsom. Loc,
Banstead UD. P Coulsdon. Retains some
vllge character.

CHIRBURY Shrops
128 SO 2698 3m ENE of Montgomery. CP,
818. Clun and Bishop's Cstle RD. P
MNTGMRY. Ch e. Sch pe. Ludlow CC. See
also Marton, Middleton, Priestweston,
Rorrington, Wotherton. Ch is nave of
former priory. Half-timbered sch, 17c.

CHIRTON Wilts
167 SU 0757 5m SE of Devizes. CP, 264.
Dvzs RD. P Dvzs. Ch e. Sch pe. Dvzs CC.

CHISBURY Wilts
157 SU 2766 4m WSW of Hungerford. Loc,
Lit Bedwyn CP.

CHISELBOROUGH Som
177 ST 4614 4m NNE of Crewkerne. CP,
253. Yeovil RD. P Stoke-sub-Hamdon.
Ch e, v. Yvl CC.

CHISELDON Wilts
157 SU 1879 4m SE of Swindon. CP, 2,598.
Highworth RD. P Swndn. Ch e, m. Sch p.
Devizes CC. See also Badbury. 1m W,
Burderop Pk, Elizn and later mansion in fine
grnds.

CHISHILL, GREAT Cambs
148 TL 4238 4m ESE of Royston. See Gt
Chshll.

CHISLEHAMPTON Oxon
158 SU 5998 7m SE of Oxford. Loc,
Stadhampton CP. Ch e. Ggn ch and hall.
Camoys Ct Farm dates from 14c.

CHISLEHURST London
161, 171 TQ 4470 3m E of Bromley. Loc,
Brmly LB. P Kent. Chslhst BC (CC). Mainly
rsdntl distr.

CHISLET Kent
173 TR 2264 4m SE of Herne Bay. CP, 684.
Bridge-Blean RD. P Canterbury. Ch e, m, v.
Sch pe. Cntrbry CC. See also Boyden Gate,
Upstreet.

CHISWELLGREEN Herts
160 TL 1304 2m SSW of St. Albans. Loc, St
Stephen CP. St Albns RD. S Herts CC (St
Albns).

CHISWICK London
160, 170 TQ 2078 1m W of Hammersmith.
Loc, Hounslow LB. Brentford and Isleworth
BC (Brntfd and Chswck). In loop of
R Thames, on N bank; C. Br. To W, C. Flyover
(M4 motorway). C. Hse (A.M.), 18c
Italianate hse. Hogarth Hse*, 17c.

CHISWORTH Derbys
101 SJ 9992 3m WSW of Glossop. CP, 230.
Chapel en le Frith RD. Ch m. Sch pm. High
Peak CC.

CHITHURST Sussex (W)
181 SU 8423 3m WNW of Midhurst. CP,
229. Mdhst RD. Ch e. Chichester CC
(Horsham).

CHITTENING TRADING ESTATE Glos
155 ST 5381 6m NW of Bristol. Loc, Brstl
CB. Brstl NW BC. Steel wks. 'Carbon black'
wks. Fabrication. Warehousing.

CHITTERING Cambs
135 TL 4970 7m SSW of Ely. Loc,
Waterbeach CP. P CAMBRIDGE. Ch b.
Sch p.

CHITTERNE Wilts
167 ST 9943 8m E of Warminster. CP, 278.
Wmnstr and Westbury RD. P Wmnstr.
Ch e2, b. Wstbry CC.

CHITTLEHAMHOLT Devon
163 SS 6420 5m SW of S Molton. CP, 190.
S Mltn RD. P Umberleigh. Ch e, v.
N Dvn CC.

CHITTLEHAMPTON Devon
163 SS 6325 5m W of S Molton. CP, 713. S
Mltn RD. P Umberleigh. Ch e, m. Sch pe.
N Dvn CC. See also Eastacott, Umberleigh. Ch
has lofty Perp twr, richly carved. Vllge has
large central square.

CHITTOE Wilts
157 ST 9566 4m SW of Calne. Loc,
Bromham CP. Ch e, m.

CHIVELSTONE Devon
187, 188 SX 7838 5m SE of Kingsbridge.
CP, 349. Kngsbrdge RD. P Kngsbrdge.
Ch e, m. Totnes CC. See also E Prawle. Ch:
remarkable scrn; plpt made from single
block of wood.

CHOBHAM Surrey
169, 170 SU 9761 3m NW of Woking. CP.
Bagshot RD. P Wkng. Ch e, v.
Sch i, pe2, s, sb. NW Srry CC (Chertsey).
See also Burrowhill. Ch has panelled oak
font.

CHOLDERTON Wilts
167 SU 2242 5m E of Amesbury. CP, 204.
Amesbury RD. P Salisbury. Ch e. Sch pe.
Slsbry CC.

CHOLESBURY Bucks
159 SP 9307 3m S of Tring.
CP(Chlsbry-cum-St Leonards), 925.
Amersham RD. Ch e. Sch pe. Chesham and
Amrshm CC (Aylesbury). See also Buckland
Cmmn.

CHOLLERFORD Nthmb
77 NY 9170 4m NNW of Hexham. Loc,
Humshaugh CP. On N Tyne, with 18c br. To
W, Chesters*, excavated rems of Roman
Wall stn.

CHOLLERTON Nthmb
77 NY 9372 5m N of Hexham. CP, 791.
Hxhm RD. Ch e, r, v. Sch pe. Hxhm CC. See
also Barrasford, Colwell, Gt Swinburne,
Gunnerton, Lit Swnbne. Ch has Roman
arcade columns.

CHOLMONDELEY Ches
109 SJ 5351 6m N of Whitchurch. CP, 238.
Nantwich RD. P Malpas. Sch p. Nntwch CC.
18c cstle and quaint ch nearby with large
family pew above nave.

CHOLSEY Berks
158 SU 5886 2m SW of Wallingford. CP,
3,107. Wllngfd RD. P Wllngfd. Ch e, b.
Sch p. Abingdon CC.

CHOLSTREY Herefs
129 SO 4659 2m W of Leominster. Loc, Lmnstr MB.

CHOP GATE Yorks (N)
86, 92 SE 5599 10m NNW of Helmsley. Loc, Bilsdale Midcable CP. Stokesley RD. P MIDDLESBROUGH, Teesside. Ch e, m. Sch pe. Richmond CC.

CHOPPINGTON Nthmb
78 NZ 2583 4m ESE of Morpeth. Loc, Bedlingtonshire UD. P. Blyth BC.

CHOPWELL Co Durham
77, 78 NZ 1158 4m N of Consett. Loc, Blaydon UD. P NEWCASTLE UPON TYNE.

CHORLEY Ches
109 SJ 5751 5m W of Nantwich. CP, 143. Nntwch RD. P Nntwch. Ch m. Nntwch CC.

CHORLEY Lancs
100 SD 5817 8m N of Wigan. MB, 31,609. P. Chly CC. Textile tn. Bthplce of Henry Tate (1819), sugar magnate and founder of Tate Gallery, London. Astley Hall*, 16c and later half-timbered hse. To NW, New Tn designated.

CHORLEY Shrops
130 SO 6983 6m S of Bridgnorth. Loc, Stottesdon CP. P Brdgnth. Ch b.

CHORLEY Staffs
120 SK 0711 3m WNW of Lichfield. CP(Farewell and Chly), 282. Lchfld RD. P Lchfld. Sch p. Lchfld and Tamworth CC.

CHORLEYWOOD Herts
159, 160 TQ 0296 2m NW of Rickmansworth. UD, 8,427. P Rckmnswth. SW Herts CC. Rsdntl.

CHORLTON Ches
110 SJ 7250 4m SSE of Crewe. CP, 92. Nantwich RD. Ch m. Nntwch CC.

CHORLTON LANE Ches
109 SJ 4547 7m WNW of Whitchurch. Loc, Chltn CP. Tarvin RD. P(Chltn), Malpas. Nantwich CC.

CHOULTON Shrops
129 SO 3788 4m E of Bishop's Cstle. Loc, Lydbury N CP.

CHOWLEY Ches
109 SJ 4756 8m SSE of Chester. CP, 51. Tarvin RD. Nantwich CC.

CHRISHALL Essex
148 TL 4439 6m E of Royston. CP, 440. Saffron Walden RD. P Rstn, Herts. Ch e, m. Sch pe. Sffrn Wldn CC. Ch: 14c brass.

CHRISTCHURCH Cambs
135 TL 4996 5m E of March. Loc, Upwell CP. P Wisbech. Ch e, m. Sch p.

CHRISTCHURCH Glos
142 SO 5712 4m E of Monmouth. Loc, W Dean CP. W Dn RD. P Coleford. W Glos CC.

CHRISTCHURCH Hants
179 SZ 1592 5m E of Bournemouth. MB, 31,373. P. Chrstchch and Lymington BC (Bnmth E and Chrstchch). See also Highcliffe, Mudeford. Rsdntl tn. Great priory ch mainly 12c. Rems of 12c cstle (A.M.) and Nmn hse (A.M.). To S, Stanpit Marsh, nature reserve.

CHRISTIAN MALFORD Wilts
157 ST 9678 4m NE of Chippenham. CP, 526. Calne and Chppnhm RD. P Chppnhm. Ch e, c. Sch pe. Chppnhm CC.

CHRISTLETON Ches
109 SJ 4465 2m ESE of Chester. CP. Chstr RD. P CHSTR. Ch e, m. Sch pe, s. City of Chstr CC.

CHRISTMAS COMMON Oxon
159 SU 7193 7m NNW of Henley. Loc, Watlington CP. To S, Wtlngtn Pk, Ggn hse in large pk. Beech woods surrounding pk (NT).

CHRISTON Som
165 ST 3757 5m SE of Weston. Loc, Loxton CP. Ch e.

CHRISTON BANK Nthmb
71 NU 2123 6m NNE of Alnwick. Loc, Embleton CP. P Alnwck.

CHRISTOW Devon
176 SX 8384 7m SW of Exeter. CP, 607. St Thomas RD. P Extr. Ch e, b, m. Sch p. Tiverton CC.

CHUDLEIGH Devon
176, 188 SX 8679 5m N of Newton Abbot. CP, 2,053. Ntn Abbt RD. P Ntn Abbt. Ch e, b, r, v2. Sch pe. Totnes CC. Former mkt tn. To S, limestone outcrop known as C. Rock.

CHUDLEIGH KNIGHTON Devon
176, 188 SX 8477 4m N of Newton Abbot.

Chulmleigh

Loc, Hennock CP. P Ntn Abbt. Ch e, c. Sch pe.

CHULMLEIGH Devon
163, 175 SS 6814 7m SSW of S Molton. CP, 960. S Mltn RD. P. Ch e, c, m, r, v. Sch p, s. N Dvn CC. See also Elstone, Week.

CHUNAL Derbys
102 SK 0391 1m S of Glossop. Loc, Charlesworth CP.

CHURCH Lancs
95 SD 7429 1m W of Accrington. UD, 5,310. P Accrngtn. Accrngtn BC. Textiles.

CHURCHAM Glos
143 SO 7618 4m W of Gloucester. CP, 739. E Dean RD. P GLCSTR. Ch e. Sch p. W Glos CC. See also Birdwood, Bulley, Oakle St.

CHURCH ASTON Shrops
119 SJ 7417 1m S of Newport. CP, 316. Wellington RD. Ch e. Sch p. The Wrekin CC.

CHURCH BRAMPTON Northants
133 SP 7165 4m NW of Northampton. CP, 164. Brixworth RD. Ch e. Daventry CC (Kettering).

CHURCH BROUGHTON Derbys.
120 SK 2033 7m E of Uttoxeter. CP, 295. Repton RD. P DERBY. Ch e, m. Sch pe. Belper CC.

CHURCH CROOKHAM Hants
169 SU 8152 3m WNW of Aldershot. Loc, Fleet UD. P Aldrsht.

CHURCHDOWN Glos
143, 144 SO 8819 3m E of Gloucester. CP, 7,075. Glcstr RD. P GLCSTR. Ch e, m, r. Sch i, p, s2. W Glos CC. See also Parton. Ch on edge of Chosen Hill at c 500ft commands wide views.

CHURCH EATON Staffs
119 SJ 8417 6m SW of Stafford. CP, 880. Stffd RD. P STFFD. Ch e. Sch pe. Stffd and Stone CC. See also High Onn, Marston. Ch Nmn to Perp; wide E window.

CHURCH END Beds
147 SP 9921 2m W of Dunstable. Loc, Totternhoe CP. Ch e. Ch made of stone from Totternhoe quarries, like several others hereabouts.

CHURCH END Beds
147 TL 1937 5m N of Hitchin. Loc, Arlesey CP. Ch e. Ch has 14c chpl with Easter sepulchre.

CHURCH END Cambs
124 TF 3909 5m W of Wisbech. Loc, Parson Drove CP. Ch e.

CHURCH END Essex
148 TL 5841 3m NE of Saffron Walden. Loc, Ashdon CP. Ch e. 1m SW, Hales Wd, nature reserve.

CHURCHEND Essex
148 TL 6322 just N of Dunmow. Loc, Gt Dnmw CP. Ch e.

CHURCHEND Essex
162 TR 0092 9m NE of Southend. Loc, Foulness CP. Rochford RD. Ch e. Sch pe. Maldon CC (SE Essex).

CHURCH END Hants
168, 169 SU 6756 4m NE of Basingstoke. Loc, Sherfield on Lodden CP. Ch e.

CHURCH END Warwicks
131 SP 2490 Ch e. 3m ENE of Coleshill. Loc, Shustoke CP.

CHURCH END Wilts
157 SU 0278 5m NNE of Calne. Loc, Lyneham CP. Ch e.

CHURCH FENTON Yorks (W)
97 SE 5136 4m SSE of Tadcaster. CP, 652. Tdcstr RD. P Tdcstr. Ch m. Sch pe. Barkston Ash CC.

CHURCH GREEN Devon
176 SY 1796 3m S of Honiton. Loc, Farway CP. Ch e.

CHURCH GRESLEY Derbys
120, 121 SK 2918 5m SE of Burton-on-Trent. Loc, Swadlincote UD. P Btn-on-Trnt, Staffs.

CHURCH HANBOROUGH Oxon
145 SP 4212 3m SSW of Woodstock. Loc, Hnbrgh CP. Witney RD. P OXFORD. Ch e. Mid-Oxon CC (Banbury). Nmn and later ch: scrn, chancel arch, shroud brass.

CHURCH HILL Ches
110 SJ 6465 1m SSW of Winsford. Loc, Wnsfd UD.

CHURCH HONEYBOURNE Worcs
144 SP 1144 5m E of Evesham. Loc,
Hnybne CP. Eveshm RD. Ch e. Sch p.
S Worcs CC.

CHURCH HOUGHAM Kent
173 TR 2740 3m WSW of Dover. Loc,
Hghm Without CP. Dvr RD. Ch e. Sch pe.
Dvr and Deal CC (Dvr).

CHURCH HOUSES Yorks (N)
86, 92 SE 6697 7m NNW of
Kirkbymoorside. Loc, Farndale E CP.
Kbmsde RD. Ch e. Thirsk and Malton CC.

CHURCHILL Devon
177 ST 2902 2m N of Axminster. Loc,
Axmnstr RD. Ch m. Honiton CC.

CHURCHILL Oxon
145 SP 2824 3m SW of Chipping Norton.
CP, 475. Chppng Ntn RD. P OXFORD.
Ch e, m. Sch pe. Banbury CC. Bthplce of
Warren Hastings, 1732; also of William Smith,
pioneer geologist, 1769, commemorated by
stone monmt.

CHURCHILL Som
165 ST 4459 4m N of Cheddar. CP, 1,435.
Axbridge RD. P BRISTOL. Ch e, m.
Sch pe, s. Weston-super-Mare CC. See also
Lr Langford. C. Ct once home of famous
Duke of Marlborough's ancestors. To S on
Mendips, Dolebury Warren, Large Iron Age
camp.

CHURCHILL Worcs
130 SO 8879 3m SSW of Stourbridge.
CP(Chchll and Blakedown), 1,273.
Kidderminster RD. P Kddrmnstr. Ch e.
Kddrmnstr CC.

CHURCHILL Worcs
143, 144 SO 9253 5m E of Worcester. CP,
28. Pershore RD. Ch e. S Worcs CC.

CHURCH KNOWLE Dorset
179 SY 9481 4m SSE of Wareham. CP, 391.
Wrhm and Purbeck RD. P Wrhm. Ch e. S
Dst CC.

CHURCH LANEHAM Notts
104 SK 8176 8m S of Gainsborough. Loc,
Lnhm CP. Ch e. Mainly Nmn ch, beside
R Trent.

CHURCH LANGTON Leics
133 SP 7293 4m N of Mkt Harborough.
Loc, E Lngtn CP. Ch e. Sch pe. Ggn rectory.

CHURCH LAWFORD Warwicks
132 SP 4476 3m W of Rugby. CP, 449.
Rgby RD. P Rgby. Ch e. Sch pe. Rgby CC.

CHURCH LAWTON Ches
110 SJ 8255 5m SSW of Congleton. CP,
1,051. Cngltn RD. Ch e. Sch pe. Knutsford
CC.

CHURCH LEIGH Staffs
120 SK 0235 4m WNW of Uttoxeter. Loc,
Lgh CP. Uttxtr RD. Ch e. Sch pe.
Burton CC.

CHURCH LENCH Worcs
144 SP 0251 5m N of Evesham. CP, 418.
Evesham RD. P Eveshm. Ch e. Sch pe.
S Worcs CC. See also Atch Lnch.

CHURCH MINSHULL Ches
110 SJ 6660 4m NW of Crewe. CP, 340.
Nantwich RD. P Nntwch. Ch e. Sch p, pe.
Nantwich CC.

CHURCH NORTON Sussex (W)
181 SZ 8695 6m S of Chichester. Loc,
Selsey CP. Ch e. Ch orig that of Slsy.

CHURCHOVER Warwicks
132 SP 5180 4m N of Rugby. CP, 647.
Rgby RD. P Rgby. Ch e. Sch pe. Rgby CC.

CHURCH PREEN Shrops
129 SO 5498 5m WSW of Much Wenlock.
CP, 89. Atcham RD. Ch e. Sch p.
Shrewsbury CC.

CHURCH PULVERBATCH Shrops
118 SJ 4302 7m SSW of Shrewsbury. CP,
322. Atcham RD. Ch e. Sch pe. Shrsbry CC.
See also Cstle Plvrbtch, Wrentnall.

CHURCHSTANTON Som
164, 176 ST 1914 5m SE of Wellington. CP,
538. Taunton RD. Ch e. Sch p. Tntn CC.
See also Stapley.

CHURCHSTOW Devon
187, 188 SX 7145 2m NW of Kingsbridge.
CP, 313. Kngsbrdge RD. P Kngsbrdge. Ch e.
Totnes CC.

CHURCH STOWE Northants
132, 133 SP 6357 5m SE of Daventry. Loc,
Stwe Nine Churches CP. Dvntry RD.
P NORTHAMPTON. Ch e. Dvntry CC
(S Nthnts).

CHURCH STREET Kent
161, 171, 172 TQ 7174 4m NNW of Rochester. Loc, Higham CP.

CHURCH STRETTON Shrops
129 SO 4593 12m S of Shrewsbury. CP, 2,707. Ludlow RD. P. Ch e, c, m, r. Sch pe, s. Ldlw CC. See also All Strttn, Lit Strttn. Late Vctrn health resort under steep hills.

CHURCHTOWN Lancs
94 SD 4843 9m NNW of Preston. Loc, Kirkland CP. Garstang RD. P Prstn. Ch e. Sch pe. N Fylde CC. In centre, mkt cross, early 19c.

CHURCH TOWN Westm
89 SD 4491 4m WSW of Kendal. Loc, Crosthwaite and Lyth CP. S Westm RD. Ch e. Sch pe. Westm CC.

CHURCH WARSOP Notts
112 SK 5668 5m NNE of Mansfield. Loc, Wsp UD. P Mnsfld. Nmn and later ch overlooks the colliery tn.

CHURCH WILNE Derbys
112, 121 SK 4431 7m ESE of Derby. CP(Draycott and Ch Wlne), 1,995. SE Derbys RD. Ch e. SE Derbys CC. Ch: Sxn font.

CHURSTON FERRERS Devon
188 SX 9056 1m W of Brixham. Loc, Torbay CB. P Brxhm.

CHURT Surrey
169 SU 8538 5m NW of Haslemere. Loc, Frensham CP. Ch e. Sch pe.

CHURTON Ches
109 SJ 4156 6m S of Chester. CP(Chtn by Aldford), 168; CP(Chtn by Farndon), 116. Tarvin RD. P CHSTR. Ch m. Nantwich CC.

CHURWELL Yorks (W)
96, 102 SE 2729 3m SSW of Leeds. Loc, Morley MB. P Mly, LDS.

CHUTE STANDEN Wilts
168 SU 3053 6m NNW of Andover. Loc, Chte CP. Pewsey RD. P Andvr, Hants. Sch pe. Devizes CC. Stndn Hse: thatched boundary wall decorated with straw birds.

CINDERFORD Glos
142, 143 SO 6513 11m WSW of Gloucester. CP, 6,918. E Dean RD. P. Ch e, b, m2, r, v3. Sch p2, s. W Glos CC. Colliery tn in Forest of Dn.

CIRENCESTER Glos
157 SP 0202 14m SSE of Cheltenham. UD, 13,022. P. Crncstr and Tewkesbury CC. See also Stratton. Mkt tn on site of Roman *Corinium.* Large mainly Perp ch at tn centre. C. Pk, 18c mansion blt by Ld Bathurst, friend of Alexander Pope. Enormous yew hedge in front of hse.

CITADILLA Yorks (N)
91 NZ 2200 3m ESE of Richmond. Loc, Brompton-on-Swale CP.

CITY OF LONDON
160 TQ 3281 2m NE of Westminster. County, 4,234. The City of Lndn and Wstmnstr S BC (The Cities of Lndn and Wstmnstr). See also Temples, Inner and Middle. Financial centre. Small area contains St Paul's Cathedral, Guildhall, Bank of England, Stock Exchange, Mansion Hse etc., as well as many modern bldngs erected since World War II.

CITY OF WESTMINSTER London
160, 170 TQ 2979. Central Lndn. See Westminster.

CITY, THE Bucks
159 SU 7896 6m WNW of High Wycombe. Loc, Radnage CP. Ch v.

CLACTON, GREAT Essex
150 TM 1716 1m N of Clacton on Sea. Loc, Clctn UD. P Clctn-on-Sea.

CLACTON ON SEA Essex
150 TM 1714 13m ESE of Colchester. UD (Clctn), 37,942. P. Harwich CC. See also Gt Clctn, Holland-on-Sea, Jaywick Sands. Resort; pier, swimming pools, holiday camp. Off-shore fishing. Three martello twrs.

CLADSWELL Worcs
131 SP 0558 3m WNW of Alcester. Loc, Inkberrow CP.

CLAINES Worcs
130 SO 8558 3m N of Worcester. Loc, N Clns CP. Droitwich RD. Ch e. Sch pe. Wcstr BC.

CLANDOWN Som
166 ST 6855 just N of Radstock. Loc,
Norton-Radstock UD. P Rdstck, Bath.
N Som CC.

CLANFIELD Hants
181 SU 6916 5m SW of Petersfield. CP,
1,464. Ptrsfld RD. P Portsmouth. Ch e, m.
Sch p. Ptrsfld CC. See also Chalton.

CLANFIELD Oxon
158 SP 2802 4m N of Faringdon. CP, 587.
Witney RD. P OXFORD. Ch e, m. Sch p.
Mid-Oxon CC (Banbury).

CLANVILLE Hants
168 SU 3148 4m NW of Andover. Loc,
Penton Grafton CP. P Andvr.

CLAPGATE Dorset
179 SU 0102 2m N of Wimborne. Loc,
Wmbne and Cranborne RD. N Dst CC.

CLAPHAM Beds
147 TL 0352 2m NNW of Bedford. CP.
Bdfd RD. P BDFD. Ch e, m. Sch pe. Bdfd
CC. Ch: large Sxn twr.

CLAPHAM London
160, 170 TQ 2975 3m S of Charing Cross.
Loc, Lambeth LB. Lmbth Central BC
(Clphm). C. Cmmn to W.

CLAPHAM Sussex (W)
182 TQ 0906 4m NW of Worthing. CP, 320.
Wthng RD. Ch e. Sch pe. Arundel CC
(Arndl and Shoreham).

CLAPHAM Yorks (W)
90 SD 7469 6m NW of Settle. CP(Clphm
cum Newby), 536. Sttle RD. P
LANCASTER. Ch e. Sch pe. Skipton CC.
See also Keasden. Stone-blt tree-lined vllge
at foot of Ingleborough (2,373ft). C. Cave*,
Gaping Ghyll, and other potholes on hillside
to N. Yorkshire Dales National Information
Centre.

CLAPPERSGATE Westm
88, 89 NY 3603 1m SW of Ambleside. Loc,
Lakes UD. Westm CC. White Craggs gdns*.

CLAPTON Glos
144 SP 1617 4m NE of Northleach. CP, 87.
N Cotswold RD. P Cheltenham. Ch e, b.
Cirencester and Tewkesbury CC.

CLAPTON Som
166 ST 6453 3m W of Radstock. Loc, Ston
Easton CP.

CLAPTON Som
177 ST 4106 3m SW of Crewkerne. Loc,
W Crewkerne CP. Chard RD. P Crkne.
Yeovil CC.

CLAPTON-IN-GORDANO Som
155, 165 ST 4773 7m W of Bristol. CP, 257.
Long Ashton RD. Ch e. Sch p, pe.
N Som CC.

CLAPWORTHY Devon
163 SS 6724 3m WSW of S. Molton. Loc,
S Mltn RD. N Dvn CC.

CLARA VALE Co Durham
78 NZ 1364 3m NE of Prudhoe. Loc,
Ryton UD.

CLARBOROUGH Notts
103 SK 7383 2m NE of Retford. CP, 498.
E Rtfd RD. P Rtfd. Ch e, m. Sch p.
Bassetlaw CC.

CLARE Suffolk (W)
149 TL 7645 6m E of Haverhill. CP, 1,328.
Clre RD. P Sudbury. Ch e, b, c, r. Sch p, s.
Bury St Edmunds CC. See also Chilton St.
Small Stour valley tn with many pargetted
hses. Handsome ch, 13c—15c. Mdvl priory*.

CLATTERCOTE Oxon
145 SP 4549 5m N of Banbury. CP(Claydon
w Clattercot), 202. Bnbry RD. Bnbry CC.

CLATWORTHY Som
164 ST 0530 8m S of Watchet. CP, 54.
Williton RD. Ch e. Bridgwater CC. Large
reservoir to W.

CLAUGHTON Lancs
89 SD 5666 6m NE of Lancaster. CP, 121.
Lunesdale RD. Ch e. Lnctr CC.

CLAUGHTON Lancs
94 SD 5342 8m N of Preston. CP, 409.
Garstang RD. P Prstn. Ch e, r. Sch pr.
N Fylde CC. Ch has oldest dated bell in
England (1296).

CLAVERDON Warwicks
131 SP 1964 5m W of Warwick. CP, 871.
Stratford-on-Avon RD. P WRWCK. Ch e, m.
Sch p. Strtford-on-Avn CC (Strtfd).

CLAVERHAM Som
155, 165 ST 4466 2m NNE of Congresbury.
Loc, Yatton CP. P BRSTL. Ch f, m.

CLAVERING Essex
148 TL 4731 6m SW of Saffron Walden. CP,
936. Sffrn Wldn RD. P Sffrn Wldn.
Ch e, m, v. Sch p. Sffrn Wldn CC. 15c ch.
Faint traces of pre-Conquest cstle.

CLAVERLEY Shrops
130 SO 7993 5m E of Bridgnorth. CP,
1,304. Brdgnth RD. P Wolverhampton,
Staffs. Ch e. Sch pe. Ludlow CC. See also
Aston, Shipley. Ch: wall-paintings of c 1200.

CLAVERTON Som
166 ST 7864 3m E of Bath. CP, 100.
Bathavon RD. Ch e. N Som CC. Rems of
terraces of Tdr mnr hse. On hill early 19c
classical mnr hse, now museum of American
domestic life.

CLAWTON Devon
174 SX 3599 3m S of Holsworthy. CP, 303.
Hlswthy RD. P Hlswthy. Ch e, m2. Sch p.
W Dvn CC (Tavistock).

CLAXBY Lincs (L)
104 TF 1194 3m N of Mkt Rasen. CP, 173.
Caistor RD. P LINCOLN. Ch e, m. Sch pe.
Gainsborough CC.

CLAXTON Norfolk
126 TG 3303 8m ESE of Norwich. CP, 170.
Loddon RD. P NRWCH, NOR 12W. Ch e.
Sch p. S Nflk CC. Thatched ch. Rems of 15c
brick cstle.

CLAXTON Yorks (N)
92, 96, 97 SE 6960 8m NE of York.
CP, 163. Flaxton RD. Ch m. Thirsk and
Malton CC.

CLAYBROOKE MAGNA Leics
132 SP 4988 4m NW of Lutterworth. CP,
459. Lttrwith RD. P(Claybrook), Rugby,
Warwickshire. Blaby CC (Harborough).

CLAYBROOK PARVA Leics
132 SP 4988 4m NW of Lutterworth. CP,
103. Lttrwith RD. Ch e. Sch pe. Blaby CC
(Harborough).

CLAY COMMON Suffolk (E)
137 TM 4780 4m NW of Southwold. Loc,
Lothingland RD. Lowestoft CC.

CLAY COTON Northants
132,133 SP 5977 6m E of Rugby. CP, 54.
Daventry RD. Ch e. Dvntry CC (S Nthnts).

CLAY CROSS Derby
111 SK 3963 5m S of Chesterfield.
UD, 9,726. P Chstrfld. NE Derby CC. Coal,
iron, engineering tn. Long rly tunnel under-
neath by George Stephenson.

CLAYDON Oxon
145 SP 4550 6m N of Banbury. CP(Cldn w
Clattercot), 202. Bnbry RD. P Bnbry.
Ch e, m. Bnbry CC.

CLAYDON Suffolk (E)
150 TM 1350 4m NNW of Ipswich. CP, 686.
Gipping RD. P Ipswch. Ch e, c. Sch p, s.
Eye CC.

CLAYGATE Surrey
170 TQ 1563 2m SE of Esher. Loc, Eshr
UD. P Eshr.

CLAYGATE CROSS Kent
171 TQ 6155 5m E of Sevenoaks. Loc,
Plaxtol CP.

CLAYHANGER Devon
164 ST 0222 4m E of Bampton. CP, 144.
Tiverton RD. P Tvtn. Ch e, m. Tvtn CC.

CLAYHANGER Staffs
120 SK 0404 4m NNE of Walsall. Loc,
Aldridge-Brownhills UD. A-B BC (Wlsll N).
Mining distr.

CLAYHIDON Devon
164 ST 1615 3m SSE of Wellington CP,
428. Tiverton RD. P Cullompton. Ch e, v.
Tvtn CC. See also Bolham Water, Rosemary
Lane.

CLAYPOLE Lincs (K)
113 SK 8549 4m SE of Newark. CP, 724.
W Kesteven RD. P Nwk, Notts. Ch e, m.
Sch pe. Grantham CC.

CLAYTON Staffs
110, 119 SJ 8543 2m S of
Newcastle-under-Lyme. Loc,
Ncstle-undr-Lme MB.

CLAYTON Sussex (E)
182 TQ 3013 6m N of Brighton. CP, 1,548.
Cuckfield RD. Ch e. Mid-Sx CC (Lewes).
See also Hassocks. Below S Downs. Partly
Saxon ch has 12c wall-paintings. Two
windmills know as Jack and Jill. C. Tunnel
(1¼m long) on London-Brighton rly has
castellated N portal.

CLAYTON Yorks (W)
103 SE 4507 7m E of Barnsley. CP(Cltn w Frickley), 189. Doncaster RD. P Dncstr. Ch m. Sch pe. Don Valley CC.

CLAYTON GREEN Lancs
94 SD 5723 5m SSE of Preston. Loc, Cltn-le-Woods CP. P Chorley. Ch r. Sch pr.

CLAYTON-LE-MOORS Lancs
95 SD 7431 2m NNW of Accrington. UD, 6,760. P Accrngtn. Accrngtn BC.

CLAYTON-LE-WOODS Lancs
94 SD 5622 5m SSE of Preston. CP, 1,880. Chorley RD. Ch m. Sch pe. Chly CC. See also Cltn Grn.

CLAYTON WEST Yorks (W)
102 SE 2510 5m NNE of Penistone. Loc, Denby Dale UD. P Huddersfield.

CLAYWORTH Notts
103 SK 7288 5m NNE of Retford. CP, 306. E Rtfd RD. P Rtfd. Ch e, m. Sch p. Bassetlaw CC.

GLEADON Co Durham
78 NZ 3862 3m SSE of S Shields. Loc, Boldon UD. P Sunderland.

CLEARBROOK Devon
187 SX 5265 6m SSE of Tavistock. Loc, Buckland Monachorum CP. P Yelverton.

CLEARWELL Glos
155, 156 SO 5708 5m SE of Monmouth. Loc, Newland CP. P Coleford. Ch e, m. Sch pe. 14c cross.

CLEASBY Yorks (N)
85 NZ 2513 3m WSW of Darlington. CP, 139. Croft RD. Ch e, m. Richmond CC.

CLEATLAM Co Durham
84 NZ 1218 5m ENE of Barnard Cstle. CP, 82. Bnd Cstle RD. Bishop Auckland CC.

CLEATOR Cumb
82 NY 0113 4m SE of Whitehaven. Loc, Cltr Moor CP. P. Ch e, r. Sch p, pr. Mining vllge. Ch(r) by Pugin.

CLEATOR MOOR Cumb
82 NY 0214 4m SE of Whitehaven. CP, 7,123. Ennerdale RD. P. Ch e, m, v. Sch pe, pr, s, sr. Whthvn CC. See also Cltr. Mining tn.

CLEAVE CAMP Cornwall
174 SS 2012 4m N of Bude. Loc, Morwenstow CP.

CLECKHEATON Yorks (W)
96, 102 SE 1925 4m NW of Dewsbury. Loc, Spenborough MB. P. Brighouse and Spnbrgh BC. Wool textile tn.

CLEEDOWNTON Shrops
129 SO 5880 6m NE of Ludlow. Loc, Stoke St Milborough CP.

CLEEHILL Shrops
129 SO 5975 5m E of Ludlow. Loc, Caynham CP. P Ldlw. Ch m. Sch p.

CLEE ST MARGARET Shrops
129 SO 5684 7m NNE of Ludlow. CP, 110. Ldlw RD. P Craven Arms. Ch e, m. Ldlw CC.

CLEETHORPES Lincs (L)
105 TA 3008 2m E of Grimsby. MB, 35,785. P. Louth CC. Resort; long pier, promenade, amusements.

CLEETON ST MARY Shrops
129, 130 SO 6178 4m WNW of Cleobury Mortimer. Loc, Bitterley CP. Ch e. Sch pe.

CLEEVE Som
155, 165 ST 4565 2m NE of Congresbury. CP, 812. Long Ashton RD. P BRSTL. Ch e, v. Sch pe. Weston-super-Mare CC.

CLEEVE HILL Glos
143, 144 SO 9826 3m NE of Cheltenham. Loc, Chtlnhm RD. P Chltnhm. Ch e, v. Cirencester and Tewkesbury CC.

CLEEVE PRIOR Worcs
144 SP 0849 5m NE of Evesham. CP, 371. Eveshm RD. P Eveshm. Ch e. Sch pe. S Worcs CC.

CLEHONGER Herefs
142 SO 4637 3m WSW of Hereford. CP, 590. Hrfd RD. P HRFD. Ch e, m, r. Sch pe. Hrfd CC. See also Gorsty Cmmn. Ch has 15c brass.

CLENCHWARTON Norfolk
124 TF 5920 2m W of King's Lynn. CP, 1,659. Marshland RD. P K's Lnn. Ch e, m. Sch p. NW Nflk CC (K's Lnn).

CLENT Worcs
130, 131 SO 9279 4m SSE of Stourbridge.

CP, 2,091. Bromsgrove RD. P Stbrdge. Ch e. Sch pe. Brmsgrve and Redditch CC (Brmsgrve). See also Holy Cross. C. Hills (NT) between indstrl Birmingham and countryside.

CLEOBRUY MORTIMER Shrops
129, 130 SO 6775 10m E of Ludlow. CP, 1,304. Ldlw RD. P Kidderminster, Worcs. Ch e, m, r. Sch p, s. Ldlw CC. Small tn on hillside running down to Rea Brook. Ch spire out of true.

CLEOBURY NORTH Shrops
129, 130 SO 6286 7m SW of Bridgnorth. CP, 110. Brdgnth RD. P Brdgnth. Ch e. Ludlow CC.

CLERKENWELL London
160 TQ 3182 2m NE of Charing Cross. Loc, Islington LB. Islngtn S and Finsbury BC (Shoreditch and Fnsbry). Mt Pleasant Post Office parcels depot to W of distr.

CLEVANCY Wilts
157 SU 0575 4m NE of Calne. Loc, Hilmarton CP.

CLEVEDON Som
155, 165 ST 4071 11m W of Bristol. UD, 14,285. P. Weston-super-Mare CC. Largely Vctrn rsdntl tn; shingle beach, small pier. 1½m E, C. Ct (NT)*, mnr hse of all periods from 14c, in terraced 18c gdns.

CLEVELEY Oxon
145 SP 3923 5m ESE of Chipping Norton. Loc, Enstone CP. Ch b.

CLEVELEYS Lancs
94 SD 3143 4m N of Blackpool. UD(Thornton Clvlys), 26,869. P Blckpl. N Fylde CC.

CLEVERTON Wilts
157 ST 9785 3m ESE of Malmesbury. CP(Lea and Clvtn), 559. Mlmsbry RD. Ch e, r. Chippenham CC.

CLEWER Som
165 ST 4451 2m SW of Cheddar. Loc, Wedmore CP.

CLEY NEXT THE SEA Norfolk
125 TG 0444 4m NW of Holt. CP, 579. Erpingham RD. P(Cley), Hlt. Ch e, m. Sch p. N Nflk CC. See also Newgate. Once busy seaport until sea defences blt early 19c.

Many attractive old hses. To S at Newgate, grand 14c—16c ch with many good brasses. Windmill. Vllge inundated in floods of 1953.

CLIBURN Westm
83 NY 5824 6m SE of Penrith. CP, 191. N Westm RD. P Pnrth, Cumberland. Ch e, m. Sch p. Westm CC.

CLIDDESDEN Hants
168, 169 SU 6349 2m S of Basingstoke. CP, 364. Bsngstke RD. P Bsngstke. Ch e, m2. Sch p. Bsngstke CC.

CLIFFE Kent
161, 171, 172 TQ 7376 5m N of Rochester. CP. Strood RD. P Rchstr. Ch e, m, v2. Sch pe. Gravesend CC. See also Clffe Wds. Between marshes and indstrl area. Ch stands high on chalky escarpment.

CLIFFE Yorks (E)
97, 98 SE 6632 3m E of Selby. CP, 768. Derwent RD. P Slby. Ch m. Sch pe. Howden CC. See also Lund, S Duffield.

CLIFF END Sussex (E)
184 TQ 8813 5m ENE of Hastings. Loc, Pett CP.

CLIFFE WOODS Kent
161, 171, 172 TQ 7373 3m N of Rochester. Loc, Cliffe CP. P Cliffe, Rchstr.

CLIFFORD Herefs
141 SO 2445 2m NNE of Hay-on-Wye. CP, 586. Dore and Bredwardine RD. Ch e. Sch p. Hereford CC. See also Priory Wd. To W, rems of 13c cstle*.

CLIFFORD Yorks (W)
97 SE 4244 3m SSE of Wetherby. CP, 1,221. Wthrby RD. P Boston Spa. Ch e, m, r, v. Sch pr. Barkston Ash CC. Very grand RC ch, to building of which the pope himself contributed money.

CLIFFORD CHAMBERS Warwicks
144 SP 1952 2m S of Stratford. CP, 398. Strtfd-on-Avon RD. P Strtfd-upon-Avn. Ch e. Sch pe. Strtfd-on-Avn CC (Strtfd).

CLIFFORD'S MESNE Glos
143 SO 7023 6m E of Ross-on-Wye. Loc, Newent RD. P Nwnt. Ch e, v. W Glos CC.

CLIFTON Beds
147 TL 1639 4m SSW of Biggleswade. CP,

1,354. Bgglswde RD. P Shefford. Ch e, b2. Sch pe. Mid-Beds CC.

CLIFTON Derbys
120 SK 1644 1m SW of Ashbourne. CP(Clftn and Compton), 518. Ashbne RD. P Ashbne. Ch e, m2. Sch pe. W Derbys CC.

CLIFTON Devon
163 SS 6041 6m SE of Ilfracombe. Loc, E Down CP.

CLIFTON Glos
155, 156, 165 ST 5673 W distr of Bristol. Loc, Brstl CB. P BRSTL 8. Brstl W BC. Brunel's famous suspension br spans Avon Gorge.

CLIFTON Lancs
94 SD 4630 5m W of Preston. CP(Newton-w-Clftn), 1,785. Fylde RD. P Prstn. S Flde CC.

CLIFTON Nthmb
78 NZ 2082 2m S of Morpeth. Loc, Stannington CP.

CLIFTON Oxon
145 SP 4831 6m SSE of Banbury. Loc, Deddington CP. Ch e, m.

CLIFTON Westm
83 NY 5326 3m SSE of Penrith. CP, 355. N Westm RD. P Pnrth, Cumberland. Ch e, m. Sch p. Westm CC. Pele twr.

CLIFTON Worcs
143 SO 8446 5m S of Worcester. Loc, Severn Stoke CP.

CLIFTON Yorks (W)
96 SE 1948 2m NNW of Otley. CP(Newall w Clftn), 197. Wharfedale RD. Ch m. Ripon CC.

CLIFTON Yorks (W)
103 SK 5296 6m SW of Doncaster. Loc, Conisbrough Pks CP. Dncstr RD. Don Valley CC.

CLIFTON CAMPVILLE Staffs
120 SK 2510 5m NE of Tamworth. CP, 431. Lichfield RD. P Tmwth. Ch e. Sch pe. Lchfld and Tmwth CC. See also Haunton. Outstanding ch, mainly 13c–14c.

CLIFTON, GREAT Cumb
82 NY 0429 3m E of Workington. See Gt Clftn.

CLIFTON HAMPDEN Oxon
158 SU 5495 3m ESE of Abingdon. CP, 476. Bullingdon RD. P Abngdn, Berks. Ch e. Sch pe. Henley CC. See also Burcot. Picturesque vllge with br over R Thames. Some caravans.

CLIFTON MAYBANK Dorset
177, 178 ST 5713 2m SE of Yeovil. CP, 75. Sherborne RD. W Dst CC.

CLIFTON REYNES Bucks
146 SP 9051 just E of Olney. CP, 96. Newport Pagnell RD. Ch e. Buckingham CC. Ch has rare wooden effigies of 13c–14c.

CLIFTON UPON DUNSMORE Warwicks
132 SP 5376 2m ENE of Rugby. CP, 1,101. Rgby RD. P(Clftn), Rgby. Ch e. Sch pe. Rgby CC.

CLIFTON UPON TEME Worcs
130 SO 7161 6m NE of Bromyard. CP, 338. Martley RD. P WORCESTER. Ch e. Sch p. Kidderminster CC.

CLIMPING Sussex (W)
181, 182 TQ 0002 2m W of Littlehampton. CP, 602. Chichester RD. Ch e. Sch pe. Arundel CC (Chchstr). Well known 12c–13c ch.

CLINT Yorks (W)
96 SE 2559 4m NW of Harrogate. CP, 455. Ripon and Pateley Br RD. Rpn CC. See also Burnt Yates.

CLINT GREEN Norfolk
125 TG 0211 3m SE of E Dereham. Loc, Yaxham CP. P Drhm.

CLIPPESBY Norfolk
126 TG 4214 7m NW of Yarmouth. Loc, Fleggburgh CP. Blofield and Flegg RD. Ch e. Ymth CC.

CLIPSHAM Rutland
123 SK 9716 7m NNW of Stamford. CP, 98. Ketton RD. P Oakham. Ch e. Rtlnd and Stmfd CC. Pleasing vllge of limestone; lmstne quarries 1m SE.

CLIPSTON Northants
133 SP 7181 4m SSW of Mkt Harborough. CP, 391. Brixworth RD. P Mkt Hbrgh, Leics. Ch e, b. Sch pe. Daventry CC (Kettering). Almshouses and sch (still used) of 1673.

CLIPSTON Notts
112, 121, 122 SK 6334 6m SE of
Nottingham. CP, 64. Bingham RD.
Rushcliffe CC (Carlton).

CLIPSTONE Notts
112 SK 6064 4m WSW of Ollerton. CP,
3,947. Southwell RD. P(Clpstne Vllge),
Mansfield. Ch m2, s. Sch p, pe. Newark CC.
See also New Clpstne. Colliery village. Rems
of mdvl royal hunting lodge for Sherwood
Forest.

CLITHEROE Lancs
95 SD 7441 9m NNE of Blackburn. MB,
13,191. P. Clthroe CC. See also Low Moor.
Mkt tn and general industry incl
agricultural-chemical plant. Rems of 12c
cstle* on mound, whence view of Pendle
Hill (1,831ft) to E.

CLIVE Shrops
118 SJ 5124 3m S of Wem. CP, 435. N
Shrops RD. P Shrewsbury. Ch e, c, v2. Sch pe.
Oswestry CC.

CLODOCK Herefs
142 SO 3227 8m N of Abergavenny. Loc,
Longtown CP. Ch e, m. 19c water mill still
in working order.

CLOFORD Som
166 ST 7243 4m SW of Frome. Loc,
Wanstrow CP. Ch e.

CLOPHILL Beds
147 TL 0838 3m E of Ampthill. CP, 1,056.
Ampthll RD. P BEDFORD. Ch e, m. Sch pe.
Mid-Beds CC.

CLOPTON Northants
134 TL 0680 5m SSE of Oundle. CP, 105.
Oundle and Thrapston RD. P Kettering.
Ch e. Wellingborough CC (Peterborough).

CLOPTON Suffolk (E)
150 TM 2254 5m NW of Woodbridge. CP,
337. Deben RD. P Wdbrdge. Ch e. Eye CC.

CLOPTON GREEN Suffolk (W)
149 TL 7654 6m N of Clare. Loc,
Wickhambrook CP.

CLOSWORTH Som
177, 178 ST 5610 4m S of Yeovil. CP, 259.
Yvl RD. Ch e. Yvl CC. See also Pendomer,
Sutton Bingham. Sttn Bnghm Reservoir to
NW.

CLOTHALL Herts
147 TL 2731 2m SE of Baldock. CP, 189.
Hitchin RD. Ch e. Htchn CC.

CLOTTON Ches
109 SJ 5263 8m ESE of Chester. Loc, Clttn
Hoofield CP. Tarvin RD. Ch m. Sch pe.
Northwich CC.

CLOUGH FOOT Yorks (W)
95 SD 9123 2m W of Todmorden. Loc,
Tdmdn MB.

CLOUGHTON Yorks (N)
93 TA 0094 4m NNW of Scarborough. CP,
573. Scbrgh RD. P Scbrgh. Ch e, m2. Sch p.
Scbrgh CC (Scbrgh and Whitby). See also
Clghtn Newlands.

CLOUGHTON NEWLANDS Yorks (N)
93 TA 0195 5m NNW of Scarborough. Loc,
Clghtn CP. P Scbrgh.

CLOVELLY Devon
174 SS 3124 9m W of Bideford. CP, 445.
Bdfd RD. P Bdfd. Ch e, m. Sch p. N Dvn
CC(Torrington). Vllge blt on steep cliffside;
small harbour at foot. Cobbled street with
steps — no wheeled vehicles. Most scenic
approach by Hobby Drive from E.

CLOWNE Derbys
103 SK 4975 6m WSW of Worksop. CP,
6,062. Clne RD. P Chesterfield.
Ch e, m, r, s, v. Sch p, s. Bolsover CC.

CLOWS TOP Worcs
130 SO 7171 5m WSW of Bewdley. Loc,
Kidderminster RD, Tenbury RD.
P Kddrmnstr. Kddrmnstr CC.

CLUN Shrops
129 SO 3080 8m W of Craven Arms. CP,
1,388. Cln and Bishop's Cstle RD. P Crvn
Arms. Ch e, m. Sch pe. Ludlow CC. See also
Bicton, Chpl Lawn, Guilden Down,
Newcastle, New Invention, Purlogue,
Whitcott Keysett. Small mkt tn among hills.
Rems of Nmn cstle. 17c almshouses.

CLUNBURY Shrops
129 SO 3780 4m WSW of Craven Arms. CP,
536. Clun and Bishop's Cstle RD. P Crvn
Arms. Ch e. Sch pe. Ludlow CC. See also
Clunton, Twitchen. Stone vllge in hilly
country.

CLUNGUNFORD Shrops
129 SO 3978 3m SW of Craven Arms. CP,

349. Clun and Bishop's Cstle RD. P Crvn Arms. Ch e, m. Ludlow CC. See also Hoptonheath.

CLUNTON Shrops
129 SO 3381 2m E of Clun. Loc, Clunbury CP. P Craven Arms. Ch m.

CLUTTON Ches
109 SJ 4654 8m SSE of Chester. CP, 119. Tarvin RD. P CHSTR. Sch pe. Nantwich CC.

CLUTTON Som
166 ST 6259 5m NW of Radstock. CP, 1,382. Clutton RD. P BRSTL. Ch e, m, v. Sch p. N Som CC.

CLYFFE PYPARD Wilts
157 SU 0776 6m NE of Calne. CP, 481. Cricklade and Wootton Bassett RD. P Swndn. Ch e, m. Sch pe. Chippenham CC. See also Bushton.

CLYST HONITON Devon
176 SX 9893 4m E of Exeter. CP, 350. St Thomas RD. P Extr. Ch e. Sch pe. Hntn CC.

CLYST HYDON Devon
176 ST 0301 8m W of Honiton. CP, 286. St Thomas RD. P Cullompton. Ch e. Sch p. Tiverton CC.

CLYST ST GEORGE Devon
176 SX 9888 5m SE of Exeter. CP, 260. St Thomas RD. P Extr. Ch e. Sch pe. Honiton CC.

CLYST ST LAWRENCE Devon
176 ST 0200 8m NE of Exeter. CP, 110. St Thomas RD. Ch e. Tiverton CC.

CLYST ST MARY Devon
176 SX 9790 4m ESE of Exeter. CP, 225. St Thomas RD. P Extr. Ch e. Sch p. Honiton CC.

COAD'S GREEN Cornwall
186 SX 2976 5m SSW of Launceston. Loc, North Hill CP. P Lncstn. Ch m. Sch p.

COAL ASTON Derbys
103, 111 SK 3679 5m S of Sheffield. Loc, Dronfield UD. P SHFFLD.

COALBROOKDALE Shrops
118, 119 SJ 6604 5m SSE of Wellington. Loc, Dawley UD. P Telford. The Wrekin CC (Ludlow). Cradle of iron industry in gorge of R Severn. Ironworks Museum.

COALEY Glos
156 SO 7701 3m NNE of Dursley. CP, 687. Dsly RD. P Dsly. Ch e, m. Sch pe. Stroud CC.

COALPIT HEATH Glos
155, 156 ST 6780 7m NE of Bristol. Loc, Sodbury RD. P BRSTL. Ch e. S Glos CC. Ch and vicarage by Butterfield.

COALPORT Shrops
119 SJ 6902 5m SW of Shifnal. Loc, Dawley UD. P Telford. The Wrekin (Ludlow). Site of former pottery wks in gorge of R Severn.

COALVILLE Leics
121 SK 4213 12m NW of Leicester. UD, 28,334. P LCSTR. Bosworth CC. See also Thringstone, Whitwick. Mining tn largely developed in 19c.

COANWOOD Nthmb
76 NY 6859 3m SSW of Haltwhistle. CP, 284. Hltwhstle RD. P Hexham. Ch f, m2. Hexham CC. See also Lambley, Stonehouse.

COAT Som
177 ST 4520 5m WSW of Ilchester. Loc, Martock CP. P Mtck.

COATE Wilts
167 SU 0461 2m E of Devizes. Loc, Bishops Cannings CP. P Dvzs.

COATES Cambs
134 TL 3097 3m E of Whittlesey. Loc, Whttlsy UD. P PETERBOROUGH. Ch e.

COATES Glos
157 SO 9700 3m W of Cirencester. CP, 377. Crncstr RD. P Crncstr. Ch e. Sch pe. Crncstr and Tewkesbury CC. 1m S, source of R Thames.

COATES, GREAT Lincs (L)
105 TA 2310 2m WNW of Grimsby. See Gt Cts.

COATHAM MUNDEVILLE Co Durham
85 NZ 2919 3m N of Darlington. CP, 169. Dlngtn RD. Ch e. Bishop Auckland CC (Sedgefield).

COBBATON Devon
163 SS 6126 5m SE of Barnstaple. Loc, Swimbridge CP. Ch m.

COBERLEY Glos
143, 144 SO 9616 4m S of Cheltenham. CP, 306. Chltnhm RD. P Chltnhm. Ch e. Sch p. Cirencester and Tewkesbury CC. See also Ullenwood.

COBHAM Kent
171 TQ 6768 4m SSE of Gravesend. CP. Strood RD. P Grvsnd. Ch e. Sch p. Grvsnd CC. See also Sole St. Ch famous for monmts, esp brasses. C. Hall, A.M. and NT, mainly Jcbn, in grnds by Repton. Owletts (NT)*, hse and gdn, late 17c.

COBHAM Surrey
170 TQ 1060 4m S of Walton-on-Thames. Loc, Esher UD. P. On R Mole; partly on A3 rd. Cedar Hse (NT)*, 15c with 18c alterations.

COBNASH Herefs
129 SO 4560 3m WNW of Leominster. Loc, Kingsland CP.

COCKAYNE HATLEY Beds
147 TL 2649 5m NE of Biggleswade. CP, 122. Bgglswde RD. Ch e. Mid-Beds CC. Ch, in pk, has French and Belgian carvings. The poet, W.E. Henley is buried here.

COCK CLARKS Essex
162 TL 8102 4m SW of Maldon. Loc, Purleigh CP. P Chelmsford. Ch m.

COCKERHAM Lancs
94 SD 4652 6m SSW of Lancaster. CP, 639. Lncstr RD. P LNCSTR. Ch e. Sch pe. Lncstr CC. 2½m WNW, rems of Cockersand Abbey, 12c–13c.

COCKERMOUTH Cumb
82 NY 1230 8m E of Workington. UD, 6,365. P. Wkngtn CC. Rems of 13c–14c cstle. In Main St, 18c hse (NT)*, bthplce of Wordsworth, 1770.

COCKERNHOE GREEN Herts
147 TL 1223 3m NE of Luton. Loc, Offley CP. Hitchin RD. P(Ccknhoe), Ltn, Beds. Ch m. Sch pe. Htchn CC.

COCKFIELD Co Durham
84 NZ 1224 7m NE of Barnard Cstle. CP, 2,121. Bnd Cstle RD. P Bishop Auckland. Ch e, c2, m, s. Sch p. Bshp Aucklnd CC.

COCKFIELD Suffolk (W)
149 TL 9054 4m N of Lavenham. CP, 712. Cosford RD. P Bury St Edmunds.

Ch e, c, m. Sch pe. Sudbury and Woodbridge CC. See also Gt Grn.

COCKFOSTERS London
160 TQ 2896 2m E of Barnet. Loc, Enfield LB. P Bnt, Herts. Southgate BC.

COCKING Sussex (W)
181 SU 8717 2m S of Midhurst. CP, 493. Mdhst RD. P Mdhst. Ch e. Sch pe. Chichester CC (Horsham). Yellow paint of cottages denotes Cowdray estate property.

COCKINGTON Devon
188 SX 8963 2m W of Torquay. Loc, Torbay CB. Cob and thatch tourist attraction.

COCKLAKE Som
165 ST 4349 3m SSW of Cheddar. Loc, Wedmore CP. P Wdmre.

COCKLEY CLEY Norfolk
125 TF 7904 3m SW of Swaffham. CP, 182. Swffhm RD. P Swffm. Ch e. SW Nflk CC. In hths of Breckland.

COCKPOLE GREEN Berks
159 SU 7981 3m ESE of Henley. Loc, Cookham RD, Wokingham RD. Windsor and Maidenhead CC (Wndsr), Wknghm CC.

COCKSHUTT Shrops
118 SJ 4329 4m SSE of Ellesmere. CP, 515. N Shrops RD. P Ellesmre. Ch e, m. Sch pe. Oswestry CC. See also English Frankton, Kenwick.

COCKTHORPE Norfolk
125 TF 9842 4m ESE of Wells. Loc, Binham CP. Ch e.

COCKWOOD Devon
176 SX 9680 3m NNE of Dawlish. Loc, Dlsh UD.

CODDENHAM Suffolk (E)
150 TM 1354 6m NNW of Ipswich. CP, 515. Gipping RD. P Ipswch. Ch e, m. Sch pe. Eye CC. Pink pargetted post office. Gryffon Hse formerly an inn. Ch has double hammerbeam angel roof. To S, Shrubland Pk, Ggn hse with Italianate gdns.

CODDINGTON Ches
109 SJ 4555 8m SSE of Chester. CP, 105. Tarvin RD. Ch e. Nantwich CC.

CODDINGTON Herefs
143 SO 7142 3m N of Ledbury. CP, 87.
Ldbry RD. P Ldbry. Ch e. Leominster CC.

CODDINGTON Notts
113 SK 8354 2m E of Newark. CP, 1,305.
Nwk RD. P Nwk. Ch e, m. Sch pe. Nwk CC.

CODFORD ST MARY Wilts
167 ST 9739 7m ESE of Warminster. Loc,
Cdfd CP. Wmnstr and Westbury RD.
P(Cdfd), Wmnstr. Ch e. Sch pe. Wstbry CC.

CODFORD ST PETER Wilts
167 ST 9639 7m ESE of Warminster. Loc,
Cdfd CP. Wmnstr and Westbury RD.
P(Cdfd), Wmnstr. Ch e. Wstbry CC. In ch,
part of 9c carved cross.

CODICOTE Herts
147 TL 2118 4m NNW of Welwyn Gdn
City. CP, 2,087. Hitchin RD. P Htchn.
Ch e, v. Sch pe. Htchn CC.

CODNOR Derbys
112 SK 4249 2m ESE of Ripley. Loc,
Heanor UD. P DERBY. Rems of 13c–14c
cstle.

CODRINGTON Glos
156 ST 7278 9m N of Bath. Loc, Dodington
CP. Ch e, b.

CODSALL Staffs
119 SJ 8603 4m NW of Wolverhampton.
CP, 6,745. Seisdon RD. P Wlvrhmptn.
Ch e, m, r. Sch p3, pe, s. SW Staff CC
(Brierley Hill). See also Cdsll Wd, Oaken.

CODSALL WOOD Staffs
119 SJ 8405 6m NW of Wolverhampton. Loc,
Cdsll CP. P Wlvrhmptn. To NE, Chillington
Hall*, (see Brewood).

COFFINSWELL Devon
188 SX 8968 3m SE of Newton Abbot. CP.
Ntn Abbt RD. Ch e. Totnes CC.

COFTON HACKETT Worcs
131 SP 0075 4m NE of Bromsgrove. CP,
5,209. Brmsgrve RD. Ch e. Brmsgrve and
Redditch CC (Brmsgrve).

COGENHOE Northants
133 SP 8360 5m E of Northampton. CP,
708. Nthmptn RD. P NTHMPTON.
Ch e, b2. Sch p. Daventry CC (S Nthnts).
See also Whitston.

COGGESHALL Essex
149, 162 TL 8522 6m E of Braintree. CP,
3,027. Brntree RD. P Colchester.
Ch e, b, c, f, m, s. Sch pe, s. Brntree CC
(Maldon). Old cloth-making tn. Many old
hses, incl Paycocke's (NT)*, c 1500.

COLAN Cornwall
185 SW 8661 4m E of Newquay. CP, 1,165.
St Austell RD. Ch e, m2. N Cnwll CC. See
also Mountjoy. Small ch has brass of Francis
Bluet, wife and twenty-two children, 1572.

COLATON RALEIGH Devon
176 SY 0787 6m NE of Exmouth. CP, 509.
St Thomas RD. P Sidmouth. Ch e, m.
Honiton CC. See also Hawkerland.

COLBURN Yorks (N)
91 SE 1999 2m SE of Richmond. CP,
2,451. Rchmnd RD. Ch e, m. Sch p.
Rchmnd CC.

COLBY Norfolk
126 TG 2231 3m NNE of Aylsham. CP,
419. Erpingham RD. Ch e, m. Sch p. N Nflk
CC. See also Banningham.

COLBY Westm
83 NY 6620 1m W of Appleby. CP, 79.
N Westm RD. Westm CC.

COLCHESTER Essex
149, 162 TL 9925 51m NE of London. MB,
76,145. P. Clchstr CC. See also Blackheath,
Mile End, Old Hth, Shrub End. Dates from
Iron Age. First Roman capital — many Rmn
rems. Huge Nmn cstle, rems now museum.
Many old bldngs but also modern tn with
engineering wks and general industry.

COLD ASH Berks
158 SU 5169 3m NE of Newbury. CP,
1,526. Nbry RD. P Nbry. Ch e, m, r. Sch pe.
Nbry CC.

COLD ASHBY Northants
132, 133 SP 6576 8m SW of Mkt
Harborough. CP, 228. Brixworth RD.
P Rugby, Warwickshire. Ch e, c. Sch p.
Daventry CC (Kettering).

COLD ASHTON Glos
156 ST 7572 5m N of Bath. CP, 242.
Sodbury RD. Ch e. S Glos CC. 16c ch and
mnr hse; in the hills.

COLD BRAYFIELD Bucks
146 SP 9252 3m E of Olney. CP, 78.
Newport Pagnell RD. Ch e. Buckingham CC.

COLDEAST Devon
176, 188 SX 8174 3m NW of Newton
Abbot. Loc, Ilsington CP. Ch v.

COLDEN Yorks (W)
95 SD 9628 2m WNW of Hebden Br. Loc,
Heptonstall CP. Sch p.

COLDEN COMMON Hants
168 SU 4722 3m NNE of Eastleigh. CP,
1,668. Winchester RD. P Wnchstr. Ch e.
Sch pe. Wnchstr CC. See also Fisher's Pond.

COLDFAIR GREEN Suffolk (E)
137 TM 4361 3m ESE of Saxmundham.
Loc, Knodishall CP. Ch m.

COLDHARBOUR Surrey
170, 182 TQ 1443 4m SSW of Dorking.
Loc, Capel CP. P Dkng. Situated high (over
700ft) in Surrey hills. To SW, Leith Hill
(NT) 965ft and highest point in SE England,
topped by 64ft twr*.

COLD HESLEDON Co Durham
85 NZ 4147 2m SW of Seaham. CP, 997.
Easington RD. Ch m. Houghton-le-Spring
CC (Easngtn).

COLD HIENDLEY Yorks (W)
102, 103 SE 3714 5m NNE of Barnsley.
CP(Havercroft w Cld Hndly), 2,792.
Hemsworth RD. Hmswth CC.

COLD HIGHAM Northants
145, 146 SP 6653 4m NNW of Towcester.
CP, 209. Tcstr RD. Ch e. Daventry CC
(S Nthnts). See also Grimscote.

COLD KIRBY Yorks (N)
92 SE 5384 5m W of Helmsley. CP, 81.
Hlmsly RD. P Thirsk. Ch e, m. Thsk and
Malton CC.

COLD NORTON Essex
162 TL 8400 4m S of Maldon. CP, 416.
Mldn RD. P Chelmsford. Ch e, v. Sch p.
Mldn CC.

COLD OVERTON Leics
122 SK 8110 3m WNW of Oakham. Loc,
Knossington CP. P Oakhm, Rutland. Ch e.

COLDRED Kent
173 TR 2746 5m NW of Dover.
CP(Shepherdswell w Cldrd), 1,238. Dvr RD.
Ch e. Dvr and Deal CC (Dvr).

COLDRIDGE Devon
175 SS 6907 10m NE of Okehampton. CP,
294. Crediton RD. P Crdtn. Ch e, v.
Tiverton CC (Torrington). See also E Leigh.
Ch: scrn, parclose scrn, plpt, bench-ends.

COLDWALTHAM Sussex (W)
181, 182 TQ 0216 2m SW of Pulborough.
CP, 661. Chanctonbury RD. Ch e. Sch pe.
Shoreham CC (Arundel and Shrhm). See also
Hardham, Watersfield.

COLE Som
166 ST 6633 1m SW of Bruton. Loc,
Pitcombe CP.

COLEBATCH Shrops
129 SO 3187 1m S of Bishop's Cstle. CP,
90. Clun and Bp's Cstle RD. Ludlow CC.

COLEBROOK Devon
176 ST 0006 5m SE of Tiverton. Loc,
Cullompton CP.

COLEBROOKE Devon
175 SS 7700 4m W of Crediton. CP, 425.
Crdtn RD. P Crdtn. Ch e. Tiverton CC
(Torrington). See also Coleford. Ch: scrn,
parclose scrn, bench-ends.

COLEBY Lincs (K)
113 SK 9760 7m S of Lincoln. CP, 389.
N Kesteven RD. P LNCLN. Ch e, m. Sch pe.
Grantham CC. Two small 18c classical
temples in grnds of 17c C. Hall.

COLEBY Lincs (L)
104 SE 8916 6m N of Scunthorpe. Loc,
W Halton CP.

COLEFORD Devon
175 SS 7701 4m WNW of Crediton. Loc,
Colebrooke CP. Ch v.

COLEFORD Glos
142 SO 5710 4m ESE of Monmouth. CP,
3,546. W Dean RD. P. Ch e, b, m, r, v2.
Sch pe. W Glos CC.

COLEFORD Som
166 ST 6848 4m S of Radstock. CP, 1,454.
Frome RD. P Bath. Ch e, m. Sch pe.
Wells CC. See also Highbury.

COLEHILL Dorset
179 SU 0200 1m NE of Wimborne. CP, 2,301. Wmbne and Cranborne RD. P Wmbne. Ch e, m. Sch p. N Dst CC. See also Canford Bottom.

COLEMAN'S HATCH Sussex (E)
183 TQ 4533 5m Se of E Grinstead. Loc, Hartfield CP. P Htfld. Ch e.

COLEMERE Shrops
118 SJ 4332 2m SE of Ellesmere. Loc, Ellesmre Rural CP. N Shrops RD. P Ellesmre. Ch e. Oswestry CC. The mere to the N is one of several in this area.

COLEMORE Hants
169, 181 SU 7030 5m S of Alton. CP(Clmre and Priors Dean), 147. Petersfield RD. Ch e. Ptrsfld CC.

COLEORTON Leics
121 SK 4017 3m NNW of Coalville. CP, 840. Ashby de la Zouch RD. P LEICESTER. Ch e, b, m. Sch p, pe. Loughborough CC. Coal mined here since Tdr times. C. Hall, formerly seat of Beaumonts, much visited by Wordsworth and other literary men. Now owned by National Coal Board.

COLERNE Wilts
156 ST 8171 6m NE of Bath. CP, 2,375. Calne and Chippenham RD. P Chppnhm. Ch e, b, c, m. Sch pe. Chppnhm CC. See also Thickwood. To NW, RAF stn. In ch, parts of 9c carved cross.

COLESBOURNE Glos
143, 144 SO 9913 6m SSE of Cheltenham. CP, 142. Cirencester RD. P Chltnhm. Ch e. Crncstr and Tewkesbury CC.

COLESDEN Beds
134 TL 1255 4m SW of St Neots. Loc, Roxton CP.

COLESHILL Berks
157 SU 2393 8m NE of Swindon. CP, 224. Faringdon RD. P Swndn, Wilts. Ch e. Sch pe. Abingdon CC. NT vllge of Cotswold stone and tiles.

COLESHILL Bucks
159 SU 9495 1m SSW of Anersham. CP, 680. Amrshm RD. P Amrshm. Ch e, b. Sch pe. Chesham and Amrshm CC (S Bucks).

COLESHILL Warwicks
131 SP 1989 8m E of Birmingham. CP, 6,786. Meriden RD. P BMNGHM. Ch e, m, r, v. Sch i, je, pr, s2, sr. Mrdn CC.

COLGATE Sussex (W)
182 TQ 2332 4m ENE of Horsham. Loc, Lr Beeding CP. P Hshm. Sch p.

COLINDALE London
160 TQ 2189 1m WNW of Hendon. Loc, Barnet LB. Hndn N BC.

COLKIRK Norfolk
125 TF 9126 2m S of Fakenham. CP, 533. Mitford and Launditch RD. P Fknhm. Ch e. Sch pe. SW Nflk CC. See also Oxwick.

COLLATON ST MARY Devon
188 SX 8660 2m W of Paignton. Loc, Torbay CB. P Pgntn.

COLLIER'S END Herts
148 TL 3720 4m N of Ware. Loc, Standon CP. P Ware.

COLLIER STREET Kent
171, 172, 184 TQ 7146 7m SSW of Maidstone. Loc, Yalding CP. P Tonbridge. Ch e. Sch pe. Orchards.

COLLIERY ROW Co Durham
85 NZ 3249 1m W of Houghton-le-Spring. Loc, Htn-le-Sprng UD. P Htn-le-Sprng.

COLLINGBOURNE DUCIS
167 SU 2453 6m SE of Pewsey. CP, 584. Psy RD. P Marlborough. Ch e, m. Sch pe. Devizes CC.

COLLINGBOURNE KINGSTON Wilts
167 SU 2355 6m SE of Pewsey. CP, 397. Psy RD. P Marlborough. Ch e, m. Sch pe. Devizes CC.

COLLINGHAM Yorks (W)
96 SE 3845 2m SSW of Wetherby. CP, 1,715. Wthrby RD. P Wthrby. Ch e, m. Sch pe. Barkston Ash CC. See also Linton. Rems of two Anglo-Saxon crosses in ch, one with runic inscriptions.

COLLINGTON Herefs
129, 130 SO 6460 3m N of Bromyard. CP, 81. Brmyd RD. Ch e. Leominster CC.

COLLINGTREE Northants
133 SP 7555 3m S of Northampton. CP, 254. Nthmptn RD. P NTHMPTN. Ch e. Sch pe. Daventry CC (S Nthnts).

COLLINS GREEN Lancs
100 SJ 5694 3m ESE of St Helens. Loc,
Burtonwood CP. P Warrington.

COLLYWESTON Northants
123 SK 9902 3m SW of Stamford. CP, 428.
Oundle and Thrapston RD. P Stmfd, Lincs.
Ch e. Sch, p. Wellingborough CC
(Peterborough). Well known for Cllwstn
roofing slates produced from locally
quarried stone.

COLMWORTH Beds
134 TL 1058 5m W of St Neots. CP, 309.
Bedford RD. P BDFD. Ch e. Sch pe. Mid-
Beds CC. See also Duck's Cross.

COLNBROOK Bucks
159, 160, 170 TQ 0277 4m ESE of Slough.
Loc, Iver CP. P Slgh. Ch e, b, m. Sch pe.
Cox's Orange Pippin, famous eating apple,
first grown here in 1820s.

COLNE Hunts
135 TL 3755 5m NE of St Ives. CP, 473. St
Ives RD. P HUNTINGDON. Ch e. Hunts CC.

COLNE Lancs
95 SD 8840 6m NE of Burnley. MB,
18,873. P. Nelson and Clne BC. See also
Laneshaw Br. Textile tn. Mobile stocks in
churchyard.

COLNE ENGAINE Essex
149 TL 8530 2m E of Halstead. CP, 581.
Hlstd RD. P Colchester. Ch e. Sch pe.
Saffron Walden CC.

COLNEY Norfolk
126 TG 1807 3m W of Norwich. CP.
Forehoe and Henstead RD. P NRWCH,
NOR 70F. Ch e. S Nflk CC (Central Nflk).

COLNEY HEATH Herts
160 TL 2005 2m SW of Hatfield. CP, 4,554.
St Albans RD. P St Albns. Ch e. Sch p.
S Herts CC (St Albns).

COLNEY STREET Herts
160 TL 1502 3m S of St Albans. Loc, St
Stephen CP. St Albns RD. P St Albns. S
Herts CC (St Albns).

COLN ROGERS Glos
157 SP 0809 6m NE of Cirencester. Loc,
Cln St Dennis CP. Ch e. Partly Saxon ch.

COLN ST ALDWYNS Glos
157 SP 1405 6m NW of Lechlade. CP, 294.
Northleach RD. P Cirencester. Ch e. Sch pe.
Crncstr and Tewkesbury CC.

COLN ST DENNIS Glos
144 SP 0810 3m SW of Northleach. CP,
202. Nthlch RD. Ch e. Cirencester and
Tewkesbury CC. See also Cln Rogers,
Fossebridge. Mainly Nmn ch.

COLSTERDALE Yorks (N)
91 SE 1381 6m W of Masham. CP, 12.
Mshm RD. Richmond CC.

COLSTERWORTH Lincs (K)
122 SK 9323 7m S of Grantham. CP, 992.
W Kesteven RD. P Grnthm. Ch e, m. Sch pe.
Rutland and Stamford CC. See also
Woolsthorpe. Ch has sundial cut by Isaac
Newton at age of nine. He was born at
Wlsthpe, qv.

COLSTON BASSETT Notts
112, 122 SK 7033 9m ESE of Nottingham.
CP, 288. Bingham RD. P NTTNGHM.
Ch e, m. Sch pe. Rushcliffe CC (Carlton).
Restored vllge cross (NT).

COLTISHALL Norfolk
126 TG 2719 2m NW of Wroxham. CP,
1,121. St Faith's and Aylsham RD. P
NORWICH, NOR 65Y. Ch e, m, s, v. Sch p.
N Nflk CC (Central Nflk). RAF stn to N.

COLTON Lancs
88, 89 SD 3186 5m NNE of Ulverston.
CP, 936. N Lonsdale RD. Ch e, b, f. Sch pe.
Morecambe and Lnsdle CC. See also Bouth,
Finsthwaite, Lake Side, Oxen Pk, Rusland.

COLTON Norfolk
125 TG 1009 5m N of Wymondham. Loc,
Marlingford CP. P NORWICH, NOR 39X.
Ch e.

COLTON Staffs
120 SK 0520 2m N of Rugeley. CP, 653.
Lichfield RD. P Rgly. Ch e. Sch pe. Lchfld
and Tamworth CC.

COLTON Yorks (W)
97 SE 5444 4m ENE of Tadcaster. CP, 155.
Tdcstr RD. P Tdcstr. Ch e. Barkston Ash CC.

COLWALL Herefs
143 SO 7342 3m SW of Malvern. CP, 2,045.

Ldbry RD. P Mlvn, Worcs. Ch e. Leominster
CC. See also Clwll Grn, Clwll Stone. 2m SE,
Herefordshire Beacon, large Iron Age hill
fort.

COLWALL GREEN Herefs
143 SO 7541 3m SSW of Malvern. Loc,
Clwll CP. P Mlvn, Worcs. Ch m.

COLWALL STONE Herefs
143 SO 7542 2m SSW of Malvern. Loc,
Clwll CP. Ch e, v. Sch pe.

COLWELL Nthmb
77 NY 9575 7m N of Hexham. Loc,
Chollerton CP. P Barrasford, Hxhm. To E,
Hallington Reservoir.

COLWICH Staffs
120 SK 0121 3m NW of Rugeley. CP,
1,844. Stafford RD. Ch e. Sch pe. Stffd and
Stone CC. See also Gt Haywood, Lit Hwd.

COLWORTH Sussex (W)
181 SU 9102 3m NW of Bognor. Loc, Oving
CP.

COLYFORD Devon
177 SY 2592 2m N of Seaton. Loc, Colyton
CP. P Cltn. Ch m.

COLYTON Devon
177 SY 2493 3m N of Seaton. CP, 1,922.
Axminster RD. P. Ch e, m, v. Sch p, s.
Honiton CC. See also Colyford. Small tn
with narrow streets and interesting old ch
with collection of monmts.

COMBE Berks
168 SU 3760 5m SSE of Hungerford. CP,
54. Hngrfd RD. P Newbury. Ch e. Nbry CC.
On S slope of Walbury Hill, ancient hill fort
and highest point in county, 974ft.

COMBE Herefs
129 SO 3463 2m ESE of Presteigne. CP, 51.
Kington RD. Leominster CC.

COMBE Oxon
145 SP 4115 2m W of Woodstock. CP, 513.
Chipping Norton RD. P OXFORD. Ch e, m.
Sch pe. Banbury CC.

COMBE DOWN Som
166 ST 7662 2m SSE of Bath. Loc, Bth CB.
P Bth. Bth BC (N Som CC). Prior Pk, great
Palladian villa blt mid-18c by Ralph Allen,
one of creators of Ggn Bath. Hse is now a
sch.

COMBE FLOREY Som
164 ST 1531 6m NW of Taunton. CP, 225.
Tntn RD. P Tntn. Ch e. Tntn CC.

COMBE HAY Som
166 ST 7359 3m S of Bath. CP, 146.
Bathavon RD. P Bth. Ch e. N Som CC.

COMBEINTEIGNHEAD Devon
176, 188 SX 9071 3m E of Newton Abbot.
Loc, Haccombe w Combe CP, Ntn Abbt RD.
P Ntn Abbt. Ch e. Totnes CC. Partly in
combe with stream running down to Teign
estuary at Coombe Cellars, former haunt of
smugglers.

COMBE MARTIN Devon
163 SS 5846 4m E of Ilfracombe. CP,
2,228. Barnstaple RD. P Ilfrcmbe.
Ch e, b, m, r. Sch p. N Dvn CC. Long
narrow tn running down to small harbour.
Mkt gardening. Red ch. Pack of Cards Inn.

COMBE MOOR Herefs
129 SO 3663 4m ESE of Presteigne. Loc,
Byton CP. Ch m.

COMBE RALEIGH Devon
176 ST 1502 1m N of Honiton. CP, 187.
Hntn RD. Ch e. Hntn CC.

COMBERBACH Ches
101 SJ 6477 2m NNW of Northwich. CP,
546. Nthwch RD. P Nthwch. Ch m. Sch i.
Nthwch CC.

COMBERFORD Staffs
120 SK 1907 2m NNW of Tamworth. Loc,
Wigginton CP.

COMBERTON Cambs
135 TL 3856 4m WSW of Cambridge. CP,
812. Chesterton RD. P CMBRDGE. Ch e, b.
Sch s. Cambs CC. Vllge college, opened
1960.

COMBERTON, GREAT Worcs
143, 144 SO 9542 2m S of Pershore. See Gt
Cmbrtn.

COMBE ST NICHOLAS Som
177 ST 3011 2m NW of Chard. CP, 867.
Chd RD. P Chd. Ch e, m. Sch pe. Yeovil CC.
See also Wadeford.

COMBROOK Warwicks
145 SP 3051 7m ESE of Stratford. CP, 140.
Strtfd-on-Avon RD. P WARWICK. Ch e.

Combrook

Strtfd-on-Avn CC (Strtfd). At S end of Compton Verney pk, with large lake. Hse is 18c; chpl (and pk?) by Capability Brown.

COMBS Derbys
111 SK 0478 3m NNW of Buxton. Loc, Chapel en le Frith CP. P Stockport, Cheshire. Ch m. High Peak CC.

COMBS Suffolk (E)
149 TL 0456 1m S of Stowmarket. CP, 460. Gipping RD. P Stwmkt. Ch e, c. Sch p. Eye CC.

COMBS FORD Suffolk (E)
136 TM 0557 just S of Stowmarket. Loc, Stwmkt UD.

COMBWICH Som
165 ST 2542 4m NW of Bridgwater. Loc, Otterhampton CP. P Brdgwtr. Ch e, m.

COME-TO-GOOD Cornwall
190 SW 8238 4m S of Truro. Loc, Feock CP. Ch f. Un-named on O.S. map. Has oldest Friends' Meeting Hse in England (1703), thatched.

COMMONDALE Yorks (N)
86 NZ 6610 5m SE of Guisborough. CP, 103. Whitby RD. P Whtby. Ch m. Cleveland and Whtby CC (Scarborough and Whtby).

COMMONMOOR Cornwall
186 SX 2469 3m N of Liskeard. Loc, St Cleer CP. P Lskd. Ch m. To SW, King Doniert's Stone (A.M.), two stones of Sxn times, originally bases of crosses.

COMMON SIDE Derbys
111 SK 3375 4m NW of Chesterfield. Loc, Barlow CP. Ch m.

COMMON, THE Wilts
167 SU 2432 7m ENE of Salisbury. Loc, Winterslow CP.

COMPSTALL Ches
101 SJ 9690 4m E of Stockport. Loc, Bredbury and Romiley UD. P Stckpt.

COMPTON Berks
158 SU 5280 6m S of Didcot. CP, 1,114. Wantage RD. P Newbury. Ch e, m. Sch pe, s. Abingdon CC. Agricultural research stn.

COMPTON Devon
188 SX 8664 3m W of Torquay. Loc, Marldon CP. C. Cstle, restored mdvl mnr hse (NT)*.

COMPTON Hants
168 SU 4625 3m S of Winchester. CP, 1,273. Wnchstr RD. P Wnchstr. Ch e. Sch pe. Wnchstr CC. See also Shawford. Nmn ch.

COMPTON Som
165 ST 4832 4m S of Glastonbury. Loc, Compton Dundon CP. Langport RD. P(Cmptn Dndn), Somerton. Sch pe. Yeovil CC. To NE, Windmill Hill (NT) and Hood monmt (see Butleigh). To SW, Dndn Hill: Iron Age camp.

COMPTON Surrey
169, 170 SU 9547 3m WSW of Guildford. CP, 937. Gldfd RD. P Gldfd. Ch e, c, v. Sch pe. Gldfd CC. Nmn ch of much interest. Watts Picture Gallery*.

COMPTON Sussex (W)
181 SU 7714 6m SSE of Petersfield. CP, 532. Chichester RD. P Chchstr. Ch e. Sch pe. Chchstr CC. See also W Marden. Pleasing downland vllge.

COMPTON ABBAS Dorset
178 ST 8618 3m S of Shaftesbury. CP, 226. Shftsbry RD. P Shftsbry. Ch e, m. N Dst CC. See also E Cmptn.

COMPTON ABDALE Glos
144 SP 0616 3m WNW of Northleach. CP, 119. Nthlch RD. P Cheltenham. Ch e. Cirencester and Tewkesbury CC.

COMPTON BASSETT Wilts
157 SU 0372 3m E of Calne. CP, 386. Clne and Chippenham RD. P Clne. Ch e. Chppnhm CC. 12c and later ch: carved stone scrn. Derelict airfield.

COMPTON BEAUCHAMP Berks
158 SU 2887 7m W of Wantage. CP, 72. Faringdon RD. Ch e. Abingdon CC. Moated Tdr mnr hse with 18c facade.

COMPTON BISHOP Som
165 ST 3955 4m WNW of Cheddar. CP, 427. Axbridge RD. P Axbrdge. Ch e. Weston-super-Mare CC. See also Cross.

COMPTON CHAMBERLAYNE Wilts
167 SU 0229 7m W of Salisbury. CP, 145. Slsbry and Wilton RD. P Slsbry. Ch e. Slsbry CC.

COMPTON DANDO Som
166 ST 6464 7m W of Bath. CP, 514.

Bathavon RD. P BRISTOL. Ch e, m2, v. Sch pe. N Som CC. See also Burnett, Chewton Keynsham, Queen Charlton.

COMPTON MARTIN Som
165, 166 ST 5457 7m N of Wells. CP, 425. Clutton RD. P BRISTOL. Ch e, m. N Som CC. Outstanding Nmn ch.

COMPTON PAUNCEFOOT Som
166 ST 6426 5m WSW of Wincanton. CP, 134. Wncntn RD. P Yeovil. Ch e. Wells CC. See also Blackford.

COMPTON VALENCE Dorset
177, 178 SY 5993 6m WNW of Dorchester. CP, 63. Dchstr RD. P Dchstr. Ch e. W Dst CC.

CONDERTON Worcs
143, 144 SO 9637 5m ENE of Tewkesbury. CP, 116. Evesham RD. S Worcs CC.

CONDICOTE Glos
144 SP 1528 3m NW of Stow-on-the-Wold. CP, 112. Cotswold RD. P Cheltenham. Ch e. Cirencester and Tewkesbury CC.

CONDOVER Shrops
118 SJ 4905 4m S of Shrewsbury. CP, 4,140. Atcham RD. P Shrsbry. Ch e. Sch pe2. Shrsbry CC. See also Dorrington, Ryton, Stapleton. Ch: monmts. C. Hall*, E-shaped 16c hse, now sch for blind children.

CONEYHURST COMMON Sussex (W)
182 TQ 1023 2m SE of Billingshurst. Loc, W Chiltington CP.

CONEYSTHORPE Yorks (N)
92 SE 7171 5m W of Malton. CP, 122. Mltn RD. P YORK. Ch e. Thirsk and Mltn CC. Estate vllge. To S, Cstle Howard*, baroque mansion by Vanbrugh, with formal gdns, lakes, temples, etc.

CONEYTHORPE Yorks (W)
96 SE 3959 3m ENE of Knaresborough. CP(Cnythpe and Clareton), 44. Nidderdale RD. Harrogate CC.

CONEY WESTON Suffolk (W)
136 TL 9578 6m ESE of Thetford. CP, 143. Thingoe RD. P Bury St Edmunds. Ch e, m. Bury St Eds CC. At bracken-covered S edge of Breckland.

CONGDON'S SHOP Cornwall
186 SX 2878 5m SW of Launceston. Loc, North Hill CP. Ch m.

CONGERSTONE Leics
120, 121 SK 3605 6m NE of Atherstone. Loc, Shackerstone CP. P Nuneaton, Warwickshire. Ch e. Sch p.

CONGHAM Norfolk
124 TF 7123 6m ENE of King's Lynn. CP, 192. Freebridge Lynn RD. P K's Lnn. Ch e. NW Nflk CC (K's Lnn).

CONGLETON Ches
110 SJ 8662 8m SW of Macclesfield. MB, 20,324. P. Mcclsfld CC. See also Key Grn, Timbersbrook. Yarn mnfg tn with three chs and several old inns. Mow Cop (qv) can be seen to S.

CONGRESBURY Som
165 ST 4363 8m ENE of Weston. CP, 1,637. Axbridge RD. P BRISTOL. Ch e, m. Sch pe. Wstn-super-Mare CC.

CONINGSBY Lincs (L)
114 TF 2258 4m SSE of Woodhall Spa. CP, 2,629. Horncastle RD. P LINCOLN. Ch e. Sch i, pe. Hncstle CC. See also Dogdyke. To S, RAF stn.

CONINGTON Cambs
134 TL 3266 3m S of St Ives. CP, 148. Chesterton RD. Ch e. Cambs CC. Ch in strange mixture of styles.

CONINGTON Hunts
134 TL 1785 8m S of Peterborough. CP, 290. Huntingdon RD. P PTRBRGH. Ch e. Hunts CC. Ch: twr.

CONISBROUGH Yorks (W)
103 SK 5198 5m WSW of Doncaster. UD, 16,800. P Dncstr. Dearne Valley CC. See also Denaby Main. 12c cstle (A.M.); unique circular keep.

CONISHOLME Lincs (L)
105 TF 4095 7m NE of Louth. CP, 71. Lth RD. Ch e, m. Lth CC. Ch: small Saxon stone sculpture; brass of 1515.

CONISTON Lancs
88, 89 SD 3097 6m SW of Ambleside. CP, 1,114. N Lonsdale RD. P. Ch e, m, r, v. Sch pe. Morecambe and Lnsdle CC. See also Bowmanstead. At NW corner of Cnstn

Water. Ruskin Museum. To SE across lake, Brantwood*, Rskn's home. To W, Cnstn Old Man, 2,635ft.

CONISTON Yorks (E)
99 TA 1535 5m NE of Hull. CP, 258. Holderness RD. P Hll. Ch m. Bridlington CC. See also Thirtleby.

CONISTON COLD Yorks (W)
95 SD 9055 6m WNW of Skipton. CP, 128. Skptn RD. P Skptn. Ch e. Skptn CC. See also Bell Busk.

CONISTONE Yorks (W)
90 SD 9867 10m N of Skipton. CP(Cnstne w Kilnsey), 103. Skptn RD. P Skptn. Ch e. Skptn CC.

CONNOR DOWNS Cornwall
189 SW 5939 3m W of Camborne. Loc, Gwinear-Gwithian CP. P Hayle. Ch m2. Sch p.

CONONLEY Yorks (W)
95 SD 9847 3m S of Skipton. CP, 869. Skptn RD. P Keighley. Ch e, b, m. Sch p. Skptn CC.

CONSALL Staffs
110 SJ 9848 5m S of Leek. CP, 199. Cheadle RD. Lk CC.

CONSETT Co Durham
77, 78 NZ 1150 12m SW of Gateshead. UD, 35,391. P. Cnstt CC. See also Delves, Ebchester, Hamsterley, High Westwood, Iveston, Leadgate, Low Wstwd, Medomsley, Shotley Br, Templetown. Iron and steel wks; coal mines.

CONSTABLE BURTON Yorks (N)
91 SE 1690 3m E of Leyburn. CP, 158. Lbn RD. P Lbn. Ch m. Sch pe. Richmond CC. C.B. Hall, mid-Ggn hse by Carr of York.

CONSTANTINE Cornwall
190 SW 7329 5m ENE of Helston. CP, 1,791. Kerrier RD. P Falmouth. Ch e, m. Sch p. Flmth and Camborne CC. See also Porth Navas, Seworgan.

CONYER Kent
172 TQ 9664 4m E of Sittingbourne. Loc, Teynham CP.

COODEN Sussex (E)
183, 184 TQ 7106 2m W of Bexhill. Loc,

Bxhll MB. Rsdntl distr. Rly runs between golf course and sandhills.

COOKBURY Devon
175 SS 4006 4m ENE of Holsworthy. CP, 89. Hlswthy RD. Ch e, m. W Dvn CC (Tavistock). To S, site of Tdr and later Dunsland Hse, (NT), burnt down in 1967.

COOKHAM Berks
159 SU 8985 3m N of Maidenhead. CP, 5,481. Ckhm RD. P Mdnhd. Ch e. Sch pe. Windsor and Mdnhd CC (Wndsr). Thames-side tourist attraction. In King's Hall, Stanley Spencer picture gallery.

COOKHAM DEAN Berks
159 SU 8684 2m SE of Marlow. Loc, Ckhm CP. P Ckhm, Maidenhead. Ch e, m. Sch pe. Much NT property in area, incl vllge grn.

COOKHAM RISE Berks
159 SU 8884 3m N of Maidenhead. Loc, Ckhm CP. Ch m2, r. Sch p.

COOKHILL Worcs
131 SP 0558 2m WNW of Alcester. Loc, Inkberrow CP. P Alcstr, Warwickshire. Ch e, b. Sch p.

COOKLEY Suffolk (E)
137 TM 3475 3m WSW of Halesworth. CP, 130. Blyth RD. Ch e. Sch pe. Eye CC.

COOKLEY Worcs
130 SO 8480 2m NNE of Kidderminster. Loc, Wolverley CP. P Kddrmnstr. Ch e, m. Sch pe. On R Stour and Staffs and Worcs Canal.

COOKLEY GREEN Oxon
159 SU 6990 6m E of Wallingford. Loc, Swyncombe CP. Henley RD. Sch pe. Hnly CC.

COOKSBRIDGE Sussex (E)
183 TQ 4013 2m N of Lewes. Loc, Hamsey CP. P Lewes.

COOKSHILL Staffs
110, 119 SJ 9443 4m ESE of Stoke-on-Trent. Loc, Caverswall CP.

COOKSMILL GREEN Essex
161 TL 6306 4m W of Chelmsford. Loc, Roxwell CP. Ch v.

COOLHAM Sussex (W)
182 TQ 1222 3m SE of Billingshurst. Loc, Shipley CP. P Horsham. Sch pe.

COOLING Kent
172 TQ 7575 5m N of Rochester. CP. Strood RD. Ch e, m. Gravesend CC. Marshes to N described by Dickens in *Great Expectations*. Now nature reserve. Ruins of 14c cstle.

COOMBE Cornwall
174 SS 2011 4m N of Bude. Loc, Morwenstow CP. NT property giving access to Duckpool Beach.

COOMBE BISSETT Wilts
167 SU 1026 3m SW of Salisbury. CP, 586. Slsbry and Wilton RD. P Slsbry. Ch e, b. Sch pe. Slsbry CC. See also Homington.

COOMBE HILL Glos
143, 144 SO 8827 4m S of Tewkesbury. Loc, Leigh CP. P GLOUCESTER. Ch m.

COOMBE KEYNES Dorset
178 SY 8484 5m WSW of Wareham. CP, 96. Wrhm and Purbeck RD. P Wrhm. Ch e. S Dst CC.

COOMBES Sussex (W)
182 TQ 1908 3m NW of Shoreham-by-Sea. CP, 66. Worthing RD. Ch e. Shrhm CC (Arundel and Shrhm). Looks across R Adur to cement wks.

COOPERSALE COMMON Essex
161 TL 4702 1m ENE of Epping. Loc, Eppng UD. P Eppng.

COPDOCK Suffolk (E)
150 TM 1142 3m WSW of Ipswich. CP, 399. Samford RD. P Ipswch. Ch e. Sch p. Sudbury and Woodbridge CC.

COPFORD GREEN Essex
149, 162 TL 9222 4m WSW of Colchester. Loc, Cpfd CP. Lexden and Winstree RD. P(Cpfd), Clchstr. Ch e, f. Sch pe. Clchstr CC. Ch: 12c Romanesque wall-paintings; very early brickwork.

COPGROVE Yorks (W)
91 SE 3463 4m SW of Boroughbridge. CP, 73. Nidderdale RD. Ch e. Harrogate CC.

COPLE Beds
147 TL 1048 3m ESE of Bedford. CP, 687. Bdfd RD. P BDFD. Ch e. Sch p. Mid-Beds CC. Ch has early 15c brass.

COPLEY Co Durham
84 NZ 0825 6m NNE of Barnard Cstle. Loc, Lynesack and Softley CP. Bnd Cstle RD. P Bishop Auckland. Ch m. Bshp Auckland CC.

COPLOW DALE Derbys
111 SK 1679 7m NNW of Bakewell. Loc, Lit Hucklow CP.

COPMANTHORPE Yorks (W)
97 SE 5646 4m SW of York. CP, 1,027. Tadcaster RD. P YK. Ch e, m. Sch p2. Barkston Ash CC.

COPPATHORNE Cornwall
174 SS 2000 4m S of Bude. Loc, Poundstock CP. 1m SE, Penfound mnr hse; see Pndstck.

COPPENHALL Staffs
119 SJ 9019 3m SSW of Stafford. CP, 140. Cannock RD. Ch e. SW Staffs CC (Cnnck).

COPPERHOUSE Cornwall
189 SW 5738 5m W of Camborne. Loc, Hayle CP. P Hle. Ch m.

COPPINGFORD Hunts
134 TL 1680 7m NW of Huntingdon. CP(Upton and Cppngfd), 262. Hntngdn RD. Hunts CC.

COPPLESTONE Devon
175 SS 7702 4m WNW of Crediton. Loc, Crdtn RD. P Crdtn. Ch m. Sch p. Tiverton CC (Torrington).

COPPULL Lancs
100 SD 5614 3m SSW of Chorley. CP, 6,332. Chly RD. P Chly. Ch e, m2, r, v. Sch i, j, pe2, pr. Chly CC. See also Cppll Moor.

COPPULL MOOR Lancs
100 SD 5513 4m SSW of Chorley. Loc, Cppll CP.

COPSALE Sussex (W)
182 TQ 1724 4m S of Horsham. Loc, Nuthurst CP. P Hshm.

COPSTER GREEN Lancs
94, 95 SD 6734 4m N of Blackburn. Loc, Salesbury CP.

COPSTON MAGNA Warwicks
132 SP 4588 4m SSE of Hinckley. CP, 54. Rugby RD. Ch e. Rgby CC.

COPT HEWICK Yorks (W)
91 SE 3471 2m E of Ripon. CP, 165. Rpn and Pateley Br RD. Ch e, m. Rpn CC.

COPTHORNE Sussex (E)
170, 182 TQ 3139 4m NE of Crawley. Loc,
Worth CP. P Crly. Ch e, r, v. Sch i, pe.

COPT OAK Leics
121 SK 4812 4m E of Coalville. Loc,
Markfield CP. Ch e.

COPYTHORNE Hants
180 SU 3014 5m SSW of Romsey. CP,
2,644. New Forest RD. Ch e, v. Sch pe. Nw
Fst CC. See also Bartley, Cadnam,
Newbridge.

CORBRIDGE Nthmb
77 NY 9864 3m E of Hexham. CP, 2,869.
Hxhm RD. P. Ch e, m3. Sch pe, s. Hxhm
CC. See also Aydon, Dilston. On N bank of
R Tyne; 17c br. Ch has Saxon twr. To W,
Roman stn of *Corstopitum* (A.M.).

CORBY Northants
133 SP 8988 7m N of Kettering. UD,
47,716. P. Kttrng CC. See also Gt Oakley.
Modern steel tn almost entirely developed
since 1950.

CORBY GLEN Lincs (K)
123 SK 9924 7m WNW of Bourne. CP, 599.
S Kesteven RD. P Grantham. Ch e, m, r.
Sch p, s. Rutland and Stamford CC.

CORBY, GREAT Cumb
76 NY 4754 5m E of Carlisle. See Gt Cby.

CORBY HILL Cumb
76 NY 4757 5m E of Carlisle. Loc, Hayton
CP. Ch m.

CORELEY Shrops
129, 130 SO 6173 4m NNE of Tenbury
Wells. CP, 384. Ludlow RD. P Ldlw. Ch e.
Sch pe. Ldlw CC.

CORES END Bucks
159 SU 9087 3m SW of Beaconsfield. Loc,
Wooburn CP. Ch v.

CORFE Som
177 ST 2319 3m S of Taunton. CP, 246.
Tntn RD. P Tntn. Ch e, b. Tntn CC.

CORFE CASTLE Dorset
179 SY 9681 4m SE of Wareham. CP,
1,381. Wrhm and Purbeck RD. P Wrhm.
Ch e, m2, v. Sch pe. S Dst CC. See also
Kingston, Norden Hth. Ruins of Nmn cstle
(A.M.) in gap of Pbck Hills. Picturesque
vllge.

CORFE MULLEN Dorset
179 SY 9798 2m WSW of Wimborne. CP,
3,235. Wmbne and Cranborne RD.
P Wmbne. Ch e, b, m, v. Sch p. N Dst CC.
See also E End.

CORFTON Shrops
129 SO 4984 4m ENE of Craven Arms. Loc,
Diddlebury CP.

CORHAMPTON Hants
168 SU 6120 10m SE of Winchester.
CP(Crhmptn and Meonstoke), 629.
Droxford RD. Ch e. Petersfield CC. Ch
mainly Saxon.

CORLEY Warwicks
132 SP 3085 4m NNW oc Coventry. CP, 858.
Meriden RD. P Cvntry. Ch e. Sch pe. Mrdn CC.
See also Crly Ash. To SE, Iron Age fort.
C. Hall may be the 'Hall Farm' in George
Eliot's *Adam Bede.*

CORLEY ASH Warwicks
132 SP 2986 5m NNW of Coventry. Loc,
Crly CP.

CORLEY MOOR Warwicks
132 SP 2885 5m NW of Coventry. Loc,
Meriden RD. Mrdn CC.

CORNARD, GREAT Suffolk (W)
149 TL 8840 1m SE of Sudbury. See Gt
Cnd.

CORNEY Cumb
88 SD 1191 4m SSE of Ravenglass. Loc,
Waberthwaite CP. Millom RD. Ch e. Whitehaven CC.

CORNFORTH Co Durham
85 NZ 3134 4m E of Spennymoor. CP, 4,006.
Sedgefield RD. Ch e, m3, s2. Sch p. Drhm CC
(Sdgfld).

CORNHILL-ON-TWEED Nthmb
64, 70 NT 8539 1m ESE of Coldstream. CP,
401. Norham and Islandshires RD. P. Ch e,
m. Sch p. Berwick-upon-Tweed CC. See also
Cstle Heaton, New Htn.

CORNHOLME Yorks (W)
95 SD 9126 2m NW of Todmorden. Loc,
Tdmdn MB. P Tdmdn, Lancs.

CORNISH HALL END Essex
148 TL 6836 6m NE of Thaxted. Loc,
Finchingfield CP. P Braintree. Ch e.

CORNSAY Co Durham
85 NZ 1443 3m SSW of Lanchester. CP,
1,350. Lnchstr RD. NW Drhm CC.

CORNSAY COLLIERY Co Durham
85 NZ 1743 3m S of Lanchester. Loc, Cnsy
CP. P DRHM. Ch s.

CORNWELL Oxon
144 SP 2727 3m W of Chipping Norton. CP,
83. Chppng Ntn RD. Ch e. Banbury CC.

CORNWOOD Devon
187,188 SX 6059 3m NW of Ivybridge. CP,
813. Plympton St Mary RD. P Ivybrdge.
Ch e. Sch pe. W Dvn CC (Tavistock). See
also Lutton. To N, wooded ravine called
'Hawns and Dendles'. 1½m SSE, Fardel,
mdvl hse, former home of Raleigh family.

CORNWORTHY Devon
188 SX 8255 4m SSE of Totnes. CP, 292.
Ttns RD. P Ttns. Ch e, m. Ttns CC. See also
Allaleigh.

CORPUSTY Norfolk
125 TG 1130 6m SSE of Holt. CP, 577.
Erpingham RD. Ch e, m. Sch p. N Nflk CC.
See also Saxthorpe.

CORRINGHAM Essex
161, 162 TQ 7083 3m SSW of Basildon. Loc,
Thurrock UD. P Stanford-le-Hope. Thrrck
BC (CC). Modern housing round ancient
centre. Ch has massive 11c bell twr.

CORRINGHAM Lincs (L)
104 SK 8791 3m E of Gainsborough. CP,
426. Gnsbrgh RD. P Gnsbrgh. Ch e, m.
Sch pe. Gnsbrgh CC. See also Aisby.

CORSCOMBE Dorset
177 ST 5205 5m SE of Crewkerne. CP, 301.
Beaminster RD. P Dorchester. Ch e.
W Dst CC. See also Toller Whelme.

CORSE Glos
143 SO 7826 4m E of Newent. CP, 463.
Nwnt RD. Ch e. Sch pe. W Glos CC.

CORSE LAWN Worcs
143 SO 8330 4m WSW of Tewkesbury. Loc,
Eldersfield CP. P GLOUCESTER. Ch m.

CORSHAM Wilts
156 ST 8670 4m SW of Chippenham. CP,
9,309. Calne and Chppnhm RD. P.
Ch e, b4, c, m, r, v2.   Sch p3, pr, sb, sg.

Chppnhm CC. See also Gastard, Neston.
Admiralty establishments. Much new
housing. Many stone hses incl almshouses.
The apparently ruined Nmn ch in Ch St is
18c folly. C. Ct*, largely mid-18c.

CORSLEY Wilts
166 ST 8246 3m WNW of Warminster. CP,
684. Wmnstr and Westbury RD. P Wmnstr.
Ch e, b, m. Sch pe. Wstbry CC. See also Csly
Hth.

CORSLEY HEATH Wilts
166 ST 8245 3m W of Warminster. Loc,
Csly CP. Ch e.

CORSTON Som
156 ST 6965 4m W of Bath. CP, 486.
Bathavon RD. P Bth. Ch e, r. Sch pe.
N Som CC.

CORSTON Wilts
156, 157 ST 9284 2m S of Malmesbury.
Loc, St Paul Mlmsbry Without CP. Mlmsbry
RD. P Mlmsbry. Ch e. Chippenham CC.

CORTON Suffolk (E)
137 TM 5497 3m N of Lowestoft. CP, 707.
Lothingland RD. P Lwstft. Ch e, m. Sch pe.
Lwstft CC.

CORTON Wilts
167 ST 9340 5m SE of Warminster. Loc,
Boyton CP. Ch b.

CORTON DENHAM Som
166 ST 6322 4m N of Sherborne. CP, 207.
Wincanton RD. P Sherborne, Dorset. Ch e.
Wells CC.

CORYTON Devon
175 SX 4583 6m N of Tavistock. CP, 111.
Tvstck RD. P Okehampton. Ch e. W Dvn CC
(Tvstck).

CORYTON Essex
161, 162 TQ 7482 4m SSE of Basildon.
Loc, Thurrock UD. P Stanford-le-Hope.
Thrrck BC (CC). Very large oil refineries.

COSBY Leics
132 SP 5494 7m SSW of Leicester. CP,
1,776. Blaby RD. P LCSTR. Ch e, b, m.
Sch p. Blby CC (Harborough).

COSELEY Staffs
130, 131 SO 9494 3m N of Dudley. Loc,
Ddly CB. P Bilston. Dldly E BC (Blstn).

COSGROVE Northants
146 SP 7942 1m N of Stony Stratford. CP,
403. Towcester RD. P Wolverton, Bucks.
Ch e, b. Sch p. Daventry CC (S Nthnts).
Meeting place of rivers and canals.

COSHAM Hants
180, 181 SU 6505 N distr of Portsmouth.
Loc, Ptsmth CB. P Ptsmth. Ptsmth N BC
(Ptsmth, Langstone).

COSSALL Notts
112,121 SK 4842 1m E of Ilkeston. CP,
1,149. Basford RD. Ch e. Sch pe. Beeston
CC (Rushcliffe). Almshouses of 1685.

COSSINGTON Leics
121, 122 SK 6013 6m N of Leicester. CP,
399. Barrow upon Soar RD. Ch e. Sch pe.
Melton CC.

COSSINGTON Som
165 ST 3540 4m NE of Bridgwater. CP,
411. Brdgwtr RD. P Brdgwtr. Ch e. Sch p.
Brdgwtr CC.

COSTESSEY Norfolk
126 TG 1711 4m NW of Norwich. CP.
Forehoe and Henstead RD. P Nrwch.
Ch e, b, m, r. Sch i, j, pr, s. S Nflk CC
(Central Nflk). See also New Cstssy.

COSTOCK Notts
121, 122 SK 5726 5m NE of
Loughborough. CP, 393. Basford RD.
P Lghbrgh, Leics. Ch e, m. Sch pe.
Rushcliffe CC. Elizn mnr hse.

COSTON Leics
122 SK 8422 6m ENE of Melton Mowbray.
Loc, Garthorpe CP. Ch e.

COSTON Norfolk
125 TG 0606 4m NW of Wymondham. Loc,
Runhall CP.

COTE Oxon
158 SP 3503 4m S of Witney. Loc, Aston
Bampton and Shifford CP. Ch b.

COTEBROOK Ches
109 SJ 5765 5m W of Winsford. Loc,
Utkinton CP. Northwich RD. P Tarporley.
Ch e, m. Nthwch CC.

COTEHILL Cumb
76 NY 4650 6m SW of Carlisle. Loc,
Wetheral CP. P Clsle. Ch e, m. Sch pe.

COTES Leics
121,122 SK 5520 1m NE of Loughborough.
CP, 67. Barrow upon Soar RD. Melton CC.

COTES Staffs
110, 119 SJ 8434 4m W of Stone. Loc,
Eccleshall CP.

COTES Westm
89 SD 4887 SSW of Kendal. Loc, Levens
CP.

COTESBACH Leics
132 SP 5382 1m SSW of Lutterworth. CP,
146. Lttrwth RD. P Rugby, Warwickshire.
Ch e. Blaby CC (Harborough).

COTGRAVE Notts
112, 121, 122 SK 6435 6m SE of
Nottingham. CP, 641. Bingham RD.
P NTTNGHM. Ch e, m. Sch i, j, p, pe.
Rushcliffe CC (Carlton).

COTHAM Notts
112 SK 7947 4m S of Newark. CP, 69.
Nwk RD. Ch e. Nwk CC. Ch monmt of 1601
to Anne Markham.

COTHELSTONE Som
164 ST 1831 5m NW of Taunton. CP, 111.
Tntn RD. Ch e. Tntn CC. Mnr hse has
arched gateway from which two of
Monmouth's followers were hanged in 1685.

COTHERIDGE Worcs
130/143 SO 7855 4m W of Worcester. CP,
249. Martley RD. P WCSTR. Ch e.
Kidderminster CC.

COTHERSTONE Yorks (N)
84 NZ 0119 3m NW of Barnard Cstle. CP,
513. Startforth RD. P Bnd Cstle, Co
Durham. Ch e, c, f, m. Richmond CC.

COTHILL Berks
158 SU 4699 3m NW of Abingdon. Loc,
Abngdn RD. P Abngdn. Ch e, b. Abngdn CC.
Ruskin Nature Reserve (NT).

COTLEIGH Devon
177 ST 2002 3m NE of Honiton. CP, 189.
Hntn RD. P Hntn. Ch e. Sch pe. Hntn CC.

COTON Cambs
135 TL 4158 2m W of Cambridge. CP, 519.
Chesterton RD. P CMBRDGE. Ch e, b.
Sch pe. Cambs CC.

COTON Northants
132, 133 SP 6771 9m NW of Northampton.
Loc, Ravensthorpe CP.

COTON Staffs
110, 119 SJ 9832 5m ESE of Stone. Loc,
Milwich CP.

COTON Staffs
119 SJ 8120 7m WSW of Stafford. Loc,
Gnosall CP. P Gnsll, STFFD.

COTON CLANFORD Staffs
119 SJ 8723 3m W of Stafford. Loc,
Seighford CP. Ch m. C.C. Hall*, 17c
half-timbered hse.

COTON IN THE CLAY Staffs
120 SK 1629 6m NW of Burton-on-Trent.
Loc, Hanbury CP.

COTON IN THE ELMS Derbys
120 SK 2415 5m S of Burton-on-Trent. CP,
463. Repton RD. P Btn-on-Trnt, Staffs.
Ch e, m. Sch pe. Belper CC.

COTTAM Lancs
94 SD 5032 3m NW of Preston. Loc,
Prstn RD. P Prstn. Ch r. Sch pr. S Flyde CC.
RC ch and sch also listed under
Woodplumpton.

COTTAM Notts
104 SK 8180 6m S of Gainsborough. CP,
67. E Retford RD. P Rtfd. Ch e, m.
Bassetlaw CC.

COTTENHAM Cambs
135 TL 4567 6m N of Cambridge. CP,
2,415. Chesterton RD. P CMBRDGE.
Ch e, b2, m, s2. Sch p, s. Cambs CC.

COTTERDALE Yorks (N)
90 SD 8393 4m NW of Hawes. Loc, High
Abbotside CP. Aysgarth RD. Ch m.
Richmond CC.

COTTERED Herts
147 TL 3129 6m ENE of Stevenage. CP,
508. Braughing RD. P Buntingford. Ch e.
Sch pe. E Herts CC. See also Throcking.
Lordship Hse, moated mnr hse of 15c and
17c.

COTTERSTOCK Northants
134 TL 0490 2m N of Oundle. CP, 75.
Oundle and Thrapston RD. Ch e.
Wellingborough CC (Peterborough). C.
Hall*, mid-17c hse with 1 :h style gables.

COTTESBROOKE Northants
133 SP 7073 9m NNW of Northampton. CP,
164. Brixworth RD. P NTHMPTN. Ch e.
Daventry CC (Kettering). C. Hall, early 18c
hse in large grnds* with lake.

COTTESMORE Rutland
122 SK 9013 4m NE of Oakham. CP, 2,445.
Oakhm RD. P Oakhm. Ch e, m. Rtlnd and
Stamford CC. Stone vllge; gives its name to
famous hunt. Ch has broach spire. Quarries
to W, airfield to N.

COTTINGHAM Northants
133 SP 8490 3m W of Corby. CP, 645.
Kettering RD. P Mkt Harborough, Leics.
Ch e, m. Sch pe. Kttrng CC.

COTTINGHAM Yorks (E)
99 TA 0432 4m NW of Hull. Loc,
Haltemprice UD. P. Hltmprce CC. N of
Baynard Cstle, of which only a mound
remains, are curious springs which vanish and
re-appear at intervals of months or years.

COTTISFORD Oxon
145, 146 SP 5831 4m S of Brackley. CP,
162. Ploughley RD. Ch e. Banbury CC
(Henley).

COTTON Suffolk (E)
136 TM 0767 5m NNE of Stowmarket. CP,
375. Hartismere RD. P Stwmkt. Ch e, m.
Eye CC.

COTTON END Beds
147 TL 0845 4m SE of Bedford. Loc,
Eastcotts CP. Bdfd RD. P BDFD. Ch b.
Sch p. Mid-Beds CC.

COTTS Devon
187 SX 4365 6m SSW of Tavistock. Loc,
Bere Ferrers CP. Ch m.

COTWALTON Staffs
110, 119 SJ 9234 2m ENE of Stone. Loc,
Stne Rural CP. Stne RD. Stafford and
Stne CC.

COUCHSMILL Cornwall
186 SX 1459 3m E of Lostwithiel. Loc,
Liskeard RD. Ch m. Bodmin CC.

COUGHTON Warwicks
131 SP 0860 2m N of Alcester. CP, 193.
Alcstr RD. P Alcstr. Ch e, r. Sch pe.
Stratford-on-Avon CC(Strtfd). Ch: glass,
monmts, bread rack in S aisle. C. Ct (NT)*,
16c hse.

COULSDON London
170 TQ 3058 4m S of Croydon. Loc, Crdn
LB. P Surrey. Crdn S BC (E Srry CC).

COULTON Yorks (N)
92 SE 6374 6m SSE of Helmsley. CP, 69.
Hlmsly RD. Thirsk and Malton CC.

COUND Shrops
118 SJ 5504 6m SE of Shrewsbury. CP,
408. Atcham RD. P Shrsbry. Ch e. Shrsbry
CC. C. Hall, early 18c mansion in pk.

COUNDON Co Durham
85 NZ 2429 2m E of Bishop Auckland. Loc,
Bshp Aucklnd UD. P Bshp Aucklnd.

COUNDON GRANGE Co Durham
85 NZ 2228 1m SE of Bishop Auckland.
Loc, Bshp Aucklnd UD.

COUNTERSETT Yorks (N)
90 SD 9187 3m ESE of Hawes. Loc,
Bainbridge CP. Ch f.

COUNTESTHORPE Leics
132, 133 SP 5895 6m S of Leicester. CP,
2,249. Blaby RD. P LCSTR. Ch e, b, m.
Sch i, j, s. Blby CC (Harborough).
Secondary sch is proving-grnd for many
advanced ideas in education.

COUNTISBURY Devon
163 SS 7449 2m E of Lynton. CP, 80.
Barnstaple RD. Ch e. Sch pe. N Dvn CC.
Hmlt at top of C. Hill and long steep
descent to Lynmouth. Views across Bristol
Channel to Wales.

COUPLAND Nthmb
64, 71 NT 9331 4m WNW of Wooler. Loc,
E w a r t   C P .   G l e n d a l e   R D .
Berwick-upon-Tweed CC. C. Cstle, 16c,
fortified early 17c.

COURTEENHALL Northants
146 SP 7653 5m S of Northampton. CP,
130. Nthmpton RD. P NTHMPTN. Ch e.
Daventry CC (S Nthnts).

COURTSEND Essex
162 TR 0293 10m ENE of Southend. Loc,
Foulness CP. Rochford RD. Maldon CC (SE
Essx).

COURTWAY Som
165 ST 2034 6m WSW of Bridgwater. Loc,
Spaxton CP. P Brdgwtr.

COUSLEY WOOD Sussex (E)
183 TQ 6533 6m SE of Tunbridge Wells.
Loc, Wadhurst CP. P Wdhst. Ch v.

COVE Devon
164 SS 9519 4m N of Tiverton. Loc, Tvtn
MB. P Tvtn.

COVE Hants
169 SU 8555 3m N of Aldershot. Loc,
Farnborough UD. P Fnbrgh.

COVEHITHE Suffolk (E)
137 TM 5281 4m NNE of Southwold. CP,
73. Lothingland RD. Ch e. Lowestoft CC.
Decayed place near coast. Present ch inside
ruins of former one.

COVEN Staffs
119 SJ 9106 5m N of Wolverhampton. Loc,
Brewood CP. P Wlvrhmptn. Ch e, m2.
Sch pe.

COVENEY Cambs
135 TL 4982 3m WNW of Ely. CP, 401. Ely
RD. P Ely. Ch e, m. Sch pe. Isle of Ely CC.
See also Wardy Hill.

COVENHAM ST BARTHOLOMEW Lincs
(L)
105 TF 3394 5m N of Louth. CP, 136. Lth
RD. P(Cynhm), Lth. Ch e, m. Lth CC. Ch
has brass of 1415.

COVENHAM ST MARY Lincs (L)
105 TF 3394 4m N of Louth. CP, 76.
Lth RD. Ch e. Lth CC.

COVENTRY Warwicks
132 SP 3379 17m ESE of Birmingham. CB,
334,839. P. BCs: Cvntry NE, NW, SE, SW,
(E, N, S). See also Allesley. Indstrl city;
motor car mnfg. Modern cathedral replaced
bldng gutted by a World War II air raid.
Pedestrian precinct in city centre. University
of Warwick to SW.

COVERACK Cornwall
190 SW 7818 10m SE of Helston. Loc, St
Keverne CP. P Hlstn. Ch m. Sch p. Fishing
vllge with small harbour; smugglers' haunt in
days of yore.

COVERHAM Yorks (N)
91 SE 1086 2m SW of Middleham.
CP(Cvrhm w Agglethorpe), 127. Leyburn
RD. Ch e. Richmond CC. Rems of 13c
abbey, partly absorbed into Ggn hse.

COVINGTON Hunts
134 TL 0570 4m ESE of Raunds. CP, 104. St Neots RD. P HUNTINGDON. Ch e. Hunts CC.

COWAN BRIDGE Lancs
89 SD 6376 2m SE of Kirkby Lonsdale. Loc, Lunesdale RD. P Carnforth. Ch m. Lancaster CC. Bronte sisters at sch here in hse close to br.

COWBEECH Sussex (E)
183 TQ 6114 4m NNE of Hailsham. Loc, Herstmonceux CP. P Hlshm.

COWBIT Lincs (H)
123 TF 2617 3m SSE of Spalding. CP, 583. Spldng RD. P Spldng. Ch e, m. Sch pe. Holland w Boston CC.

COWDEN Kent
171 TQ 4640 4m SSE of Edenbridge. CP, 863. Sevenoaks RD. P Ednbrdge. Ch e. Sch p. Svnks CC. Typical Kent/Sussex border vllge of half-timbered and weatherboard hses.

COWDEN, GREAT Yorks (E)
99 TA 2242 4m SSE of Hornsea. Loc, Mappleton CP.

COWERS LANE Derbys
111 SK 3046 3m W of Belper. Loc, Shottle and Postern CP. P DERBY.

COWES IOW
180 SZ 4995 4m N of Newport, 9m WSW of Portsmouth (by sea). UD, 18,895. P. Isle of Wight CC. See also E Cowes, Gurnard, Northwood, Whippingham. Internationally famous yachting centre with yearly regatta dating from 1814.

COWESBY Yorks (N)
91 SE 4689 5m NNE of Thirsk. CP, 63. Thsk RD. Ch e. Thsk and Malton CC.

COWFOLD Sussex (W)
182 TQ 2122 4m N of Henfield. CP, 1,275. Horsham RD. P Hshm. Ch e, r. Sch pe. Hshm and Crawley CC (Hshm). Ch has famous 15c brass.

COW HONEYBOURNE Worcs
144 SP 1143 5m E of Evesham. Loc, Hnybne CP. Eveshm RD. Ch e, m. Sch p. S Worcs CC.

COWLEY Devon
176 SX 9095 2m NNW of Exeter. Loc, Upton Pyne CP. Ch e.

COWLEY Glos
143, 144 SO 9614 5m S of Cheltenham. CP, 308. Chltnhm RD. Ch e. Cirencester and Tewkesbury CC. See also Birdlip.

COWLEY London
160 TQ 0582 1m S of Uxbridge. Loc, Hillingdon LB. P Uxbrdge, Mddx. Uxbrdge BC (CC).

COWLEY Oxon
158 SP 5404 SE distr of Oxford. Loc, Oxfd CB. P OXFD. Indstrl area blt round huge car factory. Modern shopping centre with pedestrian precinct.

COWLING Yorks (N)
91 SE 2387 2m W of Bedale. CP(Burrill w Clng), 104. Bdle RD. Thirsk and Malton CC.

COWLING Yorks (W)
95 SD 9743 5m ENE of Colne. CP, 1,685. Skipton RD. P Keighley. Ch e, b, m3. Sch p. Skptn CC.

COWLINGE Suffolk (W)
148, 149 TL 7154 6m NNE of Haverhill. CP, 270. Clare RD. P Newmarket. Ch e, c. Sch p. Bury St Edmunds CC.

COWPEN Nthmb
78 NZ 2981 1m W of Blyth. Loc, Blth MB. P Blth.

COWPLAIN Hants
181 SU 6911 3m NW of Havant. Loc, Hvnt and Waterloo UD. P Portsmouth.

COWSHILL Co Durham
84 NY 8540 9m W of Stanhope. Loc, Stnhpe CP. P Bishop Auckland.

COWTHORPE Yorks (W)
97 SE 4252 3m NNE of Wetherby. Loc, Tockwith CP. Ch e.

COXALL Herefs
129 SO 3774 5m ENE of Knighton. CP(Buckton and Cxll), 94. Leominster and Wigmore RD. Ch b. Lmnstr CC.

COXBANK Ches
110, 118, 119 SJ 6541 5m N of Mkt Drayton. Loc, Audlem CP. P Crewe. Ch m.

COXBENCH Derbys
120, 121 SK 3743 5m NNE of Derby. Loc,
Horsley CP. P DBY.

COX COMMON Suffolk (E)
137 TM 4082 3m NNE of Halesworth. Loc,
Westhall CP.

COXFORD Norfolk
125 TF 8429 4m W of Fakenham. Loc,
Tattersett CP.

COXHEATH Kent
171, 172 TQ 7451 3m SSW of Maidstone.
CP. Mdstne RD. P Mdstne. Sch p.
Mdstne CC.

COXHOE Co Durham
85 NZ 3235 5m ENE of Spennymoor. CP,
5,037. Drhm RD. P DRHM. Ch e, s.
Sch p, r, s. Drhm CC. Bthplce of Elizabeth
Barrett Browning, 1806.

COXLEY Som
165 ST 5343 2m SW of Wells. Loc, St
Cuthbert Out CP. Wlls RD. P Wlls. Ch e, m.
Sch p. Wlls CC.

COXWELL, GREAT Berks
157 SU 2693 9m NE of Swindon. See Gt
Cxwll.

COXWOLD Yorks (N)
92 SE 5377 5m N of Easingwold. CP, 176.
Easngwld RD. P YORK. Ch e, m. Sch pe.
Thirsk and Malton CC. Wide grass banks on
both sides of main street. Laurence Sterne,
author of *Tristram Shandy,* was vicar here.
To SE, Newburgh Priory, 18c mansion with
rems of monastery in grnds.

CRABBS CROSS Worcs
131 SP 0464 2m S of Redditch. Loc,
Rddtch UD. P Rddtch.

CRABTREE Sussex (W)
182 TQ 2225 4m SE of Horsham. Loc, Lr
Beeding CP.

CRACKENTHORPE Westm
83 NY 6622 2m NW of Appleby. CP, 91.
N Westm RD. Ch m. Westm CC. See also
Brampton.

CRACKINGTON HAVEN Cornwall
174 SX 1496 7m SSW of Bude. Loc, St
Gennys CP. P Bde. Resort at bottom of
steep combe. NT coastal property N and S.

CRACKLEYBANK Shrops
119 SJ 7610 2m NNE of Shifnal. Loc, Shfnl
RD. The Wrekin CC.

CRACKPOT Yorks (N)
90 SD 9796 8m NE of Hawes. Loc, Grinton
CP.

CRACOE Yorks (W)
90 SD 9760 6m N of Skipton. CP, 120.
Skptn RD. P Skptn. Sch pe. Skptn CC. See
also Threapland.

CRADLEY Herefs
143 SO 7347 3m WNW of Malvern. CP,
1,119. Bromyard RD. P Mlvn, Worcs.
Ch e, v. Sch pe. Leominster CC. See also
Ridgeway Cross, Stifford's Br, Storridge,
Westfield.

CRAFTHOLE Cornwall
186 SX 3654 5m W of Torpoint. Loc,
Sheviock CP. P Tpnt.

CRAGG Yorks (W)
96, 102 SE 0023 6m WSW of Halifax. Loc,
Hebden Royd UD. Sowerby CC.

CRAGHEAD Co Durham
78 NZ 2150 4m W of Chester-le-Street. Loc,
Stanley UD. P Stnly.

CRAISELOUND Lincs (L)
104 SK 7798 6m NNW of Gainsborough.
Loc, Haxey CP.

CRAKEHALL Yorks (N)
91 SE 2490 2m NW of Bedale. CP, 372.
Bdle RD. P Bdle. Ch e, m. Sch pe. Thirsk
and Malton CC. Stone hses round vllge grn.

CRAMBE Yorks (N)
92, 97, 98 SE 7364 5m SW of Malton. CP,
72. Mltn RD. Ch e. Thirsk and Mltn CC.
Nmn ch.

CRAMLINGTON Nthmb
78 NZ 2677 4m SW of Blyth. Loc, Seaton
Valley UD. P. Blth BC. Mining tn being
transformed by New Tn development.

CRANAGE Ches
110 SJ 7568 3m ENE of Middlewich. CP,
1,276. Congleton RD. Sch pe. Knutsford
CC.

CRANBERRY Staffs
110, 119 SJ 8236 5m WNW of Stone. Loc,
Eccleshall CP. Ch m.

CRANBORNE Dorset
179 SU 0513 6m W of Fordingbridge. CP,
560. Wimborne and Crnbne RD. P Wmbne.
Ch e, m2. Sch pe, s. N Dst CC. See also
Boveridge. Ch 13c–15c, large. Jcbn mnr hse
visited by James I.

CRANBOURNE Berks
169 SU 9272 4m SW of Windsor. Loc,
Winkfield CP. Ch e. Sch p.

CRANBROOK Kent
172, 184 TQ 7736 7m WNW of Tenterden.
CP, 4,445. Crnbrk RD. P Crnbrk.
Ch e, b, r, v3. Sch pe, s, sb, sg. Royal
Tunbridge Wells CC (Ashford). See also
Hartley, Sissinghurst. Mkt tn; large ch known
as 'Cathedral of the Weald'. Large smock-
mill still in use. 2½m NE, Glassenbury Pk,
moated 15c mnr hse; shrub gdn*.

CRANE MOOR Yorks (W)
102 SE 3001 4m ESE of Penistone. Loc,
Thurgoland CP. P SHEFFIELD. Ch m2.
Sch pe.

CRANFIELD Beds
147 SP 9542 6m WNW of Ampthill. CP,
2,501. Ampthll RD. P BEDFORD.
Ch e, b, m. Sch pe. Mid-Beds CC.

CRANFORD ST ANDREW Northants
133 SP 9277 4m ESE of Kettering. Loc,
Crnfd CP. Kttrng RD. P(Crnfd), Kttrng.
Ch e. Sch pe. Kttrng CC.

CRANFORD ST JOHN Northants
133 SP 9277 4m ESE of Kettering. Loc,
Crnfd CP. Kttrng RD. P(Crnfd), Kttrng.
Ch e. Sch pe. Kttrng CC. Two places cheek
by jowl.

CRANHAM Glos
143, 144 SO 8912 5m SE of Gloucester. CP,
460. Stroud RD. P GLCSTR. Ch e, c.
Sch pe. Strd CC.

CRANK Lancs
100 SJ 5099 3m N of St Helens. Loc,
Rainford UD. P St Helens.

CRANLEIGH Surrey
170, 182 TQ 0539 8m SE of Guildford. CP,
6,016. Hambledon RD. P. Ch e, b, m, r, v2.
Sch i, je, p, s. Gldfd CC. See also Rowly.
Much recent housing expansion. To N, boys'
public sch.

CRANMORE IOW
180 SZ 3990 3m E of Yarmouth. Loc,
Shalfleet CP. P Ymth.

CRANOE Leics
133 SP 7695 5m NNE of Mkt Harborough.
CP, 49. Mkt Hbrgh RD. P Mkt Hbrgh. Ch e.
Hbrgh CC.

CRANSFORD Suffolk (E)
137 TM 3164 2m ENE of Framlingham. CP,
174. Blyth RD. P Woodbridge. Ch e, b. Eye
CC.

CRANSLEY, GREAT Northants
133 SP 8376 3m WSW of Kettering. See Gt
Crnsly.

CRANSWICK Yorks (E)
99 TA 0252 3m S of Driffield. Loc, Hutton
Crnswck CP. P DRFFLD. Ch m2. Vllge grn
and pond.

CRANTOCK Cornwall
185 SW 7960 2m SW of Newquay. Loc,
Nquay UD. P Nquay. Separated from Nquay
by R Gannel. Spacious sands backed by
dunes, caves, rocks. Old ch.

CRANWELL Lincs (K)
113 TF 0349 3m NW of Sleaford. CP(Crnwll
and Byard's Leap), 1,673. E Kesteven RD.
P Slfd. Ch e. Sch p. Grantham CC. To W,
RAF training college. On main rd A17, stone
horseshoes recall legendary leap by horse
called Byard.

CRANWICH Norfolk
136 TL 7894 5m N of Brandon. CP, 45.
Swaffham RD. Ch e. SW Nflk CC.

CRANWORTH Norfolk
125 TF 9804 5m S of E Dereham. CP, 411.
Mitford and Launditch RD. Ch e, m. Sch p.
SW Nflk CC. See also Southburgh,
Woodrising.

CRAPSTONE Devon
187 SX 5067 4m SSE of Tavistock. Loc,
Buckland Monachorum CP. P Yelverton.

CRASTER Nthmb
71 NU 2519 6m NE of Alnwick. CP, 520.
Alnwick RD. P Alnwick. Sch pe. Berwick-
upon-Tweed CC. See also Dunstan. Fishing
vllge. 1m N on coast, ruins of Dunstanburgh
Cstle (A.M.), 14c.

CRASWALL Herefs
141 SO 2736 5m SE of Hay-on-Wye. CP,
162. Dore and Bredwardine RD. P
HEREFORD. Ch e. Hrfd CC.

CRATFIELD Suffolk (E)
137 TM 3175 5m WSW of Halesworth. CP,
270. Blyth RD. P Hlswth. Ch e. Eye CC. Ch:
seven-sacrament font.

CRATHORNE Yorks (N)
85 NZ 4407 7m S of Teesside (Stockton).
CP, 226. Stokesley RD. P Yarm. Ch e, r.
Sch p. Richmond CC.

CRAVEN ARMS Shrops
129 SO 4382 7m NW of Ludlow. Loc,
Stokesay CP. P. Ch m, r. Mileage pillar by
the 19c Crvn Arms Hotel gives distances to
various tns. Formerly rly junction for
Bishop's Cstle line, closed 1935.

CRAWCROOK Co Durham
78 NZ 1363 3m E of Prudhoe. Loc, Ryton
UD. P Rtn.

CRAWFORD Lancs
100 SD 4902 5m N of St Helens. Loc,
Skelmersdale and Holland UD. P Wigan.

CRAWLEY Hants
168 SU 4234 5m NW of Winchester. CP,
498. Wnchstr RD. P Wnchstr. Ch e, v. Sch p.
Wnchstr CC. Picturesque vllge with duck
pond.

CRAWLEY Oxon
145 SP 3412 2m NW of Witney. CP, 183.
Wtny RD. Ch e. Mid-Oxon CC (Banbury).

CRAWLEY Sussex (W)
170, 182 TQ 2636 20m N of Brighton. UD,
67,571. P. Horsham and Crly CC (Hshm).
See also Ifield, Pound Hill, Three Bridges.
Designated New Tn 1947 (pop. then under
10,000). Pedestrian precinct. Light industry.
To N, London (Gatwick) Airpt.

CRAWLEY DOWN Sussex (E)
170, 182 TQ 3437 3m W of E Grinstead.
Loc, Worth CP. P Crly. Ch e, m. Sch pe.

CRAWLEY SIDE Co Durham
84 NY 9940 just N of Stanhope. Loc,
Stnhpe CP.

CRAWSHAW BOOTH Lancs
95 SD 8125 2m N of Rawtenstall. Loc,
Rtnstll MB. P Rossendale.

CRAY Yorks (W)
90 SD 9479 8m SE of Hawes. Loc, Buckden
CP.

CRAYFORD London
161, 171 TQ 5275 1m NW of Dartford.
Loc, Bexley LB. P Dtfd, Kent. Erith and
Crfd BC. Bounded by R Cray to S, C.
Marshes and R Darent to E, R Thames to N.

CRAYKE Yorks (N)
92 SE 5670 2m E of Easingwold. CP, 393.
Easngwld RD. P YORK. Ch e, m. Sch pe.
Thirsk and Malton CC. 15c cstle, part
ruined, part incorporated in 19c hse.

CRAYS HILL Essex
161, 162 TQ 7192 3m NNW of Basildon.
Loc, Bsldn UD. P Billericay.

CRAY'S POND Oxon
158, 159 SU 6380 3m N of Pangbourne.
Loc, Goring Hth CP.

CREACOMBE Devon
164 SS 8119 10m WNW of Tiverton. CP,
52. S Molton RD. Ch e. N Dvn CC.

CREATON Northants
133 SP 7071 8m NNW of Northampton. CP,
319. Brixworth RD. P NTHMPTN. Ch e, c.
Sch p. Daventry CC. (Kettering).

CREDENHILL Herefs
142 SO 4543 4m NW of Hereford. CP,
2,481. Hrfd RD. P HRFD. Ch e. Sch pe.
Leominster CC. Ch has 14c stained glass.

CREDITON Devon
176 SS 8300 7m NW of Exeter. UD, 5,144.
P. Tiverton CC (Torrington). Ancient tn,
once seat of bishops of the South West.
Bthplce of St Boniface. Red sandstone ch.
Cider-making.

CREECH HEATHFIELD Som
177 ST 2726 4m ENE of Taunton. Loc,
Creech St Michael CP.

CREECH ST MICHAEL Som
177 ST 2725 3m E of Taunton. CP, 1,049.
Tntn RD. P Tntn. Ch e, b, v. Sch pe. Tntn
CC. See also Crch Heathfield.

CREED Cornwall
190 SW 9347 6m WSW of St Austell. CP,
203. St Astll RD. Ch e. Truro CC.

CREETING ST MARY Suffolk (E)
149 TM 0956 3m ESE of Stowmarket. CP,
493. Gipping RD. P Ipswich. Ch e. Sch pe.
Eye CC.

CREETON Lincs (K)
123 TF 0119 5m W of Bourne.
CP(Counthorpe and Crtn), 129. S Kesteven
RD. Ch e. Rutland and Stamford CC.

CREMYLL Cornwall
187 SX 4553 2m WSW of Plymouth. Loc,
Maker-w-Rame CP. St Germans RD. Bodmin
CC. Foot passenger ferry to Plmth. To S, Mt
Edgcumbe*, 16c hse rebuilt after disastrous
World War II fire; pk*.

CRESSAGE Shrops
118 SJ 5904 6m SW of Wellington. CP, 454.
Atcham RD. P Shrewsbury. Ch e. Sch pe.
Shrsbry CC.

CRESSING Essex
149, 162 TL 7920 3m SE of Braintree. CP,
1,278. Brntree RD. P Brntree. Ch e, v.
Sch p. Brntree CC (Maldon). Two 11c–14c
barns, the rems of Knights Hospitallers'
commandery.

CRESSINGHAM, GREAT Norfolk
136 TF 8501 4m W of Watton. See Gt
Crssnghm.

CRESSWELL Nthmb
78 NZ 2993 8m NE of Morpeth. CP, 181.
Mpth RD. P Mpth. Ch e. Mpth CC.

CRESSWELL Staffs
110, 119 SJ 9739 3m SW of Cheadle. Loc,
Draycott in the Moors CP.

CRESWELL Derbys
112 SK 5274 5m SW of Worksop. Loc,
Elmton CP. P Wksp, Notts. Ch e, m, r.
Sch j, pe, s, se. To E, C. Crags, limestone
cliffs; caves in gorge.

CRETINGHAM Suffolk (E)
137 TM 2260 4m WSW of Framlingham.
CP, 165. Deben RD. P Woodbridge. Ch e.
Eye CC. Ch beside R Deben; thatched roof.

CREWE Ches
109 SJ 4253 6m ENE of Wrexham. CP, 43.
Tarvin RD. Ch m. Nantwich CC.

CREWE Ches
110 SJ 7055 12m WNW of Stoke-on-Trent.
MB, 51,302. P. Crwe CC. Important rly
junction and works.

CREWKERNE Som
177 ST 4409 8m WSW of Yeovil. UD,
4,819. P. Yvl CC. Old stone-blt tn with fine
ch. Long-established sail-making industry.

CRICH Derbys
111 SK 3554 4m N of Belper. CP, 2,753.
Blpr RD. P Matlock. Ch e, m3, v.
Sch ie, j. Blpr CC. See also Fritchley,
Whatstandwell, Wheatcroft. Ch: effigies.
Tram museum.

CRICK Northants
132, 133 SP 5872 6m ESE of Rugby. CP,
780. Daventry RD. P Rgby, Warwickshire.
Ch e, v. Sch p. Dvntry CC (S Nthnts).

CRICKET MALHERBIE Som
177 ST 3611 2m S of Ilminster. Loc,
Knowle St Giles CP. Ch e.

CRICKET ST THOMAS Som
177 ST 3708 3m E of Chard. CP, 86. Chd
RD. Ch e. Yeovil CC. Ch and cottages
grouped round small mansion in extensive
grnds now Wildlife Pk*. Once home of
Nelson's admiral, Hood, whose family
monmts fill ch.

CRICKLADE Wilts
157 SU 1093 7m NW of Swindon. CP,
1,945. Crcklde and Wootton Bassett RD. P
Swndn. Ch e2, c, m. Sch pe. Chippenham
CC. Old tn, mainly stone. Large parish ch:
highly decorated 16c twr.

CRICKLEWOOD London
160 TQ 2385 2m S of Hendon. Loc, Brent
LB. Brnt E BC (Willesden E).

CRIDLING STUBBS Yorks (W)
97 SE 5221 4m E of Pontefract. CP, 199.
Osgoldcross RD. Goole CC.

CRIGGLESTONE Yorks (W)
96, 102 SE 3116 3m SSW of Wakefield. CP,
5,147. Wkfld RD. P Wkfld. Ch m4.
Sch p2, pe, s. Wkfld BC.

CRIMPLESHAM Norfolk
124 TF 6403 3m E of Downham Mkt. CP,
216. Dnhm RD. P King's Lynn. Ch e, m.
Sch p. SW Nflk CC.

CRINGLEFORD Norfolk
126 TG 1905 3m SW of Norwich. CP,
1,124. Forehoe and Henstead RD. P Nrwch.
Ch e. Sch pe. S Nflk CC (Central Nflk).

CRIPPLESTYLE Dorset
179 SU 0912 4m WSW of Fordingbridge.
Loc, Alderholt CP. Ch c.

CRIPPS CORNER Sussex (E)
184 TQ 7721 4m NNE of Battle. Loc,
Ewhurst CP.

CROCKENHILL Kent
171 TQ 5067 3m E of Orpington. Loc,
Eynsford CP. P Swanley. Ch e, bc. Sch p.

CROCKERNWELL Devon
175 SX 7592 4m N of Moretonhampstead.
Loc, Crediton RD, Okehampton RD.
P Exeter. Tiverton CC, W Dvn CC.
(Torrington).

CROCKERTON Wilts
166 ST 8642 2m SSW of Warminster. Loc,
Longbridge Deverill CP. P Wmnstr. Ch e.
Sch pe.

CROCKEY HILL Yorks (E)
97, 98 SE 6246 4m SSE of York. Loc,
Deighton CP.

CROCKHAM HILL Kent
171 TQ 4450 2m S of Westerham. Loc,
Wstrhm CP. P Edenbridge. Ch e. Sch pe. On
edge of steep hill overlooking weald. Much
NT land in area. Octavia Hill, one of the
Trust's founders, buried in churchyard. 1m
NE, Chartwell (NT)*, home of Sir Winston
Churchill, now memorial museum.

CROCKLEFORD HEATH Essex
149 TM 0426 3m ENE of Colchester. Loc,
Ardleigh CP. Ch m.

CROFT Lancs
101 SJ 6393 4m NE of Warrington. CP,
1,482. Wrrngtn RD. P Wrrngtn. Ch e, r.
Sch p, pr. Newton CC.

CROFT Leics
132 SP 5195 7m SW of Leicester. CP,
1,057. Blaby RD. P LCSTR. Ch e, v. Sch pe.
Blby CC (Harborough). Large granite
quarries.

CROFT Lincs (L)
114 TF 5061 4m WSW of Skegness. CP,
743. Spilsby RD. P Skgnss. Ch e, m.
Horncastle CC. See also Seacroft. 14c-15c
ch: very early brass.

CROFT Yorks (N)
85 NZ 2809 3m S of Darlington. CP, 480.
Crft RD. P Dlngtn, Co Durham. Ch e.
Sch pe. Richmond CC. 15c seven-arch br
over R Tees.

CROFTON Yorks (W)
96, 102, 103 SE 3717 4m SE of Wakefield.
CP, 3,640. Wkfld RD. P Wkfld. Ch e, m, r.
Sch p, s. Normanton CC. See also New
Crftn.

CROGLIN Cumb
83 NY 5747 9m SSE of Brampton. Loc,
Ainstable CP. P Carlisle. Ch e.

CROMER Herts
147 TL 2928 4m ENE of Stevenage. Loc,
Ardeley CP.

CROMER Norfolk
126 TG 2142 21m N of Norwich. UD,
5,336. P. N Nflk CC. Seaside resort. Fine ch.
Lighthouse.

CROMFORD Derbys
111 SK 2956 2m S of Matlock. Loc, Mtlck
UD. P Mtlck. Br chpl (A.M.). First
water-powered cotton mill founded here by
Arkwright, 1771.

CROMHALL Glos
156 ST 6990 8m E of Severn Rd Br. CP,
829. Thornbury RD. P Wotton-under-Edge.
Ch e, v. Sch pe. S Glos CC. See also Crmhll
Cmmn.

CROMHALL COMMON Glos
156 ST 6989 8m E of Severn Rd Br. Loc
Crmhll CP.

CROMWELL Notts
112 SK 7961 5m N of Newark. CP, 160.
Southwell RD. P Nwk. Ch e. Nwk CC.
Traces of Roman br over R Trent.

CRONDALL Hants
169 SU 7948 3m WNW of Farnham. CP,
2,503. Hartley Wintney RD. P Fnhm,
Surrey. Ch e, c, m, v. Sch p. Aldershot CC.
See also Ewshot, Mill Lane. Ch mainly Nmn;
brass of 1381.

CRONTON Lancs
100, 109 SJ 4988 2m NNW of Widnes. CP,
737. Whiston RD. P Wdns. Ch r. Sch pe, pr.
Wdns CC.

CROOK Co Durham
85 NZ 1635 5m NW of Bishop Auckland.
UD(Crk and Willington), 21,485. P.
NW Drhm CC. See also Billy Row, Fir Tree,
Helmington Row, High Grange,
Howden-le-Wear, Hunwick, Lane Ends,
Oakenshaw, Page Bank, Stanley, Sunniside,
Sunny Brow, Witton le Wear.

CROOK Westm
89 SD 4695 4m ESE of Windermere. CP,
364. S Westm RD. P Kendal. Ch e. Sch p.
Westm CC. See also Winster.

CROOKHAM Berks
168 SU 5464 5m ESE of Newbury. Loc,
Thatcham CP.

CROOKHAM Nthmb
64, 71 NT 9138 5m ESE of Coldstream.
Loc, Ford CP. P Cornhill-on-Tweed. Ch v.

CROOKHAM VILLAGE Hants
169 SU 7952 5m NW of Farnham. CP, 525.
Hartley Wintney RD. P Aldershot.
Ch e, b, m, v. Sch ie, j. Aldrsht CC.

CROOKLANDS Westm
89 SD 5383 6m SSE of Kendal. Loc,
Preston Richard CP. S Westm RD. Westm CC.

CROOME D'ABITOT Worcs
143, 144 SO 8845 7m SSE of Worcester.
CP, 280. Upton upon Severn RD. Ch e.
S Worcs CC. See also High Grn. C. Ct, large
18c mansion, decorations by Robert Adam.
Grnds (Capability Brown) with temples,
follies etc (Coade) all derelict. Hse a
convent. Ch 18c Gothic, monmts.

CROPREDY Oxon
145 SP 4646 4m N of Banbury. CP, 459.
Bnbry RD. P Bnbry. Ch e, m. Sch pe.
Bnbry CC.

CROPSTON Leics
121, 122 SK 5511 5m NNW of Leicester.
Loc, Thurcaston CP. P LCSTR. Ch v.

CROPTHORNE Worcs
143, 144 SO 9944 3m W of Evesham. CP,
545. Pershore RD. P Pshre. Ch e. Sch pe.
S Worcs CC.

CROPTON Yorks (N)
86, 92 SE 7589 4m NW of Pickering. CP,
277. Pckrng RD. P Pckrng. Ch e, m.
Scarborough CC (Thirsk and Malton). Rems
of motte-and-bailey cstle.

CROPWELL BISHOP Notts
112, 122 SK 6835 8m ESE of Nottingham.
CP, 968. Bingham RD. P NTTNGHM.
Ch e, m. Sch p. Rushcliffe CC (Carlton).

CROPWELL BUTLER Notts
112, 122 SK 6837 7m ESE of Nottingham.
CP, 482. Bingham RD. P NTTNGHM. Ch e, m.
Rushcliffe CC (Carlton).

CROSBY Cumb
81, 82 NY 0738 3m ENE of Maryport. Loc,
Crosscanonby CP. P Mrpt. Ch m2. Sch pe.

CROSBY Lancs
100 SJ 3198 5m NNW of Liverpool. MB,
57,405. P LVPL 23. Crsby BC. See also
Hightown, Seaforth.

CROSBY GARRETT Westm
83 NY 7209 3m WNW of Kirkby Stephen.
CP, 136. N Westm RD. P Kby Stphn.
Ch e, b, m. Sch p. Westm CC.

CROSBY RAVENSWORTH Westm
83 NY 6214 5m SW of Appleby. CP, 519.
N Westm RD. P Penrith, Cumberland. Ch e, m.
Sch pe. Westm CC. See also Maulds
Meaburn, Reagill.

CROSCOMBE Som
165, 166 ST 5944 3m ESE of Wells. CP,
563. Shepton Mallet RD. P Wlls. Ch e, b, v.
Sch pe. Wlls CC. Ch: Jcbn fittings and
furnishings.

CROSS Som
165 ST 4154 3m WNW of Cheddar. Loc,
Compton Bishop CP. P Axbridge.

CROSSCANONBY Cumb
81, 82 NY 0739 3m NE of Maryport. CP,
941. Cockermouth RD. Ch e. Sch pe.
Workington CC. See also Birkby, Crosby.

CROSSDALE STREET Norfolk
126 TG 2239 2m SSE of Cromer. Loc,
Northrepps CP.

CROSSGILL Lancs
89, 94 SD 5562 5m E of Lancaster. Loc,
Caton-w-Littledale CP.

CROSS GREEN Suffolk (W)
149 TL 9852 5m ENE of Lavenham. Loc,
Hitcham CP.

CROSS HANDS Glos
155, 156 ST 5585 8m N of Bristol. Loc,
Pilning and Severn Beach CP. Ch m.

CROSS HILLS Yorks (W)
96 SE 0145 4m NW of Keighley. Loc,
Glusburn CP. P Kghly. Ch m2, r. Sch s.

CROSS HOUSES Shrops
118 SJ 5407 4m SE of Shrewsbury. Loc,
Berrington CP. P Shrsbry. Ch m.

CROSS-IN-HAND Sussex (E)
183 TQ 5621 1m W of Heathfield. Loc,
Waldron CP. P Hthfld. Ch e, m. Sch pe.
Smock-mill in working order; notable
landmark.

CROSSMOOR Lancs
94 SD 4438 8m NW of Preston. Loc,
Inskip-w-Sowerby CP.

CROSS STREET Suffolk (E)
137 TM 1876 3m NE of Eye. Loc, Hoxne
CP. P(Hxne Crss St), Diss, Norfolk.

CROSSWAY GREEN Worcs
130 SO 8468 3m SE of Stourport. Loc,
Hartlebury CP. P Stpt-on-Severn.

CROSSWAYS Dorset
178 SY 7788 5m E of Dorchester. Loc,
Owermoigne CP. P Dchstr.

CROSTHWAITE GREEN Westm
89 SD 4391 5m W of Kendal. Loc, Crsthwte
and Lyth CP. S Westm RD. P(Crsthwte),
Kndl. Westm CC.

CROSTON Lancs
100 SD 4818 6m W of Chorley. CP, 1,899.
Chly RD. P Preston. Ch e, m, r.
Sch ie, pe, pm. Chly CC. Royal Umpire
Museum (old coaches, vllge grn with smithy,
rare birds, etc).

CROSTWICK Norfolk
126 TG 2516 3m WSW of Wroxham. CP,
88. St Faith's and Aylsham RD. Ch e. N
Nflk CC (Central Nflk).

CROSTWIGHT Norfolk
126 TG 3330 3m E of N Walsham. Loc,
Honing CP. Ch e.

CROUCH HILL Dorset
178 ST 7010 6m SE of Sherborne. Loc,
Holwell CP.

CROUGHTON Northants
145 SP 5433 3m SW of Brackley. CP, 964.
Brckly RD. P Brckly. Ch e, m. Sch pe.
Daventry CC (S Nthnts). Ch: 13c
wall-paintings; 15c carved bench-ends. RAF
stn to SE.

CROWAN Cornwall
189 SW 6434 4m S of Camborne. CP,
1,714. Kerrier RD. Ch e, m2. Sch p.
Falmouth and Cmbne CC. See also
Leedstown, Praze-an-Beeble, Townshend.
Ch restored by J.P. St Aubyn, whose
ancestors were squires here.

CROWBOROUGH Sussex (E)
183 TQ 5131 7m SW of Tunbridge Wells.
CP, 8,169. Uckfield RD. P.
Ch e, b3, c, m, r, s, v5. Sch i, j, pe3, pr, s.
E Grinstead CC. Rsdntl distr on edge of
Ashdown Forest. Views to S Downs.

CROWCOMBE Som
164 ST 1436 6m SE of Watchet. CP, 422.
Williton RD. P Taunton. Ch e. Sch pe.
Bridgwater CC. Ch: carved bench-ends. Ch
Hse, 16c. C. Ct, 18c.

CROWDEN Ches
102 SK 0799 4m NE of Glossop. Loc,
Tintwistle CP.

CROW EDGE Yorks (W)
102 SE 1804 4m WNW of Penistone. Loc,
Dunford CP. Pnstne RD. P SHEFFIELD.
Pnstne CC.

CROWELL Oxon
159 SU 7499 5m SSE of Thame. CP, 70.
Bullingdon RD. Ch e. Henley CC.

CROWFIELD Northants
145, 146 SP 6141 4m NNE of Brackley.
Loc, Syresham CP.

CROWFIELD Suffolk (E)
136/137/150 TM 1557 6m E of
Stowmarket. CP, 298. Gipping RD. P Ipswich.
Ch e, b. Eye CC.

CROW HILL Herefs
142, 153 SO 6326 3m NE of Ross-on-Wye.
Loc, Upton Bishop CP. Ch b.

CROWHURST Surrey
171 TQ 3947 3m S of Oxted. CP, 296.
Godstone RD. Ch e. Sch pe. E Srry CC
(Reigate). Hilltop ch with ancient yew in
churchyard. To S, C. Place, moated Tdr
mansion.

CROWHURST Sussex (E)
184 TQ 7512 4m NW of Hastings. CP. 639.
Battle RD. P Bttle. Ch e, m. Sch pe. Rye CC.

CROWHURST LANE END Surrey
171 TQ 3748 3m SSW of Oxted. Loc,
Tandridge CP. P Oxtd.

CROWLAND Lincs (H)
123 TF 2310 8m NNE of Peterborough. CP,
2,879. Spldng RD. P PTRBRGH.
Ch e, m2, s. Sch p, s. Holland w Boston CC.
See also Engine. Rems of abbey founded
716; part is present parish ch. Wide
tree-lined streets, many old hses; 14c
triangular br with sculptured figure.

CROWLAS Cornwall
189 SW 5133 3m ENE of Penzance. Loc,
Ludgvan CP. Ch m.

CROWLE Lincs (L)
104 SE 7713 8m WNW of Scunthorpe. CP.
Isle of Axholme RD. P Scnthpe.
Ch e, b, m, r. Sch p, pr, s. Gainsborough CC.
See also Ealand. Ch has fragment of Saxon
cross with runic carving.

CROWLE Worcs
130, 131 SO 9256 5m E of Worcester. CP,
480. Droitwich RD. P WCSTR. Ch e.
Sch pe. Wcstr BC.

CROWMARSH GIFFORD Oxon
158 SU 6189 just E of Wallingford. Loc,
Crmsh CP. Henley RD. P Wllngfd, Berks.
Ch e. Sch pe. Hnly CC.

CROWNTHORPE Norfolk
125 TG 0803 2m NW of Wymondham. Loc,
Wicklewood CP.

CROWTHORNE Berks
169 SU 8464 3m NW of Camberley. CP,
4,852. Easthampstead RD. P. Ch e, b, m.
Sch p, pe, s. Wokingham CC. To W,
Wellington College, 1859; to E, Broadmoor
Institution, 1863; to N, Road Research
Laboratory, 1966.

CROWTON Ches
109 SJ 5774 5m W of Northwich. CP, 371.
Nthwch RD. P Nthwch. Ch e, m. Sch pe.
Nthwch CC.

CROXALL Staffs
120 SK 1913 6m ENE of Lichfield. Loc,
Edingale CP. Ch e.

CROXDALE Co Durham
85 NZ 2636 4m S of Durham. Loc, Sunderland Br CP. P DRHM. Ch e, m, r.

CROXDEN Staffs
120 SK 0639 4m NNW of Uttoxeter. CP,
270. Uttxtr RD. Ch e. Burton CC. Rems of
EE abbey (A.M.).

CROXLEY GREEN Herts
160 TQ 0795 1m ENE of Rickmansworth.
Loc, Rckmnswth UD. P Rckmnswth. Long
triangular grn. At C. Hall Farm, large mdvl
tithe barn, over 100ft long. To N,
Redheath*, 18c hse now a sch (access
limited to facade and avenue).

CROXTON Cambs
134 TL 2459 4m E of St Neots. CP, 155.
Chesterton RD. P HUNTINGDON. Ch e.
Sch p. Cambs CC. Small estate vllge.

CROXTON Lincs (L)
104 TA 0912 6m WSW of Immingham. CP,
74. Glanford Brigg RD. Ch e. Brgg and
Scunthorpe CC (Brgg).

CROXTON Norfolk
136 TL 8786 2m N of Thetford. CP, 245.
Wayland RD. P Thtfd. Ch e, m. S Nflk CC.

CROXTON Staffs
110, 119 SJ 7831 7m E of Mkt Drayton.
Loc, Eccleshall CP. P STFFD. Ch e. Sch pe.

CROXTON KERRIAL Leics
122 SK 8329 6m SW of Grantham. CP, 524.
Melton and Belvoir RD. P Grantham, Lincs.
Ch e, m. Sch pe. Mltn CC. See also
Branston. Ch has late mdvl bench-ends.

CROYDE Devon
163 SS 4439 3m WNW of Braunton. Loc,
Georgeham CP. P Brntn. Ch b. To W beyond
sand dunes, C. Bay, large sandy beach
flanked by rocks.

CROYDON Cambs
147 TL 3149 6m NNW of Royston. CP,
229. S Cambs RD. P Rstn, Herts. Ch e, c.
Cambs CC. Burial place in 1684 of Sir
George Downing, after whom is named the
London street where the prime minister
lives.

CROYDON London
170 TQ 3265 9m S of Charing Cross. LB,
331,857. P Surrey. BCs: Crdn Central, NE,
NW, S. (Crdn NE, NW, S; E Srry CC.) See
also Addington, Addiscombe, Coulsdon,
Hooley, New Addngtn, Norbury, Norwood,
Purley, Sanderstead. Transferred from Surrey
1965. Extensive tn centre development.

CRUCKMEOLE Shrops
118 SJ 4309 4m WSW of Shrewsbury. Loc,
Pontesbury CP.

CRUCKTON Shrops
118 SJ 4310 4m WSW of Shrewsbury. Loc,
Pontesbury CP. Ch e.

CRUDGINGTON Shrops
118, 119 SJ 6318 4m NNW of Wellington.
Loc, Ercall Magna CP. Wllngtn RD.
P Telford. Sch p. The Wrekin CC.

CRUDWELL Wilts
157 ST 9592 4m NNE of Malmesbury. CP,
659. Mlmsbry RD. P Mlmsbry. Ch e. Sch pe.
Chippenham CC. See also Eastcourt.

CRUGMEER Cornwall
185 SW 9076 1m NW of Padstow. Loc,
Pdstw CP.

CRUNDALE Kent
172, 173, 184 TR 0749 6m NE of Ashford.
CP, 148. E Ashfd RD. Ch e. Ashfd CC. See
also Solestreet.

CRUWYS MORCHARD Devon
164, 176 SS 8712 5m W of Tiverton. CP,
427. Tvtn RD. Ch e, v2. Tvtn CC. See also
Pennymoor, Way Vllge. Ch and C.M. Hse
only.

CRUX EASTON Hants
168 SU 4256 7m SSW of Newbury. Loc,
Ashmansworth CP. Ch e.

CRYERS HILL Bucks
159 SU 8796 3m N of High Wycombe. Loc,
Hughenden CP. Wcmbe RD. P Hgh Wcmbe.
Wcmbe CC.

CRYSTAL PALACE London
160, 170 TQ 3471 6m SSE of Charing
Cross. Loc, Bromley LB. Beckenham BC.
High up in S Lndn; TV mast notable
landmark. Name derives from large glass
bldng orig erected in Hyde Pk to house Gt
Exhibition of 1851, later moved here but
burnt down 1936. Sports centre on site.

CUBBINGTON Warwicks
132 SP 3468 2m NE of Leamington. CP,
3,553. Warwick RD. P Lmngtn Spa.
Ch e, m, r. Sch pe, pr. Wrwck and Lmngtn
CC.

CUBERT Cornwall
185 SW 7857 3m SSW of Newquay. CP,
474. Truro RD. P Nquay. Ch e, m. Sch p.
Truro CC. See also Holywell. Ch has spire
(unusual in Cornwall), visible from afar.

CUBLEY, GREAT Derbys
120 SK 1638 5m S of Ashbourne. See Gt
Cbly.

CUBLINGTON Bucks
146 SP 8422 5m WSW of Linslade. CP, 163.
Wing RD. P Leighton Buzzard, Beds.
Ch e, m. Buckingham CC. Situated on SW
edge of Wing airfield, recommended by
Roskill Commission as third London airpt,
1970.

CUCKFIELD Sussex (E)
182 TQ 3024 2m W of Haywards Hth. UD,
25,888. P Hwds Hth. Mid-Sx CC
(E Grinstead). See also Hwds Hth, Lindfield,
Whitemans Grn. Hwds Hth is the larger
place; Cckfld still has vllge character. C. Pk,
Elizn hse much altered in 19c, now a sch;
unspoilt Elizn gatehouse at A272 roadside.

CUCKLINGTON Som
166 ST 7527 3m ESE of Wincanton. CP,
184. Wncntn RD. P Wncntn. Ch e. Wells CC.

CUCKNEY Notts
112 SK 5671 5m SSW of Worksop. CP, 249.
Wksp RD. P Mansfield. Ch e. Sch pe.
Bassetlaw CC.

CUDDESDON Oxon
158 SP 5902 6m ESE of Oxford.
CP(Cddsdn and Denton), 454. Bullingdon
RD. P OXFD. Ch e. Sch pe. Henley CC. Hse
N of ch was formerly palace of Bishops of
Oxford. To W of ch, well known theological
college. 1m E by br over R Thame, 18c
water mill in working order.

CUDDINGTON Bucks
146, 159 SP 7311 4m NNE of Thame. CP,
594. Aylesbury RD. P Aylesbury.
Ch e, b, m. Sch pe. Aylesbury CC.

CUDDINGTON Ches
109/110 SJ 6071 4m WSW of Northwich.
CP, 3,765. Nthwch RD. P Nthwch. Ch m2.
Sch p. Nthwch CC. See also Sandiway.

CUDDY HILL Lancs
94 SD 4937 6m NW of Preston. Loc,
Woodplumpton CP.

CUDHAM London
171 TQ 4459 2m E of Biggin Hill. Loc,
Bromley LB. P Sevenoaks, Kent. Orpington
BC (CC). Hilltop vllge. Large convalescent
home.

CUDLIPPTOWN Devon
175, 187 SX 5279 4m NE of Tavistock.
Loc, Peter Tavy CP.

CUDWORTH Som
177 ST 3810 3m SSE of Ilminster. CP, 65.
Chard RD. Ch e. Yeovil CC.

CUDWORTH Yorks (W)
102, 103 SE 3808 3m ENE of Barnsley.
UD, 8,838. P Bnsly. Hemsworth CC.

CUFFLEY Herts
160 TL 3002 3m W of Cheshunt. Loc,
Northaw CP. P Potters Bar. Ch b, r, v.
Sch i, j.

CULBONE Som
164 SS 8448 8m W of Minehead. Loc, Oare
CP. Ch e. Tiny and solitary mdvl ch on
wooded cliffs.

CULCHETH Lancs
101 SJ 6595 5m NE of Warrington. Loc,
Golborne UD. P Wrrngtn.

CULFORD Suffolk (W)
136 TL 8370 4m NNW of Bury St
Edmunds. CP, 637. Thingoe RD. P Bury St
Eds. Ch e. Sch pe. Bury St Eds CC. Late
18c hall, now a sch.

CULGAITH Cumb
83 NY 6129 6m E of Penrith. CP, 684.
Pnrth RD. P Pnrth. Ch e, m. Sch pe. Pnrth
and the Border CC. See also Blencarn,
Kirkland, Skirwith.

CULHAM Oxon
158 SU 5095 1m SE of Abingdon. CP, 721.
Bullingdon RD. P Abngdon, Berks. Ch e.
Sch pe. Henley CC.

CULKERTON Glos
157 ST 9395 3m NE of Tetbury. Loc,
Ashley CP. P Ttbry.

CULLERCOATS Nthmb
78 NZ 3671 N distr of Tynemouth. Loc,
Tnmth MB. P: N Shields. Fishing vllge
absorbed by Tnmth and Whitley Bay.

CULLINGWORTH Yorks (W)
96 SE 0636 3m S of Keighley. Loc, Bingley
UD. P Bradford.

CULLOMPTON Devon
176 ST 0207 5m SE of Tiverton. CP, 3,415.
Tvtn RD. P. Ch e, b, m, r, v2. Sch p, s. Tvtn
CC. See also Colebrook, Langford,
Mutterton, Westcott. Small mkt tn;
formerly a wool tn. Perp ch of interest.

CULMINGTON Shrops
129 SO 4982 4m E of Craven Arms. CP,
390. Ludlow RD. P Ldlw. Ch e. Sch pe.
Ldlw CC. 2½m NW on Callow Hill, 80ft twr
(Flounders' Folly), erected 1838 to mark
meeting point of four land boundaries.

CULMSTOCK Devon
164, 176 ST 1013 5m SSW of Wellington.
CP, 692. Tiverton RD. P Cullompton.
Ch e, f, m. Sch p. Tvtn CC. See also
Nicholashayne, Prescott.

CULPHO Suffolk (E)
150 TM 2149 4m W of Woodbridge. CP, 48.
Deben RD. Ch e. Sudbury and Wdbrdge CC.

CULVERSTONE GREEN Kent
171 TQ 6362 7m S of Gravesend. Loc,
Meopham CP. P(Clvstne), Grvsnd. Sch p.

CULVERTHORPE Lincs (K)
113, 123 TF 0240 4m SW of Sleaford.
CP(Clvthpe and Kelby), 106. E Kesteven
RD. Ch e. Grantham CC.

CULWORTH Northants
145 SP 5447 7m NE of Banbury. CP, 398.
Brackley RD. P Bnbry, Oxon. Ch e, b.
Sch pe. Daventry CC (S Nthnts).

CUMBERWORTH Lincs (L)
114 TF 5073 3m ESE of Alford. CP, 121.
Spilsby RD. Ch e, m2. Horncastle CC.

CUMMERSDALE Cumb
76 NY 3953 2m S of Carlisle. CP, 637.
Border RD. P Clsle. Sch p. Penrith and the
Bdr CC. See also Newby W.

CUMNOR Berks
158 SP 4504 3m WSW of Oxford. CP,
4,197. Abingdon RD. P OXFD. Ch e, c.
Sch pe, s. Abngdn CC. See also Farmoor,
Swinford. Amy Robsart died at former C.
Hall in 1560, possibly murdered at instigation
of her husband Robert Dudley, later Earl of
Leicester.

CUMREW Cumb
76 NY 5550 7m S of Brampton. CP, 73.
Border RD. Ch e. Penrith and the Bdr CC.

CUMWHINTON Cumb
76 NY 4552 4m SE of Carlisle. Loc,
Wetheral CP. P Clsle. Ch e. Sch p.

CUMWHITTON Cumb
76 NY 5052 7m ESE of Carlisle. CP,
325. Border RD. P Clsle. Ch e. Sch p. Penrith
and the Bdr CC. See also Hornsby.

CUNDALL Yorks(N)
91 SE 4273 4m NNE of Boroughbridge.
CP(Cndl w Leckby), 110. Wath RD. P YORK.
Ch e. Thirsk and Malton CC.

CURBAR Derbys
111 SK 2574 4m NNE of Bakewell. CP,
443. Bkwll RD. Ch e, v. Sch p. W Derbys
CC. Circular lock-up at top of vllge.

CURBOROUGH Staffs
120 SK 1212 2m N of Lichfield. CP(Cbrgh
and Elmhurst), 211. Lchfld RD. Lchfld and
Tamworth CC.

CURBRIDGE Oxon
158 SP 3308 2m WSW of Witney. CP. Wtny
RD. P Wtny. Ch m. Mid-Oxon CC
(Banbury).

CURDRIDGE Hants
180 SU 5213 3m SW of Bishop's Waltham.
CP, 1,232. Droxford RD. P
SOUTHAMPTON. Ch e, m. Sch p.
Petersfield CC.

CURDWORTH Warwicks
131 SP 1792 3m NNW of Coleshill. CP, 517.
Meriden RD. P Sutton Coldfield. Ch e, m.
Sch p. Mrdn CC.

CURLAND Som
177 ST 2717 6m SE of Taunton. CP, 133.
Tntn RD. P Tntn. Ch e, m. Tntn CC. 1m S
on edge of hills, Cstle Neroche, very large
prehistoric military earthwork.

CURRIDGE Berks
158 SU 4972 3m NNE of Newbury. Loc,
Chieveley CP. P Nbry. Ch e. Sch p.

CURRY MALLET Som
177 ST 3221 5m NNW of Ilminster. CP,
341. Langport RD. P Taunton. Ch e, b.
Sch pe. Yeovil CC.

CURRY RIVEL Som
177 ST 3925 7m NNE of Ilminster. CP,
1,633. Langport RD. P Lngpt. Ch e, v.
Sch pe. Yeovil CC. See also Hambridge. ½m
W on edge of hill, 18c monmt to Sir William
Pynsent; closed as danger to cows.

CURTISDEN GREEN Kent
171,172,184 TQ 7440 4m NW of Cranbrook.
Loc, Goudhurst CP. P Crnbrk. Ch b. Sch pe.

CURY Cornwall
189 SW 6721 4m SSE of Helston. CP, 322.
Kerrier RD. P(Cury Cross Lanes), Hlstn.
Ch e, m. Sch pe. St Ives CC. Ch has Nmn S
porch and font.

CUSOP Herefs
141 SO 2341 just SE of Hay-on-Wye. CP,
359. Dore and Bredwardine RD. Ch e.
Hereford CC.

CUTCOMBE Som
164 SS 9339 5m SW of Minehead. CP, 330.
Williton RD. Ch e. Sch pe. Bridgwater CC.
See also Luckwell Br, Wheddon Cross.

CUTNALL GREEN Worcs
130 SO 8868 5m ESE of Stourport. Loc,
Droitwich RD. P Drtwch. Sch pe.
Worcester BC.

CUTSDEAN Glos
144 SP 0830 4m ENE of Winchcombe. CP,
94. N Cotswold RD. P Cheltenham. Ch e, b.
Cirencester and Tewkesbury CC.

CUTTHORPE Derbys
111 SK 3473 3m NW of Chesterfield. Loc,
Brampton CP. Chstrfld RD. P Chstrfld.
Sch p. NE Derbys.

CUXHAM Oxon
158, 159 SU 6695 5m NE of Wallingford.
CP(Cshm w Easington), 183. Bullingdon RD.
P OXFORD. Ch e. Henley CC.

CUXTON Kent
171, 172 TQ 7066 2m SW of Rochester. CP.

Strood RD. P Rchstr. Ch e, c. Sch p.
Gravesend CC.

CUXWOLD Lincs (L)
105 TA 1701 3m E of Caistor. Loc,
Swallow CP. Ch e.

CWM HEAD Shrops
129 SO 4288 4m SSW of Ch Stretton. Loc,
Wistanstow CP. Ch e. Lone Gothic Revival
ch.

D

DACRE Cumb
83 NY 4526 4m SW of Penrith. CP, 970.
Pnrth RD. P Pnrth. Ch e, m. Pnrth and the
Border CC. See also Gt Blencow, Newbiggin,
Stainton. Cstle, 13c and later. Ch 12c and
later, with chained bible.

DACRE Yorks (W)
91 SE 1960 4m SSE of Pateley Br. CP, 471.
Ripon and Ptly Br RD. Ch e, m, v. Rpn CC.
See also Dcre Banks.

DACRE BANKS Yorks (W)
91 SE 1962 3m SE of Pateley Br. Loc, Dcre
CP.

DADDRY SHIELD Co Durham
84 NY 8937 6m W of Stanhope. Loc,
Stnhpe CP. P Bishop Auckland.

DADFORD Bucks
145, 146 SP 6638 3m NW of Buckingham.
Loc, Stowe CP. Bcknghm RD. P Bcknghm.
Bcknghm CC.

DADLINGTON Leics
132 SP 4098 3m NNW of Hinckley. Loc,
Sutton Cheney CP. Ch e.

DAGENHAM London
161 TQ 4983 4m SSW of Romford. Loc,
Barking LB. P Essex. Dgngm BC. On N bank
of Thames. Docks. Large car factory.

DAGLINGWORTH Glos
157 SO 9905 3m NW of Cirencester. CP,
381. Crncstr RD. P Crncstr. Ch e. Sch pe.
Crncstr and Tewkesbury CC. Ch partly
Saxon.

DAGNALL Bucks
147, 159 SP 9916 4m SW of Dunstable.
Loc, Edlesborough CP. P Berkhamsted,
Herts. Ch e, m. Sch p.

DAGWORTH Suffolk (E)
136 TM 0361 2m NNW of Stowmarket.
CP(Old Newton w Dgwith), 591. Gipping
RD. Eye CC.

DALBURY Derbys
120 SK 2634 6m WSW of Derby. CP(Dlbry
Lees), 151. Repton RD. P(Dlbry Ls), DBY.
Ch e. Belper CC.

DALBY Yorks (N)
92 SE 6371 7m E of Easingwold.
CP(Dlby-cum-Skewsby), 78. Easngwld RD.
Ch e. Thirsk and Malton CC.

DALBY, GREAT Leics
122 SK 7414 3m S of Melton Mowbray. See
Gt Dlby.

DALDERBY Lincs (L)
114 TF 2466 2m SSW of Horncastle. Loc,
Roughton CP. Ch e.

DALE Derbys
112,121 SK 4338 3m SW of Ilkeston.
CP(Dle Abbey). SE Derbys RD. Ch e, m.
Sch pe. SE Derbys CC. Scant rems of Nmn
abbey.

DALE HEAD Cumb
82 NY 3118 5m SE of Keswick. Loc, St
John's Castlerigg and Wythburn CP.
Cockermouth RD. P Kswck. Workington CC.

DALHAM Suffolk (E)
135 TL 7261 5m E of Newmarket. CP, 237. Mildenhall RD. P Nmkt. Ch e, m. Bury St Edmunds CC. See also Dunstall Grn. In hilly part of county. Stream runs beside main st. Derelict windmill.

DALLINGHOO Suffolk (E)
150 TM 2655 4m N of Woodbridge. CP, 211. Deben RD. P Wdbrdge. Ch e. Eye CC.

DALLINGTON Sussex (E)
183 TQ 6519 5m ESE of Heathfield. CP, 288. Battle RD. P Hthfld. Ch e, m, v. Sch pe. Rye CC.

DALLOWGILL Yorks (W)
91 SE 1971 4m NNE of Pateley Br. Loc, Laverton CP. P Ripon. Ch m. Sch p.

DALSTON Cumb
76 NY 3650 4m SSW of Carlisle. CP, 2,064. Border RD. P Clsle. Ch e, m. Sch p, pe, s. Penrith and the Bdr CC. See also Buckabank, Gaitsgill, Raughton Head, Stockdalewath.

DALSTON London
160 TQ 3384 4m NE of Charing Cross. Loc, Hackney LB. Hckny S and Shoreditch BC (Hckny Central).

DALTON Lancs
100 SD 4908 5m E of Ormskirk. CP. Wigan RD. Ch e. Sch pe. Westhoughton CC. On hill to E, Ashurst Beacon, austere twr and spire reputedly erected 1798.

DALTON Nthmb
77, 78 NZ 1172 4m W of Ponteland. Loc, Stamfordham CP. P NEWCASTLE UPON TYNE.

DALTON Westm
89 SD 5476 5m NE of Carnforth. CP, 99. S Westm RD. Westm CC.

DALTON Yorks (N)
84 NZ 1108 6m NW of Richmond. CP, 142. Rchmnd RD. P Rchmnd. Ch e, m. Rchmnd CC. To S, Cstle Steads, Iron Age fort with stone ramparts.

DALTON Yorks (N)
91 SE 4376 4m S of Thirsk. CP, 271. Thsk RD. P Thsk. Ch e, m. Thsk and Malton CC. Ch, by Butterfield, has William Morris windows.

DALTON Yorks (W)
103 SK 4594 2m ENE of Rotherham. CP, 7,426. Rthrhm RD. Ch e, m, v. Sch i, j, p, pe. Rother Valley CC.

DALTON-IN-FURNESS Lancs
88 SD 2374 4m NNE of Barrow. UD, 11,217. P. Brrw-in-Fnss BC. See also Askam-in-Fnss, Ireleth, Lindal-in-Fnss, Newton. Textiles. Dltn Cstle (NT)*, restored 14c pele twr in mkt place.

DALTON-LE-DALE Co Durham
85 NZ 4048 2m SW of Seaham. CP, 715. Easington RD. Ch e. Houghton-le-Spring CC (Easngtn).

DALTON-ON-TEES Yorks (N)
85 NZ 2908 4m S of Darlington. CP, 237. Croft RD. Richmond CC.

DALTON PIERCY Co Durham
85 NZ 4631 3m WSW of Hartlepool. CP. Stockton RD. Easington CC (Sedgefield).

DALWOOD Devon
177 ST 2400 3m WNW of Axminster. CP, 403. Axmnstr RD. P Axmnstr. Ch e, m. Sch p. Honiton CC.

DAMERHAM Hants
179 SU 1015 3m WNW of Fordingbridge. CP, 496. Ringwood and Fdngbrdge RD. P Fdngbrdge. Ch e, b, m, v. Sch pe. New Forest CC.

DAMGATE Norfolk
126 TG 4009 8m WNW of Yarmouth. Loc, Acle CP.

DANBURY Essex
162 TL 7805 5m E of Chelmsford. CP, 3,267. Chlmsfd RD. P Chlmsfd. Ch e, c, r, v3. Sch pe. Chlmsfd CC. Hilltop vllge, with rems of Danish settlement. 13c wooden effigies of knights in ch.

DANBY Yorks (N)
86 NZ 7008 6m S of Loftus. CP, 1,178. Whitby RD. P Whtby. Ch e, m2. Sch pe. Cleveland and Whtby CC (Scarborough and Whtby). See also Ainthorpe, Castleton. 1m SE, rems of 14c cstle. On hills N and S, about 1,000 small cairns, and SW large earthwork, Double Dykes. Origin and purpose of all unknown.

DANBY WISKE Yorks (N)
91 SE 3398 4m NNW of Northallerton. CP,
225. Nthlltn RD. P Nthlltn. Ch e, m.
Richmond CC.

DANEBRIDGE Ches
110 SJ 9665 6m SSE of Macclesfield. Loc,
Wincle CP. The R Dane here forms the
border with Staffs.

DANE END Herts
147 TL 3321 5m N of Hertford. Loc, Lit
Munden CP. Ware RD. P Ware. E Herts CC.

DANEHILL Sussex (E)
183 TQ 4027 5m ENE of Haywards Hth.
CP, 1,276. Uckfield RD. P Hwds Hth.
Ch e, b. Sch pe. E Grinstead CC. See also
Chelwood Gate, Furner's Grn.

DANGEROUS CORNER Lancs
100 SD 5210 5m NW of Wigan. Loc,
Wrightington CP. Wgn RD. Westhoughton
CC.

DARENTH Kent
161, 171 TQ 5671 2m SE of Dartford. CP,
5,127. Dtfd RD. P Dtfd. Ch e, v. Sch i, p.
Dtfd CC. Old vllge with Saxon ch beside R
Darent, surrounded by indstrl development.

DARESBURY Ches
100, 109 SJ 5782 4m E of Runcorn. CP.
Rncn RD. P WARRINGTON. Ch e. Sch p.
Rncn CC. Bthplce of 'Lewis Carroll'
(Charles Dodgson), 1832. Hse not now
standing.

DARFIELD Yorks (W)
103 SE 4104 5m ESE of Barnsley. UD,
7,739. P Bnsly. Dearne Valley CC.

DARGATE Kent
172, 173 TR 0761 4m E of Faversham. Loc,
Hernhill CP. P Fvshm.

DARITE Cornwall
186 SX 2569 3m N of Liskeard. Loc, St
Cleer CP. P Lskd. Sch p. Former
copper-mining vllge. 1m NE, Caradon Hill,
topped by TV mast.

DARLASTON Staffs
130, 131 SO 9796 4m ESE of
Wolverhampton. Loc, Walsall CB. P
Wednesbury. Wlsll S BC (Wdnsbry).

DARLEY Yorks (W)
96 SE 2059 5m SE of Pateley Br.
CP(Menwith w Dly), 1,160. Ripon and Ptly
Br RD. P Harrogate. Ch e, m2. Sch p. Rpn
CC.

DARLINGSCOTT Warwicks
144 SP 2342 2m NW of Shipston on Stour.
Loc, Tredington CP. P Shpstn on Str. Ch e.

DARLINGTON Co Durham
85 NZ 2914 31m S of Newcastle. CB, 85,889.
P. Dlngtn BC. See also Blackwell. Rly and br-
bldng wks. Textiles. On platform at Bank
Top Stn, George Stephenson's engine
'Locomotion'. Rly to Stockton opened 1825.

DARLISTON Shrops
118 SJ 5833 6m SSE of Whitchurch. Loc,
Prees CP. P Whtchch. Ch m.

DARLTON Notts
112 SK 7773 7m SE of Retford. CP, 146. E
Rtfd RD. Ch e. Bassetlaw CC.

DARRACOTT Devon
174 SS 2317 7m N of Bude. Loc, Welcombe
CP. Ch m.

DARRINGTON Yorks (W)
97/103 SE 4820 2m SE of Pontefract. CP,
575. Osgoldcross RD. P Pntfrct. Ch e, m.
Sch pe. Goole CC. Fine ch, mainly 13c.

DARSHAM Suffolk (E)
137 TM 4170 5m NNE of Saxmundham.
CP, 356. Blyth RD. P Sxmndhm. Ch e, m.
Eye CC.

DARTFORD Kent
161, 171 TQ 5474 16m ESE of London.
MB, 45,670. P. Dtfd CC. Indstrl Thames
estuary tn. 2½m NE, rd tunnel to Purfleet.

DARTINGTON Devon
187, 188 SX 7862 2m NW of Totnes. CP,
1,183. Ttns RD. P Ttns. Ch e. Sch pe. Ttns
CC. See also Shinner's Br, Tigley. To E, the
mdvl D. Hall*, educational and commercial
establishment run by a trust; grnds open,
hse partly open.

DARTMEET Devon
175, 187, 188 SX 6773 6m WNW of
Ashburton. Loc, Newton Abbot RD,
Tavistock RD. Totnes CC, W Dvn CC. (Ttns
CC, Tvstck CC.) At confluence of E and W
Dart.

DARTMOUTH Devon
188 SX 8751 7m SE of Totnes. MB(Clifton Dartmouth Hardness), 5,696. P. Ttns CC. Ancient tn with cstle (A.M.). Small port and resort. Royal Naval College on hill. Three ferries (two for cars) cross river to Kingswear.

DARTON Yorks (W)
102 SE 3110 3m NW of Barnsley. UD, 15,145. P Bnsly. Bnsly BC. See also Barugh, Gawber, Higham, Kexbrough, Mapplewell, Staincross.

DARWEN Lancs
94, 95 SD 6922 4m S of Blackburn. MB, 28,880. P. Dwn CC. See also Earcroft, Hoddlesden. Makes wallpapcr, paint, textiles, plastics.

DATCHET Bucks
159, 160, 170 SU 9877 2m SSE of Slough. CP, 4,282. Eton RD. P Slgh. Ch e, b, r, v. Sch pe, s. Beaconsfield CC (S Bucks). Rsdntl distr across Thames from Windsor.

DATCHWORTH Herts
147 TL 2619 4m SSE of Stevenage. CP, 1,220. Hertford RD. P Knebworth. Ch e, b. Sch pe. Htfd and Stvnge CC (Htfd). See also Bragbury End.

DAUNTSEY Wilts
157 ST 9882 4m SE of Malmesbury. CP, 467. Mlmsbry RD. P Chippenham. Ch e, s. Sch pe. Chppnhm CC. See also Dntsy Grn. Ch: monmts in Danby chpl. Doom of 16c on wooden panels. Dauntsey's boys' public sch is at W Lavington.

DAUNTSEY GREEN Wilts
157 ST 9981 5m SE of Malmesbury. Loc, Dntsy CP.

DAVENHAM Ches
110 SJ 6671 2m S of Northwich. CP, 2,149. Nthwch RD. P Nthwch. Ch e, m. Sch pe. Nthwch CC.

DAVENTRY Northants
132, 133 SP 5762 9m SSE of Rugby. MB, 11,813. P. Dvntry CC (S Nthnts). Large radio stn to E.

DAVIDSTOW Cornwall
174, 186 SX 1587 4m NE of Camelford.

CP, 368. Cmlfd RD. P Cmlfd. Ch e. N Cnwll CC. See also Tremail, Trewassa.

DAVYHULME Lancs
101 SJ 7595 5m W of Manchester. Loc, Urmston UD. P Urmstn, MNCHSTR.

DAWLEY Shrops
119 SJ 6807 12m ESE of Shrewsbury. UD, 25,935. P Telford. The Wrekin CC (The Wrkn CC, Ludlow CC). See also Coalbrookdale, Coalport, Hollinswood, Horsehay, Iron Br, Lawley, Madeley, Oldpark, Stirchley. New tn development to transform former desolation. Bthplce of Captain Webb, first swimmer of English Channel, 1875.

DAWLISH Devon
176, 188 SX 9676 7m ENE of Newton Abbot. UD, 9,505. P. Tiverton CC. See also Cockwood, Dlsh Warren, Holcombe. Resort with sandy beach; main line rly between. Bright red cliffs.

DAWLISH WARREN Devon
176, 188 SX 9778 9m ENE of Newton Abbot. Loc, Dlsh UD. P Dlsh. Sandy spit at mouth of R Exe noted for bird and plant life. Chalets and caravans abound.

DAWS HEATH Essex
162 TQ 8188 5m WNW of Southend. Loc, Benfleet UD. SE Essx CC.

DAWSMERE Lincs (H)
114, 124 TF 4430 5m NNE of Long Sutton. Loc, Gedney CP. P Spalding.

DAYLESFORD Glos
144 SP 2425 3m E of Stow-on-the-Wold. Loc, Adlestrop CP. Ch e. D. Hse, 18c hse blt for Warren Hastings, restored mid-20c by Ld Rothermere.

DEAF HILL Co Durham
85 NZ 3736 4m SW of Peterlee. Loc, Wingate CP. Ch e. Sch p.

DEAL Kent
173 TR 3752 8m NNE of Dover. MB, 25,415. P. Dvr and Dl CC (Dvr). See also Gt Mongeham, Walmer. One of the Cinque Ports; formerly busy naval and trading centre. Cstle (A.M., blt by Henry VIII. Resort; fishing, golf. Offshore, Goodwin Sands.

DEAN Cumb
82 NY 0725 4m SW of Cockermouth. CP,
710. Cockrmth RD. P Workington. Ch e.
Sch pe. Wkngtn CC. See also Branthwaite,
Deanscales, Eaglesfield, Pardshaw, Ullock.

DEAN Devon
187, 188 SX 7364 just SW of Buckfastleigh.
Loc, Dean Prior CP.

DEAN Hants
180 SU 5619 1m NNE of Bishop's Waltham.
Loc, Bshps Wlthm CP.

DEAN Som
166 ST 6744 4m E of Shepton Mallet. Loc,
Cranmore CP. Shptn Mllt RD. Ch m. Wells CC.

DEANE Hants
168 SU 5450 6m W of Basingstoke. CP, 96.
Bsngstke RD. Ch e. Bsngstke CC.

DEANLAND Dorset
179 ST 9918 9m ESE of Shaftesbury. Loc,
Sixpenny Handley CP. Ch m.

DEAN PRIOR Devon
187, 188 SX 7363 2m SSW of
Buckfastleigh. CP, 305. Totnes RD. P
Bckfstlgh. Ch e. Ttns CC. See also Dn.
Robert Herrick was vicar here.

DEAN ROW Ches
101 SJ 8781 2m E of Wilmslow. Loc,
Wlmslw UD.

DEANSCALES Cumb
82 NY 0926 3m SW of Cockermouth. Loc,
Dean CP.

DEANSHANGER Northants
146 SP 7639 2m W of Stony Stratford. CP,
1,065. Towcester RD. P Wolverton, Bucks.
Ch e, b, m. Sch p, s. Daventry CC(S Nthnts).
Chemical wks.

DEARHAM Cumb
81, 82 NZ 0736 2m E of Maryport. CP, 1,738.
Cockermouth RD. P Mrpt. Ch e, m2. Sch i, j.
Workington CC.

DEBACH Suffolk (E)
150 TM 2454 4m NNW of Woodbridge. CP,
83. Deben RD. Ch e. Eye CC. Airfield.

DEBDEN Essex
148 TL 5533 3m SSE of Saffron Walden.
CP, 665. Sffrn Wldn RD. P Sffrn Wldn. Ch
3, c, v. Sch pe. Sffrn Wldn CC. See also
Dbdn Cross. Ch: Ggn Gothic; 13c-14c rem-
nants. 1½m S, Mole Hall, moated Elizn
farmhouse with small nature reserve and
zoo*.

DEBDEN CROSS Essex
148 TL 5832 2m WNW of Thaxted. Loc,
Dbdn CP. P(Dbdn Grn), Saffron Walden.

DEBENHAM Suffolk (E)
137 TM 1763 8m ENE of Stowmarket. CP,
843. Gipping RD. P Stwmkt. Ch e, c.
Sch pe, s. Eye CC. Attractive large vllge with
main st curving up slope topped by ch.

DEDDINGTON Oxon
145 SP 4631 6m S of Banbury. CP, 1,237.
Bnbry RD. P OXFORD. Ch e, c, v.
Sch pe, s. Bnbry CC. See also Clifton,
Hempton. Large vllge in Cotswold style on
R Cherwell. Rems of Cstle (A.M.).

DEDHAM Essex
149 TM 0533 6m NE of Colchester. CP,
1,707. Lexden and Winstree RD. P Clchstr.
Ch e, m, v. Sch pe. Clchstr CC. Centre of
'Constable country' and often painted by
him. Cstle Hse*, formerly home of Sir
Alfred Munnings. 1m W, Gun Hill Place*.

DEENE Northants
133 SP 9492 4m ENE of Corby. CP, 90.
Oundle and Thrapston RD. P Cby. Ch e.
Wellingborough CC (Peterborough). D. Pk*,
ancestral home of the Brudenells. Memorials
to Ld Cardigan (a Brudenell), who led
Charge of the Light Brigade, 1854.

DEENETHORPE Northants
134 SP 9591 4m ENE of Corby. CP, 62.
Oundle and Thrapston RD. Wellingborough
CC (Peterborough).

DEEPCAR Yorks (W)
102 SK 2897 8m NNW of Sheffield. Loc,
Stocksbridge UD. P SHFFLD.

DEEPCUT Surrey
169 SU 9057 3m SE of Camberley. Loc,
Frimley and Cmbrly UD. P Cmbrly.

DEEPING GATE Hunts
123 TF 1509 7m NNW of Peterborough.
CP, 285. Ptrbrgh RD. Ch e. Ptrbrgh BC
(CC).

DEEPING ST JAMES Lincs (K)
123 TF 1509 7m NNW of Peterborough.
CP, 1,811. S Kesteven RD. P PTRBRGH.
Ch e, b, m, r.   Sch p, s.   Rutland and
Stamford CC.

DEEPING ST NICHOLAS Lincs (H)
123 TF 2115 5m SSW of Spalding.   CP,
1,834. Spldng RD. P Spldng. Ch e, m. Sch p.
Holland w Boston CC. See also Tongue End.

DEERHURST Glos
143 SO 8729 2m SW of Tewkesbury. CP,
592.   Cheltenham   RD.   Ch e.   Sch pe.
Cirencester and Tksbry CC. See also
Apperley.   Saxon ch and Odda's Chpl
(A.M.)

DEFFORD Worcs
143, 144 SO 9143 2m SW of Pershore. CP,
479. Pshre RD. P WORCESTER. Ch e.
Sch pe. S Worcs CC.

DEIGHTON Yorks (E)
97, 98 SE 6244 5m SSE of York. CP, 230.
Derwent RD. Ch m. Howden CC. See also
Crockey Hill.

DEIGHTON Yorks (N)
91 NZ 3801 5m N of Northallerton. CP, 99.
Nthlltn RD. Ch e. Rchmnd CC.

DELABOLE Cornwall
185, 186 SX 0784 2m W of Camelford. Loc,
St Teath CP. P. Ch m3. Sch p. The vast slate
quarry is famous.

DELAMERE Ches
109 SJ 5668 7m WSW of Northwich. CP,
1,193. Nthwch RD. P Nthwch. Ch e, m2.
Sch pe. Nthwch CC. To N is D. Forest.

DELPH Yorks (W)
101 SD 9807 4m ENE of Oldham. Loc,
Saddleworth UD. P Oldhm, Lancs. Weavers'
cottages.

DELVES Co Durham
84 NZ 1249 1m SE of Consett. Loc, Cnstt
UD.

DEMBLEBY Lincs (K)
113, 123 TF 0437 5m SSW of Sleaford.
CP(Aunsby and Dmblby), 160. E Kesteven
RD. Ch e. Rutland and Stamford CC.

DENABY Yorks (W)
103 SK 4899 5m NE of Rotherham. CP,
244. Doncaster RD. Sch pe. Don Valley CC.

DENABY MAIN Yorks (W)
103 SK 4999 6m NE of Rotherham. Loc,
Conisbrough UD. P Doncaster.

DENBURY Devon
188 SX 8268 3m WSW of Newton Abbot.
Loc, Torbryan CP. P Ntn Abbt. Ch e, b.
Sch p.

DENBY Derbys
111 SK 3946 3m E of Belper. CP, 1,805.
Blpr RD. P DERBY. Ch e, m2. Sch pe, s.
Blpr CC.

DENBY DALE Yorks (W)
102 SE 2208 3m NNW of Penistone. UD,
11,093. P Huddersfield. Colne Valley CC.
See also Birds Edge, Clayton W, Emley, Lr
Cumberworth, Scissett, Skelmanthorpe, Upr
Cmbrwth, Upr Dnby. Rems of Iron Age hill
fort.

DENCHWORTH Berks
158 SU 3891 3m NNW of Wantage. CP,
192. Wntge RD. P Wntge. Ch e. Sch pe.
Abingdon CC.

DENFORD Northants
134 SP 9976 1m S of Thrapston. CP, 227.
Oundle and Thrpstn RD. P Kettering. Ch e.
Wellingborough CC (Peterborough).

DENGIE Essex
162 TL 9801 9m ESE of Maldon. CP, 117.
Mldn RD. Ch e. Mldn CC.

DENHAM Bucks
160 TQ 0487 2m NNW of Uxbridge. CP,
6,861. Eton RD. P(Dnhm Grn), Dnhm,
Uxbrdge, Middx. Ch e, m, r, v. Sch p3, s.
Beaconsfield CC (S Bucks). Densely
populated rsdntl distr. Has old ch and a
few old hses.

DENHAM Suffolk (E)
137 TM 1974 3m E of Eye. CP, 167.
Hartismere RD. P Diss, Norfolk. Ch e.
Eye CC.

DENHAM Suffolk (W)
136 TL 7561 6m WSW of Bury St
Edmunds. CP, 114. Thingoe RD. Ch e. Bury
St Eds CC. Earthwork of cstle. Ch:
Lewkenor monmts.

DENHOLME Yorks (W)
96 SE 0633 6m W of Bradford. UD, 2,587.
P Brdfd. Keighley BC.

DENMEAD Hants
180, 181 SU 6512 5m NW of Havant. CP, 2,863. Droxford RD. P Portsmouth. Ch e, v. Sch p. Petersfield CC. See also Anthill Cmmn.

DENNINGTON Suffolk (E)
137 TM 2867 2m N of Framlingham. CP, 474. Blyth RD. P Woodbridge. Ch e, m. Sch pe. Eye CC. Ch has massive flint twr and porch; spacious clear-glass interior. Bench-ends.

DENNY LODGE Hants
180 SU 3305 3m NE of Brockenhurst. CP, 667. New Forest RD. Nw Frst CC.

DENSHAW Yorks (W)
101 SD 9710 5m ESE of Rochdale. Loc, Saddleworth UD. P Delph, Oldham, Lancs.

DENSTON Suffolk (W)
149 TL 7652 5m N of Clare. CP, 153. Clare RD. P Newmarket. Ch e, v. Bury St Edmunds CC. Ch carved pews. Hall, 16c and 18c.

DENSTONE Staffs
120 SK 1040 5m N of Uttoxeter. CP, 649. Uttxtr RD. P Uttxtr. Ch e, m. Sch pe. Burton CC. To W, D. College (Woodard Foundation), boys' public sch.

DENT Yorks (W)
90 SD 7087 4m SE of Sedbergh. CP, 680. Sdbgh RD. P Sdbgh. Ch e, m4, v. Sch pe. Skipton CC. See also Gawthrop, Lea Yeat, Stone Hse. Only vllge in Dentdale. Stone hses and some cobbled streets. To SE, Whernside, 2,414ft, highest point in W Riding.

DENTON Co Durham
85 NZ 2119 5m NW of Darlington. CP, 79. Dlngtn RD. Ch e. Sch pe. Bishop Auckland CC (Sedgefield).

DENTON Hunts
134 TL 1487 7m SSW of Peterborough. CP(Dntn and Caldecote), 89. Norman Cross RD. Ch e. Hunts CC.

DENTON Kent
173 TR 2147 7m N of Folkestone. CP(Cntn w Wootton), 311. Dover RD. P Canterbury. Ch e, r, v. Dvr and Deal CC (Dvr).

DENTON Lancs
101 SJ 9295 6m ESE of Manchester. UD, 38,107. P MNCHSTR. Mnchstr, Gorton BC. See also Haughton Grn. Carpet-mnfg, hat-mnfg.

DENTON Lincs (K)
113, 122 SK 8632 4m WSW of Grantham. CP, 361. W Kesteven RD. P Grnthm. Ch e, m. Sch pe. Rutland and Stamford CC. Stone-blt estate vllge. Almshouses of 1653.

DENTON Norfolk
137 TM 2788 4m W of Bungay. CP, 325. Depwade RD. P Harleston. Ch e, v. Sch pe. S Nflk CC.

DENTON Northants
133 SP 8357 5m ESE of Northampton. CP, 414. Nthmptn RD. P NTHMPTN. Ch e, b. Sch p. Daventry CC (S Nthnts).

DENTON Oxon
158 SP 5902 6m ESE of Oxford. CP(Cuddesdon and Dntn), 454. Bullingdon RD. Henley CC.

DENTON Sussex (E)
183 TQ 4502 1m NE of Newhaven. Loc, Nwhvn UD.

DENTON Yorks (W)
96 SE 1448 2m ENE of Ilkley. CP, 123. Wharfedale RD. Ch e. Ripon CC. D. Hall, 18c hse by Carr of York, in setting above R Wharfe with moors rising behind.

DENVER Norfolk
124 TF 6101 1m S of Downham Mkt. CP, 817. Dnhm RD. P Dnhm Mkt. Ch e. Sch pe. SW Nflk CC. 1m SW, D. Sluice, control point of complex Fenland drainage system.

DENWICK Nthmb
71 NU 2014 1m ENE of Alnwick. CP, 451. Alnwck RD. Berwick-upon-Tweed CC.

DEOPHAM Norfolk
125 TG 0400 4m W of Wymondham. CP, 476. Forehoe and Henstead RD. P Wndhm. Ch e, m. Sch p. S Nflk CC (Central Nflk). See also Hackford. Ch has fine Perp twr.

DEOPHAM GREEN Norfolk
136 TM 0499 3m N of Attleborough. Loc, Dphm CP.

DEPDEN Suffolk (W)
136/149 TL 7757 6m SW of Bury St Edmunds. CP, 176. Clare RD. Ch e. Bury St Eds CC. Par incl highest point in Sfflk (420ft).

DEPTFORD London
161, 171 TQ 3776 4m SE of Lndn Br. Loc, Lewisham LB. Dptfd BC. On S bank of Thames. Dickens lived here 1837—9. D. Power Stn beside river.

DEPTFORD Wilts
167 SU 0138 10m NW of Salisbury. Loc, Wylye CP.

DERBY Derbys
120, 121 SK 3536 35m NNE of Birmingham. CB, 219,348. P(DBY). Dby N BC, Dby S BC. Mnfg, engineering and rly city; capital of county. Cathedral mainly by James Gibbs, 1725.

DERRILL Devon
174 SS 3003 2m W of Holsworthy. Loc, Pyworthy CP. Ch m.

DERRINGSTONE Kent
173 TR 2049 6m SE of Canterbury. Loc, Barham CP.

DERRINGTON Staffs
119 SJ 8922 2m W of Stafford. Loc, Seighford CP. P STFFD. Ch e.

DERRY HILL Wilts
157 ST 9570 3m SE of Chippenham. Loc, Calne and Chppnhm RD. P Clne. Ch e. Sch pe. Chppnhm CC. Grand 19c gates of Bowood Pk (see Clne).

DERRYTHORPE Lincs (L)
104 SE 8208 4m WSW of Scunthorpe. Loc, Keadby w Althorpe CP.

DERSINGHAM Norfolk
124 TF 6830 8m NE of King's Lynn. CP, 2,026. Docking RD. P K's Lnn. Ch e, m. Sch pe, se. NW Nflk CC (K's Lnn).

DESBOROUGH Northants
133 SP 8083 5m NW of Kettering. UD, 5,294. P Kttrng. Kttrng CC. Small mnfg tn.

DESFORD Leics
121 SK 4703 7m W of Leicester. CP, 2,300. Mkt Bosworth RD. P LCSTR. Ch e, v. Sch p. Bswth CC. See also Botcheston.

DETCHANT Nthmb
64, 71 NU 0836 2m NW of Belford. Loc, Middleton CP.

DETLING Kent
172 TQ 7958 3m NE of Maidstone. CP, 748. Hollingbourn RD. P Mdstne. Ch e. Sch pe. Mdstne CC. Below ridge of N Downs. Kent County Show ground at top of hill.

DEUXHILL Shrops
130 SO 6987 4m SSW of Bridgnorth. CP, 26. Brdgnth RD. Ludlow CC.

DEVIZES Wilts
167 SU 0061 10m SE of Chippenham. MB, 10,170. P. Dvzs CC. Old but busy mkt tn; many Ggn hses. Large central square. Museum of Wilts prehistory.

DEVONPORT Devon
187 SX 4554 W distr of Plymouth. Loc, Plmth CB. P Plmth. Plmth, Dvnpt BC. Naval dockyards. Tn hall modelled on Parthenon. Bthplce of Captain Scott, Antarctic explorer, 1868.

DEVORAN Cornwall
190 SW 7939 4m SSW of Truro. Loc, Feock CP. P Truro. Ch e, m. Sch p.

DEWLISH Dorset
178 SY 7798 7m NE of Dorchester. CP, 220. Dchstr RD. P Dchstr. Ch e, m. W Dst CC. D Hse*, early 18c; limited opening.

DEWSBURY Yorks (W)
96, 102 SE 2421 5m W of Wakefield. CB, 51,310. P. Dsbry BC. Wool textile tn.

DIAL POST Sussex (W)
182 TQ 1519 7m S of Horsham. Loc, W Grinstead CP. P Hshm.

DIBDEN Hants
180 SU 4007 4m NW of Fawley. CP, 9,803. New Forest RD. P SOUTHAMPTON. Ch e, m. Sch i, j, p, s. Nw Frst CC. See also Hythe. 13c ch mostly destroyed in World War II, now rebuilt.

DICKLEBURGH Norfolk
137 TM 1682 3m NE of Diss. CP, 789. Depwade RD. P Dss. Ch e, b. Sch pe. S Nflk CC. See also Rushall.

DIDBROOK Glos
144 SP 0531 3m NE of Winchcombe. Loc,
Stanway CP. Ch e. Two cottages show cruck
construction.

DIDCOT Berks
158 SU 5290 10m S of Oxford. CP, 11,212.
Wallingford RD. P. Ch e, m, r, v.
Sch i2, j2, pe, s2, sg. Abingdon CC.

DIDDINGTON Hunts
134 TL 1965 3m N of St Neots. CP, 119. St
Nts RD. Ch e. Hunts CC.

DIDDLEBURY Shrops
129 SO 5085 5m ENE of Craven Arms. CP,
621. Ludlow RD. P Crvn Arms. Ch e.
Sch pe. Ldlw CC. See also Bouldon,
Corfton, Gt Sutton, Lit Sttn, Peaton,
Westhope. Ch partly Saxon. Grey stone
vllge.

DIDLEY Herefs
142 SO 4532 6m SW of Hereford. Loc, St
Devereux CP.

DIDMARTON Glos
156 ST 8287 6m SW of Tetbury. CP, 278.
Ttbry RD. P Badminton. Ch e, c. Stroud
CC. See also Oldbury on the Hill. Mdvl ch
replaced by Vctrn one.

DIDWORTHY Devon
187, 188 SX 6862 4m SW of Buckfastleigh.
Loc, Brent CP.

DIGBY Lincs (K)
113 TF 0854 6m N of Sleaford. CP, 426.
E Kesteven RD. P LINCOLN. Ch e, m.
Sch p, pe. Grantham CC.

DIGGLE Yorks (W)
102 SE 0008 6m ENE of Oldham. Loc,
Saddleworth UD. P Dobcross, Oldhm,
Lancs.

DIGMOOR Lancs
100 SD 4905 5m ESE of Ormskirk. Loc,
Skelmersdale and Holland UD. Large
housing development for Sklmsdle New Tn.

DIGSWELL Herts
147 TL 2314 1m N of Welwyn Gdn City.
Loc, Wlwn Gdn Cty UD. P Wlwn. Vllge
below Wlwn rly viaduct carrying main line
from King's Cross to the North over R
Mimram. (Rly narrows to two tracks on
viaduct).

DILHAM Norfolk
126 TG 3325 4m SE of N Walsham. CP,
294. Smallburgh RD. Ch e, m. Sch pe. N
Nflk CC.

DILHORNE Staffs
110, 119 SJ 9743 6m ESE of
Stoke-on-Trent. CP, 577. Cheadle RD. P Stke-
on-Trnt. Ch e, m. Sch pe. Leek CC. See also
Godleybrook.

DILLINGTON Hunts
134 TL 1365 4m NW of St Neots. Loc,
Gt Staughton CP.

DILSTON Nthmb
77 NY 9763 1m SW of Corbridge. Loc,
Cbrdge CP.

DILTON Wilts
166 ST 8649 2m SSW of Westbury. Loc,
Wstbry UD, Warminster and Wstbry RD.
P Wstbry. Wstbry CC.

DILTON MARSH Wilts
166 ST 8449 2m SW of Westbury. CP,
1,339. Warminster and Wstbry RD. P(Dltn),
Wstbry. Ch e, b. Sch i, je. Wstbry CC.

DILWYN Herefs
142 SO 4154 6m WSW of Leominster. CP,
780. Weobley RD. P HEREFORD. Ch e, m.
Sch pe. Lmnstr CC. See also Barewood,
Haven, Luntley, Sollers Dlwn.

DIMPLE Lancs
95, 101 SD 7015 4m NNW of Bolton. Loc,
Turton UD. Darwen CC.

DINDER Som
165, 166 ST 5744 2m ESE of Wells. CP,
198. Wlls RD. P Wlls. Ch e. Sch pe. Wlls CC.
Stone vllge with fine ch, mnr hse, cottages,
stream.

DINEDOR Herefs
142 SO 5336 3m SE of Hereford. CP, 260.
Hrfd RD. Ch e. Hrfd CC. Rems of World
War II ordnance factory and many dumps.

DINGLEY Northants
133 SP 7787 2m E of Mkt Harborough. CP,
85. Kettering RD. P Mkt Hbrgh, Leics. Ch e.
Kttrng CC.

DINNINGTON Nthmb
78 NZ 2073 3m E of Ponteland. CP, 1,573.
Cstle Ward RD. P NEWCASTLE UPON
TYNE. Ch e, m. Hexham CC. See also
Mason. To SW, NE Regional Airpt.

DINNINGTON Som
177 ST 4012 3m ESE of Ilminster. CP, 69.
Chard RD. Ch e, m. Yeovil CC.

DINNINGTON Yorks (W)
103 SK 5285 6m NW of Worksop. CP(Dnngtn
St John's), 7,514. Kiveton Pk RD.
P SHEFFIELD. Ch e, m3, r, s, v. Sch p, pr, s.
Rother Valley CC.

DINTON Bucks
146, 159 SP 7711 4m WSW of Aylesbury.
CP(Dntn w Ford and Upton), 651.
Aylesbury RD. P Aylesbury. Ch e. Sch pe.
Aylesbury CC. See also Westlington. Ch has
Nmn doorway. Stocks and whipping-post
still standing, also 18c folly.

DINTON Wilts
167 SU 0131 8m W of Salisbury. CP, 493.
Slsbry and Wilton RD. P Slsbry. Ch e, m.
Sch pe. Slsbry CC. See also Baverstock.
Several old hses; vllge largely NT, incl
Phillipps Hse* (now holiday home for
YWCA), blt 1816, and Lit Clarendon, late
15c.

DINWORTHY Devon
174 SS 3115 8m NNW of Holsworthy. Loc,
Bradworthy CP.

DIPTFORD Devon
187, 188 SX 7256 5m WSW of Totnes. CP,
308. Ttns RD. P Ttns. Ch e. Sch pe. Ttns
CC.

DIPTON Co Durham
78 NZ 1553 3m ENE of Consett. Loc,
Stanley UD. P NEWCASTLE UPON TYNE.

DIRT POT Nthmb
84 NY 8546 12m SSW of Hexham. Loc,
Allendale CP. Hxhm RD. Hxhm CC.

DISEWORTH Leics
121 SK 4524 6m WNW of Loughborough.
Loc, Long Whatton CP. P DERBY.
Ch e, b, m. Sch pe.

DISHFORTH Yorks (N)
91 SE 3873 5m ENE of Ripon. CP, 1,492.
Wath RD. P Thsk. Ch e, m. Sch p, pe. Thsk
and Malton CC. Large RAF stn.

DISLEY Ches
101 SJ 9784 6m SE of Stockport. CP,
3,920. Dsly RD. P Stckpt. Ch e, b, f, m2.

Sch p. Mcclsfld CC. In large deer pk 2m S,
Lyme Hall (NT)*, Elizn and later. To N, D.
Tunnel (rly), over 2m long.

DISS Norfolk
136 TM 1180 14m S of Wymondham. UD,
4,477. P. S Nflk CC. Small mkt tn. Mere,
with public gdns, near tn centre. 1¼m E,
Frenze ch, with famous 15c brasses.

DISTINGTON Cumb
82 NY 0023 3m S of Workington. CP,
2,824. Ennerdale RD. P Wkngtn. Ch e, m.
Sch i, j, s. Whitehaven CC. See also Pica.

DITCHEAT Som
166 ST 6236 4m WNW of Bruton. CP, 608.
Shepton Mallet RD. P Shptn Mllt. Ch e.
Sch p. Wells CC. See also Alhampton,
Wraxall.

DITCHINGHAM Norfolk
137 TM 3391 1m N of Bungay. CP, 1,059.
Loddon RD. P Bngy, Suffolk. Ch e. Sch pe.
S Nflk CC. D. Hall has grnds with lake, by
Capability Brown. Hsptl, sch, training centre
(All Hallows), run by religious community.

DITCHLING Sussex (E)
182 TQ 3215 3m SSE of Burgess Hill. CP,
1,644. Chailey RD. P Hassocks.
Ch e, f, r, v2. Sch pe. Lewes CC. Vllge below
S Downs; 1½m S, D. Beacon, 813ft. 16c
Anne of Cleves Hse in vllge.

DITTERIDGE Wilts
156 ST 8169 5m NE of Bath. Loc, Box CP.
Ch e.

DITTISHAM Devon
188 SX 8654 3m NNW of Dartmouth. CP,
508. Totnes RD. P Dtmth. Ch e, v. Ttns CC.
See also Capton. Colour-washed thatched
cottages. Plum orchards. Ch: font, scrn,
plpt.

DITTON Kent
171, 172 TQ 7158 4m WNW of Maidstone.
CP, 1,962. Malling RD. P Mdstne. Ch e.
Sch pe. Tonbridge and Mllng CC
(Sevenoaks). Paper mills.

DITTON Lancs
100, 109 SJ 4985 1m W of Widnes. Loc,
Wdns MB. P Wdns.

DITTON GREEN Cambs
135 TL 6558 3m S of Newmarket. Loc,
Woodditton CP.

DITTON PRIORS Shrops
129, 130 SO 6089 7m WSW of Bridgnorth.
CP, 617. Brdgnth RD. P Brdgnth. Ch e, m2.
Sch pe. Ludlow CC. See also Middleton
Priors. Grey stone vllge under Brown Clee
Hill.

DOBCROSS Yorks (W)
101 SD 9906 4m ENE of Oldham. Loc,
Saddleworth UD. P Oldham. Ch e. Weavers'
cottages.

DOBWALLS Cornwall
186 SX 2165 3m W of Liskeard. Loc,
Lskd RD. P Lskd. Ch m. Sch p. Bodmin CC.

DOCCOMBE Devon
175 SS 7786 2m ENE of
Moretonhampstead. Loc, Mtnhmpstd CP.
P Newton Abbot.

DOCKING Norfolk
125 TF 7637 6m ESE of Hunstanton. CP,
1,593. Dckn RD. P King's Lynn. Ch e, m2.
Sch pe. NW Nflk CC (K's Lnn).

DOCKLOW Herefs
129 SO 5657 4m E of Leominster. CP, 143.
Lmnstr and Wigmore RD. Ch e. Lmnstr CC.

DOCKRAY Cumb
83 NY 3921 9m SW of Penrith. Loc,
Matterdale CP. Pnrth RD. P Pnrth. Pnrth
and the Border CC. To SSE, Aira Force,
well-known beauty spot, subject of
Wordsworth poem.

DODDENHAM Worcs
130 SO 7556 6m W of Worcester. CP, 263.
Martley RD. Ch e. Kidderminster CC.

DODDINGHURST Essex
161 TQ 5899 3m N of Brentwood. CP,
1,843. Epping and Ongar RD. P Brntwd.
Ch e. Sch pe. Brntwd and Ongr CC
(Chigwell).

DODDINGTON Cambs
135 TL 3990 3m N of Chatteris. CP, 1,325.
N Witchford RD. P March. Ch e, m. Sch p.
Isle of Ely CC. See also Primrose Hill.

DODDINGTON Ches
110 SJ 7047 5m S of Crewe. CP, 51.
Nantwich RD. Ch e. Nntwch CC.

DODDINGTON Kent
172 TQ 9357 5m SSE of Sittingbourne. CP,
540. Swale RD. P Sttngbne. Ch e. Sch p.
Faversham CC.

DODDINGTON Lincs (K)
113 SK 9070 5m W of Lincoln. CP(Dddngtn
and Whisby), 352. N Kesteven RD.
P LNCLN. Ch e. Grantham CC. D. Hall*,
Elizn mansion.

DODDINGTON Nthmb
64, 71 NT 9932 3m N of Wooler. CP, 229.
Glendale RD. Ch e.
Berwick-upon-Tweed CC. See also Fenton
Tn, Nesbit. Cup-and-ring marked rocks, and
British camp, on Dod Law.

DODDINGTON Shrops
129, 130 SO 6176 4m W of Cleobury
Mortimer. Loc, Hopton Wafers CP.
P Kidderminster,Worcs. Ch e.

DODDINGTON, GREAT Northants
133 SP 8864 2m SSW of Wellingborough.
See Gt Dddngtn.

DODDISCOMBSLEIGH Devon
176 SX 8586 6m SW of Exeter. CP, 169.
St Thomas RD. P Extr. Ch e. Sch p.
Tiverton CC. Ch: 15c stained glass.

DODFORD Northants
132, 133 SP 6160 3m ESE of Daventry. CP,
162. Dvntry RD. Ch e. Dvntry CC. Ch has
many monmts and brasses to Cressy and de
Keynes families.

DODFORD Worcs
130, 131 SO 9372 2m NW of Bromsgrove.
CP(Ddfd w Grafton), 664. Brmsgrve RD.
P Brmsgrve. Ch e, b. Sch p. Brmsgrve and
Redditch CC (Brmsgrve).

DODINGTON Glos
156 ST 7480 10m N of Bath. CP, 326.
Sodbury RD. Ch e. S Glos CC. See also
Codrington, Wapley. D. Hse*, 18c hse in
large pk laid out by Capability Brown.

DODINGTON Som
164 ST 1740 7m ESE of Watchet. Loc,
Holford CP. Ch e. D. Mnr, Elizn hse with
great hall.

DODLESTON Ches
109 SJ 3661 4m SW of Chester. CP, 405.
Chstr RD. P CHSTR. Ch e. Sch pe. City of
Chstr CC. Sir Thomas Egerton, Ld
Chancellor, d 1617, lived at the Old Hall,
now a farmhouse.

DODWORTH Yorks (W)
102 SE 3105 2m WSW of Barnsley. UD,
4,551. P Bnsly. Penistone CC.

DOE LEA Derbys
112 SK 4566 6m SE of Chesterfield. Loc,
Ault Hucknall CP. P Chstrfld. Ch m.

DOGDYKE Lincs (K) and (L)
114 TF 2055 5m S of Woodhall Spa. CP,
248, E Kesteven RD; loc, Coningsby CP.
P LINCOLN. Sch p. Grantham CC,
Horncastle CC. See also Chpl Hill.

DOGMERSFIELD Hants
169 SU 7852 5m NW of Farnham. CP, 343.
Hartley Wintney RD. P Basingstoke. Ch e.
Sch pe. Bsngstke CC (Aldershot).

DOG VILLAGE Devon
176 SX 9896 5m ENE of Exeter. Loc,
Broad Clyst CP. Ch b.

DOLPHINHOLME Lancs
94 SD 5153 6m SSE of Lancaster. Loc,
Ellel CP. P LNCSTR. Ch e, m. Sch pe.

DOLTON Devon
163, 175 SS 5712 6m SE of Torrington. CP,
415. Trrngtn RD. P Winkleigh. Ch e, b, m, v.
Sch pe. W Dvn CC (Trrngtn). Ch: font.

DONCASTER Yorks (W)
103 SE 5703 17m NE of Sheffield.
CB, 82,505. P. Dncstr BC. Indstrl tn; rly
locomotive wks. Racecourse where St Leger
is run. (Grandstand by Carr of York, 1776.)
To W, Cusworth Hall*, 18c hse, now
museum, in large grnds; lake.

DONHEAD ST ANDREW Wilts
166, 167 ST 9124 4m ENE of Shaftesbury.
CP, 428. Mere and Tisbury RD. P(Dnhd),
Shftsbry, Dorset. Ch e. Sch pe.
Westbury CC.

DONHEAD ST MARY Wilts
166, 167 ST 9024 3m ENE of Shaftesbury.
CP, 934. Mere and Tisbury RD. Ch e, m, v.
Westbury CC. See also Charlton, Ludwell.

DONINGTON Lincs (H)
114, 123 TF 2035 9m NNW of Spalding.
CP, 1,948. Spldng RD. P Spldng. Ch e, m, v.
Sch pe, s. Holland w Boston CC.

DONINGTON Shrops
119 SJ 8004 4m ESE of Shifnal. CP, 3,428.
Shfnl RD. Ch e. The Wrekin CC.

DONINGTON ON BAIN Lincs (L)
105 TF 2383 6m WSW of Louth. CP, 289.
Lth RD. P Lth. Ch e, m. Sch p. Lth CC. 1m
W, Belmont TV transmitter; 1m E, Stenigot
radar stn.

DONISTHORPE Leics
120, 121 SK 3114 3m WSW of Ashby de la
Zouch. CP(Oakthorpe and Dnsthpe), 2,435.
Ashby de la Zch RD. P Burton-on-Trent,
Staffs. Ch e, m2. Sch p. Loughborough CC.

DONKEY TOWN Surrey
169 SU 9360 4m E of Camberley. Loc, West
End CP.

DONNINGTON Berks
158 SU 4668 1m N of Newbury. CP (Shaw
cum Dnngtn), 2,091. Nbry RD. P Nbry.
Ch e. Nbry CC. Ruined twin-towered
gatehouse of D. Cstle (A.M.), twice besieged
by parliamentarians in Civil War, 1644–6.

DONNINGTON Glos
144 SP 1928 2m N of Stow-on-the-Wold.
CP, 117. N Cotswold RD. Cirencester and
Tewkesbury CC.

DONNINGTON Herefs
143 SO 7034 2m S of Ledbury. CP, 89.
Ldbry RD. Ch e. Leominster CC.

DONNINGTON Shrops
118 SJ 5807 6m ESE of Shrewsbuy. Loc,
Wroxeter CP. P Telford. Ch m.

DONNINGTON Shrops
119 SJ 7013 2m N of Oakengates. Loc,
Lilleshall CP. Ch e, r. Sch i, j.

DONNINGTON Sussex (W)
181 SU 8502 2m S of Chichester. CP,
1,398. Chchstr RD. Ch e. Chchstr CC. View
of Chchstr Cathedral.

DONYATT Som
177 ST 3314 1m WSW of Ilminster. CP,
353. Chard RD. P Ilminstr. Ch e. Sch p.
Yeovil CC. This and many a neighbouring
vllge blt of golden-yellow stone produced by
nearby quarries.

DORCHESTER Dorset
178 SY 6990 7m N of Weymouth. MB,
13,737. P. W Dst CC. Mkt tn and county
capital. Once important Roman stn.
On S side, Max Gate, Thomas Hardy's home.
Judge Jeffreys' lodgings in High St.

DORCHESTER Oxon
158 SU 5794 4m NNW of Wallingford. CP.
Bullingdon RD. P(Dchstr-on-Thames),
OXFORD. Ch e, r. Sch p, pe, s. Henley CC.
On R Thame near junction with Thames.
Vllge with several old hses and famous mdvl
abbey.

DORDON Warwicks
120 SK 2600 4m SE of Tamworth. CP.
Atherstone RD. P Tmwth, Staffs.
Ch e, c, m. Sch p. Meriden CC.

DORKING Surrey
170 TQ 1649 5m W of Reigate. UD, 22,354,
P. Dkng CC. See also Brockham, Mickleham,
N Holmwood, Westcott, W Humble. Rsdntl
tn at S end of gap in N Downs. To NE, Box
Hill (NT); 4m SSW, Leith Hill (NT), 965ft
and highest point in SE England, topped by
64ft twr* (see also Coldharbour).

DORMANS LAND Surrey
171 TQ 4042 3m N of E Grinstead. Loc,
Lingfield CP. P Lngfld. Ch e, b. Sch p.
Greathed Mnr*, Vctrn hse.

DORMINGTON Herefs
142 SO 5840 5m E of Hereford. CP, 123.
Hrfd RD. Ch e. Hrfd CC.

DORMSTON Worcs
130, 131 SO 9857 9m E of Worcester. CP,
74. Pershore RD. Ch e. S Worcs CC. Moat
Fm, typical Worcs half-timbered hse of
1663.

DORNEY Bucks
159 SU 9279 3m W of Slough. CP, 805.
Eton RD. P Windsor, Berks. Ch e. Sch p.
Beaconsfield CC (S Bucks). See also
Boveney.

DORRIDGE Warwicks
131 SP 1575 3m SSE of Solihull. Loc, Slhll
CB. P Slhll.

DORRINGTON Lincs (K)
113 TF 0852 5m NNE of Sleaford. CP, 408.
E Kesteven RD. P LINCOLN. Ch e, m, v.
Sch pe. Grantham CC.

DORRINGTON Shrops
118 SJ 4702 6m S of Shrewsbury. Loc,
Condover CP. P Shrsby. Ch e, v. Sch pe.

DORSINGTON Warwicks
144 SP 1349 5m SW of Stratford. CP, 94.

Strtfd-on-Avon RD. P Strtfd-upon-Avn.
Ch e. Strtfd-on-Avn CC (Strtfd).

DORSTONE Herefs
142 SO 3141 5m E of Hay-on-Wye. CP,301.
Dore and Bredwardine RD. P HEREFORD.
Ch e, m. Hrfd CC. See also Bage. 1m N,
Arthur's Stone (A.M.), neolithic chambered
tomb.

DORTON Bucks
146, 159 SP 6814 5m NNW of Thame. CP,
128. Aylesbury RD. Ch e. Aylesbury CC.

DOSTHILL Staffs
120/131 SK 2100 3m S of Tamworth. Loc,
Tmwth MB. P Tmwth. Lichfield and
Tmwth CC (Meriden). Formerly in
Warwicks.

DOTTERY Dorset
177 SY 4595 2m N of Bridport. Loc,
Beaminster RD, Brdpt RD. W Dst CC.

DOUBLEBOIS Cornwall
186 SX 1965 3m W of Liskeard. Loc,
Lskd CP. Lskd RD.

DOUGHTON Glos
156 ST 8791 1m SSW of Tetbury. Loc,
Ttbry Upton CP. D. Mnr and D. Hse,
characteristic Cotswold bldngs.

DOULTING Som
166 ST 6443 2m E of Shepton Mallet. CP,
538. Shptn Mllt RD. P Shptn Mllt. Ch e.
Sch pe. Wells CC. Large quarries producing
stone long used in Som bldngs, incl Wells
Cathedral and Glastonbury Abbey.

DOUSLAND Devon
187 SX 5368 5m SE of Tavistock. Loc,
Meavy CP. P Yelverton.

DOVE HOLES Derbys
111 SK 0778 3m NNE of Buxton. Loc,
Chapel en le Frith CP. P Bxtn. Ch m.
Sch pe. High Peak CC.

DOVENBY Cumb
81, 82 NY 0933 2m NW of Cockermouth.
Loc, Bridekirk CP. P Cckrmth.

DOVER Kent
173 TR 3141 15m SE of Canterbury. MB,
34,322. P. Dvr and Deal CC (Dvr). Channel
port with large modern docks for freight
and passengers, dominated by high white
cliffs and cstle (A.M.). Oldest of Cinque
Ports.

DOVERCOURT Essex
150 TM 2531 1m SSW of Harwich. Loc, Hrwch MB. P Hrwch. Resort with long under-cliff walk and good sands. Modern indstrl development.

DOVERDALE Worcs
130 SO 8666 3m NW of Droitwich. CP, 78. Drtwch RD. Ch e. Worcester BC.

DOVERIDGE Derbys
120 SK 1134 2m E of Uttoxeter. CP, 893. Ashbourne RD. P DERBY. Ch e, m. Sch p. W Derbys CC.

DOWARD, GREAT Herefs
142 SO 5516 4m NE of Monmouth. Loc, Whitchurch CP.

DOWBRIDGE Lancs
94 SD 4331 7m WNW of Preston. Loc, Kirkham UD, Fylde RD. S Flde CC.

DOWDESWELL Glos
144 SP 0019 4m ESE of Cheltenham. CP, 192. Northleach RD. Ch e. Cirencester and Tewkesbury CC.

DOWLAND Devon
163, 175 SS 5610 7m SE of Torrington. CP, 83. Trrngtn RD. Ch e. W Dvn CC (Trrngtn).

DOWLISH WAKE Som
177 ST 3712 2m SE of Ilminster. CP, 228. Chard RD. P Ilmnstr. Ch e. Yeovil CC.

DOWN AMPNEY Glos
157 SU 0997 6m SE of Cirencester. CP, 445. Crncstr RD. P Crncstr. Ch e. Sch pe. Crncstr and Tewkesbury CC. Bthplce of Vaughan Williams, composer. D.A. Hse*, Tdr and later.

DOWNDERRY Cornwall
186 SX 3153 4m E of Looe. Loc, St Germans CP. P Torpoint. Ch m. Sch pe.

DOWNE London
171 TQ 4361 2m NNE of Biggin Hill. Loc, Bromley LB. P Orpington, Kent. Orpngtn BC(CC). Vllge in green belt. Restored 13c ch; shingled spire. Down Hse*, once home of Charles Darwin, contains Darwin relics.

DOWNEND Berks
158 SU 4775 5m N of Newbury. Loc, Chieveley CP.

DOWNEND IOW
180 SZ 5387 2m SE of Newport. Loc, Isle of Wight RD, Npt MB. Isle of Wt CC.

DOWNGATE Cornwall
186 SX 3672 2m N of Callington. Loc, Stokeclimsland CP. P Cllngtn. Ch m.

DOWNHAM Cambs
135 TL 5283 3m NNW of Ely. CP, 1,800. Ely RD. Ch e, b2, m2. Sch pe. Isle of Ely CC. See also Pymore.

DOWNHAM Essex
161, 162 TQ 7295 4m E of Billericay. Loc, S Hanningfield CP. Ch e. Sch pe.

DOWNHAM Lancs
95 SD 7844 3m ENE of Clitheroe. CP, 181. Clthroe RD. P Clthroe. Ch e. Sch pe. Cthroe CC. Stone vllge.

DOWNHAM Nthmb
64, 70 NT 8634 4m SSE of Coldstream. Loc, Carham CP.

DOWNHAM MARKET Norfolk
124 TF 6103 10m S of King's Lynn. UD, 3,608. P. SW Nflk CC.

DOWN HATHERLEY Glos
143 SO 8622 3m NE of Gloucester. CP, 432. Glcstr RD. Ch e. W Glos CC.

DOWNHEAD Som
166 ST 6945 5m W of Frome. CP, 113. Shepton Mallet RD. Ch e, m. Wells CC.

DOWNHOLME Yorks (N)
91 SE 1197 4m WSW of Richmond. CP, 65. Rchmnd RD. P Rchmnd. Ch e. Rchmnd CC. 1½m SE, Walburn Hall, interesting 16c fortified hse.

DOWNLEY Bucks
159 SU 8495 2m NW of High Wycombe. Loc, W Wcmbe CP. Wcmbe RD. P Hgh Wcmbe. Ch e. Sch p. Wcmbe CC.

DOWN ST MARY Devon
175 SS 7404 6m WNW of Crediton. CP, 323. Crdtn RD. P Crdtn. Ch e. Tiverton CC (Torrington).

DOWNSIDE Som
166 ST 6244 1m N of Shepton Mallet. Loc, Shptn Mllt UD.

DOWNSIDE Som
166 ST 6450 4m SW of Radstock. Loc,
Chilcompton CP. Ch e. Sch je. To SW,
Blacker's Hill Camp, Iron Age promontory
camp with 40ft ramparts. (For D. Abbey see
Stratton on the Fosse).

DOWNSIDE Surrey
170 TQ 1058 4m WNW of Leatherhead.
Loc, Esher UD. P Cobham.

DOWN THOMAS Devon
187 SX 5050 3m SSE of Plymouth. Loc,
Wembury CP. P Plmth. Ch m.

DOWNTON Hants
179 SZ 2693 4m WSW of Lymington. Loc,
Lmngtn MB. P Lmngtn.

DOWNTON Wilts
167 SU 1821 6m SSE of Salisbury. CP,
1,796. Slsbry and Wilton RD. P Slsbry.
Ch e, b, m2, r. Sch pe, s. Slsbry CC. See also
Charlton, Wick. The Moot, early 18c brick
house; in grnds, reconstructed earthwork,
possibly Saxon meeting place. Tannery in
vllge.

DOWNTON ON THE ROCK Herefs
129 SO 4273 5m W of Ludlow. CP(Dntn),
90. Leominster and Wigmore RD. P Ldlw,
Salop. Ch e. Lmnstr CC. D. Cstle, romantic
18c 'Gothic' cstle; classical interior,
remarkable furnishings and pictures.

DOWSBY Lincs (K)
123 TF 1129 6m N of Bourne. CP, 177.
S Kesteven RD. P Bne. Ch e. Sch pe.
Rutland and Stamford CC.

DOXFORD Nthmb
71 NU 1823 6m N of Alnwick. Loc,
Newton-by-the-Sea CP. Alnwck RD.
Berwick-upon-Tweed CC.

DOYNTON Glos
156 ST 7274 6m NNW of Bath. CP, 365.
Sodbury RD. P BRISTOL. Ch e. S Glos CC.

DRAKES BROUGHTON Worcs
143, 144 SO 9248 2m NNW of Pershore.
CP(Drks Brghtn and Wadborough), 625.
Pshre RD. P Pshre. Ch e, m. Sch pe.
S Worcs CC.

DRAUGHTON Northants
133 SP 7676 7m W of Kettering. CP, 77.
Brixworth RD. Ch e. Daventry CC (Kttrng).

DRAUGHTON Yorks (W)
96 SE 0352 3m E of Skipton. CP, 118.
Skptn RD. P Skptn. Ch m. Skptn CC.

DRAX Yorks (W)
97, 98 SE 6726 5m SE of Selby. CP, 266.
Slby RD. P Slby. Ch e. Sch p.
Barkston Ash CC. Large power stn.

DRAYCOTE Warwicks
132 SP 4470 5m SW of Rugby. CP(Bourton
and Drcte), 281. Rgby RD. Rgby CC. D.
Reservoir to S.

DRAYCOTT Derbys
112, 121 SK 4433 6m ESE of Derby.
CP(Drctt and Church Wilne), 1,995.
SE Derbys RD. P DBY. Ch e, m. Sch p.
SE Derbys CC.

DRAYCOTT Glos
144 SP 1835 3m NNW of Moreton-in-Marsh.
Loc, Blockley CP. P Mtn-in-Msh. Ch b.

DRAYCOTT Som
165 ST 4750 2m SE of Cheddar. Loc,
Rodney Stoke CP. P Chddr. Ch e, m.
Sch pe. Stone quarries. Strawberry-growing
area.

DRAYCOTT IN THE CLAY Staffs
120 SK 1528 5m SE of Uttoxeter. CP, 965.
Uttxtr RD. P DERBY. Ch m, r. Sch pe.
Burton CC.

DRAYCOTT IN THE MOORS Staffs
110, 119 SJ 9840 7m ESE of
Stoke-on-Trent. CP, 841. Cheadle RD. Ch r.
Sch p. Leek CC. See also Cresswell.

DRAYTON Berks
158 SU 4794 2m SW of Abingdon. CP,
1,916. Abngdn RD. P Abngdn. Ch e, b, m.
Sch p. Abngdn CC.

DRAYTON Leics
133 SP 8392 5m WNW of Corby. CP, 112.
Mkt Harborough RD. Ch e. Hbrgh CC.

DRAYTON Norfolk
126 TG 1813 4m NW of Norwich. CP,
1,346. St Faith's and Aylsham RD.
P NRWCH, NOR 52X. Ch e, m. Sch pe.
N Nflk CC (Central Nflk).

DRAYTON Oxon
145 SP 4241 2m WNW of Banbury. CP.
Bnbry RD. P Bnbry. Ch e. Bnbry CC.

DRAYTON Som
177 ST 4024 7m NNE of Ilminster. CP,
306. Langport RD. P Lngpt. Ch e.
Yeovil CC.

DRAYTON Worcs
130, 131 SO 9076 5m E of Kidderminster.
Loc, Chaddesley Corbett CP.

DRAYTON BASSETT Staffs
120 SK 1900 3m SSW of Tamworth. CP,
767. Lichfield RD. P Tmwth. Ch e. Sch p.
Lchfld and Tmwth CC.

DRAYTON BEAUCHAMP Bucks
146, 159 SP 9012 2m WNW of Tring. CP,
141. Aylesbury RD. Ch e. Aylesbury CC.

DRAYTON PARSLOW Bucks
146 SP 8328 4m SW of Bletchley. CP, 406.
Winslow RD. P Bltchly. Ch e, b, m. Sch p.
Buckingham CC.

DRAYTON ST LEONARD Oxon
158 SU 5996 4m N of Wallingford. CP, 281.
Bullingdon RD. P OXFORD. Ch e, m.
Henley CC.

DREWSTEIGNTON Devon
175 SX 7390 3m NNW of
Moretonhampstead. CP, 625.
Okhmpton RD. P Exeter. Ch e, v. Sch p.
W Dvn CC (Torrington). Granite hilltop
vllge. 1m SW, Lutyens-designed Cstle Drogo.
1m SE, Fingle Br, beauty spot. 2m W,
Spinsters' Rock, Bronze Age cromlech or
megalithic tomb.

DRIFFIELD Glos
157 SU 0799 4m ESE of Cirencester. CP,
158. Crncstr RD. Ch e. See also Harnhill. Ch has
monmts to members of Hanger family with
cautiously worded epitaphs.

DRIFFIELD Yorks (E)
99 TA 0257 12m SW of Bridlington. UD,
7,899. P. Howden CC. Old mkt tn. Ch has
notable Perp twr. Canal; chalk stream, D.
Beck, with good trout fishing.

DRIFT Cornwall
189 SW 4328 2m WSW of Penzance. Loc,
Sancreed CP.

DRIGG Cumb
88 SD 0699 2m SE of Seascale. CP(Drgg
and Carleton), 563. Millom RD. Ch e.

Sch pe. Whitehaven CC. To W, D. Dunes and
nature reserve.

DRIGHLINGTON Yorks (W)
96, 102 SE 2229 4m SE of Bradford. Loc,
Morley MB. P Brdfd.

DRIMPTON Dorset
177 ST 4105 3m SSW of Crewkerne. Loc,
Broadwindsor CP. P Beaminster. Ch e.

DRINKSTONE Suffolk (W)
136 TL 9561 6m WNW of Stowmarket. CP,
347. Thedwastre RD. P Bury St Edmunds.
Ch e, m. Sch pe. Bury St Eds CC. See also
Drnkstne Grn. Post-mill dated 1689.

DRINKSTONE GREEN Suffolk (W)
136 TL 9560 6m WNW of Stowmarket.
Loc, Drnkstne CP.

DROINTON Staffs
120 SK 0226 6m ENE of Stafford. Loc,
Stowe CP.

DROITWICH Worcs
130, 131 SO 8693 6m NNE of Worcester.
MB, 12,766. P. Wcstr BC. Spa tn; saline and
radio-active springs. Much subsidence due to
extraction of salt. RC Byzantine ch with
mosaics. To E, Chateau Impney,
Vctrn-French mansion now hotel. To W,
Westwood Hse, Tdr hse now flats.

DRONFIELD Derbys
103, 111 SK 3578 5m S of Sheffield. UD,
17,826. P SHFFLD. NE Derbys CC. See also
Coal Aston. Coal, iron and steel works. Ch
partly 14c. Several 18c hses.

DRONFIELD WOODHOUSE Derbys
111 SK 3278 5m SSW of Sheffield. Loc,
Drnfld UD. P SHFFLD.

DROXFORD Hants
180 SU 6018 3m E of Bishop's Waltham.
CP, 606. Drxfd RD. P SOUTHAMPTON.
Ch e, m. Sch p. Petersfield CC.

DROYLSDEN Lancs
101 SJ 9098 4m E of Manchester. UD,
24,134. PMNCHSTR. Ashton-under-Lyne BC.

DRUMBURGH Cumb
75 NY 2659 3m NE of Kirkbride. Loc,
Bowness CP. Wigton RD. P Carlisle. Sch i.
Penrith and the Border CC. Rems of early
16c cstle blt of Roman stones.

DRYBECK Westm
83 NY 6615 3m SSW of Appleby. Loc,
Hoff CP.

DRYBROOK Glos
142, 143 SO 6417 2m N of Cinderford. CP,
2,832. E Dean RD. P. Ch e, c, m2. Sch p.
W Glos CC. See also Brierley, Ruardean Hill,
Rdn Woodside.

DRY DODDINGTON Lincs (K)
113 SK 8546 6m SE of Newark.
CP(Westborough and Dry Dddngtn), 262.
W Kesteven RD. Ch e. Grantham CC.

DRY DRAYTON Cambs
135 TL 3862 5m WNW of Cambridge. CP,
450. Chesterton RD. P CMBRDGE.
Ch e, m2. Sch pe. Cambs CC.

DUCKINGTON Ches
109 SJ 4951 7m NNW of Whitchurch. CP,
65. Tarvin RD. Nantwich CC.

DUCKLINGTON Oxon
158 SP 3507 1m S of Witney. CP. Wtny RD.
P Wtny. Ch e, b. Sch pe. Mid-Oxon CC
(Banbury).

DUCK'S CROSS Beds
134 TL 1156 5m WSW of St Neots. Loc,
Colmworth CP.

DUDDENHOE END Essex
148 TL 4636 5m W of Saffron Walden. Loc,
Elmdon CP. P Sffrn Wldn.

DUDDINGTON Northants
123 SK 9800 5m SW of Stamford. CP, 184.
Oundle and Thrapston RD. Ch e, v.
Wellingborough CC (Peterborough).

DUDDLESWELL Sussex (E)
183 TQ 4627 4m N of Uckfield. Loc,
Maresfield CP. P Uckfld. On Ashdown
Forest.

DUDDO Nthmb
64 NT 9342 8m SSW of
Berwick-upon-Tweed. CP, 268. Norham and
Islandshires RD. P BRWCK-UPN-TWD.
Ch e. Brwck-upn-Twd CC.

DUDDON Ches
109 SJ 5164 7m E of Chester. CP, 234.
Tarvin RD. P Tarporley. Ch e, m.
Northwich CC.

DUDDON BRIDGE Cumb
88 SD 1988 5m NNE of Millom. Loc, Mllm
Without CP. Mllm RD. Whitehaven CC.

DUDLESTON Shrops
118 SJ 3438 4m WNW of Ellesmere. Loc,
Ellesmre Rural CP.   N Shrops RD.
P Ellesmre. Ch e, m. Sch pe. Oswestry CC.

DUDLESTON HEATH Shrops
118 SJ 3636 2m WNW of Ellesmere. Loc,
Ellesmre Rural CP. N Shrops RD.
P Ellesmre. Ch e, m. Oswestry CC.

DUDLEY Nthmb
78 NZ 2673 6m N of Newcastle. Loc,
Longbenton UD. P.

DUDLEY Staffs
130, 131 SO 9490 8m WNW of
Birmingham. CB, 185,535. P Worcs.
Ddly E BC, Ddly W BC. (Brierley Hill CC,
Bilston BC, Ddly BC.) See also Brierley Hill,
Coseley, Sedgley. Ironworks and general
industry.

DUFFIELD Derbys
120, 121 SK 3443 5m N of Derby. CP.
Belper RD. P DBY. Ch e, b, m. Sch p, pe, s.
Blpr CC. Subterranean rems of large Nmn
cstle (A.M.).

DUFTON Westm
83 NY 6925 3m N of Appleby. CP, 249.
N Westm RD. P Appleby. Ch e, m. Sch p.
Westm CC.

DUGGLEBY Yorks (E)
92, 93 SE 8767 6m ESE of Malton. Loc,
Kirby Grindalythe CP. P Mltn. Ch m.

DUKINFIELD Ches
101 SJ 9497 6m E of Manchester. MB,
17,294. P. Stalybridge and Hyde CC.

DULCOTE Som
165, 166 ST 5644 1m SE of Wells. Loc, St
Cuthbert Out CP. Wlls RD. Wlls CC.

DULFORD Devon
176 ST 0705 7m NW of Honiton. Loc,
Broadhembury CP.

DULLINGHAM Cambs
135 TL 6357 3m SSW of Newmarket. CP,
520. Nmkt RD. P Nmkt, Suffolk.
Ch e, c, m. Sch p. Cambs CC. Several
thatched hses.

DULOE Beds
134 TL 1560 2m W of St Neots. Loc, Staploe CP.

DULOE Cornwall
186 SX 2358 4m SSW of Liskeard. CP, 549. Lskd RD. P Lskd. Ch e, m. Sch pe. Bodmin CC. See also Herodsfoot. Ch: monmts and unusual plan; stone circle; holy well.

DULVERTON Som
164 SS 9127 10m NNW of Tiverton. CP, 1,393. Dlvtn RD. P. Ch e, m, r, v. Sch pe, s. Taunton CC. See also Battleton.

DULWICH London
160, 170 TQ 3374 4m S of Lndn Br. Loc, Southwark LB. Dlwch BC. At centre, D. Vllge retains vllge atmosphere. To S, D. Pk and College (founded early 17c). D. Art Gallery, by Soane 1811–13, restored after severe damage in World War II.

DUMBLETON Glos
144 SP 0136 5m S of Evesham. CP, 477. Cheltenham RD. P Evshm, Worcs. Ch e. Sch p. Cirencester and Tewkesbury CC. See also Gt Washbourne, Wormington.

DUMMER Hants
168 SU 5846 5m SW of Basingstoke. CP(Dmmr w Kempshott), 409. Bsngstke RD. P Bsngstke. Ch e. Sch pe. Bsngstke CC.

DUNBALL Som
165 ST 3141 3m N of Bridgwater. Loc, Puriton CP. P Brdgwtr.

DUNCHIDEOCK Devon
176 SX 8787 4m SW of Exeter. CP, 98. St Thomas RD. P Exeter. Ch e. Tiverton CC. Ch and a few cottages. 1m S, prominent belvedere twr (Lawrence Cstle), erected 1788.

DUNCHURCH Warwicks
132 SP 4871 3m SSW of Rugby. CP, 1,842. Rgby RD. P Rgby. Ch e, b, m. Sch pe. Rgby CC. Some old hses incl one in which Gunpowder Plotters met in 1605.

DUNCOTE Northants
145, 146 SP 6750 2m NW of Towcester. Loc, Greens Norton CP.

DUNCTON Sussex (W)
181, 182 SU 9617 5m ESE of Midhurst. CP, 291. Petworth RD. P Ptwth. Ch e2, r. Sch pe. Chichester CC (Horsham). View of wooded downs to S.

DUNDON Som
165 ST 4832 5m SSW of Glastonbury. Loc, Compton Dundon CP. Langport RD. P(Cmptn Dndn), Somerton. Ch e. Yeovil CC. See Compton.

DUNDRAW Cumb
82 NY 2149 3m WNW of Wigton. CP, 158. Wgtn RD. Penrith and the Border CC. See also Kelsick.

DUNDRY Som
155, 156, 165 ST 5566 4m SSW of Bristol. CP, 790. Long Ashton RD. P BRSTL. Ch e, b2. Sch pe. N Som CC. Bird's eye view of Brstl from ch twr orig blt as landmark for ships by Merchant Venturers in 1484.

DUNFORD BRIDGE Yorks (W)
102 SE 1502 6m W of Penistone. Loc, Dnfd CP. Pnstne RD. P SHEFFIELD. Ch m. Pnstne CC.

DUNGENESS Kent
184 TR 0916 11m ESE of Rye. Loc, Lydd MB. Shingle, shacks, two lighthouses, two nuclear power stns; nature reserve. W terminus of Romney Hythe and Dymchurch Light Rly.

DUNHAM Notts
113 SK 8174 10m WNW of Lincoln. CP, 261. E Retford RD. Bassetlaw CC. P(Dnhm-on-Trnt), Newark. Ch e, m. Sch pe.

DUNHAM, GREAT Norfolk
125 TF 8714 5m NE of Swaffham. See Gt Dnhm.

DUNHAM-ON-THE-HILL Ches
109 SJ 4772 6m NE of Chester. CP, 589. Chstr RD. P(Dnhm Hll), WARRINGTON. Ch e, m2. Sch p. City of Chstr CC.

DUNHAMPTON Worcs
130 SO 8466 4m NW of Droitwich. Loc, Ombersley CP.

DUNHAM TOWN Ches
101 SJ 7487 2m W of Altrincham. Loc, Dnhm Massey CP. Bucklow RD. P Altrnchm. Ch e. Knutsford CC.

DUNHAM WOODHOUSES Ches
101 SJ 7288 3m W of Altrincham. Loc,
Dnhm Massey CP. Bucklow RD.
P Altrnchm. Ch m. Knutsford CC.

DUNHOLME Lincs (L)
104 TF 0279 6m NNE of Lincoln. CP, 847.
Welton RD. P LNCLN. Ch e, m. Sch pe.
Gainsborough CC.

DUNKERTON Som
166 ST 7159 3m NNE of Radstock. CP,
555. Bathavon RD. P Bath. Ch e.
N Som CC. See also Tunley, Withyditch. In
coal-mining area.

DUNKESWELL Devon
176 ST 1407 5m N of Honiton. CP, 352.
Hntn RD. P Hntn. Ch e, b, m. Hntn CC. See
also Abbey.

DUNKESWICK Yorks (W)
96 SE 3046 5m S of Harrogate. Loc,
Harewood CP.

DUNKIRK Kent
172, 173 TR 0758 4m ESE of Faversham.
CP, 657. Swale RD. Ch e. Sch p.
Fvrshm CC.

DUNK'S GREEN Kent
171 TQ 6152 4m NNE of Tonbridge. Loc,
Malling RD. P Tnbrdge. Ch c. Tnbrdge and
Mllng CC (Sevenoaks).

DUNLEY Worcs
130 SO 7869 2m SW of Stourport. Loc,
Astley CP. P Stpt-on-Severn.

DUNMOW Essex
148 TL 6222 9m E of Bishop's Stortford.
CP(Gt Dnmw), 3,827. Dnmw RD. P.
Ch e, b, r, v2. Sch pe, s. Saffron Walden CC.
See also Churchend. Bacon factory recalls
ancient, perhaps Nmn, 'Dnmw Flitch'
ceremony.

DUNNINGTON Warwicks
144 SP 0653 7m NNE of Eveham. Loc,
Salford Priors CP. P Alcester. Ch b. Sch pe.

DUNNINGTON Yorks (E)
97, 98 SE 6752 4m E of York. CP, 983.
Derwent RD. P YK. Ch e, m. Sch pe.
Howden CC.

DUNNINGTON Yorks (E)
99 TA 1552 4m NW of Hornsea. Loc,
Bewholme CP. Ch e, m.

DUNNOCKSHAW Lancs
95 SD 8127 4m SSW of Burnley. CP, 309.
Bnly RD. Sch p. Clitheroe CC.

DUNSBY Lincs (K)
123 TF 1026 4m N of Bourne. CP, 163.
S Kesteven RD. P Bne. Ch e. Rutland and
Stamford CC.

DUNSCROFT Yorks (W)
103 SE 6509 6m NE of Doncaster. Loc,
Hatfield CP. P Dncstr. Ch e, m. Sch p.

DUNSDALE Yorks (N)
86 NZ 6018 4m S of Redcar. Loc,
Guisborough UD. P Gsbrgh.

DUNSDEN GREEN Oxon
159 SU 7377 3m NNE of Reading. Loc, Eye
and Dunsden CP. Henley RD. P(Dnsdn),
Rdng, Berks. Ch e. Sch pe. Hnly CC.

DUNSFOLD Surrey
169, 170, 182 TQ 0036 8m S of Guildford.
CP, 883. Hambledon RD. P Godalming.
Ch e, b. Sch pe. Gldfd CC.

DUNSFORD Devon
176 SX 8189 4m ENE of
Moretonhampstead. CP, 572. St
Thomas RD. P Exeter. Ch e, b. Sch p.
Tiverton CC. Cob and thatch. Ch: Fulford
monmt.

DUNSLEY Yorks (N)
86 NZ 8511 3m W of Whitby.
CP(Newholm-cum-Dnsly), 206. Whtby RD.
Cleveland and Whtby CC (Scarborough and
Whtby).

DUNSMORE Bucks
159 SP 8605 4m ENE of Princes
Risborough. Loc, Aylesbury RD,
Wycombe RD. Aylesbury CC
(Aylesbury CC, Wcmbe CC).

DUNSOP BRIDGE Yorks (W)
94, 95 SD 6650 7m NW of Clitheroe. Loc,
Bowland Forest High CP. Blnd RD.
P Clthroe, Lancs. Ch e. Skipton CC.

DUNSTABLE Beds
147 TL 0121 4m W of Luton. MB, 31,790.
P. S Beds CC. Modern mkt and indstrl tn at
crossing of Roman Watling Street and more
ancient Icknield Way. SW are D. Downs
(NT), famous for gliding.

DUNSTALL Staffs
120 SK 1820 4m WSW of Burton-on-Trent.
CP, 262. Tutbury RD. Ch e. Btn CC.

DUNSTALL GREEN Suffolk (W)
135 TL 7460 7m ESE of Newmarket. Loc,
Dalham CP.

DUNSTAN Nthmb
71 NU 2419 6m NE of Alnwick. Loc,
Craster CP. Ch m.

DUNSTER Som
164 SS 9943 2m SE of Minehead. CP, 958.
Williton RD. P Mnhd. Ch e, m. Sch p.
Bridgwater CC. Show vllge. Cstle*, priory
ch, dovecote*. Wide main st lined with old
stone hses; yarn mkt and butter cross (both
A.M.). Conygar Twr, 18c folly, on hill to
NW.

DUNS TEW Oxon
145 SP 4528 8m S of Banbury. CP, 278.
Bnbry RD. P OXFORD. Ch e. Sch p.
Bnbry CC.

DUNSTON Lincs (K)
113 TF 0662 8m SE of Lincoln. CP, 495.
N Kesteven RD. P LNCLN. Ch e, m. Sch pe.
Grantham CC. 3½m W, D. Pillar, erected
18c as beacon for travellers. Lamp replaced
1810 by statue of George III removed in
World War II.

DUNSTON Norfolk
126 TG 2202 4m S of Norwich. Loc, Stoke
Holy Cross CP. Ch e.

DUNSTON Staffs
119 SJ 9217 3m S of Stafford. CP, 427.
Cannock RD. P STFFD. Ch e. Sch pe.
SW Staffs CC (Cnnck).

DUNSTONE Devon
175, 187, 188 SX 7175 5m NW of
Ashburton. Loc, Widecombe in the
Moor CP. Ch m.

DUNSTONE Devon
187 SX 5951 4m SW of Ivybridge. Loc,
Yealmpton CP.

DUNSVILLE Yorks (N)
103 SE 6407 5m NE of Doncaster. Loc,
Hatfield CP. P Dncstr. Ch m. Sch p.

DUNSWELL Yorks (E)
99 TA 0735 4m NNW of Hull. Loc,
Haltemprice UD. P Hll. Hltmprce CC.

DUNTERTON Devon
186 SX 3779 5m SE of Launceston. CP, 59.
Tavistock RD. Ch e. W Dvn CC (Tvstck).

DUNTISBOURNE ABBOTS Glos
157 SO 9707 5m NW of Cirencester. CP,
211. Crncstr RD. Ch e. Crncstr and
Tewkesbury CC. See also Dntsbne Leer.
Many old bldngs.

DUNTISBOURNE LEER Glos
157 SO 9707 5m NW of Cirencester. Loc,
Dntsbne Abbots CP. Attractive hmlt with a
ford.

DUNTISBOURNE ROUSE Glos
157 SO 9806 3m NW of Cirencester. CP, 82.
Crncstr RD. Ch e. Crncstr and
Tewkesbury CC. See also Middle Dntsbne.
Interesting ch of many periods. 14c cross in
churchyard.

DUNTISH Dorset
178 ST 6906 7m SSE of Sherborne. Loc,
Buckland Newton CP.

DUNTON Beds
147 TL 2344 3m E of Biggleswade. CP, 437.
Bgglswde RD. P Bgglswde. Ch e, b. Sch ie.
Mid-Beds CC.

DUNTON Bucks
146 SP 8224 6m W of Linslade. CP, 76.
Winslow RD. Ch e. Buckingham CC.

DUNTON Norfolk
125 TF 8830 3m W of Fakenham. CP.
Walsingham RD. Ch e, m. NW Nflk CC
(N Nflk). See also Shereford, Toftrees.

DUNTON BASSETT Leics
132 SP 5490 4m N of Lutterworth. CP,
591. Lttrwth RD. P RUGBY. Ch e, m.
Sch p. Blaby CC (Harborough).

DUNTON GREEN Kent
171 TQ 5157 2m NW of Sevenoaks. CP,
1,840. Svnks RD. P Svnks. Ch e, c, v. Sch p.
Svnks CC.

DUNTON WAYLETTS Essex
161 TQ 6590 3m SSW of Billericay. Loc,
Basildon UD.

DUNWICH Suffolk (E)
137 TM 4770 4m SSW of Southwold. CP,
157. Blyth RD. P Saxmundham. Ch e.
Eye CC. Once thriving port, submerged by
sea. Walls of mdvl priory on crumbling cliffs
formerly enclosed vllge cricket ground.

DURDAR Cumb
76 NY 4051 3m S of Carlisle. Loc, St Cuthbert Without CP. Border RD. Penrith and the Bdr CC.

DURHAM Co Durham
85 NZ 2742 14m S of Newcastle. MB(Drhm and Framwellgate), 24,744. P(DRHM). Drhm CC. City on cliffs over double loop of R Wear. Cathedral, largely Nmn. Mdvl cstle. University. Gulbenkian Museum of Oriental art.

DURLEIGH Som
165 ST 2736 2m WSW of Bridgwater. CP, 125. Brdgwtr RD. Ch e. Brdgwtr CC. Large lake (reservoir) to W. W Bower mnr hse, Tdr, retains thatched dovecote with orig mud nesting niches.

DURLEY Hants
180 SU 5116 3m W of Bishop's Waltham. CP, 873. Droxford RD. P SOUTHAMPTON. Ch e, m. Sch pe. Petersfield CC. See also Dly St.

DURLEY Wilts
167 SU 2364 5m SE of Marlborough. Loc, Burbage CP. P Mlbrgh.

DURLEY STREET Hants
180 SU 5217 2m W of Bishop's Waltham. Loc, Durley CP.

DURNFORD, GREAT Wilts
167 SU 1338 3m SSW of Amesbury. See Gt Dnfd.

DURRINGTON Wilts
167 SU 1544 2m N of Amesbury. CP, 4,737. Amesbury RD. P Salisbury. Ch e, c, s, r. Sch ie, je, s. Slsbry CC. See also Larkhill. Surrounded by Army establishments.

DURSLEY Glos
156 ST 7597 7m SW of Stroud. CP, 4,744. Dsly RD. P. Ch e, m, r, v2. Sch i, je, s2. Strd CC. Small Cotswold mkt tn; woollen manufacture.

DURSTON Som
177 ST 2928 5m ENE of Taunton. CP, 137. Tntn RD. P Tntn. Ch e. Tntn CC.

DURWESTON Dorset
178 ST 8508 2m NW of Blandford. CP, 340. Blndfd RD. P Blndfd Forum. Ch e, m.

Sch pe. N Dst CC. 'Transportation tablet' on br over R Stour. ('Any person wilfully injuring ...bridge...liable to be transported for life.')

DUSTON Northants
133 SP 7261 2m W of Northampton. Loc, Nthmptn CB. P NTHMPTON. Ch c, r. Nthmptn S BC (S Nthnts CC).

DUTON HILL Essex
148 TL 6026 3m S of Thaxted. Loc, Gt Easton CP. P Dunmow.

DUTTON Ches
100, 109 SJ 5779 4m SE of Runcorn. CP. Rncn RD. P WARRINGTON. Sch p. Rncn CC.

DUXFORD Cambs
148 TL 4746 6m NNW of Saffron Walden. CP, 1,398. S Cambs RD. P CAMBRIDGE. Ch e2, v. Sch pe. Cambs CC. Large, rambling. Two ancient chs; modern factory at S edge. D. Chpl (A.M.), near Whittlesford stn, 13c. Gdns* of D. Mill, which is mentioned in Domesday.

DYE HOUSE Nthmb
77 NY 9358 3m S of Hexham. Loc, Hexhamshire Low Quarter CP. Hxhm RD. Ch m. Hxhm CC.

DYKE Lincs (K)
123 TF 1022 2m NNE of Bourne. Loc, Bne UD. P Bne.

DYMCHURCH Kent
173 TR 1029 5m SW of Hythe. CP, 1,739. Romney Marsh RD. P Rmny Msh. Ch e, m, r. Sch p. Folkestone and Hthe CC. Between Rmny Msh and enormous sea wall. Holiday centre; famous light rly to Rmny, Hthe, and Dungeness. Martello twr.

DYMOCK Glos
143 SO 7031 4m S of Ledbury. CP, 1,212. Newent RD. P. Ch e. Sch pe. W Glos CC. See also Bromsberrow Hth, Greenway, Preston, Ryton. Nmn ch.

DYRHAM Glos
156 ST 7375 7m N of Bath. CP(Drhm and Hinton), 238. Sodbury RD. P Chippenham, Wilts. Ch e. S Glos CC. D. Pk (NT)*, 17c—18c hse.

E

EAGLAND HILL Lancs
94 SD 4345 9m NE of Blackpool. Loc, Pilling CP.

EAGLE Lincs (K)
113 SK 8767 7m WSW of Lincoln. CP(Eagle and Swinethorpe), 463. N Kesteven RD. P LNCLN. Ch e, m. Sch p. Grantham CC.

EAGLESCLIFFE Co Durham
85 NZ 4215 3m SW of Teesside (Stockton). Loc, Stcktn RD. P STCKTN-ON-TEES, Tssde. Ch m. Easingtn CC (Sedgefield).

EAGLESFIELD Cumb
82 NY 0928 2m SW of Cockermouth. Loc, Dean CP. P Cckrmth. Ch m. Sch pe. Bthplace (1766) of John Dalton, founder of Atomic Theory.

EAKRING Notts
112 SK 6762 4m SSE of Ollerton. CP, 601. Southwell RD. P Newark. Ch e, m2. Nwk CC.

EALAND Lincs (L)
104 SE 7811 7m W of Scunthorpe. Loc, Crowle CP. P Scnthpe. Ch m.

EALING London
160 TQ 1780 8m W of Charing Cross. LB, 299,450. BCs: Acton, Ealng N, Southall (Actn, Ealng N, Ealng S, Sthll). See also Actn, Greenford, Hanwell, Northolt, Perivale, Sthll.

EAMONT BRIDGE Westm
83 NY 5228 1m SSE of Penrith. CP(Yanwath and Eamnt Br), 237. N Westm RD. P Pnrth. Ch e. Westm CC. 1m E, Brougham Cstle (A.M.), impressive rems of 12c–14c cstle restored mid-17c. Ch is SE of Eamnt Br next to former Brghm Hall.

EARBY Yorks (W)
95 SD 9046 4m NNE of Colne. UD, 4,816. P Clne, Lancs. Skipton CC. See also Kelbrook.

EARCROFT Lancs
94, 95 SD 6824 2m S of Blackburn. Loc, Darwen MB.

EARDINGTON Shrops
130 SO 7290 2m SSE of Bridgnorth. CP, 285. Brdgnth RD. P Brdgnth. Ludlow CC.

EARDISLAND Herefs
129 SO 4158 5m W of Leominster. CP, 474. Weobley RD. P Lmnstr. Ch e, m. Sch pe. Lmnstr CC. Many timbered hses. 1m S, Burton Ct*, mainly 18c hse incorporating parts of earlier bldngs incl 14c great hall.

EARDISLEY Herefs
142 SO 3149 7m NE of Hay-on-Wye. CP, 656. Kington RD. P HEREFORD. Ch e, m2. Sch pe. Leominster CC. See also Hurstway Cmmn. Ch: 12c carved font.

EARDISTON Shrops
118 SJ 3725 6m ESE of Oswestry. Loc, Ruyton-XI-Towns CP. Ch e. Ch blt 1860 as private chpl for Pradoe, brick hse in pk to W.

EARDISTON Worcs
130 SO 6968 6m E of Tenbury Wells. Loc, Lindridge CP. P Tnbry Wlls.

EARITH Hunts
135 TL 3874 5m ENE of St Ives. CP, 619. St Ives RD. P HUNTINGDON. Ch e, m. Hunts CC. To NE, experimental track for hovercraft project.

EARLE Nthmb
71 NT 9826 1m S of Wooler. CP, 101. Glendale RD. Berwick-upon-Tweed CC.

EARLESTOWN Lancs
100 SJ 5795 4m E of St Helens. Loc, Newton-le-Willows UD. P Ntn-le-Wllws. Rly and general engineering.

EARLS BARTON Northants
133 SP 8563 4m SW of Wellingborough. CP(Earl Btn), 2,699. Wllngbrgh RD. P NORTHAMPTON. Ch e, b2, m, r. Sch p. Wllngbrgh CC. Ch has fine Saxon twr.

EARLS COLNE Essex
149 TL 8628 3m ESE of Halstead. CP, 2,106. Hlstd RD. P Colchester. Ch e, b, f. Sch p, s. Saffron Walden CC. Large ironworks. Vctrn hse occupies site of 12c priory.

EARL'S COURT London
160, 170 TQ 2578 3m WSW of Charing Cross. Loc, Kensington and Chelsea LB. Chlsea BC (Knsngtn S). Exhibition hall (Warwick Rd).

EARL'S CROOME Worcs
143 SO 8742 6m N of Tewkesbury. CP, 274. Upton upon Severn RD. P WORCESTER. Ch e. Sch pe. S Worcs CC.

EARL'S GREEN Suffolk (E)
136 TM 0366 5m N of Stowmarket. Loc, Hartismere RD. Eye CC.

EARL SHILTON Leics
132 SP 4697 3m NE of Hinckley. Loc, Hnckly UD. P LCSTR. Hosiery and footwear mnfg.

EARL SOHAM Suffolk (E)
137 TM 2363 3m W of Framlingham. CP, 468. Blyth RD. P Woodbridge. Ch e, b. Eye CC. Pink and white painted hses. Row of poplars. Ch has double hammerbeam roof.

EARL STERNDALE Derbys
111 SK 0967 4m SSE of Buxton. Loc, Hartington Middle Quarter CP. Bakewell RD. P Bxtn. Ch m. Sch pe. W Derbys CC. Cynical inn sign of The Quiet Woman depicts woman standing headless.

EARL STONHAM Suffolk (E)
136 TM 1159 4m E of Stowmarket. CP(Stnhm Earl), 492. Gipping RD. Ch e, v. Sch p, pe. Eye CC. Ch: hammerbeam roof.

EARLSWOOD Warwicks
131 SP 1174 4m SW of Solihull. Loc, Tanworth CP. P Slhll. Ch e, m.

EARNLEY Sussex (W)
181 SZ 8196 6m SSW of Chichester. CP, 261. Chchstr RD. Ch e. Chchstr CC.

EARSDON Nthmb
78 NZ 3272 2m W of Whitley Bay. Loc, Seaton Valley UD. P Whtly Bay. Blyth BC.

EARSHAM Norfolk
137 TM 3289 1m SW of Bungay. CP, 622. Depwade RD. P Bngy, Suffolk. Ch s. Sch pe. S Nflk CC.

EARSWICK Yorks (N)
97, 98 SE 6257 3m NNE of York. CP, 233. Flaxton RD. Thirsk and Malton CC.

EARTHAM Sussex (W)
181 SU 9309 6m NE of Chichester. CP, 139. Chchstr RD. Ch e. Chchstr CC. Small vllge of flint and brick.

EARTHCOTT GREEN Glos
155, 156 ST 6585 6m SE of Severn Rd Br. Loc, Alveston CP.

EASBY Yorks (N)
86 NZ 5708 3m E of Stokesley. CP, 72. Stksly RD. Ch e, m. Richmond CC. On hill 1m N, Captain Cook monmt.

EASBY Yorks (N)
91 NZ 1800 1m ESE of Richmond. CP, 112. Rchmnd RD. Ch e. Rchmnd CC. 13c–14c abbey (A.M.) beside R Swale.

EASEBOURNE Sussex (W)
181 SU 8922 just NE of Midhurst. CP, 2,023. Mdhst RD. P Mdhst. Ch e. Sch pe. Chichester CC (Horsham). Cowdray estate vllge, denoted by yellow paint on hses.

EASENHALL Warwicks
132 SP 4679 4m NW of Rugby. CP, 135. Rgby RD. Rgby CC.

EASHING Surrey
169 SU 9443 2m W of Godalming. Loc, Shackleford CP. Old cottages (NT), and 13c br in two parts (NT) over R Wey.

EASINGTON Bucks
146, 159 SP 6810 3m NNW of Thame. Loc, Chilton CP.

EASINGTON Co Durham
85 NZ 4143 2m NNW of Peterlee. CP, 9,953. Easngtn RD. P Ptrlee. Ch e, m, r, s, v. Sch pe. Easngtn CC. See also Easngtn Colliery.

EASINGTON Nthmb
64, 71 NU 1234 1m NE of Belford. CP, 199. Blfd RD. Berwick-upon-Tweed CC. See also Spindlestone, Waren Mill.

EASINGTON Oxon
158, 159 SU 6697 6m NE of Wallingford. CP(Cuxham w Easngtn), 183. Bullingdown RD. Ch e. Henley CC.

EASINGTON Yorks (E)
105 TA 3919 7m SE of Withernsea. CP, 553. Holderness RD. P Hull. Ch e, m. Sch pe. Bridlington CC. See also Kilnsea, Out Newton.

EASINGTON Yorks (N)
86 NZ 7418 2m E of Loftus. Loc, Lfts UD. P Saltburn-by-the-Sea.

EASINGTON COLLIERY Co Durham
85 NZ 4343 2m N of Peterlee. Loc,
Easngtn CP. P Ptrlee. Ch e, b, m, r, v2.
Sch ig, p.

EASINGTON LANE Co Durham
85 NZ 3646 5m WSW of Seaham. Loc,
Hetton UD. P Httn-le-Hole.

EASINGWOLD Yorks (N)
92 SE 5269 12m NNW of York. CP, 2,686.
Easngwld RD. P YK. Ch e, m2, r, s. Sch p, s.
Thirsk and Malton CC. Small mkt tn. Large
cobbled square with pleasant bldngs; in the
middle, startling Vctrn tn hall.

EASOLE STREET Kent
173 TR 2652 6m SW of Sandwich. Loc,
Nonington CP.

EASTACOMBE Devon
163 SS 5329 3m SSW of Barnstaple. Loc,
Tawstock CP. Ch b.

EASTACOTT Devon
163 SS 6223 6m WSW of S Molton. Loc,
Chittlehampton CP.

EAST ADDERBURY Oxon
145 SP 4735 3m SSE of Banbury. CP.
Bnbry RD. Ch e, m, r. Sch pe. Bnbry CC.
One vllge with W Addrbry but divided by
A41 rd.

EAST ALLINGTON Devon
187, 188 SX 7648 3m NE of Kingsbridge.
CP, 418. Knsbrdge RD. P Totnes. Ch e, m.
Sch p. Ttns CC.

EAST ANSTEY Devon
164 SS 8626 3m WSW of Dulverton. CP,
206. S Molton RD. P Tiverton. Ch e. Sch p.
N Dvn CC.

EAST APPLETON Yorks (N)
91 SE 2395 5m SE of Richmond. CP
(Apptn E and W), 73. Rchmnd RD.
Rchmnd CC.

EAST ASHLING Sussex (W)
181 SU 8207 3m NW of Chichester. Loc,
Funtington CP.

EAST AYTON Yorks (N)
93 SE 9985 4m SW of Scarborough. CP,
704. Scbrgh RD. P Scbrgh. Ch e, m. Sch p.
Scbrgh CC (Scbrgh and Whitby). Rems of
pele twr just NW.

EAST BARKWITH Lincs (L)
105 TF 1681 6m SE of Mkt Rasen. CP, 238.
Horncastle RD. P LINCOLN Ch e. Sch pe.
Hncstle CC.

EAST BARMING Kent
171, 172 TQ 7254 2m WSW of Maidstone.
Loc, Brmng CP. Mdstne RD. P(Bmng),
Mdstne. Ch e. Sch p. Mdstne CC.

EAST BARNBY Yorks (N)
86 NZ 8212 4m WNW of Whitby. Loc,
Bnby CP. Whtby RD. Cleveland and
Whitby CC (Scarborough and Whtby).

EAST BARNET London
160 TQ 2794 1m SE of Barnet. Loc,Bnt LB.
P Bnt, Herts. Chipping Bnt BC (Bnt CC).

EAST BARSHAM Norfolk
125 TF 9133 3m N of Fakenham. Loc,
Bshm CP. Walsingham RD. P Fknhm.
Ch e, m. Sch p. NW Nflk CC (N Nflk). Tdr
brick mnr hse with handsome gateway.

EAST BECKHAM Norfolk
126 TG 1539 2m S of Sheringham. CP, 45.
Erpingham RD. Ch e. N Nflk CC.

EAST BERGHOLT Suffolk (E)
149 TM 0734 3m NW of Manningtree. CP,
1,903. Samford RD. P Colchester. Essex.
Ch e, m, v. Sch pe, s. Sudbury and
Woodbridge CC. Bthplce of John Constable,
1776. Flatford Mill and Willy Lott's Cottage
(NT). Ch bells housed in cage in churchyard.

EAST BIERLEY Yorks (W)
96 SE 1929 3m SE of Bradford. Loc,
Spenborough MB. P Brdfd. Brighouse and
Spnbrgh BC.

EAST BILNEY Norfolk
125 TF 9519 4m NNW of E Dereham. Loc,
Beetley CP. P Drhm. Ch e.

EAST BLATCHINGTON Sussex (E)
183 TQ 4800 just N of Seaford. Loc,
Sfd UD.

EAST BOLDRE Hants
180 SU 3700 5m ESE of Brockenhurst.
CP,774. New Forest RD. Ch e. Sch pe. Nw
Frst CC. See also E End.

EASTBOURNE Sussex (E)
183 TV 6198 19m E of Brighton. CB,
70,495. P. Eastbne CC. See also Hampden
Pk. Seaside resort. To W, Beachy Head,
575ft chalk cliff. Lighthouse offshore.

EAST BRADENHAM Norfolk
125 TF 9208 5m SW of E Dereham. Loc,
Brdnhm CP. Swaffham RD. P Thetford.
Ch e, m. SW Nflk CC.

EAST BRENT Som
165 ST 3452 6m S of Weston. CP, 904.
Axbridge RD. P Highbridge. Ch e, m.
Sch i, je. Wstn-super-Mare CC. See also
Rooks Br. To S, Brnt Knoll, isolated
conical hill topped by Iron Age fort. Ch:
spire.

EAST BRIDGE Suffolk (E)
137 TM 4566 5m ENE of Saxmundham.
Loc, Theberton CP. Ch m.

EAST BRIDGFORD Notts
112, 122 SK 6943 8m E of Nottingham. CP,
906. Bingham RD. P NTTNGHM. Ch e, m.
Sch pe. Rushcliffe CC (Carlton). Above
R Trent. To S, site of Roman tn,
Margidunum, on Fosse Way (A46).

EAST BUCKLAND Devon
163 SS 6731 4m NNW of S Molton. CP, 70.
S Mltn RD. Ch e. N Dvn CC.

EAST BUDLEIGH Devon
176 SY 0684 5m ENE of Exmouth. CP,
164. St Thomas RD. P Budleigh Salterton.
Ch e, v2. Sch pe. Honiton CC. Thatched
cottages and stream beside main street
running up to 15c ch. 1m W, 16c Hayes
Barton*. bthplace of Sir Walter Raleigh,
1552.

EASTBURN Yorks (W)
96 SE 0244 3m NW of Keighley.
CP(Steeton W Eastbn), 2,463. Skipton RD.
P Kghly. Ch m, v. Sch p. Kghly BC.

EAST BURTON Dorset
178 SY 8387 6m W of Wareham, Loc,
Wool CP. To W on Winfrith Hth, Atomic
Energy Establishment.

EASTBURY Berks
158 SU 3477 6m N of Hungerford. Loc,
Lambourn CP. P Newbury. Ch e, m.
Thatched cottages.

EASTBURY Herts
160 TQ 0992 3m ESE of Rickmansworth.
Loc, Rckmnswth UD.

EAST BUTTERWICK Lincs (L)
104 SE 8305 5m SW of Scunthorpe. CP,
223. Glanford Brigg RD. P Scnthpe.
Ch e, m2. Brgg and Scnthpe CC (Brgg).
Below dyke containing R Trent.

EASTBY Yorks (W)
96 SE 0154 3m NE of Skipton. CP(Embsay
w Eastby), 1,060. Skptn RD. Skptn CC.

EAST CARLETON Norfolk
126/137 TG 1801 5m SW of Norwich. CP,
238. Forehoe and Henstead RD. Ch e.
S Nflk CC (Central Nflk).

EAST CARLTON Northants
133 SP 8389 4m W of Corby. CP, 237.
Kettering RD. P Mkt Harborough, Leics.
Ch e. Kttrng CC.

EAST CHALDON Dorset
178 SY 7983 8m SE of Dorchester.
Alternative name for Chaldon Herring, qv.
P Dchstr.

EAST CHALLOW Berks
158 SU 3888 1m W of Wantage. CP, 789.
Wntge RD. P Wntge. Ch e, m. Sch pe.
Abingdon CC.

EAST CHEVINGTON Nthmb
71 NZ 2699 3m S of Amble. CP, 3,570.
Morpeth RD. Ch e. Mpth CC. See also
Broomhill, Chvngtn Drift, Red Row, S
Brmhll.

EAST CHILTINGTON Sussex (E)
183 TQ 3615 4m NW of Lewes. CP, 632.
Chailey RD. Ch e. Lws CC.

EAST CHINNOCK Som
177 ST 4913 4m WSW of Yeovil. CP, 357.
Yvl RD. P Yvl. Ch e, m. Yvl CC.

EAST CHISENBURY Wilts
167 SU 1452 5m SSW of Pewsey. Loc,
Enford CP.

EASTCHURCH Kent
172 TQ 9871 7m NE of Sittingbourne. Loc,
Queenborough-in-Sheppey MB. P Sheerness.
Site of first aerodrome in Britain.

EAST CLANDON Surrey
170 TQ 0651 4m ENE of Guildford. CP,
317. Gldfd RD. P Gldfd. Ch e. Dorking CC.
Brick-and-timber cottages. To E, Hatchlands
(NT)*, 18c hse blt for Admiral Boscawen 'at
the expense of the enemies of his country'.
Interior decorations by Robert Adam.

EAST CLAYDON Bucks
146 SP 7325 6m SSE of Buckingham. CP,
256. Winslow RD. Ch e. Sch p.
Bcknghm CC. See also Botolph Claydon.
Many old hses, incl the Elizn White Hse.

EAST COKER Som
177, 178 ST 5412 3m SSW of Yeovil. CP,
1,514. Yvl RD. P Yvl. Ch e, v. Sch p.
Yvl CC. See also N Ckr. Blt of Ham stone.
To SE, Sutton Bingham Reservoir.

EASTCOMBE Glos
156, 157 SO 8904 3m E of Stroud. Loc,
Bisley-w-Lypiatt CP. P Strd. Ch e, b.
Sch p, s.

EAST COMBE Som
164 ST 1631 6m NW of Taunton. Loc,
Bishop's Lydeard CP.

EAST COMPTON Dorset
178 ST 8718 3m S of Shaftesbury. Loc,
Compton Abbas CP. Ch e.

EAST COTE Cumb
75 NY 1155 1m NNE of Silloth. Loc,
Sllth CP.

EASTCOTE Northants
146 SP 6854 3m N of Towcester. Loc,
Pattishall CP. Ch b.

EASTCOTE Warwicks
131 SP 1979 3m E of Solihull. Loc,
Barston CP. Eastcte Hse, 17c. Wharley Hall,
17c. Eastcte Hall has 15c hall.

EASTCOTT Cornwall
174 SS 2515 7m NNE of Bude. Loc,
Morwenstow CP. Ch m.

EASTCOTT Wilts
167 SU 0255 4m SSE of Devizes. Loc,
Easterton CP.

EAST COTTINGWITH Yorks (E)
97, 98 SE 7042 7m SW of Pocklington. Loc,
Cttngwth CP. Pcklngtn RD. P YORK.
Ch e, m. Howden CC.

EAST COULSTON Wilts
167 ST 9554 5m ENE of Westbury. CP,
118. Warminster and Wstbry RD. Ch e.
Wstbry CC.

EASTCOURT Wilts
157 ST 9792 4m NE of Malmesbury. Loc,
Crudwell CP. P Mlmsbry.

EAST COWES IOW
180 SZ 5095 just E of Cowes across river.
Loc, Cowes UD. P. Osborne Hse (A.M.),
Queen Victoria's home designed by Prince
Albert; now partly convalescent home for
ex-service officers. Norris Cstle, 18c 'Nmn'
by James Wyatt. Much holiday
development.

EAST COWICK Yorks (W)
97, 98 SE 6621 5m WSW of Goole. Loc,
Snaith and Cwck CP. P Gle. Ch e. Sch pe.

EAST COWTON Yorks (N)
91 NZ 3003 7m NW of Northallerton. CP,
337. Nthlltn RD. P Nthlltn. Ch e, m. Sch pe.
Richmond CC.

EAST CRAMLINGTON Nthmb
78 NZ 2776 4m SW of Blyth. Loc, Seaton
Valley UD. Blth BC.

EAST CRANMORE Som
166 ST 6843 4m E of Shepton Mallet. Loc,
Cranmore CP. Shptn Mllt RD. Ch e.
Wells CC.

EAST CURTHWAITE Cumb
83 NY 3348 5m E of Wigton. Loc,
Border RD, Wgtn RD. Penrith and the
Bdr CC.

EAST DEAN Hants
167 SU 2726 6m NW of Romsey. CP, 223.
Rmsy and Stockbridge RD. Ch e.
Winchester CC.

EASTDEAN Sussex (E)
183 TV 5597 4m W of Eastbourne. CP, 937.
Hailsham RD. P Eastbne. Ch e. Eastbne CC.
NT land to S and W, incl chalk cliffs known
as The Seven Sisters, and Birling Gap.

EAST DEAN Sussex (W)
181 SU 9013 6m NNE of Chichester. CP,
304. Chchstr RD. P Chchstr. Ch e, c.
Chchstr CC. In Lavant valley N of
Goodwood.

EAST DEREHAM Norfolk
125 TF 9913 15m W of Norwich. UD,
9,391. P(Drhm). SW Nflk CC. See also
Toftwood Cmmn. Mkt place flanked by 18c
hses. Large mdvl ch and detached bell twr.
Bonner's Cottages, early 16c, pargeted, now
museum of local history. Engineering wks.

EAST DITCHBURN Nthmb
71 NU 1421 6m NNW of Alnwick. Loc,
Eglingham CP.

EAST DOWN Devon
163 SS 6041 6m SE of Ilfracombe. CP, 213.
Barnstaple RD. Ch e, m. N Dvn CC. See also
Clifton.

EAST DRAYTON Notts
104 SK 7775 6m SE of Retford. CP, 158.
E Rtfd RD. P Rtfd. Ch e, m. Bassetlaw CC.

EAST END Dorset
179 SY 9998 2m SW of Wimborne. Loc,
Corfe Mullen CP. P Wmbne. Ch m.

EASTEND Essex
162 TQ 9492 4m ENE of Rochford. Loc,
Paglesham CP. P Pglshm, Rchfd.

EAST END Hants
168 SU 4161 5m SW of Newbury. Loc,
E Woodhay CP. P Nbry, Berks.

EAST END Hants
180 SZ 3697 3m ENE of Lymington. Loc,
E Boldre CP. P Lmngtn. Ch c.

EAST END Herts
148 TL 4527 5m NNW of Bishop's
Stortford. Loc, Furneux Pelham CP.

EAST END Kent
172, 184 TQ 8335 3m WNW of Tenterden.
Loc, Benenden CP.

EAST END Norfolk
126 TG 5114 4m N of Yarmouth. Loc,
Ormesby St Margaret w Scratby CP.

EAST END Oxon
145 SP 3914 4m NE of Witney. Loc,
N Leigh CP. P Wtny. Ch m.

EASTER COMPTON Glos
155, 156 ST 5782 6m N of Bristol. Loc,
Almondsbury CP. P BRSTL. Ch m. Sch p.

EASTERGATE Sussex (W)
181 SU 9405 6m E of Chichester. CP,
1,146. Chchstr RD. P Chchstr. Ch e. Sch pe.
Arundel CC (Chchstr).

EASTERTON Wilts
167 SU 0255 4m SSE of Devizes. CP, 472.
Dvzs RD. P Dvzs. Ch e. Sch pe. Dvzs CC.
See also Eastcott.

EASTERTOWN Som
165 ST 3454 5m SSE of Weston. Loc,
Lympsham CP.

EAST FARLEIGH Kent
171, 172 TQ 7353 2m SW of Maidstone.
CP. Mdstne RD. P Mdstne. Ch e. Sch p.
Mdstne CC. Mdvl br over R Medway.

EAST FARNDON Northants
133 SP 7184 2m SSW of Mkt Harborough.
CP, 259. Brixworth RD. P Mkt Hbrgh,
Leics. Ch e. Daventry CC (Kettering).

EAST FERRY Lincs (L)
104 SK 8199 6m N of Gainsborough. CP,
96. Gnsbrgh RD. P Gnsbrgh. Ch e, m.
Gnsbrgh CC.

EASTFIELD Yorks (N)
93 TA 0483 3m S of Scarborough. Loc,
Scbrgh MB.

EAST GARSTON Berks
158 SU 3676 6m NNE of Hungerford. CP,
490. Hngrfd RD. P Newbury. Ch e, m.
Nbry CC. Thatched cottages under the
downs.

EASTGATE Co Durham
84 NY 9538 3m W of Stanhope. Loc,
Stnhpe CP. P Bishop Auckland. Ch m.

EAST GINGE Berks
158 SU 4486 3m ESE of Wantage. Loc,
W Hendred CP.

EAST GRAFTON Wilts
167 SU 2560 6m E of Pewsey. Loc,
Grftn CP. Marlborough and Ramsbury RD.
P Mlbrgh. Ch e. Sch pe. Devizes CC. Stone
and timbered thatched cottages round grn.

EAST GRIMSTEAD Wilts
167 SU 2227 5m ESE of Salisbury. Loc,
Grmstd CP. Slsbry and Wilton RD. Ch e.
Slsbry CC.

EAST GRINSTEAD Sussex (E)
171, 183 TQ 3939 8m E of Crawley. UD,
18,569. P. E Grnstd CC. See also
Ashurstwood. Shopping centre and rsdntl tn
on busy A22 rd.

EAST GULDEFORD Sussex (E)
184 TQ 9321 1m NE of Rye. CP, 90.
Battle RD. Ch e. Rye CC.

EAST HADDON Northants
132, 133 SP 6668 7m NW of Northampton.
CP, 402. Brixworth RD. P NTHMPTN. Ch e.
Sch pe. Daventry CC (Kettering).

EAST HAGBOURNE Berks
158 SU 5388 1m S of Didcot. CP, 938.
Wllngfd RD. P Ddct. Ch e, m. Sch pe.
Abingdon CC. Thatch, tile-hanging,
half-timbering. At W end, a restored 15c
cross, topped by Jcbn dial.

EAST HALTON Lincs (L)
99/104 TA 1319 4m NNW of Immingham.
CP, 664. Glanford Brigg RD. P Grimsby.
Ch e, m. Sch p. Brgg and Scunthorpe CC
(Brgg).

EASTHAM Ches
100, 109 SJ 3680 6m SSE of Birkenhead.
Loc, Bebington MB. P Wirral. Docks at
seaward end of Manchester Ship Canal.

EAST HAM London
161 TQ 4283 8m ENE of Charing Cross.
Loc, Newham LB. Nwhm NE BC,
Nwhm S BC (Barking, E Hm N, E Hm S,
W Hm N, W Hm S, Woolwich E).

EASTHAM Worcs
129, 130 SO 6568 4m E of Tenbury Wells.
CP, 236. Tnbry RD. Ch e. Sch pe.
Kidderminster CC.

EASTHAMPSTEAD Berks
169 SU 8667 1m S of Bracknell. Loc,
Brcknll CP. P Brcknll. Ch e, b. Sch pe.

EAST HANNEY Berks
158 SU 4192 4m NNE of Wantage. CP, 541.
Wntge RD. P Wntge. Ch e, v. Sch pe.
Abingdon CC.

EAST HANNINGFIELD Essex
162 TL 7701 5m SE of Chelmsford. CP,
516. Chlmsfd RD. P Chlmsfd. Ch e, v.
Sch pe. Chlmsfd CC.

EAST HARDWICK Yorks (W)
103 SE 4618 2m S of Pontefract. CP, 152.
Osgoldcross RD. P Pntfrct. Sch p. Goole CC.

EAST HARLING Norfolk
136 TL 9986 6m SW of Attleborough. Loc,
Hlng CP. Wayland RD. P NORWICH, NOR
12X. Ch e, f, m. Sch p. S Nflk CC.
Outstanding mainly 15c ch: stained glass,
scrn, monmts.

EAST HARLSEY Yorks (N)
91 SE 4299 5m NE of Northallerton. CP,
240. Nthlltn RD. P Nthlltn. Ch e, m. Sch pe.
Richmond CC.

EAST HARPTREE Som
165, 166 ST 5655 7m N of Wells. CP, 550.
Clutton RD. P BRISTOL. Ch e, m, r.
Sch pe. N Som CC.

EAST HARTFORD Nthmb
78 NZ 2679 3m WSW of Blyth. Loc, Seaton
Valley UD. P(Htfd Colliery), Cramlington.
Blth BC.

EAST HARTING Sussex (W)
SU 7919 4m SE of Petersfield. Loc,
Htng CP. Midhurst RD. Chichester CC
(Horsham).

EAST HATCH Wilts
166, 167 ST 9228 5m NE of Shaftesbury.
Loc, W Tisbury CP. Mere and Tsbry RD.
Westbury CC.

EAST HATLEY Cambs
147 TL 2850 7m ENE of Biggleswade. Loc,
Htly CP. S Cambs RD. Ch e. Cambs CC. Ch
completed 1961. (14c ch still standing but
not in use.)

EAST HAUXWELL Yorks (N)
91 SE 1693 4m ENE of Leyburn. CP, 39.
Lbn RD. Ch e. Richmond CC.

EAST HECKINGTON Lincs (K)
113, 123 TF 1944 8m E of Sleaford. Loc,
E Kesteven RD. P Boston. Sch pe.
Grantham CC.

EAST HEDLEYHOPE Co Durham
85 NZ 1540 3m ENE of Tow Law. Loc,
Hdlhpe CP. Lanchester RD. P Bishop
Auckland. Ch m. NW Drhm CC.

EAST HENDRED Berks
158 SU 4688 4m E of Wantage. CP, 1,303.
Wntge RD. P Wntge. Ch e, m, r2, v.
Sch pe, pr. Abingdon CC. Thatch,
half-timbering. H. Hse is mdvl, with 13c
chpl.

EAST HESLERTON Yorks (E)
93 SE 9276 9m ENE of Malton. Loc,
Hslrtn CP. Norton RD. Ch e, m.
Howden CC.

EAST HOATHLY Sussex (E)
183 TQ 5216 4m SE of Uckfield. CP, 737.
Hailsham RD. P Lewes. Ch e. Sch pe.
Lws CC (Eastbourne). On a ridge with long
view to N. Trug baskets made here.

EAST HOLME Dorset
178, 179 SY 8986 2m WSW of Wareham.
CP, 55. Wrhm and Purbeck RD. Ch e.
S Dst CC. Ch in pk; hse incorporates rems of
former priory.

EASTHOPE Shrops
129 SO 5695 5m SW of Much Wenlock. CP,
101. Bridgnorth RD. P Mch Wnlock. Ch e.
Ludlow CC.

EASTHORPE Essex
149, 162 TL 9121 6m WSW of Colchester.
Loc, Copford CP. Lexden and Winstree RD.
Ch e. Clchstr CC.

EAST HORRINGTON Som
165, 166 ST 5846 2m ENE of Wells. Loc, St
Cuthbert Out CP. Wlls RD. P Wlls. Ch e.
Wlls CC.

EAST HORSLEY Surrey
170 TQ 0952 5m WSW of Leatherhead. CP,
3,466. Guildford RD. P Lthrhd. Ch e, v.
Dorking CC. Ch: brasses.

EAST HUNTSPILL Som
165 ST 3444 4m SE of Burnham. CP, 784.
Bridgwater RD. Ch e, m. Sch p. Brdgwtr CC.
See also Bason Br.

EAST HYDE Beds
147 TL 1217 2m N of Harpenden. Loc,
Hde CP. Luton RD. P Ltn. Ch e. S Beds CC.

EAST ILSLEY Berks
158 SU 4981 6m SSW of Didcot. CP, 415.
Wantage RD. P Newbury. Ch e, b. Sch p.
Abingdon CC.

EASTINGTON Glos
144 SP 1213 1m SE of Northleach.
CP(Nthlch w Eastngtn), 1,248. Nthlch RD.
Cirencester and Tewkesbury CC.

EASTINGTON Glos
156 SO 7705 5m W of Stroud. CP, 1,399.
Gloucester RD. P Stonehouse. Ch e, b, m.
Sch p. Strd CC. See also Nupend.

EAST KEAL Lincs (L)
114 TF 3763 8m ESE of Horncastle. CP,
256. Spilsby RD. P Splsby. Ch e, m.
Hncstle CC.

EAST KENNETT Wilts
157 SU 1167 5m W of Marlborough. CP, 91.
Mlbrgh and Ramsbury RD. Sch pe.
Devizes CC.

EAST KESWICK Yorks (W)
96 SE 3644 4m W of Wetherby. CP, 734.
Wthrby RD. P LEEDS. Ch e, m. Sch pe.
Barkston Ash CC.

EAST KIRKBY Lincs (L)
114 TF 3362 7m SE of Horncastle. CP, 244.
Spilsby RD. P Splsby. Ch e, m. Sch pe.
Hncstle CC.

EAST KNAPTON Yorks (E)
92, 93 SE 8875 7m ENE of Malton. Loc,
Scampston CP.

EAST KNIGHTON Dorset
178 SY 8185 7m W of Wareham. Loc,
Winfrith Newburgh CP.

EAST KNOYLE Wilts
166, 167 ST 8830 5m NNE of Shaftesbury.
CP, 750. Mere and Tisbury RD. P Salisbury.
Ch e, c, m. Sch pe. Westbury CC. See also
Milton, Pertwood. Ch, mainly EE and 19c:
decorations designed by Christopher Wren's
father, then rector.

EAST KYLOE Nthmb
64, 71 NU 0539 5m NW of Belford. Loc,
Kyloe CP. Norham and Islandshires RD.
Berwick-upon-Tweed CC.

EAST LAMBROOK Som
177 ST 4318 5m NE of Ilminster. Loc,
Kingsbury Episcopi CP. P: S Petherton.
Ch e. E Lmbrk Mnr*, 15c–16c hse in fine
gdns.

EAST LANGDON Kent
173 TR 3346 3m NNE of Dover. Loc,
Lngdn CP. Dvr RD. Ch e. Sch p. Dvr and
Deal CC (Dvr).

EAST LANGTON Leics
133 SP 7292 3m N of Mkt Harborough. CP,
361. Mkt Hbrgh RD. P Mkt Hbrgh.
Hbrgh CC. See also Ch Lngtn.

EAST LAVANT Sussex
181 SU 8608 2m N of Chichester. Loc,
Lvnt CP. Chchstr RD. P(Lvnt), Chchstr.
Ch e. Sch pe. Chchstr CC. By R Lvnt; view
N to Downs.

EAST LAVINGTON Sussex (W)
181 SU 9416 4m SSW of Petworth. CP,
254. Midhurst RD. Ch e. Chichester CC
(Horsham).

EAST LAYTON Yorks (N)
85 NZ 1609 6m N of Richmond. CP, 75.
Rchmnd RD. P Rchmnd. Ch e. Rchmnd CC.

EASTLEACH MARTIN Glos
157 SP 2005 4m N of Lechlade. Loc,
Eastlch CP. Northleach RD. Ch e. Sch pe.
Cirencester and Tewkesbury CC.

EASTLEACH TURVILLE Glos
157 SP 1905 4m N of Lechlade. Loc,
Eastlch CP. Northleach RD. P Cirencester.
Ch e, m. Sch pe. Crncstr and
Tewkesbury CC. Eastlch Martin and Eastlch
Tvlle are twin Cotswold hmlts each with an
ancient ch. R Leach flows between.

EAST LEAKE Notts
121, 122 SK 5526 4m NNE of
Loughborough. CP, 2,856. Basford RD.
P Lghbrgh, Leics. Ch e, b, m, r. Sch p2, s.
Rushcliffe CC. Ch contains vamping horn
nearly 8ft long, one of six in England.

EAST LEARMOUTH Nthmb
64, 70 NT 8637 2m SE of Coldstream. Loc,
Carham CP.

EASTLEIGH Devon
163 SS 4827 2m ENE of Bideford. Loc,
Westleigh CP. Ch m.

EAST LEIGH Devon
175 SS 6905 9m NE of Okehampton. Loc,
Coldridge CP. P Crediton.

EASTLEIGH Hants
180 SU 4519 5m NNE of Southampton.

MB, 45,320. P. Eastlgh CC. See also
Bishopstoke, Chandler's Ford. Rly junction
and wks. Borough incl Sthmptn Airpt to S.

EAST LEXHAM Norfolk
125 TF 8516 5m NNE of Swaffham. Loc,
Lxhm CP. Mitford and Launditch RD. Ch e.
SW Nflk CC.

EAST LILBURN Nthmb
71 NU 0423 4m SE of Wooler. Loc,
L l b n C P. G l e n d a l e R D.
Berwick-upon-Tweed CC.

EASTLING Kent
172 TQ 9656 4m SW of Faversham. CP,
353. Swale RD. P Fvshm. Ch e, m. Sch p.
Fvshm CC.

EAST LISS Hants
181 SU 7727 4m NE of Petersfield. Loc,
Lss CP.

EAST LOOE Cornwall
186 SX 2553 7m S of Liskeard. See Looe.

EAST LOUND Lincs (L)
104 SK 7899 6m NNW of Gainsborough.
Loc, Haxey CP.

EAST LULWORTH Dorset
178 SY 8582 5m SW of Wareham. CP, 291.
Wrhm and Purbeck RD. P Wrhm. Ch e, r.
S Dst CC. Ruined 16c cstle; ch r, 1786, in
grnds — first Roman Catholic ch allowed to
be blt after Reformation.

EAST LUTTON Yorks (E)
93 SE 9469 9m NW of Driffield. Loc,
Lttns CP. Norton RD. Howden CC.

EAST LYDFORD Som
165, 166 ST 5731 7m SE of Glastonbury.
Loc, Lydford CP. Shepton Mallet RD. Ch e.
Wells CC.

EAST MALLING Kent
171, 172 TQ 7057 4m W of Maidstone.
CP(E Mllng and Larkfield), 5,142.
Mllng RD. P Mdstne. Ch e, m. Sch pe, s.
Tonbridge and Mllng CC (Sevenoaks). See
also New Hythe. Vllge grn famous in cricket
history. Horticultural Research Centre at
Brabourne, ½m N.

EAST MARDEN Sussex (W)
181 SU 8014 7m NNW of Chichester. Loc,
Marden CP. Chichester RD. Ch e.

Chchstr CC. In a hollow; flint cottages. Well has thatched cover. Plain 13c ch.

EAST MARKHAM Notts
112 SK 7473 5m SSE of Retford. CP, 839. E Rtfd RD. P Newark. Ch e, m. Sch p. Bassetlaw CC. Large mdvl ch.

EAST MARTON Yorks (W)
95 SD 9050 5m W of Skipton. Loc, Mtns Both CP. Skptn RD. P Skptn. Ch e. Sch pe. Skptn CC.

EAST MEON Hants
181 SU 6722 4m W of Petersfield. CP, 1,438. Ptrsfld RD. P Ptrsfld. Ch e, c, m. Sch pe. Ptrsfld CC. 15c Ct Hse beside fine Nmn ch. Stream runs at side of vllge street.

EAST MERSEA Essex
149, 162 TM 0514 8m SSE of Colchester. CP, 276. Lexden and Winstree RD. P Clchstr. Ch e. Clchstr CC. On island between mouths of rivers Colne and Blackwater. S. Baring Gould rector here 1870–81.

EAST MOLESEY Surrey
170 TQ 1468 2m WSW of Kingston. Loc, Esher UD. P.

EAST MORTON Yorks (W)
96 SE 1042 3m ENE of Keighley. Loc, Kghly MB.

EAST NESS Yorks (N)
92 SE 6978 6m ESE of Helmsley. Loc, Nss CP. Kirkbymoorside RD. Thirsk and Malton CC.

EASTNOR Herefs
143 SO 7337 1m E of Ledbury. CP, 333. Ldbry RD. P Ldbry. Ch e. Sch pe. Leominster CC. Vctrn vllge. Eastnr Cstle*, neo-Nmn of 1808 in fine grnds.

EAST NORTON Leics
122 SK 7800 5m W of Uppingham. CP, 95. Billesdon RD. P LCSTR. Ch e. Harborough CC (Melton).

EAST OAKLEY Hants
168 SU 5750 4m W of Basingstoke. Loc, Oakley CP.

EASTOFT Lincs (L) and Yorks (W)
104 SE 8016 3m NE of Crowle. CP, 366, Isle of Axholme RD; CP, 37, Goole RD. P Scunthorpe, Lincs. Ch e, m. Sch pe. Gainsborough CC, Gle CC.

EAST OGWELL Devon
176, 188 SX 8370 2m SW of Newton Abbot. Loc, Ogwll CP. P Ntn Abbt. Ch e.

EASTON Devon
175 SX 7188 3m NW of Moretonhampstead. Loc, Chagford CP.

EASTON Dorset
178 SY 6971 on Isle of Portland, S of Weymouth. Loc, Ptlnd UD. P Ptlnd.

EASTON Hants
168 SU 5132 3m NE of Winchester. Loc, Itchen Valley CP. Wnchstr RD. P Wnchstr. Ch e, m. Wnchstr CC.

EASTON Hunts
134 TL 1371 6m W of Huntingdon. CP, 90. Hntngdn RD. Ch e. Hunts CC.

EASTON IOW
180 SZ 3486 2m SSW of Yarmouth. Loc, Freshwater CP. P(Frshwtr Bay), Frshwtr.

EASTON Lincs (K)
122 SK 9326 6m S of Grantham. CP, 128. W Kesteven RD. Rutland and Stamford CC.

EASTON Norfolk
125 TG 1310 6m WNW of Norwich. CP, 437. Forehoe and Henstead RD. P NRWCH, NOR 54X. Ch e, m. Sch pe. S Nflk CC (Central Nflk).

EASTON Som
165 ST 5147 3m NW of Wells. Loc, St Cuthbert Out CP. Wlls RD. P Wlls. Ch e. Wlls CC.

EASTON Suffolk (E)
137 TM 2858 3m S of Framlingham. CP, 289. Blyth RD. P Woodbridge. Ch e. Sch p. Eye CC. *Cottages ornés.*

EASTON, GREAT Essex
148 TL 6125 3m NNW of Dunmow. See Gt Eastn, Essex.

EASTON, GREAT Leics
133 SP 8493 4m NW of Corby. See Gt Eastn, Leics.

EASTON GREY Wilts
156, 157 ST 8887 3m W of Malmesbury. CP, 110. Mlmsbry RD. P Mlmsbry. Ch e. Chippenham CC.

EASTON-IN-GORDANO Som
155 ST 5175 5m WNW of Bristol. CP,
4,130. Long Ashton RD. P BRSTL.
Ch e, bc, m. Sch pe. N Som CC. See also
Ham Grn, Pill.

EASTON MAUDIT Northants
133 SP 8858 6m S of Wellingborough. CP,
108. Wllngbrgh RD. Ch e. Wllngbrgh CC.

EASTON ON THE HILL Northants
123 TF 0104 2m SW of Stamford. CP, 419.
Oundle and Thrapston RD. P(Eastn), Stmfd,
Lincs. Ch e. Sch pe. Wellingborough CC
(Peterborough). Blt of Collyweston stone.
15c priest's hse (NT).

EASTON ROYAL Wilts
167 SU 2060 3m E of Pewsey. CP, 256.
Psy RD. P Psy. Ch e, m. Sch p. Devizes CC.

EAST ORCHARD Dorset
178 ST 8317 4m SSW of Shaftesbury. CP,
105. Shftsbry RD. P Shftsbry. Ch e, m.
Sch pe. N Dst CC.

EAST ORD Nthmb
64 NT 9851 2m SW of
Berwick-upon-Tweed. Loc, Ord CP. Norham
and Islandshires RD. P BRWCK-UPN-TWD.
Brwck-upn-Twd CC.

EAST PANSON Devon
174 SX 3692 5m NNE of Launceston. Loc,
St Giles on the Hth CP.

EAST PECKHAM Kent
171 TQ 6648 5m ENE of Tonbridge. CP,
2,006. Malling RD. P Tnbrdge. Ch e, b, m, s.
Sch p. Tnbrdge and Mllng CC (Sevenoaks).
See also Hale St.

EAST PENNARD Som
165, 166 ST 5937 4m SSW of Shepton
Mallet. CP, 321. Shptn Mllt RD.
P Shptn Mllt. Ch e. Wells CC.

EAST PORINGLAND Norfolk
137 TG 2701 5m SSE of Norwich. Loc,
Plnd CP. Forehoe and Henstead RD.
P(Plnd), Nrwch. Ch e. Sch p. S Nflk CC
(Central Nflk).

EAST PORTLEMOUTH Devon
187, 188 SX 7438 4m S of Kingsbridge. CP,
239. Kngsbrdge RD. P Salcombe. Ch e, m.
Ttns CC.

EAST PRAWLE Devon
187, 188 SX 7836 6m SSE of Kingsbridge.
Loc, Chivelstone CP. P Kngsbrdge.

EAST PRESTON Sussex (W)
182 TQ 0602 3m E of Littlehampton. CP,
4,039. Worthing RD. P Lttlhmptn. Ch e, r.
Sch p. Arundel CC (Arndl and Shoreham).
See also Angmering-on-Sea.

EAST PUTFORD Devon
174 SS 3616 8m N of Holsworthy. CP, 102.
Bideford RD. Ch e. N Dvn CC (Torrington).

EAST QUANTOXHEAD Som
164 ST 1343 4m E of Watchet. CP, 146.
Williton RD. Ch e. Sch p. Bridgwater CC.
Show vllge between Quantocks and sea. Ct
Hse, property of Luttrells for over 700
years.

EAST RAINTON Co Durham
85 NZ 3347 1m SSW of
Houghton-le-Spring. Loc, Hetton UD.
P Htn-le-Sprng.

EAST RAVENDALE Lincs (L)
105 TF 2399 6m SSW of Grimsby. CP, 43.
Grmsby RD. Ch e. Sch pe. Louth CC.

EAST RAYNHAM Norfolk
125 TF 8825 3m SSW of Fakenham. Loc,
Rnhm CP. Walsingham RD. Ch e.
NW Nflk CC (N Nflk). Rnhm Hall, 17c, seat
of Townshend family.

EASTREA Cambs
134 TL 2997 2m E of Whittlesey. Loc,
Whttlsy UD.

EAST RETFORD Notts
103 SK 7081 18m WNW of Lincoln. MB,
18,402. P(Rtfd). Bassetlaw CC.

EAST RIGTON Yorks (W)
96 SE 3643 4m SSW of Wetherby. Loc,
Bardsey cum Rgtn CP.

EASTRINGTON Yorks (E)
97, 98 SE 7929 5m NE of Goole. CP, 602.
Howden RD. P Gle. Ch e, m. Sch p.
Hdn CC. See also Portington.

EAST ROUNTON Yorks (N)
91 NZ 4203 7m NE of Northallerton. CP,
116. Stokesley RD. P(Rntn), Nthlltn. Ch e.
Richmond CC.

EAST RUDHAM Norfolk
125 TF 8328 6m W of Fakenham. CP, 679.
Docking RD. P King's Lynn. Ch e, m.
Sch pe. NW Nflk CC (K's Lnn).

EAST RUNTON Norfolk
126 TG 1942 1m W of Cromer. Loc,
Rntn CP. Erpingham RD. P Crmr. Ch m.
N Nflk CC.

EAST RUSTON Norfolk
126 TG 3427 4m ESE of N Walsham. CP,
431. Smallburgh RD. P NORWICH, NOR
18Z. Ch e, m. Sch p. N Nflk CC.

EASTRY Kent
173 TR 3054 2m SW of Sandwich. CP,
2,059. Eastry RD. P Sndwch. Ch e, b, m.
Sch p, pe. Dover and Deal CC (Dvr).

EAST SHEFFORD Berks
158 SU 3874 5m NE of Hungerford. CP, 88.
Hngrfd RD. Ch e, m. Newbury CC.

EAST SLEEKBURN Nthmb
78 NZ 2883 2m NW of Blyth. Loc,
Bedlingtonshire UD. Blth BC.

EAST SOMERTON Norfolk
126 TG 4719 8m NNW of Yarmouth. Loc,
Smtn CP. Blofield and Flegg RD. Sch p.
Ymth CC.

EAST STOCKWITH Lincs (L)
104 SK 7994 3m NNW of Gainsborough.
CP, 261. Gnsbrgh RD. P Gnsbrgh. Ch e, m.
Sch p. Gnsbrgh CC.

EAST STOKE Dorset
178 SY 8786 3m W of Wareham. CP, 419.
Wrhm and Purbeck RD. P Wrhm. Ch e.
Sch pe. S Dst CC. See also W Holme.

EAST STOKE Notts
112 SK 7549 4m SW of Newark. CP, 211.
Nwk RD. Ch e. Sch pe. Nwk CC. Site of
Roman stn *Ad Pontem* to N along Fosse
Way. To S, site of Battle of Stke Field,
1487.

EAST STOUR Dorset
166 ST 7922 4m W of Shaftesbury. CP,
384. Shftsbry RD. P Gillingham. Ch e, m.
N Dst CC. See also Knapp Corner.

EAST STOURMOUTH Kent
173 TR 2662 5m NW of Sandwich. Loc,
Stmth CP. Eastry RD. Dover and Deal CC
(Dvr).

EAST STRATTON Hants
168 SU 5440 8m NE of Winchester. Loc,
Micheldever CP. P Wnchstr. Ch e, m.

EAST STUDDAL Kent
173 TR 3149 4m WSW of Deal. Loc,
Sutton CP. P Dover.

EAST TAPHOUSE Cornwall
186 SX 1863 4m W of Liskeard. Loc, St
Pinnock CP. P Lskd.

EAST THIRSTON Nthmb
71 NZ 1999 5m WSW of Amble. Loc,
Thstn CP. Morpeth RD. Mpth CC.

EAST TILBURY Essex
161, 171 TQ 6877 3m ENE of Tilbury. Loc,
Thurrock UD. P Grays. Thrrck BC (CC).
Thames-side indstrl. Shoe factory. Coal Hse
Fort blt by Gordon of Khartoum.

EAST TISTED Hants
169, 181 SU 7032 4m S of Alton. CP, 180.
Altn RD. P Altn. Ch e. Sch pe.
Petersfield CC. Early 19c estate vllge.

EAST TORRINGTON Lincs (L)
104 TF 1483 4m SE of Mkt Rasen. Loc,
Legsby CP. Ch e.

EAST TUDDENHAM Norfolk
125 TG 0711 6m ESE of E Dereham. CP,
423. Mitford and Launditch RD. P Drhm.
Ch e. SW Nflk CC.

EAST TYTHERLEY Hants
168 SU 2929 6m NNW of Romsey. CP, 243.
Rmsy and Stockbridge RD. Ch e.
Winchester CC.

EAST TYTHERTON Wilts
157 ST 9674 3m E of Chippenham. Loc,
Bremhill CP. P(Tthtn), Chppnhm. Ch v.
Sch p. Ch, 18c, blt by Moravians who
settled here c 1740.

EAST VILLAGE Devon
176 SS 8405 3m N of Crediton. Loc,
Sandford CP. Ch m.

EASTVILLE Lincs (L)
114 TF 4056 9m NNE of Boston. CP, 294.
Spilsby RD. Ch e, m. Sch p. Horncastle CC.

EAST WALTON Norfolk
124 TF 7416 8m ESE of King's Lynn. CP,
117. Freebridge Lynn RD. P K's Lnn.
Ch e, m. Sch pe. NW Nflk CC (K's Lnn).

EASTWELL Leics
122 SK 7728 6m NNE of Melton Mowbray.
Loc, Eaton CP. P Mltn Mbry. Ch e, r.
13c—14c ch almost unrestored.

EAST WELLOW Hants
168 SU 3020 3m W of Romsey. Loc,
Wllw CP. Rmsy and Stockbridge RD. Ch e.
Eastleigh CC. (Winchester). Burial place of
Florence Nightingale.

EASTWICK Herts
148, 161 TL 4311 1m NW of Harlow. CP,
157. Ware RD. Ch e. E Herts CC. Ch: 13c
effigy of knight.

EAST WINCH Norfolk
124 TF 6916 5m ESE of King's Lynn. CP,
504. Freebridge Lynn RD. P K's Lnn.
Ch e, m. Sch pe. NW Nflk CC (K's Lnn). See
also W Bilney.

EAST WITTERING Sussex (W)
181 SZ 8096 6m SSW of Chichester. CP,
1,850. Chchstr RD. P Chchstr. Ch e, c.
Sch p. Chchstr CC. Bungalows and caravans.
Shingle beach.

EAST WITTON Yorks (N)
91 SE 1486 2m SE of Middleham.
CP(E Wttn Tn), 194. Leyburn RD. P Lbn.
Ch e, m. Sch pe. Richmond CC. 1½m SE,
Jervaulx Abbey*, rems of 12c Cistercian
monastic hse.

EASTWOOD Notts
112 SK 4646 5m ESE of Ripley. UD,
10,864. P NOTTINGHAM. Beeston CC
(Ashfield). Bthplce of D.H. Lawrence.

EASTWOOD Yorks (W)
95 SD 9625 2m ENE of Todmorden. Loc,
Tdmdn MB. P Tdmdn, Lancs.

EAST WOODBURN Nthmb
77 NY 9086 5m ENE of Bellingham. Loc,
Corsenside CP. Bllnghm RD. Hexham CC.

EAST WOODHAY Hants
168 SU 4061 5m SW of Newbury. CP,
1,859. Kingsclere and Whitchurch RD.
Ch e, v. Sch pe. Basingstoke CC. See also
Ball Hill, Broad Laying, \E End, N End,
Woolton Hill.

EAST WOODLANDS Som
166 ST 7944 3m SSE of Frome. Loc,
Selwood CP. Frme RD. Ch e. Wells CC.

EAST WORLDHAM Hants
169 SU 7538 2m ESE of Alton. Loc,
Wldhm CP. Altn RD. Ch e. Sch pe.
Petersfield CC.

EAST WORLINGTON Devon
163, 175 SS 7713 9m SSE of S Molton. CP,
260. S Mltn RD. P Crediton. Ch e, m2.
Sch p. N Dvn CC. See also W Wlngtn.

EAST WRETHAM Norfolk
136 TL 9190 5m NE of Thetford. Loc,
Wrthm CP. Wayland RD. Ch e. S Nflk CC.

EAST YOULSTONE Devon
174 SS 2715 7m NNE of Bude. Loc,
Bradworthy CP.

EATHORPE Warwicks
132 SP 3969 5m ENE of Leamington. CP,
111. Warwick RD. P Lmngtn Spa. Wrwck
and Lmngtn CC.

EATON Berks
158 SP 4403 4m WSW of Oxford.
CP(Appleton w Eaton), 756. Abingdon RD.
Abngdn CC.

EATON Ches
109 SJ 5763 6m WSW of Winsford. Loc,
Rushton CP. P Tarporley. Sch p.

EATON Ches
110 SJ 8765 2m NNE of Congleton. CP,
257. Macclesfield RD. Sch pe. Mcclsfld CC.

EATON Leics
122 SK 7929 7m NNE of Melton Mowbray.
CP, 571. Mltn and Belvoir RD. P Grantham,
Lincs. Ch e, m. Sch pe. Mltn CC. See also
Eastwell, Goadby Marwood.

EATON Notts
103 SK 7178 2m S of Retford. CP, 254.
E Rtfd RD. Ch e. Bassetlaw CC.

EATON Shrops
129 SO 4989 4m SE of Ch Stretton.
CP(Eatn-under-Heywood), 253.
Ludlow RD. Ch e. Ldlw CC. See also
Ticklerton.

EATON BISHOP Herefs
142 SO 4438 4m W of Hereford. CP, 375.
Hrfd RD. P HRFD. Ch e, m. Hrfd CC. Ch:
14c stained glass.

EATON BRAY Beds
147 SP 9620 3m W of Dunstable. CP, 1,509. Luton RD. P Dnstble. Ch e, b, m, s. Sch p. S Beds CC. Ch has famous 13c interior.

EATON CONSTANTINE Shrops
118 SJ 6006 5m SW of Wellington. Loc, Leighton CP. P Shrewsbury. Ch e. Sch pe.

EATON HASTINGS Berks
157 SU 2698 11m NE of Swindon. CP, 110. Faringdon RD. P Frngdn. Ch e. Abingdon CC.

EATON SOCON Hunts
134 TL 1658 1m SW of St Neots. Loc, St Nts UD. P HUNTINGDON. Hunts CC (Mid-Beds). Old lock-up on grn.

EATON UPON TERN Shrops
118, 119 SJ 6523 6m WNW of Newport. Loc, Stoke upn Tn CP.

EBBERSTON Yorks (N)
92, 93 SE 8982 6m ESE of Pickering. CP, 466. Pckrng RD. P Scarborough. Ch e, m. Sch p. Scbrgh CC (Scbrgh and Whitby). Ebbstn Hall*, early 18c Palladian-style mansion with water gdn. To N, King Alfred's cave, in which neolithic rems were found.

EBBESBOURNE WAKE Wilts
167 ST 9924 8m E of Shaftesbury. CP (Ebbesborne Wake), 227. Salisbury and Wilton RD. P (Ebbesbourne), Slsbry. Ch e, v. Sch pe. Slsbry CC. See also Fifield Bavant.

EBCHESTER Co Durham
77, 78 NZ 1055 3m N of Consett. Loc, Cnstt UD. P Cnstt.

EBFORD Devon
176 SX 9887 5m SE of Exeter. Loc, Woodbury CP.

EBRINGTON Glos
144 SP 1840 2m E of Chipping Campden. CP, 563. N Cotswold RD. P Chppng Cmpdn. Ch e. Sch pe. Cirencester and Tewkesbury CC. See also Charingworth. Hidcote Boyce.

ECCHINSWELL Hants
168 SU 4959 5m SSE of Newbury. CP (Ecchnswll and Sydmonton), 1,072. Kingsclere and Whitchurch RD. P Nbry, Berks. Ch e, v. Sch pe. Basingstoke CC.

ECCLES Kent
171, 172 TQ 7260 4m NNW of Maidstone. Loc, Aylesford CP. P Mdstne. Ch m, s. Large Roman villa.

ECCLES
101 SJ 7798 4m W of Manchester. MB, 38,413. P MNCHSTR. Eccls BC. Here Bridgewater Canal is carried over Mnchstr Ship Canal by swing br. Modern shopping area N of mkt place. Royal Ordnance Factory at Patricoft.

ECCLESFIELD Yorks (W)
102, 103 SK 3594 4m N of Sheffield. CP. Wortley RD. P SHFFLD. Ch e, m5, r, v. Sch i, j2, p2, pr2, s. Penistone CC. See also Chapeltown, Grenoside, High Grn. Very large 15c ch. Rems of Benedictine priory.

ECCLESHALL Staffs
119 SJ 8329 5m SW of Stone. CP, 5,028. Stne RD. P STAFFORD. Ch e, m, r, v. Sch p, se. Stffd and Stne CC. See also Chatcull, Cotes, Cranberry, Croxton, Fairoak, Millmeece, Offleyhay, Slindon, Sturbridge, Sugnall, Wetwood. Cstle, dismantled in 19c, was former residence of Bishops of Lichfield.

ECCLES ROAD Norfolk
136 TM 0190 4m SSW of Attleborough. Loc, Quidenham CP. Ch e. Sch pe. To SW, motor racing circuit on disused airfield.

ECCLESTON Ches
109 SJ 4162 2m S of Chester. CP, 261. Chstr RD. P CHSTR. Ch e. Sch pe. City of Chstr CC. Eaton Hall, 1m S, no longer standing, was home of the Grosvenors, later Dukes of Westminster. Ecclstn Square, London, is named after vllge.

ECCLESTON Lancs
100 SD 5117 4m W of Chorley. CP, 2,149. Chly RD. P Chly. Ch e, m, r. Sch pe. Chly CC. See also Ecclstn Grn.

ECCLESTON Lancs
100 SJ 4895 2m W of St Helens. CP, 8,192. Whiston RD. Ch e3. Sch i, j, pr. Huyton CC.

ECCLESTON, GREAT Lancs
94 SD 4240 8m ENE of Blackpool. See Gt Ecclstn.

ECCLESTON GREEN Lancs
100 SD 5216 4m W of Chorley. Loc, Ecclstn CP.

ECCUP Yorks (W)
96 SE 2842 5m N of Leeds. Loc, Lds CB. Lds NW BC. Large reservoir.

ECKINGTON Derbys
103 SK 4379 7m SE of Sheffield. CP. Chesterfield RD. P SHFFLD. Ch e, m7, r, S2, v2. Sch i, j, pe, pr. NE Derbys CC. See also Highlane, Marshlane, Renishaw, Ridgeway, Spinkhill. 12c–13c ch contains Sitwell monmts.

ECKINGTON Worcs
143, 144 SO 9241 3m SSW of Pershore. CP, 803. Pshre RD. P Pshre. Ch e. Sch pe. S Worcs CC. Ch has 17c monmt to Hanfords of Woollas Hall, 17c stone mnr hse 1½m SE on Bredon Hill.

ECKWORTHY Devon
163 SS 4017 6m W of Torrington. Loc, Buckland Brewer CP.

ECTON Northants
133 SP 8263 5m ENE of Northampton.CP, 461. Wellingborough RD. Ch e, b. Sch p. Wllngbrgh CC.

EDALE Derbys
102, 111 SK 1285 9m NNE of Buxton. CP, 361. Chapel en le Frith RD. P SHEFFIELD. Ch e. Sch pe. High Peak CC. See also Barber Booth. S end of 250 mile Pennine Way, which traverses Kinder Scout (2½m NW), summit of The Peak.

EDBURTON Sussex
182 TQ 2311 4m E of Steyning. Loc, Upr Beeding CP. Ch e. Tiny vllge under the Downs.

EDDERSIDE Cumb
82 NY 1045 5m S of Silloth. Loc, Holme St Cuthbert CP.

EDDISTONE Devon
174 SS 2421 10m NNE of Bude. Loc, Hartland CP. Ch m.

EDENBRIDGE Kent
171 TQ 4446 8m SW of Sevenoaks. CP, 5,242. Svnks RD. P. Ch e, b3, m, r2. Sch p, pv, s. Svnks CC. See also Marlpit Hill, Marsh Grn. Mkt tn with light indstrl development.

EDENFIELD Lancs
95, 101 SD 7919 5m N of Bury. Loc, Ramsbottom UD. P Rmsbttm, Bury.

EDENHALL Cumb
83 NY 5632 3m ENE of Penrith. Loc, Langwathby CP. Ch e. Glass cup of the Musgraves of Eden Hall (demolished), known as "The Luck of Edn Hll', is now in the Victoria and Albert Museum, London.

EDENHAM Lincs (K)
123 TF 0621 2m WNW of Bourne. CP, 399. S Kesteven RD. P Bne. Ch e. Sch pe. Rutland and Stamford CC. See also Grimsthorpe. Ch has many monmts to Willoughby de Ersby family (Dukes of Ancaster), of Grmsthpe, qv.

EDENSOR Derbys
111 SK 2570 2m ENE of Bakewell. CP, 166. Bkwll RD. P Bkwll. Ch e. W Derbys CC. Estate vllge of Chatsworth Hse* across R Derwent to E. The 17c–19c hse is palatial home of Dukes of Devonshire.

EDENTHORPE Yorks (W)
103 SE 6206 4m NE of Doncaster. CP, 2,824. Dncstr RD. P Dncstr. Ch v. Sch p. Don Valley CC.

EDEN VALE Co Durham
85 NZ 4237 2m S of Peterlee. Loc, Cstle Edn CP.

EDGBASTON Warwicks
131 SP 0684 2m SSW of Birmingham. Loc, Bmnghm CB. P BMNGHM 15. Bmnghm, Edgbstn BC. Bmnghm University is here.

EDGCOTE Northants
145 SP 5048 5m NNE of Banbury. CP, 76. Brackley RD. Ch e. Daventry CC (S Nthnts). Edgcte Mnr, 18c hse.

EDGCOTT Bucks
145, 146 SP 6722 6m E of Bicester. CP, 143. Buckingham RD. P Aylesbury. Ch e. Bcknghm CC.

EDGE Co Durham
84 NZ 0726 6m NNE of Barnard Cstle. Loc, Lynesack and Softley CP. Bnd Cstle RD. Bishop Auckland CC.

EDGE Shrops
118 SJ 3908 6m WSW of Shrewsbury. Loc, Pontesbury CP.

EDGEBOLTON Shrops
118 SJ 5721 6m SE of Wem. Loc, Shawbury CP. Ch m.

EDGE END Glos
142 SO 5913 4m W of Cinderford. Loc,
W Dean CP. W Dn RD. Ch m. W Glos CC.

EDGEFIELD Norfolk
125 TG 0934 3m SSE of Holt. CP, 397.
Erpingham RD. P(Edgfld Grn), Melton
Constable. Ch e, m. Sch p. N Nflk CC. See
also Ramsgate St.

EDGEWORTH Glos
157 SO 9406 5m WNW of Cirencester. CP,
129. Crncstr RD. P Stroud. Ch e. Crncstr
and Tewkesbury CC.

EDGMOND Shrops
119 SJ 7219 1m WNW of Newport. CP,
1,239. Wellington RD. P Npt. Ch e, m2.
Sch pe. The Wrekin CC. See also Adeney,
Edgmnd Marsh.

EDGMOND MARSH Shrops
119 SJ 7120 2m WNW of Newport. Loc,
Edgmnd CP.

EDGTON Shrops
129 SO 3885 3m NW of Craven Arms. CP,
86. Clun and Bishop's Cstle RD.
P Crvn Arms. Ch e, m. Ludlow CC.

EDGWARE London
160 TQ 2092 10m NW of Charing Cross.
Loc, Barnet LB. P Middx. Hndn N BC.

EDGWORTH Lancs
95, 101 SD 7416 5m NNE of Bolton. Loc,
Turton UD. P Ttn, Bltn. Darwen CC.

EDINGALE Staffs
120 SK 2112 5m N of Tamworth. CP, 365.
Lichfield RD. P Tmwth. Ch e. Sch pe.
Lchfld and Tmwth CC. See also Croxall.

EDINGLEY Notts
112 SK 6655 8m W of Newark. CP, 241.
Southwell RD. P Nwk. Ch e, m. Nwk CC.

EDINGTHORPE Norfolk
126 TG 3232 3m ENE of N Walsham. Loc,
Bacton CP. P: N Wlshm. Ch e.

EDINGTON Som
165 ST 3839 6m ENE of Bridgwater. CP,
462. Brdgwtr RD. P Brdgwtr. Ch e, v.
Sch pe. Brdgwtr CC. See also Edngtn Burtle.
Possible site of Battle of Ethandun, 878, in
which King Alfred defeated Danes. (But see
Edngtn, Wilts.)

EDINGTON Wilts
166, 167 ST 9253 4m ENE of Westbury.
CP, 575. Warminster and Wstbry RD.
P Wstbry. Ch e, m. Sch p. Wstbry CC.
Possible site of Battle of Ethandun, 878.
(But see Edngtn, Som.) Outstanding 14c ch.

EDINGTON BURTLE Som
165 ST 3943 7m WNW of Glastonbury.
Loc, Edington CP. Sch pe.

EDITHMEAD Som
165 ST 3249 1m E of Burnham. Loc,
Burnham Without CP. Axbridge RD.
Weston-super-Mare CC.

EDITH WESTON Rutland
122 SK 9205 5m ESE of Oakham. CP,
2,064. Oakhm RD. P Oakhm. Ch e. Rtlnd
and Stamford CC. Once owned by Edith,
wife of Edward the Confessor.

EDLESBOROUGH Bucks
147 SP 9719 3m WSW of Dunstable. CP,
1,334. Wing RD. P Dnstble, Beds. Ch e, m.
Sch p. Buckingham CC. See also Dagnall. Ch
has outstanding woodwork and brasses.

EDLINGHAM Nthmb
71 NU 1109 6m SW of Alnwick. CP, 265.
Alnwck RD. P Alnwck. Ch e.
Berwick-upon-Tweed CC. See also
Abberwick. Partly Nmn ch; ruined 14c cstle.
Moors all round.

EDLINGTON Lincs (L)
114 TF 2371 2m NW of Horncastle. CP,
105. Hncstle RD. Ch e. Hncstle CC.

EDMONDBYERS Co Durham
77/84 NZ 0150 6m W of Consett. CP, 180.
Weardale RD. P Cnstt. Ch e. NW Drhm CC.
Remote moorland vllge with small Nmn ch
containing woodwork from various sources
incl organ case of St Mary Redcliffe, Bristol.
To N, Derwent Reservoir.

EDMONDSHAM Dorset
179 SU 0611 6m WSW of Fordingbridge.
CP, 156. Wimborne and Cranborne RD.
P Wmbne. Ch e.

EDMONDSLEY Co Durham
85 NZ 2349 3m SW of Chester-le-Street. CP,
1,239. Chstr-le-Strt RD. P DRHM. Ch m.
Sch p. Chstr-le-Strt CC.

EDMONDTHORPE Leics
122 SK 8517 5m N of Oakham. Loc,
Wymondham CP. P Melton Mowbray. Ch e.
Ch: 17c monmts.

EDMONTON London
160 TQ 3493 9m NNE of Charing Cross.
Loc, Enfield LB. Edmntn BC. Indstrl distr.
To E, Lee Valley Recreational Pk
development N of sewage wks.

EDNASTON Derbys
120 SK 2342 5m SE of Ashbourne. Loc,
Brailsford CP. E. Mnr*, by Lutyens; gdn*.

EDSTASTON Shrops
118 SJ 5132 2m N of Wem. Loc, Wm
Rural CP. N Shrops RD. Ch e. Oswestry CC.
Telford br over branch of Shropshire Union
Canal. Ch has three notable Nmn doorways.

EDSTONE, GREAT Yorks (N)
92 SE 7084 6m W of Pickering. See Gt
Edstne.

EDVIN LOACH Herefs
129, 130 SO 6658 2m N of Bromyard. CP,
18. Brmyd RD. Ch e. Leominster CC.

EDWALTON Notts
112, 121, 122 SK 5935 4m SSE of
Nottingham. Loc, W Bridgford UD.
P NTTNGHM. Rushcliffe CC
(Nttnghm S BC).

EDWARDSTONE Suffolk (W)
149 TL 9442 4m E of Sudbury. CP, 299.
Cosford RD. Ch e, v. Sdbry and
Woodbridge CC.

EDWINSTOWE Notts
112 SK 6266 2m W of Ollerton. CP, 3,666.
Southwell RD. P Mansfield. Ch e, m2.
Sch p, pe. Newark CC. In Sherwood Forest.
Robin Hood and Maid Marian said to have
been married in the ch.

EDWORTH Beds
147 TL 2240 3m SE of Biggleswade. CP, 48.
Bgglswde RD. Ch e. Mid-Beds CC.

EDWYN RALPH Herefs
129, 130 SO 6457 2m NNW of Bromyard.
CP, 111. Brmyd RD. P Brmyd. Ch e.
Leominster CC.

EFFINGHAM Surrey
170 TQ 1153 4m WSW of Leatherhead. CP,
2,402. Guildford RD. P Lthrhead. Ch e, m,
r. Sch p, s. Dorking CC.

EFFORD Devon
176 SS 8901 3m E of Crediton. Loc,
Shobrooke CP.

EGERTON Kent
172, 184 TQ 9047 3m WSW of Charing. CP,
773. W Ashford RD. P Ashfd. Ch e, b.
Sch pe. Ashfd CC. See also Forstal.

EGERTON Lancs
101 SD 7114 4m N of Bolton. Loc,
Turton UD. P Bromley Cross, Bltn.
Darwen CC.

EGGESFORD Devon
163, 175 SS 6811 9m SSW of S Molton. CP,
89. Crediton RD. Ch e. Tiverton CC
(Torrington). First Forestry Commission
trees planted here in 1919.

EGGINGTON Beds
147 SP 9525 2m E of Leighton Buzzard.
CP, 301. Luton RD. P Lghtn Bzzd. Ch e, m.
Sch i. S Beds CC.

EGGINGTON Derbys
120 SK 2628 4m NNE of Burton-on-Trent.
CP, 355. Repton RD. P DERBY. Ch e, m.
Sch p. Belper CC.

EGGLESCLIFFE Co Durham
85 NZ 4213 4m SSW of Teesside
(Stockton). CP, 2,113. Stcktn RD.
P STCKTN-ON-TEES, Tssde. Ch e, m.
Sch p3, pe s. Easington CC (Sedgefield).
Mdvl br over R Tees.

EGGLESTON Co Durham
84 NZ 0023 5m NW of Barnard Cstle. CP,
352. Bnd Cstle RD. P Bnd Cstle. Ch e, m.
Sch p. Bishop Auckland CC.

EGHAM Surrey
160, 169, 170 TQ 0171 2m W of Staines.
UD, 30,510. P. NW Srry CC (Chertsey).
See also Englefield Grn, Thorpe, Virginia
Water. On R Thames. To NW, Runnymede
(see Wraysbury); Magna Carta Memorial;
RAF Memorial; President Kennedy
Memorial.

EGLETON Rutland
122 SK 8707 1m SE of Oakham. CP, 82.
Oakhm RD. P Oakhm. Ch e. Rtlnd and
Stamford CC. Basically Nmn ch of
exceptional interest.

EGLINGHAM Nthmb
71 NU 1019 6m NW of Alnwick. CP, 361.
Alnwck RD. P Alnwck. Ch e. Sch pe.
Berwick-upon-Tweed CC. See also
E Ditchburrn, N Charlton, S Chltn,
W Dtchbn. Gdns* of 16c—18c hall.

EGLOSHAYLE Cornwall
185, 186 SX 0072 just E of Wadebridge. CP,
376. Wdbrdge and Padstow RD. P Wdbrdge.
Ch e, m2. N Cnwll CC. See also Washaway.

EGLOSKERRY Cornwall
174, 186 SX 2786 4m WNW of Launceston.
CP, 292. Lncstn RD. P Lncstn. Ch e, m.
Sch p. N Cnwll CC. See also Tregeare.

EGMANTON Notts
112 SK 7368 5m E of Ollerton. CP, 183.
Southwell RD. P Newark. Ch e, m. Nwk CC.

EGREMONT Cumb
82 NY 0110 5m SSE of Whitehaven. CP,
6,943. Ennerdale RD. P. Ch e2, m, r, v2.
Sch i, p, pr, s. Whthvn CC. See also Moor
Row. Rems of Nmn cstle.

EGTON Yorks
86 NZ 8006 6m WSW of Whitby. CP, 674.
Whtby RD. P Whtby. Ch e, m. Sch pe.
Cleveland and Whtby CC (Scarborough and
Whtby). See also Egtn Br.

EGTON BRIDGE Yorks (N)
86 NZ 8005 7m WSW of Whitby. Loc,
Egtn CP. Ch r. Sch pr.

EIGHT ASH GREEN Essex
149 TL 9425 3m W of Colchester. CP, 856.
Lexden and Winstree RD. P Clchstr. Ch m.
Sch pe. Clchstr CC.

ELBERTON Glos
155, 156 ST 6088 2m ESE of Severn Rd Br.
Loc, Aust CP. Ch e.

ELBURTON Devon
187 SX 5353 3m ESE of Plymouth. Loc,
Plmth CB. P Plymstock, Plmth. Plmth,
Sutton BC (Tavistock CC).

ELCOMBE Wilts
157 SU 1380 3m SSW of Swindon. Loc,
Wroughton CP.

ELDERNELL Cambs
134 TL 3198 3m ENE of Whittlesey. Loc,
Whttlsy UD.

ELDERSFIELD Worcs
143 SO 8031 6m W of Tewkesbury. CP,
477. Upton upon Severn RD. Ch e. Sch pe.
S Worcs CC. See also Corse Lawn. Pigeon
Hse Farm has moat and dovecote.

ELDON Co Durham
85 NZ 2327 2m SE of Bishop Auckland.
Loc, Shildon UD. P(Eldn Lane), Bshp
Aucklnd.

ELDROTH Yorks (W)
90 SD 7665 4m WNW of Settle. Loc,
Lawkland CP.

ELDWICK Yorks (W)
96 SE 1240 4m E of Keighley. Loc,
Bingley UD. P Bngly.

ELEMORE VALE Co Durham
85 NZ 3545 3m SSE of Houghton-le-Spring.
Loc, Hetton UD.

ELFORD Staffs
120 SK 1810 4m E of Lichfield. CP, 399.
Lchfld RD. P Tamworth. Ch e. Sch p.
Lchfld and Tmwth CC. Ch: monmts.

ELHAM Kent
173 TR 1743 6m NNW of Folkestone. CP,
1,151. Elhm RD. P Canterbury. Ch e, m.
Sch pe. Flkstne and Hythe CC. Stream-side
vllge. 2m SE, Acrise Place, mainly Elizn
brick mansion in large pk.

ELING Hants
180 SU 3612 3m W of Southampton. CP,
18,387. New Forest RD. Ch e. Nw Frst CC
(Eastleigh). See also Ashurst, Calmore,
Testwood, Totton. The orig vllge has
ancient toll br across Bartley Water owned
by Winchester College.

ELKESLEY Notts
103 SK 6875 4m SSW of Retford. CP, 843.
E Rtfd RD. P Rtfd. Ch e, m. Sch p
Bassetlaw CC.

ELKSTONE Glos
143, 144 SO 9612 6m S of Cheltenham. CP,
170. Cirencester RD. P Chltnhm. Ch e.
Crncstr and Tewkesbury CC. Well preserved
Nmn ch.

ELLAND Yorks (W)
96, 102 SE 1021 3m SSE of Halifax. UD,
17,817. P. Sowerby CC. See also Greetland,
Holywell Grn, Sowood Grn, Stainland. Wool
textile tn.

ELLASTONE Staffs
120 SK 1143 5m WSW of Ashbourne. CP, 234. Uttoxeter RD. P Ashbne, Derbyshire. Ch e. Sch pe. Burton CC.

ELLEL Lancs
94 SD 4856 3m S of Lancaster. CP. Lncstr RD. Ch e. Sch pe. Lncstr CC. See also Dolphinholme, Galgate.

ELLENHALL Staffs
119 SJ 8426 5m WNW of Stafford. CP, 159. Stffd RD. P STFFD. Ch e. Stffd and Stone CC. See also Lawnhead.

ELLEN'S GREEN Kent
170, 182 TQ 0935 6m NW of Horsham. Loc, Ewhurst CP.

ELLERBECK Yorks (N)
91 SE 4396 4m ENE of Northallerton. CP, 69. Nthlltn RD. Richmond CC.

ELLERBY Yorks (N)
86 NZ 8014 6m WNW of Whitby. CP, 39. Whtby RD. Cleveland and Whtby CC (Scarborough and Whtby).

ELLERDINE HEATH Shrops
118, 119 SJ 6122 7m NNW of Wellington. Loc, Ercall Magna CP. Wllngtn RD. P(Ellrdne), Telford. Ch m2. Sch p. The Wrekin CC.

ELLERKER Yorks (E)
98 SE 9229 8m SSE of Mkt Weighton. CP, 324. Beverley RD. P Brough. Ch e, m. Haltemprice CC.

ELLERTON Yorks (E)
97, 98 SE 7039 7m NE of Selby. CP, 285. Howden RD. P YORK. Ch e. Hdn CC. See also Aughton.

ELLERTON Yorks (N)
91 SE 2597 5m ESE of Richmond. CP(Ellrtn-on-Swale), 112. Rchmnd RD. Rchmnd CC. Rems of Cistercian abbey.

ELLESBOROUGH Bucks
159 SP 8306 3m NE of Princes Risborough. CP, 819. Wycombe RD. Ch e. Sch p. Aylesbury CC (Wcmbe). See also Butler's Cross, Nash Lee, N Lee. To S over Beacon Hill, Chequers, prime minister's 16c country hse.

ELLESMERE Shrops
118 SJ 3934 8m ENE of Oswestry. CP (Ellesmre Urban), 2,261. N Shrops RD. P. Ch e, c, m, r. Sch p, s. Oswstry CC. The mere (114 acres), one of several in district, imparts seaside resort atmosphere in summer.

ELLESMERE PORT Ches
100, 109 SJ 4077 7m N of Chester. MB, 61,556. P Wirral. Bebington and Ellesmre Pt BC (Wrrl CC). See also Childer Thornton, Gt Sutton, Hooton, Ince, Lit Sttn, Whitby. Docks on Manchester Ship Canal. Large oil refinery at Stanlow.

ELLINGHAM Hants
179 SU 1408 2m N of Ringwood. CP, 595. Rngwd and Fordingbridge RD. Ch e. New Forest CC. See also Blashford, Linford, Linwood, Moyles Ct. 1m E, Moyles Ct, 17c brick hse, now sch.

ELLINGHAM Norfolk
137 TM 3592 2m NE of Bungay. CP, 363. Loddon RD. Ch e. Sch pe. S Nflk CC.

ELLINGHAM Nthmb
71 NU 1725 6m SE of Belford. CP, 430. Blfd RD. Ch e, r. Sch pe. Berwick-upon-Tweed CC. See also Chathill, Newham, Preston.

ELLINGHAM, GREAT Norfolk
136 TM 0196 2m NW of Attleborough. See Gt Ellnghm.

ELLINGSTRING Yorks (N)
91 SE 1783 4m WNW of Masham. CP, 62. Mshm RD. P Ripon. Richmond CC.

ELLINGTON Hunts
134 TL 1671 5m W of Huntingdon. CP, 289. Hntngdn RD. P HNTNGDN. Ch e. Hunts CC.

ELLINGTON Nthmb
78 NZ 2791 6m NE of Morpeth. CP, 1,197. Mpth RD. P Mpth. Sch p. Mpth CC. See also Linton Colliery.

ELLISFIELD Hants
168, 169 SU 6345 4m S of Basingstoke. CP, 218. Bsngstke RD. P Bsngstke. Ch e. Bsngstke CC.

ELLISTOWN Leics
121 SK 4310 2m S of Coalville. Loc, Ibstock CP. P LEICESTER. Ch e, r.

ELLOUGH Suffolk (E)
137 TM 4486 3m SSE of Beccles. CP, 79.
Wainford RD. Ch e. Lowestoft CC.

ELLOUGHTON Yorks (E)
98 SE 9428 10m W of Hull. CP, 3,174.
Beverley RD. P Brough. Ch e, c.
Haltemprice CC. See also Brough. SW, on
the Humber: bird sanctuary.

ELLWOOD Glos
155, 156 SO 5908 6m ESE of Monmouth.
Loc, W Dean CP. W Dn RD. Ch m2, v.
Sch p. W Glos CC.

ELM Cambs
124 TF 4707 2m SSE of Wisbech. CP,
2,492. Wsbch RD. P Wsbch. Ch e. Sch pe3.
Isle of Ely CC. See also Friday Br. Black
Horse Inn, 1665.

ELMBRIDGE Worcs
130, 131 SO 8967 3m N of Droitwich. CP,
303. Drtwch RD. Ch e. Worcester BC.

ELMDON Essex
148 TL 4639 5m W of Saffron Walden. CP,
490. Sffrn Wldn RD. P Sffrn Wldn. Ch e.
Sch pe. Sffrn Wldn CC. See also Br Grn
Duddenhoe End. Deeply rural.

ELMDON Warwicks
131 SP 1783 7m ESE of Birmingham. Loc,
Solihull CB, Meriden RD. P(Elmdn Hth),
Slhll. Slhll BC (CC), Mrdn CC. Intntl airpt
(Bmnghm).

ELMERS END London
171 TQ 3668 3m W of Bromley. Loc,
Brmly LB. Beckenham BC.

ELMESTHORPE Leics
132 SP 4696 3m ENE of Hinckley. CP, 361.
Blaby RD. Ch e. Blby CC (Harborough).
Site of deserted mdvl vllge still clearly
discernible.

ELM, GREAT Som
166 ST 7449 2m NW of Frome. See Gt Elm.

ELMHURST Staffs
120 SK 1112 2m N of Lichfield.
CP(Curborough and Elmhst), 211.
Lchfld RD. Sch p. Lchfld and
Tamworth CC.

ELMLEY CASTLE Worcs
143, 144 SO 9841 4m WSW of Evesham.

CP, 310. Pershore RD. P Pshre. Ch e.
Sch pe. S Worcs CC. See also Kersoe. Vllge
with stream beside main st. Ch: monmts.

ELMLEY LOVETT Worcs
130 SO 8669 4m ESE of Stourport. CP,
265. Droitwich RD. Ch e. Worcester BC.

ELMORE Glos
143 SO 7815 4m SW of Gloucester. CP,
303. Glcstr RD. P GLCSTR. Ch e. Sch pe.
Stroud CC. See also Elmre Back, Farleys
End. In loop of R Severn. Elmre Ct*,
mainly Elizn hse.

ELMORE BACK Glos
143 SO 7616 4m WSW of Gloucester. Loc,
Elmre CP. Timber-framed cottages.

ELMSCOTT Devon
174 SS 2321 10m N of Bude. Loc,
Hartland CP. P Htlnd, Bideford. Ch m.

ELMSETT Suffolk (W)
149 TM 0546 3m NE of Hadleigh. CP, 363.
Cosford RD. P Ipswich. Ch e, m. Sch pe.
Sudbury and Woodbridge CC.

ELMSTEAD Essex
149 TM 0626 4m E of Colchester. CP, 854.
Tendring RD. P Clchstr. Ch e, m2. Sch pe.
Harwich CC. See also Elmstd Mkt.

ELMSTEAD MARKET Essex
149, 162 TM 0624 4m E of Colchester. Loc,
Elmstd CP.

ELMSTONE Kent
173 TR 2660 5m WNW of Sandwich. Loc,
Preston CP. Ch e.

ELMSTONE HARDWICKE Glos
143, 144 SO 9226 3m NNW of Cheltenham.
CP, 235. Chltnhm RD. Ch e. Cirencester and
Tewkesbury CC. Vllge situated partly in
Uckington CP, incl ch.

ELMSWELL Suffolk (W)
136 TL 9863 5m NW of Stowmarket. CP,
1,177. Thedwastre RD. P Bury St Edmunds.
Ch e, b, m. Sch p. Bury St Eds CC.

ELMSWELL Yorks (E)
98 SE 9958 2m WNW of Driffield. Loc,
Garton CP.

ELMTON Derbys
112 SK 5073 6m SW of Worksop. CP,
6,788. Clowle RD. Ch e. Bolsover CC. See
also Creswell.

ELSDON Nthmb
77 NY 9393 3m E of Otterburn. CP, 249.
Rothbury RD. P NEWCASTLE UPON
TYNE. Ch e. Sch pe.
Berwick-upon-Tweed CC. Large grn; hills all
round. 14c fortified parsonage.

ELSECAR Yorks (W)
102, 103 SE 3800 5m SSE of Barnsley. Loc,
Hoyland Nether UD. P Bnsly.

ELSENHAM Essex
148 TL 5326 4m NE of Bishop's Stortford.
CP, 832. Saffron Walden RD. P Bshp's
Sttfd, Herts. Ch e, f. Sch pe. Sffrn Wldn CC.
Partly Nmn ch. Stansted airpt nearby.

ELSFIELD Oxon
145/158 SP 5410 3m NNE of Oxford. CP,
113. Bullingdon RD. P OXFD. Ch e.
Mid-Oxon CC (Henley).

ELSHAM Lincs (L)
104 TA 0312 4m NE of Brigg. CP, 257.
Glanford Brgg RD. P Brgg. Ch e, r. Brgg and
Scunthorpe CC (Brgg).

ELSING Norfolk
125 TG 0516 4m ENE of E Dereham. CP,
251. Mitford and Launditch RD. P Drhm.
Ch e, m. Sch p. SW Nflk CC. Ch: brass of
1347 considered one of finest in England.

ELSLACK Yorks (W)
95 SD 9349 4m WSW of Skipton. CP, 94.
Skptn RD. P Skptn. Sch p. Skptn CC.

ELSTEAD Surrey
169 SU 9043 4m W of Godalming. CP,
2,163. Hambledon RD. P Gdlmng. Ch e, c.
Sch pe. Farnham CC. Old br spans R Wey.
Ggn water mill on site of mdvl one.

ELSTED Sussex (W)
181 SU 8119 5m ESE of Petersfield. CP,
188. Midhurst RD. P Mdhst. Ch e, v. Sch pe.
Chichester CC (Horsham).

ELSTON Notts
112 SK 7648 5m SW of Newark. CP, 390.
Nwk RD. P Nwk. Ch e. Sch pe. Nwk CC.

ELSTONE Devon
163 SS 6716 6m SSW of S Molton. Loc,
Chulmleigh CP.

ELSTOW Beds
147 TL 0547 2m S of Bedford. CP, 629.

Bdfd RD. P BDFD. Ch e, bc. Sch p, s.
Mid-Beds CC. John Bunyan, 1628–88, born
here. Ch has brass of an abbess.

ELSTREE Herts
160 TQ 1795 1m SW of Borehamwood. CP.
Elstree RD. P Brhmwd. Ch e, c. Sch pe.
S Herts CC (Barnet CC, SW Herts CC). See
also Brhmwd. Film studios.

ELSTRONWICK Yorks (E)
99 TA 2232 8m ENE of Hull. CP, 289.
Holderness RD. P Hll. Ch m.
Bridlington CC. See also Lelley.

ELSWICK Lancs
94 SD 4238 7m E of Blackpool. CP, 465.
Fylde RD. P Preston. Ch c. S Flde CC.

ELSWORTH Cambs
134 TL 3163 5m S of St Ives. CP, 476.
Chesterton RD. P CAMBRIDGE. Ch e, b2.
Sch pe. Cambs CC.

ELTERWATER Westm
88, 89 NY 3204 3m W of Ambleside. Loc,
Lakes UD. Westm CC.

ELTHAM London
161, 171 TQ 4374 4m SE of Greenwich.
Loc, Grnwch LB. Woolwich W BC. Elthm
Palace (A.M.). Winter Gdn*, Avery Hill.

ELTISLEY Cambs
134 TL 2759 5m E of St Neots. CP, 253.
Chesterton RD. P HUNTINGDON. Ch e, m.
Cambs CC. Large grn-cum-cricket-grnd.
Oliver Cromwell's sister Jane married in ch
in 1636.

ELTON Ches
100, 109 SJ 4575 7m NE of Chester. CP,
478. Chstr RD. P CHSTR. Ch m. Sch p. City
of Chstr CC.

ELTON Co Durham
85 NZ 4017 3m WSW of Teesside
(Stockton). CP. Stcktn RD. Ch e.
Easington CC (Sedgefield). Tiny ch, partly
Nmn.

ELTON Derbys
111 SK 2260 5m W of Matlock. CP, 444.
Bakewell RD. P Mtlck. Ch e, m2, v. Sch pe.
W Derbys CC.

ELTON Herefs
129 SO 4570 4m SW of Ludlow. CP, 51.
Leominster and Wigmore RD. Ch e.
Lmnstr CC.

ELTON Hunts
134 TL 0893 5m NE of Oundle. CP, 550.
Norman Cross RD. P PETERBOROUGH.
Ch e, m. Sch pe. Hunts CC. Ch: twr,
monmts. Eltn Hall has Tdr gateway.

ELTON Notts
112, 122 SK 7638 9m W of Grantham. CP,
67. Bingham RD. P NOTTINGHAM. Ch e.
Rushcliffee CC (Carlton).

ELTRINGHAM Nthmb
77, 78 NZ 0862 1m W of Prudhoe. Loc,
Prdhoe UD.

ELVASTON Derbys
112, 121 SK 4132 4m SE of Derby. CP.
SE Derbys RD. Ch e. SE Derbys CC. See
also Ambaston, Thulston. E. Cstle*,
originally 17c, redesigned by James Wyatt
early 19c. Grnds* contain lake and famous
topiary work.

ELVEDEN Suffolk (W)
136 TL 8179 4m SW of Thetford. CP, 370.
Mildenhall RD. P Thtfd, Norfolk. Ch e.
Sch pe. Bury St Edmunds CC. Breckland
vllge in forestry area. Ggn hall altered in
Indian style 19c, much enlarged early 20c.
Iveagh estate.

ELVINGTON Kent
173 TR 2750 6m W of Deal. Loc, Eythorne
CP. P Dover. Ch r, v. Sch p. Mining vllge.

ELVINGTON Yorks (E)
97, 98 SE 7047 7m ESE of York. CP, 386.
Derwent RD. P YK. Ch e, m. Sch pe.
Howden CC.

ELWICK Co Durham
85 NZ 4532 3m W of Hartlepool. CP.
Stockton RD. P Htlpl. Ch e. Sch pe.
Easington CC (Sedgefield).

ELWICK Nthmb
64, 71 NU 1136 2m NNE of Belford. Loc,
Middleton CP.

ELWORTH Ches
110 SJ 7361 1m W of Sandbach. Loc,
Sndbch UD. P Sndbch.

ELWORTHY Som
164 ST 0834 5m S of Watchet. CP, 82.

Williton RD. Ch e. Bridgwater CC. 1m SE,
Willett's Twr, folly of 1820 blt to look like
ruined ch.

ELY Cambs
135 TL 5480 15m NNE of Cambridge. UD,
9,969. P. Isle of Ely CC. See also
Chettisham, Prickwillow, Queen Adelaide,
Stuntney. Vast cathedral, Norman to Perp;
visible at great distance across Fens. Tn was
home of Oliver Cromwell for ten years.

EMBERTON Bucks
146 SP 8849 1m S of Olney. CP, 465.
Newport Pagnell RD. P Olney. Ch e. Sch p.
Buckingham CC.

EMBLETON Co Durham
85 NZ 4229 6m WSW of Hartlepool. CP, 80.
Sedgefield RD. Drhm CC (Sdgfld).

EMBLETON Cumb
82 NY 1730 3m E of Cockermouth. CP,
306. Cckrmth RD. P Cckrmth. Ch e, m.
Sch pe. Workington CC.

EMBLETON Nthmb
71 NU 2322 7m NNE of Alnwick. CP, 562.
Alnwck RD. P Alnwck. Ch e, m, v. Sch pe.
Berwick-upon-Tweed CC. See also Christon
Bank. 1m E, Embltn Bay; the sand and rock
coast from here to N is NT. At S end of
Bay, Dunstanburgh Cstle (see Craster).

EMBOROUGH Som
166 ST 6151 5m WSW of Radstock. CP,
154. Shepton Mallet RD. P Bath. Ch e.
Wells CC.

EMBSAY Yorks (W)
96 SE 0053 2m NE of Skipton. CP(Embsay
w Eastby), 1,060. Skptn RD. P Skptn.
Ch e, m, v. Sch pe. Skptn CC.

EMERY DOWN Hants
180 SU 2808 just W of Lyndhurst. Loc,
New Forest RD. P Lndhst. Ch e.
Nw Frst CC.

EMLEY Yorks (W)
102 SE 2413 5m S of Dewsbury. Loc,
Denby Dale UD. P Huddersfield.

EMMINGTON Oxon
159 SP 7402 3m SE of Thame. Loc,
Chinnor CP. Ch e.

EMNETH Norfolk
124 TF 4807 2m SE of Wisbech. CP, 1,886.
Marshland RD. P Wsbch, Cambs. Ch e, m2.
Sch ie, j. NW Nflk CC (King's Lynn). See
also Gaultree, Holly End.

EMNETH HUNGATE Norfolk
124 TF 5107 4m ESE of Wisbech. Loc,
Emneth CP.

EMPINGHAM Rutland
122/123 SK 9508 5m W of Stamford. CP,
643. Oakham RD. P Oakhm. Ch e, m. Rtlnd
and Stmfd CC. Large basically 13c ch in
attractive vllge. 2m NE, site of lost vllge of
Hardwick, and of Battle of Losecoat Field,
1470.

EMPSHOTT Hants
169, 181 SU 7531 6m SSE of Alton. Loc,
Hawkley CP. P Liss. Ch e.

EMSWORTH Hants
181 SU 7406 2m E of Havant. Loc, Hvnt
and Waterloo UD. P. Yachting; oyster
fisheries.

ENBORNE Berks
158 SU 4365 3m WSW of Newbury. CP,
553. Nbry RD. Ch e, m2. Sch pe. Nbry CC.

ENDERBY Leics
132 SP 5399 5m SW of Leicester. CP,
4,024. Blaby RD. P LCSTR. Ch e, c, m, v.
Sch p, s. Blby CC (Harborough).

ENDMOOR Westm
89 SD 5384 5m SSE of Kendal. Loc,
Preston Richard CP. S Westm RD. P Kndl.
Sch pe. Westm CC.

ENDON Staffs
110 SJ 9253 6m NNE of Stoke-on-Trent.
CP(Endn and Stanley), 2,697. Leek RD.
P Stke-on-Trent. Ch e, m. Sch pe, s. Lk CC.
See also Endn Bank.

ENDON BANK Staffs
110 SJ 9253 6m NNE of Stoke-on-Trent.
Loc, Endn and Stanley CP. Ch e.

ENFIELD London
160 TQ 3296 10m N of Charing Cross. LB,
266,788. P Middx. BCs: Edmonton,
Enfld N, Southgate (Edmntn, Enfld E,
Enfld W, Sthgte). See also Botany Bay,

Cockfosters, Edmntn, Fortyhill, Palmer's
Grn, Ponders End, Sthgte, Winchmore Hill.
Indstrl distr. Lee Valley Reservoirs to E.
Forty Hall* (Forty Hill), 17c.

ENFORD Wilts
167 SU 1351 6m SSW of Pewsey. CP, 685.
Psy RD. P Psy. Ch e, b, m. Sch pe.
Devizes CC. See also E Chisenbury.

ENGINE COMMON Glos
156 ST 6984 9m ESE of Severn Rd Br. Loc,
Sodbury RD. S Glos CC.

ENGINE, THE Lincs (H)
123 TF 2508 7m NE of Peterborough. Loc,
Crowland CP.

ENGLEFIELD Berks
158 SU 6272 3m S of Pangbourne. CP, 186.
Bradfield RD. P Reading. Ch e. Sch pe.
Newbury CC. Site of skirmish between
Alfred and the Danes in 870.

ENGLEFIELD GREEN Surrey
160, 169, 170 SU 9971 1m W of Egham.
Loc, Eghm UD. P Eghm. To NE,
Runnymede; see Eghm, Wraysbury.

ENGLISH BICKNOR Glos
142 SO 5815 5m ENE of Monmouth. CP,
457. W Dean RD. P Coleford. Ch e. Sch pe.
W Glos CC. Largely Nmn ch is inside rems
of motte and bailey.

ENGLISHCOMBE Som
166 ST 7162 3m SW of Bath. CP, 351.
Bathavon RD. P Bth. Ch e, m. Sch p.
N Som CC. See also Inglesbatch. To NE,
section of Wansdyke, ancient earthwork (see
Stanton Priors).

ENGLISH FRANKTON Shrops
118 SJ 4529 4m W of Wem. Loc,
Cockshutt CP.

ENHAM ALAMEIN Hants
168 SU 3649 3m N of Andover. Loc,
Andvr MB. P Andvr. Rehabilitation centre
for war-disabled set up in 1920s. Name
changed from Knight's Enham 1945.

ENMORE Som
165 ST 2334 4m WSW of Bridgwater. CP,
253. Brdgwtr RD. P Brdgwtr. Ch e, v.
Sch pe. Brdgwater CC. Enmre Cstle blt late
18c in pseudo-mdvl style; part survives.

ENNERDALE BRIDGE Cumb
82 NY 0715 6m ESE of Whitehaven. Loc,
Ennrdle and Kinniside CP. Ennrdle RD.
P Cleator. Ch e. Sch pe. Whthvn CC.

ENSDON Shrops
118 SJ 4016 6m WNW of Shrewsbury. Loc,
Montford CP.

ENSIS Devon
163 SS 5626 4m S of Barnstaple. Loc,
Tawstock CP.

ENSON Staffs
119 SJ 9428 4m NNE of Stafford. CP(Salt
and Ensn), 357. Stffd RD. Stffd and
Stone CC.

ENSTONE Oxon
145 SP 3724 4m ESE of Chipping Norton.
CP, 927. Chppng Ntn RD. P OXFORD.
Ch e, m, r. Sch p. Banbury CC. See also
Cleveley, Gagingwell, Lidstone. R Glyme
divides vllges into two: Ch Enstne and Neat
Enstne. 14c tithe barn. Ch has library of
chained books.

ENVILLE Staffs
130 SO 8286 5m WNW of Stourbridge. CP,
515. Seisdon RD. P Stbrdge, Worcs. Ch e.
Sch pe. SW Staffs CC (Brierley Hill).

EPPERSTONE Notts
112 SK 6548 7m NE of Nottingham. CP,
455. Southwell RD. P NTTNGHM. Ch e, m.
Sch pe. Newark CC.

EPPING Essex
161 TL 4602 5m S of Harlow. UD, 11,681.
P. Eppng Forest CC (Eppng). See also
Coopersale Cmmn, Fiddlers Hmlt. Mostly
rsdntl for London. Eppng Forest property
of City of Lndn.

EPPING GREEN Essex
161 TL 4305 2m NW of Epping. Loc,
Eppng Upland CP. P Eppng. Ch c.

EPPING GREEN Herts
160 TL 2906 4m SSW of Hertford. Loc, Lit
Berkhamsted CP. P HTFD.

EPPING UPLAND Essex
161 TL 4404 2m NW of Epping. CP, 808.
Eppng and Ongar RD. Ch e. Eppng
Forest CC (Eppng). See also Eppng Grn.

EPPLEBY Yorks (N)
85 NZ 1713 7m W of Darlington. CP, 232.

Richmond RD. P Rchmnd. Ch m. Sch pe.
Rchmnd CC.

EPSOM Surrey
170 TQ 2060 3m SW of Sutton. UD(Epsm
and Ewell), 72,054. P. Epsm and Ewell BC
(Epsm CC). Famous racecourse to SE.

EPWELL Oxon
145 SP 3540 6m W of Banbury. CP, 184.
Bnbry RD. P Bnbry. Ch e, m. Bnbry CC.

EPWORTH Lincs (L)
104 SE 7803 8m SW of Scunthorpe. CP,
1,975. Isle of Axholme RD. P Doncaster,
Yorkshire. Ch e, b, m2. Sch p, pe, s.
Gainsborough CC. Childhood home of John
and Charles Wesley. Old rectory* belongs to
Methodist Ch.

ERIDGE GREEN Sussex (E)
171, 183 TQ 5535 3m SW of Tunbridge
Wells. Loc, Frant CP. P TNBRDGE WLLS.
Ch e. Estate vllge at NW corner of Eridge
Pk.

ERISWELL Suffolk (W)
135 TL 7278 7m SW of Brandon. CP, 262.
Mildenhall RD. P Brndn. Ch e, m. Sch pe.
Bury St Edmunds CC.

ERITH London
161, 171 TQ 5177 3m NW of Dartford.
Loc, Bexley LB. P Kent. Erith and
Crayford BC. Indstrl distr on S bank of
Thames; cables, electrical equipment, etc.
Brick wks and sand and gravel wks on
marshes to E. Thamesmead housing
development to NW.

ERLESTOKE Wilts
167 ST 9653 5m SW of Devizes. CP, 226.
Dvzs RD. P Dvzs. Ch e. Sch pe. Dvzs CC.
Many hses decorated with 18c sculpture.
Erlestke Pk is a detention centre.

ERMINGTON Devon
187, 188 SX 6353 2m S of Ivybridge. CP,
1,245. Plympton St Mary RD. P Ivybridge.
Ch e, m, r, v. Sch p. W Dvn CC (Tavistock).
See also Lee Mill Estate. Ch has crooked
spire.

ERPINGHAM Norfolk
126 TG 1931 3m N of Aylsham. CP, 451.
Erpnghm RD. P NORWICH, NOR 46Y.
Ch e, v. Sch pe. N Nflk CC. See also
Calthorpe. Ch: brass, c 1415.

ERWARTON Suffolk (E)
150 TM 2134 7m SE of Ipswich.
CP(Arwarton), 154. Samford RD. P Ipswch.
Ch e. Sudbury and Woodbridge CC.
Extraordinary Jcbn gateway to hall.

ERYHOLME Yorks (N)
85 NZ 3209 4m SE of Darlington. CP, 153.
Croft RD. Ch e. Richmond CC.

ESCOMB Co Durham
85 NZ 1830 1m WNW of Bishop Auckland.
Loc, Bshp Aucklnd UD. P Bshp Aucklnd.
Saxon ch.

ESCRICK Yorks (E)
97, 98 SE 6243 6m SSE of York. CP, 443.
Derwent RD. P YK. Ch e. Sch pe.
Howden CC. Escrck Pk, 18c mansion, now
girls' public sch. Famous rhododendron
wds.

ESH Co Durham
85 NZ 1944 3m SE of Lanchester. CP,
5,728. Lnchstr RD. P DRHM. Ch e, r2.
Sch p, pe, pr. NW Drhm CC. See also Langley
Pk, Quebec.

ESHER Surrey
170 TQ 1364 4m SW of Kingston. UD,
64,186. P. Eshr BC (CC). See also Claygate,
Cobhm, Downside, E Molesey, Long
Ditton, Oxshott, Stoke D'Abernon, Thames
Dttn, W Mlsy. Busy rsdntl and shopping tn.
To N, Sandown Pk racecourse. To SW,
Claremont*, 18c hse now a sch, and Clmnt
Wds (NT)*, parkland laid out in 18c by
William Kent.

ESHOLT Yorks (W)
96 SE 1840 5m NNE of Bradford. Loc,
Brdfd CB. P Shipley. Brdfd N BC. Eshlt
Hall, early 18c hse, now part of Brdfd
sewage wks.

ESHOTT Nthmb
71 NZ 2097 6m SW of Amble. Loc,
Thirston CP. Morpeth RD. Ch m. Mpth CC.

ESHTON Yorks (W)
95 SD 9356 4m NW of Skipton. CP, 50.
Skptn RD. Skptn CC.

ESH WINNING Co Durham
85 NZ 1941 5m W of Durham. Loc,
Brandon and Byshottles UD. P DRHM.
Sch p.

ESKDALE GREEN Cumb
88 NY 1400 6m E of Seascale. Loc,
Eskdle CP. Millom RD. P(Eskdle),
Holmrook. Ch e. Sch pe. Whitehaven CC.

ESPRICK Lancs
94 SD 4036 6m E of Blackpool. Loc,
Greenhalgh-w-Thistleton CP. Sch pe.

ESSENDINE Rutland
123 TF 0412 4m NNE of Stamford. CP,
151. Ketton RD. P Stmfd, Lincs. Ch e.
Rtlnd and Stmfd CC. On exceptionally fast
stretch of rly line.

ESSENDON Herts
160 TL 2708 3m E of Hatfield. CP.
Htfld RD. P Htfld. Ch e. Sch pe. Welwyn
and Htfld CC (Hertford). Ch: Wedgwood
font, 1780.

ESSINGTON Staffs
119 SJ 9603 4m NW of Walsall. CP, 4,109.
Cannock RD. P Wolverhampton. Ch e, m2.
Sch p, pe. SW Staffs (Cnnck).

ESTON Yorks (N)
86 NZ 5518 4m ESE of Teesside
(Middlesborough). Loc, Tssde CB.
P MDDLSBRGH, Tssde. Tssde, Redcar BC.

ESWORTHY Devon
164 SS 8722 5m W of Bampton. Loc,
Oakford CP.

ETAL Nthmb
64, 71 NT 9239 5m E of Coldstream. Loc,
Ford CP. P Cornhill-on-Tweed. Ch e, v.
Vllge of charm on R Till. Rems of 14c cstle.

ETCHILHAMPTON Wilts
167 SU 0460 3m ESE of Devizes. CP, 161.
Dvzs RD. P Dvzs. Ch e. Sch pe. Dvzs CC.

ETCHINGHAM Sussex (E)
183, 184 TQ 7126 7m NNW of Battle. CP,
674. Bttle RD. P. Ch e, m. Sch pe. Rye CC.
Large 14c ch: brasses. Haremere Hall*, Jcbn
hse containing Oriental treasures.

ETCHINGHILL Kent
173 TR 1639 3m N of Hythe. Loc,
Lyminge CP.

ETCHINGHILL Staffs
120 SK 0218 1m W of Rugeley. Loc,
Rgly UD. P Rgly. On E edge of Cannock
Chase.

ETHERLEY DENE Co Durham
85 NZ 1928 1m W of Bishop Auckland.
Loc, Bshp Aucklnd UD. P Bshp Aucklnd.

ETON Bucks
159, 160, 170 SU 9677 2m SSW of Slough.
UD, 3,954. P Windsor, Berks. Etn and
Slgh BC. Home of famous public sch, with
some fine bldngs*, esp the chpl.

ETON WICK Bucks
159 SU 9478 2m WSW of Slough. Loc,
Etn UD. P Windsor, Berks. Sch pe.

ETTINGTON Warwicks
144 SP 2648 6m SE of Stratford. CP, 716.
Strtfd-on-Avon RD. P Strtfd-upon-Avn.
Ch e, f, m. Sch pe. Strtfd-on-Avn CC
(Strtfd).

ETTON Hunts
123 TF 1406 6m NW of Peterborough. CP,
161. Ptrbrgh RD. P PTRBRGH. Ch e.
Ptrbrgh BC (CC). Stone Fenside vllge. Tdr
mnr hse. 1¼m S, moated Woodcroft Cstle,
13c and later, besieged in Civil War.

ETTON Yorks (E)
98 SE 9843 4m NW of Beverley. CP, 313.
Bvrly RD.   P Bvrly. Ch e, m.
Haltemprice CC. Ch has very fine Nmn twr
arch.

ETWALL Derbys
120 SK 2631 6m WSW of Derby. CP, 1,866.
Repton RD. Ch e, m. Sch p, s. Belper CC.
E. Hsptl, almshouses of 1681.

EUSTON Suffolk (W)
136 TL 8979 3m SE of Thetford. CP, 214.
Thingoe RD. P Thtfd, Norfolk. Ch e. Bury
St Edmunds CC. Grafton estate.

EUXTON Lancs
100 SD 5519 2m NW of Chorley. CP, 3,265.
Chly RD. P Chly. Ch e, m, r. Sch pe, pr.
Chly CC. See also Shaw Grn.

EVEDON Lincs (K)
113 TF 0947 2m ENE of Sleaford.
CP (Ewerby and Evedn), 308.
E Kesteven RD. Ch e. Grantham CC.

EVENLEY Northants
145, 146 SP 5834 1m S of Brackley. CP,
377. Brckly RD. P Brckly. Ch e.
Daventry CC (S Nthnts).

EVENLODE Glos
144 SP 2229 2m SSE of Moreton-in-Marsh.
CP, 202. N Cotswold RD. P Mtn-in-Msh.
Ch e. Cirencester and Tewkesbury CC.
Crafts exhibition in Old Sch.

EVENWOOD Co Durham
85 NZ 1525 4m SW of Bishop Auckland.
CP(Evnwd and Barony), 3,156. Barnard
Cstle RD. P Bshp Aucklnd. Ch e, c, m6.
Sch p, pe. Bshp Aucklnd CC.

EVERCREECH Som
166 ST 6438 3m NW of Bruton. CP, 1,394.
Shepton Mallet RD. P Shptn Mllt. Ch e, m.
Sch pe. Wells CC. See also Chesterblade,
Stoney Stratton. Famous ch twr.

EVERDON Northants
132, 133 SP 5957 3m SSE of Daventry. CP,
364. Dvntry RD. P Dvntry. Ch e. Sch p.
Dvntry CC (S Nthnts). See also Lit Evrdn.

EVERINGHAM Yorks (E)
98 SE 8042 4m S of Pocklington. CP, 302.
Pcklngtn RD. P YORK. Ch e, r.
Howden CC. Evrnghhm Pk is one of the
Duke of Norfolk's seats.

EVERLEIGH Wilts
167 SU 2053 5m SSE of Pewsey. CP, 202.
Psy RD. Ch e. Sch pe. Devizes CC.

EVERSDEN, GREAT Cambs
148 TL 3653 6m SW of Cambridge. See Gt
Evrsdn.

EVERSHOLT Beds
147 SP 9932 4m SW of Ampthill. CP, 450.
Ampthll RD. P Bletchley, Bucks. Ch e, m.
Sch p. Mid-Beds CC.

EVERSHOT Dorset
177, 178 ST 5704 7m S of Yeovil. CP, 258.
Beaminster RD. P Dorchester. Ch e, v.
Sch pe. W Dst CC.

EVERSLEY Hants
169 SU 7762 8m SSE of Reading. CP,
1,170. Hartley Wintney RD. P Basingstoke.
Ch e, b. Sch pe. Bsngstke CC (Aldershot).
See also Evrsley Cross. Charles Kingsley
rector here 1844—75, buried in churchyard.

EVERSLEY CROSS Hants
169 SU 7961 9m SSE of Reading. Loc,
Eversley CP.

EVERTON Beds
147 TL 2051 4m NNE of Biggleswade. CP, 215. Bgglswde RD. P Sandy. Ch e. Sch p. Mid-Beds CC. Part of vllge formerly in Hunts (Hunts CC).

EVERTON Hants
180 SZ 2994 2m WSW of Lymington. Loc, Lmngtn MB. P Lmngtn.

EVERTON Notts
103 SK 6991 6m N of Retford. CP, 575. E Rtfd RD. P Doncaster, Yorkshire. Ch e, m. Sch p. Bassetlaw CC.

EVESBATCH Herefs
143 SO 6848 5m SSE of Bromyard. CP, 88. Brmyd RD. Ch e. Leominster CC.

EVESHAM Worcs
144 SP 0343 13m SE of Worcester. MB, 13,847. P. S Worcs CC. Centre of fruit and vegetable growing area, Vale of Evshm. Riverside gdns beside R Avon; many boats. Two old chs, rems of Benedictine abbey*. Site of battle 1265.

EWDEN VILLAGE Yorks (W)
102 SK 2796 7m NW of Sheffield. Loc, Stockbridge UD.

EWELL Surrey
170 TQ 2163 4m SSE of Kingston. UD(Epsom and Ewell), 72,054. P Epsm. Epsm and Ewell BC (Epsm CC). See also Worcester Pk.

EWELL MINNIS Kent
173 TR 2743 4m WNW of Dover. Loc, Alkham CP.

EWELME Oxon
158, 159 SU 6491 3m ENE of Wallingford. CP, 542. Bullingdon RD. P OXFORD. Ch e. Sch pe. Henley CC. Watercress beds. Perp ch: 11ft wooden font cover; tomb of Alice Chaucer. 15c sch and almshouses.

EWEN Glos
157 SU 0097 3m SSW of Cirencester. Loc, Kemble CP.

EWERBY Lincs (K)
113 TF 1247 4m ENE of Sleaford. CP(Ewrby and Evedon), 308. E Kesteven RD. P Slfd. Ch e, m. Sch pe. Grantham CC.

EWHURST Surrey
170, 182 TQ 0940 7m SW of Dorking. CP, 2,169. Hambledon RD. P Cranleigh. Ch e, v. Sch pe. Guildford CC. See also Ellen's Grn.

EWHURST Sussex (E)
184 TQ 7924 6m NNE of Battle. CP, 799. Bttle RD. P Robertsbridge. Ch e. Rye CC. See also Cripps Corner, Staple Cross.

EWORTHY Devon
175 SX 4495 9m W of Okehampton. Loc, Germansweek CP. Ch m.

EWSHOT Hants
169 SU 8149 3m W of Aldershot. Loc, Crondall CP. P Farnham, Surrey. Ch e. Sch p.

EWYAS HAROLD Herefs
142 SO 3828 11m NNE of Abergavenny. CP, 504. Dore and Bredwardine RD. P HEREFORD. Ch e, b, m. Sch p. Hrfd CC.

EXBOURNE Devon
175 SS 6001 4m NNE of Okehampton. CP, 282. Okhmpton RD. P Okhmptn. Ch e, m. Sch pe. W Dvn CC (Torrington).

EXBRIDGE Devon and Som
164 SS 9324 3m SSE of Dulverton. Alternative spelling for Exebridge, qv.

EXBURY Hants
180 SU 4200 3m SW of Fawley. CP(Exbury and Lepe), 273. New Forest RD. P SOUTHAMPTON. Ch e. Nw Frst CC. Woodland gdns*, surrounding modern Exbury Hse.

EXEBRIDGE Devon and Som
164 SS 9324 3m SSE of Dulverton. Loc, Tiverton RD, Dlvtn RD. P Dlvtn. Tvtn CC, Taunton CC.

EXELBY Yorks (N)
91 SE 2987 2m ESE of Bedale. CP(Exlby, Leeming and Newton), 2,097. Bdle RD. Ch m. Sch pe. Thirsk and Malton CC. See also Londonderry.

EXETER Devon
176 SX 9192 64m SW of Bristol. CB, 95,598. P. Extr BC. See also Alphington, Pinhoe, Topsham, Whipton. Ancient city and county capital, much damaged in World War II. Cathedral: Dec; Nmn twrs. 15c guildhall. Scant rems of Nmn Rougemont Cstle.

EXFORD Som
164 SS 8538 9m SW of Minehead. CP, 453.
Dulverton RD. P Mnhd. Ch e, m. Sch pe.
Taunton CC. Hunting centre.

EXHALL Warwicks
131 SP 1055 2m SSE of Alcester. CP, 162.
Alcstr RD. P Alcstr. Ch e, m2. Sch p2, pr.
Stratford-on-Avon CC (Strtfd).

EXMINSTER Devon
176 SX 9487 3m SSE of Exeter. CP, 3,302.
St Thomas RD. P Extr. Ch e, m, v. Sch p.
Tiverton CC.

EXMOUTH Devon
176 SY 0080 9m SE of Exeter. UD, 25,815.
P. Honiton CC. See also Littleham. Resort
with sandy beaches. 2m N, A La Ronde*,
late 18c hse of curious architecture.

EXNING Suffolk (W)
135 TL 6265 2m NW of Newmarket. Loc,
Nmkt UD. P Nmkt.

EXTON Devon
176 SX 9886 6m SE of Exeter. Loc,
Woodbury CP. P Extr.

EXTON Hants
168 SU 6120 10m SE of Winchester. CP,
244. Droxford RD. Ch e. Petersfield CC.

EXTON Rutland
122 SK 9211 4m ENE of Oakham. CP, 703.
Oakhm RD. P Oakhm. Ch e, r. Rtlnd and
Stamford CC. Ch: monmts.

EXTON Som
164 SS 9233 4m N of Dulverton. CP, 248.
Dlvtn RD. Ch e. Taunton CC.

EYAM Derbys
111 SK 2176 5m N of Bakewell. CP, 987.
Bkwll RD. P SHEFFIELD. Ch e, m, v.
Sch pe. W Derbys CC. Famous as the Plague
Village of 1665–6, when 259 persons died.
Well-dressing.

EYDON Northants
145 SP 5450 8m NE of Banbury. CP, 335.
Brackley RD. P Rugby, Warwickshire.
Ch e, m. Daventry CC (S Nthnts).

EYE Herefs
129 SO 4963 3m N of Leominster. CP(Eye,
Moreton and Ashton), 192. Lmnstr and
Wigmore RD. Ch e. Lmnstr CC. Eye Mnr*,
17c Renaissance hse; plaster ceilings,
woodwork. 1m E, Berrington Hall (NT)*,
18c hse by Henry Holland in grnds by
Capability Brown.

EYE Hunts
123 TF 2202 3m NE of Peterborough. CP,
2,364. Ptrbrgh RD. P PTRBRGH. Ch e, m.
Sch pe. Ptrbrgh BC (CC).

EYE Suffolk (E)
136 TM 1473 4m SSE of Diss. MB, 1,659.
P. Eye CC. Smallest borough in England.
Slight rems of cstle. Splendid 15c ch.

EYEWORTH Beds
147 TL 2545 4m E of Biggleswade. CP, 89.
Bgglswde RD. Ch e. Mid-Beds CC.

EYHORNE STREET Kent
172 TQ 8354 5m E of Maidstone. Loc,
Hollingbourne CP. Ch b.

EYKE Suffolk (E)
150 TM 3151 3m NE of Woodbridge. CP,
280. Deben RD. P Wdbrdge. Ch e. Sch pe.
Eye CC. Airfields in vicinity.

EYNESBURY Hunts
134 TL 1859 just S of St Neots. Loc, St
Nts UD. P St Nts, HUNTINGDON.
Hunts CC. Ch: twr, bench-ends.

EYNSFORD Kent
171 TQ 5465 7m N of Sevenoaks. CP,
3,185. Dartford RD. P Dtfd. Ch e, b. Sch p.
Svnks CC (Dtfd). See also Crockenhill. On
R Darent. Cstle (A.M.). To E, Lullingstone
Roman villa (A.M.). 1m S, L. Cstle*, 18c
hse with 16c gateway.

EYNSHAM Oxon
158 SP 4309 5m E of Witney. CP, 2,628.
Wtny RD. P OXFORD. Ch e, b, m, r, v.
Sch p, s. Mid-Oxon CC (Banbury). See also
Barnard Gate.

EYPE Dorset
177 SY 4491 1m SW of Bridport. Loc,
Symondsbury CP. P Brdpt. Ch e.

EYTHORNE Kent
173 TR 2849 5m NNW of Dover. CP, 1,805.
Eastry RD. P Dvr. Ch e, b. Dvr and Deal CC
(Dvr). See also Barfreston, Elvington.

EYTON Herefs
129 SO 4761 2m NNW of Leominster. CP,
112. Lmnstr and Wigmore RD. Ch e.
Lmnstr CC.

EYTON UPON THE WEALD MOORS
Shrops
118, 119 SJ 6514 2m N of Wellington. CP,
122. Wllngtn RD. P(Eytn), Telford. Ch e.
The Wrekin CC.

EYWORTH Beds
147 TL 2545 4m E of Biggleswade.
Alternative spelling for Eyeworth, qv.

F

FACCOMBE Hants
168 SU 3958 8m NNE of Andover. CP, 112.
Andvr RD. Ch e. Winchester CC
(Basingstoke).

FACEBY Yorks (N)
91 NZ 4903 10m NE of Northallerton. CP,
116. Stokesley RD. Ch e, m. Richmond CC.

FADDILEY Ches
109 SJ 5953 4m W of Nantwich. CP, 159.
Nntwch RD. P Nntwch. Ch m. Sch p.
Nntwch CC.

FADMOOR Yorks (N)
86, 92 SE 6789 5m NE of Helmsley. CP,
112. Kirkbymoorside RD. Ch m. Thirsk and
Malton CC.

FAILAND Som
155, 165 ST 5271 4m W of Bristol. Loc,
Wraxall CP. P BRSTL. Ch m2. Sch pe.

FAILSWORTH Lancs
101 SD 9002 3m SW of Oldham. UD,
22,640. P MANCHESTER. Mnchstr,
Openshaw BC. See also Woodhouses. Textile
tn.

FAIRBURN Yorks (W)
97 SE 4727 3m ENE of Castleford. CP, 701.
Osgoldcross RD. P Knottingley. Ch e, m.
Sch p. Goole CC.

FAIRFIELD Worcs
130, 131 SO 9475 3m N of Bromsgrove.
Loc, Belbroughton CP. P Brmsgrve. Ch e.
Sch p.

FAIRFORD Glos
157 SP 1501 8m E of Cirencester. CP,
1,602. Crncstr RD. P. Ch e, c, r. Sch pe, s.
Crncstr and Tewkesbury CC. Perp 'wool' ch
with famous stained glass. To S, large
airfield with attendant bldngs.

FAIRLIGHT Sussex (E)
184 TQ 8712 4m ENE of Hastings. CP, 866.
Battle RD. P Hstngs. Ch e. Rye CC. With F.
Cove a suburb of Hstngs. Fine cliff scenery.

FAIRMILE Devon
176 SY 0897 5m WSW of Honiton. Loc,
Ottery St Mary UD, Hntn RD. Hntn CC.
To S, Cadhay*, 16c hse.

FAIR OAK Hants
180 SU 4918 3m E of Eastleigh. CP, 1,858.
Winchester RD. P Eastlgh. Ch e, v. Sch j, p, s.
Wnchstr CC. See also Horton Hth.

FAIROAK Staffs
110, 119 SJ 7632 6m E of Mkt Drayton.
Loc, Eccleshall CP.

FAIRSEAT Kent
171 TQ 6261 7m NE of Sevenoaks. Loc,
Stansted CP. P Svnks.

FAIRSTEAD Essex
149, 162 TL 7616 4m WNW of Witham. CP,
262. Braintree RD. Ch e. Brntree CC
(Maldon). Ch has 13c twr and
wall-paintings.

FAIRSTEAD Norfolk
126 TG 2823 4m S of N Walsham. Loc,
Scottow CP.

FAIRWARP Sussex (E)
183 TQ 4626 4m N of Uckfield. Loc,
Maresfield CP. P Uckfld. Ch e.

FAIRY CROSS Devon
163 SS 4024 3m WSW of Bideford. Loc,
Alwington CP. P Bdfd.

FAKENHAM Norfolk
125 TF 9129 11m NNW of E Dereham. CP,
3,753. Walsingham RD. P.
Ch e, b, c, m, r, s, v. Sch p, s2. NW Nflk CC
(N Nflk). Old tn blt round mkt square.
Printing wks.

FALDINGWORTH Lincs (L)
104 TF 0684 4m SW of Mkt Rasen. CP,
248. Welton RD. P Mkt Rasen. Ch e, m.
Sch p. Gainsborough CC.

FALFIELD Glos
156 ST 6893 8m ENE of Severn Rd Br. CP,
545. Thornbury RD. P Wotton-under-Edge.
Ch e, v. S Glos CC.

FALKENHAM Suffolk (E)
150 TM 2939 3m N of Felixtowe. CP, 140.
Deben RD. Ch e, v. Sudbury and
Woodbridge CC.

FALMER Sussex (E)
183 TQ 3508 4m NE of Brighton. CP, 205.
Chailey RD. P Brghtn. Ch e. Sch pe.
Lewes CC. At bottom of hill towards
Brghtn, University of Sussex. Bldngs mostly
by Sir Basil Spence.

FALMOUTH Cornwall
190 SW 8092 9m SE of Redruth. MB,
17,883. P. Flmth and Camborne CC. Resort,
port with large natural anchorage (Carrick
Rds); entrance guarded by Pendennis Cstle
(A.M.), Tudor fort.

FALSTONE Nthmb
76 NY 7287 8m WNW of Bellingham. CP,
345. Bllnghm RD. P Hexham. Ch e. Sch p.
Hxhm CC. See also Plashetts. On the
N Tyne in Kielder Forest.

FANGDALE BECK Yorks (N)
86, 92 SE 5794 7m NNW of Helmsley. Loc,
Bilsdale Midcable CP. Stokesley RD.
P MIDDLESBROUGH, Teesside. Ch e2.
Richmond CC.

FANGFOSS Yorks (E)
97, 98 SE 7653 4m NW of Pocklington. CP,
306. Pcklngtn RD. P YORK. Ch e, m.
Sch pe. Howden CC. See also Bolton.

FARCET Hunts
134 TL 2094 3m S of Peterborough. CP,
1,236. Norman Cross RD. P PTRBRGH.
Ch e, m2, s. Sch pe. Hunts CC. Brick-mnfg.

FAR DUCKMANTON Derbys
112 SK 4472 4m E of Chesterfield. Loc,
Staveley UD.

FAREHAM Hants
180 SU 5706 6m NW of Portsmouth. UD,
80,296. P. Frhm BC (Gosport and Frhm).
See also Burridge, Funtley, Hill Head,
Lock's Hth, Lr Swanwick, Pk Gate, Peel
Cmmn, Portchester, Sarisbury, Stubbington,
Swnwck, Titchfield, Wallington, Warsash.
Old mkt tn and port now part of Ptsmth
conurbation. Naval shore establishments.

FAREWELL Staffs
120 SK 0811 3m NW of Lichfield. CP(Frwll
and Chorley), 282. Lchfld RD. Lchfld and
Tamworth CC.

FAR FOREST Worcs
130 SO 7275 4m W of Bewdley. Loc,
Rock CP. P Kidderminster. Ch e. Sch pe.

FARINGDON Berks
158 SU 2895 10m NE of Swindon. CP(Gt
Frngdn), 3,389. Frngdn RD. P.
Ch e, b, m, v. Sch p, sg. Abingdon CC.
Limestone mkt tn.

FARINGTON Lancs
94 SD 5425 3m S of Preston. CP, 4,434.
Prstn RD. P Leyland, Prstn. Ch e, m, r.
Sch p, pe. S Fylde CC.

FARLAM Cumb
76 NY 5558 2m SE of Brampton. CP, 670.
Border RD. Ch e, m. Penrith and the
Bdr CC. See also Hallbankgate, Tindale.

FARLEIGH Som
155, 165 ST 4969 6m WSW of Bristol. Loc,
Backwell CP. Ch b.

FARLEIGH Surrey
171 TQ 3760 1m NE of Warlingham.
CP(Chelsham and Frlgh). Godstone RD.
P Wlnghm. Ch e. E Srry CC (Reigate).

FARLEIGH GREEN Kent
171, 172 TQ 7252 3m SW of Maidstone.
Loc, W Frlgh CP.

FARLEIGH HUNGERFORD Som
166 ST 8057 3m W of Trowbridge. Loc,
Norton St Philip CP. P Bath. Ch e. Rems of
14c cstle (A.M.). Chpl, with monmts of
Hngrfd family, now armour museum.

FARLEIGH WALLOP Hants
168 SU 6246 3m SSW of Basingstoke. CP,
194. Bsngstke RD. P Bsngstke. Ch e.
Bsngstke CC. See also Broadmere.

FARLESTHORPE Lincs (L)
114 TF 4774 2m SE of Alford. CP, 49.
Spilsby RD. Ch e, m. Horncastle CC.

FARLETON Lancs
89 SD 5767 7m NE of Lancaster. CP(Hornby-
w-Fltn), 483. Lunesdale RD. Lncstr CC.

FARLETON Westm
89 SD 5381 5m WNW of Kirkby Lonsdale.
Loc, Beetham CP.

FARLEY Staffs
120 SK 0644 4m E of Cheadle. CP, 264.
Chdle RD. Ch m. Leek CC.

FARLEY Wilts
167 SU 2229 5m E of Salisbury. CP(Pitton)
and Farley), 534. Slsbry and Wilton RD.
P Slsbry. Ch e, m. Sch pe. Slsbry CC. Ch and
Fox Almshouses blt 1681, possibly designed
by Wren.

FARLEY GREEN Surrey
170 TQ 0645 5m SE of Guildford. Loc,
Albury CP. To W on F. Hth, site of Roman
temple.

FARLEY HILL Berks
169 SU 7465 6m SSE of Reading. Loc,
Swallowfield CP. P Rdng. Ch e. Sch p.

FARLEYS END Glos
143 SO 7715 4m WSW of Gloucester. Loc,
Elmore CP.

FARLINGTON Yorks (N)
92 SE 6167 10m N of York. CP, 118.
Easingwold RD. P YK. Thirsk and
Malton CC.

FARLOW Shrops
129, 130 SO 6480 4m NNW of Cleobury
Mortimer. CP, 206. Bridgnorth RD.
P Kidderminster, Worcs. Ch e, m. Sch pe.
Ludlow CC. See also Oreton.

FARMBOROUGH Som
166 ST 6660 4m NNW of Radstock. CP,
800. Clutton RD. P Bath. Ch e, m2. Sch pe.
N Som CC.

FARMCOTE Glos
144 SP 0629 2m E of Winchcombe. Loc,
Temple Guiting CP. Ch e.

FARMINGTON Glos
144 SP 1315 1m E of Northleach. CP, 151.
Nthlch RD. P Cheltenham. Ch e. Cirencester
and Tewkesbury CC. Pump hse on grn,
presented by people of Fmngtn, U.S.A, in
19c.

FARMOOR Berks
158 SP 4506 2m SE of Eynsham. Loc,
Cumnor CP. P OXFORD.

FARNBOROUGH Berks
158 SU 4381 SSE of Wantage. CP, 116.
Wntge RD. P Wntge. Ch e. Abingdon CC.
Highest vllge in county (700ft).

FARNBOROUGH Hants
169 SU 8754 2m N of Aldershot. UD,
41,233. P. Aldrsht CC. See also Cove, Fox
Lane, W Hth. Military tn; some mid-20c
indstrl development. Biennial air display.

FARNBOROUGH London
171 TQ 4464 2m SW of Orpington. Loc,
Bromley LB. P Orpngtn, Kent. Orpngtn BC
(CC).

FARNBOROUGH Warwicks
145 SP 4349 6m N of Banbury. CP, 225.
Southam RD. P Bnbry, Oxon. Ch e. Sch pe.
Stratford-on-Avon CC (Strtfd).

FARNCOMBE Surrey
169, 170 SU 9745 1m NE of Godalming.
Loc, Gdlmng MB. P Gdlmng. Rsdntl distr.
To W, Charterhouse, boys' public sch.

FARNDISH Beds
133 SP 9263 3m SW of Rushden. Loc,
Podington CP. Ch e. Small mainly 12c ch.

FARNDON Ches
109 SJ 4154 6m ENE of Wrexham. CP, 818.
Tarvin RD. P CHESTER. Ch e, c2. Sch pe.
Nantwich CC. Bthplce of John Speed,
cartographer, 1552.

FARNDON Notts
112 SK 7651 2m SW of Newark. CP, 1,609.
Nwk RD. P Nwk. Ch e, m2. Sch pe.
Nwk CC.

FARNHAM Dorset
179 ST 9515 8m NE of Blandford. CP, 149.
Blndfd RD. P Blndfd Forum. Ch e, m.
N Dst CC. Pitt-Rivers Museum, founded by
General Pitt-Rivers (see also Tollard Royal).

FARNHAM Essex
148 TL 4724 2m NNW of Bishop's
Stortford. CP, 433. Saffron Walden RD.
P Bshp's Sttfd, Herts. Ch e, v. Sch pe. Sffrn
Wldn CC. See also Fnhm Grn.

FARNHAM Suffolk (E)
137 TM 3660 2m SW of Saxmundham. CP,
118. Blyth RD. P Sxmndhm. Ch e. Eye CC.
Ch on hill overlooking Alde valley. S wall
leans alarmingly despite buttresses.

FARNHAM Surrey
169 SU 8446 3m SW of Aldershot. UD,
31,175. P. Fnhm CC. See also Folly Hill,
Hale, Hth End, Rowledge, Runfold, Upr
Hle. Many Ggn hses. Cstle (A.M.).

FARNHAM Yorks (W)
91 SE 3460 2m N of Knaresborough. CP,
106. Nidderdale RD. Ch e. Harrogate CC.
Ch has Nmn chancel.

FARNHAM COMMON Bucks
159, 160 SU 9684 3m N of Slough. Loc,
Fnhm Royal CP. P Slgh. Ch v. Sch p.

FARNHAM GREEN Essex
148 TL 4625 3m NNW of Bishop's
Stortford. Loc, Fnhm CP.

FARNHAM ROYAL Bucks
159, 160 SU 9683 2m N of Slough. CP,
3,563. Eton RD. P Slgh. Ch e3, r. Sch pe.
Beaconsfield CC (S Bucks).

FARNHILL Yorks (W)
96 SE 0046 4m SSE of Skipton. CP, 526.
Skptn RD. Ch m. Skptn CC.

FARNINGHAM Kent
171 TQ 5466 5m SSE of Dartford. CP,
1,373. Dtfd RD. P Dtfd. Ch e. Sch pe.
Sevenoaks CC (Dtfd). Largely 18c;
by-passed by main rd. Old flour mill by
R Darent.

FARNLEY Yorks (W)
96 SE 2148 2m NNE of Otley. CP, 140.
Wharfedale RD. Ch e. Sch pe. Ripon CC. F.
Hall, 18c classical mansion by Carr of York

incorporating Elizn hse. Turner painted
many watercolours of it.

FARNLEY TYAS Yorks (W)
102 SE 1612 3m SSE of Huddersfield. Loc,
Kirkburton UD. P Hddsfld.

FARNSFIELD Notts
112 SK 6456 7m ESE of Mansfield. CP,
1,624. Southwell RD. P Newark. Ch e, m, v.
Sch p, pe. Nwk CC.

FARNWORTH Lancs
100, 109 SJ 5187 1m N of Widnes. Loc,
Wdns MB. P Wdns.

FARNWORTH Lancs
101 SD 7306 2m SE of Bolton. MB, 26,841.
P Bltn. Fnwth BC (CC). Coal, iron, textiles.

FARRINGDON Devon
176 SY 0191 6m E of Exeter. CP, 251. St
Thomas RD. Ch e. Honiton CC.

FARRINGDON Hants
169 SU 7135 3m S of Alton. CP, 522.
Altn RD. P Altn. Ch e. Sch pe.
Petersfield CC. 'Massey's Folly', red brick
Victrn edifice blt by former rector as vllge
hall and sch.

FARRINGTON Dorset
178 ST 8415 6m NNW of Blandford. Loc,
Iwerne Courtney CP. Ch e.

FARRINGTON GURNEY Som
166 ST 6255 4m W of Radstock. CP, 646.
Clutton RD. P BRISTOL. Ch e, m. Sch pe.
N Som CC.

FAR SAWREY Lancs
88, 89 SD 3795 5m ESE of Coniston. Loc,
Claife CP. N Lonsdale RD. P Ambleside,
Westmorland. Ch e. Morecambe and
Lnsdle CC.

FARSLEY Yorks (W)
96 SE 2135 4m ENE of Bradford. Loc,
Pudsey MB. P Pdsy.

FARTHINGHOE Northants
145 SP 5339 4m WNW of Brackley. CP,
351. Brckly RD. P Brckly. Ch e, m. Sch p.
Daventry CC (S Nthnts).

FARTHINGSTONE Northants
132, 133/145, 146 SP 6155 5m SSE of
Daventry. CP, 145. Dvntry RD.
P Towcester. Ch e. Dvntry CC (S Nthnts).

FARWAY Devon
176 SY 1895 3m SSE of Honiton. CP, 198.
Hntn RD. P Colyton. Ch e, m. Sch pe.
Hntn CC. See also Ch Grn.

FATFIELD Co Durham
78 NZ 3053 2m NE of Chester-le-Street.
Loc, Harraton CP. Chstr-le-Strt RD.
P Washington. Ch e, m. Chstr-le-Strt CC.

FAUGH Cumb
76 NY 5055 7m E of Carlisle. Loc,
Hayton CP.

FAULKBOURNE Essex
149, 162 TL 7917 2m NW of Witham. CP,
129. Braintree RD. P Wthm. Ch e.
Brntree CC (Maldon). 15c brick fortified
mnr hse.

FAULKLAND Som
166 ST 7354 3m E of Radstock. Loc,
Hemington CP. P Bath. Ch m.

FAULSGREEN Shrops
118 SJ 5932 5m W of Mkt Drayton. Loc,
Prees CP. Ch e.

FAVERSHAM Kent
172 TR 0161 7m ESE of Sittingbourne.
MB, 14,807. P. Fvrshm CC. See also
Ospringe, Preston. Mkt tn and small port;
some light industry. Guildhall 16c with 19c
additions. Restored gunpowder mill*.
Freemasons' Hall*, 16c.

FAWDINGTON Yorks (N)
91 SE 4372 5m NNE of Boroughbridge. CP,
15. Thirsk RD. Thsk and Malton CC.

FAWFIELDHEAD Staffs
111 SK 0763 6m S of Buxton. CP, 355.
Leek RD. Ch m2. Lk CC.

FAWKHAM GREEN Kent
171 TQ 5865 7m SW of Gravesend. Loc,
Fkhm CP. Dartford RD. P(Fkhm), Dtfd.
Ch e. Sch pe. Sevenoaks CC (Dtfd).

FAWLER Berks
158 SU 3288 5m W of Wantage. Loc,
Kingston Lisle CP. Ch m.

FAWLER Oxon
145 SP 3717 2m SSE of Charlbury. CP.
Chipping Norton RD. Banbury CC.

FAWLEY Berks
158 SU 3981 4m S of Wantage. CP, 181.
Wntge RD. P Wntge. Ch e. Sch pe.
Abingdon CC. See also S Fawley. The
'Marygreen' of Hardy's *Jude the Obscure.*

FAWLEY Bucks
159 SU 7586 3m N of Henley. CP, 382.
Wycombe RD. P(Fwly Grn),
Hnly-on-Thames, Oxon. Ch e. Wcmbe CC.
To SE beside Thames, F. Ct, attributed to
Wren.

FAWLEY Hants
180 SU 4503 6m SSE of Southampton. CP,
7,685. New Forest RD. P STHMPTN.
Ch e, m, v. Sch p. Nw Frst CC. See also
Blackfield, Calshot, Hardley, Holbury,
Langley. Large oil refinery and power stn.
To S at Ashlett, tide mill of 1818.

FAWLEY CHAPEL Herefs
142 SO 5929 3m N of Ross-on-Wye. Loc,
Brockhampton CP. Ch e.

FAXFLEET Yorks (E)
98 SE 8624 7m E of Goole. Loc,
Blacktoft CP.

FAYGATE Sussex (W)
182 TQ 2134 3m SW of Crawley. Loc,
Horsham RD. P Hshm. Ch m. Hshm and
Crly CC (Hshm).

FAZELEY Staffs
120 SK 2001 1m S of Tamworth. CP,
3,946. Lichfield RD. P Tmwth. Ch e, m.
Sch p. Lchfld and Tmwth CC. See also
Bonehill. On A5 rd at crossing of
Birmingham and Fzly Canal.

FEARBY Yorks (N)
91 SE 1981 2m W of Masham. CP, 121.
Mshm RD. P Ripon. Richmond CC.

FEARNHEAD Lancs
101 SJ 6390 3m NE of Warrington.
CP(Poulton-w-Fnhd), 6,378. Wrrngtn RD.
P Wrrngtn. Ch m, r, v. Sch p. Newton CC.

FEATHERSTONE Staffs
119 SJ 9405 4m NNE of Wolverhampton.
CP, 2,170. Cannock RD. P Wlvrhmptn.
Ch m. Sch p. SW Staffs CC (Cnnck). To SW,
Moseley Old Hall (NT)*, Elizn hse orig
half-timbered, encased in brick in 19c;
refuge of Charles II after Battle of
Worcester.

FEATHERSTONE Yorks (W)
97 SE 4220 3m S of Castleford. UD,
15,242. P Pontefract. Pntfrct and Cstlfd BC
(Pntfrct). See also Ackton, Purston Jaglin,
Snydale, Streethouse.

FECKENHAM Worcs
131 SP 0061 4m SSW of Redditch. Loc,
Rddtch UD. P Rddtch.

FEERING Essex
149, 162 TL 8720 5m NE of Witham. CP,
953. Braintree RD. P Colchester. Ch e, v.
Sch pe. Brntree CC (Maldon). Constable
often stayed at rectory. Ch contains his
painting of Risen Christ previously at
Manningtree.

FEETHAM Yorks (N)
90 SD 9898 12m WSW of Richmond. Loc,
Melbecks CP. Reeth RD. Rchmnd CC.

FELBRIDGE Surrey
171 TQ 3739 1m NW of E Grinstead. CP,
1,372. Godstone RD. P: E Grnstd, Sussex.
Ch e. Sch p. E Srry CC (Reigate).

FELBRIGG Norfolk
126 TG 2039 2m SSW of Cromer. CP, 177.
Erpingham RD. Ch e. N Nflk CC. To W, F.
Hall (NT)*, 17c mansion in grnds by Repton.
Ch, in hall grnds, has many good brasses.

FELCOURT Surrey
171 TQ 3841 2m N of E Grinstead. Loc,
Lingfield CP. P: E Grnstd, Sussex.

FELDEN Herts
160 TL 0404 2m SSW of Hemel Hempstead.
Loc, Hml Hmpstd MB.

FELIXKIRK Yorks (N)
91 SE 4684 3m NE of Thirsk. CP, 88.
Thsk RD. Ch e. Thsk and Malton,CC.

FELIXSTOWE Suffolk (E)
150 TM 3034 11m SE of Ipswich. UD,
18,888. P. Sudbury and Woodbridge CC.
See also Walton. Container port. Resort.

FELLING Co Durham
78 NZ 2762 1m E of Gateshead. UD,
38,595. P Grshd 10. Gtshd E BC.

FELMERSHAM Beds
134 SP 9957 6m NNW of Bedford. CP, 376.
Bdfd RD. P BDFD. Ch e, m. Sch p.

Bdfd CC. 'Finest EE ch in county.' Beside
the Ouse.

FELMINGHAM Norfolk
126 TG 2529 2m WSW of N Walsham. CP,
402. Smallburgh RD. P: N Wlshm. Ch e, m.
N Nflk CC.

FELPHAM Sussex (W)
181, 182 SZ 9599 1m E of Bognor. Loc,
Bgnr Regis UD. P Bgnr Rgs.

FELSHAM Suffolk (W)
136 TL 9457 5m NNE of Lavenham. CP,
303. Thedwastre RD. P Bury St Edmunds.
Ch e. Bury St Eds CC.

FELSTED Essex
148 TL 6720 3m ESE of Dunmow. CP,
2,056. Dnmw RD. P Dnmw. Ch e, c. Sch p.
Saffron Walden CC. See also Bannister Grn,
Hartford End. Scattered vllge of pleasing
hses. Boys' public sch founded 1564. Partly
Nmn ch. Sugar factory.

FELTHAM London
160, 170 TQ 1073 3m SW of Hounslow.
Loc, Hnslw LB. P Middx. Flthm and
Heston BC (Flthm).

FELTHORPE Norfolk
126 TG 1617 7m NNW of Norwich. CP,
400. St Faith's and Aylsham RD.
P NRWCH, NOR 83X. Ch e, v. Sch pe.
N Nflk CC (Central Nflk).

FELTON Herefs
142 SO 5748 7m NE of Hereford. CP, 113.
Bromyard RD. Ch e. Leominster CC.

FELTON Nthmb
71 NU 1800 8m S of Alnwick. CP, 718.
Alnwck RD. P Morpeth. Ch e, m, r. Sch pe.
Berwick-upon-Tweed CC.

FELTON Som
155, 165 ST 5265 6m SW of Bristol. Loc,
Winford CP. P BRSTL. Ch e, c. Sch pe. Brstl
Airpt to W.

FELTON BUTLER Shrops
118 SJ 3917 7m WNW of Shrewsbury. Loc,
Gt Ness CP.

FELTWELL Norfolk
135 TL 7190 5m NW of Brandon. CP,
3,192. Downham RD. P Thetford.
Ch e2, m2. Sch pe. SW Nflk CC. See also
Fltwll Anchor.

FELTWELL ANCHOR Norfolk
135 TL 6289 4m ENE of Littleport. Loc,
Fltwll CP.

FENAY BRIDGE Yorks (W)
96, 102 SE 1815 3m E of Huddersfield.
Loc, Kirkburton UD. P Hddsfld.

FENCE Lancs
95 SD 8237 2m W of Nelson. Loc,
Burnley RD. P Bnly. Ch e. Sch pe.
Clitheroe CC. F. Hse, 14c.

FENCE HOUSES Co Durham
78 NZ 3150 2m WNW of
Houghton-le-Spring. Loc, Htn-le-Sprng UD.
P Htn-le-Sprng.

FENCOTE Yorks (N)
91 SE 2893 4m NNE of Bedale. CP(Kirkby
Fleetham w Fncte), 397. Bdle RD. Ch m.
Thirsk and Malton CC.

FENCOTT Oxon
145, 146 SP 5716 4m S of Bicester.
CP(Fnctt and Murcott), 134. Ploughley RD.
Mid-Oxon CC (Henley).

FENDIKE CORNER Lincs (L)
114 TF 4560 7m WSW of Skegness. Loc,
Thorpe St Peter CP. Ch m.

FEN DITTON Cambs
135 TL 4860 3m ENE of Cambridge. CP,
674. Chesterton RD. P CMBRDGE. Ch e.
Sch p. Cambs CC. Suburb carefully
maintaining riverside vllge character.

FEN DRAYTON Cambs
134 TL 3368 3m SE of St Ives. CP, 489.
Chesterton RD. P CAMBRIDGE. Ch e, m.
Sch p. Cambs CC. Hse in Church St
occupied by Dutch engineer Vermuyden
while reclaiming Fens bears inscription
'1713. Niet Zonder Arbyt' (nothing without
work).

FEN END Warwicks
131 SP 2275 7m NNW of Warwick. Loc,
Balsall CP. Meriden RD. P Kenilworth.
Mrdn CC.

FENISCOWLES Lancs
94, 95 SD 6425 3m SW of Blackburn. Loc,
Livesey CP. Blckbn RD. P Blckbn. Ch e, m.
Sch p. Darwen CC.

FENITON Devon
176 SY 1099 4m W of Honiton. CP, 320.
Hntn RD. P Hntn. Ch e, b. Sch pe. Hntn CC.

FENNY BENTLEY Derbys
111 SK 1750 2m N of Ashbourne. CP, 156.
Ashbne RD. P Ashbne. Ch e. Sch pe.
W Derbys CC. 15c mnr hse incorporates
rems of earlier twr.

FENNY BRIDGES Devon
176 SY 1198 4m WSW of Honiton. Loc,
Ottery St Mary UD, Hntn RD. Hntn CC.

FENNY COMPTON Warwicks
145 SP 4152 8m NNW of Banbury. CP, 520.
Southam RD. P Leamington Spa. Ch e, m2.
Sch pe. Stratford-on-Avon CC (Strtfd). To E
beside rly, F.C. 'Tunnel' on the Oxford
Canal; now a cutting since removal of
tunnel's top in 1868.

FENNY DRAYTON Leics
132 SP 3597 3m E of Atherstone. Loc,
Witherley CP. P Nuneaton, Warwickshire.
Ch e. Ch: Purefoy monmts, 16c and 17c.
Much modern rsdntl development.

FENNY STRATFORD Bucks
146 SP 8834 just NE of Bletchley. Loc,
Bltchly UD.

FENROTHER Nthmb
78 NZ 1792 4m NNW of Morpeth. Loc,
Tritlington CP.

FENSTANTON Hunts
134 TL 3168 2m S of St Ives. CP, 1,061. St
Ives RD. P HUNTINGDON. Ch e, b, c.
Sch p. Hunts CC. Old lock-up-cum-clock
-twr.

FENTON Cumb
76 NY 5056 6m E of Carlisle. Loc,
Hayton CP. Ch m.

FENTON Hunts
134 TL 3279 1m SE of Warboys. CP(Pidley
cum Fntn), 376. St Ives RD. Hunts CC.

FENTON Lincs (K)
113 SK 8750 5m ESE of Newark. CP, 63.
W Kesteven RD. Ch e. Grantham CC.

FENTON Lincs (L)
104 SK 8476 9m SSE of Gainsborough. CP,
214. Gnsbrgh RD. Ch m. Gnsbrgh CC.

FENTON Staffs
110, 119 SJ 8944 SE distr of
Stoke-on-Trent. Loc, Stke-on-Trnt CB.
P Stke-on-Trnt. S-on-T S BC. Pottery distr.

FENTON TOWN Nthmb
64, 71 NT 9733 4m NNW of Wooler. Loc,
Doddington CP.

FENWICK Nthmb
64 NU 0640 5m NNW of Belford. Loc,
Kyloe CP. Norham and Islandshires RD.
Berwick-upon-Tweed CC.

FENWICK Nthmb
77, 78 NZ 0572 7m NE of Corbridge. Loc,
Matfen CP.

FENWICK Yorks (W)
103 SE 5916 6m WNW of Thorne. CP, 145.
Doncaster RD. Ch e, m. Sch p. Don
Valley CC.

FEOCK Cornwall
190 SW 8238 4m S of Truro. CP, 2,157.
Truro RD. P Truro. Ch m. Sch pe.
Truro CC. See also Carnon Downs,
Come-to-Good, Devoran, Penpoll. Thatch.
Stocks in churchyard have seven holes.
To NE, Trelissick Hse; gdns (NT)*.

FERNDOWN Dorset
179 SU 0700 4m E of Wimborne. Loc,
Hampreston CP. P Wmbne. Ch c. Sch p, s.
Rsdntl; Bournemouth overspill.

FERNHAM Berks
158 SU 2991 2m S of Faringdon. CP, 151.
Frngdn RD. P Frngdn. Ch e. Sch pe.
Abingdon,CC.

FERNHILL HEATH Worcs
130 SO 8759 3m NNE of Worcester. Loc,
N Claines CP. Droitwich RD. P WCSTR.
Wcstr BC.

FERNHURST Sussex (W)
169, 181 SU 8928 3m S of Haslemere. CP,
2,549. Midhurst RD. P Hslmre, Surrey.
Ch e, v2. Sch p. Chichester CC (Horsham).
See also Camelsdale, Kingsley Grn. Under
Blackdown. Ch restored 19c by Salvin, who
lived at hse called Hawksfold.

FERNILEE Derbys
111 SK 0178 4m NW of Buxton. Loc,
Whaley Bridge UD.

FERRENSBY Yorks (W)
91 SE 3660 3m NNE of Knaresborough. CP,
105. Nidderdale RD. Ch m. Harrogate CC.

FERRING Sussex (W)
182 TQ 0902 3m W of Worthing. CP, 3,449.
Wthng RD. P Wthng. Ch e. Sch pe.
Arundel CC (Arndl and Shoreham).

FERRYBRIDGE Yorks (W)
97 SE 4824 2m NE of Pontefract. Loc,
Knottingley UD. P Knttngly. Power stn of
the Yorkshire Electricity Board.

FERRYHILL Co Durham
85 NZ 2832 6m S of Durham. CP, 10,562.
Sedgefield RD. P. Ch e2, b, m2, r2, s, v2.
Sch p2, s. Drhm CC (Sdgfld).

FERRYHILL STATION Co Durham
85 NZ 3031 3m ESE of Spennymoor. Loc,
Sedgefield RD. Ch m. Sch p. Drhm CC
(Sdgfld).

FERSFIELD Norfolk
136 TM 0683 4m NW of Diss. Loc,
Bressingham CP. P Dss. Ch e, m.

FETCHAM Surrey
170 TQ 1455 1m W of Leatherhead. Loc,
Lthrhd UD. P Lthrhd.

FEWSTON Yorks (W)
96 SE 1954 6m N of Otley. CP, 159.
Wharfedale RD. P Harrogate. Ch e, m.
Sch p. Ripon CC. Reservoirs. To S, Swinsty
Hall, small 16c mnr hse.

FIDDINGTON Glos
143, 144 SO 9231 2m SE of Tewkesbury.
Loc, Ashchurch CP.

FIDDINGTON Som
165 ST 2140 6m WNW of Bridgwater. CP,
241. Brdgwtr RD. Ch e, b. Brdgwtr CC.

FIDDLEFORD Dorset
178 ST 8013 7m NW of Blandford. Loc,
Sturminster RD. Ch m. N Dst CC.

FIDDLERS HAMLET Essex
161 TL 4701 1m SE of Epping. Loc,
Eppng UD.

FIELD Staffs
120 SK 0233 4m W of Uttoxeter. Loc,
Leigh CP. Uttxtr RD. Burton CC.

FIELD BROUGHTON Lancs
88, 89 SD 3881 3m NNW of Grange-over-Sands. Loc, Brghtn E CP. N Lonsdale RD. Ch e. Morecambe and Lnsdle CC.

FIELD DALLING Norfolk
125 TG 0039 4m W of Holt. CP, 323. Walsingham RD. P Hlt. Ch e, m. Sch p. NW Nflk CC (N Nflk). See also Saxlingham.

FIELD HEAD Leics
121 SK 4909 5m SE of Coalville. Loc, Groby CP.

FIFEHEAD MAGDALEN Dorset
166 ST 7821 5m W of Shaftesbury. CP, 92. Sturminster RD. P Gillingham. Ch e. N Dst CC. Perp ch with 13c twr.

FIFEHEAD NEVILLE Dorset
178 ST 7610 8m WNW of Blandford. CP, 149. Sturminster RD. P Stmnstr Newton. Ch e. N Dst CC.

FIFIELD Berks
159 SU 9076 4m W of Windsor. Loc, Bray CP. P Maidenhead. Ch v.

FIFIELD Oxon
144 SP 2318 4m N of Burford. CP, 212. Chipping Norton RD. P OXFORD. Ch e. Banbury CC.

FIFIELD BAVANT Wilts
167 SU 0125 9m WSW of Salisbury. Loc, Ebbesborne Wake CP. Ch e. Ch is one of smallest in England.

FIGHELDEAN Wilts
167 SU 1547 4m N of Amesbury. CP, 793. Amesbury RD. P Salisbury. Ch e, m. Sch pe. Slsbry CC.

FIGHTING COCKS Co Durham
85 NZ 3414 3m E of Darlington. Loc, Dlngtn RD. Bishop Auckland CC (Sedgefield).

FILBY Norfolk
126 TG 4613 5m NW of Yarmouth. CP, 489. Blofield and Flegg RD. P Gt Ymth. Ch e, m. Sch p. Ymth CC. On edge of F. Broad.

FILEY Yorks (E)
93 TA 1180 7m SE of Scarborough. UD, 5,337. P. Bridlington CC. Old fishing vllge, now holiday resort. F. Brigg, mile-long reef covered at high tide.

FILGRAVE Bucks
146 SP 8748 3m N of Newport Pagnell. CP(Tyringham w Flgrve), 181. Npt Pgnll RD. Ch e. Sch pe. Buckingham CC.

FILKINS Oxon
157 SP 2304 3m NNE of Lechlade. CP(Flkns and Broughton Poggs), 482. Witney RD. P Lchlde, Glos. Ch e, m. Sch pe. Mid-Oxon CC (Banbury). Small museum of domestic articles. Vllge lock-up*.

FILLEIGH Devon
163 SS 6628 4m WNW of S Molton. CP, 209. S Mltn RD. P Barnstaple. Ch e. Sch p. N Dvn CC.

FILLEIGH Devon
163 SS 7410 9m NW of Crediton. Loc, Lapford CP.

FILLINGHAM Lincs (L)
104 SK 9485 10m N of Lincoln. CP, 198. Gainsborough RD. P Gnsbrgh. Ch e, m. Gnsbrgh CC. John Wycliffe was rector, 1361–8. F. Cstle, late 18c Gothic, visible across lake.

FILLONGLEY Warwicks
132 SP 2887 6m NNW of Coventry. CP, 1,533. Meriden RD. P Cvntry. Ch e, m. Sch pe. Mrdn CC.

FILTON Glos
155, 156 ST 6079 4m N of Bristol. CP, 12,297. Sodbury RD. P BRSTL. Ch e, m, r, s, v. Sch p3, s2. S Glos CC. Aeroplane factory.

FIMBER Yorks (E)
92, 98 SE 8960 9m WNW of Driffield. CP, 133. Drffld RD. Ch e, m. Howden CC.

FINBOROUGH, GREAT Suffolk (E)
136 TM 0157 2m WSW of Stowmarket. See Gt Fnbrgh.

FINCHAM Norfolk
124 TF 6806 5m ENE of Downham Mkt. CP, 500. Dnhm RD. P King's Lynn. Ch e, m2. Sch pe. SW Nflk CC.

FINCHAMPSTEAD Berks
169 SU 7963 4m SSW of Wokingham. CP, 2,731. Wknghm RD. P Wknghm. Ch e, b, v. Sch p, pe. Reading S CC (Wknghm). See also

Wick Hill. To E, F. Ridges (NT), walks and views, whence avenue of Wellingtonias marches towards Crowthorne.

FINCHDEAN Hants
181 SU 7312 4m NNE of Havant. Loc, Rowlands Cstle CP. To N, St Hubert's Chpl, Idsworth, 12c with fine 14c wall-paintings.

FINCHINGFIELD Essex
148 TL 6832 5m ENE of Thaxted. CP, 1,130. Braintree RD. P Brntree. Ch e, m, v. Sch pe. Brntree CC (Maldon). See also Cornish Hall End, Howe St. Much visited picturesque vllge: post-mill, green, pond, stream. 2m E, Wethersfield RAF/US air base.

FINCHLEY London
160 TQ 2590 7m NNW of Charing Cross. Loc, Barnet LB. Fnchly BC. Rsdntl distr.

FINDERN Derbys
120, 121 SK 3030 4m SW of Derby. CP. Repton RD. P DBY. Ch e, m. Sch p. Belper CC.

FINDON Sussex (W)
182 TQ 1208 4m NNW of Worthing. CP, 1,289. Worthing RD. P Wthg. Ch e, v. Sch pe. Shoreham CC (Arundel and Shrhm). See also N End. 1m E on Downs, Iron Age fort known as Cissbury Ring (NT).

FINEDON Northants
133 SP 9171 3m NNE of Wellingborough. Loc, Wllngbrgh UD. P Wllngbrgh.

FINGAL STREET Suffolk (E)
137 TM 2169 5m ESE of Eye. Loc, Worlingworth CP.

FINGEST Bucks
159 SU 7791 5m N of Henley. CP(Fngst and Lane End), 2,063. Wycombe RD. Ch e, v. Wcmbe CC. The much photographed ch has Nmn twr with unusual roof.

FINGHALL Yorks (N)
91 SE 1889 4m E of Leyburn. CP, 115. Lbn RD. P Lbn. Ch e, m. Richmond CC.

FINGRINGHOE Essex
149, 162 TM 0220 4m SSE of Colchester. CP, 580. Lexden and Winstree RD.

P Clchstr. Ch e, m. Sch pe. Clchstr CC. 15c ch with wall-paintings.

FINMERE Oxon
145, 146 SP 6333 4m W of Buckingham. CP, 282. Ploughley RD. P BCKNGHM. Ch e. Sch pe. Banbury CC (Henley).

FINNINGHAM Suffolk (E)
136 TM 0669 6m SW of Eye. CP, 328. Hartismere RD. P Stowmarket. Ch e, m. Sch pe. Eye CC.

FINNINGLEY Notts
103 SK 6799 7m ESE of Doncaster. CP, 917. E Retford RD. P Dncstr, Yorkshire. Ch e, m. Sch p2, pe. Bassetlaw CC. In Fenland on borders of Lincs, Notts, Yorks.

FINSBURY London
160 TQ 3182 2m NE of Charing Cross. Loc, Islington LB. Islngtn S and Fnsbry BC (Shoreditch and Fnsbry). To N of F. Square in City Rd, Wesley's Chpl, founded by John Wesley 1778, rebuilt 1899.

FINSTALL Worcs
130, 131 SO 9770 1m ESE of Bromsgrove. Loc, Stoke Prior CP. P Brmsgrve. Ch e.

FINSTHWAITE Lancs
88, 89 SD 3687 8m NE of Ulverston. Loc, Colton CP. P Ulvstn. Ch e. Sch pe. On wooded hill to S, early 19c twr commemorating English naval victories.

FINSTOCK Oxon
145 SP 3616 2m S of Charlbury. CP, 467. Chipping Norton RD. P OXFORD. Ch e, m. Sch pe. Banbury CC.

FIRBECK Yorks (W)
103 SK 5688 6m NNW of Worksop. CP, 255. Kiveton Pk RD. P Wksp, Notts. Ch e. Rother Valley CC.

FIRBY Yorks (E)
92 SE 7466 4m SW of Malton. CP, 67. Norton RD. Howden CC. See also Kirkham.

FIRBY Yorks (N)
91 SE 2686 1m S of Bedale. CP, 34. Bdle RD. Thirsk and Malton CC.

FIRGROVE Lancs
101 SD 9113 1m E of Rochdale. Loc, Rchdle CB, Milnrow UD. P Rchdle. Rchdle BC, Heywood and Royton CC.

FIRSBY Lincs (L)
114 TF 4563 7m W of Skegness. CP, 199.
Spilsby RD. Ch e, m. Horncastle CC.

FIR TREE Co Durham
85 NZ 1434 2m SW of Crook. Loc, Crk and
Willington UD. P Crk.

FISHBOURNE IOW
180 SZ 5592 2m W of Ryde. Loc, Rde MB.

FISHBOURNE Sussex
See New Fshbne and Old Fshbne.

FISHBURN Co Durham
85 NZ 3632 2m NNE of Sedgefield. CP,
2,853. Sdgfld RD. P STOCKTON-ON-TEES,
Teesside. Ch m. Sch i, j. Drhm CC (Sdgfld).

FISHER'S POND Hants
168 SU 4820 2m NE of Eastleigh. Loc,
Colden Cmmn CP. P Eastlgh.

FISHER STREET Sussex (W)
169, 181 SU 9531 3m ESE of Haslemere.
Loc, Northchapel CP.

FISHERTON DE LA MERE Wilts
167 SU 0038 11m NW of Salisbury. Loc,
Wylye CP. Ch e.

FISHLAKE Yorks (W)
103 SE 6513 2m W of Thorne. CP, 611.
Thne RD. P Doncaster. Ch e, m. Sch pe.
Goole CC.

FISHLEY Norfolk
126 TG 3911 7m SE of Wroxham.
CP(Upton w Fshly), 429. Blofield and
Flegg RD. Ch e. Ymth CC.

FISHPOND BOTTOM Dorset
177 SY 3698 4m NNE of Lyme Regis. Loc,
Whitechurch Canonicorum CP. Ch v.

FISHPOOL Notts
112 SK 5655 4m SSE of Mansfield. Loc,
Blidworth CP.

FISHTOFT Lincs (H)
114, 124 TF 3642 3m ESE of Boston. CP,
3,236. Bstn RD. P Bstn. Ch e, m2. Sch pe.
Holland w Bstn CC.

FISHTOFT DROVE Lincs (L)
114 TF 3148 3m NNW of Boston. Loc,
Frithville CP.

FISKERTON Lincs (L)
113 TF 0472 4m E of Lincoln. CP, 567.
Welton RD. P LNCLN. Ch e, m. Sch pe.
Gainsborough CC.

FISKERTON Notts
112 SK 7351 4m WSW of Newark.
CP(Fskrtn cum Morton), 353.
Southwell RD. P Sthwll. Ch m. Nwk CC.
Beside wide loop of R Trent.

FITTLETON Wilts
167 SU 1449 5m N of Amesbury. CP, 277.
Psy RD. Ch e. Sch pe. Devizes CC.

FITTLEWORTH Sussex (W)
181, 182 TQ 0119 3m SE of Petworth. CP,
863. Ptwth RD. P Pulborough. Ch e, b.
Sch pe. Chichester CC (Horsham).

FITTON END Cambs
124 TF 4212 3m NW of Wisbech. Loc,
Newton CP.

FITZ Shrops
118 SJ 4417 4m NW of Shrewsbury. Loc,
Pimhill CP. Atcham RD. Ch e. Shrsbry CC.

FITZHEAD Som
164 ST 1228 5m N of Wellington. CP, 229.
Wllngtn RD. P Taunton. Ch e. Tntn CC.

FITZWILLIAM Yorks (W)
103 SE 4115 5m SW of Pontefract. Loc,
Hemsworth UD. P Pntfrct.

FIVE ASH DOWN Sussex (E)
183 TQ 4723 2m N of Uckfield. Loc,
Uckfld RD. P Uckfld. Ch v. E Grinstead CC.

FIVE ASHES Sussex (E)
183 TQ 5524 6m ENE of Uckfield. Loc,
Mayfield CP. P Mayfld. Sch pe.

FIVEHEAD Som
177 ST 3522 5m N of Ilminster. CP, 423.
Langport RD. P Taunton. Ch e, b. Sch pe.
Yeovil CC. See also Swell.

FIVE OAK GREEN Kent
171 TQ 6445 4m E of Tonbridge. Loc,
Capel CP. P Tnbrdge. Ch c.

FIVE OAKS Sussex (W)
182 TQ 0928 2m NNE of Billingshurst. Loc,
Bllngshst CP. P Bllngshst.

FLACKWELL HEATH Bucks
159 SU 8990 3m SE of High Wycombe.
Loc, Chepping Wcmbe CP. Wcmbe RD.
P Hgh Wcmbe. Ch m. Sch i, j. Wcmbe CC.

FLADBURY Worcs
143, 144 SO 9946 3m E of Pershore. CP,
582. Pshre RD. P Pshre. Ch e. Sch pe.
S Worcs CC. Ch: 15c brasses; 14c stained
glass (vestry window).

FLAGG Derbys
111 SK 1368 5m W of Bakewell. CP, 197.
Bkwll RD. P Buxton. Ch m, v. Sch p.
W Derbys CC.

FLAMBOROUGH Yorks (E)
93 TA 2270 4m ENE of Bridlington. CP,
1,706. Brdlngtn RD. P Brdlngtn. Ch e, m2.
Sch pe. Brdlngtn CC. Immense chalk cliffs,
dramatic coastal scenery, sea birds (see
Bempton). Old chalk-blt beacon twr and
lighthouse* at F. Head. To W, Dane's Dyke,
which despite name is a prehistoric defensive
rampart. Ch has 15c carved oak scrn, and
rood loft (see Hubberholme).

FLAMSTEAD Herts
147, 160 TL 0714 3m W of Harpenden. CP,
1,221. Hemel Hempstead RD. P St Albans.
Ch e, m. Sch p. Hml Hmpstd CC. Ch: mdvl
wall-paintings, uncovered in 1930s.

FLANSHAM Sussex (W)
181, 182 SU 9601 2m NE of Bognor. Loc,
Yapton CP. P Bgnr Regis.

FLASBY Yorks (W)
95 SD 9456 4m NW of Skipton. CP(Flsby
w Winterburn), 110. Skptn RD. Skptn CC.

FLASH Staffs
111 SK 0267 4m SSW of Buxton. Loc,
Quarnford CP. Leek RD. Ch m. Sch pe.
Lk CC. At over 1500ft among steep hills in
Peak Distr National Pk.

FLAUNDEN Herts
159, 160 TL 0100 4m E of Chesham. CP,
202. Hemel Hempstead RD. P Hml Hmpstd.
Ch e, b. Hml Hmpstd CC. Ch is first work of
Sir G.G. Scott, 1838.

FLAWBOROUGH Notts
112, 122 SK 7842 7m S of Newark. CP, 42.
Bingham RD. Ch e. Rushcliffe CC (Carlton).

FLAWITH Yorks (N)
91 SE 4865 5m E of Boroughbridge. CP, 61.
Easingwold RD. Thirsk and Malton CC.

FLAX BOURTON Som
155, 165 ST 5069 5m WSW of Bristol. CP,
334. Long Ashton RD. P BRSTL. Ch e.
Sch pe. N Som CC.

FLAXBY Yorks (W)
96 SE 3957 3m E of Knaresborough. CP,
53. Nidderdale RD. Harrogate CC.

FLAXLEY Glos
143 SO 6915 2m ENE of Cinderford. Loc,
Blaisdon CP. Ch e. F. Abbey, 17c–18c hse
incorporating parts of earlier monastery.
To W, Iron Age fort in Welshbury Wd.

FLAXTON Yorks (N)
92, 97, 98 SE 6862 8m NE of York. CP,
284. Flaxton RD. P YK. Ch e, m. Sch pe.
Thirsk and Malton CC.

FLECKNEY Leics
132, 133 SP 6493 7m NW of Mkt
Harborough. CP, 1,495. Mkt Hbrgh RD.
P LEICESTER. Ch e, b2. Sch pe. Hbrgh CC.

FLECKNOE Warwicks
132 SP 5163 4m W of Daventry. Loc,
Wolfhampcote CP. Rugby RD. P Rgby.
Ch e, m. Rgby CC.

FLEDBOROUGH Notts
113 SK 8172 10m W of Lincoln. CP, 64.
E Retford RD. Ch e. Bassetlaw CC.

FLEET Dorset
178 SY 6380 3m W of Weymouth. CP, 100.
Dorchester RD. Ch e. S Dst CC. On N shore
of 8m long lake (The Fleet) enclosed on
S side by Chesil Beach (or Bank).

FLEET Hants
169 SU 8053 4m NW of Aldershot. UD,
21, 362. P Aldrsht. Aldrsht CC. See also Ch
Crookham.

FLEET Lincs (H)
124 TF 3823 2m ESE of Holbeach. CP,
1,489. E Elloe RD. P Spalding. Ch e, m.
Sch p2. Holland w Boston CC. See also Flt
Hargate. Ch has detached twr and spire.

FLEETHAM Nthmb
71 NU 1928 6m SE of Belford. Loc, Beadnell CP.

FLEET HARGATE Lincs (H)
124 TF 3925 2m E of Holbeach. Loc, Flt CP. Ch b.

FLEETWOOD Lancs
94 SD 3348 8m NNE of Blackpool. MB, 28,584. P. N Fylde CC. Tn orig laid out by Decimus Burton, 19c. Important fishing port. Chemicals and plastics factory. Radar stn. Computer centre.

FLEMPTON Suffolk (W)
136 TL 8169 4m NW of Bury St Edmunds. CP, 151. Thingoe RD. P Bury St Eds. Ch e. Bury St Eds CC.

FLETCHERTOWN Cumb
82 NY 2042 5m SW of Wigton. Loc, Allhallows CP. Wgtn RD. P Carlisle. Ch e, m. Sch pe. Penrith and the Border CC..

FLETCHING Sussex (E)
183 TQ 4223 3m NW of Uckfield. CP, 902. Uckfld RD. P Uckfld. Ch e. Sch pe. E Grinstead CC. Edward Gibbon, historian, buried in Nmn and later ch. 14c brass. To W, Sheffied Pk, hse by James Wyatt with gdns (NT)*, pk and lake. From Shffld Pk Stn, Bluebell Rly* runs to Horsted Keynes, 4m NNW.

FLEXBURY Cornwall
174 SS 2007 just N of Bude. Loc, Bde-Stratton UD. P Bde.

FLEXFORD Surrey
169 SU 9350 4m E of Aldershot. Loc, Normandy CP.

FLIMBY Cumb
81, 82 NY 0233 2m SSW of Maryport. Loc, Mrpt UD. P Mrpt.

FLIMWELL Sussex (E)
183 TQ 7131 3m W of Hawkhurst. Loc, Ticehurst CP. P Wadhurst. Ch e, b.

FLINTHAM Notts
112 SK 7445 6m SSW of Newark. CP, 1,208. Bingham RD. P Nwk. Ch e, m. Sch p. Rushcliffe CC (Carlton).

FLINTON Yorks (E)
99 TA 2236 7m S of Hornsea. Loc, Humbleton CP. Ch m.

FLITCHAM Norfolk
124 TF 7226 8m NE of King's Lynn. CP(Fltchm w Appleton), 301. Freebridge Lynn RD. P K's Lnn. Ch e, m. Sch pe. NW Nflk CC (K's Lnn).

FLITTON Beds
147 TL 0635 2m SE of Ampthill. CP, 572. Ampthll RD. P BEDFORD. Ch e. Mid-Beds CC.

FLITWICK Beds
147 TL 0334 2m S of Ampthill. CP, 3,604. Ampthll RD. P BEDFORD. Ch e, b2, m, v. Sch p2. Mid-Beds CC.

FLIXBOROUGH Lincs (L)
104 SE 8715 3m NNW of Scunthorpe. CP, 449. Glanford Brigg RD. P Scnthpe. Ch e. Brgg and Scnthpe CC (Brgg). Steel and chemical wks.

FLIXTON Lancs
101 SJ 7494 6m WSW of Manchester. Loc, Urmston UD. P Urmstn, MNCHSTR.

FLIXTON Suffolk (E)
137 TM 3186 2m SW of Bungay. CP, 98. Wainford RD. P Bngy. Ch e. Sch pe. Lowestoft CC.

FLIXTON Yorks (E)
93 TA 0479 5m W of Filey. Loc, Folkton CP. P Scarborough. Ch m.

FLOCKTON Yorks (W)
102 SE 2314 4m S of Dewsbury. Loc, Kirkburton UD. P Wakefield.

FLODDEN Nthmb
64, 71 NT 9235 6m NW of Wooler. Loc, Ford CP.

FLOOKBURGH Lancs
88, 89 SD 3675 3m WSW of Grange-over-Sands. Loc, Lr Holker CP. N Lonsdale RD. P Grnge-over-Snds. Ch e. Sch ie. Morecambe and Lnsdle CC.

FLORDON Norfolk
137 TM 1897 6m SE of Wymondham. CP, 218. Forehoe and Henstead RD. P NORWICH, NOR 68W. Ch e. S Nflk CC (Central Nflk).

FLORE Northants
132, 133 SP 6460 5m ESE of Daventry. CP, 927. Dvntry RD. P NORTHAMPTON. Ch e, c. Sch pe. Dvntry CC (S Nthnts).

FLOWTON Suffolk (E)
149 TM 0846 5m WNW of Ipswich. CP, 101. Gipping RD. Ch e. Eye CC.

FLUSHING Cornwall
190 SW 8033 just N of Falmouth, across river. Loc, Mylor CP. P Flmth. Ch e, m2, r. Sch pe.

FLYFORD FLAVELL Worcs
143, 144 SO 9854 8m E of Worcester. CP, 118. Pershore RD. P WCSTR. Ch e. Sch p. S Worcs CC.

FOBBING Essex
161, 162 TQ 7183 3m S of Basildon. Loc, Thurrock UD. P Stanford-le-Hope. Thrrck BC(CC). Ch has tall 15c twr.

FOCKERBY Yorks (W)
104 SE 8419 6m NE of Crowle. CP, 62. Goole RD. Gle CC.

FOGGATHORPE Yorks (E)
97, 98 SE 7537 8m WSW of Mkt Weighton. CP, 221. Howden RD. P Selby. Ch m. Sch p. Hdn CC. See also Harlthorpe, Laytham.

FOLE Staffs
120 SK 0437 4m NW of Uttoxeter. Loc, Cheadle RD, Uttxtr RD. Ch m. Leek CC, Burton CC.

FOLKE Dorset
178 ST 6513 3m SSE of Sherborne. CP, 325. Shbne RD. Ch e. Sch pe. W Dst CC. See also Allweston.

FOLKINGHAM Lincs (K)
113, 123 TF 0733 8m E of Grantham. CP, 462. S Kesteven RD. P Sleaford. Ch e, m. Sch pe. Rutland and Stamford CC. Ggn hses round large square. Classical style 'Hse of Correction' blt 1825.

FOLKESTONE Kent
173 TR 2236 15m SSE of Canterbury. MB, 43,760. P. Flkstne and Hythe CC. See also Sandgate. Channel port and resort. High white cliffs; view to France.

FOLKINGTON Sussex (E)
183 TQ 5603 4m NW of Eastbourne. CP, 73. Hailsham RD. Ch e. Lewes CC (Eastbne).

FOLKSWORTH Hunts
134 TL 1489 6m SSW of Peterborough. CP(Flkswth and Washingley), 291. Norman Cross RD. Ch e. Sch pe. Hunts CC.

FOLKTON Yorks (E)
93 TA 0579 4m W of Filey. CP, 477. Bridlington RD. Ch e. Sch pe. Brdlngtn CC. See also Flixton.

FOLLIFOOT Yorks (W)
96 SE 3452 3m SE of Harrogate. CP, 386. Nidderdale RD. P Hrrgte. Ch e, m, r. Sch pe, pr. Hrrgte CC. Rsdntl for Hrrgte, Leeds, Bradford.

FOLLY GATE Devon
175 SX 5797 2m NNW of Okehampton. Loc, Inwardleigh CP. P Okhmptn. Ch m.

FOLLY HILL Surrey
169 SU 8348 2m SW of Aldershot. Loc, Farnham UD. P Fnhm.

FONTHILL GIFFORD Wilts
166, 167 ST 9231 7m NNE of Shaftesbury. CP, 210. Mere and Tisbury RD. Ch e. Westbury CC. On W edge of F. Pk (see Bishop's Fnthll).

FONTMELL MAGNA Dorset
178 ST 8616 4m S of Shaftesbury. CP, 541. Shftsbry RD. P Shftsbry. Ch e. Sch pe. N Dst CC. See also Bedchester. Ch: gargoyles, carvings on parapet.

FONTWELL Sussex (W)
181 SU 9407 6m ENE of Chichester. Loc, Chchstr RD. P Arundel. Arndl CC (Chchstr).

FOOLOW Derbys
111 SK 1976 5m NNW of Bakewell. CP, 108. Bkwll RD. Ch v. W Derbys CC.

FORCETT Yorks (N)
85 NZ 1712 7m W of Darlington. CP(Fctt and Carkin), 152. Richmond RD. Ch e. Sch pe. Rchmnd CC. F. Pk, early Ggn hse; dovecote and grotto in grnds. To S, Stanwick Fortifications (A.M.), vast complex of military earthworks associated with anti-Roman rebellions of 1c.

FORD Bucks
159 SP 7709 4m SW of Aylesbury. CP(Dinton-w-Fd and Upton), 651. Aylesbury RD. Ch b. Aylesbury CC.

FORD Devon
163 SS 4024 3m WSW of Bideford. Loc,
Alwington CP.

FORD Glos
144 SP 0829 4m E of Winchcombe. Loc,
Temple Guiting CP.

FORD Nthmb
64, 71 NT 9437 7m NNW of Wooler. CP,
775. Glendale RD. P BERWICK-UPON
-TWEED. Ch e. Sch pe. Brwck-upn-Twd CC.
See also Crookham, Etal, Flodden,
Kimmerston.

FORD Shrops
118 SJ 4113 5m W of Shrewsbury. CP, 641.
Atcham RD. P Shrsbry. Ch e, m. Sch pe.
Shrsbry CC.

FORD Staffs
111 SK 0653 5m ESE of Leek. Loc,
Grindon CP.

FORD Sussex (W)
181, 182 SU 9903 2m SSW of Arundel. CP,
268. Chichester RD. Ch e. Arndl CC
(Chchstr). Open prison on site of former
airfield.

FORD Wilts
156 ST 8474 5m W of Chippenham. Loc,
N Wraxall CP. P Chppnhm. Ch e.

FORDCOMBE Kent
171 TQ 5240 4m W of Tunbridge Wells.
Loc, Penshurst CP. P Tnbrdge Wlls. Ch e.
Sch pe.

FORD END Essex
148 TL 6716 4m SE of Dunmow. Loc, Gt
Waltham CP. P Chelmsford. Ch e. Sch pe.
1m NW, mdvl wayside chpl.

FORDHAM Cambs
135 TL 6370 5m N of Newmarket. CP,
1,709. Nmkt RD. P Ely. Ch e, c, m. Sch pe.
Cambs CC. See also Landwade.

FORDHAM Essex
149 TL 9228 5m WNW of Colchester. CP,
379. Lexden and Winstree RD. P Clchstr.
Ch e, v. Sch pe. Clchstr CC.

FORDHAM Norfolk
135 TL 6199 2m S of Downham Mkt. CP,
148. Dnhm RD. Ch e. SW Nflk CC.

FORDINGBRIDGE Hants
179 SU 1414 10m S of Salisbury. CP,
4,567. Ringwood and Fdngbrdge RD. P.
Ch e, c2, m, r, s. Sch p, s. New Forest CC.
See also Bickton, Blissford, Godshill,
Hungerford, Hyde, N Gorley, Sandleheath,
Stuckton. Old br spans R Avon.

FORDON Yorks (E)
93 TA 0475 5m SW of Filey. Loc, Wold
Newton CP. Ch e.

FORDSTREET Essex
149 TL 9226 5m WNW of Colchester. Loc,
Lexden and Winstree RD. Clchstr CC.

FORD STREET Som
164 ST 1518 2m SSE of Wellington. Loc,
Wllngtn Without CP. Wllngtn RD.
Taunton CC.

FORDWELLS Oxon
145 SP 3013 4m NW of Witney. Loc,
Chipping Norton RD, Wtny RD. Ch m.
Banbury CC, Mid-Oxon CC. (Bnbry.)

FORDWICH Kent
173 TR 1859 2m NE of Canterbury. CP,
166. Bridge-Blean RD. Ch e. Cntrbry CC.
On R Stour and once port for Cntrbry.
Many boats. 16c tn hall on quay.

FOREMARK Derbys
120, 121 SK 3326 6m SSW of Derby. CP,
76. Repton RD. Ch e. Belper CC.

FOREST Co Durham
84 NY 8729 6m WNW of
Middleton-in-Teesdale. CP(Frst and Frith),
257. Barnard Cstle RD. P(Frst-in-Tsdle),
Bnd Cstle. Ch e, m2. Sch p. Bishop
Auckland CC. See also Harwood, Langdon
Beck. To SE in this parish, High Force,
well known waterfall of R Tees.

FORESTBURN GATE Nthmb
71 NZ 0696 3m S of Rothbury. Loc,
Hollinghill CP. Rthbry RD.
Berwick-upon-Tweed CC.

FOREST GREEN Surrey
170, 182 TQ 1241 4m ENE of Cranleigh.
Loc, Dorking and Horley RD. P Dkng. Ch c.
Dkng CC.

FOREST HEAD Cumb
76 NY 5857 4m SE of Brampton. Loc,
Border RD. Penrith and the Bdr CC.

FOREST HILL Oxon
158 SP 5807 5m E of Oxford. CP(Frst Hll w Shotover), 741. Bullingdon RD. P OXFD. Ch e, m. Mid-Oxon CC (Henley). The poet Milton was married in the ch.

FOREST ROW Sussex (E)
171, 183 TQ 4235 3m SE of E Grinstead. CP, 3,523. Uckfield RD. P. Ch e, b2, r. Sch pe. E Grnstd CC. See also Hammerwood. At N edge of Ashdown Forest. Ashdn Hse, 18c hse 1m E across R Medway, now boys' preparatory sch. To W, Weir Wd Reservoir.

FORESTSIDE Sussex (W)
181 SU 7512 5m NNE of Havant. Loc, Stoughton CP. P Rowland's Cstle, Hants. Ch,e.

FOREST TOWN Notts
112 SK 5662 2m ENE of Mansfield. Loc, Mnsfld Woodhouse UD. P Mnsfld.

FORMBY Lancs
100 SD 3007 6m SSW of Southport. UD, 23,501. P LIVERPOOL. Crosby BC (Ormskirk CC). See also Freshfield. Rsdntl tn of mainly 19c bldngs. Once a fishing vllge; now separated from sea by sand dunes.

FORNCETT END Norfolk
136 TM 1493 5m SSE of Wymondham. Loc, Fnctt CP. Depwade RD. Ch m. S Nflk CC.

FORNCETT ST MARY Norfolk
137 TM 1693 6m SE of Wymondham. Loc, Fnctt CP. Depwade RD. P NORWICH, NOR 86W. Ch e, m. S Nflk CC.

FORNCETT ST PETER Norfolk
137 TM 1692 6m SSE of Wymondham. Loc, Fnctt CP. Depwade RD. P NORWICH, NOR 84W. Ch e. Sch pe. S Nflk CC.

FORNHAM ALL SAINTS Suffolk (W)
136 TL 8367 2m NNW of Bury St Edmunds. CP, 400. Thingoe RD. Ch e, b. Bury St Eds CC.

FORNHAM ST MARTIN Suffolk (W)
136 TL 8567 2m N of Bury St Edmunds. CP, 464. Thingoe RD. P Bury St Eds. Ch e. Bury St Eds CC.

FORSBROOK Staffs
110, 119 SJ 9641 6m ESE of Stoke-on-Trent. CP, 3,055. Cheadle RD. Ch e, m. Sch ie. Leek CC. See also Blythe Marsh, Boundary.

FORSTAL, THE Kent
172, 184 TQ 8946 4m WSW of Charing. Loc, Egerton CP.

FORSTON Dorset
178 SY 6695 4m NNW of Dorchester. Loc, Charminster CP.

FORTHAMPTON Glos
143 SO 8532 2m W of Tewkesbury. CP, 216. Gloucester RD. P GLCSTR. Ch e. W Glos CC. Several half-timbered thatched cottages.

FORTON Lancs
94 SD 4851 6m S of Lancaster. CP, 850. Garstang RD. P Preston. Ch e, c, m, r. Sch p. N Flyde CC. See also Hollins Lane.

FORTON Shrops
118 SJ 4216 5m WNW of Shrewsbury. Loc, Montford CP.

FORTON Som
177 ST 3307 1m SE of Chard. Loc, Chd CP. Chd RD. Ch m. Yeovil CC.

FORTON Staffs
119 SJ 7521 2m NNE of Newport. CP, 400. Stafford RD. Ch e. Stffd and Stone CC. See also Sutton. To SE across Shrops Union Canal, Aqualate Mere, mile-long lake.

FORTUNESWELL Dorset
178 SY 6873 on Isle of Portland, S of Weymouth. Loc, Ptlnd UD. Ch blt by convict labour, 1872.

FORTY FEET BRIDGE Hunts
134 TL 3087 2m NNE of Ramsey. Loc, Rmsy UD. P HUNTINGDON. Br spans Forty Foot Drain blt by Vermuyden, the Dutch engineer.

FORTY GREEN Bucks
159 SU 9291 1m NW of Beaconsfield. Loc, Penn CP.

FORTYHILL London
160 TQ 3398 1m NE of Enfield. Loc, Enfld LB. Enfld N BC (Enfld W).

FORWARD GREEN Suffolk (E)
136 TM 0959 3m E of Stowmarket. Loc,
Stonham Earl CP. Gipping RD. P Stwmkt.
Eye CC.

FOSBURY Wilts
168 SU 3158 7m S of Hungerford.
CP(Tidcombe and Fsbry), 112. Marlborough
and Ramsbury RD. Ch e. Devizes CC.

FOSDYKE Lincs (H)
114, 123 TF 3133 7m S of Boston. CP, 483.
Bstn RD. P Bstn. Ch e, m. Sch pe. Holland
w Bstn CC.

FOSSEBRIDGE Glos
144 SP 0811 3m SW of Northleach. Loc,
Coln St Dennis CP. P Cheltenham.

FOSTER STREET Essex
161 TL 4809 3m ESE of Harlow. Loc,
N Weald Bassett CP.

FOSTON Derbys
120 SK 1931 6m E of Uttoxeter. CP(Fstn
and Scropton), 668. Repton RD. P DERBY.
Belper CC.

FOSTON Lincs (K)
113, 122 SK 8542 6m NW of Grantham.
CP, 319. W Kesteven RD. P Grnthm. Ch e.
Sch pe. Grnthm CC.

FOSTON Yorks (N)
92 SE 6965 7m SW of Malton. CP, 96.
Mltn RD. Ch e. Sch pe. Thirsk and Mltn CC.
F. Old Rectory*, brick hse of 1813 blt by
Sidney Smith, rector here 2806–29.

FOSTON ON THE WOLDS Yorks (E)
99 TA 1055 5m ESE of Driffield. CP(Fstn),
346. Drffld RD. P Drffld. Ch e. Howden CC.
See also Brigham, Gembling.

FOTHERBY Lincs (L)
105 TF 3191 3m NNW of Louth. CP, 238.
Lth RD. P Lth. Ch e, m. Lth CC.

FOTHERINGAY Northants
134 TL 0693 3m NNE of Oundle. CP, 172.
Oundle and Thrapston RD.
P PETERBOROUGH. Ch e. Sch pe.
Wellingborough CC (Ptrbrgh). Only mounds
mark site of cstle where Mary, Queen of
Scots, was imprisoned, and executed in
1587. 14c ch with lantern twr survives from
collegiate foundation destroyed in 16c.

FOULBY Yorks (W)
96, 102, 103 SE 3917 4m ESE of
Wakefield. CP(Huntwick w Flby and
Nostell), 300. Hemsworth RD. Hmswth CC.
To SE, Nostell Priory (NT)*, 18c mansion
in large grnds; lake beside main rd.

FOULDEN Norfolk
136 TL 7699 7m SSW of Swaffham. CP,
246. Swffhm RD. P Thetford. Ch e. Sch pe.
SW Nflk CC.

FOULRIDGE Lancs
95 SD 8942 1m N of Colne. CP, 1,253.
Burnley RD. P Clne. Ch e, m2. Sch pe.
Clitheroe CC. Sailing (Clne Reservoir).

FOULSHAM Norfolk
125 TG 0324 8m ESE of Fakenham. CP,
734. St Faith's and Aylsham RD.
P Dereham. Ch e, b, m. Sch p. N Nflk CC
(Central Nflk). Ggn hses round mkt place,
mostly blt after great fire of 1771.

FOUR ASHES Suffolk (E)
136 TM 0070 8m NNW of Stowmarket.Loc,
Walsham-le-Willows CP.

FOUR CROSSES Staffs
119 SJ 9509 2m WSW of Cannock. Loc,
Hatherton CP. Cross-rds on A5.

FOUR ELMS Kent
171 TQ 4648 2m NE of Edenbridge. Loc,
Hever CP. P Ednbrdge. Ch e, v. Sch p.

FOUR FORKS Som
165 ST 2337 4m W of Bridgwater. Loc,
Spaxton CP.

FOUR GOTES Cambs
124 TF 4516 4m N of Wisbech. Loc, Tydd
St Giles CP.

FOUR LANES Cornwall
189 SW 6938 2m SSW of Redruth. Loc,
Camborne–Rdrth UD. P Rdrth.

FOURLANES END Ches
110 SF 8059 3m ESE of Sandbach. Loc,
Congleton RD. Knutsford CC.

FOUR MARKS Hants
168, 169 SU 6634 4m SW of Alton. CP,
1,616. Altn RD. P Altn. Ch e, r, v. Sch pe.
Petersfield CC. See also Kitwood.

FOUR OAKS Sussex (E)
184 TQ 8624 5m NW of Rye. Loc,
Beckley CP.

FOUR OAKS Warwicks
131 SP 2480 6m W of Coventry. Loc,
Berkswell CP.

FOURSTONES Nthmb
77 NY 8968 4m NW of Hexham. Loc,
Wardem CP. P Hxhm.

FOUR THROWS Kent
184 TQ 7729 1m ESE of Hawkhurst. Loc,
Hkhst CP. P Hkhst.

FOVANT Wilts
167 SU 0028 9m W of Salisbury. CP, 486.
Slsbry and Wilton RD. P Slsbry. Ch e, v.
Sch pe. Slsbry CC. Large regimental badges
cut in chalk during World War I on hillside
to S.

FOWEY Cornwall
186 SX 1251 5m SSE of Lostwithiel. MB(St
Austell w Fwy), 32,252. P. Truro CC
(Bodmin). Tn with steep, narrow, congested
streets. Resort with busy harbour; port for
china clay exports.

FOWLMERE Cambs
148 TL 4245 5m NE of Royston. CP, 591.
S Cambs RD. P Rstn, Herts. Ch e, v. Sch p.
Cambs CC.

FOWNHOPE Herefs
142 SO 5834 6m SE of Hereford. CP, 724.
Hrfd RD.   P HRFD.   Ch e, b, v.   Sch pe.
Hrfd CC. Ch: 12c carved tympanum.

FOXCOMBE HILL Berks
158 SP 4901 3m N of Abingdon. Loc,
Abngdn RD. Abngdn CC.

FOX CORNER Surrey
169, 170 SU 9654 4m NNW of Guildford.
Loc, Pirbright CP. P Gldfd.

FOXEARTH Essex
149 TL 8344 2m WSW of Long Melford. CP,
256. Halstead RD. Ch e. Sch pe. Saffron
Walden CC.

FOXFIELD Lancs
88 SD 2185 4m NE of Millom. Loc,
Broughton W CP. N Lonsdale RD.
Morecambe and Lnsdle CC.

FOXHAM Wilts
157 ST 9777 4m NE of Chippenham. Loc,
Bremhill CP. P Chppnhm. Ch e, m.

FOXHOLE Cornwall
185, 190 SW 9654 4m WNW of St Austell.
Loc, St Stephen-in-Brannel CP. St Astll RD.
P St Astll. Ch m. Sch p. Truro CC.

FOXHOLES Yorks (E)
93 TA 0173 8m SW of Filey. CP, 237.
Norton RD. P Driffield. Ch e, m.
Howden CC. See also Butterwick.

FOX LANE Hants
169 SU 8557 2m SW of Camberley. Loc,
Farnborough UD.

FOXLEY Norfolk
125 TG 0321 6m NNE of E Dereham. CP,
180. Mitford and Launditch RD. P Drhm.
Ch e. SW Nflk CC.

FOXLEY Wilts
156, 157 ST 8985 3m WSW of Malmesbury.
Loc, Norton CP. Ch e.

FOXT Staffs
111 SK 0348 4m NNE of Cheadle. Loc,
Ipstones CP. P Stoke-on-Trent. Ch e, m.
Sch p.

FOXTON Cambs
148 TL 4148 6m NE of Royston. CP, 643.
S Cambs RD. P Rstn, Herts. Ch e, m. Sch p.
Cambs CC.

FOXTON Leics
133 SP 7090 3m NW of Mkt Harborough.
CP, 364. Mkt Hbrgh RD. P Mkt Hbrgh.
Ch e, b. Sch p. Hbrgh CC. To W, staircase
locks on Grand Union Canal.

FOXTON Yorks (N)
91 SE 4296 4m ENE of Northallerton. Loc,
Thimbleby CP.

FOXUP Yorks (W)
90 SD 8776 9m NNE of Settle. Loc, Halton
Gill CP.

FOXWIST GREEN Ches
110 SJ 6268 3m NW of Winsford. Loc,
Wnsfd UD.

FOY Herefs
142 SO 5928 3m N of Ross-on-Wye. CP,
206. Rss and Whitchurch RD. Ch e.
Hereford CC. See also Hole-in-the-Wall.

FRADDON Cornwall
185 SW 9158 7m ESE of Newquay. Loc, St
Enoder CP. P St Columb. Ch m.

FRADLEY Staffs
120 SK 1613 4m NE of Lichfield. Loc,
Alrewas CP. P Lchfld. Ch e. Sch p. Disused
airfield across Coventry Canal near its
junction with Trent and Mersey Canal (F.
Junction).

FRADSWELL Staffs
110, 119 SJ 9931 6m ESE of Stone. CP,
182. Stafford RD. P STFFD. Ch e. Stffd
and Stne CC.

FRAISTHORPE Yorks (E)
99 TA 1561 4m SSW of Bridlington. Loc,
Barmston CP. Ch e.

FRAMFIELD Sussex (E)
183 TQ 4920 2m ESE of Uckfield. CP,
1,703. Uckfld RD. P Uckfld. Ch e, b, v.
Sch pe. E Grinstead CC. See also Blackboys.

FRAMINGHAM EARL Norfolk
126 TG 2702 5m SE of Norwich. CP, 249.
Forehoe and Henstead RD. P NRWCH,
NOR 44W. Ch e, m. Sch s. S Nflk CC
(Central Nflk).

FRAMINGHAM PIGOT Norfolk
126 TG 2703 4m SE of Norwich. CP, 188.
Forehoe and Henstead RD. Ch e. S Nflk CC
(Central Nflk).

FRAMLINGHAM Suffolk (E)
137 TM 2863 9m N of Woodbridge. CP,
2,005. Blyth RD. P Wdbrdge. Ch e, m, v3.
Sch pe, s, sg. Eye CC. See also Brabling Grn.
Small country tn. Extensive rems of
12c–13c cstle (A.M.); Tdr chimneys. Ch:
Howard monmts. Agricultural college.

FRAMPTON Dorset
178 SY 6295 5m WNW of Dorchester. CP,
367. Dchstr RD. P Dchstr. Ch e. Sch p.
W Dst CC.

FRAMPTON Lincs (H)
114, 123 TF 3239 3m S of Boston. CP,
1,154. Bstn RD. P Bstn. Ch e, m. Holland
w Bstn CC. See also Sandholme.

FRAMPTON COTTERELL Glos
155, 156 ST 6681 8m NE of Bristol. CP,
3,786. Sodbury RD. P BRSTL.
Ch e, cm, m, v. Sch i, j, pe. S Glos CC.

FRAMPTON MANSELL Glos
156, 157 SO 9202 6m W of Cirencester.
Loc, Sapperton CP. P Stroud. Ch e, b.

FRAMPTON ON SEVERN Glos
156 SO 7407 7m WNW of Stroud. CP,
1,096. Gloucester RD. P GLCSTR. Ch e, v.
Sch pe. Strd CC. Vllge has vast grn.

FRAMSDEN Suffolk (E)
137 TM 1959 6m WSW of Framlingham.
CP, 350. Gipping RD. P Stowmarket.
Ch e, b. Eye CC. Post-mill in working order.

FRAMWELLGATE MOOR Co Durham
85 NZ 2644 2m N of Durham. CP, 3,639.
Drhm RD. P DRHM. Ch m3. Sch p, s.
Drhm CC. See also Pity Me.

FRANCHE Worcs
130 SO 8178 1m NNW of Kidderminster.
Loc, Kddrmnstr MB. P Kddrmnstr.

FRANKBY Ches
100, 109 SJ 2486 5m WSW of Birkenhead.
Loc, Hoylake UD. P West Kirby, Wirral.

FRANKLEY Worcs
130, 131 SO 9980 3m SE of Halesowen. CP,
178. Bromsgrove RD. Ch e. Brmsgrve and
Redditch CC (Brmsgrve). Reservoirs to N
and W. To S, F. Beeches (NT), hilltop
beechwood.

FRANKTON Warwicks
132 SP 4270 6m SW of Rugby. CP, 321.
Rgby RD. P Rgby. Ch e. Rgby CC.

FRANSHAM, GREAT Norfolk
125 TF 8913 6m W of E Dereham. See Gt
Frnshm.

FRANT Sussex (E)
171, 183 TQ 5935 3m S of Tunbridge Wells.
CP, 1,445. Uckfield RD. P TNBRDGE
WLLS. Ch e. Sch pe. E Grinstead CC. See
also Bells Yew Grn, Eridge Grn. Handsome
vllge with large roadside grn. Views to N
over Eridge Pk and far beyond.

FRATING Essex
149, 162 TM 0822 6m ESE of Colchester.
CP, 323. Tendring RD. P Clchstr. Ch e.
Harwich CC.

FRATING GREEN Essex
149, 162 TM 0923 6m ESE of Colchester.
Loc, Frtng CP.

FRATTON Hants
180, 181 SU 6500 inner distr of
Portsmouth. Loc, Ptsmth CB. Ptsmth S BC.

FREATHY Cornwall
186 SX 3952 3m SW of Torpoint. Loc, St
John CP.

FRECKENHAM Suffolk (W)
135 TL 6672 6m NNE of Newmarket. CP,
677. Mildenhall RD. P Bury St Edmunds.
Ch e, m. Sch pe. Bury St Eds CC.

FRECKLETON Lancs
94 SD 4228 7m W of Preston. CP, 3,309.
Fylde RD. P Prstn. Ch e, m. Sch p, pe.
S Flde CC.

FREEBY Leics
122 SK 8020 3m E of Melton Mowbray. CP,
353. Mltn and Belvoir RD. Ch e, c. Mltn CC.
See also Brentingby, Saxby, Stapleford,
Wyfordby.

FREELAND Oxon
145 SP 4112 4m ENE of Witney. CP, 654.
Wtny RD. P OXFORD. Ch e, m. Sch pe.
Mid-Oxon CC (Banbury).

FREETHORPE Norfolk
126 TG 4105 7m W of Yarmouth. CP, 491.
Blofield and Flegg RD. P NORWICH, NOR
66Z. Ch e. Sch p. Ymth CC. See also Frthpe
Cmmn, Wickhampton.

FREETHORPE COMMON Norfolk
126 TG 4004 8m W of Yarmouth. Loc,
Frthpe CP. Ch m.

FREISTON Lincs (H)
114, 124 TF 3743 3m E of Boston. CP,
1,254. Bstn RD. P Bstn. Ch e, m. Holland
w Bstn CC. See also Halltoft End, Scrane
End. Large 11c–12c ch is rems of priory.

FREMINGTON Devon
163 SS 5132 3m W of Barnstaple. CP,
4,409. Bnstple RD. P Bnstple. Ch e, m, v.
Sch p. N Dvn CC. See also Bickington,
Holmacott, Yelland.

FREMINGTON Yorks (N)
90 SE 0499 8m W of Richmond. CP(Reeth,
Frmngtn and Healaugh), 540. Rth RD.
Rchmnd CC.

FRENCHAY Glos
155, 156 ST 6477 5m NE of Bristol. Loc,
Brstl CB, Sodbury RD. P Fishponds,
BRSTL. Ch e, f, m, v. Brstl NE BC,
S Glos CC. Retains vllge character despite
proximity to Brstl.

FRENCHBEER Devon
175 SX 6785 5m W of Moretonhampstead.
Loc, Chagford CP.

FRENSHAM Surrey
169 SU 8441 4m S of Farnham. CP, 2,478.
Hambledon RD. P Fnhm. Ch e, c2. Sch pe.
Fnhm CC. See also Churt, Millbridge,
Rushmoor, Spreakley. F. Ponds to E and S
are large lakes. F. Cmmn (NT).

FRESHFIELD Lancs
100 SD 2908 6m SSW of Southport. Loc,
Formby UD. P Fmby, LIVERPOOL.

FRESHFORD Som
166 ST 7860 4m SE of Bath. CP, 594.
Bathavon RD. P Bth. Ch e, b, m. Sch pe.
N Som CC. Vllge on wooded banks of
R Frome.

FRESHWATER IOW
180 SZ 3487 2m SSW of Yarmouth. CP,
3,537. Isle of Wight RD and CC. P.
Ch e2, b2, c, m. Sch pe. See also Easton,
Norton, Ntn Grn. Ch has 14c brass. 1m SW,
Farringford, home of Tennyson; now hotel.
1½m SW, Tnnsn Down (NT) and monmt.

FRESSINGFIELD Suffolk (E)
137 TM 2677 8m W of Halesworth. CP,
711. Hartismere RD. P Diss, Norfolk.
Ch e, b, m. Sch pe. Eye CC. Se also Lit
Whittingham Grn.

FRESTON Suffolk (E)
150 TM 1639 3m S of Ipswich. CP, 204.
Samford RD. Ch e. Sudbury and
Woodbridge CC.

FRETHERNE Glos
156 SO 7309 8m WNW of Stroud.
CP(Frthne w Saul), 718. Gloucester RD.
Ch e, c. Strd CC. See also Upr Framilode.

FRETTENHAM Norfolk
126 TG 2417 3m W of Wroxham. CP, 288.
St Faith's and Aylsham RD. P NORWICH,
NOR 02Y. Ch e, m. Sch p. N Nflk CC
(Central Nflk).

FRIAR'S GATE Sussex (E)
183 TQ 4933 2m NW of Crowborough. Loc,
Withyham CP.

FRIDAY BRIDGE Cambs
124 TF 4604 3m S of Wisbech. Loc,
Elm CP. P Wsbch. Ch e, m. Sch p.

FRIDAYTHORPE Yorks (E)
98 SE 8759 9m W of Driffield. CP, 218.
Drffld RD. P Drffld. Ch e, m. Sch p.
Howden CC. 500ft up, blt round grn with
two ponds. Ch has Nmn doorway.

FRIERN BARNET London
160 TQ 2793 3m SE of Barnet. Loc,
Bnt LB. Finchley BC.

FRIESTHORPE Lincs (L)
104 TF 0783 4m SSW of Mkt Rasen. CP,
51. Welton RD. Ch e. Gainsborough CC.

FRIESTON Lincs (K)
113 SK 9347 8m N of Grantham. Loc,
Caythorpe CP.

FRIETH Bucks
159 SU 7990 4m NW of Marlow. Loc,
Hambleden CP. P Henley-on-Thames, Oxon.
Ch e. Sch pe.

FRILFORD Berks
158 SU 4497 4m W of Abingdon. CP, 245.
Abngdn RD. Ch m. Sch pe. Abngdn CC.

FRILSHAM Berks
158 SU 5373 6m NE of Newbury. CP.
Bradfield RD. Ch e. Nbry CC.

FRIMLEY Surrey
169 SU 8758 2m S of Camberley.
UD(Frmly and Cmbrly), 44,784. P Cmbrly.
NW Srry CC (Woking). See also Deepcut,
Frmly Grn, Mytchett.

FRIMLEY GREEN Surrey
169 SU 8856 3m SSE of Camberley. Loc,
Frmly and Cmbrly UD. P Cmbrly.

FRING Norfolk
124 TF 7334 5m SE of Hunstanton. CP,
112. Docking RD. Ch e. NW Nflk CC
(King's Lynn).

FRINGFORD Oxon
145, 146 SP 6028 4m NNE of Bicester. CP,
379. Ploughley RD. P Bcstr. Ch e. Sch pe.
Banbury CC (Henley).

FRINSTED Kent
172 TQ 8957 4m S of Sittingbourne. CP,
109. Hollingbourn RD. Ch e. Maidstone CC.

FRINTON Essex
150 TM 2319 5m NE of Clacton. UD(Frntn
and Walton), 12,431. P(Frntn-on-Sea).
Harwich CC. See also Gt Holland, Kirby
Cross, Kby-le-Soken. Resort, fine sands,
fishing.

FRISBY ON THE WREAKE Leics
122 SK 6917 4m WSW of Melton Mowbray.
CP(Frsby), 647. Mltn and Belvoir RD.
P Mltn Mbry. Ch e, m. Sch pe. Mltn CC. See
also Kirby Bellars.

FRISKNEY Lincs (L)
114 TF 4655 8m SW of Skegness. CP,
1,524. Spilsby RD. P Boston. Ch e, m2.
Sch pe. Horncastle CC.

FRISTON Suffolk (E)
137 TM 4160 3m SE of Saxmundham. CP,
658. Blyth RD. P Sxmndhm. Ch e, b. Sch p.
Eye CC.

FRISTON Sussex (E)
183 TV 5598 4m W of Eastbourne. CP, 241.
Hailsham RD. Ch e. Eastbne CC. Downland
vllge. Gliding.

FRITCHLEY Derbys
111 SK 3552 3m WNW of Ripley. Loc,
Crich CP. P DERBY. Ch m, v2.

FRITHAM Hants
179 SU 2314 9m SW of Romsey. Loc,
Bramshaw CP. P Lyndhurst. Ch v.

FRITH COMMON Worcs
130 SO 6869 6m E of Tenbury Wells. Loc,
Lindridge CP. P Tnbry Wlls.

FRITHELSTOCK Devon
163 SS 4619 2m W of Torrington. CP, 297.
Trrngtn RD. Ch e, m. W Dvn CC (Trrngton).
Rems of 13c priory.

FRITHELSTOCK STONE Devon
163 SS 4518 3m W of Torrington. Loc,
Frthlstck CP. P Trrngtn. Ch b.

FRITHVILLE Lincs (L)
114 TF 3150 4m N of Boston. CP, 627.
Spilsby RD. P Bstn. Ch e, m2. Sch p.
Horncastle CC. See also Fishtoft Drove.

FRITTENDEN Kent
172, 184 TQ 8141 4m NE of Cranbrook.
CP, 783. Crnbrk RD. P Crnbrk. Ch e, b, v.
Sch pe. Royal Tunbridge Wells CC
(Ashford).

FRITTON Norfolk
137 TM 2292 7m WNW of Bungay. Loc,
Morning Thorpe CP. Ch e.

FRITTON Suffolk (E)
137 TG 4600 6m SW of Yarmouth. CP,
192. Lothingland RD. P Gt Ymth, Norfolk.
Ch e. Lowestoft CC. To E, F. Decoy, 3m
long lake with wooded banks.

FRITWELL Oxon
145 SP 5229 6m NW of Bicester. CP, 570.
Ploughley RD. P Bcstr. Ch e, v. Sch pe.
Banbury CC (Henley). Mnr hse of 1619.

FRIZINGTON Cumb
82 NY 0317 4m E of Whitehaven.
CP(Arlecdon and Frzngtn), 4,094.
Ennerdale RD. P. Ch e, m, r. Sch p, pe, pr.
Whthvn CC.

FROCESTER Glos
156 SO 7803 4m W of Stroud. CP, 206.
Gloucester RD. Ch e. Strd CC. F. Ct, mainly
14c with later additions incl half-timbered
gatehouse; visited by Elizabeth I, 1574. Well
preserved 14c tithe barn.

FRODESLEY Shrops
118 SJ 5101 7m S of Shrewsbury. CP, 157.
Atcham RD. Ch e. Shrsbry CC.

FRODSHAM Ches
100, 109 SJ 5177 3m S of Runcorn. CP,
5,661. Rncn RD. P WARRINGTON.
Ch e, bc, m4, r. Sch ie2, j, p, s. Rncn CC.
Busy small tn on edge of marshes. Bear's
Paw, 17c inn.

FROGGATT Derbys
111 SK 2476 5m NNE of Bakewell. CP,
168. Bkwll RD. Ch v. W Derbys CC.

FROGHALL Staffs
111 SK 0247 3m N of Cheadle. Loc,
Ipstones CP. P Stoke-on-Trent.

FROGMORE Devon
187, 188 SX 7742 3m ESE of Kingsbridge.
Loc, Kngsbrdge RD. P Kngsbrdge.
Totnes CC.

FROGMORE Hants
169 SU 8460 2m W of Camberley. Loc,
Yateley CP. P Cmbrly, Surrey. Sch i.

FROLESWORTH Leics
132 SP 5090 5m NNW of Lutterworth. CP,
181. Lttrwth RD. Ch e. Blaby CC
(Harborough). 18c almshouses.

FROME Som
166 ST 7747 11m S of Bath. UD, 13,384. P.
Wells CC. Steep mdvl streets, 18c wool
merchants' hses. Industries still incl wool;
also plastics, paint, brewing.

FROME ST QUINTIN Dorset
177, 178 ST 5902 9m SSE of Yeovil. CP,
129. Dorchester RD. Ch e. W Dst CC.

FROMES HILL Herefs
143 SO 6846 5m SSE of Bromyard. Loc,
Bishop's Frome CP. P Ledbury. Ch e, c.

FROME VAUCHURCH Dorset
177, 178 SY 5997 7m NW of Dorchester.
CP, 143. Dchstr RD. Ch e. W Dst CC.

FROSTENDEN Suffolk (E)
137 TM 4781 4m NNW of Southwold. CP,
283. Lothingland RD. Ch e. Sch pe.
Lowestoft CC.

FROSTERLEY Co Durham
84 NZ 0236 6m W of Tow Law. Loc,
Stanhope CP. P Bishop Auckland. Ch e, m2.
Black limestone known as 'Frosterley
marble' quarried here.

FROXFIELD Wilts
158 SU 2968 3m W of Hungerford. CP, 293.
Marlborough and Ramsbury RD. P Mlbrgh.
Ch e. Devizes CC. Brick almshouses of 1694
with later additions.

FROXFIELD GREEN Hants
181 SU 7025 3m WNW of Petersfield.
CP(Frxfld), 854. Ptrsfld RD. P(Frxfld),
Ptrsfld. Ch e. Sch pe. Ptrsfld CC.

FROYLE Hants
169 SU 7542 3m NE of Alton. CP, 734.
Altn RD. P(Upr Frle), Altn. Ch e. Sch pe.
Petersfield CC. See also Lr Frle. Ld Mayor
Trelour's sch for handicapped children.

FRYERNING Essex
161 TL 6400 5m NE of Brentwood.
CP(Ingatestone and Frnng), 3,549.

Fryton

Chelmsford RD. Ch e. Chlmsfd CC. Rsdntl development round 15c ch.

FRYTON Yorks (N)
92 SE 6875 6m WNW of Malton. CP, 52. Mltn RD. Thirsk and Mltn CC.

FULBECK Lincs (K)
113 SK 9450 8m WNW of Sleaford. CP, 546. W Kesteven RD. P Grantham. Ch e, m. Sch pe. Grnthm CC. Ch: monmts. F. Hall early Ggn, seat of Fane family.

FULBOURN Cambs
135 TL 5156 5m ESE of Cambridge. CP, 2,906. Chesterton RD. P CMBRDGE. Ch e2, c. Sch p. Cambs CC.

FULBROOK Oxon
144 SP 2512 just NE of Burford. CP, 429. Witney RD. Ch e. Sch pe. Mid-Oxn CC (Banbury).

FULFORD Staffs
110, 119 SJ 9538 4m NE of Stone. CP. Stne RD. P Stoke-on-Trent. Ch e, m. Sch p. Stafford and Stne CC. See also Blythe Br, Saverley Grn.

FULFORD Yorks (E)
97, 98 SE 6149 2m SSE of York. CP, 2,339. Derwent RD. P YK. Ch e, m. Sch pe, s. Howden CC.

FULHAM London
160, 170 TQ 2577 4m WSW of Charing Cross. Loc, Hammersmith LB. Flhm BC. On N bank of Thames in loop of river; Putney and Wandsworth Brs. At N end of Ptny Br, F. Palace, residence of Bishop of Lndn.

FULKING Sussex (E)
182 TQ 2411 4m E of Steyning. CP, 241. Cuckfield RD. P Henfield. Mid-Sx CC (Lewes).

FULLER'S MOOR Ches
109 SJ 4954 8m NNW of Whitchurch. Loc, Broxton CP.

FULLER STREET Essex
148, 149, 162 TL 7416 5m W of Witham. Loc, Braintree RD, Chelmsford RD. Brntree CC. (Maldon CC, Chlmsfd CC.)

FULLERTON Hants
168 SU 3739 4m S of Andover. Loc, Wherwell CP.

FULLETBY Lincs (L)
114 TF 2973 3m NE of Horncastle. CP, 97. Hncstle RD. P Hncstle. Ch e. Hncstle CC.

FULL SUTTON Yorks (E)
97, 98 SE 7455 5m NW of Pocklington. CP, 109. Pcklngtn RD. P YORK. Ch e, m. Howden CC.

FULMER Bucks
159, 160 SU 9985 4m NNE of Slough. CP, 602. Eton RD. P Slgh. Ch e. Sch p. Beaconsfield CC (S Bucks).

FULMODESTONE Norfolk
125 TF 9930 5m E of Fakenham. CP(Fulmodeston), 449. Walsingham RD. P Fknhm. Ch e, m. Sch p. NW Nflk CC (N Nflk). See also Barney.

FULNETBY Lincs (L)
104 TF 0979 6m S of Mkt Rasen. CP, 38. Welton RD. Gainsborough CC.

FULSTOW Lincs (L)
105 TF 3297 6m N of Louth. CP, 344. Lth RD. P Lth. Ch e, m. Sch p. Lth CC.

FULWOOD Lancs
94 SD 5331 1m N of Preston. UD, 21,741. P Prstn. Prstn N BC. See also Sharoe Grn.

FULWOOD Notts
112 SK 4757 4m WSW of Mansfield. Loc, Sutton in Ashfield UD.

FUNTINGTON Sussex (W)
181 SU 8008 4m WNW of Chichester. CP, 1,222. Chchstr RD. Ch e. Sch p. Chchstr CC. See also E Ashling, W Ashling, W Stoke, Woodend. Flint and brick vllge S of S Downs.

FUNTLEY Hants
180 SU 5608 1m N of Fareham. Loc, Frhm UD. P Frhm. To N, county mental hospital. To W, rems of 18c ironworks.

FURNER'S GREEN Sussex (E)
183 TQ 4026 5m E of Haywards Hth. Loc, Danehill CP. P Uckfield.

FURNESS VALE Derbys
111 SK 0083 1m NNW of Whaley Br. Loc, Whly Br UD. P Stockport, Cheshire.

FURNEUX PELHAM Herts
148 TL 4327 5m NW of Bishop's Stortford. CP, 399. Braughing RD. P Buntingford. Ch e. Sch pe. E Herts CC. See also E End.

FURZEHILL Devon
163 SS 7245 3m S of Lynton. Loc,
Lntn UD.

FYFET Som
177 ST 2314 6m S of Taunton. Loc,
Otterford CP.

FYFIELD Berks
158 SU 4298 5m W of Abingdon. CP(Ffld
and Tubney), 514. Abngdn RD. P Abngdn.
Ch e, b. Sch pe. Abngdn CC. Limestone
vllge, once famous for Matthew Arnold's
'Fyfield elm', no longer standing. 14c mnr
hse.

FYFIELD Essex
161 TL 5606 3m NNE of Ongar. CP, 488.
Epping and Ongr RD. P Ongr. Ch e, v.
Sch pe, s. Brentwood and Ongr CC
(Chigwell).

FYFIELD Hants
168 SU 2946 4m WNW of Andover. CP,
314. Andvr RD. Ch e. Winchester CC
(Basingstoke).

FYFIELD Wilts
157 SU 1468 3m W of Marlborough. CP,
146. Mlbrgh and Ramsbury RD. Ch e.
Devizes CC. F. Down is nature reserve.

FYLING THORPE Yorks (N)
93 NZ 9405 5m SE of Whitby. Loc,
Fylingdales CP. Whtby RD. P Whtby.
Sch pe. Cleveland and Whtby CC
(Scarborough and Whtby). On Fylingdales
Moor, SW, Defence Ministry Early Warning
Radar Stn. Many small prehistoric cairns,
presumably burial chambers, and large
rampart and·ditch.

G

GADDESBY Leics
122 SK 6813 5m SW of Melton Mowbray.
CP, 658. Mltn and Belvoir RD. P LCSTR.
Ch e, m. Sch p. Mltn CC. See also Ashby
Folville, Barsby. Outstanding 13c—14c ch:
mdvl bench-ends; 19c equestrian monmt.

GADDESDEN, GREAT Herts
147, 159, 160 TL 0211 3m NNW of Hemel
Hempstead. See Gt Gddsdn.

GAGINGWELL Oxon
145 SP 4025 6m NNW of Woodstock. Loc,
Enstone CP.

GAILEY Staffs
119 SJ 9110 4m W of Cannock. Loc,
Penkridge CP. P STAFFORD. Ch e. Sch pe.
M6 and A5 intersection. Mining subsidence.
Circular lock-keeper's twr by Staffs and
Worcs Canal. Reservoir.

GAINFORD Co Durham
85 NZ 1716 7m WNW Darlington.
CP, 1,130. Barnard Cstle RD. P Dlngtn.
Ch e, m, r. Sch pe. Bishop Auckland CC.
13c ch above R Tees.

GAINSBOROUGH Lincs (L)
104 SK 8190 15m NW of Lincoln.
UD, 17,420. P. Gnsbrgh CC. Inland port;
engineering wks. The 'St Oggs' of George
Eliot's *The Mill on the Floss.*

GAINSFORD END Essex
148, 149 TL 7235 6m NW of Halstead. Loc,
Toppesfield CP.

GAITSGILL Cumb
83 NY 3846 8m ESE of Wigton. Loc,
Dalston CP.

GALGATE Lancs
94 SD 4855 4m S of Lancaster. Loc,
Ellel CP. P LNCSTR. Ch m.

GALHAMPTON Som
166 ST 6329 4m SW of Bruton. Loc,
N Cadbury CP. P Yeovil. Ch v.

GALLEY COMMON Warwicks
132 SP 3192 3m W of Nuneaton. Loc,
Nntn MB. P Nntn.

GALLEY END Essex
161, 162 TL 7103 2m SSE of Chelmsford.
Loc, Gt Baddow CP.

GALLEYWOOD Essex
161, 162 TL 7002 3m S of Chelmsford.
Loc, Gt Baddow CP. P Chlmsfd. Ch e, m.
Sch i, pe.

GALLOPING GREEN Co Durham
78 NZ 2758 3m SSE of Gateshead. Loc,
Lamesley CP.

GALMPTON Devon
187, 188 SX 6940 4m SW of Kingsbridge.
Loc, S Huish CP. P Kngsbrdge.

GALMPTON Devon
188 SX 8856 2m W of Brixham. Loc,
Torbay CB. P Brxhm.

GALPHAY Yorks (W)
91 SE 2572 4m WNW of Ripon. Loc,
Azerley CP. P Rpn. Ch m. Sch p.

GAMBLESBY Cumb
83 NY 6139 8m NE of Penrith. Loc,
Glassonby CP. P Pnrth. Ch e, m. Sch p.

GAMELSBY Cumb
75 NY 2552 3m N of Wigton. Loc,
Aikton CP.

GAMLINGAY Cambs
147 TL 2352 6m NE of Biggleswade.
CP, 1,622. S Cambs RD. P Sandy, Beds.
Ch e, b, m2. Sch p, s. Cambs CC. Once
larger place almost burnt out in 1600. Has
modern vllge college.

GAMSTON Notts
103 SK 7176 3m S of Retford. CP, 210.
E Rtfd RD. P Rtfd. Ch e. Bassetlaw CC.

GAMSTON Notts
112, 121, 122 SK 6037 3m SE of
Nottingham. CP, 143. Bingham RD. Ch b.
Sch pe. Rushcliffe CC (Carlton).

GANAREW Herefs
142 SO 5216 2m NNE of Monmouth.
CP, 110. Ross and Whitchurch RD. Ch e.
Hereford CC. To E, Lit Doward Camp, Iron
Age hill fort.

GANSTEAD Yorks (E)
99 TA 1434 5m NE of Hull. Loc, Bilton CP.

GANTHORPE Yorks (N)
92 SE 6870 6m W of Malton. CP, 67.
Mltn RD. Thirsk and Mltn CC.

GANTON Yorks (E)
93 SE 9877 8m WSW of Filey. CP, 240.
Norton RD. P Scarborough. Ch e, m.
Sch pe. Howden CC. See also Potter
Brompton. Well known golf course.

GARBOLDISHAM Norfolk
136 TM 0081 7m W of Diss. CP, 511.
Wayland RD. P Dss. Ch e, m. Sch pe.
S Nflk CC. 1m W on G. Hth, section of
earthwork known as Devil's Ditch.

GARE HILL Som and Wilts
166 ST 7840 5m S of Frome. Loc,
Frme RD, Mere and Tisbury RD. Ch e, m.
Wells CC, Westbury CC.

GARFORD Berks
158 SU 4296 5m W of Abingdon. CP, 140.
Abngdn RD. Ch e. Sch pe. Abngdn CC.

GARFORTH Yorks (W)
97 SE 4033 7m E of Leeds. UD, 25,296.
P LDS. Barkston Ash CC. See also Allerton
Bywater, Kippax. Coal-mining distr.

GARGRAVE Yorks (W)
95 SD 9354 4m WNW of Skipton.
CP, 1,432. Skptn RD. P Skptn. Ch e, m.
Sch i, je. Skptn CC.

GARNETT BRIDGE Westm
89 SD 5299 4m N of Kendal. Loc,
S Westm RD. Westm CC.

GARRAS Cornwall
189, 190 SW 7023 4m SE of Helston. Loc,
Mawgan-in-Meneage CP, Kerrier RD. Ch m.
Sch p. St Ives CC.

GARRIGILL Cumb
84 NY 7441 4m SSE of Alston. CP(Alstn w
Grrgll), 2,105. Alstn w Grrgll RD. P Alstn.
Ch e, m2, v. Penrith and the Border CC.

GARRISTON Yorks (N)
91 SE 1592 3m ENE of Leyburn. CP, 23.
Lbn RD. Richmond CC.

GARSDALE HEAD Yorks (W)
90 SD 7892 6m WNW of Hawes. Loc,
Gsdle CP. Sedbergh RD. P(Gsdle). Sdbgh.
Ch e, m. Sch pe. Skipton CC. Here is one of
loneliest and wildest stretches of
Settle—Carlisle rly.

GARSDON Wilts
157 ST 9687 2m E of Malmesbury. Loc,

Lea and Cleverton CP. Ch e, m. Ch: 17c monmt to Sir Laurence Washington, ancestor of George Wshngtn, bears family arms of stars and stripes (cf Sulgrave, Wickhamford).

GARSHALL GREEN Staffs
110, 119 SJ 9634 4m E of Stone. Loc, Milwich CP.

GARSINGTON Oxon
158 SP 5802 5m SE of Oxford. CP, 930. Bullingdon RD. P OXFD. Ch e. Sch pe. Henley CC. Small 16c mnr hse.

GARSTANG Lancs
94 SD 4945 10m S of Lancaster. CP, 2,134. Gstng RD. P Preston. Ch e, c, m, r. Sch p, pe, s. N Fylde CC.

GARSWOOD Lancs
100 SJ 5599 3m NE of St Helens. Loc, Ashton-in-Makerfield UD. P Wigan.

GARTHORPE Leics
122 SK 8320 5m E of Melton Mowbray. CP, 140. Mltn and Belvoir RD. Ch e. Mltn CC. See also Coston.

GARTHORPE Lincs (L)
104 SE 8419 6m NE of Crowle. CP, 323. Isle of Axholme RD. P Scunthorpe. Ch e, m. Sch pe. Gainsborough CC.

GARTON Yorks (E)
99 TA 2635 7m NW of Withernsea. Loc, E Gtn CP. Holderness RD. Ch e, m. Bridlington CC. See also Elmswell.

GARTON-ON-THE-WOLDS Yorks (E)
98 SE 9859 3m NW of Driffield. CP, 425. Drffld RD. P Drffld. Ch e, m. Sch pe. Howden CC. Nmn ch, much restored, 1½m NW on Gtn Hill, monmt of 1865 to Sir Tatton Sykes of Sledmere, qv.

GARVESTONE Norfolk
125 TG 0107 4m SSE of E Dereham. CP, 492. Mitford and Launditch RD. P NORWICH, NOR 29X. Ch e, m. Sch p. SW Nflk CC. See also Reymerston, Thuxton.

GARWAY Herefs
142 SO 4522 7m NNW of Monmouth. CP, 340. Ross and Whitchurch RD. P HEREFORD. Ch e, b. Sch p. Hrfd CC. See also Lit Garway. Nmn ch; twr joined to it by 17c passage. Circular dovecote sole rems of Knights Templar's commandery.

GARWAY HILL Herefs
142 SO 4425 10m SSW of Hereford. Loc, Orcop CP. P HRFD. Ch m.

GASPER Wilts
166 ST 7633 5m E of Bruton. CP(Stourton w Gspr), 302. Mere and Tisbury RD. Westbury CC.

GASTARD Wilts
156, 157 ST 8868 4m SW of Chippenham. Loc, Corsham CP. P Cshm. Sch pe.

GASTHORPE Norfolk
136 TL 9780 7m E of Thetford. Loc, Riddlesworth CP. Wayland RD. P Diss. S Nflk CC.

GATCOMBE IOW
180 SZ 4985 3m S of Newport. CP, 309. Isle of Wight RD and CC. Ch e. See also Chillerton. G. Hse (NT), mid-18c hse, formerly home of Worsley family.

GATEBECK Westm
89 SD 5485 5m SSE of Kendal. Loc, Preston Patrick CP. S Westm RD. Westm CC.

GATE BURTON Lincs (L)
104 SK 8382 5m SSE of Gainsborough. CP, 74. Gnsbrgh RD. Ch e. Gnsbrgh CC. 18c gazebo temple in pk of hall.

GATEFORTH Yorks (W)
97 SE 5628 4m WSW of Selby. CP, 205. Slby RD. Ch e. Barkston Ash CC. G. Hall is sanatorium.

GATE HELMSLEY Yorks (N)
97, 98 SE 6955 6m ENE of York. CP, 214. Flaxton RD. P YK. Ch e, m. Thirsk and Malton CC.

GATELEY Norfolk
125 TF 9624 4m SE of Fakenham. CP, 79. Mitford and Launditch RD. Ch e. SW Nflk CC.

GATENBY Yorks (N)
91 SE 3287 4m E of Bedale. CP, 35. Bdle RD. P Northallerton. Thirsk and Malton CC.

GATESHEAD Co Durham
78 NZ 2563 just S of Newcastle. CB, 94,457. P. BCs: Gtshd E, Grshd W. 19c indstrl tn. To SW, Team Valley Trading Estate, developed initially between the two world wars.

GATES HEATH Ches
109 SJ 4760 6m SE of Chester. Loc,
Golborne Bellow CP. Tarvin RD.
Nantwich CC.

GATHURST Lancs
100 SD 5307 3m WNW of Wigan. Loc,
Orrell UD.

GATLEY Ches
101 SJ 8488 3m WSW of Stockport.
UD(Cheadle and Gtly), 60,648. P Chdle.
Chdle BC(CC).

GATTON Surrey
170 TQ 2753 2m NE of Reigate. Loc,
Rgte MB.

GATWICK (London Airport) Surrey
170, 182 TQ 2841 1m S of Horley. Loc,
Charlwood CP. P(Lndn[Gtwck] Airpt), Hly.

GAULBY Leics
122 SK 6901 7m ESE of Leicester. CP, 80.
Billesdon RD. Ch e. Harborough CC
(Melton).

GAULTREE Norfolk
124 TF 4907 3m SE of Wisbech. Loc,
Emneth CP.

GAUNT'S COMMON Dorset
179 SU 0205 4m N of Wimborne. Loc,
Wmbne and Cranborne RD. P Wmbne.
Sch p. N Dst CC.

GAUTBY Lincs (L)
113 TF 1772 5m WNW of Horncastle.
CP, 74. Hncstle RD. Ch e. Hncstle CC.

GAWBER Yorks (W)
102 SE 3207 1m NW of Barnsley. Loc,
Darton UD. P Bnsly.

GAWCOTT Bucks
146 SP 6831 2m SSW of Buckingham. Loc,
Bcknghm MB. P BCKNGHM. Sch p.
Entirely rural although within the borough.

GAWSWORTH Ches
110 SJ 8969 3m SW of Macclesfield.
CP, 1,375. Mcclsfld RD. P Mcclsfld.
Ch e, m. Mcclsfld CC. See also Warren. Ch
and old rectory, 15c; old hall* 16c; new hall
18c.

GAWTHROP Yorks (W)
89 SD 6987 4m SE of Sedbergh. Loc,
Dent CP.

GAWTHWAITE Lancs
88 SD 2784 4m NNW of Ulverston. Loc,
Subberthwaite CP. N Lonsdale RD.
Morecambe and Lnsdle CC.

GAYDON Warwicks
145 SP 3654 6m SW of Southam.
CP, 1,055. Sthm RD. P WARWICK. Ch e.
Sch p, pe. Stratford-on-Avon CC (Strtfd).

GAYHURST Bucks
146 SP 8446 2m NW of Newport Pagnell.
CP, 39. Npt Pgnll RD. Ch e. Buckingham CC.
G. Hse originally blt in 16c and given by
Elizabeth I to Drake, who, however, im-
mediately disposed of it. Later the home of
Everard Digby, conspirator in Gunpowder
Plot, 1605, for which he was executed.

GAYLE Yorks (N)
90 SD 8789 just S of Hawes. Loc, Hws CP.
Ch m.

GAYLES Yorks (N)
84 NZ 1207 5m NW of Richmond. CP. 104.
Rchmnd RD. Rchmnd CC.

GAY STREET Sussex (W)
182 TQ 0820 3m NE of Pulborough. Loc,
W Chiltington CP.

GAYTON Ches
100, 108, 109 SJ 2780 6m SSW of
Birkenhead. Loc, Wirral UD. Wrrl CC.

GAYTON Norfolk
124 TF 7217 7m E of Kings's Lynn.
CP, 883. Freebridge Lynn RD. P K's Lnn.
Ch e, m. Sch pe. NW Nflk CC(K's Lnn). See
also Gtn Thorpe.

GAYTON Northants
146 SP 7054 4m N of Towcester. CP, 404.
Tcstr RD. P NORTHAMPTON. Ch e. Sch pe.
Daventry CC(S Nthnts).

GAYTON Staffs
119 SJ 9828 5m NE of Stafford. CP, 156.
Stffd RD. P STFFD. Ch e. Stffd and
Stone CC.

GAYTON LE MARSH Lincs (L)
105 TF 4284 5m W of Mablethorpe.
CP, 148. Louth RD. P Alford. Ch e, m.
Lth CC.

GAYTON THORPE Norfolk
124 TF 7418 8m E of King's Lynn. Loc,
Gtn CP. Ch e, m.

GAZELEY Suffolk (W)
135 TL 7264 5m E of Newmarket. CP, 370.
Mildenhall RD. P Nmkt. Ch e, v. Sch pe.
Bury St Edmunds CC.

GEDDING Suffolk (W)
136 TL 9558 6m W of Stowmarket.
CP, 126. Thedwastre RD. Ch e. Bury
St Edmunds CC.

GEDDINGTON Northants
133 SP 8983 3m NNE of Kettering.
CP, 1,361. Kttrng RD. P Kttrng. Ch e, c.
Sch pe. Kttrng CC. Fine square with mdvl
ch, br, hses; in centre one of three surviving
orig Eleanor crosses (A.M.). Others at
Hardingstone and Waltham Cross.

GEDNEY Lincs (H)
124 TF 4024 2m WNW of Long Sutton.
CP, 2,073. E Elloe RD. P Spalding. Ch e.
Sch p. Holland w Boston CC. See also
Dawsmere, Gdny Drove End, Gdny Dyke.
Impressive 13c–14c ch.

GEDNEY DROVE END Lincs (H)
124 TF 4529 4m NNE of Long Sutton. Loc,
Gdny CP. P Spalding. Ch e, m. Sch p.

GEDNEY DYKE Lincs (H)
124 TF 4126 2m NNW of Long Sutton.
Loc, Gdny CP. P Spalding. Ch m.

GEDNEY HILL Lincs (H)
123 TF 3311 8m W of Wisbech. CP, 426.
E Elloe RD. P Spalding. Ch e, b. Sch pe.
Holland w Boston CC.

GEE CROSS Ches
101 SJ 9593 4m NE of Stockport. Loc,
Hyde MB. P Hde.

GELDESTON Norfolk
137 TM 3991 2m WNW of Beccles. CP, 338.
Loddon RD. P Bccls, Suffolk. Ch e.
S Nflk CC.

GELSTON Lincs (K)
113 SK 0145 6m N of Grantham. Loc,
Hough-on-the-Hill CP.

GEMBLING Yorks (E)
99 TA 1157 6m E of Driffield. Loc,
Foston CP. Sch p.

GENTLESHAW Staffs
120 SK 0511 4m S of Rugeley. Loc,
Longdon CP. P Rgly. Ch e. Sch p.

GEORGE GREEN Bucks
159, 160 SU 9981 2m ENE of Slough. Loc,
Wexham CP. Eton RD. P Slgh. Beaconsfield CC (S Bucks).

GEORGEHAM Devon
163 SS 4639 3m NW of Braunton. CP,
1,018. Barnstaple RD. P Brntn. Ch e, b.
Sch pe. N Dvn CC. See also Croyde,
N Buckland, Pickwell.

GEORGE NYMPTON Devon
163 SS 7023 2m SSW of S Molton. CP, 181.
S Mltn RD. P: S Mltn. Ch m. N Dvn CC.

GERMANSWEEK Devon
175   SX 4394 9m W of Okehampton.
CP, 130. Okhmpton RD. P Beaworthy.
Ch e, b. W Dvn CC (Torrington). See also
Eworthy.

GERMOE Cornwall
189 SW 5829 5m WNW of Helston. CP, 399.
Kerrier RD. P Penzance. Ch e, m, r. Sch p.
St Ives CC. In churchyard, curious small
mdvl(?) bldng, origin and purpose unknown.

GERRANS Cornwall
190 SW 8735 2m NE of St Mawes across
river. CP, 909. Truro RD. Ch m2, v. Sch p.
Truro CC. See also Bohortha, Porthscatho,
Trevithian.

GERRARDS CROSS Bucks
159, 160 TQ 0088 4m ESE of Beaconsfield.
CP, 5,851. Eton RD. P. Ch e, c, m.
Sch pe. Bcnsfld CC. (S Bucks).

GESTINGTHORPE Essex
149 TL 8138 4m WSW of· Sudbury.
CP, 382. Halstead RD. P Hlstd. Ch e.
Saffron Walden CC.

GIDDING, GREAT Hunts
134 TL 1183 6m SE of Oundle. See Gt
Gddng.

GIDEA PARK London
161 TQ 5390 1m NE of Romford. Loc,
Havering LB. Rmfd BC.

GIDLEIGH Devon
175   SX   6788   5 m   WNW   of

Moretonhampstead. CP, 117. Okehampton RD. P Newton Abbot. Ch e. W Dvn CC (Torrington). Granite ch and timy 13c–14c cstle, on E edge of Dartmoor.

GIGGLESWICK Yorks (W)
90 SD 8164 just NW of Settle. CP, 980. Sttle RD. P Sttle. Ch e. Sch p. Skipton CC. See also Stackhouse. In limestone country of Craven district. Quarries.Boys' public sch. 1m N, G. Scar; beyond, hills with many caves and potholes.

GILBERDYKE Yorks (E)
98 SE 8329 6m ENE of Goole. CP, 1,129. Howden RD. P Brough. Ch m. Sch p. Hdn CC. See also Hive, Sandholme, Scalby, Staddlethorpe.

GILCRUX Cumb
82 NY 1138 5m E of Maryport. CP, 341. Cockermouth RD. P Carlisle. Ch e, m. Sch pe. Workington CC.

GILDERSOME Yorks (W)
96, 102 SE 2429 4m SW of Leeds. Loc, Morley MB. P Mly, LDS.

GILDINGWELLS Yorks (W)
103 SK 5585 4m NNW of Worksop. CP, 75. Kiveton Pk RD. Rother Valley CC.

GILESGATE MOOR Co Durham
85 NZ 2942 1m E of Durham. Loc, Belmont CP. Drhm RD. P DRHM. Ch r. Sch p2. Drhm CC.

GILLAMOOR Yorks (N)
86, 92 SE 6890 3m NNW of Kirkbymoorside. CP, 144. Kbmsde RD. P YORK. Ch e, m2. Sch pe. Thirsk and Malton CC.

GILLING EAST Yorks (N)
92 SE 6177 4m S of Helmsley. CP, 187. Hlmsly RD. P YORK. Ch e, r. Sch pe. Thirsk and Malton CC. G. Cstle, 14c–18c hse, now preparatory sch for Ampleforth College (RC); Elizn great hall*, fine grnds.

GILLINGHAM Dorset
166 ST 8026 4m NW of Shaftesbury. CP, 3,619. Shftsbry RD. P. Ch e, b, m, r. Sch p, s. N Dst CC. See also Huntingford, Milton on Stour, Wyke Marsh. Mkt and indstrl tn.

GILLINGHAM Kent
172 TQ 7767 30m ESE of London.

MB, 86,714. P. Gllnghm BC. See also Rainham, Wigmore.

GILLINGHAM Norfolk
137 TM 4191 1m NW of Beccles. CP, 468. Loddon RD. P Bccls, Suffolk. Ch e, r. Sch pe. S Nflk CC.

GILLING WEST Yorks (N)
85/91 NZ 1805 3m NNE of Richmond. CP(Gllng w Hartforth and Sedbury), 665. Rchmnd RD. P Rchmnd. Ch e. Sch pe. Rchmnd CC. To S, Aske Hall, mansion of all dates from 15c to 20c. To SE of hall, Oliver's Ducket, Gothic folly.

GILLOW HEATH Staffs
110 SF 8858 3m SSE of Congleton. Loc, Biddulph UD.

GILL'S GREEN Kent
184 TQ 7532 1m N of Hawkhurst. Loc, Hkhst CP. P Hkhst.

GILMONBY Yorks (N)
84 NY 9913 4m SW of Barnard Cstle. CP, 52. Startforth RD. Richmond CC.

GILMORTON Leics
132, 133 SP 5787 3m NE of Lutterworth. CP, 432. Lttrwth RD. P Rugby, Warwickshire. Ch e, c. Sch pe. Blaby CC (Harborough).

GILSLAND Cumb and Nthmb
76 NY 6366 5m WNW of Haltwhistle. Loc, Border RD. Hltwhstle RD. P Carlisle. Ch e. Sch pe. Penrith and the Border CC, Hexham CC. Vllge became a spa in 19c when sulphur and chalybeate springs were discovered.

GILSTON Herts
148, 161 TL 4413 2m N of Harlow. CP, 210. Ware RD. Ch e. E Herts CC.

GIMINGHAM Norfolk
126 TG 2836 4m N of N Walsham. CP, 482. Erpingham RD. P NORWICH, NOR 34Y. Ch e. Sch pe. N Nflk CC.

GIPPING Suffolk (E)
136 TM 0763 3m NNE of Stowmarket. CP, 97. Gppng RD. Ch e. Eye CC.

GIPSEY BRIDGE Lincs (L)
114 TF 2849 5m NW of Boston. Loc, Thornton le Fen CP. Spilsby RD. P Bstn. Ch m. Sch p. Horncastle CC.

GIRSBY Yorks (N)
85 NZ 3508 6m SE of Darlington. CP, 47.
Croft RD. Ch e. Richmond CC.

GIRTON Cambs
135 TL 4262 3m NW of Cambridge.
CP, 3,115. Chesterton RD. P CMBRDGE.
Ch e, b. Sch p. Cambs CC. Cmbrdge suburb
with one of the university's three women's
colleges.

GIRTON Notts
113 SK 8266 8m NNE of Newark. CP, 129.
Nwk RD. Ch m. Nwk CC.

GISBURN Yorks (W)
95 SD 8248 7m NE of Clitheroe. CP, 414.
Bowland RD. P Clthroe, Lancs. Ch e. Sch p.
Skipton CC.

GISLEHAM Suffolk (E)
137 TM 5188 4m SSW of Lowestoft.
CP, 524. Lothingland RD. Ch e. Sch s.
Lwstft CC.

GISLINGHAM Suffolk (E)
136 TM 0771 5m WSW of Eye. CP, 329.
Hartismere RD. P Eye. Ch e, m, v. Sch pe.
Eye CC.

GISSING Norfolk
136 TM 1485 4m NNE of Diss. CP, 254.
Depwade RD. P Dss. Ch e, m. Sch p.
S Nflk CC.

GITTISHAM Devon
176 SY 1398 2m WSW of Honiton. CP, 262.
Hntn RD. P Hntn. Ch e. Hntn CC.

GIVENDALE, GREAT Yorks (E)
98 SE 8153 3m NNE of Pocklington. Loc,
Millington CP.

GLAISDALE Yorks (N)
86 NZ 7705 8m WSW of Whitby. CP, 879.
Whtby RD. P Whtby. Ch e, m3. Sch p.
Cleveland and Whtby CC (Scarborough and
Whtby). See also Houlsyke, Lealholm.

GLANDFORD Norfolk
125 TG 0441 3m NW of Holt.
CP (Letheringsett w Glndfd), 274.
Erpingham RD. Ch e. N Nflk CC. Model
vllge and ch, reproducing in miniature many
mdvl E Anglian ch styles, all blt c 1900.
Shell museum.

GLANTON Nthmb
71 NU 0714 7m W of Alnwick. CP, 247.
Alnwck RD. P Alnwck. Ch v2. Sch p.
Berwick-upon-Tweed CC. See also Glntn
Pike.

GLANTON PIKE Nthmb
71 NU 0514 8m W of Alnwick. Loc,
Glntn CP.

GLANVILLES WOOTTON Dorset
178 ST 6708 6m SSE of Sherborne.
CP, 196. Sturminster RD. P Shbne. Ch e, m.
N Dst CC.

GLAPTHORN Northants
134 TL 0290 2m NW of Oundle. CP, 222.
Oundle and Thrapston RD. Ch e. Sch pe.
Wellingborough CC (Peterborough).

GLAPWELL Derbys
112 SK 4766 5m NW of Mansfield.
CP, 1,676. Blackwell RD. P Chesterfield.
Ch m. Bolsover CC.

GLASCOTE Staffs
120 SK 2203 1m ESE of Tamworth. Loc,
Tmwth MB. P Tmwth. Lichfield and
Tmwth CC (Meriden).

GLASSHOUSE HILL Glos
143 SO 7020 8m W of Gloucester. Loc,
Taynton CP.

GLASSHOUSES Yorks (W)
91 SE 1764 1m SE of Pateley Br. Loc, High
and Low Bishopside CP. Ripon and Ptly
Br RD. P Harrogate. Ch m. Sch p. Rpn CC.

GLASSON Cumb
75 NY 2560 3m NNE of Kirkbride. Loc,
Bowness CP. Wigton RD. Penrith and the
Border CC.

GLASSON Lancs
94 SD 4456 4m SSW of Lancaster. Loc,
Thurnham CP. Lncstr RD. P (Glssn
Dock), LNCSTR. Ch e. Sch pe. Lncstr CC.
Dock blt late 18c to serve Lncstr.

GLASSONBY Cumb
83 NY 5738 7m NE of Penrith. CP, 299.
Pnrth RD. Ch m. Sch pe. Pnrth and the
Border CC. See also Gamblesby. To S, two
stone circles: Long Meg and her Daughters
(59 stones), and Little Meg (11 stones).

Glaston

GLASTON Rutland
122 SK 8900 2m E of Uppingham. CP, 145.
Uppnghm RD. P Uppnghm. Ch e. Rtlnd and
Stamford CC.

GLASTONBURY Som
165 ST 5039 13m E of Bridgwater.
MB, 6,571. P. Wells CC. Ancient centre of
Christian culture and pilgrimage; also
Arthurian legends. Rems of 13c abbey*.
Tribunal Hse (A.M.), museum. To E, G. Tor
(NT), steep conical hill topped by ruined ch.

GLATTON Hunts
134 TL 1586 8m SSW of Peterborough.
CP, 146. Norman Cross RD.
P HUNTINGDON. Ch e. Hunts CC. Partly
Nmn ch: notable twr, bench-ends. Thatched
cottages.

GLAZEBROOK Lancs
101 SJ 6992 6m ENE of Warrington.
CP(Rixton-w-Glzbrk), 1,583. Wrrngtn RD.
P Wrrngtn. Ch m2. Newton CC.

GLAZEBURY Lancs
101 SJ 6797 7m NE of Warrington. Loc,
Golborne UD. P Wrrngtn.

GLAZELEY Shrops
130 SO 7088 3m SSW of Bridgnorth.
CP, 30. Brdgnth RD. Ch e. Ludlow CC.

GLEASTON Lancs
88 SD 2570 4m ENE of Barrow. Loc,
Aldingham CP. P Ulverston. Ch c.

GLEMHAM, GREAT Suffolk (E)
137 TM 3461 3m WSW of Saxmundham.
See Gt Glmhm.

GLEMSFORD Suffolk (W)
149 TL 8248 3m NW of Long Melford.
CP, 1,365. Mlfd RD. P Sudbury.
Ch e, b2, m. Sch p. Sdbry and
Woodbridge CC.

GLENFIELD Leics
121 SK 5406 3m WNW, of Leicester.
CP(Glenfields). Blaby RD. P LCSTR.
Ch e, m. Sch i, ie, j2. Blby CC (Harborough).

GLEN, GREAT Leics
132, 133 SP 6597 6m SE of Leicester. See
Gt Gln.

GLEN PARVA Leics
132, 133 SP 5698 4m S of Leicester. CP.
Blaby RD. Ch e. Sch p. Blby CC
(Harborough).

GLENRIDDING Westm
83 NY 3816 8m N of Ambleside. Loc,
Lakes UD. P Penrith, Cumberland.
Westm CC.

GLENTHAM Lincs (L)
104 TF 0090 7m W of Mkt Rasen. CP, 283.
Caistor RD. P LINCOLN. Ch e, m2. Sch p.
Gainsborough CC.

GLENTWORTH Lincs (L)
104 SK 9488 8m E of Gainsborough.
CP, 462. Gnsbrgh RD. P Gnsbrgh. Ch e, m.
Sch p. Gnsbrgh CC. Ruins of great hse blt
by Wray family; Wray monmts in ch.

GLEWSTONE Herefs
142 SO 5522 3m WSW of Ross-on-Wye.
Loc, Marston CP. P Rss-on-Wye.

GLINTON Hunts
123 TF 1505 5m NNW of Peterborough.
CP, 1,067. Ptrbrgh RD. P PTRBRGH.
Ch e, m. Sch pe, s. Ptrbrgh BC (CC). Old
stone vllge with unharmonious modern
accretions. Ch: 15c spire; gargoyles.

GLOOSTON Leics
133 SP 7595 6m N of Mkt Harborough.
CP, 48. Mkt Hbrgh RD. Ch e. Hbrgh CC.

GLOSSOP Derbys
102 SK 0394 13m E of Manchester.
MB, 24,147. P. High Peak CC. See also
Hadfield.

GLOUCESTER Glos
143 SO 8318 32m NNE of Bristol.
CB, 90,134. P(GLCSTR). Glcstr BC. See
also Hucclecote, Longlevens. Indstrl city on
R Severn. Nmn to Perp cathedral with
cloisters. 15c New Inn has galleried
courtyard.

GLUSBURN Yorks (W)
96 SE 0044 4m WNW of Keighley.
CP, 2,816. Skipton RD. P Kghly. Ch b.
Sch p. Skptn CC. See also Cross Hills. Stone
Gappe, 18c hse, is original of Gateshead Hall
in *Jane Eyre*.

GLYMPTON Oxon
145 SP 4221 3m NNW of Woodstock.

CP, 126. Chipping Norton RD. P OXFORD. Ch e. Banbury CC.

GLYNDE Sussex (E)
183 TQ 4508 3m ESE of Lewes. CP, 238. Chailey RD. P Lws. Ch e. Lws CC. G Place*, 16c hse blt round courtyard. To N, Glyndebourne, Elizn hse added to in 19c and 20c; opera hse opened 1934. Annual opera season in summer.

GNOSALL Staffs
119 SJ 8220 6m WSW of Stafford. CP, 2,482. Stffd RD. P STFFD. Ch e, m. Sch p, pe, s. Stffd and Stone CC. See also Bromstead Hth, Coton, Knightley, Moreton, Outwoods. Impressive Nmn and later ch.

GOADBY Leics
133 SP 7598 7m N of Mkt Harborough. CP, 56. Billesdon RD. Ch e. Hbrgh CC (Melton).

GOADBY MARWOOD Leics
122 SK 7826 5m NNE of Melton Mowbray. Loc, Eaton CP. P Mltn Mbry. Ch e, m. 14c ch: Dec windows, mdvl glass. Large find of Roman coins in 1953.

GOATACRE Wilts
157 SU 0177 4m N of Calne. Loc, Hilmarton CP. Ch m.

GOATHILL Dorset
178 ST 6717 3m E of Sherborne. CP, 25. Shbne RD. Ch e. W Dst CC.

GOATHLAND Yorks (N)
86, 92 NZ 8301 7m SW of Whitby. CP, 474. Whtby RD. P Whtby. Ch e, m. Sch p. Cleveland and Whtby CC (Scarborough and Whtby). See also Beck Hole. High moorland vllge with grn. Many waterfalls, incl Mallyan Spout and Nellie Ayre Force S of vllge. 2½m SW, Roman rd (A.M.) on Wheeldale Moor.

GOATHURST Som
165 ST 2534 3m SW of Bridgwater. CP, 260. Brdgwtr RD. P Brdgwtr. Ch e. Brdgwtr CC.

GOBOWEN Shrops
118 SJ 3033 3m NNE of Oswestry. CP(Selattyn and Gbwn), 1,830. Oswstry RD. P Oswstry. Ch e, c, m, r. Sch p. Oswstry CC. Army camp. Orthopaedic hsptl.

GODALMING Surrey
169, 170, 182 SU 9643 4m SSW of Guildford. MB, 18,634. P Farnham CC. See also Farncombe. Rsndtl and shopping tn. Tn Hall, early 19c, now museum.

GODINGTON Oxon
145, 146 SP 6427 5m NE of Bicester. CP, 44. Ploughley RD. Ch e. Banbury CC (Henley).

GODLEYBROOK Staffs
110, 119 SJ 9744 6m E of Stoke-on-Trent. Loc, Dilhorne CP.

GODMANCHESTER Hunts
134 TL 2470 1m SSE of Huntingdon. MB(Hntngdn and Gdmnchstr), 16,540. P HNTNGDN. Hunts CC. Separated from Hntngdn by R Ouse, spanned, however, by 13c br. Charter granted 1212. Several old hses incl Tdr grammar sch.

GODMANSTON Dorset
178 SY 6697 5m NNW of Dorchester. CP(Godmanstone), 121. Dchstr RD. P(Gdmnstne), Dchstr. Ch e. W Dst CC. The Smith's Arms has some claim to title of England's smallest inn; licence granted by Charles II who had his horse shod here.

GODMERSHAM Kent
172, 173 TR 0650 6m NE of Ashford. CP, 310. E Ashfd RD. P Canterbury. Ch e. Ashfd CC. G. Pk belonged to Jane Austen's brother; she stayed here often. Landscape and formal gdns*.

GODNEY Som
165 ST 4742 3m NNW of Glastonbury. CP, 227. Wells RD. P Wlls. Ch e. Wlls CC. On boggy 'moors' where peat is dug. Nearby, site of prehistoric lake vllge; finds in Glstnbry and Taunton Museums. (See also Meare, Ulrome.)

GODOLPHIN CROSS Cornwall
189 SW 6031 4m NW of Helston. Loc, Breage CP. P Brge, Hlstn. Ch e, m. To NW, G. Hse*, Tdr and later.

GODSHILL Hants
179 SU 1715 2m E of Fordingbridge. Loc, Fdngbrdge CP. P Fdngbrdge. Ch v. Sch pe.

GODSHILL IOW
180 SZ 5281 3m W of Shanklin. CP, 945. Isle of Wight RD and CC. P Ventnor.

Ch e, m2. Sch p. See also Roud. To S, Appuldurcombe Hse (A.M.), ruin of early 18c home of Worsley family.

GODSTONE Surrey
170 TQ 3451 6m E of Reigate. CP, 5,510. Gdstne RD. P. Ch e, b. Sch p, pe. E SrryCC(Rgte). See also Blindley Hth. Large grn beside A22 rd, with pond.

GOFF'S OAK Herts
160 TL 3203 2m W of Cheshunt. Loc, Chshnt UD. P Waltham Cross.

GOLANT Cornwall
186 SX 1254 2m N of Fowey. Loc, St Sampson CP. St Austell RD. P Fwy. Ch e, m. Bodmin CC.

GOLBERDON Cornwall
186 SX 3271 2m NW of Callington. Loc, South Hill CP. P Cllngtn. Ch m.

GOLBORNE Lancs
101 SJ 6098 6m N of Warrington. UD, 28,178. P Wrrngtn. Newton CC. See also Culcheth, Glazebury, Kenyon, Lowton, Ltn Cmmn, Twiss Grn. Colliery. Textiles.

GOLCAR Yorks (W)
96, 102 SE 0915 3m W of Huddersfield. Loc, Colne Valley UD. P Hddsfld. Clne Vlly CC.

GOLDEN CROSS Sussex (E)
183 TQ 5312 4m WNW of Hailsham. Loc, Chiddingly CP. P Hlshm.

GOLDEN GREEN Kent
171 TQ 6348 3m ENE of Tonbridge. Loc, Hadlow CP. P Tnbrdge.

GOLDEN POT Hants
169 SU 7043 3m N of Alton. Loc, Shalden CP.

GOLDEN VALLEY Glos
143, 144 SO 9022 3m W of Cheltenham. Loc, Staverton CP.

GOLDERS GREEN London
160 TQ 2488 1m ESE of Hendon. Loc, Barnet LB. Hndn S BC.

GOLDHANGER Essex
162 TL 9008 4m ENE of Maldon. CP, 506. Mldn RD. P Mldn. Ch e. Sch p. Mldn CC.

GOLDSBOROUGH Yorks (N)
86 NZ 8314 4m NW of Whitby. Loc, Lythe CP. To NW, Roman signal stn.

GOLDSBOROUGH Yorks (W)
96 SE 3856 2m ESE of Knaresborough. CP, 161. Nidderdale RD. P Knsbrgh. Ch e. Sch pe. Harrogate CC. 18c estate vllge. G. Hall, 17c mansion with 18c alterations. Hoard of Viking silver found at G. incl coins struck in Samarkand.

GOLDSITHNEY Cornwall
189 SW 5430 5m E of Penzance. Loc, Perranuthnoe CP. P Pnznce. Ch m. Sch i.

GOLDTHORPE Yorks (W)
103 SE 4604 7m ESE of Barnsley. Loc, Dearne UD. P Rotherham. Hemsworth CC.

GOLDWORTHY Devon
174 SS 3922 5m WSW of Bideford. Loc, Parkham CP. Ch m.

GOMELDON Wilts
167 SU 1835 5m NE of Salisbury. Loc, Idmiston CP. Sch p.

GOMERSAL Yorks (W)
96, 102 SE 2026 4m NW of Dewsbury. Loc, Spenborough MB. P Cleckheaton. Brighouse and Spnbrgh CC.

GOMSHALL Surrey
170 TQ 0847 5m W of Dorking. Loc, Shere CP. P Guildford. Ch v. Vllge under N Downs, on busy narrow rd. Tannery.

GONALSTON Notts
112 SK 6847 8m NE of Nottingham. CP, 92. Southwell RD. P NTTNGHM. Ch e. Newark CC.

GONERBY, GREAT Lincs (K)
113, 122 SK 8938 2m NNW of Grantham. See Gt Gnrby.

GOOD EASTER Essex
148, 161 TL 6212 6m S of Dunmow. CP, 349.   Chelmsford RD.   P Chlmsfd. Ch e, v. Braintree CC (Chlmsfd).

GOODERSTONE Norfolk
125/136 TF 7602 6m SW of Swaffham. CP, 337. Swffhm RD. P King's Lynn. Ch e, m. Sch pe. SW Nflk CC.

GOODLEIGH Devon
163 SS 5934 3m E of Barnstaple. CP, 219.
Bnstple RD. P Bnstple. Ch e, m, v. Sch pe.
N Dvn CC.

GOODMANHAM Yorks (E)
98 SE 8943 1m NE of Mkt Weighton.
CP, 222. Pocklington RD. P YORK.
Ch e, m. Howden CC. Mainly Nmn ch,
supposedly on site of pagan temple
destroyed by chief priest when he was
converted and the North of England became
christianised c mid-7c.

GOODMAYES London
161 TQ 4686 4m WSW of Romford. Loc,
Redbridge LB. P Ilford, Essex. Ilfd S BC.

GOODNESTONE Kent
172, 173 TR 0461 2m E of Faversham.
CP, 58. Swale RD. Ch e. Fvrshm CC.

GOODNESTONE Kent
173 TR 2554 5m WSW of Sandwich.
CP, 414. Eastry RD. P Canterbury. Ch e.
Sch pe. Dover and Deal CC (Dvr). See also
Chillenden, Knowlton. In pk of G. Hse,
often visited by Jane Austen. Brasses in ch.

GOODRICH Herefs
142 SO 5719 4m SSW of Ross-on-Wye.
CP, 510. Rss and Whitchurch RD.
P Rss-on-Wye. Ch e. Sch pe. Hereford CC.
To N, G. Castle (A.M.), massive 12c–14c
rems. To E, scant rems of Flanesford Priory.

GOODRINGTON Devon
188 SX 8958 1m S of Paignton. Loc,
Torbay CB. P Pgntn. Famous stretch of
sand.

GOODWORTH CLATFORD Hants
168 SU 3642 2m S of Andover. CP, 510.
Andvr RD. P Andvr. Ch e Sch pe.
Winchester CC (Basingstoke).

GOOLE Yorks (W)
97, 98 SE 7423 17m NE of Doncaster.
MB, 18,066. P. Gle CC. At confluence of
rivers Don and Ouse. Docks, and two very
high water twrs.

GOOLEFIELDS Yorks (W)
97, 98 SE 7520 2m SSE of Goole. CP, 176.
Gle RD. Gle CC.

GOONBELL Cornwall
190 SW 7249 5m NNE of Redruth. Loc,
St Agnes CP. P St Agnes. Ch m.

GOONHAVERN Cornwall
185, 190 SW 7853 5m SSW of Newquay.
Loc, Perranzabuloe CP. P Truro. Ch m.
Sch p.

GOOSEHAM Cornwall
174 SS 2216 7m N of Bude. Loc,
Morwenstow CP.

GOOSEY Berks
158 SU 3591 4m NW of Wantage. CP, 122.
Wntge RD. Ch e. Abingdon CC.

GOOSNARGH Lancs
94 SD 5536 5m NNE of Preston. CP, 1,176.
Prstn RD. P Prstn. Ch e, r. Sch p, pe, pr.
S Fylde CC. See also Inglewhite, White
Chpl.

GOOSTREY Ches
110 SJ 7770 6m SSE of Knutsford.
CP, 940. Congleton RD. P Crewe. Ch e, m.
Sch pe. Kntsfd CC.

GOREFIELD Cambs
124 TF 4112 3m WNW of Wisbech. Loc,
Leverington CP. P Wsbch. Ch e, c, v. Sch p.

GORING Oxon
158 SU 5980 5m S of Wallingford.
CP, 2,157. Henley RD. P Reading, Berks.
Ch e, r, v. Sch pe. Hnly CC. Small tn on
R Thames between Chilterns and Berks
Downs. Mainly Nmn ch has late 13c bell.
Icknield Way crosses R Thames here.

GORING-BY-SEA Sussex (W)
182 TQ 1102 2m W of Worthing. Loc,
Wthng MB. P Wthng.

GORING HEATH Oxon
158, 159 SU 6579 2m NE of Pangbourne.
CP, 935. Henley RD. P Reading, Berks.
Sch pe. Hnly CC. See also Cray's Pond,
Whitchurch Hill.

GORLESTON ON SEA Norfolk
126 TG 5203 S distr of Yarmouth. Loc,
Gt Ymth CB. P Gt Ymth. Resort. Ch has
very early (1320) military brass.

GORRAN CHURCHTOWN Cornwall
190 SW 9942 6m SSW of St Austell. Loc,
St Goran CP. St Astll RD. P(Grrn), St Astll.
Ch e. Truro CC. Large ch with tall twr
stands high; font, bench-ends.

GORRAN HAVEN Cornwall
190 SX 0141 7m S of St Austell. Loc,

St Goran CP. St Astll RD. P Grrn, St Astll. Ch e, m. Sch p. Truro CC. Small bathing place and fishing vllge.

GORSLEY Glos
143 SO 6825 5m E of Ross-on-Wye. Loc, Newent RD. P Rss-on-Wye, Herefordshire. Ch e. W Glos CC.

GORSLEY COMMON Herefs
142, 143 SO 6725 5m E of Ross-on-Wye. Loc, Linton CP. Ch b. Sch pe.

GORSTY COMMON Herefs
142 SO 4437 4m WSW of Hereford. Loc, Clehonger CP.

GORSTY HILL Staffs
120 SK 1029 3m S of Uttoxeter. Loc, Marchington CP. Ch m.

GOSBECK Suffolk (E)
150 TM 1655 7m N of Ipswich. CP, 213. Gipping RD. Ch e. Eye CC.

GOSBERTON Lincs (H)
114, 123 TF 2431 6m N of Spalding. CP, 2,226. Spldng RD. P Spldng. Ch e, b, m. Sch p. Holland w Boston CC. See also Risegate, Westhorpe.

GOSBERTON CLOUGH Lincs (H)
123 TF 1929 6m NNW of Spalding. Loc, Gsbtn CP. P Spldng. Ch e, m. Sch p.

GOSFIELD Essex
149 TL 7829 2m WSW of Halstead. CP, 831. Hlstd RD. P Hlstd. Ch e. Sch p. Saffron Walden CC. Ch: monmts, 15c brass. G. Hall*, Tdr and 18c mansion visited by Elizabeth I.

GOSFORD Oxon
145 SP 4913 5m NNW of Oxford. CP(Gsfd and Water Eaton), 1,260. Ploughley RD. Sch s. Mid-Oxon CC (Banbury).

GOSFORTH Cumb
88 NY 0603 2m NE of Seascale. CP, 893. Ennerdale RD. P Sscle. Ch e, m. Sch pe. Whitehaven CC. 10c cross, 15ft high, in churchyard.

GOSFORTH Nthmb
78 NZ 2468 2m N of Newcastle. UD, 26,826. P NCSTLE UPON TYNE 3. Wallsend BC. Mainly rsdntl suburb. To Ncstle Racecourse in G. Pk.

GOSMORE Herts
147 TL 1827 1m S of Hitchin. Loc, Ippollitts CP.

GOSPEL END Staffs
130. 131 SO 9093 3m SSW of Wolverhampton. Loc, Himley CP. P Dudley, Worcs. SW Staffs CC (Bilston BC). Mining vllge.

GOSPEL OAK London
160 TQ 2885 4m NNW of Charing Cross. Loc, Camden LB. St Pancras N BC. Distr S of Parliament Hill on Hampstead Hth; name recalls tree where gospel was read during beating of bounds.

GOSPORT Hants
180 SZ 6199 2m W of Portsmouth. MB, 75,947. P. Gspt BC (Gspt and Fareham). See also Alverstoke, Bridgemary, Hardway, Lee-on-the-Solent. Naval centre. Establishments incl RN victualling yard and Haslar Hsptl. Rems of 17c–18c defence wks and Palmerston forts of 1850s (mostly occupied by Navy — see also Ptsmth). Foot passenger ferry to Ptsmth.

GOSWICK Nthmb
64 NU 0545 6m SE of Berwick-upon-Tweed. Loc, Ancroft CP.

GOTHAM Notts
112, 121, 122 SK 5330 7m SSW of Nottingham. CP, 1,434. Basford RD. P NTTNGHM. Ch e, m 2. Sch p. Rushcliffe CC. Gypsum mines.

GOTHERINGTON Glos
143, 144 SO 9629 5m N of Cheltenham. CP, 457. Chltnhm RD. P Chltnhm. Ch e, m. Sch p. Cirencester and Tewkesbury CC.

GOUDHURST Kent
171, 172, 183, 184 TQ 7237 4m WNW of Cranbrook. CP, 2,767. Crnbrk RD. P Crnbrk. Ch e, m, r, v. Sch pe. Royal Tunbridge Wells CC (Ashford). See also Curtisden Grn, Kilndown. Hilltop vllge, partly NT, overlooking Weald. Hop gdns, orchards. Ch: brasses, monmts. ½m NE, Ladham Hse; shrub gdn*. 1½m SW, Finchcocks, 18c brick mansion. 1½m S, Bedgebury Pk, early 19c mansion, and National Pinetum*.

GOULCEBY Lincs (L)
105 TF 2579 6m N of Horncastle. CP, 93.
Hncstle RD. P Louth. Ch e. Hncstle CC.

GOVETON Devon
187, 188 SX 7546 2m NE of Kingsbridge.
Loc, Buckland-tout-Saints CP. P Kngsbrdge.

GOWDALL Yorks (W)
97, 98 SE 6222 6m S of Selby. CP, 211.
Goole RD. Ch m. Gle CC.

GOXHILL Lincs (L)
99 TA 1021 4m E of Barton-upon-Humber.
CP, 1,192.   Glanford Brigg RD.
P Barrow-on-Hmbr. Ch e, m. Sch p. Brgg
and Scunthorpe CC (Brgg).

GOXHILL Yorks (E)
99 TA 1844 2m SW of Hornsea. Loc,
Hatfield CP. Holderness RD. Ch e.
Bridlington CC.

GRAFFHAM Sussex (W)
181 SU 9217 4m SE of Midhurst. CP, 503.
Mdhst RD. P Petworth. Ch e. Sch p.
Chichester CC (Horsham). Wooded
downland country. G. Down to S rises to
over 700ft.

GRAFHAM Hunts
134 TL 1669 6m N of St Neots. CP, 184.
St Nts RD. P HUNTINGDON. Ch e.
Hunts CC. On edge of huge modern
reservoir, G. Water; sailing, fishing, nature
reserve.

GRAFTON Herefs
142 SO 4937 2m SSW of Hereford. CP, 145.
Hrfd RD. Ch e. Sch s. Hrfd CC.

GRAFTON Oxon
157 SP 2600 4m E of Lechlade. CP(Grftn
and Radcot), 63. Witney RD. Mid-Oxon CC
(Banbury).

GRAFTON Shrops
118 SJ 4319 5m NW of Shrewsbury. Loc,
Pimhill CP. Atcham RD. Sch p. Shrsbry CC.

GRAFTON Worcs
129 SO 5761 5m SSW of Tenbury Wells.
Loc, Bockleton CP.

GRAFTON Worcs
143, 144 SO 9837 6m ENE of Tewkesbury.
Loc, Beckford CP.

GRAFTON Yorks (W)
91, 97 SE 4163 3m SSE of Boroughbridge.
CP(Marton cum Grftn), 344.
Nidderdale RD. P YORK. Ch m. Sch pe.
Harrogate CC.

GRAFTON FLYFORD Worcs
130, 131 SO 9655 7m E of Worcester.
CP, 144.   Pershore RD. P WCSTR. Ch e.
S Worcs CC.

GRAFTON REGIS Northants
146 SP 7546 4m ESE of Towcester.
CP, 174. Tcstr RD. P Tcstr. Ch e.
Daventry CC (S Nthnts). See also Alderton.
Royal connection was a hunting lodge.
Elizabeth Woodville, who married Edward
IV, lived at Grfton. Oak tree under which
they met survives.

GRAFTON UNDERWOOD Northants
133 SP 9280 4m ENE Kettering. CP, 131.
Kttrng RD. P Kttrng. Ch e. Kttrng CC.
Many-bridged stream flows through vllge of
stone and thatched cottages.

GRAFTY GREEN Kent
172, 184 TQ 8748 5m W of Charing. Loc,
Hollingbourn RD. P Maidstone. Ch b.
Mdstne CC.

GRAIN Kent
172 TQ 8876 10m ENE of Rochester. Loc,
Isle of Grn CP. Strood RD. P(Isle of
Grn), Rchstr. Ch e, c, r. Sch pe.
Gravesend CC. Oil refinery.

GRAINSBY Lincs (L)
105 TF 2799 6m S of Grimsby. CP, 87.
Louth RD. Ch e, m. Lth CC.

GRAINTHORPE Lincs (L)
105 TF 3897 7m NNE of Louth. CP, 520.
Lth RD. P Lth. Ch e, m2. Sch p. Lth CC.

GRAMPOUND Cornwall
190 SW 9348 6m WSW of St Austell.
CP, 412. St Astll RD. P Truro. Ch m2.
Sch pe; Truro CC. On R Fal. (Grampound =
Grand Pont.)

GRAMPOUND ROAD Cornwall
185, 190 SW 9150 6m W of St Austell. Loc,
Truro RD. P Truro. Ch m. Sch pe. Truro CC.
Grown up round rly stn.

GRANBOROUGH Bucks
146 SP 7625 7m SE of Buckingham. CP, 261.

Winslow RD. P Bletchley. Ch e, m. Bcknghm CC.

GRANBY Notts
112, 122 SK 7536 10m W of Grantham. CP, 264. Bingham RD. P NOTTINGHAM. Ch e, m. Rushcliffe CC (Charlton). See also Sutton.

GRANDBOROUGH Warwicks
132 SP 4966 5m S of Rugby. CP, 313. Rgby RD. P Rgby. Ch e, m. Sch pe. Rgby CC.

GRANGE Ches
100, 109 SJ 2386 6m W of Birkenhead. Loc, Hoylake UD. P West Kirby, Wirral.

GRANGE Cumb
82 NY 2517 4m S of Keswick. Loc, Borrowdale CP. Ch e, m.

GRANGE MOOR Yorks (W)
96, 102 SE 2216 5m E of Huddersfield. Loc, Kirkburton UD. P Wakefield.

GRANGE-OVER-SANDS Lancs
89 SD 4077 11m SW of Kendal. UD(Grnge), 3,627. P. Morecambe and Lonsdale CC. See also Kents Bank. Mcmbe Bay resort.

GRANGE VILLA Co Durham
78 NZ 2352 3m W of Chester-le-Street. Loc, Pelton CP. P Chstr-le-Strt.

GRANSDEN, GREAT Hunts
134 TL 2755 6m ESE of St Neots. See Gt Grnsdn.

GRANSMOOR Yorks (E)
99 TA 1259 6m E of Driffield. Loc, Burton Agnes CP.

GRANTCHESTER Cambs
135 TL 4355 2m SSW of Cambridge. CP, 418. Chesterton RD. P CMBRDGE. Ch e. Sch pe. Cambs CC. Rupert Brooke, poet, lived at The Old Vicarage. Modern part in Stulpfield Rd area.

GRANTHAM Lincs (K)
113, 122 SK 9135 21m E of Nottingham. MB, 27,913. P. Grnthm CC. Ancient tn; fine 12c–14c ch with 281ft spire. Many old hses. Agricultural machinery wks.

GRAPPENHALL Ches
101 SJ 6386 3m SE of Warrington. CP, 7,746. Runcorn RD. P Wrrngtn, Lancs. Ch e, m. Sch p, pe. Rncn CC. See also Thelwall.

GRASBY Lincs (L)
104 TA 0804 3m NW of Caistor. CP, 292. Cstr RD. P Barnetby. Ch e, m. Sch pe. Gainsborough CC. Vicarage and sch blt by Charles Tennyson, brother of the poet and vicar here 1837–77.

GRASMERE Westm
83 NY 3307 3m NW of Ambleside. Loc, Lakes UD. P Amblsde. Westm CC. Dove Cottage*, once home of Wordsworth, and Wdswth Museum, at Town End, to SE.

GRASSCROFT Yorks (W)
101 SD 9704 3m E of Oldham. Loc, Saddleworth UD. P Oldhm.

GRASSINGTON Yorks (W)
90 SE 0064 8m N of Skipton. CP, 1,131. Skptn RD. P Skptn. Ch c, m. Sch pe s. Skptn CC. Wharfedale vllge with wide main street running up hill. G. Hall, 13c hse. In immediate vicinity manv round and disc barrows, Iron Age hut circles and fortifications, and on hillsides clearly defined lynchets.

GRASSMOOR Derbys
112 SK 4067 3m SSE of Chesterfield. Loc, Hasland CP. Chstrfld RD. P Chstrfld. Ch m. NE Derbys CC.

GRASSTHORPE Notts
112 SK 7967 9m N of Newark. CP, 53. Southwell RD. Nwk CC.

GRATELEY Hants
167 SU 2741 6m WSW of Andover. CP(Grately), 463. Andvr RD. P Andvr. Ch e. Sch p. Winchester CC (Basingstoke).

GRATWICH Staffs
120 SK 0231 4m WSW of Uttoxeter. Loc, Kingstone CP. Ch e.

GRAVELEY Cambs
134 TL 2563 5m S of Huntingdon. CP, 204. Chesterton RD. P HNTNGDN. Ch e. Cambs CC.

GRAVELEY Herts
147 TL 2327 2m N of Stevenage. CP, 400.
Hitchin RD. P Htchn. Ch e, m. Sch pe.
Htchn CC.

GRAVENEY Kent
172, 173 TR 0562 3m ENE of Faversham.
CP, 305. Swale RD. P Fvrshm. Ch e. Sch p.
Fvrshm CC. Ch: 14c and 15c brasses.
Ancient 40ft rowing boat, perhaps over
1000 years old, found 1970 at Hammond's
Drain on G. Marshes.

GRAVESEND Kent
161, 171 TQ 6474 8m E of Dartford.
MB, 54,044. P. Grvsnd CC. Part of
Thames-side indstrl complex: factories,
wharves, shipping.

GRAYINGHAM Lincs (L)
104 SK 9496 8m SW of Brigg. CP, 106.
Gainsborough RD. Ch e. Gnbrgh CC.

GRAYRIGG Westm
89 SD 5797 5m NE of Kendal. CP, 166.
S Westm RD. P Kndl. Ch e. Sch pe.
Westm CC.

GRAYS Essex
161, 171 TQ 6177 2m NW of Tilbury. Loc,
Thurrock UD. P. Thrrck BC (CC).
Dockyards, warehouses, factories.

GRAYSHOTT Hants
169 SU 8735 3m NW of Haslemere.
CP, 1,636. Alton RD. Ch e, m, r2. Sch pe.
Petersfield CC.

GRAYSWOOD Surrey
169, 181 SU 9134 1m NE of Haslemere.
Loc, Hslmre UD. P Hslmre.

GREASBROUGH Yorks (W)
103 SK 4195 N distr of Rotherham. Loc,
Rthrhm CB. P Rthrhm.

GREASBY Ches
100, 109 SJ 2587 4m W of Birkenhead.
Loc, Hoylake UD. P Upton, Wirral.

GREASLEY Notts
112 SK 4947 7m NW of Nottingham.
CP, 5,351. Basford RD. Ch e, b, c, m, v.
Sch p. Beeston CC (Rushcliffe). See also
Watnall Chaworth. Slight rems of G. Cstle,
14c.

GREAT ABINGTON Cambs
148 TL 5348 6m N of Saffron Walden.
CP, 593. S Cambs RD. P(Abngtn), Cmbrdge.
Ch e. Sch p. Cambs CC. Joined on to Lit A.
Ch has monument to Sir William Walton,
who 'changed this life for a beter' in 1639.

GREAT ADDINGTON Northants
134 SO 9575 3m SW of Thrapston. CP, 213.
Oundle and Thrpstn RD. P Kettering. Ch e.
Sch pe. Wellingborough CC (Peterborough).

GREAT ALNE Warwicks
131 SP 1159 2m NE of Alcester. CP, 354.
Alcstr RD. P Alcstr. Ch e. Sch p.
Stratford-on-Avon CC (Strtfd).

GREAT ALTCAR Lancs
100 SD 3206 1m ESE of Formby.
CP(Altcr), 1,404. W Lancs RD. Ch e.
Crosby BC (Ormskirk CC).

GREAT AMWELL Herts
148, 161 TL 3712 1m SE of Ware.
CP, 2,396. Ware RD. Ch e. Sch pe.
E Herts CC. See also Hertford Hth. Monmt
to Sir Hugh Myddleton erected by Robert
Mylne, 1800. Both men were associated
with the creation of the 'New River'
supplying water to London.

GREAT ASBY Westm
83 NY 6813 5m S of Appleby. Loc,
Asby CP. N Westm RD. P Appleby.
Ch e, b, m. Sch pe. Westm CC. Rectory
incorporates pele twr. Many prehistoric
earthworks on surrounding hills.

GREAT ASHFIELD Suffolk (W)
136 TM 0068 6m NNW of Stowmarket.
CP, 334. Thedwastre RD. P Bury
St Edmunds. Ch e, m. Bury St Eds CC.

GREAT AYTON Yorks (N)
86 NZ 5510 5m SW of Guisborough.
CP, 3,451. Stokesley RD.
P MIDDLESBROUGH, Teesside.
Ch e2, f, m, v. Sch i, ie, j. Richmond CC.
Captain Cook went to school here. Small
museum*. 2m NE, cairns, hut circles,
earthworks have yielded Iron Age rems.

GREAT BADDOW Essex
161, 162 TL 7204 2m SE of Chelmsford.
CP, 9,647. Chlmsfd RD. P Chlmsfd. Ch e, c.
Sch i2, j2, p, s. Chlmsfd CC. See also Galley
End, Galleywood. Large modern
development 'The Vineyards' grafted on to
mainly 19c rsdntl vllge.

GREAT BADMINTON Glos
156 ST 8082 8m WSW of Malmesbury.
CP, 347. Sodbury RD. P(Bdmntn). Ch e.
Sch pe. S Glos CC. B. Hse*, 17c and later, in
large pk where well known three-day horse
trials are held annually. Seat of Duke of
Beaufort.

GREAT BARDFIELD Essex
148 TL 6730 4m E of Thaxted. CP, 952.
Braintree RD. P Brntree. Ch e, f, m, r.
Sch p. Brntree CC (Saffron Walden).
Picturesque vllge with stream.

GREAT BARFORD Beds
147 TL 1252 3m NW of Sandy. CP, 788.
Bedford RD. P BDFD. Ch e, m. Sch p.
Mid-Beds CC. 15c br over Ouse.

GREAT BARRINGTON Glos
144 SP 2013 3m WNW of Burford. Loc,
Brrngtn CP. Northleach RD. P OXFORD.
Ch e. Sch pe. Cirencester and
Tewkesbury CC. Quarries here supplied
stone for famous bldngs all over S England.

GREAT BARROW Ches
109 SJ 4768 4m ENE of Chester. Loc,
Brrw CP. Chstr RD. P CHSTR. Ch e. m.
Sch pe. City of Chstr CC.

GREAT BARTON Suffolk (W)
136 TL 8967 3m NE of Bury St Edmunds.
CP, 979. Thingoe RD. P Bury St Eds.
Ch e, b. Sch pe. Bury St Eds CC.

GREAT BARUGH Yorks (N)
92 SE 7479 4m SW of Pickering. CP(Brgh,
Gt and Lit), 153. Pckrg RD. Ch e, m.
Scarborough CC (Thirsk and Malton).

GREAT BAVINGTON Nthmb
77 NY 9880 10m N of Corbridge. Loc,
Bvngtn CP. Bellingham RD. Ch v.
Hexham CC.

GREAT BEALINGS Suffolk (E)
150 TM 2348 2m W of Woodbridge. CP, 236.
Deben RD. P Wdbrdge. Ch e. Sudbury
and Wdbrdge CC. Considerable housing
development. Ch: bench-ends, Jcbn plpt;
row of limes and a cedar outside.

GREAT BEDWYN Wilts
167 SU 2764 5m SW of Hungerford.
CP, 849. Marlborough and Ramsbury RD.
P Mlbrgh. Ch e, m. Sch pe. Devizes CC. On
Kennet and Avon Canal; pumping stn* with

original engines of 1810. Stonemason's
museum.

GREAT BENTLEY Essex
150 TM 1121 6m NW of Clacton.
CP, 1,155. Tendring RD. P Colchester.
Ch e, m. Harwich CC. See also Aingers Grn.
Very large grn. 12c ch.

GREAT BILLING Northants
133 SP 8162 4m ENE of Northampton.
Loc, Bllng CP. Nthmptn RD. P NTHMPTN.
Ch e, m, r. Sch pe. Daventry CC (S Nthnts).

GREAT BIRCHAM Norfolk
125 TF 7632 8m SE of Hunstanton. Loc,
Bchm CP. Docking RD. P King's Lynn.
Ch e, m. Sch pe. NW Nflk CC (K's Lnn).

GREAT BLAKENHAM Suffolk (E)
150 TM 1150 5m NW of Ipswich. CP, 435.
Gipping RD. P Ipswch. Ch e, b. Eye CC.
Cement wks etc.

GREAT BLENCOW Cumb
83 NY 4532 4m WNW of Penrith. Loc,
Dacre CP. P(Blncw), Pnrth.

GREAT BOLAS Shrops
118, 119 SJ 6421 6m N of Wellington.
CP(Bolas Magna), 246. Wllngtn RD.
P Telford. Ch e. Sch pe. The Wrekin CC.

GREAT BOOKHAM Surrey
170 TQ 1354 2m WSW of Leatherhead.
Loc, Lthrhd UD. P Lthrhd. To S, Polesden
Lacey (NT)*, Rgncy hse in fine grnds.

GREAT BOURTON Oxon
145 SP 4545 3m N of Banbury. Loc,
Btn CP. Bnbry RD. P Bnbry. Ch e, m.
Bnbry CC.

GREAT BOWDEN Leics
133 SP 7488 1m NE of Mkt Harborough.
Loc, Mkt Hbrgh UD. P Mkt Hbrgh.

GREAT BRADLEY Suffolk (W)
148 TL 6653 5m N of Haverhill. CP, 230.
Clare RD. P Newmarket. Ch e. Bury
St Edmunds CC. Ch has Tdr brick porch;
infant Stour flows past.

GREAT BRAXTED Essex
149, 162 TL 8614 2m E of Witham.
CP, 322. Maldon RD. P Wthm. Ch e.
Mldn CC.

GREAT BRICETT Suffolk (E)
149 TM 0350 5m N of Hadleigh. CP, 305.
Gipping RD. P Ipswich. Ch e. Eye CC.
Aircraft noise from Wattisham Airfield.

GREAT BRICKHILL Bucks
146 SP 9030 3m SE of Bletchley. CP, 536.
Wing RD. P Bltchly. Ch e, m. Sch pe.
Buckingham CC.

GREAT BRIDGEFORD Staffs
119 SJ 8827 3m NW of Stafford. Loc,
Seighford CP. P STFFD.

GREAT BRINGTON Northants
132, 133 SP 6665 6m WNW of
Northampton. Loc, Brngtn CP.
Brixworth RD. P NTHMPTN. Ch e.
Daventry CC (Kettering). Washington graves
(see Lit Brngtn, Sulgrave). 13c ch full of
monmts to Spencer family of Althorp (see
Harlestone).

GREAT BROMLEY Essex
149 TM 0826 4m SSW of Manningtree.
CP, 780. Tendring RD. P Colchester.
Ch e, m. Sch pe. Harwich CC. Outstanding
15c ch; brass. Gt B. Hall now a Cheshire
Home.

GREAT BUDWORTH Ches
101 SJ 6677 2m N of Northwich. CP, 367.
Runcorn RD. P Nthwch. Ch e. Sch pe.
Rncn CC.

GREAT BURDON Co Durham
85 NZ 3116 2m NE of Darlington. CP, 62.
Dlngtn RD. Bishop Auckland CC
(Sedgefield).

GREAT BURSTEAD Essex
161 TQ 6892 1m S of Billericay. Loc,
Basildon UD.

GREAT BUSBY Yorks (N)
85 NZ 5205 2m S of Stokesley. CP, 76.
Stksly RD. Richmond CC.

GREAT CANFIELD Essex
148 TL 5918 3m SW of Dunmow. CP, 363.
Dnmw RD. P Dnmw. Ch e. Saffron
Walden CC. See also Bacon End. Partly Nmn
ch with wall-paintings. Rems of motte and
bailey cstle.

GREAT CARLTON Lincs (L)
105 TF 4185 5m ESE of Louth. CP, 167.
Lth RD. P Lth. Ch e, m. Sch pe. Lth CC.

GREAT CASTERTON Rutland
123 TF 0009 2m NW of Stamford. CP, 287.
Ketton RD. P Stmfd, Lincs. Ch e. Rtlnd and
Stmfd CC. Stone vllge on site of Roman tn.
EE ch. Bypassed by Gt N Rd.

GREAT CHALFIELD Wilts
166 ST 8663 3m N of Trowbridge. Loc,
Atworth CP. Ch e. Moated mnr hse (NT)*
of c 1480.

GREAT CHART Kent
172, 184 TQ 9842 2m W of Ashford.
CP, 969. W Ashfd RD. P Ashfd. Ch e, m.
Sch p. Ashfd CC. Ch brasses. 1½m SE,
Yardhurst*, Kentish hall c1450.

GREAT CHATWELL Staffs
119 SJ 7914 4m SE of Newport. Loc,
Blymhill CP. P Npt, Salop.

GREAT CHESTERFORD Essex
148 TL 5042 4m NNW of Saffron Walden.
CP, 659. Sffrn Wldn RD. P Sffrn Wldn.
Ch e, c. Sch pe. Sffrn Wldn CC.

GREAT CHEVERELL Wilts
167 ST 9854 5m SSW of Devizes. CP(Chvrll
Magna), 319. Dvzs RD. P Dvzs. Ch e, b.
Sch pe. Dvzs CC.

GREAT CHISHILL Cambs
148 TL 4238 4m ESE of Royston. Loc, Gt
and Lit Chshll CP. S Cambs RD. P Rstn,
Herts. Ch e. Sch p. Cambs CC. Vllge on hill,
with wide views. Transferred from Essex in
1890s 'for reasons of administrative
convenience'.

GREAT CLACTON Essex
150 TM 1716 1m N of Clacton on Sea. Loc,
Clctn UD. P Clctn-on-Sea.

GREAT CLIFTON Cumb
82 NY 0429 3m E of Workington.
CP, 1,635. Cockermouth RD. P Wkngtn.
Ch m. Sch i. Wkngtn CC.

GREAT COATES Lincs (L)
105 TA 2310 2m WNW of Grimsby. Loc,
Grmsby CB. P Grmsby. Grmsby BC
(Louth CC).

GREAT COMBERTON Worcs
143, 144 SO 9542 2m S of Pershore.
CP, 201. Pshre RD. Ch e. S Worcs CC.
Thatched half-timbered cottages.

GREAT CORBY Cumb
76 NY 4754 5m E of Carlisle. Loc, Wetheral CP. P Clsle. Ch m. Sch p. To S, Cby Cstle, 14c and later.

GREAT CORNARD Suffolk (W)
149 TL 8840 1m SE of Sudbury. CP, 2,416. Melford RD. P Sdbry. Ch e. Sch p2. Sdbry and Woodbridge CC.

GREAT COWDEN Yorks (E)
99 TA 2242 4m SSE of Hornsea. Loc, Mappleton CP.

GREAT COXWELL Berks
157 SU 2693 9m NE of Swindon. CP, 195. Faringdon RD. P Frngdn. Ch e. Abingdon CC. At N end, tithe ban (NT)*, 152ft long and 48ft high, blt by monks of Beaulieu in 13c.

GREAT CRANSLEY Northants
133 SP 8376 3m WSW of Kettering. Loc, Crnsly CP. Kttrng RD. P(Crnsly), Kttrng. Ch e. Kttrng CC.

GREAT CRESSINGHAM Norfolk
136 TF 8501 4m W of Watton. CP, 271. Swaffham RD. P Thetford. Ch e, m. Sch pe. SW Nflk CC.

GREAT CUBLEY Derbys
120 SK 1638 5m S of Ashbourne. Loc, Cbly CP. Ashbne RD. Ch e, m. W Derbys CC.

GREAT DALBY Leics
122 SK 7414 3m S of Melton Mowbray. Loc, Burton and Dlby CP. Mltn and Belvoir RD. P Mltn Mbry. Ch e, m. Sch p. Mltn CC.

GREAT DODDINGTON Northants
133 SP 8864 2m SSW of Wellingborough. CP, 730. Wllngbrgh RD. P Wllngbrgh. Ch e. Sch p. Wllngbrgh CC.

GREAT DOWARD Herefs
142 SO 5516 4m NE of Monmouth. Loc, Whitchurch CP.

GREAT DRIFFIELD Yorks (E)
99 TA 0257 12m SW of Bridlington. UD (Drffld), 7,899. P (Drffld). Howden CC. mkt tn. Ch has notable Perp twr. Canal; chalk stream, D. Beck, with good trout fishing.

GREAT DUNHAM Norfolk
125 TF 8714 5m NE of Swaffham. CP, 310. Mitford and Launditch RD. P King's Lynn. Ch e, m. Sch p. SW Nflk CC.

GREAT DUNMOW Essex
148 TL 6222 9m E of Bishop's Stortford. CP, 3,827. Dnmw RD. P(Dnmw). Ch e, b, r, v2. Sch pe, s. Saffron Walden CC. See also Churchend. Bacon factory recalls ancient, perhaps Nmn, 'Dnmw Flitch' ceremony.

GREAT DURNFORD Wilts
167 SU 1338 3m SSW of Amesbury. Loc, Dnfd CP. Amsbry RD. P Salisbury. Ch e. Sch pe. Slsbry CC.

GREAT EASTON Essex
148 TL 6125 3m NNW of Dunmow. CP, 691. Dnmw RD. P Dnmw. Ch e. Sch pe. Saffron Walden CC. See also Duton Hill.

GREAT EASTON Leics
133 SP 8493 4m NW of Corby. CP, 408. Mkt Harborough RD. P Mkt Hbrgh. Ch e, m. Hbrgh CC.

GREAT ECCLESTON Lancs
94 SD 4240 8m ENE of Blackpool. CP, 721. Garstang RD. P Preston. Ch e, m, r. Sch pe, pr. N Flyde CC.

GREAT EDSTONE Yorks (N)
92 SE 7084 6m W of Pickering. CP, 113. Kirkbymoorside RD. P YORK. Ch e, m. Thirsk and Malton CC.

GREAT ELLINGHAM Norfolk
136 TM 0196 2m NW of Attleborough. CP, 680. Wayland RD. P Attlbrgh. Ch e, b, m. Sch p. S Nflk CC.

GREAT ELM Som
166 ST 7449 2m NW of Frome. CP(Elm), 163. Frme RD. P Frme. Ch e. Wells CC.

GREAT EVERSDEN Cambs
148 TL 3653 6m SW of Cambridge. CP, 184. S Cambs RD. P CMBRDGE. Ch e. Cambs CC.

GREAT FINBOROUGH Suffolk (E)
136 TM 0157 2m WSW of Stowmarket. CP, 381. Gipping RD. P Stwmkt. Ch e, c. Sch pe. Eye CC. See also High St Grn.

GREATFORD Lincs (K)
123 TF 0811 5m NE of Stamford. CP, 151.
S Kesteven RD. P Stmfd. Ch e. Sch pe.
Rutland and Stmfd CC.

GREAT FRANSHAM Norfolk
125 TF 8913 6m W of E Dereham. Loc,
Frnsham CP. Mitford and Launditch RD.
Ch e, m. SW Nflk CC. Ch has 15c brasses.

GREAT GADDESDEN Herts
147, 159, 160 TL 0211 3m NNW of Hemel
Hempstead. CP, 1,016. Hml Hmpstd RD.
Ch e, b, m. Sch pe. Hml Hmpstd CC. See
also Jockey End, Water End.

GREAT GIDDING Hunts
134 TL 1183 6m SE of Oundle. CP, 239.
Huntingdon RD. P HNTNGDN. Ch e, b, m.
Sch pe. Hunts CC.

GREAT GIVENDALE Yorks (E)
98 SE 8153 3m NNE of Pocklington. Loc,
Millington CP.

GREAT GLEMHAM Suffolk (E)
137 TM 3461 3m WSW of Saxmundham.
CP, 227. Blyth RD. P Sxmndhm. Ch e, m.
Sch pe. Eye CC. Ch has seven-sacrament
font and angel roof. Derelict airfield at top
of hill.

GREAT GLEN Leics
132, 133 SP 6597 6m SE of Leicester.
CP, 1,223. Billesdon RD. P LCSTR.
Ch e, m. Sch pe. Harborough CC (Melton).

GREAT GONERBY Lincs (K)
113, 122 SK 8938 2m NNW of Grantham.
CP, 1,128. W Kesteven RD. P Grnthm.
Ch e, m3. Sch pe. Grnthm CC.

GREAT GRANSDEN Hunts
134 TL 2755 6m ESE of St Neots. CP, 476.
St Nts RD. P Sandy, Beds. Ch e, b. Sch pe.
Hunts CC.

GREAT GREEN Suffolk (W)
149 TL 9155 4m N of Lavenham. Loc,
Cockfield CP.

GREAT HABTON Yorks (N)
92 SE 7576 3m NNW of Malton. CP, 103.
Mltn RD. P Mltn. Ch e, m. Thirsk and
Mltn CC.

GREAT HALE Lincs (K)
113, 123 TF 1442 5m ESE of Sleaford.
CP, 554. E Kesteven RD. P Slfd. Ch e, m.
Sch pe. Grantham CC.

GREAT HALLINGBURY Essex
148 TL 5119 2m SE of Bishop's Stortford.
CP, 1,001. Dunnow RD. P Bshp's
Sttfd, Herts. Ch e. Sch pe. Saffron
Walden CC.

GREATHAM Co Durham
85 NZ 4927 3m SSW of Hartlepool.
CP, 1,416. Stockton RD. P Htlpl. Ch e, v.
Sch pe. Easington CC (Sedgefield). To SE,
large salt wks.

GREATHAM Hants
169, 181 SU 7730 5m NNE of Petersfield.
CP, 428. Ptrsfld RD. Ch e. Sch p.
Ptrsfld CC.

GREATHAM Sussex
182 TQ 0416 2m S of Pulborough. Loc,
Parham CP. Chanctonbury RD. Ch e.
Shoreham CC (Arundel and Shrhm).

GREAT HAMPDEN Bucks
159 ST 8402 3m E of Princes Risborough.
CP(Gt and Lit Hmpdn), 331. Wycombe RD.
Ch e. Sch pe. Aylesbury CC (Wcmbe). See
also Hmpdn Row. H. Hse, rebuilt 1754,
formerly home of John Hmpdn who defied
Charles I.

GREAT HANWOOD Shrops
118 SJ 4409 4m WSW of Shrewsbury. CP.
Atcham RD. P(Hnwd), Shrsbry. Ch e, m.
Sch pe. Shrsbry CC.

GREAT HARROWDEN Northants
133 SP 8870 2m NNW of Wellingborough.
CP. Wllngbrgh RD. Ch e, r. Wllngbrgh CC.

GREAT HARWOOD Lancs
95 SD 7332 4m NE of Blackburn.
UD, 11,000. P Blckbn. Clitheroe CC.
Aero-engineering, textiles, mining. To NE,
Martholme, with restored Tdr gatehouse*.
(Interior shown by appointment only.)

GREAT HASELEY Oxen
158, 159 SP 6401 5m SW of Thame.
CP, 550. Bullingdon RD. P OXFORD. Ch e.
Sch pe. Henley CC. See also Lit Hsly. Old
hses and fine Nmn to Perp ch. 2½m NW,
Rycote Chpl (A.M.).

GREAT HATFIELD Yorks (E)
99 TA 1842 3m SSW of Hornsea. Loc,
Htfld CP. Holderness RD. P Hull. Ch m.
Bridlington CC.

GREAT HAYWOOD Staffs
119, 120 SJ 9922 4m NW of Rugeley. Loc, Colwich CP. P STAFFORD. Ch e, r, v. Sch pe, pr. To SW across R Trent, Shugborough (NT)*, 18c hse in pk containing neo-Grecian monmts.

GREAT HECK Yorks (W)
97 SE 5921 7m SSW of Selby. Loc, Hck CP. Osgoldcross RD. Ch m. Goole CC.

GREAT HENNY Essex
149 TL 8637 2m S of Sudbury. CP, 168. Halstead RD. P Sdbry, Suffolk. Ch e. Saffron Walden CC.

GREAT HINTON Wilts
166, 167 ST 9059 3m WNW of Trowbridge. CP, 149. Warminster and Westbury RD. Ch m. Wstbry CC.

GREAT HOCKHAM Norfolk
136 TL 9592 6m WSW of Attleborough. CP(Hckhm), 359. Wayland RD. P Thetford. Ch e, m. Sch p. S Nflk CC.

GREAT HOLLAND Essex
150 TM 2119 4m NE of Clacton. Loc, Frinton and Walton UD. P Frntn-on-Sea.

GREAT HORKESLEY Essex
149 TL 9730 4m NNW of Colchester. CP, 1,072. Lexden and Winstree RD. P Clchstr. Ch e. Sch pe. Clchstr CC. See also Hksly Hth.

GREAT HORMEAD Herts
148 TL 4030 7m NW of Bishop's Stortford. Loc, Hrmd CP. Braughing RD. Ch e. Sch pe. E Herts CC. Thatched cottages in vllge st.

GREAT HORWOOD Bucks
146 SP 7731 5m ESE of Buckingham. CP, 596. Winslow RD. P Bletchley. Ch e, c. Sch pe. Bcknghm CC.

GREAT HOUGHTON Northants
133 SP 7958 3m ESE of Northampton. CP, 301. Nthmptn RD. P NTHMPTN. Ch e. Daventry CC (S Nthnts).

GREAT HOUGHTON Yorks (W)
103 SE 4306 5m E of Barnsley. CP, 2,265. Hemsworth RD. P Bnsly. Ch m, v. Sch p, pe. Hmswth CC.

GREAT HUCKLOW Derbys
111 SK 1777 6m NNW of Bakewell. CP, 131. Bkwll RD. Ch m, v. Sch pe. W Derbys CC. Gliding centre.

GREAT KELK Yorks (E)
99 TA 1058 5m E of Driffield. Loc, Klk CP. Drffld RD. Ch m. Howden CC.

GREAT KIMBLE Bucks
159 SP 8206 2m NE of Princes Risborough. CP(Gt and Lit Kmble), 807. Wycombe RD. Ch e. Sch pe. Aylesbury CC (Wcmbe). See also Kmble Wick.

GREAT KINGSHILL Bucks
159 SU 8797 3m NNE of High Wycombe. Loc, Hughenden CP. Wcmbe RD. Ch m. Sch pe. Wcmbe CC.

GREAT LANGTON Yorks (N)
91 SE 2996 5m WNW of Northallerton. CP, 81. Nthlltn RD. P Nthlltn. Ch e, m. Sch pe. Richmond CC.

GREAT LEIGHS Essex
148, 149, 162 TL 7217 4m SSW of Braintree. CP(Gt and Lit Lghs), 1,018. Chelmsford RD. P Chlmsfd. Ch e, v. Sch p. Brntree CC (Chlmsfd). Ch has round Nmn twr, rare in Essex. To NW, reservoir; fishing.

GREAT LIMBER Lincs (L)
104 TA 1308 5m NNE of Caistor. CP, 332. Cstr RD. Ch e, m. Gainsborough CC. Estate vllge on edge of Brocklesby (qv) Pk. Pelham mausoleum*.

GREAT LINFORD Bucks
146 SP 8542 2m WSW of Newport Pagnell. CP, 283. Npt Pgnll RD. P Npt Pgnll. Ch e. Sch pe. Buckingham CC.

GREAT LIVERMERE Suffolk (W)
136 TL 8871 5m NNE of Bury St Edmunds. CP, 207. Thingoe RD. P Bury St Eds. Ch e. Bury St Eds CC. Large lake or 'mere' remains in pk of hse demolished in 19c.

GREAT LONGSTONE Derbys
111 SK 2071 2m NNW of Bakewell. CP, 589. Bkwll RD. P Bkwll. Ch e, m. Sch pe. W Derbys CC.

GREAT LUMLEY Co Durham
85 NZ 2949 2m SE of Chester-le-Street. CP, 2,426. Chstr-le-Strt RD. P Chstr-le-Strt. Ch e, m2, v. Sch i, j. Chstr-le-Strt CC.

GREAT MALVERN Worcs
143 SO 7745 7m SW of Worcester. See Malvern.

GREAT MAPLESTEAD Essex
149 TL 8034 2m N of Halstead. CP, 331. Hlstd RD. P Hlstd. Ch e. Sch pe. Saffron Walden CC. Ch has 17 monmts to Dyne family.

GREAT MASSINGHAM Norfolk
125 TF 7922 9m WSW of Fakenham. CP 832. Freebridge Lynn RD. P King's Lynn. Ch e, m. Sch pe. NW Nflk CC (K's Lnn).

GREAT MELTON Norfolk
125 TG 1206 4m NNE of Wymondham. CP, 175. Forehoe and Henstead RD. Ch e. S Nflk CC (Central Nflk). See also High Grn.

GREAT MILTON Oxon
158 SP 6202 8m ESE of Oxford. CP, 778. Bullingdon RD. P OXFD. Ch e, m2. Sch pe. Mid-Oxon CC (Henley).

GREAT MISSENDEN Bucks
159 SP 8901 4m W of Chesham. CP, 5,737. Amersham RD. P. Ch e, b, m, r. Sch pe, s. Chesham and Amrshm CC (Aylesbury). See also Heath End, Prestwood, S Heath.

GREAT MITTON Yorks (W)
95 SD 7139 3m SW of Clitheroe. CP, 149. Bowland RD. Ch e. Skipton CC. Fine 13c–15c ch.

GREAT MONGEHAM Kent
173 TR 3451 2m W of Deal. Loc, Dl MB. P Dl.

GREAT MOSS Lancs
100 SD 5203 4m WSW of Wigan. Loc, Billinge-and-Winstanley UD.

GREAT MUSGRAVE Westm
84 NY 7613 3m N of Kirkby Stephen. Loc, Msgrve CP. N Westm RD. P Kby Stphn. Ch e. Sch pe. Westm CC.

GREAT NESS Shrops
118 SJ 3918 7m NW of Shrewsbury. CP, 774. Atcham RD. Ch e. Shrsbry CC (Oswestry). See also Felton Butler, Nesscliff, Wilcott.

GREAT OAKLEY Essex
150 TM 1927 6m ESE of Manningtree. CP, 680. Tendring RD. P Harwich. Ch e, m. Sch pe. Hrwch CC. See also Stone's Grn.

GREAT OAKLEY Northants
133 SP 8785 3m SW of Corby. Loc, Cby UD. P Cby.

GREAT OFFLEY Herts
147 TL 1427 3m WSW of Hitchin. Loc, Offley CP. Htchn RD. P(Offley), Htchn. Ch e, m. Sch pe. Htchn CC.

GREAT ORMSIDE Westm
83 NY 7017 2m SSE of Appleby. Loc, Ormsde CP. N Westm RD. Ch e. Westm CC.

GREAT ORTON Cumb
75 NY 3254 5m WSW of Carlisle. Loc, Ortn CP. Border RD. P Clsle. Ch e. Sch p. Penrith and the Bdr CC.

GREAT OUSEBURN Yorks (W)
91, 97 SE 4461 5m SE of Boroughbridge. CP, 347. Nidderdale RD. P YORK. Ch e, c. Sch p. Harrogate CC. See also Branton Grn.

GREAT OXENDON Northants
133 SP 7383 2m S of Mkt Harborough. CP, 245. Brixworth RD. P(Oxndn), Mkt Hbrgh, Leics. Ch e. Daventry CC (Kettering).

GREAT OXNEY GREEN Essex
161 TL 6606 3m W of Chelmsford. Loc, Writtle CP.

GREAT PARNDON Essex
161 TL 4308 1m SW of Harlow. Loc, Hlw UD. P Hlw.

GREAT PAXTON Hunts
134 TL 2063 3m NE of St Neots. CP, 396. St Nts RD. P HUNTINGDON. Ch e, v. Sch pe. Hunts CC.

GREAT PLUMPTON Lancs
94 SD 3833 5m ESE of Blackpool. Loc, Westby-w-Plmptns CP.

GREAT PLUMSTEAD Norfolk
126 TG 3009 5m E of Norwich. CP(Gt and Lit Plmstd), 1,695. Blofield and Flegg RD. P NRWCH, NOR 51Z. Ch e. Sch p. Yarmouth CC (Central Nflk).

GREAT PONTON Lincs (K)
113, 122 SK 9230 4m S of Grantham.
CP, 322. W Kesteven RD. P Grnthm.
Ch e, m. Sch pe. Rutland and Stamford CC.
Ch: 16c twr.

GREAT PRESTON Yorks (W)
97 SE 4029 3m NNW of Castleford. CP(Gt
and Lit Prstn), 1,078. Tadcaster RD.
P Woodlesford, LEEDS. Ch e. Sch ie, j.
Normanton CC.

GREAT RAVELEY Hunts
134 TL 2581 3m SW of Ramsey. Loc,
Upwood and the Raveleys CP.

GREAT RISSINGTON Glos
144 SP 1917 5m NW of Burford. CP, 308.
N Cotswold RD. P Cheltenham. Ch e. Sch p.
Cirencester and Tewkesbury CC.

GREAT ROLLRIGHT Oxon
145 SP 3231 3m N of Chipping Norton.
Loc, Rllrght CP. Chppng Ntn RD. P Chppng
Ntn. Ch e. Sch pe. Banbury CC. 2m WSW,
Rllrght Stones (A.M.), ancient stone circle,
sometimes known as King's Men. To S
thereof, small Perp ch of Lit Rllrght.

GREAT RYBURGH Norfolk
125 TF 9527 3m SE of Fakenham. CP, 484.
Walsingham RD. P Fknhm. Ch e, m, s.
Sch pe. NW Nflk CC (N Nflk).

GREAT RYLE Nthmb
71 NU 0212 7m NNW of Rothbury. Loc,
Alnham CP.

GREAT SALING Essex
148, 149 TL 7025 4m WNW of Braintree.
CP, 299. Brntree RD. Ch e. Brntree CC
(Maldon).

GREAT SALKELD Cumb
83 NY 5536 5m NNE of Penrith. CP, 377.
Pnrth RD. P Pnrth. Ch e, m. Sch pe. Pnrth
and the Border CC. Ch has massive twr blt
in 14c to ward off Scots.

GREAT SAMPFORD Essex
148 TL 6435 3m NE of Thaxted. CP, 341.
Saffron Walden RD. P Sffrn Wldn. Ch e, b.
Sch p. Sffrn Wldn CC.

GREAT SANKEY Lancs
100, 109 SJ 5688 2m W of Warrington.
CP, 5,857. Wrrngtn RD. P Wrrngtn. Ch e.
Sch p3. Newton CC.

GREAT SAREDON Staffs
119 SJ 9508 2m WSW of Cannock. Loc,
Srdn CP. Cnnck RD. SW Staffs CC (Cnnck).

GREAT SAUGHALL Ches
109 SJ 3670 4m NW of Chester. Loc,
Sghll CP. Chstr RD. P(Sghll), CHSTR.
Ch e, m, v. Sch pe. City of Chstr CC.

GREAT SAXHAM Suffolk (W)
136 TL 7862 4m W of Bury St Edmunds.
CP, 189. Thingoe RD. P Bury St Eds. Ch e.
Bury St Eds CC.

GREAT SHEFFORD Berks
158 SU 3875 5m NE of Hungerford. Loc,
W Shffd CP. Hngrfd RD. P Newbury.
Ch e, m. Sch pe. Nbry CC. Ch has only
round Nmn twr in county.

GREAT SHELFORD Cambs
148 TL 4652 4m S of Cambridge.
CP, 3,761. Chesterton RD. P CMBRDGE.
Ch e, b. Sch pe. Cambs CC.

GREAT SMEATON Yorks (N)
91 NZ 3404 7m NNW of Northallerton.
CP, 173. Nthlltn RD. P Nthlltn. Ch e. Sch p.
Richmond CC.

GREAT SNORING Norfolk
125 TF 9434 4m NNE of Fakenham.
CP, 247. Walsingham RD. P Fknhm.
Ch e, m. Sch pe. NW Nflk CC (N Nflk).
Rectory (exterior*) has Tdr brickwork with
terra cotta decoration, c 1500.

GREAT SOMERFORD Wilts
157 ST 9682 3m SE of Malmesbury.
CP, 504. Mlmsbry RD. P Chippenham.
Ch e, m, v. Sch pe. Chppnhm CC. See also
Startley.

GREAT SOUDLEY Shrops
119 SJ 7228 5m SE of Mkt Drayton. Loc,
Cheswardine CP. P Mkt Drtn. Ch m.

GREAT STAINTON Co Durham
85 NZ 3322 6m NE of Darlington. CP, 87.
Dlngtn RD. Ch e. Bishop Auckland
CC(Sedgefield).

GREAT STAMBRIDGE Essex
162 TQ 8991 4m N of Southend.
CP(Stmbrdge), 499. Rochford RD. P Rchfd.
Ch e. Sch p. Maldon CC (SE Essx).

GREAT STAUGHTON Hunts
134 TL 1264 5m NW of St Neots. CP, 985.
St Nts RD. P HUNTINGDON. Ch e, bv.
Sch p. Hunts CC. See also Dillington, Stghtn
Highway. Ch : monmts. 17c vllge cross with
sundial.

GREAT STEEPING Lincs (L)
114 TF 4364 8m W of Skegness. CP, 156.
Spilsby RD. P Splsby. Ch e, m. Sch p.
Horncastle CC.

GREAT STONAR Kent
173 TR 3359 1m N of Sandwich. Loc,
Sndwch MB.

GREATSTONE-ON-SEA Kent
184 TR 0823 10m E of Rye. Loc, New
Romney MB. P(Grtstne), New Rmny.
Resort. Sandy beach.

GREAT STRICKLAND Westm
83 NY 5522 5m SSE of Penrith. CP, 194.
N Westm RD. P Pnrth, Cumberland.
Ch e, m. Westm CC.

GREAT STUKELEY Hunts
134 TL 2174 2m NNW of Huntingdon. Loc,
The Stukeleys CP. Hntngdn RD.
P HNTNGDN. Ch e. Hunts CC.

GREAT STURTON Lincs (L)
105 TF 2176 5m NW of Horncastle. CP, 57.
Hncstle RD. Ch e. Hncstle CC.

GREAT SUTTON Ches
100, 109 SJ 3775 1m WSW of Ellesmere
Port. Loc, Ellesmre Pt MB. P Lit
Sttn, Wirral.

GREAT SUTTON Shrops
129 SO 5183 5m N of Ludlow. Loc,
Diddlebury CP.

GREAT SWINBURNE Nthmb
77 NY 9375 7m N of Hexham. Loc,
Chollerton CP.

GREAT TEW Oxon
145 SP 3929 5m ENE of Chipping Norton.
CP, 261. Chppng Ntn RD. P OXFORD.
Ch e. Sch p. Banbury CC. Estate vllge of
honey-coloured stone hses ; several thatched
roofs.

GREAT TEY Essex
149 TL 8925 6m W of Colchester. CP, 476.
Lexden and Winstree RD. P Clchstr. Ch e.
Sch pe. Clchstr CC.

GREAT THURLOW Suffolk (W)
148 TL 6750 3m N of Haverhill. CP, 239.
Clare RD. Ch e. Bury St Edmunds CC.
Handsome vllge. Ggn hall next to ch, with
large gdn.

GREAT TORRINGTON Devon
163 SS 4919 5m SSE of Bideford.
MB, 3,536. P(Trrngton). W Dvn CC
(Trrngtn). Hilltop tn. Perp ch blown up
1646, rebuilt 1651.

GREAT TOSSON Nthmb
71 NU 0200 2m WSW of Rothbury. Loc,
Tssn CP. Rthbry RD. Berwick-upon
-Tweed CC.

GREAT TOTHAM Essex
149, 162 TL 8613 3m ESE of Witham.
CP, 1,291. Maldon RD. P Mldn. Ch e, c, v.
Sch p. Mldn CC.

GREAT URSWICK Lancs
88 SD 2774 3m SSW of Ulverston. Loc,
Urswick CP. N Lonsdale RD. P Ulvstn.
Ch e, v. Sch pe. Morecambe and Lnsdle CC.

GREAT WACTON Herefs
129, 130 SO 6256 3m NW of Bromyard.
CP(Wctn), 66. Brmyd RD. Ch e.
Leominster CC.

GREAT WAKERING Essex
162 TQ 9487 4m ENE of Southend.
CP, 3,109. Rochford RD. P Sthnd-on-Sea.
Ch e, c, m, r, s, v3. Sch p. Maldon CC
(SE Essx).

GREAT WALDINGFIELD Suffolk (W)
149 TL 9143 3m NE of Sudbury. CP, 458.
Melford RD. P Sdbry. Ch e, v. Sch pe. Sdbry
and Woodbridge CC. Old vllge is grouped
round ch; new large housing estates on
main rd to Sudbury, ending in disused
airfield.

GREAT WALSINGHAM Norfolk
125 TF 9437 4m SSE of Wells. CP, 554.
Wlsnghm RD. P Wlsnghm. Ch e, m.
NW Nflk CC (N Nflk). Outstanding 14c ch.

GREAT WALTHAM Essex
148, 161 TL 6913 4m N of Chelmsford.
CP. Chlmsfd RD. P Chlmsfd. Ch e, m, v.
Sch pe. Braintree CC (Chlmsfd). See also
Ford End, Howe St. Nmn and 15c ch.
Langley Pk, early Ggn hse with handsome
lodge and pk.

GREAT WARLEY Essex
161 TQ 5890 2m SSW of Brentwood. Loc,
Brntwd UD. P Brntwd. Highly decorated ch
blt 1902.

GREAT WASHBOURNE Glos
143, 144 SO 9834 6m E of Tewkesbury.
Loc, Dumbleton CP. Ch e.

GREAT WELDON Northants
133 SP 9289 2m E of Corby. Loc, Wldn CP.
Kettering RD. P Cby. Ch e. Sch pe.
Kttrng CC. Famous bldng stone, said to
have been used for old St Paul's, produced
here. Ch has lantern twr which used to guide
travellers in surrounding forests.

GREAT WELNETHAM Suffolk (W)
136 TL 8859 4m SSE of Bury St Edmunds.
CP(Gt Whelnetham), 444. Thingoe RD.
Ch e. Sch pe. Bury St Eds CC.

GREAT WENHAM Suffolk (E)
149 TM 0738 4m SE of Hadleigh. CP(Wnhm
Magna), 177. Samford RD.
P Colchester, Essex. Ch e, v. Sudbury and
Woodbridge CC.

GREAT WHITTINGTON Nthmb
77 NZ 0070 4m NNE of Corbridge. Loc,
Whttngtn CP. Hexham RD. P NEWCASTLE
UPON TYNE. Ch m. Sch p. Hxhm CC.

GREAT WIGBOROUGH Essex
149, 162 TL 9614 5m E of Tiptree. CP(Gt
and Lit Wgbrgh), 215. Lexden and
Winstree RD. Ch e. Colchester CC.

GREAT WILBRAHAM Cambs
135 TL 5457 6m E of Cambridge. CP, 448.
Chesterton RD. P CMBRDGE. Ch e, b.
Sch pe. Cambs CC.

GREAT WILNE Derbys
112, 121 SK 4430 7m ESE of Derby.
CP(Shardlow and Gt Wlne), 922.
SE Derbys RD. Ch e, m. SE Derbys CC.

GREAT WISHFORD Wilts
167 SU 0835 5m NW of Salisbury. CP, 298.
Slsbry and Wilton RD. Ch e. Sch pe.
Slsbry CC. Almshouses of 1628; sch of 1722.

GREAT WITCOMBE Glos
143, 144 SO 9114 5m SSW of Cheltenham.
CP, 108. Chltnhm RD. Ch e. Cirencester and
Tewkesbury CC. Roman villa (A.M.).

GREAT WITLEY Worcs
130 SO 7566 5m SW of Stourport. CP, 399.
Martley RD. P WORCESTER. Ch e. Sch pe.
Kidderminster CC. Wtly Ct, 1m SE, ruined
palatial Ggn mansion. Ch alongside; interior
a rococo riot.

GREAT WOLFORD Warwicks
144 SP 2434 3m ENE of Moreton-in-Marsh.
CP, 154. Shipston on Stour RD. P Shpstn
on Str. Ch e. Sch p. Stratford-on-Avon CC
(Strtfd).

GREAT WOOLSTONE Bucks
146 SP 8738 3m N of Bletchley. Loc,
Wlstne-cum-Willen CP. Newport Pagnell RD.
Ch e. Buckingham CC.

GREATWORTH Northants
145, 146 SP 5542 4m NW of Brackley.
CP, 532. Brckly RD. P Banbury, Oxon.
Ch e, m. Sch p. Daventry CC (S Nthnts). See
also Halse. Radio stn.

GREAT WRATTING Suffolk (W)
148 TL 6848 2m NE of Haverhill. CP, 176.
Clare RD. P Hvrhll. Ch e. Bury
St Edmunds CC.

GREAT WYMONDLEY Herts
147 TL 2128 2m E of Hitchin. Loc,
Wmndly CP. Htchn RD. Ch e. Htchn CC.
Ch: Nmn nave and apsidal chancel.

GREAT WYRLEY Staffs
119 SJ 9907 2m SSE of Cannock.
CP, 5,567. Cnnck RD. P Walsall. Ch e, m2.
Sch j, p2, s. SW Staffs CC (Cnnck). See also
Landywood.

GREAT WYTHEFORD Shrops
118 SJ 5719 6m NE of Shrewsbury. Loc,
Shawbury CP.

GREAT YARMOUTH Norfolk
126 TG 5207 18m E of Norwich.
CB, 50,152. P. Ymth CC. See also Gorleston

on Sea. Centre for herring fishing industry. Resort. Many interesting bldngs and chs; rems of old fortifications. To W, Breydon Water, large tidal lake.

GREAT YELDHAM Essex
149 TL 7638 4m S of Clare. CP, 738. Halstead RD. P Hlstd. Ch e, b. Sch pe. Saffron Walden CC. See also Pool St.

GREENBANK Lancs
94 SD 5254 5m SE of Lancaster. Loc, Over Wyresdale CP. Lncstr RD. Lncstr CC.

GREENDYKES Nthmb
71 NU 0628 4m SW of Belford. Loc, Chatton CP.

GREENFIELD Beds
147 TL 0534 2m SE of Ampthill. Loc, Amptll RD. P BEDFORD. Ch m. Sch pe. Mid-Beds CC.

GREENFIELD Yorks (W)
101 SD 9904 5m E of Oldham. Loc, Saddleworth UD. P Oldhm, Lancs.

GREENFORD London
160 TQ 1482 3m NW of Ealing. Loc, Ealing LB. P Middx. Ealng N BC.

GREEN, GREAT Suffolk (W)
149 TL 9155 4m N of Lavenham. Loc, Cockfield CP.

GREENHALGH Lancs
94 SD 4035 6m E of Blackpool. CP(Grnhlgh-w-Thistleton), 466. Fylde RD. Ch v. S Flde CC. See also Esprick.

GREENHAM Berks
158 SU 4865 1m SE of Newbury. CP, 1,206. Nbry RD. Ch e, b. Nbry CC.

GREENHAM Som
164 ST 0720 4m W of Wellington. Loc, Stawley CP. P Wllngton. G. Barton, mnr hse of c 1400. 1½m N, Cothay*, late 15c mnr hse.

GREEN HAMMERTON Yorks (W)
97 SE 4556 6m NNE of Wetherby. CP, 497. Nidderdale RD. P YORK. Ch e, m. Sch pe. Harrogate CC.

GREENHAUGH Nthmb
77 NY 7987 4m NW of Bellingham. Loc, Tarset CP. Bllngham RD. P Hexham. Sch p. Hxhm CC.

GREENHEAD Nthmb
76 NY 6665 3m WNW of Haltwhistle. CP, 355. Hltwhstle RD. P Carlisle, Cumberland. Ch e, m. Sch pe. Hexham CC. On the rd and rly from Newcastle to Carlisle, and close to the Roman Wall.

GREENHITHE Kent
161, 171 TQ 5875 3m E of Dartford. Loc, Swanscombe UD. P. Part of Thames-side indstrl complex. Anchorage of HMS Worcester, wooden sailing ship.

GREENHOLME Westm
83 NY 5905 9m NE of Kendal. Loc, Orton CP. Ch m.

GREENHOW HILL Yorks (W)
91 SE 1164 3m WSW of Pateley Br. Loc, Bewerley CP. P Ptly Br, Harrogate. Ch e. Rems of mining and smelting wks.

GREENMOUNT Lancs
100 SD 7714 3m NW of Bury. Loc, Tottington UD. P Bury.

GREENODD Lancs
88, 89 SD 3182 3m NE of Ulverston. Loc, Edton w Newland CP. N Lonsdale RD. P Ulvstn. Morecambe and Lnsdle CC.

GREEN ORE Som
165, 166 ST 5750 4m NE of Wells. Loc, St Cuthbert Out CP. Wlls RD. Wlls CC. Sculpture of Romulus and Remus by Italian prisoner of war 1945, near main rd.

GREENSIDE Co Durham
78 NZ 1462 3m E of Prudhoe. Loc, Ryton UD. P Rtn.

GREENS NORTON Northants
145, 146 SP 6649 2m NW of Towcester. CP, 726. Tcstr RD. P Tcstr. Ch e, m. Sch pe. Daventry CC (S Nthnts). See also Duncote.

GREENSTEAD GREEN Essex
149 TL 8227 2m SSE of Halstead. CP(Grnstd Grn and Hlstd Rural), 657. Hlstd RD. P Hlstd. Saffron Walden CC.

GREENSTED Essex
161 TL 5302 just W of Ongar. Loc, Ongr CP. Ch e. Nave of ch blt of oak tree trunks, some over 1,000 years old.

GREEN STREET Herts
160 TQ 1998 4m WSW of Potters Bar. Loc,
Elstree RD. S Herts CC.

GREEN STREET GREEN London
171 TQ 4563 2m SSW of Orpington. Loc,
Bromley LB. P Orpngtn, Kent.
Orpngtn BC (CC).

GREEN, THE Cumb
88 SD 1784 3m N of Millom. Loc, Mllm
Without CP. Mllm RD. P Mllm. Whitehaven CC.

GREENWAY Glos
143 SO 7033 3m S of Ledbury. Loc,
Dymock CP. P Dmck.

GREENWICH London
161, 171 TQ 3877 4m SSE of Lndn Br.
LB, 216,441. BCs: Grnwch; Woolwich E;
Wlwch W. See also Blackheath, Charlton,
Eltham, Kidbrooke, Plumstead, Shooters
Hill, Wlwch. On S bank of Thames. Royal
Naval College on site of former royal palace;
Painted Hall*(Wren), chpl*. National
Maritime Museum. Old Royal Observatory*.

GREET Glos
144 SP 0230 1m N of Winchcombe. Loc,
Wnchcmbe CP.

GREETE Shrops
129 SO 5770 2m NW of Tenbury Wells.
CP, 123. Ludlow RD. Ch e. Ldlw CC.

GREETHAM Lincs (L)
114 TF 3070 3m E of Horncastle. CP, 85.
Hncstle RD. Ch e. Sch pe. Hncstle CC.

GREETHAM Rutland
122 SK 9214 6m NE of Oakham. CP, 423.
Oakhm RD. P Oakhm. Ch e, m. Rtlnd and
Stamford CC.

GREETLAND Yorks (W)
96, 102 SE 0821 3m S of Halifax. Loc,
Elland UD. P Hlfx.

GREINTON Som
165 ST 4136 6m WSW of Glastonbury.
CP, 101. Brdgwtr RD. Ch e. Brdgwtr CC.

GRENDON Northants
133 SP 8760 5m S of Wellingborough.
CP, 346. Wllngbrgh RD.
P NORTHAMPTON. Ch e, c. Sch pe.
Wllngbrgh CC. G. Hall is now county youth
centre.

GRENDON Warwicks
120, 121 SK 2800 2m NW of Atherstone.
CP, 1,460. Athrstne RD. P Athrstne.
Ch e, m. Sch pe. Meriden CC.

GRENDON COMMON Warwicks
131 SP 2799 3m WNW of Atherstone. Loc,
Athrstne RD. Meriden CC.

GRENDON GREEN Herefs
129 SO 5957 6m E of Leominster. Loc,
Grndn Bishop CP. Bromyard RD. Ch e.
Lmnstr CC.

GRENDON UNDERWOOD Bucks
146 SP 6820 6m E of Bicester. CP, 570.
Aylesbury RD. P Aylesbury. Ch e. Sch p.
Aylesbury CC. Grndn Psychiatric Prison.

GRENOSIDE Yorks (W)
102 SK 3394 4m NNW of Sheffield. Loc,
Ecclesfield CP. P SHFFLD. Ch e, m3. Sch p.

GRESHAM Norfolk
126 TG 1638 3m S of Sheringham. CP, 363.
Erpingham RD. P NORWICH, NOR 23Y.
Ch e, m. Sch p. N Nflk CC. Rems of G.
Cstle, home in 15c of Paston family, famed
for 'Paston Letters'.

GRESSENHALL Norfolk
125 TF 9615 2m NW of E Dereham.
CP, 617. Mitford and Launditch RD.
P Drhm. Ch e, m. Sch pe. SW Nflk CC. See
also Grssnhll Grn.

GRESSENHALL GREEN Norfolk
125 TF 9616 3m NW of E Dereham. Loc,
Grssnhll CP.

GRESSINGHAM Lancs
89 SD 5769 5m E of Carnforth. CP, 138.
Lunesdale RD. Ch e. Lancaster CC.

GRETA BRIDGE Yorks (N)
84 NZ 0813 3m SE of Barnard Cstle. Loc,
Startforth RD. P Bnd Cstle, Co Durham.
Richmond CC. On site of Roman fort near
confluence of rivers Tees and Greta. Dickens
stayed at coaching inn here on way to
investigate 'Yorkshire Schools' at Bowes, qv.
Rokeby Hall, 18c hse associated with Sir
Walter Scott and painted by Turner. 2m
NW, Egglestone Abbey (A.M.).

GRETTON Glos
144 SP 0030 2m NW of Winchcombe. Loc,
Wnchcmbe CP. P Cheltenham. Ch e, m.
Sch p.

GRETTON Northants
133 SP 8994 3m N of Corby. CP, 888.
Kettering RD. P Cby. Ch e, b. Sch p.
Kttrng CC. 1½m SE, Kirby Hall (A.M.),
partly restored ruins of 16c–17c mansion,
largely by Inigo Jones.

GREWELTHORPE Yorks (W)
91 SE 2376 6m NW of Ripon. CP, 397. Rpn
and Pateley Br RD. P Rpn. Ch e, m. Sch pe.
Rpn CC.

GREYSOUTHEN Cumb
82 NY 0729 3m WSW of Cockermouth.
CP, 509. Cckrmth RD. P Cckrmth. Ch m.
Sch pe. Workington CC.

GREYSTOKE Cumb
83 NY 4430 5m W of Penrith. CP, 517.
Pnrth RD. P Pnrth. Ch e. Sch p. Pnrth and
the Border CC. See also Lit Blencow. Vctrn
cstle by Salvin in large pk.

GREYWELL Hants
169 SU 7151 5m E of Basingstoke. CP, 258.
Hartley Wintney RD. P Bsngstke. Ch e.
Bsngstke CC (Aldershot).

GRIGGHALL Westm
89 SD 4691 3m W of Kendal. Loc,
Underbarrow and Bradleyfield CP.

GRIMEFORD VILLAGE Lancs
101 SD 6112 4m SE of Chorley. Loc,
Anderton CP. Chly RD. Chly CC.

GRIMETHORPE Yorks (W)
103 SE 4109 5m ENE of Barnsley. Loc,
Brierley CP. P Bnsly. Ch e, m, r, v. Sch i, s2.
Colliery.

GRIMLEY Worcs
130 SO 8360 4m N of Worcester. CP, 573.
Martley RD. P WCSTR. Ch e. Sch pe.
Kidderminster CC. See also Moseley, Sinton
Grn.

GRIMOLDBY Lincs (L)
105 TF 3988 4m E of Louth. CP, 825.
Lth RD. P Lth. Ch e, m2. Sch p. Lth CC. To
S, Manby airfield.

GRIMPO Shrops
118 SJ 3626 5m ESE of Oswestry. Loc,
W Felton CP. Ch c.

GRIMSARGH Lancs
94 SD 5834 4m NE of Preston. CP, 835.
Prstn RD. P Prstn. Ch e, c. Sch pe.
S Fylde CC.

GRIMSBY Lincs (L)
105 TA 2709 16m SE of Hull. CB, 95,685.
P. Grmsby BC. See also Gt Coates. Largely
Vctrn tn; important centre of North Sea
fishing industry. with large docks,
warehouses, fish mkt.

GRIMSCOTE Northants
145, 146 SP 6553 4m NNW of Towcester.
Loc, Cold Higham CP.

GRIMSCOTT Cornwall
174 SS 2606 3m E of Bude. Loc,
Launcells CP. P Bde. Ch m.

GRIMSTHORPE Lincs (K)
123 TF 0423 4m WNW of Bourne. Loc,
Edenham CP. P Bne. G. Cstle, vast pile by
Vanbrugh in vast pk, seat of Duke of
Ancaster.

GRIMSTON Leics
122 SK 6821 5m WNW of Melton Mowbray.
CP, 339. Mltn and Belvoir RD. P Mltn Mbry.
Ch e, m. Sch pe. Mltn CC. See also Saxelby.

GRIMSTON Norfolk
124 TF 7222 6m E of King's Lynn.
CP, 1132. Freebridge Lynn RD. P K's Lnn.
Ch e, m. Sch p2. NW Nflk CC (K's Lnn). See
also Pott Row.

GRIMSTONE Dorset
178 SY 6494 4m NW of Dorchester. Loc,
Stratton CP.

GRINACOMBE MOOR Devon
175 SX 4191 7m NE of Launceston. Loc,
Broadwoodwidger CP. Ch m.

GRINDALE Yorks (E)
93 TA 1371 4m NW of Bridlington.
CP, 138. Brdlngtn RD. Ch e. Brdlngtn CC.

GRINDLEFORD Derbys
111 SK 2477 6m NNE of Bakewell. Loc,
Eyam Woodlands CP. Bkwll RD.
P SHEFFIELD. Ch m. Sch p. W Derbys CC.

GRINDLETON Yorks (W)
95 SD 7545 3m NNE of Clitheroe. CP, 671.
Bowland RD. P Clthroe, Lancs. Ch e, f, m.
Sch pe, s. Skipton CC.

GRINDLEY BROOK Ches and Shrops
118 SJ 5243 2m NW of Whitchurch. Loc,
Tarvin RD, N Shrops RD. P Whtchch, Salop.
Nantwich CC, Oswestry CC.

GRINDLOW Derbys
111 SK 1877 6m NNW of Bakewell. CP, 36.
Bkwll RD. W Derbys CC.

GRINDON Staffs
111 SK 0854 7m ESE of Leek. CP, 232.
Lk RD. P Lk. Ch e. Sch pe. Lk CC. See also
Ford.

GRINGLEY ON THE HILL Notts
103 SK 7390 5m W of Gainsborough.
C P , 6 9 0 . E R e t f o r d R D .
P Doncaster, Yorkshire. Ch e, m3. Sch pe.
Bassetlaw CC. Commands very wide views
to S.

GRINSDALE Cumb
76 NY 3658 2m WNW of Carlisle. Loc,
Beaumont CP. Ch e.

GRINSHILL Shrops
118 SJ 5223 3m S of Wem. CP, 272.
N Shrops RD. P Shrewsbury. Ch e. Sch pe.
Oswestry CC. Supplies a greenish sandstone
from which many local bldngs have been
made.

GRINTON Yorks (N)
90 SE 0498 8m WSW of Richmond.
CP, 178. Reeth RD. P Rchmnd. Ch e.
Rchmnd CC. See also Crackpot.

GRISTHORPE Yorks (N)
93 TA 0882 2m WNW of Filey. CP, 235.
Scarborough RD. P Filey. Ch m. Sch pe.
Scbrgh CC (Scbrgh and Whitby).

GRISTON Norfolk
136 TL 9499 7m WNW of Attleborough.
CP, 763. Wayland RD. P Thetford. Ch e.
S Nflk CC.

GRITTENHAM Wilts
157 SU 0382 7m ESE of Malmesbury. Loc,
Brinkworth CP.

GRITTLETON Wilts
156 ST 8580 6m NW of Chippenham.
CP, 4 3 2. Calne and Chppnhm RD.
P Chppnhm. Ch e, b. Sch p. Chppnhm CC.
See also Leigh Delamere, Littleton Drew.

GRIZEBECK Lancs
88 SD 2385 5m NW of Ulverston. Loc,
Kirkby Ireleth CP. N Lonsdale RD.
P Kkby-in-Furness. Sch p. Morecambe and
Lnsdle CC.

GRIZEDALE Lancs
88, 89 SD 3394 3m SE of Coniston. Loc,
Satterthwaite CP. Name also of beck and of
surrounding forest.

GROBY Leics
121 SK 5207 4m WNW of Leicester.
CP, 3,035. Mkt Bosworth RD. P LCSTR.
Ch e, c. Sch p. Bswth CC. See also Field
Head. To N, G. Pool, largest natural lake in
Leics. Granite quarries.

GROOMBRIDGE Kent and Sussex (E)
171, 183 TQ 5337 4m WSW of Tunbridge
Wells. Loc, Tonbridge RD, Uckfield RD.
P TNBRDGE WLLS. Ch e, m. Sch pe. Royal
Tnbrdge Wlls CC (Tonbridge),
E Grinstead CC. The old Grmbrdge and the
17c G. Place are in Kent; shops etc in
Sussex.

GROSMONT Yorks (N)
86 NZ 8205 6m SW of Whitby. Loc,
Eskdaleside cum Ugglebarnby CP.
Whitby RD. P Whtby. Ch e, m. Sch pe.
Cleveland and Whtby CC (Scarborough and
Whtby).

GROTON Suffolk (W)
149 TL 9541 4m W of Hadleigh. CP, 201.
Cosford RD. Ch e. Sudbury and
Woodbridge CC.

GROTTON Yorks (W)
101 SD 9604 3m E of Oldham. Loc,
Saddleworth UD.

GROVE Berks
158 SU 4090 2m N of Wantage. CP, 1,845.
Wntge RD. P Wntge. Ch e, b, m. Sch i, pe.
Abingdon CC.

GROVE Bucks
146 SP 9222 2m S of Leighton Buzzard.
CP, 12. Wing RD. Ch e. Buckingham CC.

GROVE Dorset
178 SY 6972 on Isle of Portland, S of
Weymouth. Loc, Ptlnd UD.

GROVE Kent
173 TR 2361 6m ENE of Canterbury. Loc,
Wickhambreaux CP.

GROVE Notts
103 SK 7379 2m ESE of Retford. CP, 103.
E Rtfd RD. Ch e. Bassetlaw CC. G. Hall,
mainly 18c by Carr of York.

GRUNDISBURGH Suffolk (E)
150 TM 2250 3m WNW of Woodbridge.
CP, 930. Deben RD. P Wdbrdge. Ch e, b.
Sch p. Eye CC. Many new hses. Ch with
famous double hammerbeam angel roof,
wall-painting, 18c red brick twr.

GUARLFORD Worcs
143 SO 8145 2m E of Malvern. CP, 257.
Upton upon Severn RD. Ch e. S Worcs CC.

GUESTLING GREEN Sussex (E)
184 TQ 8513 4m NE of Hastings. Loc,
Gstlng CP. Battlle RD. P Hstngs. Ch e, m.
Sch pe. Rye CC.

GUESTWICK Norfolk
125 TG 0627 7m S of Holt. CP, 166.
St Faith's and Aylsham RD. P Dereham.
Ch e, v. N Nflk CC (Centrall Nflk).

GUIDE Lancs
95 SD 7025 SE distr of Blackburn. Loc,
Blckbn CB. P Blckbn. Blckbn BC.

GUIDE POST Nthmb
78 NZ 2585 4m E of Morpeth. Loc,
Bedlingtonshire UD. Blyth BC.

GUILDEN DOWN Shrops
129 SO 3082 1m N of Clun. Loc, Cln CP.

GUILDEN MORDEN Cambs
147 TL 2744 6m E of Biggleswade. CP, 566.
S Cambs RD. P Royston, Herts. Ch e, v.
Sch pe. Cambs CC.

GUILDEN SUTTON Ches
109 SJ 4468 3m ENE of Chester. CP.
Chstr RD. P CHSTR. Ch e, m2. Sch pe. City
of Chstr CC.

GUILDFORD Surrey
169, 170 SU 9949 27m SW of London.
MB, 56,887. P. Gldfd CC. See also Onslow
Vllge, Stoughton. County tn. Well known
steep High St. Rems of cstle keep*. Modern
cathedral on Stag Hill, and Surrey
University development.

GUILSBOROUGH Northants
132, 133 SP 6773 9m NNW of
Northampton. CP, 459. Brixworth RD.
P NTHMPTN. Ch e, b. Sch pe, s.
Daventry CC (S Nthnts). Restored grammar
sch of 1668.

GUISBOROUGH Yorks (N)
86 NZ 6116 5m SW of Saltburn.
UD, 13,852. P. Cleveland and Whitby CC
(Clvlnd). See also Dunsdale, Hutton
Lowcross, Newton, Upleatham. Rems of
12c Augustinian priory (A.M.).

GUISELEY Yorks (W)
96 SE 1941 6m NNE of Bradford. Loc,
Aireborough UD. P LEEDS. Pudsey BC.
Indstrl, incl pram-mnfg. Elizn rectory,
formerly moated.

GUIST Norfolk
125 TF 9925 6m SE of Fakenham. CP, 270.
Mitford and Launditch RD. P Dereham.
Ch e. Sch pe. SW Nflk CC.

GUITING POWER Glos
144 SP 0924 5m SE of Winchcombe.
CP, 303. N Cotswold RD. P Cheltenham.
Ch e, b. Sch pe. Cirencester and
Tewkesbury CC.

GULVAL Cornwall
189 SW 4831 1m NE of Penzance. Loc,
Pnznce MB. B. P Pnznce. Ch e. In
flower-growing area.

GUMLEY Leics
133 SP 6890 4m WNW of Mkt Harborough.
CP, 106. Mkt Hbrgh RD. P Mkt Hbrgh.
Ch e. Hbrgh CC.

GUNBY Lincs (K)
122 SK 9121 9m S of Grantham. CP(Gnby
and Stainby), 162. W Kesteven RD. Ch e, m.
Rutland and Stamford CC.

GUNBY Lincs (L)
114 TF 4666 7m WNW of Skegness. CP, 43.
Spilsby RD. Ch e. Horncastle CC. G. Hall
(NT)*, William and Mary brick hse in formal
gdns.

GUNDLETON Hants
168 SU 6133 8m WSW of Alton. Loc,
Bishops Sutton CP.

GUNN Devon
163 SS 6333 5m E of Barnstaple. Loc,
Swimbridge CP.

GUNNERSBURY London
160, 170 TQ 1978 2m W of Hammersmith.
Loc, Hounslow LB. Brentford and
Isleworth BC (Brntfd and Chiswick). G.
Pk*, early 19c hse now museum, in large pk.

GUNNERSIDE Yorks (N)
90 SD 9598 7m NE of Hawes. Loc, Melbecks CP. Reeth RD. P Richmond. Ch m. Sch pm. Rchmnd CC.

GUNNERTON Nthmb
77 NY 9075 7m NNW of Hexham. Loc, Chollerton CP. P Hxhm.

GUNNESS Lincs (L)
104 SE 8411 3m W of Scunthorpe. CP, 767. Glanford Brigg RD. P Scnthpe. Ch e, m. Sch pe. Brgg and Scnthpe CC (Brgg).

GUNNISLAKE Cornwall
175, 187 SX 4371 4m SW of Tavistock. Loc, Calstock CP. P. Ch m, r, s, v. Sch p. Former centre of mining industry. New Br, c 1320, spans Tamar.

GUNTHORPE Norfolk
125 TG 0134 5m WSW of Holt. CP, 310. Walsingham RD. P Melton Constable. Ch e, m2. NW Nflk (N Nflk). See also Bale.

GUNTHORPE Notts
112, 122 SK 6844 7m ENE of Nottingham. CP, 472. Southwell RD. P NTTNGHM. Ch e, m. Sch pe. Newark CC. Trentside vllge; boating.

GUNTHORPE Rutland
122 SK 8605 2m SSE of Oakham. CP, 33. Oakhm RD. Rtlnd and Stmfd CC.

GUNWALLOE Cornwall
189 SW 6522 3m S of Helston. CP, 215. Kerrier RD. P Hlstn. Ch e. St Ives CC. In two parts: Ch Cove, with ch on beach, and G. Fishing Cove to N.

GURNARD IOW
180 SZ 4795 1m W of Cowes. Loc, Cowes UD. P Cowes.

GURNEY SLADE Som
166 ST 6249 4m N of Shepton Mallet. Loc, Binegar CP. P Bath.

GUSSAGE ALL SAINTS Dorset
179 SU 0010 7m N of Wimborne. CP, 180. Wmbne and Cranborne RD. P Wmbne. Ch e. N Dst CC.

GUSSAGE ST ANDREW Dorset
179 ST 9714 8m NE of Blandford. Loc, Sixpenny Handley CP. Ch e. Ch formerly chpl of nunnery founded by King Alfred's daughter.

GUSSAGE ST MICHAEL Dorset
179 ST 9811 7m ENE of Blandford. CP, 190. Wimborne and Cranborne RD. P Wmbne. Ch e. N Dst CC.

GUSTON Kent
173 TR 3244 2m N of Dover. CP, 1,236. Dvr RD. Ch e. Sch pe. Dvr and Deal CC (Dvr).

GUYHIRN Cambs
124 TF 4003 4m NNW of March. Loc, Wisbech RD. P Wsbch. Ch m. Isle of Ely CC.

GUY'S MARSH Dorset
166 ST 8420 2m SW of Shaftesbury. Loc, Cann CP.

GUYZANCE Nthmb
71 NU 2103 3m W of Amble. Loc, Acklington CP.

GWEEK Cornwall
189, 190 SW 7026 3m E of Helston. Loc, Kerrier RD. P Hlstn. Ch m. Falmouth and Camborne CC.

GWENNAP Cornwall
190 SW 7340 3m ESE of Redruth. CP, 1,095. Truro RD. P Rdrth. Ch e, m2. Falmouth and Camborne CC. Among once prosperous, now derelict, tin and copper mines. To NW, c 1m E of Redruth, G.Pit, large amphitheatre now terraced, where Wesley used to preach.

GWINEAR Cornwall
189 SW 5937 4m WSW of Camborne. CP(Gwnr-Gwithian), 1,693. W Penwith RD. P Hayle. Ch e, m3. Sch p. Falmouth and Cmbne CC. See also Carnhell Grn, Connor Downs.

GWITHIAN Cornwall
189 SW 5841 4m WNW of Camborne. CP(Gwinear-Gwthn), 1,693. W Penwith RD. P Hayle. Ch m. Falmouth and Cmbne CC. Sandy beaches to W, rocky slate cliffs to N incl Godrevy Point (NT).

H

HABBERLEY Shrops
118 SJ 3903 8m SW of Shrewsbury. Loc,
Pontesbury CP. Ch e. Late 16c hall. Defunct
lead mines in vicinity.

HABBERLEY Worcs
130 SO 8077 2m W of Kidderminster. Loc,
Kddrmnstr Foreign CP. Kddrmnstr RD.
Kddrmnstr CC.

HABROUGH Lincs (L)
104/105 TA 1413 3m W of Immingham.
CP, 367. Grimsby RD. P. Ch e, m.
Louth CC.

HABTON, GREAT Yorks (N)
92 SE 7576 3m NNW of Malton. See Gt
Hbtn.

HACCOMBE Devon
176, 188 SX 8970 3m ESE of Newton
Abbot. CP(Hccmbe w Combe), 398. Ntn
Abbt RD. Ch e. Totnes CC. Ch: monmts.

HACCONBY Lincs (K)
123 TF 1025 3m N of Bourne.
CP(Haconby), 279. S Kesteven RD. P Bne.
Ch e, b. Sch p. Rutland and Stamford CC.
See also Stainfield.

HACEBY Lincs (K)
113, 123 TF 0336 6m SSW of Sleaford.
CP(Newton and Hcby), 134.
E Kesteven RD. Ch e. Rutland and
Stamford CC.

HACHESTON Suffolk (E)
137 TM 3059 3m SSE of Framlingham.
CP, 389. Blyth RD. P Woodbridge. Ch e.
Eye CC. Long drawn out vllge. Ch on its
own along Wickham Mkt rd.

HACKFORD Norfolk
125 TG 0702 3m WNW of Wymondham.
Loc, Deopham CP. Ch e, m.

HACKFORTH Yorks (N)
91 SE 2493 4m NNW of Bedale. CP, 130.
Bdle RD. P Bdle. Sch pe. Thirsk and
Malton CC.

HACKLETON Northants
133/146 SP 8055 5m SE of Northampton.
CP, 914. Nthmptn RD. Ch b. Sch p.
Daventry CC (S Nthnts). See also Horton,
Piddington. Memorial chpl of William Carey,
first English Protestant missionary in India,
founder of Baptist Mssnry Society, 1792.

HACKNESS Yorks (N)
93 SE 9690 5m WNW of Scarborough.
CP, 102. Scbrgh RD. P Scbrgh. Ch e. Sch pe.
Scbrgh CC (Scbrgh and Whitby). Estate
village with Ggn hall. Ch partly Saxon.

HACKNEY London
161 TQ 3685 5m NE of Charing Cross.
LB, 216,659. BCs: Hckny Central, Hckny N
and Stoke Newington, Hckny S and
Shoreditch (Bethnal Grn, Hckny Cntrl, Stke
Nwngtn and Hckny N, Shdtch and
Finsbury). See also Dalston, Homerton,
Shdtch, Stke Nwngtn. In Lndn's East End.
H. Marshes in Lee Valley to E. Victoria Pk
to S is partly in borough.

HACKTHORN Lincs (L)
104 SK 9982 7m NNE of Lincoln. CP, 232.
Welton RD. P LNCLN. Ch e, m. Sch pe.
Gainsborough CC.

HACKTHORPE Westm
83 NY 5423 5m SSE of Penrith. Loc,
Lowther CP. N Westm RD.
P Pnrth, Cumberland. Westm CC. On edge
of Lthr Pk.

HACONBY Lincs (K)
123 TF 1025 3m N of Bourne. Alternative
spelling for Hacconby, qv.

HADDENHAM Bucks
159 SP 7408 3m NE of Thame. CP, 2,240.
Aylesbury RD. P Aylesbury. Ch e, b, m, r.
Sch p, pe. Aylesbury CC.

HADDENHAM Cambs
135 TL 4675 6m WSW of Ely. CP, 1,701.
Ely RD. P Ely. Ch e, b2, m. Sch p. Isle of
Ely CC. See also Aldreth, Hill Row.

HADDINGTON Lincs (K)
113 SK 9163 6m SW of Lincoln.
CP(Auburn Hddngtn and
S Hykeham), 755. N Kesteven RD.
Grantham CC.

HADDISCOE Norfolk
137 TM 4497 4m NNE of Beccles. CP, 472.
Loddon RD. P NORWICH, NOR 29W.
Ch e, m. S Nflk CC. See also Thorpe.

HADDON Hunts
134 TL 1392 5m SW of Peterborough.
CP, 66. Norman Cross RD. Ch e. Hunts CC.

HADEMORE Staffs
120 SK 1708 4m ESE of Lichfield. Loc,
Fisherwick CP. Lchfld RD. Lchfld and
Tamworth CC.

HADFIELD Derbys
102 SK 0296 2m NNW of Glossop. Loc,
Glssp MB. P Hyde, Cheshire.

HADHAM CROSS Herts
148 TL 4218 4m WSW of Bishop's
Stortford. Loc, Much Hdhm CP. Ch c.

HADHAM FORD Herts
148 TL 4321 3m W of Bishop's Stortford.
Loc, Lit Hdhm CP.

HADLEIGH Essex
162 TQ 8187 5m W of Southend. Loc,
Benfleet UD. P Bnflt. SE Essx CC. Rems of
Nmn cstle (A.M.), painted by Constable
1829.

HADLEIGH Suffolk (W)
149 TM 0242 9m W of Ipswich. UD, 5,101.
P Ipswch. Sudbury and Woodbridge CC.
Small tn of charm, once famous for cloth.
15c guildhall*. Ch: scrns, brasses.

HADLEY Shrops
118, 119 SJ 6712 2m ENE of Wellington.
CP, 5,088. Wllngtn RD. P Telford.
Ch e, m3, v. Sch i, j, s. The Wrekin CC.

HADLEY END Staffs
120 SK 1320 6m ENE of Rugeley. Loc,
Yoxall CP.

HADLOW Kent
171 TQ 6349 4m NE of Tonbridge.
CP, 2,305. Tnbrdge RD. P Tnbrdge. Ch e, b.
Sch p. Tnbrdge and Malling CC (Tnbrdge).
See also Barnes St, Golden Grn. 170ft twr
is rems of 19c Gothic cstle.

HADLOW DOWN Sussex (E)
183 TQ 5324 4m ENE of Uckfield. CP, 736.
Uckfld RD. P Uckfld. Ch e, v. Sch pe.
E Grinstead CC.

HADNALL Shrops
118 SJ 5220 5m NNE of Shrewsbury.
CP, 431. N Shrops RD. P Shrsbry. Ch e.
Sch pe. Oswestry CC.

HADSTOCK Essex
148 TL 5544 4m NNE of Saffron Walden.
CP, 298. Sffrn Wldn RD. P CAMBRIDGE.
Ch e. Sffrn Wldn CC.

HADZOR Worcs
130, 131 SO 9162 1m ESE of Droitwich.
CP, 305. Drtwch RD. Ch e, r. Worcester BC.
H. Hse, classical, 1827, now RC college.

HAFFENDEN QUARTER Kent
172, 184 TQ 8840 8m W of Ashford. Loc,
Smarden CP.

HAGGATE Lancs
95 SD 8735 3m NE of Burnley. Loc,
Briercliffe CP. Bnly RD. Ch e, b.
Clitheroe CC.

HAGGERSTON Nthmb
64 NU 0443 6m SSE of
Berwick-upon-Tweed. Loc, Ancroft CP.

HAGLEY Herefs
142 SO 5641 3m E of Hereford. Loc,
Lugwardine CP.

HAGLEY Worcs
130, 131 SO 9180 2m S of Stourbridge.
CP, 3,421. Bromsgrove RD. P Stbrdge.
Ch e, v. Sch p, sr. Brmsgrve and
Redditch CC. H. Hall, Ggn; ornamental
bldngs in grnds.

HAGWORTHINGHAM Lincs (L)
114 TF 3469 5m E of Horncastle. CP, 240.
Hncstle RD. P Spilsby. Ch e. Sch pe.
Hncstle CC.

HAIGH Lancs
101 SD 6009 3m NNE of Wigan. CP, 781.
Wgn RD. P Wgn. Ch e. Sch pe.
Westhoughton CC. See also Red Rock.

HAIGHTON GREEN Lancs
94 SD 5634 4m NE of Preston. Loc,
Hghtn CP. Prstn RD. S Fylde CC.

HAILE Cumb
82 NY 0308 7m SSE of Whitehaven.
CP, 157. Ennerdale RD. Ch e. Whthvn CC.

HAILES Glos
144 SP 0430 2m NE of Winchcombe. Loc,
Stanway CP. Ch e. Rems of Cistercian
abbey* founded in 1246 by younger son of
King John; museum.

HAILEY Herts
148, 161 TL 3710 2m SSE of Ware. Loc,
Hoddesdon UD. P HERTFORD.

HAILEY Oxon
145 SP 3512 2m N of Witney. CP.
Wtny RD. P Wtny. Ch e, m. Sch pe.
Mid-Oxon CC (Banbury).

HAILSHAM Sussex (E)
183 TQ 5909 7m N of Eastbourne.
CP, 5,955. Hlshm RD. P. Ch e, b, c, m, r, v2.
Sch i, j, s. Lewes CC (Eastbne). See also
Magham Down.

HAIL WESTON Hunts
134 TL 1662 2m NW of St Neots. CP, 315.
St Nts RD. P HUNTINGDON. Ch e, b.
Hunts CC.

HAINAULT London
161 TQ 4591 1m SE of Chigwell. Loc,
Redbridge LB. P Ilford, Essex. Ilfd N BC
(Ilfd N BC, Chgwll CC).

HAINFORD Norfolk
126 TG 2218 4m WNW of Wroxham.
CP, 643. St Faith's and Aylsham RD.
P NORWICH, NOR 85X. Ch e, m. Sch pe.
N Nflk CC (Central Nflk). See also
Waterloo.

HAINTON Lincs (L)
105 TF 1884 5m SE of Mkt Rasen. CP, 209.
Louth RD. P LINCOLN. Ch e, r. Sch p.
Lth CC. In ch Heneage Chpl with monmts
to Hnge family, owners of vllge and hall
since 14c. Grnds by Capability Brown.

HAISTHORPE Yorks (E)
99 TA 1264 3m WSW of Bridlington. Loc,
Carnaby CP. Ch m.

HALAM Notts
112 SK 6754 8m W of Newark. CP, 312.
Southwell RD. P Nwk. Ch e, m. Sch pe.
Nwk CC.

HALBERTON Devon
164, 176 ST 0012 3m E of Tiverton.
CP, 1,268. Tvtn RD. P Tvtn. Ch e, m. Sch p.
Tvtn CC. See also Ash Thomas. Vllge in two
parts: Hr Tn and Lr Tn. Ch has notable
scrns, one rood and two parclose.

HALE Ches
101 SJ 7786 1m S of Altrincham.
UD, 17,030. P Altrnchm. Knutsford CC. See
also Halebarns. Largely rsdntl.

HALE Hants
179 SU 1918 4m NE of Fordingbridge.
CP, 572. Ringwood and Fdngbrdge RD.
P Fdngbrdge. Ch e. Sch p. New Forest CC.
See also N Charford. H. Pk*, baroque Ggn
hse with portraits and tapestries.

HALE Lancs
100, 109 SJ 4682 3m SW of Widnes.
CP, 630. Whiston RD. P LIVERPOOL 24.
Ch e. Sch pe. Wdns CC. Inn sign recalls
local 9ft giant John Middleton, 1578–1627.

HALE Surrey
169 SU 8448 2m SW of Aldershot. Loc,
Farnham UD.

HALEBARNS Ches
101 SJ 7985 2m SE of Altrincham. Loc,
Hale UD. P Altrnchm.

HALE, GREAT Lincs (K)
113, 123 TF 1442 5m ESE of Sleaford. See
Gt Hle.

HALES Norfolk
137 TM 3897 5m NNW of Beccles. CP, 317.
Loddon RD. P NORWICH, NOR 31W.
Ch e, m. Sch p. S Nflk CC. Nmn thatched
ch. Colourful new vllge centre.

HALES Staffs
110, 119 SJ 7133 3m E of Mkt Drayton.
Loc, Tyrley CP. Newcastle-under-Lyme RD.
P Mkt Drtn, Salop. Ch e. Sch p. N-u-L BC.

HALESOWEN Worcs
130, 131 SO 9683 7m WSW of Birmingham.
MB, 53,933. P. Hlswn and Stourbridge BC.
In mining area; iron and steel wks.

HALE STREET Kent
171 TQ 6749 6m ENE of Tonbridge. Loc,
E Peckham CP. Ch v.

HALESWORTH Suffolk (E)
137 TM 3877 8m SSW of Beccles. UD, 3,250.
P. Lowestoft CC. Small tn with long narrow
main st called Thoroughfare. R Blyth once
navigable here — witness Quay St.

HALEWOOD Lancs
100, 109 SJ 4585 4m W of Widnes.
CP, 3,791. Whiston RD. P LIVERPOOL 26.
Ch e. Sch ir2, jr2, p4, pe, pr, s, sbr, sgr.
Wdns CC. Car assembly plant to S covers
350 acres.

HALFORD Shrops
129 SO 4383 just NE of Craven Arms.
CP, 167. Ludlow RD. Ch e. Ldlw CC.

HALFORD Warwicks
144 SP 2645 7m SE of Stratford. CP, 293.
Shipston on Stour RD. P Shpstn on Str.
Ch e. Sch p. Stratford-on-Avon CC (Strtfd).
On R Stour and the Fosse Way. Ch: Nmn
tympanum over N door.

HALFPENNY GREEN Staffs
130 SO 8291 7m E of Bridgnorth. Loc,
Bobbington CP. Airfield to S used for civil
flying sch and parachute jumping.

HALFWAY HOUSE Shrops
118 SJ 3411 8m ENE of Welshpool. Loc,
Atcham RD. P Shrsbry. Shrsbry CC.

HALFWAY HOUSES Kent
172 TQ 9372 6m NNE of Sittingbourne.
Loc, Queenborough-in-Sheppey MB.
P Sheerness.

HALIFAX Yorks (W)
96, 102 SE 0925 6m SW of Bradford. CB,
91,171. P. Hlfx BC. See also Luddenden.
Indstrl, esp textiles. Forest of chimneys in
deep Calder valley.

HALLAND Sussex (E)
183 TQ 5016 4m SE of Uckfield. Loc,
E Hoathly CP. P Lewes. Ch v. 1m W,
Bentley Wildfowl Collection*.

HALLATON Leics
133 SP 7896 5m WSW of Uppingham.
CP, 424. Mkt Harborough RD. P Mkt
Hbrgh. Ch e, c. Sch pe. Hbrgh CC. Large
Nmn-Dec ch. Many old hses. Rems of motte
and bailey cstle blt to protect local iron
workings.

HALLATROW Som
166 ST 6357 4m WNW of Radstock. Loc,
High Littleton CP. P BRISTOL.

HALLBANKGATE Cumb
76 NY 5859 3m ESE of Brampton. Loc,
Farlam CP. P Brmptn. Ch m. Sch p.

HALL DUNNERDALE Lancs
88 SD 2195 6m WSW of Coniston. Loc,
Dnnrdle-w-Seathwaite CP. N Lonsdale RD.
Morecambe and Lnsdle CC.

HALLEN Glos
155, 156 ST 5580 5m NNW of Bristol. Loc,
Almondsbury CP. P BRSTL. Ch e.

HALLGARTH Co Durham
85 NZ 3243 4m E of Durham. Loc,
Pittington CP.

HALLING Kent
171, 172 TQ 7064 4m SW of Rochester.
CP, 2,157. Strood RD. Ch e, b. Sch p.
Gravesend CC. See also Upr Hllng.

HALLINGBURY, GREAT Essex
148 TL 5119 2m SE of Bishop's Stortford.
See Gt Hllngbry.

HALLINGTON Lincs (L)
105 TF 3085 2m SW of Louth. CP, 57.
Lth RD. Lth CC.

HALLINGTON Nthmb
77 NY 9875 7m N of Corbridge. Loc,
Whittington, CP. Hexham RD. Ch m.
Hxhm CC. To W, H. Reservoir.

HALLOUGHTON Notts
112 SK 6851 7m W of Newark. CP, 53.
Southwell RD. Ch e. Nwk CC.

HALLOW Worcs
130 SO 8258 3m NW of Worcester.
CP, 1,204. Martley RD. P WCSTR. Ch e, v.
Sch pe. Kidderminster CC. See also
Shoulton.

HALLSANDS Devon
188 SX 8138 6m SE of Kingsbridge. Loc,
Stokenham CP. P Kngsbrdge. Small fishing
vllge. Shoreside cottages derelict since gale
of 1917.

HALL'S GREEN Herts
147 TL 2728 3m NE of Stevenage. Loc,
Weston CP.

HALLTOFT END Lincs (H)
114 TF 3645 3m ENE of Boston. Loc,
Freiston CP. Ch m.

HALLWORTHY Cornwall
174, 186 SX 1887 5m ENE of Camelford.
Loc, Cmlfd RD, Launceston RD.
N Cnwll CC.

HALMER END Staffs
110 SJ 7949 5m WNW of Stoke-on-Trent.
Loc, Audley Rural CP. P Stke-on-Trnt.
Ch m2, v. Sch s.

HALMORE Glos
156 SO 6902 5m NW of Dursley. Loc,
Thornbury RD. P Berkeley. Ch m.
S Glos CC.

HALNAKER Sussex (W)
181 SU 9008 4m NE of Chichester. Loc,
Boxgrove CP. Main rd hmlt. To N, ruins of
H. Hse, mdvl mnr hse, containing gdns* of
Lit Hlnkr, modern hse in classical style.

HALSALL Lancs
100 SD 3710 3m WNW of Ormskirk.
CP, 1,960. W Lancs RD. Ch e, m. Sch pe.
Ormskk CC. See also Shirdley Hill.

HALSE Northants
145, 146 SP 5640 3m NNW of Brackley.
Loc, Greatworth CP.

HALSE Som
164 ST 1427 5m WNW of Taunton.
CP, 284. Tntn RD. P Tntn. Ch e, m.
Tntn CC.

HALSE TOWN Cornwall
189 SW 5038 1m SSW of St Ives. Loc,
St Ives MB. P St Ives. Childhood home of
Sir Henry Irving, actor. To E, Knill Monmt,
erected 1782 by Sir John Knill as monmt to
himself.

HALSHAM Yorks (E)
99 TA 2727 4m W of Withernsea. CP, 263.
Holderness RD. P Hull. Ch e, m.
Bridlington CC.

HALSINGER Devon
163 SS 5138 2m NE of Braunton. Loc,
Brntn CP.

HALSTEAD Essex
149 TL 8130 6m NE of Braintree.
UD, 7,621. P. Saffron Walden CC. Ch has

14c Bourchier family tombs. Courtauld's
silk mill of 1826 beside river. Blue Br Hse*,
16c—17c hse in perfect orig condition.

HALSTEAD Kent
171 TQ 4861 4m SSE of Orpington.
CP, 1,582. Sevenoaks RD. P Svnks. Ch e.
Sch p. Svnks CC.

HALSTEAD Leics
122 SK 7505 7m WSW of Oakham. Loc,
Tilton CP. Ch m.

HALSTOCK Dorset
177, 178 ST 5308 5m SSW of Yeovil.
CP, 339. Beaminster RD. P Yvl, Somerset.
Ch e. Sch p. W Dst CC.

HALTHAM Lincs (L)
114 TF 2463 4m SSW of Horncastle.
CP, 102. Hncstle RD. Ch e. Hncstle CC.

HALTON Bucks
146 SP 8710 4m SE of Aylesbury.
CP, 3,132. Aylesbury RD. P Aylesbury.
Ch e. Sch p. Aylesbury CC.

HALTON Ches
100, 109 SJ 5381 1m E of Runcorn. Loc,
Rncn UD. P Rncn. Ruined Nmn cstle stands
on rocky eminence.

HALTON Lancs
89 SD 5065 3m NE of Lancaster.
CP(Hltn-w-Aughton), 1,486. Lunesdale RD.
P LNCSTR. Ch e, c. Sch pe. Lncstr CC. 11c
churchyard cross.

HALTON EAST Yorks (W)
96 SE 0453 4m ENE of Skipton. CP, 72.
Skptn RD. Ch m. Skptn CC.

HALTON GILL Yorks (W)
90 SD 8876 9m NNE of Settle. CP, 37.
Sttle RD. Ch e. Skipton CC. See also Foxup.

HALTON HOLEGATE Lincs (L)
114 TF 4165 7m SSW of Alford. CP, 389.
Spilsby RD. P Splsby. Ch e, m. Sch pe.
Horncastle CC. Twr windmill to SW.

HALTON LEA GATE Nthmb
76 NY 6558 5m SW of Haltwhistle. Loc,
Hartleyburn CP. Hltwhstle RD.
P Carlisle, Cumberland. Hexham CC.

HALTON WEST Yorks (W)
95 SD 8454 6m SSE of Settle. CP, 99.
Sttle RD. Skipton CC.

HALTWHISTLE Nthmb
76 NY 7064 14m W of Hexham. CP, 3,475.
Hltwhstle RD. P. Ch e, m2, r, s, v2.
Sch i, pe, s. Hxhm CC. Mkt tn for now
worked out coal-mining area. On S Tyne.

HALVERGATE Norfolk
126 TG 4206 6m W of Yarmouth. CP, 440.
Blofield and Flegg RD. Ch e, m. Sch p.
Ymth CC. See also Tunstall.

HALWELL Devon
187, 188 SX 7753 5m SSW of Totnes.
CP, 219. Ttns RD. Ch e. Sch p. Ttns CC. See
also Washbourne.

HALWILL Devon
175 SX 4299 6m ESE of Holsworthy.
CP, 407. Hlswthy RD. Ch e, b2. W Dvn CC
(Tavistock).

HALWILL JUNCTION Devon
175 SS 4400 7m ESE of Holsworthy. Loc,
Hlswthy RD, Okehampton RD. W Dvn CC
(Tavistock CC, Torrington CC). Erstwhile
dividing point of the Atlantic Coast Express.

HAM Glos
156 ST 6898 9m NE of Severn Rd Br.
CP(Hm and Stone), 1,103. Thornbury RD.
S Glos CC. See also Bevington.

HAM Kent
173 TR 3254 2m S of Sandwich. Loc,
Northbourne CP. Ch e.

HAM London
160, 170 TQ 1771 2m S of Richmond. Loc,
R c h m n d   u p o n   T h a m e s LB.
P Rchmnd, Surrey. Rchmnd BC. Aircraft
factory to S. To N beside R Thames, H.
Hse*, Jcbn and later (NT and Victoria and
Albert Museum).

HAM Wilts
168 SU 3363 4m S of Hungerford. CP, 170.
Marlborough and Ramsbury RD. P Mlbrgh.
Ch e. Sch pe. Devizes CC.

HAMBLE Hants
180 SU 4806 5m SE of Southampton.
CP, 3,001. Winchester RD. P STHMPTN.
Ch e. Sch ie, j, s. Eastleigh CC. Yachting and
boat-building centre for centuries. Now also
aircraft factories and flying training
establishments.

HAMBLEDEN Bucks
159 SU 7886 3m NNE of Henley.
C P , 1 , 5 3 0 .   W y c o m b e R D .
P Hnly-on-Thames, Oxon. Ch e, v. Sch pe.
Wcmbe CC. See also Frieth, Mill End,
Rockwell End, Skirmett. 17c mnr hse.

HAMBLEDON Hants
180, 181 SU 6414 7m NW of Havant.
CP, 1,019. Droxford RD. P Portsmouth.
Ch e, m. Sch p. Petersfield CC. See also
Chidden. To NE, Broadhalfpenny Down,
where H. Cricket Club instituted in 18c. To
N on Windmill Down, vineyard and wine
press*.

HAMBLEDON Surrey
169, 170, 182 SU 9638 3m S of Godalming.
CP, 1,486. Hmbldn RD. P Gdlmng. Ch e.
Sch pe. Guildford CC.

HAMBLETON Lancs
94 SD 3742 6m NE of Blackpool. CP, 836.
Garstang RD. P Blckpl. Ch e, c. Sch p.
N Fylde CC.

HAMBLETON Rutland
122 SK 9007 3m ESE of Oakham. CP, 171.
Oakhm RD. P Oakhm. Ch e. Rtlnd and
Stamford CC. Consists of Upr, Middle, and
Nether H. Upr H. has the ch; Middle has the
Jcbn Old Hall.

HAMBLETON Yorks (W)
97 SE 5530 4m WSW of Selby. CP, 495.
Slby RD. P Slby. Ch m. Sch pe. Barkston
Ash CC.

HAMBRIDGE Som
177 ST 3921 5m NE of Ilminster. Loc,
Curry Rivel CP. P Langport. Ch e, m. Sch p.

HAMBROOK Glos
155, 156 ST 6378 5m NE of Bristol. Loc,
Winterbourne CP. P BRSTL. Sch p.

HAMBROOK Sussex (W)
181 SU 7806 5m W of Chichester. Loc,
Chchstr RD. P Chchstr. Chchstr CC.

HAMERINGHAM Lincs (L)
114 TF 3167 3m ESE of Horncastle.
CP, 56. Hncstle RD. Ch e. Hncstle CC.

HAMERTON Hunts
134 TL 1379 8m NW of Huntingdon.
CP, 130. Hntngdn RD. P HNTNGDN. Ch e.
Hunts CC.

HAM GREEN Som
155, 156 ST 5375 4m NW of Bristol. Loc,
Easton-in-Gordano CP.

HAM GREEN Worcs
131 SP 0163 3m SSW of Redditch. Loc,
Rddtch UD.

HAMMER Sussex (W)
169, 181 SU 8732 1m SW of Haslemere.
Loc, Linchmere CP. P Hslmre. Ch c.

HAMMERSMITH London
160, 170 TQ 2278 5m WSW of Charing
Cross. LB, 184,935. BCs: Fulham,
Hmmrsmth N. (Barons Ct, Flhm,
Hmmrsmth N). See also Flhm, Shepherd's
Bush. On N bank of Thames; H. Br.
H. Flyover carries A4 rd over H. Br Rd.

HAMMERWICH Staffs
120 SK 0607 3m WSW of Lichfield.
CP, 2,408. Lchfld RD. P Walsall. Ch e, m.
Sch p. Lchfld and Tamworth CC.

HAMMERWOOD Sussex (E)
171 TQ 4339 3m E of E Grinstead. Loc,
Forest Row CP. Ch e.

HAMMOON Dorset
178 ST 8114 7m NW of Blandford. CP, 42.
Sturminster RD. Ch e. N Dst CC. Name
derived from William de Moion, owner of
the mnr, who fought at Battle of Hastings.

HAMPDEN, GREAT Bucks
159 ST 8402 3m E of Princes Risborough.
See Gt Hmpdn.

HAMPDEN PARK Sussex (E)
183 TQ 6002 2m N of Eastbourne. Loc,
Eastbne CB. P Eastbne.

HAMPDEN ROW Bucks
159 SP 8401 3m ESE of Princes
Risborough. Loc, Gt and Lit Hmpdn CP.
P Gt Missenden.

HAMPNETT Glos
144 SP 0915 1m NW of Northleach.
CP, 103. Nthlch RD. Ch e. Cirencester and
Tewkesbury CC. Restored Nmn ch.

HAMPOLE Yorks (W)
103 SE 5010 6m NW of Doncaster. CP, 214.
Dncstr RD. P Dncstr. Don Valley CC. See
also Skelbrooke.

HAMPRESTON Dorset
179 SZ 0598 5m NNW of Bournemouth.
CP, 6,534. Wimborne and Cranborne RD.
Ch e. Sch pe. N Dst CC. See also Ferndown,
Longham, Stapehill, Trickett's Cross.

HAMPSTEAD London
160 TQ 2685 4m NW of Charing Cross. Loc,
Camden LB. Hmpstd BC. Rsdntl distr.
H. Hth, large open space on high grnd.
Kenwood Hse*, 18c, by Robert Adam.
Fenton Hse (NT)*, late 17c. Keats Hse and
Museum.

HAMPSTEAD NORRIS Berks
158 SU 5276 7m NNE of Newbury. CP.
Wantage RD. P Nbry. Ch e. Sch pe.
Abingdon CC.

HAMPSTHWAITE Yorks (W)
96 SE 2558 4m NW of Harrogate. CP, 565.
Nidderdale RD. P Hrrgte. Ch e, m, v. Sch pe.
Hrrgte CC.

HAMPTON London
170 TQ 1469 3m W of Kingston. Loc,
Richmond upon Thames LB. P Middx.
Twickenham BC. On N bank of Thames. To
E, Bushey Pk; to SE, H. Ct Pk, with
H. Ct Palace (A.M.), blt by Cardinal Wolsey
in 16c; 17c additions by Wren.

HAMPTON Shrops
130 SO 7486 4m SSE of Bridgnorth. Loc,
Chelmarsh CP.

HAMPTON BISHOP Herefs
142 SO 5538 3m ESE of Hereford. CP, 373.
Hrfd RD. P HRFD. Ch e. See also Tupsley.
Hrfd CC. Almost encircled by rivers Wye
and Lugg.

HAMPTON GAY Oxon
145 SP 4816 7m NNW of Oxford.
CP (Hmptn Gay and Poyle), 142.
Ploughley RD. Ch e. Mid-Oxon CC
(Banbury). Farm and a row of cottages. Ch
at some distance via vestigial track.

HAMPTON HEATH Ches
109 SJ 4949 6m NNW of Whitchurch. Loc,
Hmptn CP. Tarvin RD. Ch m. Nantwich CC.

HAMPTON IN ARDEN Warwicks
131 SP 2080 3m E of Solihull. CP, 1,332.
Meriden RD. P Slhll. Ch e, v. Sch pe.
Mrdn CC. Handsome vllge with old hses;
packhorse br to SE.

HAMPTON LOADE Shrops
130 SO 7486 4m SSE of Bridgnorth. Loc,
Quatt Malvern CP.

HAMPTON LOVETT Worcs
130, 131 SO 8865 2m NNW of Droitwich.
CP. Drtwch RD. Ch e. Worcester BC.

HAMPTON LUCY Warwicks
131 SP 2557 4m ENE of Stratford. CP, 512.
Strtfd-on-Avon RD. P WARWICK. Ch e.
Sch pe. Strtfd-on-Avn CC (Strtfd). Fine
early 19c ch. Thatched vllge pump.
Charlecote Pk to S - see Chlcte.

HAMPTON ON THE HILL Warwicks
131 SP 2564 2m W of Warwick. Loc,
Budbrooke CP. P WRWCK. Ch e, r.

HAMPTON POYLE Oxon
145 SP 5015 6m N of Oxford. CP(Hmptn
Gay and Ple), 142. Ploughley RD. Ch e. Mid-
Oxon CC (Banbury).

HAMPTON WAFER Herefs
129 SO 5757 5m ESE of Leominster.
CP, 20. Lmnstr and Wigmore RD.
Lmnstr CC.

HAMPTON WICK London
170 TQ 1769 just W of Kingston. Loc,
Richmond upon Thames LB.
P Kngstn-upn-Thms, Surrey.
Twickenham BC. At E edge of Bushey Pk.

HAMPTWORTH Wilts
179 SU 2419 9m SE of Salisbury. Loc,
Redlynch CP. Ch m2.

HAMSEY Sussex (E)
183 TQ 4012 2m N of Lewes. CP, 753
Chailey RD. Ch e. Sch p. Lws CC. See also
Cooksbridge, Offham.

HAMSEY GREEN Surrey
171 TQ 3559 4m S of Croydon. Loc,
Caterham and Warlingham UD. P South
Crdn.

HAMSTALL RIDWARE Staffs
120 SK 1019 4m ENE of Rugeley. CP, 286.
Lichfield RD. P Rgly. Ch e. Sch p. Lchfld
and Tamworth CC. Fine mdvl ch and Elizn
mnr hse with unusual gatehouse.

HAMSTEAD IOW
180 SZ 4091 3m ENE of Yarmouth. Loc,
Shalfleet CP.

HAMSTEAD MARSHALL Berks
158 SU 4165 4m WSW of Newbury.
CP, 168. Nbry RD. P Nbry. Ch e. Nbry CC.

HAMSTERLEY Co Durham
77, 78 NZ 1156 4m N of Consett. Loc,
Cnstt UD. P(Hmstly
Colliery), NEWCASTLE UPON TYNE.

HAMSTERLEY Co Durham
84 NZ 1131 6m WNW Bishop Auckland.
CP, 343. Barnard Cstle RD. P Bshp
Aucklnd. Ch e, b, m. Sch p. Bshp
Aucklnd CC.

HAMSTREET Kent
184 TR 0033 6m S of Ashford. Loc,
Orlestone CP. P Ashfd. Ch m.

HAM STREET Som
165, 166 ST 5534 4m SE of Glastonbury.
Loc, Baltonsborough CP.

HAMWORTHY Dorset
179 SY 9991 1m W of Poole. Loc, Ple MB.
P Ple. Power stn.

HANBURY Staffs
120 SK 1727 5m NW of Burton-on-Trent.
CP, 518. Tutbury RD. Ch e, m. Sch pe.
Btn CC. See also Coton in the Clay.

HANBURY Worcs
130, 131 SO 9663 4m E of Droitwich.
CP, 834. Drtwch RD. P Bromsgrove. Ch e.
Sch pe. Worcester BC. Ch: Vernon monmts.
H. Hall (NT)*, brick, early 18c; painted hall,
plasterwork. Mere Hall, mdvl black and
white.

HANCHURCH Staffs
110, 119 SJ 8441 3m S of
Newcastle-under-Lyme. Loc,
Swynnerton CP. P Stoke-on-Trent.

HANDCROSS Sussex (E)
182 TQ 2629 4m S of Crawley. Loc,
Slaugham CP. P Haywards Hth. Sch p. To
SE, Nymans (NT), with 30-acre gdns*.

HANDFORTH Ches
101 SJ 8583 1m NNE of Wilmslow. Loc,
Wlmslw UD. P Wlmslw. H. Hall,
half-timbered 16c hse, to E opposite
housing estate.

HANDLEY Ches
109 SJ 4657 7m SE of Chester. CP, 206.

Tarvin RD. P CHSTR. Ch e. Sch p. Nantwich CC. See also Milton Grn.

HANDSACRE Staffs
120 SK 0916 3m ESE of Rugeley. CP(Armitage w Hndsacre), 2,302. Lichfield RD. Ch m. Sch p. Lchfld and Tamworth CC.

HANFORD Dorset
178 ST 8411 4m NW of Blandford. CP, 46. Sturminster RD. Ch e. N Dst CC.

HANGING LANGFORD Wilts
167 SU 0337 8m NW of Salisbury. Loc, Steeple Lngfd CP.

HANHAM Glos
155, 156 ST 6472 4m E of Bristol. Loc, Kingswood UD. P Kngswd, BRSTL.

HANKELOW Ches
110 SJ 6745 4m SSE of Nantwich. CP, 206. Nntwch RD. P Crewe. Ch m2. Sch pe. Nntwch CC.

HANKERTON Wilts
157 ST 9790 3m NE of Malmesbury. CP, 178. Mlmsbry RD. P Mlmsbry. Ch e, b. Chippenham CC.

HANKHAM Sussex (E)
183 TQ 6105 4m N of Eastbourne. Loc, Westham CP. Ch m. Sch p.

HANLEY Staffs
110 SJ 8847 N distr of Stoke-on-Trent. Loc, Stke-on-Trnt CB. P Stke-on-Trnt. S-on-T Central BC. Pottery distr. Bthplce of Arnold Bennett and one of his *Five Towns* ('Hanbridge').

HANLEY CASTLE Worcs
143 SO 8342 4m ESE of Malvern. CP, 1,249. Upton upon Severn RD. P WORCESTER. Ch e, r. Sch ie, s. S Worcs CC. Severn End, restored 17c black and white hse; contemporary outbldngs, terraced gdns.

HANLEY CHILDE Worcs
129, 130 SO 6565 4m ESE of Tenbury Wells. Loc, Hnly CP. Tnbry RD. Ch e. Kidderminster CC.

HANLEY SWAN Worcs
143 SO 8142 3m SE of Malvern. Loc, Hnly Cstle CP. P WORCESTER. Ch e. Sch je.

HANLEY WILLIAM Worcs
129, 130 SO 6765 5m ESE of Tenbury Wells. Loc, Hnly CP. Tnbry RD. Ch e. Kidderminster CC.

HANLITH Yorks (W)
90 SD 9061 5m ESE of Settle. CP, 25. Sttle RD. Skipton CC.

HANNAH Lincs (L)
105 TF 5079 4m NE of Alford. CP(Hnnh cum Hagnaby), 56. Louth RD. Ch e. Lth CC.

HANNINGTON Hants
168 SU 5355 7m WNW of Basingstoke. Loc, Kingsclere CP. P Bsngstke. Ch e, m. Sch pe.

HANNINGTON Northants
133 SP 8171 5m WNW of Wellingborough. CP, 117. Brixworth RD. Ch e. Daventry CC (Kettering).

HANNINGTON Wilts
157 SU 1793 6m NNE of Swindon. CP, 236. Highworth RD. P Swndn. Ch e. Devizes CC. See also Hnnngtn Wick.

HANNINGTON WICK Wilts
157 SU 1795 7m N of Swindon. Loc, Hnngtn CP.

HANSLOPE Bucks
146 SP 8046 4m N of Wolverton. CP, 1,032. Newport Pagnell RD. P Wlvtn. Ch e, m, v. Sch p. Buckingham CC. See also Long St. Ch: high 15c twr and spire; Nmn chancel.

HANTHORPE Lincs (K)
123 TF 0824 3m NNW of Bourne. Loc, Morton CP.

HANWELL London
160 TQ 1580 1m W of Ealing. Loc, Ealng LB. Ealng N BC, Southall BC. H. Viaduct, famous rly viaduct by Brunel, carries main line over valley of R Brent.

HANWELL Oxon
145 SP 4343 2m NNW of Banbury. CP, 218. Bnbry RD. P Bnbry. Ch e, m. Bnbry CC.

HANWOOD, GREAT Shrops
118 SJ 4409 4m WSW of Shrewsbury. See Gt Hnwd.

HANWORTH London
160, 170 TQ 1271 4m SW of Richmond.

Loc, Hounslow LB. P Feltham, Middx.
Flthm and Heston BC (Flthm).

HANWORTH Norfolk
126 TG 1935 4m SSW of Cromer. CP, 196.
Erpingham RD. P NORWICH, NOR 38Y.
Ch e. N Nflk CC.

HAPPISBURGH Norfolk
126 TG 3831 6m E of N Walsham. CP, 784.
Smallburgh RD. P NORWICH, NOR 25Z.
Ch e, m. Sch pe. N Nflk CC. See also
Walcott, Whimpwell Grn. 18c lighthouse.

HAPPISBURGH COMMON Norfolk
126 TG 3728 6m E of N Walsham. Loc,
Hsbrgh CP.

HAPSFORD Ches
109 SJ 4774 6m NE of Chester. CP, 99.
Chstr RD. City of Chstr CC.

HAPTON Lancs
95 SD 7931 3m W of Burnley. CP, 1,713.
Bnly RD. P Bnly. Ch e, m, r. Sch p, pe.
Clitheroe CC.

HAPTON Norfolk
137 TM 1796 5m SE of Wymondham. Loc,
Tharston CP. P NORWICH, NOR 69W.
Ch e. Sch pe.

HARBERTON Devon
187, 188 SX 7758 2m WSW of Totnes.
CP, 897. Ttns RD. P Ttns. Ch e, m. Ttns CC.
See also Belsford, Harbertonford. Ch: scrn,
plpt.

HARBERTONFORD Devon
187, 188 SX 7856 3m SSW of Totnes. Loc,
Harberton CP. P Ttns. Ch e, m. Sch pe.

HARBLEDOWN Kent
173 TR 1358 1m W of Canterbury.
CP, 1,839. Bridge-Blean RD. Ch e.
Cntrbry CC.

HARBOROUGH MAGNA Warwicks
132 SP 4779 3m NNW of Rugby; CP, 379.
Rgby RD. P Rgby. Ch e. Sch pe. Rgby CC.

HARBOTTLE Nthmb
71 NT 9304 8m WNW of Rothbury.
CP, 200. Rthbry RD. P Morpeth. Ch v.
Sch pe. Berwick-upon-Tweed CC. See also
Holystone, Sharperton. In upr Coquetdale.
Rems of Nmn cstle.

HARBRIDGE Hants
179 SU 1410 3m S of Fordingbridge.
CP (Hbrdge and Ibsley), 662. Ringwood and
Fdngbrdge RD. Ch e. New Forest CC. See
also S Gorley.

HARBURY Warwicks
132 SP 3759 3m WSW of Southam.
CP, 1,378. Sthm RD. P Leamington Spa.
Ch e, m. Sch pe. Stratford-on-Avon CC
(Strtfd).

HARBY Leics
112, 122 SK 7431 7m N of Melton
Mowbray. CP (Clawson and Hby), 1,846.
Mltn and Belvoir RD. P Mltn Mbry. Ch e, m.
Sch pe. Mltn CC.

HARBY Notts
113 SK 8770 6m W of Lincoln. CP, 266.
Newark RD. P Nwk. Ch e, m. Sch p.
Nwk CC. Eleanor, queen of Edward I, died
here.

HARCOMBE Devon
176 SY 1590 3m NE of Sidmouth. Loc,
Sdmth UD.

HARDEN Yorks (W)
96 SE 0838 2m SE of Keighley. Loc,
Bingley UD. P Bngly. On hill to SE,
St David's Ruin, 18c folly.

HARDHAM Sussex (W)
182 TQ 0317 1m SW of Pulborough. Loc,
Coldwaltham CP. Ch e. 11c–12c ch with
famous wall-paintings.

HARDINGHAM Norfolk
125 TG 0403 5m WNW of Wymondham.
CP, 326. Mitford and Launditch RD.
P Norwich. Ch e, m. Sch pe. SW Nflk CC.

HARDINGSTONE Northants
133 SP 7657 2m SSE of Northampton.
CP, 1,488. Nthmptn RD. P NTHMPTN.
Ch e, b. Sch p. Daventry CC (S Nthnts). One
of the three surviving orig Eleanor crosses is
here. (Others at Geddington and Waltham
Cross.)

HARDINGS WOOD Staffs
110 SJ 8254 6m NNW of Stoke-on-Trent.
Loc, Kidsgrove UD.

HARDINGTON Som
166 ST 7452 4m NW of Frome. Loc,
Hemington CP. Ch e.

HARDINGTON MANDEVILLE Som
177 ST 5111 4m SW of Yeovil. CP, 358.
Yvl RD. P Yvl. Ch e, m. Yvl CC.

HARDLEY Hants
180 SU 4304 2m NW of Fawley. Loc,
Fwly CP. Ch m, v. Sch s.

HARDLEY STREET Norfolk
137 TG 3801 7m NNW of Beccles. Loc,
Langley w Hardley CP. Loddon RD. Ch e.
Sch p. S Nflk CC.

HARDMEAD Bucks
146 SP 9347 4m ENE of Newport Pagnell.
CP, 98. Npt Pgnll RD. Ch e.
Buckingham CC.

HARDROW Yorks (N)
90 SD 8691 1m NNW of Hawes. Loc, High
Abbotside CP. Aysgarth RD. Ch e.
Richmond CC. On Pennine Way. To N,
Hardraw Force, 90ft waterfall.

HARDSTOFT Derbys
112 SK 4463 6m SSE of Chesterfield. Loc,
Ault Hucknall CP.

HARDWAY Hants
180 SU 6001 1m N of Gosport. Loc,
Gspt MB. P Gspt.

HARDWAY Som
166 ST 7133 2m E of Bruton. Loc,
Brewham CP. Wncntn RD. Wells CC.

HARDWICK Bucks
146 SP 8019 3m N of Aylesbury. CP, 248.
Aylesbury RD. P Aylesbury. Ch e. Sch pe.
Aylesbury CC.

HARDWICK Cambs
135 TL 3758 5m W of Cambridge. CP, 460.
Chesterton RD. P CMBRDGE. Ch e.
Cambs CC.

HARDWICK Norfolk
137 TM 2290 W of Bungay. Loc,
Shelton CP. P NORWICH, NOR 76W. Ch e.

HARDWICK Northants
133 SP 8569 3m WNW of Wellingborough.
CP, 61. Wllngbrgh RD. Ch e. Wllngbrgh CC.

HARDWICK Notts
103 SK 6375 4m SE of Worksop. Loc,
Wksp MB. P Wksp.

HARDWICK Oxon
145, 146 SP 5729 4m N of Bicester.
CP(Hdwck w Tusmore), 85. Ploughley RD.
Ch e. Banbury CC (Henley).

HARDWICK Oxon
158 SP 3706 3m SSE of Witney.
CP(Hdwck-w-Yelford), 85. Wtny RD. Ch e.
Mid-Oxon CC (Banbury).

HARDWICKE Glos
143 SO 7912 4m SW of Gloucester.
CP, 861. Glcstr RD. P GLCSTR. Ch e.
Sch pe. Stroud CC.

HARDWICKE Glos
143, 144 SO 9027 4m NNW of Cheltenham.
Loc, Elmstone Hardwicke CP. Chltnhm RD.
Cirencester and Tewkesbury CC.

HAREBY Lincs (L)
114 TF 3365 5m SE of Horncastle. CP, 30.
Spilsby RD. Ch e. Hncstle CC.

HAREFIELD London
160 TQ 0590 4m N of Uxbridge. Loc,
Hillingdon LB. P Uxbrdge, Middx.
Uxbrdge BC (CC). Ch: monmts, brasses.
Countess of Derby's Almhouses, 1600.

HARE HATCH Berks
159 SU 8077 6m WSW of Maidenhead. Loc,
Wargrave CP.

HARESCOMBE Glos
143 SO 8310 3m N of Stroud. CP, 263.
Gloucester RD. Ch e. Strd CC.

HARESFIELD Glos
143 SO 8110 5m SSW of Gloucester.
CP, 432. Glcstr RD. P Stonehouse. Ch e.
Sch pe. Stroud CC. To SE, H. Beacon (NT)
within Iron Age fort; viewpoint.

HARE STREET Herts
148 TL 3929 7m SSE of Royston. Loc,
Hormead CP. Braughing RD. P Buntingford.
E Herts CC.

HAREWOOD Yorks (W)
96 SE 3245 7m NNE of Leeds. CP, 1,338.
Wetherby RD. P LDS. Ch e. Sch pe.
Barkston Ash CC. See also Dunkeswick,
Weardley, Wike. Estate vllge. H. Hse*, 18c
mansion by Carr of York; grnds laid out by
Capability Brown. Rems of cstle on N slope
overlooking Wharfedale.

HAREWOOD END Herefs
142 SO 5226 5m WNW of Ross-on-Wye.
Loc, Rss and Whitchurch RD.
P HEREFORD. Hrfd CC.

HARFORD Devon
187, 188 SX 6359 2m N of Ivybridge.
CP, 115. Plympton St Mary RD. Ch e.
W Dvn CC (Tavistock).

HARGRAVE Ches
109 SJ 4862 6m ESE of Chester. Loc,
Foulk Stapleford CP. Tarvin RD. P CHSTR.
Ch e, m. Northwich CC.

HARGRAVE Northants
134 TL 0370 3m SE of Raunds. CP, 207.
Oundle and Thrapston RD.
P Wellingborough. Ch e, m. Wllngbrgh CC.

HARGRAVE Suffolk (W)
136 TL 7760 6m WSW of Bury
St Edmunds. CP, 228. Thingoe RD. P Bury
St Eds. Ch e, m. Bury St Eds CC.

HARGRAVE GREEN Suffolk (W)
136 TL 7759 6m WSW of Bury
St Edmunds. Loc, Hgrve CP.

HARKER Cumb
76 NY 3960 3m N of Carlisle. Loc,
Rockcliffe CP.

HARKSTEAD Suffolk (E)
150 TM 1834 6m SSE of Ipswich. CP, 304.
Samford RD. P Ipswch. Ch e. Sch pe.
Sudbury and Woodbridge CC.

HARLASTON Staffs
120 SK 2110 4m N of Tamworth. CP, 264.
Lichfield RD. P Tmwth. Ch e. Sch pe.
Lchfld and Tmwth CC.

HARLAXTON Lincs (K)
113, 122 SK 8832 3m SW of Grantham.
CP, 406. W Kesteven RD. P Grnthm. Ch e.
Sch pe. Rutland and Stamford CC. H. Mnr,
vast ornate 19c edifice by Salvin; numerous
outbuildings. Some cottages in vllge in similar
style.

HARLESTON Norfolk
137 TM 2483 7m SW of Bungay.
CP (Redenhall w Hlstn), 1,809.
Depwade RD. P. Ch e, c, m. S Nflk CC.

HARLESTON Suffolk (E)
136 TM 0160 2m WNW of Stowmarket.
CP, 136. Gipping RD. Ch e. Eye CC.

HARLESTONE Northants
133 SP 7064 4m NW of Northampton. CP.
Brixworth RD. P NTHMPTN. Ch e, b.
Sch p. Daventry CC (Kettering). To W,
Althorp Pk*, 16c hse with later additions
and alterations, seat of Spencer family since
1508. Grnds laid out by Le Nôtre.

HARLE SYKE Lancs
95 SD 8635 3m NE of Burnley. Loc,
Briercliffe CP. Bnly RD. P Bnly.
Clitheroe CC.

HARLEY Shrops
118 SJ 5901 2m WNW of Much Wenlock.
CP, 150. Atcham RD. Ch e. Shrewsbury CC.

HARLINGTON Beds
147 TL 0330 5m S of Ampthill. CP, 862.
Ampthll RD. P Dunstable. Ch e, m. Sch p.
Mid-Beds CC.

HARLINGTON London
160, 170 TQ 0877 4m SSE of Uxbridge.
Loc, Hillingdon LB. P Hayes, Middx. Hayes
and Hlngtn BC. Ch has Nmn S doorway;
brasses, Easter sepulchre.

HARLOW Essex
148, 161 TL 4410 22m NNE of London.
UD, 77,666. P. Hlw CC (Epping). See also
Gt Parndon, Potter St. New tn, blt 1947
onwards to plans of Sir F. Gibberd: large
traffic-free mkt place with bronze statue;
11-storey tn hall with observation platform;
sports centre. (Pop. of new tn 57,791.)

HARLOW HILL Nthmb
77, 78 NZ 0768 4m NNW of Prudhoe. Loc,
Stamfordham CP. Ch m. On line of Roman
Wall. To W, chain of reservoirs for
Newcastle.

HARLTHORPE Yorks (E)
97, 98 SE 7437 8m ENE of Selby. Loc,
Foggathorpe CP.

HARLTON Cambs
148 TL 3852 6m SW of Cambridge.
CP, 285. Chesterton RD. P CMBRDGE.
Ch e. Cambs CC. Lofty ch, with Vctrn font
erected by Cmbrdge Camden Society to
replace the 'ridiculous pagan vase'
previously used.

HARMAN'S CROSS Dorset
179 SY 9880 3m WNW of Swanage. Loc,
Worth Matravers CP. P Swnge.

HARMBY Yorks (N)
91 SE 1289 1m ESE of Leyburn. CP, 191.
Lbn RD. Ch m. Richmond CC.

HARMER GREEN Herts
147 TL 2516 2m NNE of Welwyn Gdn City.
Loc, Wlwn CP.

HARMERHILL Shrops
118 SJ 4922 6m N of Shrewsbury. Loc,
Myddle CP. P Shrsbry. Ch v. Sch pe.

HARMONDSWORTH London
160, 170 TQ 0577 4m S of Uxbridge. Loc,
Hillingdon LB. Hayes and Harlington BC
(Uxbrdge CC). Mnr Farm Tithe Barn (A.M.),
190ft by 36ft. 1½m SE, Lndn (Heathrow)
Airpt.

HARMSTON Lincs (K)
113 SK 9762 6m S of Lincoln. CP, 763.
N Kesteven RD. P LNCLN. Ch e, m. Sch pe.
Grantham CC.

HARNHILL Glos
157 SP 0600 3m ESE of Cirencester. Loc,
Driffield CP. Ch e.

HAROLD WOOD London
161 TQ 5590 3m WSW of Brentwood. Loc,
Havering LB. P Romford, Essex.
Upminster BC (Hornchurch).

HAROME Yorks (N)
92 SE 6482 2m ESE of Helmsley. CP, 269.
Hlmsly RD. P YORK. Ch e, m. Sch pe.
Thirsk and Malton CC.

HARPENDEN Herts
147, 160 TL 1314 5m SSE of Luton.
UD, 24,161. P. St Albans CC (Hemel
Hempstead). See also Hatching Grn. Mainly
rsdntl.

HARPFORD Devon
176 SY 0990 3m NW of Sidmouth.
CP, 1,021. St Thomas RD. Ch e. Hntn CC.
See also Burrow, Newton Poppleford, Venn
Ottery.

HARPHAM Yorks (E)
99 TA 0961 5m ENE of Driffield. CP, 424.
Drffld RD. P Drffld. Ch e, m. Howden CC.
See also Lowthorpe, Ruston Parva.

HARPLEY Norfolk
125 TF 7825 9m WSW of Fakenham.
CP, 364. Freebridge Lynn RD. P King's
Lynn. Ch e, m. Sch pe. NW Nflk CC (K's
Lnn).

HARPLEY Worcs
130 SO 6861 5m NNE of Bromyard. Loc,
Lr Sapey CP.

HARPOLE Northants
133 SP 6960 4m W of Northampton.
CP, 1,097. Nthmptn RD. P NTHMPTN.
Ch e, b, m. Sch pe. Daventry CC (S Nthnts).

HARPSDEN Oxon
159 SU 7680 1m S of Henley. CP, 431.
Hnly RD. Ch e. Sch pe. Hnly CC. Ch: 16c
brass.

HARPSWELL Lincs (L)
104 SK 9389 7m E of Gainsborough.
CP, 198. Gnsbrgh RD. Ch e. Gnsbrgh CC.
RAF stn to N; many gliders.

HARPUR HILL Derbys
111 SK 0671 1m S of Buxton. Loc,
Bxtn MB. P Bxtn.

HARRIETSHAM Kent
172 TQ 8652 7m ESE of Maidstone.
CP, 1,152. Hollingbourn RD. P Mdstne.
Ch e. Sch pe. Mdstne CC.

HARRINGTON Cumb
82 NX 9925 2m S of Workington. Loc,
Wkngtn MB. P Wkngtn. Reclamation work
to convert despoiled indstrl area for
provision of seaside amenities.

HARRINGTON Lincs (L)
114 TF 3671 6m WSW of Alford. CP, 48.
Spilsby RD. Ch e. Horncastle CC.

HARRINGTON Northants
133 SP 7780 6m W of Kettering. CP, 143.
Kttrng RD. P NORTHAMPTON. Ch e.
Kttrng CC. In ch, a vamping horn, formerly
used to summon congregation and
accompany singing - one of few surviving in
England.

HARRINGWORTH Northants
133 SP 9197 4m ESE of Uppingham.
CP, 158. Oundle and Thrapston RD.
P Corby. Ch e, v. Wellingborough CC
(Peterborough). To W, Welland rly viaduct,
82 arches.

HARRISEAHEAD Staffs
110 SF 8655 7m N of Stoke-on-Trent. Loc,
Kidsgrove UD. P Stke-on-Trnt.

HARROGATE Yorks (W)
96 SE 3055 14m N of Leeds. MB, 62,290.
P. Hrrgte CC. See also Pannal. Rsdntl, spa,
and conference tn, almost entirely Vctrn.
To W, Harlow Car Gdns*; ornamental, rare
and experimental plants. To SE, Rudding
Pk*, Rgncy hse in grnds by Repton.

HARROLD Beds
133 SP 9456 5m NE of Olney. CP, 956.
Bedford RD. P BDFD. Ch e, r, v2. Sch p, s.
Bdfd CC. Has 18c octagonal mkt hse and old
circular lock-up.

HARROW London
160 TQ 1588 10m WNW of Charing Cross.
LB, 202,718. P Middx. BCs: Hrrw
Central, E, W. See also Pinner, Stanmore,
Wealdstone' H. Sch, well known boys'
public sch founded in 16c, is at
H.-on-the-Hill.

HARROWBARROW Cornwall
186 SX 3969 2m E of Callington. Loc,
Calstock CP. P Cllngtn. Ch m. Sch p.

HARROWDEN Beds
147 TL 0747 2m SE of Bedford. Loc,
Eastcotts CP. Bdfd RD. P BDFD. Ch m.
Mid-Beds CC.

HARROWDEN, GREAT Northants
133 SP 8870 2m NNW of Wellingborough.
See Gt Hrrwdn.

HARROW STREET Suffolk (W)
149 TL 9537 6m ESE of Sudbury. Loc,
Leavenheath CP. Melford RD. Sdbry and
Woodbridge CC.

HARSTON Cambs
148 TL 4250 5m SSW of Cambridge.
CP, 1,186. Chesterton RD. P CMBRDGE.
Ch e, b. Sch p. Cambs CC.

HARSTON Leics
113, 122 SK 8331 5m WSW of Grantham.
Loc, Belvoir CP. P Grnthm, Lincs. Ch e.
Ironworks in area. Iron Age and Anglo-
Saxon rems unearthed in 1930s.

HART Co Durham
85 NZ 4634 3m NW of Hartlepool. CP.
Stockton RD. P Htlpl. Ch e. Sch p.

Easington CC (Sedgefield). Unrestored ch of
various periods.

HARTBURN Nthmb
77, 78 NZ 0886 7m W of Morpeth. CP, 185.
Mpth RD. P Mpth. Ch e. Sch p. Mpth CC.
See also High Angerton, Low Angrtn. Fine
13c ch.

HARTEST Suffolk (W)
149 TL 8352 4m NNW of Long Melford.
CP, 360. Mlfd RD. P Bury St Edmunds.
Ch e, v3. Sch pe. Sudbury and
Woodbridge CC.

HARTFIELD Sussex (E)
171, 183 TQ 4735 6m ESE of E Grinstead.
CP, 1,953. Uckfield RD. P. Ch e, m. Sch pe.
E Grnstd CC. See also Coleman's Hatch,
Holtye, Upr Htfld. Pleasant vllge below
Ashdown Forest. Lychgate of ch attached
to side of 16c cottage.

HARTFOOT LANE Dorset
178 ST 7602 8m WSW of Blandford. Loc,
Blndfd RD, Dorchester RD. N Dst CC,
W Dst CC.

HARTFORD Ches
110 SJ 6372 1m SW of Northwich.
CP, 2,272. Nthwch RD. P Nthwch. Ch e, m.
Sch p, sb, sg, sr. Nthwch CC.

HARTFORD Hunts
134 TL 2572 1m NE of Huntingdon. Loc,
Hntngdn and Godmanchester MB.
P HNTNGDN.

HARTFORDBRIDGE Hants
169 SU 7757 3m NW of Fleet. Loc, Hartley
Wintney CP.

HARTFORD END Essex
148 TL 6817 5m SE of Dunmow. Loc,
Felsted CP. P Chelmsford.

HARTFORTH Yorks (N)
85 NZ 1706 3m N of Richmond. CP(Gilling
w Htfth and Sedbury), 665. Rchmnd RD.
Rchmnd CC.

HARTHILL Ches
109 SJ 5055 8m WNW of Nantwich. CP, 66.
Tarvin RD. P CHESTER. Ch e. Sch p.
Nntwch CC.

HARTHILL Yorks (W)
103 SK 4980 6m W of Worksop. CP(Hthll

w Woodall), 1,458.   Kiveton Pk RD.
P SHEFFIELD. Ch e, m.   Sch p.   Rother
Valley CC.

HARTINGTON Derbys
111 SK 1260 7m SW of Bakewell.
CP(Htngtn Town Quarter), 396.
Ashbourne RD. P Buxton.   Ch e, m.
Sch p, pe. W Derbys CC.

HARTLAND Devon
174 SS 2624 12m NNE of Bude. CP, 1,326.
Bideford RD. P Bdfd. Ch e, m2, r. Sch p.
N Dvn CC (Torrington). See also Eddistone,
Elmscott, Meddon, Philham, S Hole, Stoke,
Titchberry. Ch, at Stke, has 130ft Perp twr.
2½m NW, H. Point; lighthouse*.

HARTLEBURY Worcs
130 SO 8470 2m E of Stourport. CP, 2,401.
Droitwich RD. P Kidderminster. Ch e.
Sch pe, s. Worcester BC. See also Crossway
Grn, Lincomb. H. Cstle*, 15c–18c moated
hse, residence of Bishops of Wcstr. Hurd
library added 1780. One wing now Worcs
County museum. Picnic area.

HARTLEPOOL Co Durham
85   NZ   5032   9m   NNE   of
Teesside(Stockton). CB, 96,898. P. Htlpl BC
(The Htlpls). See also Seaton Carew. Coal
and iron port. Shipbuilding. Steel wks.
Nuclear power stn.

HARTLEY Kent
171 TQ 6166 5m SSW of Gravesend.
CP, 2,388. Dartford RD. P Dtfd. Ch e, c, r.
Sevenoaks CC (Dtfd).

HARTLEY Kent
184 TQ 7534 2m SW of Cranbrook. Loc,
Crnbrk CP. P Crnbrk. Ch c.

HARTLEY Nthmb
78 NZ 3475 3m NNW of Whitley Bay. Loc,
Whtly Bay MB.

HARTLEY Westm
84 NY 7808 just E of Kirkby Stephen.
CP, 129. N Westm RD. Westm CC.

HARTLEY WESPALL Hants
169 SU 6958 6m NE of Basingstoke.
CP, 155. Bsngstke RD. P Bsngstke. Ch e.
Bsngstke CC. Ch has timbered wall dating
from 14c.

HARTLEY WINTNEY Hants
169 SU 7656 8m NW of Farnham.
CP, 2,808. Htly Wntny RD. P Basingstoke.
Ch e, b, m, r2.   Sch p.   Bsngstke CC
(Aldershot). See also Hartfordbridge,
Phoenix Grn, W Grn.

HARTLINGTON Yorks (W)
90 SE 0361 7m NNE of Skipton. CP, 59.
Skptn RD. Skptn CC.

HARTLIP Kent
172 TQ 8364 4m W of Sittingbourne.
CP, 572. Swale RD. P Sttngbne. Ch e, m.
Sch pe. Faversham CC. Orchards.

HARTON Yorks (N)
92, 97, 98 SE 7062 8m SW of Malton.
CP, 94. Flaxton RD. Sch pe. Thirsk and
Mltn CC.

HARTPURY Glos
143 SO 7925 5m NNW of Gloucester.
CP, 763. Newent RD. P GLCSTR. Ch e, m.
Sch pe. W Glos. Large stone tithe barn.

HARTSHEAD Yorks (W)
96, 102 SE 1822 4m W of Dewsbury. Loc,
Spenborough MB. P Liversedge. Brighouse
and Spnbrgh BC.

HARTSHILL Warwicks
132 SP 3293 3m WNW of Nuneaton.
CP, 2,583. Atherstone RD.   P Nntn.
Ch e, f, m2. Sch i, j, s. Meriden CC. Slight
rems of mdvl cstle.

HARTSHORNE Derbys
120, 121 SK 3221 4m NW of Ashby de la
Zouch.   CP, 3,918.   Repton RD.
P Burton-on-Trent, Staffs. Ch e, m. Sch pe.
Belper CC.

HARTSOP Westm
83 NY 4013 6m NNE of Ambleside. Loc,
Lakes UD. Westm CC.

HARTWELL Northants
146 SP 7850 6m E of Towcester. CP, 588.
Northampton RD. P NTHMPTN. Ch e, m.
Sch pe. Daventry CC (S Nthnts).

HARVEL Kent
171 TQ 6563 7m S of Gravesend. Loc,
Meopham CP. P Grvsnd.

HARVINGTON Worcs
130 SO 8774 3m ESE of Kidderminster.
Loc, Chaddesley Corbett CP. Ch r. H. Hall
(NT)*, Elizn, moated; priests' hiding holes.

HARVINGTON Worcs
144 SP 0548 3m NNE of Evesham. CP, 735.
Evshm RD. P Eveshm. Ch e. Sch pe.
S Worcs CC. See also Hvngtn Cross.

HARVINGTON CROSS Worcs
144 SP 0549 4m N of Evesham. Loc,
Hvngtn CP.

HARWELL Berks
158 SU 4989 2m W of Didcot. CP, 2,214.
Wantage RD. P Ddct. Ch e, m. Sch p.
Abingdon CC. To SW, Atomic Energy
Research Establishment.

HARWICH Essex
150 TM 2632 17m ENE of Colchester.
MB, 14,892. P. Hrwch CC. See also Dovercourt. Port for Continental passenger and
containerised freight traffic (see also Parke-
ston). In mdvl times important naval and
defensive strongpoint.

HARWOOD Co Durham
84 NY 8133 10m NW of Middleton in
Teesdale. Loc, Forest and Frith CP.
P Barnard Cstle. Ch e, m.

HARWOOD DALE Yorks (N)
93 SE 9695 7m NW of Scarborough.
CP, 115. Scbrgh RD. P Scbrgh. Ch e, m.
Scbrgh CC (Scbrgh and Whitby).

HARWOOD, GREAT Lancs
95 SD 7332 4m NE of Blackburn. See Gt
Hwd.

HARWORTH Notts
103 SK 6191 8m NNE of Worksop.
CP, 8,289. Wksp RD. P Doncaster, Yorkshire.
Ch e, r. Sch pe. Bassetlaw CC. See also
Bircotes.

HASCOMBE Surrey
169, 170, 182 SU 9939 3m SSE of
Godalming. CP, 294. Hambledon RD.
P Gdlmng. Ch e. Guildford CC. 1m NNW,
Winkworth Arboretum (NT)*, hillside
planted with rare trees and flowering shrubs.

HASELBECH Northants
133 SP 7177 6m S of Mkt Harborough.
CP, 78. Brixworth RD. Ch e. Daventry CC
(Kettering).

HASELBURY PLUCKNETT Som
177 ST 4710 2m ENE of Crewkerne.
CP, 615. Yeovil RD. P Crkne. Ch e, m.
Sch pe. Yvl CC.

HASELEY Warwicks
131 SP 2367 4m NW of Warwick. CP, 223.
Wrwck RD. Ch e. Wrwck and
Leamington CC. See also Hsly Knob.

HASELEY, GREAT Oxon
158, 159 SP 6401 5m SW of Thame. See Gt
Hsly.

HASELEY KNOB Warwicks
131 SP 2371 5m NNW of Warwick. Loc,
Hsly CP. P WRWCK.

HASELOR Warwicks
131 SP 1257 2m E of Alcester. CP, 221.
Alcstr RD. P Alcstr. Ch e. Sch p.
Stratford-on-Avon CC (Strtfd). See also
Walcot.

HASELTON Glos
144 SP 0818 3m NW of Northleach.
Alternative name for Hazleton, qv.

HASFIELD Glos
143 SO 8227 6m N of Gloucester. CP, 175.
Glcstr RD. P GLCSTR. Ch e. W Glos CC.

HASKAYNE Lancs
100 SD 3508 4m E of Formby. Loc,
Downholland CP. W Lancs RD. P Ormskirk.
Sch pe. Ormskirk CC.

HASKETON Suffolk (E)
150 TM 2450 2m NW of Woodbridge.
CP, 436. Deben RD. P Wdbrdge. Ch e.
Sudbury and Wdbrdge CC. Ch has round
flint twr with octagonal top.

HASLAND Derbys
111 SK 3969 1m SSE of Chesterfield. Loc,
Chstrfld MB. P Chstrfld.

HASLEMERE Surrey
169, 181 SU 9032 12m SSW of Guildford.
UD, 13,252. P. Farnham CC. See also
Grayswood, Hindhead, Shottermill. Tn in
hilly country in SW corner of county under
Blackdown, 918ft (in Sussex). Much NT
property in area.

HASLINGDEN Lancs
95 SD 7823 4m SSE of Accrington.
MB, 14,953. P Rossendale. Rssndle BC. See
also Helmshore. Textile tn.

HASLINGFIELD Cambs
148 TL 4052 5m SW of Cambridge.
CP, 855. Chesterton RD. P CMBRDGE.
Ch e, m. Sch pu. Cambs CC.

HASLINGTON Ches
110 SJ 7355 2m E of Crewe. CP, 2,879.
Nantwich RD. P Crwe. Ch e, b, c, m3. Sch p.
Crwe CC. See also Winterley.

HASSALL Ches
110 SJ 7657 4m ENE of Crewe. CP, 218.
Congleton RD. Knutsford CC.

HASSALL GREEN Ches
110 SJ 7858 5m ENE of Crewe. Loc,
Betchton CP. Congleton RD. P Sandbach.
Ch m. Sch pm. Knutsford CC.

HASSELL-STREET Kent
172, 173, 184 TR 0946 6m ENE of
Ashford. Loc, Hastingleigh CP.

HASSINGHAM Norfolk
126 TG 3605 9m ESE of Norwich. Loc,
Strumpshaw CP. Ch e.

HASSOCKS Sussex (E)
182 TQ 2915 3m SSW of Burgess Hill. Loc,
Clayton CP. P. Ch c. Sch i, j, s.

HASSOP Derbys
111 SK 2272 2m N of Bakewell. CP, 125.
Bkwll RD. P Bkwll. Ch r. W Derbys CC.

HASTINGLEIGH Kent
172, 173, 184 TR 0944 6m ENE of
Ashford. CP, 218. E Ashfd RD. P Ashfd.
Ch e. Ashfd CC. See also Hassell St.

HASTINGS Sussex (E)
184 TQ 8109 32m E of Brighton.
CB, 72,169. P. Hstngs BC. See also Ore,
St Leonards. Resort. Cinque port. Rems of
Nmn cstle* on cliff top. Famous battle of
1066 fought at Battle, qv, 5m NW.

HASTINGWOOD Essex
161 TL 4807 3m SE of Harlow. Loc,
N Weald Bassett CP. P Hlw.

HASTOE Herts
159 SP 9109 1m S of Tring. Loc, Trng UD.

HASWELL Co Durham
85 NZ 3743 4m NW of Peterlee. CP, 5,661.
Easington RD. P DRHM. Ch e, m2, s. Sch p.
Easngtn CC. See also Hswll Plough,
S Hetton.

HASWELL PLOUGH Co Durham
85 NZ 3742 4m WNW of Peterlee. Loc,
Hswll CP. Ch m.

HATCH Beds
147 TL 1547 1m SW of Sandy. Loc,
Northill CP.

HATCH Hants
168, 169 SU 6752 2m E of Basingstoke.
Loc, Basing CP.

HATCH BEAUCHAMP Som
177 ST 3020 5m SE of Taunton. CP, 470.
Tntn RD. P Tntn. Ch e, b. Sch pe. Tntn CC.

HATCHING GREEN Herts
147, 160 TL 1312 1m S of Harpenden. Loc,
Hpndn UD.

HATCHMERE Ches
109 SJ 5571 6m W of Northwich. Loc,
Norley CP.

HATCLIFFE Lincs (L)
105 TA 2100 6m SSW of Grimsby. CP, 131.
Grmsby RD. P Grmsby. Ch e, m. Lth CC.

HATFIELD Herefs
129 SO 5959 6m E of Leominster. CP, 141.
Lmnstr and Wigmore RD. P Lmnstr. Ch e.
Lmnstr CC.

HATFIELD Herts
160 TL 2308 5m E of St Albans. CP.
Htfld RD. P. Ch e, c, m2, r2, v2.
Sch i4, j4, p4, s5, sg. Welwyn and Htfld CC
(Hertford). See also Lemsford, Newgate St,
Stanborough. New tn (pop. 25,211) to SW
of old tn. In latter, H. Hse*, early 17c, in
large pk. Aircraft factory on W side of tn.

HATFIELD Yorks (W)
103 SE 6609 7m NE of Doncaster.
CP, 11,344. Thorne RD. P Dncstr.
Ch e, m3, v. Sch p2, pe, s. Goole CC. See
also Dunscroft, Dunsville, Htfld Woodhouse.

HATFIELD BROAD OAK Essex
148 TL 5416 5m SE of Bishop's Stortford.
CP, 2,083. Dunmow RD. P Bshp's
Sttfd, Herts. Ch e. Sch pe. Saffron
Walden CC. See also Htfld Hth. 18c library
beside ch which incorporates rems of 12c
priory.

HATFIELD, GREAT Yorks (E)
99 TA 1842 3m SSW of Hornsea. See Gt
Htfld.

HATFIELD HEATH Essex
148 TL 5215 5m SSE of Bishop's Stortford.

Hatfield Peverel

Loc, Htfld Broad Oak CP. P Bshp's Sttfd, Herts. Ch e, c. Sch p.

HATFIELD PEVEREL Essex
162 TL 7911 3m SW of Witham. CP, 2,850. Braintree RD. P Chelmsford. Ch e, m, s. Sch pe. Brntree CC (Maldon). See also Nounsley.

HATFIELD WOODHOUSE Yorks (W)
103 SE 6708 7m ENE of Doncaster. Loc, Htfld CP. P Dncstr. Ch m. Sch p.

HATFORD Berks
158 SU 3394 3m E of Faringdon. CP, 107. Frngdn RD. Ch e. Abingdon CC.

HATHERDEN Hants
168 SU 3450 3m NNW of Andover. Loc, Tangley CP. P Andvr. Ch e. Sch pe.

HATHERLEIGH Devon
175 SS 5404 7m NNW of Okehampton. CP, 984. Okhmptn RD. P Okhmptn. Ch e, b, m. Sch p. W Dvn CC (Torrington). George Inn, 15c.

HATHERN Leics
121 SK 5022 3m NW of Loughborough. Loc, Lghbrgh MB. P Lghbrgh. Whatton Hse*, blt 1800, in extensive grnds.

HATHEROP Glos
157 SP 1505 5m NW of Lechlade. CP, 204. Cirencester RD. P Crncstr. Ch e. Sch pe. Crncstr and Tewkesbury CC.

HATHERSAGE Derbys
111 SK 2381 8m WSW of Sheffield. CP, 1,522. Bakewell RD. P SHFFLD. Ch e, m2, r. Sch pe, pr. W Derbys CC. The 'Morton' of *Jane Eyre*. Burial place of Little John, follower of Robin Hood.

HATHERTON Ches
110 SJ 6847 4m SE of Nantwich. CP, 313. Nntwch RD. P Nntwch. Ch m2, r. Nntwch CC.

HATHERTON Staffs
119 SJ 9510 1m W of Cannock. CP, 530. Cnnck RD. Ch e, m. SW Staffs CC (Cnnck). See also Four Crosses.

HATLEY ST GEORGE Cambs
147 TL 2751 7m NE of Biggleswade. Loc, Htly CP. S Cambs RD. P Sandy, Beds. Ch e. Cambs CC. Estate vllge for H. Pk. Buff Wd is

nature reserve owned by Cambridge University; part open without permit.

HATT Cornwall
186 SX 3962 3m NW of Saltash. Loc, Botusfleming CP. P Sltsh.

HATTINGLEY Hants
168, 169 SU 6437 5m WSW of Alton. Loc, Medstead CP.

HATTON Ches
100, 109 SJ 5982 4m S of Warrington. CP, 340. Runcorn RD. P WRRNGTN. Rncn CC.

HATTON Derbys
120 SK 2130 4m NNW of Burton-on-Trent. CP, 1,462. Repton RD. P DERBY. Ch m2, v. Sch p, s. Belper CC.

HATTON Lincs (L)
105 TF 1776 7m NW of Horncastle. CP, 135. Horncastle RD. Ch e. Hncstle CC.

HATTON Warwicks
131 SP 2367 3m WNW of Warwick. CP, 1,835. Wrwck RD. P WRWCK. Ch e. Sch p. Wrwck and Leamington CC. A number of locks on Grand Union Canal to S. County Mental Hsptl to E.

HAUGHAM Lincs (L)
105 TL 3381 4m S of Louth. CP, 53. Lth RD. Ch e. Lth CC.

HAUGH HEAD Nthmb
71 NU 0026 1m SSE of Wooler. Loc, Glendale RD. Berwick-upon-Tweed CC.

HAUGHLEY Suffolk (E)
136 TM 0262 3m NW of Stowmarket. CP, 978. Gipping RD. P Stwmkt. Ch e, c. Sch pe. Eye CC. See also Hghly Grn. Large mound remains from Nmn cstle. H. Pk*, restored 17 hse.

HAUGHLEY GREEN Suffolk (E)
136 TM 0364 4m NNW of Stowmarket. Loc, Hghly CP.

HAUGHTON Notts
112 SK 6872 4m NNE of Ollerton. CP, 43. E Retford RD. Bassetlaw CC.

HAUGHTON Shrops
118 SJ 3727 6m ESE of Oswestry. Loc, W Felton CP. Ch m.

HAUGHTON Shrops
118 SJ 5516 4m ENE of Shrewsbury. Loc,
Upton Magna CP.

HAUGHTON Staffs
119 SJ 8620 4m WSW of Stafford. CP, 567.
Stffd RD. P STFFD. Ch e. Sch pe. Stffd and
Stone CC. See also Allimore Grn.

HAUGHTON GREEN Lancs
101 SJ 9393 3m NE of Stockport. Loc,
Denton UD. P Dntn, MANCHESTER.

HAUGHTON MOSS Ches
109 SJ 5756 6m NW of Nantwich. Loc,
Hghtn CP. Nntwch RD. Nntwch CC.

HAUNTON Staffs
120 SK 2310 5m NNE of Tamworth. Loc,
Clifton Campville CP. Ch r.

HAUXLEY Nthmb
71 NU 2803 1m SE of Amble. CP, 702.
Alnwick RD. Berwick-upon-Tweed CC. See
also Low Hxly, Radcliffe. The parish
includes Coquet Island.

HAUXTON Cambs
148 TL 4352 4m SSW of Cambridge.
CP, 484. Chesterton RD. P CMBRDGE.
Ch e. Sch p. Cambs CC. Ch partly Nmn.
Fertilizer factory on main rd.

HAVANT Hants
181 SU 7106 6m NE of Portsmouth.
UD(Hvnt and Waterloo), 108,999. P. Hvnt
and Wtrloo BC (Ptsmth, Langstone).
Bedhampton, Cowplain, Emsworth,
Lngstne, N Hayling, Purbrook, S Hlng,
Waterlooville. Part of Ptsmth conurbation.
Leigh Pk, modern housing estate for Ptsmth
overspill.

HAVEN Herefs
142 SO 4054 7m WSW of Leominster. Loc,
Dilwyn CP.

HAVEN SIDE Yorks (E)
99 TA 3021 5m SSW of Withernsea. Loc,
Patrington CP.

HAVENSTREET IOW
180 SZ 5690 2m SW of Ryde. Loc,
Rde MB. P Rde.

HAVERCROFT Yorks (W)
102, 103 SE 3914 6m NNE of Barnsley.

CP(Hvrcrft w Cold Hiendley), 2,792.
Hemsworth RD. P Ryhill, Wakefield. Ch v.
Sch i. Hmswth CC.

HAVERHILL Suffolk (W)
148 TL 6745 16m SE of Cambridge.
UD, 12,430. P. Bury St Edmunds CC. Red
brick indstrl tn. Much new housing.

HAVERIGG Cumb
88 SD 1678 1m SW of Millom. Loc,
Mllm CP. P Mllm. Ch m. Sch p.

HAVERING-ATTE-BOWER London
161 TQ 5193 3m N of Romford. Loc,
Hvrng LB. P Rmfd, Essex. Rmfd BC. Vllge
grn imparts rural air. 18c stocks and
whipping post.

HAVERING'S GROVE Essex
161 TQ 6494 2m W of Billericay. Loc,
Brentwood UD.

HAVERSHAM Bucks
146 SP 8242 1m NE of Wolverton.
CP(Hvshm-cum-Lit Linford), 795. Newport
Pagnell RD. P Wlvtn. Ch e. Sch p.
Buckingham CC.

HAVERTHWAITE Lancs
88, 89 SD 3483 5m NE of Ulverston.
CP, 805. N Lonsdale RD. P Ulvstn. Ch e.
Sch p, pe. Morecambe and Lnsdle CC. See
also Backbarrow.

HAWES Yorks (N)
90 SD 8789 13m SE of Kirkby Stephen.
CP, 1,137. Aysgarth RD. P. Ch e, c, m.
Sch p. Richmond CC. See also Appersett,
Burtersett, Gayle. Mkt tn in
Upr Wensleydale.

HAWFORD Worcs
130 SO 8460 3m N of Worcester. Loc,
Ombersley CP.

HAWKCHURCH Devon
177 ST 3400 3m ENE of Axminster.
CP, 539. Axmnstr RD. P Axmnstr. Ch e.
Sch pe. Honiton CC.

HAWKEDON Suffolk (W)
149 TL 7953 5m NNE of Clare. CP, 142.
Clre RD. P Bury St Edmunds. Ch e.
Bury St Eds CC.

HAWKERIDGE Wilts
166 ST 8653 2m N of Westbury. Loc,
Heywood CP. P Wstbry. Ch c.

HAWKERLAND Devon
176 SY 0588 4m WNW of Sidmouth. Loc,
Colaton Raleigh CP.

HAWKESBURY Glos
156 ST 7686 9m WSW of Tetbury.
CP, 1,355. Sodbury RD. Ch e, m. Sch pe.
S Glos CC. See also Hksbry Upton,
Hillesley, Lit Badminton, Tresham. Fine ch
and churchyard yew hedge. To N, 19c H.
Monmt commemorates Ld Edward
Somerset.

HAWKESBURY UPTON Glos
156 ST 7886 8m WSW of Tetbury. Loc,
Hksbry CP. P Badminton. Ch c, m.

HAWKHILL Nthmb
71 NU 2212 2m E of Alnwick. Loc,
Lesbury CP.

HAWKHURST Kent
184 TQ 7630 4m SSW of Cranbrook.
CP, 3,526. Crnbrk RD. P. Ch e, b3, m, r.
Sch pe. Royal Tunbridge Wells CC
(Ashford). See also Four Throws, Gill's Grn,
Moor. Once centre of Wealden iron
industry. Home of William Penn, founder of
Pennsylvania.

HAWKHURST MOOR Kent
184 TQ 7529 just S of Hawkhurst. See
Moor, The.

HAWKINGE Kent
173 TR 2239 2m N of Folkestone.
CP, 1,428. Elham RD. Ch e. Sch p. Flkstne
and Hythe CC. See also Up Hill.

HAWKLEY Hants
169, 181 SU 7429 4m N of Petersfield.
CP, 430. Ptrsfld RD. P Liss. Ch e. Sch pe.
Ptrsfld CC. See also Empshott.

HAWKRIDGE Som
164 SS 8630 4m WNW of Dulverton. Loc,
Withypoole CP. Ch e. Many Bronze
Age barrows on surrounding moorland. 1m
N, Tarr Steps (NT), clapper br across
R Barle, perhaps oldest br in England.
(Reconstructed after floods of 1952.)

HAWKSHEAD Lancs
88, 89 SD 3598 3m E of Coniston. CP, 633.
N Lonsdale RD. P Ambleside, Westmorland.
Ch e, m. Sch p. Morecambe and Lnsdle CC.
See also Hkshd Hill, Out Gate. Ct Hse

(NT)*, formerly part mdvl priory. Folk
Museum of Rural Crafts. Wordsworth went
to sch in vllge.

HAWKSHEAD HILL Lancs
88, 89 SD 3398 2m ENE of Coniston. Loc,
Hkshd CP. Ch b.

HAWKSWICK Yorks (W)
90 SD 9570 12m N of Skipton. CP, 36.
Settle RD. Skptn CC.

HAWKSWORTH Notts
112, 122 SK 7543 7m SSW of Newark.
CP, 118. Bingham RD. P NOTTINGHAM.
Ch e. Rushcliffe CC (Carlton).

HAWKSWORTH Yorks (W)
96 SE 1641 6m N of Bradford. Loc,
Aireborough UD. P Guiseley, LEEDS.
Pudsey BC.

HAWKWELL Essex
162 TQ 8492 5m NNW of Southend.
CP, 6,274. Rochford RD. P Hockley.
Ch e, b, r, v. Sch j, p2. Maldon CC
(SE Essx).

HAWLEY Hants
169 SU 8558 2m SW of Camberley.
CP, 3,757. Hartley Wintney RD. Ch e.
Sch p. Aldershot CC. See also Blackwater.

HAWLEY Kent
161, 171 TQ 5571 2m SSE of Dartford.
Loc, Sutton-at-Hone CP. P Dtfd.

HAWLING Glos
144 SP 0623 4m SE of Winchcombe.
CP, 168. Cheltenham RD. Ch e, m.
Cirencester and Tewkesbury CC.

HAWNBY Yorks (N)
86, 92 SE 5489 6m NW of Helmsley.
CP, 68. Hlmsly RD. P YORK. Ch e, m.
Thirsk and Malton CC.

HAWORTH Yorks (W)
96 SE 0337 3m SSW of Keighley. Loc,
Kghly MB. P Kghly. Moorland tn, famous as
home of Brontë family. H. Parsonage* is
Brontë museum. H. Stn rly museum.

HAWSKER Yorks (N)
86, 93 NZ 9207 3m SE of Whitby.
CP(Hskr-cum-Stainsacre), 494. Whtby RD.
P(High Hskr), Whtby. Ch e, m. Cleveland
and Whtby CC (Scarborough and Whtby).

HAWSTEAD Suffolk (W)
136 TL 8559 3m S of Bury St Edmunds.
CP, 248. Thingoe RD. Ch e. Bury
St Eds CC. Ch: monmts.

HAWTHORN Co Durham
85 NZ 4145 2m SSW of Seaham. CP, 349.
Easington RD. P Shm. Ch e. Easngtn CC.

HAWTHORN Wilts
156 ST 8469 5m WSW of Chippenham. Loc,
Box CP. P.

HAWTHORN HILL Berks
159 SU 8774 5m S of Maidenhead. Loc,
Warfield CP.

HAWTON Notts
112 SK 7851 2m SSW of Newark. CP, 66.
Nwk RD. Ch e. Nwk CC. Ch: chancel,
containing elaborate 14c Easter sepulchre.

HAXBY Yorks (N)
97, 98 SE 6058 4m N of York. CP, 2,407.
Flaxton RD. P YK. Ch e. Sch p. Thirsk and
Malton CC.

HAXEY Lincs (L)
104 SK 7699 7m NNW of Gainsborough.
CP, 2,069. Isle of Axholme RD.
P Doncaster, Yorkshire. Ch e, m. Sch pe.
Gnsbrgh CC. See also Craiselound, E Lound,
Low Burnham, Westwoodside.

HAYDOCK Lancs
100 SJ 5697 4m E of St Helens.
UD, 14,180. P St Helens. Newton CC. At
intersection of M6 motorway and E Lancs
Rd. H. Pk Racecourse to NE.

HAYDON Dorset
178 ST 6715 2m ESE of Sherborne. CP, 48.
Shbne RD. Ch e. W Dst CC.

HAYDON BRIDGE Nthmb
77 NY 8464 6m W of Hexham. Loc,
Hdn CP. Hxhm RD. P Hxhm. Ch e, c, m, r.
Sch pe, s. Hxhm CC. Astride the S Tyne,
crossed by 18c br oft repaired.

HAYDON WICK Wilts
157 SU 1387 3m NNW of Swindon.
CP, 564. Highworth RD. P Swndn. Sch p2.
Devizes CC.

HAYES London
160 TQ 0981 3m SE of Uxbridge. Loc,
Hillingdon LB. P Middx. Hayes and
Harlington BC.

HAYES London
171 TQ 4066 2m S of Bromley. Loc,
Brmly LB. P Brmly, Kent.
Ravensbourne BC (Brmly). Large cmmn.

HAYFIELD Derbys
102, 111 SK 0386 4m S of Glossop.
CP, 2,518. Chapel en le Frith RD.
P Stockport, Cheshire. Ch e, m3, v. Sch p.
High Peak CC. See also Birch Vale. Textile
mnfg tn.

HAYLE Cornwall
189 SW 5537 6m WSW of Camborne.
CP, 4,830. W Penwith RD. P. Ch m, r, s, v.
Sch s. Falmouth and Cmbne CC. See also
Angarrack, Copperhouse, Phillack. Mnfg tn
and port. Bungalow tn to N, thence 3m of
sands to NE.

HAYNES Beds
147 TL 0841 6m SSE of Bedford. CP, 801.
Ampthill RD. P BDFD. Ch e, b, m. Sch p.
Mid-Beds CC. See also Silver End.

HAYTON Cumb
76 NY 5057 3m SSW of Brampton.
CP, 1,350. Border RD. P Carlisle. Ch e.
Sch pe. Penrith and the Bdr CC. See also
Corby Hill, Faugh, Fenton, How, Talkin.

HAYTON Cumb
82 NY 1041 5m NE of Maryport. CP(Htn
and Mealo), 214. Wigton RD.
P Aspatria, Carlisle. Ch e. Penrith and the
Border CC.

HAYTON Notts
103 SK 7284 3m NE of Retford. CP, 292.
E Rtfd RD. Ch e, m. Bassetlaw CC.

HAYTON Yorks (E)
98 SE 8245 2m SSE of Pocklington.
CP, 272. Pcklngtn RD. P YORK. Ch e.
Howden CC. See also Burnby.

HAYTON'S BENT Shrops
129 SO 5180 4m N of Ludlow. Loc,
Stanton Lacy CP. P Ldlw. Ch m.

HAYTOR VALE Devon
175, 187, 188 SX 7777 5m NNE of
Ashburton. Loc, Ilsington CP.
P(Haytor) Newton Abbot. 1m W, Haytor,
most accessible of Dartmoor tors and
prominent landmark from E.

HAYWARDS HEATH Sussex (E)
182 TQ 3323 12m N of Brighton. Loc, Cuckfield UD. P. Rsdntl and shopping centre.

HAYWOOD Herefs
142 SO 4835 4m SSW of Hereford. CP, 174. Hrfd RD. Hrfd CC.

HAYWOOD, GREAT Staffs
119, 120 SJ 9922 4m NW of Rugeley. See Gt Hwd.

HAZELBURY BRYAN Dorset
178 ST 7408 8m SE of Sherborne. CP, 553. Sturminster RD. P Stmnstr Newton. Ch e, m. Sch p. N Dst CC. See also Kingston.

HAZELEY Hants
169 SU 7459 9m S of Reading. Loc, Mattingley CP.

HAZEL GROVE Ches
101 SJ 9286 3m SE of Stockport. UD(Hzl Grve and Bramhall), 39,534. P Stckpt. Hzl Grve BC (Cheadle CC). See also Woodford.

HAZELSLADE Staffs
120 SK 0212 4m SSW of Rugeley. Loc, Cannock UD. P Cnnck. Cnnck CC. At S edge of Cnnck Chase.

HAZELWOOD Derbys
111 SK 3246 2m SW of Belper. CP, 291. Blpr RD. P Duffield, DERBY. Ch e. Sch pe. Blpr CC.

HAZLEMERE Bucks
159 SU 8995 2m NE of High Wycombe. Loc, Hughenden CP. Wcmbe RD. P Hgh Wcmbe. Ch e, v. Sch p, pe. Wcmbe CC.

HAZLERIGG Nthmb
78 NZ 2371 5m N of Newcastle. CP, 1,543. Cstle Ward RD. P NWCSTLE UPON TYNE. Hexham CC.

HAZLETON Glos
144 SP 0818 3m NW of Northleach. CP, 185. Nthlch RD. P Cheltenham. Ch e. Cirencester and Tewkesbury CC. See also Salperton.

HEACHAM Norfolk
124 TF 6737 2m S of Hunstanton. CP, 2,680. Docking RD. P King's Lynn. Ch e, m. Sch p. NW Nflk CC (K's Lnn).

Extensive lavender fields in vicinity; lavender water made here.

HEADBOURNE WORTHY Hants
168 SU 4832 2m N of Winchester. CP, 823. Wnchstr RD. Ch e, m. Wnchstr CC. Saxon ch; good 15c brass.

HEADCORN Kent
172, 184 TQ 8344 6m NE of Cranbrook. CP, 1,782. Hollingbourn RD. P Ashford. Ch e, b, m. Sch p. Maidstone CC. Many half-timbered bldngs, incl 15c cloth hall.

HEADINGLEY Yorks (W)
96 SE 2736 2m NW of Leeds. Loc, Lds CB. P LDS 8. Lds NW BC. Rsdntl distr. Cricket grnd of test match status.

HEADINGTON Oxon
158 SP 5407 E distr of Oxford. Loc, Oxfd CB. P OXFD. Rsdntl suburb. Well known quarries, no longer extant, provided stone for many Oxfd colleges. Ch has Nmn chancel arch.

HEADLAM Co Durham
85 NZ 1818 7m WNW of Darlington. CP, 63. Barnard Cstle RD. Bishop Auckland CC.

HEADLESS CROSS Worcs
131 SP 0365 1m S of Redditch. Loc, Rddtch UD. P Rddtch.

HEADLEY Hants
168 SU 5162 4m SE of Newbury. Loc, Kingsclere CP. P Nbry, Berks. Ch e, b.

HEADLEY Hants
169 SU 8236 5m WNW of Haslemere. CP, 3,010. Alton RD. P Bordon. Ch e, m2, r. Sch pe. Petersfield CC. See also Land of Nod, Standford.

HEADLEY Surrey
170 TQ 2054 3m ESE of Leatherhead. CP, 725. Dorking and Horley RD. P Epsom. Ch e, c. Sch pe. Dkng CC.

HEADON Notts
103 SK 7477 4m SE of Retford. CP(Hdn cum Upton), 177. E Rtfd RD. Ch e, m. Bassetlaw CC.

HEADS NOOK Cumb
76 NY 4955 6m E of Carlisle. Loc, Border RD. P Clsle. Penrith and the Bdr CC.

HEAGE Derbys
111 SK 3750 2m W of Ripley. Loc, Rply UD. P DERBY.

HEALAUGH Yorks (N)
90 SE 0199 12m W of Richmond CP(Reeth, Fremington and Hlgh), 540 Rth RD. P Rchmnd. Ch m. Rchmnd CC.

HEALAUGH Yorks (W)
97 SE 5047 3m NNE of Tadcaster. CP, 225. Tdcstr RD. P Tdcstr. Ch e. Barkston Ash CC. Nmn ch. Rems of Augustinian priory incorporated in farm bldngs 1½m SW.

HEALD GREEN Ches
101 SJ 8485 3m N of Wilmslow. Loc, Cheadle and Gatley UD. P Chdle.

HEALEY Lancs
95, 101 SD 8816 2m NNW of Rochdale. Loc. Whitworth UD. P Rchdle.

HEALEY Nthmb
77 NZ 0158 4m SSE of Corbridge. CP, 192. Hexham RD. Ch e. Hxhm CC. See also Minsteracres.

HEALEY Yorks (N)
91 SE 1880 3m W of Masham. CP, 132. Mshm RD. Ch e, m. Sch pe. Richmond CC.

HEALING Lincs (L)
105 TA 2110 3m WNW of Grimsby. CP. Grmsby RD. P Grmsby. Ch e, m. Sch p, s. Louth CC.

HEAMOOR Cornwall
189 SW 4631 1m NW of Penzance. Loc, Pnznce MB. P Pnznce.

HEANOR Derbys
112 SK 4346 4m NW of Ilkeston. UD, 24.352. P. Ilkstn CC. See also Codnor, Loscoe.

HEANTON PUNCHARDON Devon
163 SS 5035 1m SE of Braunton. CP, 931. Barnstaple RD. Ch e. N Dvn CC.

HEAPHAM Lincs (L)
104 SK 8788 4m ESE of Gainsborough. CP, 97. Gnsbrgh RD. Ch e, m. Gnsbrgh CC.

HEASLEY MILL Devon
163 SS 7332 4m NNE of S Molton. Loc, N Mltn CP. P: S Mltn. Ch m.

HEATH Derbys
112 SK 4466 5m SE of Chesterfield. CP, 2,131. Chstrfld RD. P Chstrfld. Ch e, r. Sch p. NE Derbys CC.

HEATH Yorks (W)
96, 102 SE 3520 1m ESE of Wakefield. CP(Warmfield cum Hth), 983. Wkfld RD. Sch pe. Normanton CC. H. Hall, mid 18c hse by Carr of York. Other interesting old hses round adjoining cmmn.

HEATH AND REACH Beds
146 SP 9228 2m N of Leighton Buzzard. CP, 922. Luton RD. P Lghtn Bzzd. Ch e, b, m. Sch pe. S Beds CC.

HEATH COMMON Sussex (W)
182 TQ 1114 1m E of Storrington. Loc, Washington CP. P Pulborough.

HEATHCOTE Derbys
111 SK 1460 7m SW of Bakewell. Loc, Hartington Nether Quarter CP. Ashbourne RD. W Derbys CC.

HEATH END Bucks
159 SU 8898 4m NNE of High Wycombe. Loc, Gt Missenden CP.

HEATH END Hants
168 SU 5862 7m ESE of Newbury. Loc, Tadley CP. Ch e.

HEATH END Surrey
169 SU 8449 1m SW of Aldershot. Loc, Farnham UD. P Fnhm.

HEATHER Leics
120, 121 SK 3910 4m SSE of Ashby de la Zouch. CP, 646. Ashby de la Zch RD. P LEICESTER. Ch e, m. Sch p. Loughborough CC.

HEATHFIELD Devon
176, 188 SX 8375 3m NNW of Newton Abbot. Loc, Bovey Tracey CP. P Ntn Abbt. Ch b. Sch pe. Brick and pottery works.

HEATHFIELD Som
164 ST 1626 4m WNW of Taunton. Loc, Norton Fitzwarren CP. Ch e.

HEATHFIELD Sussex (E)
183 TQ 5821 12m S of Tunbridge Wells. CP, 3,244, and loc, Waldron CP. Hailsham RD. P. Ch e, c, r, v. Sch pe, s. Rye CC. See also Broad Oak, Cade St, Old Hthfld.

HEATH HAYES Staffs
120 SK 0110 2m E of Cannock. Loc,
Cnnck UD. P Cnnck. Cnnck CC.
Coal-mining distr.

HEATH HILL Shrops
119 SJ 7614 3m SSE of Newport. Loc,
Sheriffhales CP.

HEATH HOUSE Som
165 ST 4146 5m SSW of Cheddar. Loc,
Wedmore CP. Ch m.

HEATHROW London (airpt)
160, 170 TQ 0775 14m WSW of Charing
Cross. Loc, Hillingdon LB.
P(Lndn[Hthrw] Airpt Central), Hounslow,
Middx. Hayes and Harlington BC
(Uxbridge CC).

HEATH, THE Suffolk (W)
149 TL 9043 2m NE of Sudbury. Loc, Gt
Waldingfield CP.

HEATLEY Ches
101 SJ 7088 4m W of Altrincham. Loc,
Lymm UD. P(Htly Heath), Lmm.

HEATON Lancs
89, 94 SD 4460 2m E of Heysham.
CP(Hth-w-Oxcliffe), 267. Lancaster RD.
Lncstr CC.

HEATON Staffs
110 SJ 9562 4m NNW of Leek. CP, 295.
Lk RD. Ch m2. Lk CC.

HEATON'S BRIDGE Lancs
100 SD 4011 2m NNW of Ormskirk. Loc,
Scarisbrick CP. P Ormskk.

HEAVERHAM Kent
171 TQ 5758 4m NE of Sevenoaks. Loc,
Kemsing CP.

HEBBURN Co Durham
78 NZ 3164 4m ENE of Gateshead. UD,
23,597. P. Jarrow BC.

HEBDEN Yorks (W)
90 SE 0263 9m W of Pateley Br. CP, 221.
Skipton RD. P Skptn. Ch e, m. Sch pe.
Skptn CC.

HEBDEN BRIDGE Yorks (W)
95 SD 9827 7m WNW of Halifax. Loc,
Hbdn Royd UD. P. Sowerby CC.

HEBRON Nthmb
78 NZ 1989 2m N of Morpeth. CP, 635.
Mpth RD. Ch e. Mpth CC.

HECKFIELD Hants
169 SU 7260 8m S of Reading. CP, 397.
Hartley Wintney RD. P Basingstoke. Ch e.
Sch pe. Bsngstke CC (Aldershot). To NW
on H. Hth, Wellington monmt.

HECKFIELD GREEN Suffolk (E)
137 TM 1876 3m ENE of Eye. Loc,
Hoxne CP.

HECK, GREAT Yorks (W)
97 SE 5921 7m SSW of Selby. See Gt Hck.

HECKINGTON Lincs (K)
113, 123 TF 1444 5m ESE of Sleaford.
CP, 1,691. E Kesteven RD. P Slfd.
Ch e, b, m, v. Sch pe. Grantham CC. Large
splendid 14c Dec ch. Eight-sailed twr windmill* of 1830 in working order.

HECKMONDWIKE Yorks (W)
96, 102 SE 2123 2m NW of Dewsbury.
UD, 9,361. P. Brighouse and Spenborough BC.
Textile mnfg tn, mostly carpets and blankets.

HEDDINGTON Wilts
157 ST 9966 3m S of Calne. CP, 325. Clne
and Chippenham RD. P Clne. Ch e. Sch pe.
Chppnhm CC.

HEDDON-ON-THE-WALL Nthmb
78 NZ 1366 7m WNW of Newcastle.
CP, 1,331. Cstle Ward CP. P NCSTLE UPON
TYNE. Ch e, m. Sch pe. Hexham CC. On
the Roman Wall. Ancient ch, partly Saxon.

HEDENHAM Norfolk
137 TM 3193 3m NW of Bungay. CP, 195.
Loddon RD. P Bngy, Suffolk. Ch e.
S Nflk CC.

HEDGE END Hants
180 SU 4912 5m E of Southampton.
CP, 4,464. Winchester RD. P STHMPTN.
Ch e, c, m, r, s, v. Sch i, j, s. Eastleigh CC.

HEDGERLEY Bucks
159, 160 SU 9687 SE of Beaconsfield.
CP, 846. Eton RD. P Slough. Ch e.
Bcnsfld CC (S Bucks).

HEDLEY ON THE HILL Nthmb
77, 78 NZ 0759 3m SSW of Prudhoe.
CP(Hdly), 154. Hexham RD.

P(Hdly), Stocksfield. Ch m. Hxhm CC. Over 700ft up. Views to Scottish border on a clear day.

HEDNESFORD Staffs
120 SK 0012 2m NE of Cannock. Loc, Cnnck UD. P Cnnck. Cnnck CC. Coal-mining distr.

HEDON Yorks (E)
99 TA 1828 6m E of Hull. MB, 2,600. P Hll. Bridlington CC. Prosperous seaport in mdvl times. Outstanding 12c ch known as 'King of Holderness' (Patrington is 'Queen'). 15c civic mace one of oldest in England. Cross commemorating Henry IV's landing at Ravenspur in Humber estuary 1399.

HEDSOR Bucks
159 SU 9187 3m SW of Beaconsfield. CP, 127. Wycombe RD. Ch e. Sch pe. Bcnsfld CC (Wcmbe).

HEGDON HILL Herefs
142 SO 5853 7m SE of Leominster. Loc, Pencombe w Grendon Warren CP.

HEIGHINGTON Co Durham
85 NZ 2422 5m NNW of Darlington. CP, 1,758. Dlngtn RD. P Dlngtn. Ch e, m. Sch pe. Bishop Auckland CC (Sedgefield). See also Redworth. Mainly Nmn ch.

HEIGHINGTON Lincs (K)
113 TF 0369 4m ESE of Lincoln. CP, 1,325. N Kesteven RD. P LNCLN. Ch e, m2. Sch p, pe. Grantham CC.

HELE Devon
163 SS 5347 1m E of Ilfracombe. Loc, Ilfrcmbe UD. P Ilfrcmbe.

HELE Devon
176 SS 9902 7m SSE of Tiverton. Loc, St Thomas RD, Tvtn RD. P Exeter. Tvtn CC.

HELFORD Cornwall
190 SW 7526 6m E of Helston. Loc, Manaccan CP. P Hlstn. Boating vllge. Foot passenger ferry across H. River to H. Passage.

HELHOUGHTON Norfolk
125 TF 8626 4m SW of Fakenham. CP, 212. Walsingham RD. P Fknhm. Ch e, m. NW Nflk CC (N Nflk).

HELIONS BUMPSTEAD Essex
148 TL 6541 3m SSW of Haverhill. CP, 366. Halstead RD. P Hvrhll, Suffolk. Ch e, v. Saffron Walden CC.

HELLAND Cornwall
185, 186 SX 0771 3m N of Bodmin. CP, 234. Wadebridge and Padstow RD. P Bdmn. Ch e, m. Bdmn CC.

HELLESDON Norfolk
126 TG 2010 2m NW of Norwich. CP. St Faith's and Aylsham RD. Ch e, s, v. Sch p3, s. N Nflk CC (Central Nflk).

HELLIDON Northants
132 SP 5158 4m SW of Daventry. CP, 141. Dvntry RD. P Dvntry. Ch e, m. Dvntry CC (S Nthnts).

HELLIFIELD Yorks (W)
95 SD 8556 5m SSE of Settle. CP, 1,014. Sttle RD. P Skptn. Ch e, b, m. Sch p. Skptn CC.

HELLINGLY Sussex (E)
183 TQ 5812 2m N of Hailsham. CP, 4,111. Hlshm RD. P Hlshm. Ch e, b, m. Sch p. Lewes CC (Eastbourne). See also Horsebridge, Upr Dicker. Horselunges, restored 16c half-timbered hse. 1m E, county mental hsptl.

HELLINGTON Norfolk
126 TG 3103 6m ESE of Norwich. CP, 85. Loddon RD. Ch e. S Nflk CC.

HELMDON Northants
145, 146 SP 5843 4m N of Brackley. CP, 481. Brckly RD. P Brckly. Ch e, b. Sch p. Daventry CC (S Nthnts).

HELMINGHAM Suffolk (E)
137 TM 1857 6m N of Ipswich. CP, 224. Gipping RD. P Stowmarket. Ch e. Sch p. Eye CC. H. Hall, in deer pk, Tdr and later; home of the Tollemaches.

HELMINGTON ROW Co Durham
85 NZ 1835 1m W of Willington. Loc, Crook and Wllngtn UD. P Crk.

HELMSHORE Lancs
95 SD 7821 1m S of Haslingden. Loc, Hslngdn MB. P Rossendale. Hlmshre Indstrl Museum displays early textile machinery. Hlmshre Stn Rly Museum.

HELMSLEY Yorks (N)
92 SE 6183 12m E of Thirsk. CP, 1,324. Hlmsly RD. P YORK. Ch e, m2, r. Sch pe, pm. Thirsk and Malton CC. See also Carlton. Mkt tn blt round large cobbled square. 12c cstle (A.M.). Duncombe Pk, partly 18c mansion, seat of Earls of Feversham, now girls' sch. Formal terraced gdns* with classical-style temples.

HELPERBY Yorks (N)
91 SE 4369 4m NE of Boroughbridge. CP, 439. Easingwold RD. P YORK. Ch m. Thirsk and Malton CC.

HELPERTHORPE Yorks (E)
93 SE 9570 9m NW of Driffield. Loc, Luttons CP. Norton RD. Ch e, m. Howden CC. Stream and duckpond by roadside.

HELPRINGHAM Lincs (K)
113, 123 TF 1340 5m SE of Sleaford. CP, 671. E Kesteven RD. P Slfd. Ch e, m. Sch p. Rutland and Stamford CC.

HELPSTON Hunts
123 TF 1205 6m NW of Peterborough. CP, 641. Ptrbrgh RD. P PTRBRGH. Ch e, m. Sch p. Ptrbrgh BC(CC). Vctrn monmt on grn commemorates John Clare, 19c local poet.

HELSBY Ches
100, 109 SJ 4875 5m SSW of Runcorn. CP, 3,634. Rncn RD. P WARRINGTON. Ch e, m, r. Sch p, sb, sg. Rncn CC. To S is H. Hill (part NT), site of Iron Age fort and with views over Mersey and to Welsh mts.

HELSTON Cornwall
189 SW 6527 15m SW of Truro. MB, 9,827. P. St Ives CC. See also Porthleven. Mkt tn of Lizard peninsula. Former tin-mining centre. Furry Dance, origin unknown, takes place May 8th.

HELSTONE Cornwall
185, 186 SX 0881 2m SW of Camelford. Loc, Cmlfd CP. P Cmlfd. Ch m.

HELTON Westm
83 NY 5122 5m S of Penrith. Loc, Askham CP. Ch m.

HELWITH BRIDGE Yorks (W)
90 SD 8169 4m N of Settle. Loc, Horton in Ribblesdale CP.

HEMBLINGTON Norfolk
126 TG 3411 5m SE of Wroxham. CP, 211. Blofield and Flegg RD. Ch e, v. Sch p. Yarmouth CC. Ch has wall-paintings of life of St Christopher.

HEMEL HEMPSTEAD Herts
160 TL 0507 7m NNW of Watford. MB, 69,371. P. Hml Hmpstd CC. See also Bourne End, Felden, Piccotts End. Indstrl and rsdntl new tn developed to E of old tn. Pop. of new tn 69,966.

HEMINGBROUGH Yorks (E)
97, 98 SE 6730 4m ESE of Selby. CP, 693. Derwent RD. P Slby. Ch e, m. Sch p. Howden CC. Notable 12c–14c ch with tall twr.

HEMINGBY Lincs (L)
114 TF 2374 3m NNW of Horncastle. CP, 188. Hncstle RD. P Hncstle. Ch e. Sch pe. Hncstle CC. Early 18c sch and almshouses, now cottages.

HEMINGFIELD Yorks (W)
102, 103 SE 3901 4m SE of Barnsley. Loc, Wombwell UD. P Bnsly.

HEMINGFORD ABBOTS Hunts
134 TL 2871 3m E of Huntingdon. CP, 628. St Ives RD. P HNTNGDN. Ch e. Sch pe. Hunts CC. Spired ch beside R Ouse.

HEMINGFORD GREY Hunts
134 TL 2970 4m E of Huntingdon. CP, 1,435. St Ives RD. P HNTNGDN. Ch e, c. Sch p. Hunts CC. Old hses; water mill. On R Ouse.

HEMINGSTONE Suffolk (E)
150 TM 1553 6m N of Ipswich. CP, 184. Gipping RD. Ch e. Eye CC.

HEMINGTON Leics
121 SK 4528 4m SSW of Long Eaton. CP(Lockington-Hmngtn), 529. Cstle Donington RD. P DERBY. Loughborough CC.

HEMINGTON Northants
134 TL 0985 4m SE of Oundle. CP, 79. Oundle and Thrapston RD. P PETERBOROUGH. Ch e. Wellingborough CC (Ptrbrgh).

HEMINGTON Som
166 ST 7253 3m ESE of Radstock. CP, 563.

Frome RD. Ch e, m. Sch p. Wells CC. See also Faulkland, Hardington. To NW, Turner's Twr, 180ft, folly blt 1885 to outdo column in Ammerdown Pk (see Kilmersdon).

HEMLEY Suffolk (E)
150 TM 2842 4m S of Woodbridge. CP, 50. Deben RD. Ch e. Sudbury and Wdbrdge CC. Close to R Deben where there is a landing place.

HEMPNALL Norfolk
137 TM 2494 7m WNW of Bungay. CP, 768. Depwade RD. P NORWICH, NOR 64W. Ch e, m. Sch p. S Nflk CC. See also Hmpnll Grn.

HEMPNALL GREEN Norfolk
137 TM 2492 6m WNW of Bungay. Loc, Hmpnll CP.

HEMPSTEAD Essex
148 TL 6338 5m NNE of Thaxted. CP, 403. Saffron Walden RD. P Sffrn Wldn. Ch e, m. Sffrn Wldn CC. Ch: tomb of William Harvey (1657), discoverer of circulation of the blood.

HEMPSTEAD Norfolk
125 TG 1037 2m ESE of Holt. CP, 201. Erpingham RD. P Hlt. Ch e, m. N Nflk CC.

HEMPSTEAD Norfolk
126 TG 4028 8m ESE of N Walsham. Loc, Lessingham CP. Ch e. Sch p.

HEMPTON Norfolk
125 TF 9129 1m SW of Fakenham. CP, 428. Walsingham RD. NW Nflk CC (N Nflk). P(Hmptn Grn), Fknhm. Ch e.

HEMPTON Oxon
145 SP 4431 5m S of Banbury. Loc, Deddington CP. Ch e, c.

HEMSBY Norfolk
126 TG 4917 6m NNW of Yarmouth. CP, 1,099. Blofield and Flegg RD. P Gt Ymth. Ch e, c, m, r. Sch p. Ymth CC. See also Newport.

HEMSWELL Lincs (L)
104 SK 9390 7m E of Gainsborough. CP, 1,656. Gnsbrgh RD. P Gnsbrgh. Ch e, m. Sch p. Gnsbrgh CC. RAF stn. Gliders. In vllge street, old maypole topped by fox weather vane.

HEMSWORTH Yorks (W)
103 SE 4213 6m SSW of Pontefract. UD, 14,856. P Pntfrct. Hmswth CC. See also Fitzwilliam, Kinsley.

HEMYOCK Devon
164, 176 ST 1313 5m S of Wellington. CP, 1,063. Tiverton RD. P Cullompton. Ch e, b, m, r. Sch p. Tvtn CC.

HENBURY Ches
110 SJ 8873 2m W of Macclesfield. CP, 424. Mcclsfld RD. Ch e. Sch pe. Mcclsfld CC.

HENDON London
160 TQ 2289 7m NW of Charing Cross. Loc, Barnet LB. Hndn N BC, Hndn S BC.

HENFIELD Sussex (W)
182 TQ 2116 7m N of Shoreham-by-Sea. CP, 2,906. Chanctonbury RD. P. Ch e, b, c, r. Sch pe. Shrhm CC (Arundel and Shrhm). See also Oreham Cmmn. Large hsing estate to W of main rd.

HENGOED Shrops
118 SJ 2833 3m N of Oswestry. Loc, Selattyn and Gobowen CP. P Oswstry. Ch e, m.

HENGRAVE Suffolk (W)
136 TL 8268 3m NNW of Bury St Edmunds. CP, 188. Thingoe RD. P Bury St Eds. Ch e. Bury St Eds CC. H. Hall, large Tdr hse, now RC convent sch.

HENHAM Essex
148 TL 5428 4m WSW of Thaxted. CP, 729. Saffron Walden RD. P Bishop's Stortford, Herts. Ch e, v. Sch p. Sffrn Wldn CC.

HENLEY Dorset
178 ST 6904 9m SSE of Sherborne. Loc, Buckland Newton CP. Ch b.

HENLEY Som
165 ST 4332 6m SW of Glastonbury. Loc, High Ham CP. Ch v.

HENLEY Suffolk (E)
150 TM 1551 4m N of Ipswich. CP, 253. Gipping RD. P Ipswich. Ch e. Sch p. Eye CC. Once tiny place much enlarged by estate of modern hses with landscape windows.

HENLEY Sussex (W)
181 SU 8925 3m N of Midhurst. Loc,
Mdhst RD. Chichester CC (Horsham).

HENLEY-IN-ARDEN Warwicks
131 SP 1565 7m NNW of Stratford.
CP, 1,353. Strtfd-on-Avon RD. P Solihull.
Ch e, b, m. Sch p, s. Strtfd-on-Avn CC
(Strtfd). Long high st. Several old bldngs,
incl restored 15c half-timbered guildhall*.

HENLEY-ON-THAMES Oxon
159 SU 7682 7m NNE of Reading.
MB, 11,402. P. Hnly CC. River resort. Many
Ggn hses. Annual regatta first week in July.

HENLOW Beds
147 TL 1738 4m S of Biggleswade.
CP, 3,682. Bgglswde RD. P. Ch e, m.
Sch p, pe. Mid-Beds CC.

HENNOCK Devon
176 SX 8380 6m NNW of Newton Abbot.
CP, 954. Ntn Abbt RD. P Ntn Abbt.
Ch e, m. Sch p. Totnes CC. See also
Chudleigh Knighton.

HENNY, GREAT Essex
149 TL 8637 2m S of Sudbury. See
Gt Hnny.

HENNY STREET Essex
149 TL 8738 2m S of Sudbury. Loc,
Halstead RD. Saffron Walden CC.

HENSALL Yorks (W)
97 SE 5923 6m SSW of Selby. CP, 315.
Osgoldcross RD. P Goole. Ch e, m. Sch p.
Gle CC.

HENSHAW Nthmb
77 NY 7664 4m E of Haltwhistle. CP, 652.
Hltwhstle RD. Ch e, m. Sch pe. Hexham CC.

HENSINGHAM Cumb
82 NX 9816 1m SE of Whitehaven. Loc,
Whthvn MB. P Whthvn.

HENSTEAD Suffolk (E)
137 TM 4986 5m SE of Beccles. CP(Hnstd
w Hulver Street), 351. Lothingland RD.
Ch e. Lowestoft CC.

HENSTRIDGE Som
178 ST 7219 6m ENE of Sherborne.
CP, 1,127. Wincanton RD. P Templecombe.
Ch e, m, v. Sch pe. Wells CC. See also
Hnstrdge Ash, Hnstrdge Marsh, Yenston.

HENSTRIDGE ASH Som
166 ST 7220 5m S of Wincanton. Loc,
Henstridge CP.

HENSTRIDGE MARSH Som
166 ST 7420 6m SSE of Wincanton. Loc,
Henstridge CP.

HENTON Oxon
159 SP 7602 3m W of Princes Risborough.
Loc, Chinnor CP.

HENTON Som
165 ST 4945 3m W of Wells. Loc,
Wookey CP. P Wlls. Ch e.

HENWOOD Cornwall
186 SX 2673 6m WNW of Callington. Loc,
Linkinhorne CP. P Liskeard. Ch m.

HEPBURN Nthmb
71 NU 0624 5m ESE of Wooler. Loc,
Chillingham CP.

HEPPLE Nthmb
71 NT 9800 5m WSW of Rothbury.
CP, 190. Rthbry RD. P Morpeth.
Berwick-upon-Tweed CC. Coquetdale vllge
among moors.

HEPSCOTT Nthmb
78 NZ 2284 2m SE of Morpeth. CP, 464.
Mpth RD. P Mpth. Mpth CC.

HEPTONSTALL Yorks (W)
95 SD 9828 just NW of Hebden Br.
CP, 1,361. Hepton RD. P Hbdn Br.
Ch e, b, m2. Sch p. Sowerby CC. See also
Colden, Slack.

HEPWORTH Suffolk (W)
136 TL 9874 9m WSW of Diss. CP, 371.
Thingoe RD. P Dss, Norfolk. Ch e, m.
Sch pe. Bury St Edmunds CC.

HEPWORTH Yorks (W)
102 SE 1606 6m SSE of Huddersfield. Loc,
Holmfirth UD. P Hddsfld.

HEREFORD Herefs
142 SO 5140 45m SW of Birmingham.
MB, 46,503. P(HRFD). Hrfd CC. See also
Tupsley. County and cathedral tn. Three
Choirs Festival every third year. Famous
stock market. Many interesting old hses.
Cider factory.

HERMITAGE Berks
158 SU 5073 5m NNE of Newbury. CP.
Nbry RD. P Nbry. Ch e. Sch p. Nbry CC
(Abingdon).

HERMITAGE Dorset
178 ST 6406 6m S of Sherborne. CP, 83.
Shbne RD. Ch e, v. W Dst CC.

HERMITAGE Sussex (W)
181 SU 7505 3m E of Havant. Loc,
Southbourne CP. Ch v.

HERNE Kent
173 TR 1865 2m S of Herne Bay. Loc, Hne
Bay UD. P Hne Bay.

HERNE BAY Kent
173 TR 1768 7m NNE of Canterbury.
UD, 25,117. P. Cntrbry CC. See also
Broomfield, Hne, Hillborough, Reculver.
Seaside resort, mainly Vctrn.

HERNE HILL London
160, 170 TQ 3274 4m S of Lndn Br. Loc,
Lambeth LB. Norwood BC.

HERNHILL Kent
172, 173 TR 0660 3m E of Faversham.
CP, 687. Swale RD. Ch e, m. Sch pe.
Fvrshm CC. See also Dargate.

HERODSFOOT Cornwall
186 SX 2160 4m SW of Liskeard. Loc,
Duloe CP. P Lskd. Ch e.

HERONGATE Essex
161 TQ 6391 3m SE of Brentwood. Loc,
Brntwd UD. P Brntwd.

HERONSGATE Herts
159, 160 TQ 0294 2m W of
Rickmansworth. Loc, Rckmnswth UD.

HERRIARD Hants
168, 169 SU 6646 4m SSE of Basingstoke.
CP, 292. Bsngstke RD. P Bsngstke. Ch e.
Sch pe. Bsngstke CC. See also Southrope. H.
Pk Gdns*, surrounding a now demolished
early 18c mansion.

HERRINGFLEET Suffolk (E)
137 TM 4797 6m NW of Lowestoft.
CP, 262. Lothingland RD. Ch e. Lwstft CC.
Rems of St Olave's Priory to NW. Old
smock mill down by R Waveney. Ch has
thatched roof and round Nmn twr.

HERRINGSWELL Suffolk (W)
135 TL 7169 6m NE of Newmarket.
C P , 2 7 3 . Mildenhall R D .
P Bury St Edmunds. Ch e. Bury St Eds CC.

HERSDEN Kent
173 TR 2062 4m NE of Canterbury. Loc,
Bridge-Blean RD. P Cntrbry. Ch e, m, r.
Sch p. Cntrbry CC.

HERSHAM Surrey
1 7 0 TQ 1 1 6 4 2 m S S E of
Walton-on-Thames. Loc, Wltn and
Weybridge UD. P Wltn-on-Thms.

HERSTMONCEUX Sussex (E)
183 TQ 6312 4m NE of Hailsham.
CP, 1,922. Hlshm RD. P Hlshm. Ch e, f, v.
Sch pe. Rye CC. See also Cowbeech. H.
Cstle, restored 15c bldng, houses the Royal
Observatory formerly at Greenwich; grnds*.

HERTFORD Herts
147, 160 TL 3212 6m E of Welwyn Gdn
City. MB, 20,379. P(HTFD). Htfd and
Stevenage CC. See also Hertingfordbury.
Scant rems of Nmn cstle; present cstle dates
from 1500. Used as municipal offices.

HERTFORD HEATH Herts
148, 161 TL 3510 2m S of Ware. Loc,
Gt Amwell CP. P HTFD. Ch v. Sch p.
To E, Haileybury College, boys' public sch.

HERTINGFORDBURY Herts
147, 160 TL 3012 1m W of Hertford. Loc,
Htfd MB; CP, 746, Htfd RD. Htfd and
Stevenage CC(Htfd). See also Letty Grn.

HESKETH BANK Lancs
94 SD 4423 7m WSW of Preston. Loc,
Hskth-w-Becconsall CP. W Lancs RD.
P Prstn. Ch e, m. Sch pe. Ormskirk CC.

HESKETH LANE Lancs
94, 95 SD 6141 8m W of Clitheroe. Loc,
Chipping CP. P Preston.

HESKET NEWMARKET Cumb
83 NY 3438 8m SE of Wigton. Loc,
Caldbeck CP. P Wgtn. Ch m. Sch p. Spacious
main street, reminiscent of Yorks, climbing
slope.

HESKIN GREEN Lancs
100 SD 5315 4m WSW of Chorley. Loc,

Hesleden

Hskn CP. Chly RD. P(Hskn), Chly. Ch m.
Sch pe. Chly CC.

HESLEDEN Co Durham
85 NZ 4438 2m S of Peterlee. Loc, Monk
Hsldn CP. P Hartlepool. Ch m2. Sch p.

HESLINGTON Yorks (E)
97, 98 SE 6250 2m ESE of York. CP.
Derwent RD. P YK. Ch e, m. Sch je.
Howden CC. University of Yk.

HESSAY Yorks (W)
97 SE 5253 5m W of York. CP, 104.
Nidderdale RD. Ch m. Barkston Ash CC.

HESSENFORD Cornwall
186 SX 3057 6m SE of Liskeard. Loc,
St Germans CP. P Torpoint. Ch e, m.

HESSETT Suffolk (W)
136 TL 9361 5m ESE of Bury St Edmunds.
CP, 276. Thedwastre RD. P Bury St Eds.
Ch e. Bury St Eds CC. Fine 14c−15c ch:
glass.

HESSLE Yorks (E)
99 TA 0326 5m WSW of Hull. Loc,
Haltemprice UD. P. Hltmprce CC.

HESSLE Yorks (W)
103 SE 4317 3m SSW of Pontefract.
CP(Hssle and Hill Top), 129.
Hemsworth RD. Hmswth CC.

HEST BANK Lancs
89 SD 4666 3m N of Lancaster. Loc,
Lncstr RD. P LNCSTR. Ch c. Morecambe
and Lonsdale CC.

HESTON London
160, 170 TQ 1377 1m N of Hounslow. Loc,
Hnslw LB. P Hnslw, Middx. Feltham and
Hstn BC (Hstn and Isleworth). To E,
Osterley Pk (NT)*, 16c and 18c hse;
decoration by Robert Adam.

HESWALL Ches
100, 108, 109 SJ 2681 6m SW of
Birkenhead. Loc, Wirral UD. P Wrrl.
Wrrl CC.

HETHE Oxon
145, 146 SP 5929 4m N of Bicester. CP,
296. Ploughley RD. P Bcstr. Ch e, m, r.
Sch pe. Banbury CC (Henley).

HETHERSETT Norfolk
126 TG 1504 4m NE of Wymondham.
CP, 1,613. Forehoe and Henstead RD.
P NORWICH, NOR 42X. Ch e, m. Sch pe.
S Nflk CC (Central Nflk).

HETHERSGILL Cumb
76 NY 4767 5m NW of Brampton. CP, 443.
Border RD. P Carlisle. Ch e, m. Sch pe.
Penrith and the Bdr CC. See also
Boltonfellend.

HETHPOOL Nthmb
70 NT 8928 6m W of Wooler. Loc,
Kirknewton CP.

HETT Co Durham
85 NZ 2836 4m S of Durham. CP, 148.
Drhm RD. Drhm CC.

HETTON Yorks (W)
95 SD 9658 5m NNW of Skipton. CP, 83.
Skptn RD. P Skptn. Ch m. Skptn CC.

HETTON LE HILL Co Durham
85 NZ 3545 3m S of Houghton-le-Spring.
Loc, Pittington CP.

HETTON-LE-HOLE Co Durham
85 NZ 3547 6m NE of Durham. UD
(Httn), 16,871. P. Houghton-le-Spring CC.
See also Easington Lane, E Rainton,
Elemore Vale, High Moorsley, Low Msly.

HEUGH Nthmb
77, 78 NZ 0873 5m W of Ponteland. Loc,
Stamfordham CP. Ch m.

HEVENINGHAM Suffolk (E)
137 TM 3372 5m SW of Halesworth.
CP, 145. Blyth RD. P Hlswth. Ch e. Eye CC.
H. Hall*, large Palladian mansion by Sir
Robert Taylor and James Wyatt in pk laid
out by Capability Brown.

HEVER Kent
171 TQ 4744 2m SE of Edenbridge.
CP, 1,062. Sevenoaks RD. Ch e. Sch pe.
Svnks CC. See also Four Elms. H. Cstle*,
fortified Tdr mnr, moated, once home of
Boleyn family and much visited by
Henry VIII. Restored, and gdns* created, by
1st Ld Astor c. 1920. Brass in ch to Thomas
Boleyn.

HEVERSHAM Westm
89 SD 4983 6m S of Kendal. CP, 484.

S Westm RD. P Milnthorpe. Ch e. Sch pe, s. Westm CC. See also Leasgill.

HEVINGHAM Norfolk
126 TG 1921 4m S of Aylsham. CP, 676. St Faith's and Aylshm RD. P NORWICH, NOR 04Y. Ch e. Sch p. N Nflk CC (Central Nflk). See also Buxton Hth.

HEWELSFIELD Glos
155, 156 SO 5602 6m NNE of Chepstow. CP, 380. Lydney RD., P Ldny. Ch e. W Glos CC. See also Brockweir.

HEWISH Som
165 ST 3964 3m W of Congresbury. Loc, Axbridge RD. P Weston-super-Mare. Ch e. Sch pe. W-s-M CC.

HEWISH Som
177 ST 4208 2m SW of Crewkerne. Loc, W Crkne CP. Chard RD. Yeovil CC.

HEXHAM Nthmb
77 NY 9364 20m W of Newcastle. UD, 9,799. P. Hxhm CC. See also Low Gate. Mkt tn on R Tyne, with splendid abbey ch.

HEXTABLE Kent
161, 171 TQ 5170 3m SSW of Dartford. Loc, Swanley CP. P Swnly. Ch v. Sch p.

HEXTON Herts
147 TL 1030 5m W of Hitchin. CP, 157. Htchn RD. P Htchn. Ch e, m. Sch p. Htchn CC. To SW on Barton Hills, Ravensburgh Cstle, Iron Age fort, on county boundary.

HEXWORTHY Devon
175, 187, 188 SX 6572 7m WNW of Ashburton. Loc, Lydford CP.

HEYBRIDGE Essex
161 TQ 6498 just SW of Ingatestone. Loc, Chelmsford RD. Chlmsfd CC.

HEYBRIDGE Essex
162 TL 8508 just N of Maldon. Loc, Mldn UD. P Mldn. 19c ironworks. Nmn ch.

HEYBRIDGE BASIN Essex
162 TL 8707 1m E of Maldon. Loc, Mldn UD. Canal with wharves and barges. Caravan sites.

HEYBROOK BAY Devon
187 SX 4948 4m SSE of Plymouth. Loc, Wembury CP.

HEYDON Cambs
148 TL 4340 5m E of Royston. CP, 151. S Cambs RD. P Rstn, Herts. Ch e. Cambs CC. Stands on ridge; wide view to N. Ch completely restored after severe air raid damage in World War II.

HEYDON Norfolk
125 TG 1127 5m W of Aylsham. CP, 176. St Faith's and Aylshm RD. P NORWICH, NOR 11Y. Ch e. N Nflk CC (Central Nflk). Picturesque hses round vllge grn.

HEYDOUR Lincs (K)
113, 123 TF 0039 5m SW of Sleaford. CP(Haydor), 220. W Kesteven RD. Ch e. Sch pe. Grantham CC.

HEYSHAM Lancs
89, 94 SD 4161 2m SSW of Morecambe. MB(Morecambe and Hshm), 41,863. P Mcmbe. Mcmbe and Lonsdale CC. Resort; port for N Ireland. Oil refinery. Chemicals factory.

HEYSHOTT Sussex (W)
181 SU 8918 2m SSE of Midhurst. CP, 399. Mdhst RD. P Mdhst. Ch e. Chichester CC (Horsham). Downland views, esp from Ambersham Cmmn, 1m NE.

HEYTESBURY Wilts
166, 167 ST 9242 4m ESE of Warminster. CP, 526. Wmnstr and Westbury RD. P Wmnstr. Ch e. Sch pe. Wstbry CC. See also Tytherington. 17c–18c almshouses. Octagonal lock-up.

HEYTHROP Oxon
145 SP 3527 2m E of Chipping Norton. CP, 308. Chppng Ntn RD. Ch e. Banbury CC

HEYWOOD Lancs
101 SD 8510 3m WSW of Rochdale. MB, 30,418. P. Hwd and Royton CC. Engineering and textiles.

HEYWOOD Wilts
166 ST 8753 2m N of Westbury. CP, 490. Warminster and Wstbry RD. Ch e. Sch pe. Wstbry CC. See also Hawkeridge.

HIBALDSTOW Lincs (L)
104 SE 9702 3m SSW of Brigg. CP, 1,142.
Glanford Brgg RD. P Brgg. Ch e, m. Sch p.
Brgg and Scunthorpe CC (Brgg).

HICKLETON Yorks (W)
103 SE 4805 6m WNW of Doncaster.
CP, 102. Dncstr RD. P Dncstr. Ch e. Sch pe.
Don Valley CC.

HICKLING Norfolk
126 TG 4124 9m ESE of N Walsham.
CP, 750. Smallburgh RD.
P NORWICH, NOR 31Z. Ch e, m2. Sch pe.
N Nflk CC. To S, H. Broad; part is nature
reserve.

HICKLING Notts
122 SK 6929 7m NW of Melton Mowbray.
CP, 385. Bingham RD. P Mltn Mbry, Leics.
Ch e, m Rushcliffe CC (Carlton). Ch
contains Saxon coffin lid.

HICKLING GREEN Norfolk
126 TG 4123 9m SE of N Walsham. Loc,
Hcklng CP.

HICKLING HEATH Norfolk
126 TG 4022 9m SE of N Walsham. Loc,
Hcklng CP.

HIDCOTE BARTRIM Glos
144 SP 1742 3m NE of Chipping Campden.
Loc, Ebrington CP. H. Mnr, 17c hse (NT),
with formal gdns*.

HIDCOTE BOYCE Glos
144 SP 1742 2m NE of Chipping Campden.
Loc, Ebrington CP.

HIGH ACKWORTH Yorks (W)
103 SE 4417 3m SSW of Pontefract. Loc,
Ackwth CP. Hemsworth RD.
P (Ackwth), Pntfrct. Ch e. Sch pe.
Hmswth CC. To S, 18c Friends' sch.

HIGHAM Derbys
111 SK 3959 3m NNW of Alfreton.
CP (Shirland and Hghm), 5,196.
Chesterfield RD. P DERBY. NE Derbys CC.

HIGHAM Kent
161, 171, 172 TQ 7171 3m NW of
Rochester. CP. Strood RD. P Rchstr.
Ch e, c. Sch p. Gravesend CC. See also Ch
St, Hghm Upshire. To S, Gadshill, home of
Dickens 1857–70.

HIGHAM Lancs
95 SD 8036 3m WSW of Nelson.
CP (Hghm-w-W Close Booth), 503.
Burnley RD. P Bnly. Ch m. Sch pe.
Clitheroe CC.

HIGHAM Suffolk (E)
149 TM 0335 4m S of Hadleigh. CP, 162.
Samford RD. P Colchester, Essex. Ch e.
Sudbury and Woodbridge CC.

HIGHAM Suffolk (W)
135 TL 7465 7m E of Newmarket. CP, 205.
Mildenhall RD. P Bury St Edmunds. Ch e.
Bury St Eds CC.

HIGHAM Yorks (W)
102 SE 3107 2m WNW of Barnsley. Loc,
Darton UD. P Bnsly.

HIGHAM FERRERS Northants
134 SP 9668 1m N of Rushden. MB, 4,700.
P Wellingborough. Wllngbrgh CC. Footwear
factories. 12c–13c ch with fine 14c chantry
chpl.

HIGHAM GOBION Beds
147 TL 1032 5m WNW of Hitchin. CP, 28.
Ampthill RD. Ch e. Mid-Beds CC.

HIGHAM ON THE HILL Leics
132 SP 3895 3m WNW of Hinckley.
CP, 723. Mkt Bosworth RD.
P Nuneaton, Warwickshire. Ch e, m. Sch pe.
Bswth CC.

HIGHAMPTON Devon
175 SS 4804 9m E of Holsworthy. CP, 170.
Okehampton RD. P Beaworthy. Ch e, m.
Sch p. W Dvn CC (Torrington).

HIGHAM UPSHIRE Kent
161, 171, 172 TQ 7171 3m NW of
Rochester. Loc, Hghm CP.

HIGH ANGERTON Nthmb
77, 78 NZ 0985 7m W of Morpeth. Loc,
Hartburn CP.

HIGH BEACH Essex
161 TQ 4097 4m SW of Epping. Loc,
Waltham Holy Cross UD. Eppng Forest CC
(Eppng).

HIGH BENTHAM Yorks (W)
89 SD 6669 7m SE of Kirkby Lonsdale.
Loc, Bnthm CP. Settle RD. Ch e, f, m, r.
Sch p. Skipton CC.

HIGH BICKINGTON Devon
163 SS 6020 8m WSW of S Molton.
CP, 410. Torrington RD. P Umberleigh.
Ch e, m, v. Sch pe. W Dvn CC (Trrngtn). Ch:
16c bench-ends.

HIGH BRAY Devon
163 SS 6934 6m NNW of S Molton.
CP, 150. Barnstaple RD. Ch e. Sch pe.
N Dvn CC. See also Lydcott.

HIGHBRIDGE Som
165 ST 3247 2m SE of Burnham. Loc,
Bnhm-on-Sea UD. P. Confusion of rds,
garages, indstrl plant.

HIGHBROOK Sussex (E)
183 TQ 3630 6m SSW of E Grinstead. Loc,
W Hoathly CP. Ch e.

HIGHBURTON Yorks (W)
102 SE 1912 4m SE of Huddersfield. Loc,
Kirkburton UD.

HIGHBURY London
160 TQ 3185 3m NNE of Charing Cross.
Loc, Islingtôn LB. Islngtn Central BC
(Islngtn E).

HIGHBURY Som
166 ST 6849 3m S of Radstock. Loc,
Coleford CP.

HIGH BUSTON Nthmb
71 NU 2308 4m SE of Alnwick. Loc,
Alnmouth CP.

HIGH CALLERTON Nthmb
78 NZ 1670 1m S of Ponteland. Loc,
Pntlnd CP.

HIGH CASTERTON Westm
89 SD 6278 just E of Kirkby Lonsdale. Loc,
Csttn CP.

HIGH CATTON Yorks (E)
97, 98 SE 7153 7m E of York. Loc,
Cttn CP. Pocklington RD. Ch m.
Howden CC.

HIGHCLERE Hants
168 SU 4360 5m SSW of Newbury.
CP, 547. Kingsclere and Whitchurch RD.
P Nbry, Berks. Ch e. Sch p. Basingstoke CC.
H. Cstle, Vctrn-Elizn hse designed by Barry.
Grnds, laid out by Capability Brown, belong
to earlier, 18c, hse.

HIGHCLIFFE Hants
179 SZ 2193 3m E of Christchurch. Loc,
Chrstchch MB. P Chrstchch.

HIGH COGGES Oxon
158 SP 3709 1m ESE of Witney. Loc,
S Leigh CP.

HIGH CONISCLIFFE Co Durham
85 NZ 2215 4m W of Darlington. CP, 266.
Dlngtn RD. P Dlngtn. Ch e, m. Sch pe.
Bishop Auckland CC (Sedgefield).

HIGH CROSS Hants
181 SU 7126 3m NW of Petersfield. Loc,
Froxfield CP. Ptrsfld RD. Ch e. Ptrsfld CC.

HIGH CROSS Herts
148 TL 3618 3m N of Ware. Loc,
Standon CP. P Ware. Ch e. Sch pe.

HIGH CROSS BANK Derbys
120, 121 SK 2817 5m SSE of
Burton-on-Trent. Loc, Cstle Gresley CP.

HIGH DUBMIRE Co Durham
85 NZ 3349 just W of Houghton-le-Spring.
Loc, Htn-le-Sprng UD.

HIGH EASTER Essex
148, 161 TL 6214 4m S of Dunmow.
CP, 271. Dnmw RD. P Chelmsford. Ch e, c.
Saffron Walden CC.

HIGH ELLINGTON Yorks (N)
91 SE 1983 2m NW of Masham. CP(Ellngtn
Hgh and Low), 84. Mshm RD. Ch m.
Richmond CC.

HIGHER ASHTON Devon
176 SX 8584 6m SW of Exeter. Loc,
Ashtn CP. St Thomas RD. Ch e. Tvtn CC.

HIGHER BALLAM Lancs
94 SD 3630 5m SE of Blackpool. Loc,
Westby-w-Plumptons CP.

HIGHER BOCKHAMPTON Dorset
178 SY 7292 3m ENE of Dorchester. Loc,
Stinsford CP. Bthplce of Thomas Hardy,
1840. The hse (NT)* has small collection of
Hardy relics.

HIGHER BRUCKLAND Devon
177 SY 2893 3m W of Lyme Regis. Loc,
Axmouth CP.

HIGH ERCALL Shrops
118 SJ 5917 5m NW of Wellington. Loc, Ercll Magna CP. Wllngtn RD. P Telford. Ch e, m. Sch p. The Wrekin CC. Royalist stronghold in Civil War. Poultry-rearing distr. Flat country. Ercall pronounced 'arkle'.

HIGHERFORD Lancs
95 SD 8640 1m N of Nelson. Loc, Barrowford UD.

HIGHER PENWORTHAM Lancs
94 SD 5128 1m WSW of Preston. Loc, Pnwthm CP. Prstn RD. P(Pnwthm), Prstn. Ch e, c, m2, r2. Sch i, p2, pe3, pr2, s, sg. S Fylde CC.

HIGHER TOWN St Martin's, Isles of Scilly
189 SV 9215. Loc, St Mtn's CP. P(St Mtn's). Ch e, m.

HIGHER WALTON Ches
100, 109 SJ 5985 2m SSW of Warrington. Loc, Wltn CP. Runcorn RD. P WRRNGTN. Ch e. Rncn CC.

HIGHER WALTON Lancs
94 SD 5827 3m ESE of Preston. Loc, Wltn-le-Dale UD. P Prstn.

HIGHER WHEELTON Lancs
94, 95 SD 6122 6m SW of Blackburn. Loc, Whltn CP.

HIGHER WHITLEY Ches
101 SJ 6180 5m S of Warrington. Loc, Whtly CP. Runcorn RD. P WRRNGTN. Ch m. Sch p. Rncn CC.

HIGHER WRAXALL Dorset
177, 178 ST 5601 8m NE of Bridport. Loc, Wrxll CP. Beaminster RD. W Dst CC.

HIGHER WYCH Ches
118 SJ 4943 3m WNW of Whitchurch. Loc, Wigland CP. Tarvin RD. Ch m. Nantwich CC.

HIGH ETHERLEY Co Durham
85 NZ 1628 3m WSW of Bishop Auckland. Loc, Ethrly CP. Barnard Cstle RD. P Bshp Aucklnd. Ch e. Bishop Auckland CC.

HIGHFIELD Co Durham
78 NZ 1458 7m WSW of Gateshead. Loc, Blaydon UD. P Rowlands Gill.

HIGHFIELDS Cambs
135 TL 3558 6m W of Cambridge. Loc, Caldecote CP.

HIGH GARRETT Essex
149 TL 7726 3m NNE of Braintree. Loc, Brntree and Bocking UD. P Brntree. Foley Hse (formerly Folly Hse), home of Samuel Courtauld, mid-19c silk manufacturer who blt Bckng and Halstead mills, qv.

HIGHGATE London
160 TQ 2887 4m NNW of Charing Cross. Loc, Camden LB, Haringey LB. St Pancras N BC, Hornsey BC. H. Ponds at E edge of Hampstead Hth. Well known cemetery (1838), burial place of Karl Marx, George Eliot, Christina Rossetti.

HIGHGATE Yorks (W)
103 SE 5819 7m NW of Thorne. Loc, Balne CP. Osgoldcross RD. P(Blne), Goole. Gle CC.

HIGH GRANGE Co Durham
85 NZ 1731 2m S of Crook. Loc, Crk and Willington UD. P Crk.

HIGH GRANTLEY Yorks (W)
91 SE 2370 5m WSW of Ripon. Loc, Grntly CP. Rpn and Pateley Br RD. P(Grntly), Rpn. Ch e, m. Sch p. Rpn CC. G. Hall, 18c mansion perhaps by Carr of York, now adult education college.

HIGH GREEN Norfolk
125 TG 1305 3m NNE of Wymondham. Loc, Gt Melton CP. Ch b.

HIGH GREEN Worcs
143 SO 8745 6m S of Worcester. Loc, Croome D'Abitot CP. P WCSTR.

HIGH GREEN Yorks (W)
102 SE 1915 3m ESE of Huddersfield. Loc, Kirkburton UD.

HIGH GREEN Yorks (W)
102 SK 3397 5m S of Barnsley. Loc, Ecclesfield CP. P SHEFFIELD. Ch m.

HIGH HALDEN Kent
172, 184 TQ 8937 2m N of Tenterden. CP, 931. Tntdn RD. P Ashford. Ch e, m. Sch pe. Ashfd CC.

HIGH HALSTOW Kent
172 TQ 7875 5m NNE of Rochester.

CP, 944. Strood RD. P Rchstr. Ch e. Sch p. Gravesend CC. Mainly indstrl. Nature reserve N of vllge.

HIGH HAM Som
165 ST 4231 7m SW of Glastonbury. CP, 633. Langport RD. P Lngpt. Ch e, m. Sch pe. Yeovil CC. See also Henley, Low Hm.

HIGH HARRINGTON Cumb
82 NY 0025 2m S of Workington. Loc, Wkngtn MB. P Wkngtn.

HIGH HARTINGTON Nthmb
77 NZ 0288 11m W of Morpeth. Loc, Rothley CP.

HIGH HATTON Shrops
118, 119 SJ 6124 7m SSW of Mkt Drayton. Loc, Stanton upon Hine Hth CP. Sch pe.

HIGH HESKET Cumb
83 NY 4744 9m SSE of Carlisle. Loc, Hskt CP. Penrith RD. Ch m. Sch pe. Pnrth and the Border CC.

HIGH HESLEDEN Co Durham
85 NZ 4538 2m SE of Peterlee. Loc, Monk Hsldn CP.

HIGH HOYLAND Yorks (W)
102 SE 2710 5m NNE of Penistone. CP, 141. Pnstne RD. P Barnsley. Ch e, m. Pnstne CC.

HIGH HUNSLEY Yorks (E)
98 SE 9535 6m SE of Weighton. Loc, Rowley CP.

HIGH HURSTWOOD Sussex (E)
183 TQ 4926 3m NNE of Uckfield. Loc, Buxted CP. P Uckfld. Ch e. Sch pe.

HIGH HUTTON Yorks (N)
92 SE 7568 3m SW of Malton. Loc, Httns Ambo CP. Mltn RD. Ch e. Thirsk and Mltn CC.

HIGH KILBURN Yorks (N)
92 SE 5179 6m ESE of Thirsk. CP(Klbn Hgh and Low), 229. Thsk RD. Thsk and Malton CC.

HIGH LANE Ches
101 SJ 9585 5m SE of Stockport. Loc, Marple UD. P Stckpt.

HIGH LANE Herefs
129, 130 SO 6760 4m NNE of Bromyard. Loc, Wolferlow CP.

HIGH LAVER Essex
161 TL 5208 4m NNW of Ongar. CP, 407. Epping and Ongr RD. P Ongr. Ch e. Brentwood and Ongr CC (Chigwell). Tablet in ch to John Locke, 17c philosopher, who lived here.

HIGHLEADON Glos
143 SO 7723 5m NW of Gloucester. Loc, Rudford CP. Ch m. Notable tithe barn.

HIGH LEGH Ches
101 SJ 7084 5m NW of Knutsford. CP, 866. Bucklow RD. P Kntsfd. Ch e. Kntsfd CC. See also Sworton Heath.

HIGHLEIGH Sussex (W)
181 SZ 8498 4m S of Chichester. Loc, Sidlesham CP.

HIGH LEVEN Yorks (N)
85 NZ 4412 4m S of Teeside (Stockton). Loc, Stokesley RD. Ch m. Richmond CC.

HIGHLEY Shrops
130 SO 7483 6m S of Bridgnorth. CP, 2,145. Brdgnth RD. P Brdgnth. Ch e, b, m, v. Sch p. Ludlow CC. See also Woodhill. Colliery vllge of brick.

HIGH LITTLETON Som
166 ST 6458 3m NW of Radstock. CP, 1,413. Clutton RD. P BRISTOL. Ch e, m. Sch pe. N Som CC. See also Hallatrow.

HIGH LORTON Cumb
82 NY 1625 4m SE of Cockermouth. Loc, Ltn CP. Cckrmth RD. Ch m. Sch p. Workington CC.

HIGH MARISHES Yorks (N)
92 SE 8178 4m S of Pickering. Loc, Mrshs CP. Pckrng RD. Scarborough CC (Scbrgh and Whitby).

HIGH MARNHAM Notts
113 SK 8070 10m W of Lincoln. Loc, Mnhm CP. E Retford RD. Bassetlaw CC.

HIGH MELTON Yorks (W)
103 SE 5001 4m W of Doncaster. CP, 261. Dncstr RD. P Dncstr. Ch e. Don Valley CC.

HIGH MICKLEY Nthmb
77, 78 NZ 0761 2m SW of Prudhoe. Loc,
Prdhoe UD.

HIGHMOOR Oxon
159 SU 7084 4m WNW of Henley. CP, 349.
Hnly RD. P(Hghmr Cross), Hnly-on-Thames.
Ch e. Hnly CC.

HIGH MOORSLEY Co Durham
85 NZ 3345 2m S of Houghton-le-Spring.
Loc, Hetton UD.

HIGHNAM Glos
143 SO 7819 3m WNW of Gloucester.
CP, 607. Glcstr RD. P GLCSTR   Ch e.
Sch pe. W Glos CC.

HIGH NEWTON Lancs
89 SD 4082 3m N of Grange-over-Sands.
Loc, Upr Allithwaite CP. N Lonsdale RD.
Sch pe. Morecambe and Lnsdle CC.

HIGH NEWTON-BY-THE-SEA Nthmb
71 NU 2325 8m NNE of Alnwick. Loc,
Ntn-by-the-Sea CP. Alnwck RD.
P(Ntn-by-the-Sea), Alnwck.
Berwick-upon-Tweed CC.

HIGH OFFLEY Staffs
119 SJ 7826 5m NNE of Newport. CP, 634.
Stafford RD. Ch e. Sch pe. Stffd and
Stone CC. See also Shebdon, Woodseaves.

HIGH ONGAR Essex
161 TL 5603 1m NE of Ongar. CP. Epping
and Ongr RD. P Ongr. Ch e, v. Sch p.
Brentwood and Ongr CC (Chigwell). See
also Nine Ashes, Norton Hth.

HIGH ONN Staffs
119 SJ 8216 5m ESE of Newport. Loc,
Ch Eaton CP.

HIGH RODING Essex
148 TL 6017 3m SSW of Dunmow. CP(Hgh
Roothing), 330. Dnmw RD. P Dnmw. Ch e.
Saffron Walden CC. One of eight Rodings,
pronounced 'roothing'.

HIGH SPEN Co Durham
78 NZ 1359 8m WSW of Gateshead. Loc,
Blaydon UD. P Rowlands Gill.

HIGHSTED Kent
172 TQ 9061 2m S of Sittingbourne. Loc,
Sttngbne and Milton UD.

HIGH STREET GREEN Suffolk (E)
149 TM 0055 3m WSW of Stowmarket.
Loc, Gt Finborough CP.

HIGHTOWN Lancs
100 SD 3003 3m S of Formby. Loc,
Crosby MB. P LIVERPOOL. Large housing
development to S.

HIGH TOYNTON Lincs (L)
114 TF 2869 1m E of Horncastle. CP, 81.
Hncstle RD. Ch e. Hncstle CC.

HIGH URPETH Co Durham
78 NZ 2354 3m NW of Chester-le-Street.
Loc, Urpth CP. Chstr-le-Strt RD.
Chstr-le-Strt CC.

HIGHWAY Wilts
157 SU 0474 4m NE of Calne. Loc,
Hilmarton CP.

HIGHWEEK Devon
176, 188 SX 8472 1m NW of Newton
Abbot. Loc, Ntn Abbt UD. P Ntn Abbt. To
S on A381, Bradley Mnr (NT)*, small 15c
mnr hse in valley of R Lemon.

HIGH WESTWOOD Co Durham
77, 78 NZ 1155 3m NNE of Consett. Loc,
Cnstt UD. P(Wstwd), NEWCASTLE UPON
TYNE.

HIGH WORSALL Yorks (N)
85 NZ 3809 7m SSW of Teesside(Stockton).
CP, 57. Stokesley RD. Richmond CC.

HIGHWORTH Wilts
157 SU 2092 6m NNE of Swindon.
CP, 3,451. Hghwth RD. P Swndn.
Ch e, m2, r, v. Sch p, s.   Devizes CC. See
also Sevenhampton. 17c and 18c stone hses.
Carpet factory.

HIGH WRAY Lancs
88, 89 NY 3700 3m S of Ambleside. Loc,
Claife CP. N Lonsdale RD. Morecambe and
Lnsdle CC. Above W shore of Lake,
Windermere.

HIGH WYCH Herts
148, 161 TL 4614 3m N of Harlow.
CP, 625. Braughing RD. P Sawbridgeworth.
Ch e. Sch pe. E Herts CC.

HIGH WYCOMBE Bucks
159 SU 8692 28m WNW of London.
MB, 59,298. P. Wcmbe CC. Indstrl tn noted

for furniture mnftre. 2m WNW, W Wcmbe Pk (NT)*, 18c hse in ornamental pk. Golden ball on twr of W Wcmbe ch said to have seating for eight.

HILBOROUGH Norfolk
136 TF 8200 5m S of Swaffham. CP, 219. Swffhm RD. P Thetford. Ch e. Sch pe. SW Nflk CC. See also Bodney.

HILDENBOROUGH Kent
171 TQ 5648 2m NW of Tonbridge. CP, 5,012. Tnbrdge RD. P Tnbrdge. Ch e, v. Sch p2, pe. Tnbrdge and Malling CC (Tnbrdge).

HILDERSHAM Cambs
148 TL 5448 6m N of Saffron Walden. CP, 165. S Cambs RD. Ch e. Cambs CC. Ch has outstanding 14c brass.

HILDERSTONE Staffs
110, 119 SJ 9434 3m E of Stone. CP, 364. Stne RD. P Stne. Ch e, m. Sch pe. Stafford and Stne CC.

HILDERTHORPE Yorks (E)
93 TA 1765 just S of Bridlington. Loc, Brdlngtn MB.

HILFIELD Dorset
178 ST 6305 7m S of Sherborne. CP, 76. Shbne RD. Ch e. W Dst CC.

HILGAY Norfolk
135 TL 6298 3m S of Downham Mkt. CP, 1,343. Dnhm RD. P Dnhm Mkt. Ch e, m2. Sch p, pe. SW Nflk CC. See also Ten Mile Bank.

HILL Glos
155, 156 ST 6495 6m NE of Severn Rd Br. CP, 120. Thornbury RD. Ch e. S Glos CC.

HILLAM Yorks (W)
97 SE 5028 5m ENE of Castleford. CP, 284. Osgoldcross RD. P LEEDS. Ch m. Goole CC.

HILLBECK Westm
84 NY 7915 just N of Brough. CP, 26. N Westm RD. Westm CC.

HILLBOROUGH Kent
173 TR 2168 2m E of Herne Bay. Loc, Hne Bay UD.

HILLBROW Sussex (W)
181 SU 7926 3m NE of Petersfield. Loc, Rogate CP.

HILLBUTTS Dorset
179 ST 9901 1m WNW of Wimborne. Loc, Pamphill CP. P Wmbne.

HILL CHORLTON Staffs
110, 119 SJ 7939 5m SW of Newcastle-under-Lyme. CP(Chpl and Hll Chltn), 455. Ncstle-undr-Lyme RD. Ch m. N-u-L BC.

HILL COTTAGES Yorks (N)
86, 92 SE 7097 10m NW of Pickering. Loc, Rosedale E Side CP. Pckrng RD. P(Rsdle E), Rsdle Abbey, Pckrng. Scarborough CC (Thirsk and Malton).

HILL CROOME Worcs
143, 144 SO 8840 5m N of Tewkesbury. CP, 171. Upton upon Severn RD. Ch e. S Worcs CC.

HILL DYKE Lincs (H) and (L)
114 TF 3547 3m NNE of Boston. Loc, Bstn RD. Spilsby RD. Holland w Bstn CC, Horncastle CC.

HILL END Co Durham
84 NZ 0136 7m WSW of Tow Law. Loc, Stanhope CP.

HILLESDEN Bucks
146 SP 6828 3m S of Buckingham. CP, 199. Bcknghm RD. P BCKNGHM. Ch e. Sch pe. Bcknghm CC.

HILLESLEY Glos
156 ST 7689 8m WSW of Tetbury. Loc, Hawkesbury CP. P Wotton-under-Edge. Ch e, b. Sch pe.

HILLFARANCE Som
164 ST 1624 3m W of Taunton. Loc, Oake CP. P Tntn. Ch e.

HILL HEAD Hants
180 SU 5402 3m SW of Fareham. Loc, Frhm UD. P Frhm.

HILLIARD'S CROSS Staffs
120 SK 1412 3m NE of Lichfield. Loc, Alrewas CP.

HILLINGDON London
160 TQ 0782 14m W of Charing Cross.
LB, 234,718. P Middx. BCs: Hayes and
Harlington, Ruislip-Northwood, Uxbridge.
(Uxbridge CC, Hayes and Hlngtn BC,
Rslp-Nthwd BC.) See also Cowley,
Harefield, Hlngtn, Harmondsworth, Hayes,
Heathrow, Ickenham, Longford, Nthwd,
Rslp, Rslp Cmmn, Sipson, Uxbrdge,
W Drayton, Yiewsley.

HILLINGTON Norfolk
124 TF 7125 7m ENE of King's Lynn.
CP, 236. Freebridge Lynn RD. P K's Lnn.
Ch e. Sch p. NW Nflk CC (K's Lnn).

HILL RIDWARE Staffs
120 SK 0817 2m E of Rugeley. Loc,
Mavesyn Rdwre CP. P Rgly. Sch p.

HILL ROW Cambs
135 TL 4575 6m WSW of Ely. Loc,
Haddenham CP.

HILLS TOWN Derbys
112 SK 4769 just SE of Bolsover. Loc,
B l s v r U D , B l a c k w e l l R D .
P Blsvr, Chesterfield.

HILL, THE Cumb
88 SD 1783 2m N of Millom. Loc, Mllm
W i t h o u t C P . M l l m R D . Ch e.
Whitehaven CC.

HILL TOP Hants
180 SU 4003 4m W of Fawley. Loc, New
Forest RD. Nw Frst CC.

HILMARTON Wilts
157 SU 0175 3m NNE of Calne. CP, 743.
Clne and Chippenham RD. P Clne. Ch e.
Sch p. Chppnhm CC. See also Clevancy,
Goatacre, Highway.

HILPERTON Wilts
166 ST 8759 1m NE of Trowbridge.
CP, 1,170. Bradford and Melksham RD.
P Trwbrdge. Ch e, b, m. Sch pe.
Westbury CC.

HILPERTON MARSH Wilts
166 ST 8659 1m NE of Trowbridge. Loc,
Hlptn CP. P Trwbrdge.

HILSTON Yorks (E)
99 TA 2833 5m NW of Withernsea. Loc,
Roos CP. Ch e. On hill to NW, Storr's Twr,
18c landmark for sailors.

HILTON Co Durham
85 NZ 1621 5m SSW of Bishop Auckland.
CP, 79. Barnard Cstle RD. Bshp
Aucklnd CC.

HILTON Derbys
120 SK 2430 4m N of Burton-on-Trent.
CP, 968. Repton RD. P DERBY. Ch m.
Sch p. Belper CC.

HILTON Dorset
178 ST 7803 7m WSW of Blandford.
CP, 371. Blndfd RD. P Blndfd Forum. Ch e.
Sch pe. N Dst CC. See also Hr Anstey,
Lit Anstey, Lr Anstey, Anstey Cross.

HILTON Hunts
134 TL 2866 5m SE of Huntingdon.
CP, 318. St Ives RD. P HNTNGDN. Ch e, m.
Hunts CC. 17c turf maze.

HILTON Shrops
130 SO 7795 4m ENE of Bridgnorth. Loc,
Worfield CP. P Brdgnth.

HILTON Westm
84 NY 7320 3m E of Appleby. Loc,
Murton CP. P Appleby. Ch e, m.

HILTON Yorks (N)
85 NZ 4611 5m S of Teesside (Stockton).
CP, 118. Stokesley RD. P Yarm. Ch e.
Richmond CC.

HIMBLETON Worcs
130, 131 SO 9458 4m SE of Droitwich.
CP, 287. Drtwch RD. P Drtwch. Ch e.
Sch pe. Worcester BC.

HIMLEY Staffs
130 SO 8791 4m W of Dudley. CP.
Seisdon RD. Ch e. See also Gospel End.
SW Staffs CC (Brierley Hill CC, Bilston BC).
To SE, Holbeche Hse, last refuge of
Gunpowder Plot conspirators. To NE, H.
Hall, 18c—19c mansion, now a college, in
large pk*.

HINCASTER Westm
89 SD 5184 5m S of Kendal. CP, 130.
S Westm RD. Westm CC.

HINCKLEY Leics
132 SP 4293 4m ENE of Nuneaton.
UD, 47,982. P. Bosworth CC. See also
Barwell, Burbage, Earl Shilton, Stoke
Golding. A centre of hosiery industry. First
stocking-frame in Leics installed here in
1640.

HINDERCLAY Suffolk (W)
136 TM 0276 6m WSW of Diss. CP, 195.
Thedwastre RD. P Dss, Norfolk. Ch e, m.
Bury St Edmunds CC.

HINDERWELL Yorks (N)
86 NZ 7916 5m ESE of Loftus. CP, 2,412.
Whitby RD. P Saltburn-by-the-Sea. Ch e, m.
Sch p. Cleveland and Whtby CC
(Scarborough and Whtby). See also Port
Mulgrave, Runswick, Staithes. Resort.

HINDFORD Shrops
118 SJ 3333 4m NE of Oswestry. Loc,
Whittington CP.

HINDHEAD Surrey
169 SU 8835 2m NNW of Haslemere. Loc,
Hslmre UD. P. At over 800ft among hths
and wds. Much NT property in area, esp
Gibbet Hill and Devil's Punchbowl to E.

HINDLEY Lancs
101 SD 6104 2m ESE of Wigan.
UD, 24,307. P Wgn. Westhoughton CC. See
also Hndly Grn. Coal-mining, rubber-mnfg.

HINDLEY GREEN Lancs
101 SD 6403 4m ESE of Wigan. Loc,
Hndly UD. P Wgn. Asbestos factory.

HINDLIP Worcs
130 SO 8758 3m NE of Worcester. CP, 268.
Droitwich RD. Ch e. Sch pe. Worcester BC.

HINDOLVESTON Norfolk
125 TG 0329 6m SSW of Holt. CP, 396.
Walsingham RD. P Dereham. Ch e, m. Sch p.
NW Nflk CC (N Nflk).

HINDON Wilts
166, 167 ST 9132 7m NNE of Shaftesbury.
CP, 514. Mere and Tisbury RD. P Salisbury.
Ch e, c, m. Sch pe. Westbury CC.

HINDRINGHAM Norfolk
125 TF 9836 6m NE of Fakenham.
CP, 530. Walsingham RD. P Fknhm.
Ch e, m. Sch pe. NW Nflk CC (N,Nflk). See
also Lr Grn. 16c moated hall.

HINGHAM Norfolk
125/136 TG 0202 6m W of Wymondham.
CP, 1,388. Forehoe and Henstead RD.
P NORWICH, NOR 23X. Ch e, m, v2. Sch p.
S Nflk CC (Central Nflk). Many attractive
18c hses.

HINSTOCK Shrops
119 SJ 6926 5m SSE of Mkt Drayton.
CP, 691. Mkt Drtn RD. P Mkt Drtn.
Ch e, m. Sch p. Oswestry CC. See also
Lockleywood.

HINTLESHAM Suffolk (E)
149 TM 0843 4m E of Hadleigh. CP, 464.
Samford RD. P Ipswich. Ch e, m. Sch pe.
Sudbury and Woodbridge CC. Hall*, Elizn
and later; annual Festival of the Arts.

HINTON Glos
156 SO 6803 6m NW of Dursley. CP, 1,818.
Thornbury RD. S Glos CC. See also
Newtown, Purton, Sharpness.

HINTON Glos
156 ST 7376 7m N of Bath. CP(Dyrham
and Hntn), 238. Sodbury RD. Ch v.
S Glos CC.

HINTON Hants
179 SZ 2095 4m ENE of Christchurch. Loc,
Chrstchch E CP. Ringwood and
Fordingbridge RD. P Chrstchch. Ch e. New
Forest CC.

HINTON Northants
145 SP 5352 7m SSW of Daventry. Loc,
Woodford cum Membris CP. Dvntry RD.
Ch m. Dvntry CC (S Nthnts).

HINTON AMPNER Hants
168 SU 5927 7m E of Winchester. Loc,
Bramdean CP. Ch e. Sch pe.

HINTON BLEWETT Som
165, 166 ST 5956 8m NNE of Wells.
CP, 180. Clutton RD. Ch e. N Som CC. See
also S Widcombe.

HINTON CHARTERHOUSE Som
166 ST 7758 4m SSE of Bath. CP, 440.
Bathavon RD. P Bth. Ch e. Sch pe.
N Som CC. To NE, rems of Carthusian
priory*, founded 1232 and second oldest in
England. (Witham, Som, founded 1178.)

HINTON, GREAT Wilts
166, 167 ST 9059 3m WNW of Trowbridge.
See Gt Hntn.

HINTON-IN-THE-HEDGES Northants
145, 146 SP 5536 1m W of Brackley.
CP, 93. Brckly RD. Ch e. Daventry CC
(S Nthnts).

HINTON MARSH Hants
168 SU 5827 7m E of Winchester. Loc,
Wnchstr RD. Wnchstr CC.

HINTON MARTELL Dorset
179 SU 0106 4m N of Wimborne. CP, 300.
Wmbne and Cranborne RD. P Wmbne. Ch e.
Sch pe. N Dst CC.

HINTON ON THE GREEN Worcs
144 SP 0240 2m SSW of Evesham. CP, 268.
Eveshm RD. P Eveshm. Ch e. S Worcs CC.

HINTON PARVA Dorset
179 SU 0004 3m N of Wimborne. CP, 69.
Wmbne and Cranborne RD. Ch e. N Dst CC.

HINTON PARVA Wilts
157 SU 2383 5m E of Swindon. Loc,
Bishopstone CP. P Swndn. Ch e.

HINTON ST GEORGE Som
177 ST 4212 2m NW of Crewkerne.
CP, 417. Chard RD. P. Ch e, v. Sch pe.
Yeovil CC. Stone vllge. Ch: Poulett family
monmts and vast pew.

HINTON ST MARY Dorset
178 ST 7816 9m NW of Blandford. CP, 192.
Sturminster RD. P Stmnstr Newton. Ch e.
N Dst CC. Roman mosaic floor
discovered, 1963.

HINTON WALDRIST Berks
158 SU 3798 6m ENE of Faringdon.
CP, 232. Frngdn RD. P Frngdn. Ch e.
Abingdon CC. Moated mnr hse.

HINTS Staffs
120 SK 1503 3m W of Tamworth.
CP, 325. Lichfield RD. P Tmwth. Ch e.
Lchfld and Tmwth CC.

HINWICK Beds
133 SP 9361 4m SSW of Rushden. Loc,
Podington CP. H. Hall*, early 18c hse in pk.

HINXHILL Kent
172, 173, 184 TR 0442 2m E of Ashford.
CP, 43. E Ashfd RD. Ch e. Ashfd CC.

HINXTON Cambs
148 TL 4945 5m NNW of Saffron Walden.
CP, 282. S Cambs RD. P Sffrn Wldn, Essex.
Ch e, v. Cambs CC.

HINXWORTH Herts
147 TL 2340 4m SE of Biggleswade.

CP, 241. Hitchin RD. P Baldock. Ch e, m.
Htchn CC.

HIPPERHOLME Yorks (W)
96, 102 SE 1225 2m E of Halifax. Loc,
Brighouse MB. P Hlfx.

HIPSWELL Yorks (N)
91 SE 1898 2m SSE of Richmond.
CP, 4,271. Rchmnd RD. Ch e. Sch pe.
Rchmnd CC.

HIRST Nthmb
78 NZ 2887 5m E of Morpeth. Loc,
Ashington UD.

HIRST COURTNEY Yorks (W)
97, 98 SE 6124 5m S of Selby. CP, 146.
Slby RD. P Slby. Sch p. Barkston Ash CC.

HISCOTT Devon
163 SS 5426 4m S of Barnstaple. Loc,
Tawstock CP. Ch b, m.

HISTON Cambs
135 TL 4363 3m N of Cambridge.
CP, 3,258. Chesterton RD. P CMBRDGE.
Ch e2, b, m, s2. Sch j. Cambs CC. Hexagonal
smock mill.

HITCHAM Suffolk (W)
149 TL 9851 4m ENE of Lavenham.
CP, 579. Cosford RD. P Ipswich. Ch e.
Sch pe. Sudbury and Woodbridge CC. See
also Cross Grn.

HITCHIN Herts
147 TL 1829 8m NE of Luton. UD, 28,680.
P. Htchn CC. Old mkt tn of pleasing aspect.

HITHER GREEN London
161, 171 TQ 3874 5m SE of Lndn Br. Loc,
Lewisham LB. Lwshm E BC (Lwshm N).

HITTISLEIGH Devon
175 SX 7395 6m NNW of
Moretonhampstead. CP, 111. Crediton RD.
Ch e, m. Tiverton CC (Torrington).

HIVE Yorks (E)
98 SE 8231 7m NE of Goole. Loc,
Gilberdyke CP.

HIXON Staffs
120 SK 0025 5m ENE of Stafford. Loc,
Stowe CP. P STFFD. Ch e, m. Sch pe, s.

HOADEN Kent
173 TR 2659 4m WNW of Sandwich. Loc,
Ash CP.

HOAR CROSS Staffs
120 SK 1323 7m W of Burton-on-Trent.
Loc, Tutbury RD, Uttoxeter RD.
P Btn-on-Trnt. Ch e. Sch pe. Btn CC. Ch,
19c, by G.F. Bodley, to W near H. Hse.

HOARWITHY Herefs
142 SO 5429 5m NW of Ross-on-Wye. Loc,
Hentland CP. Rss and Whitchurch RD.
P HEREFORD. Ch e, v. Hrfd CC. Vctrn
Italianate ch.

HOATH Kent
173 TR 2064 3m SE of Herne Bay. CP, 323.
Bridge-Blean RD. P Canterbury. Ch e. Sch p.
Cntrbry CC. Mining area.

HOBSON Co Durham
78 NZ 1755 7m SW of Gateshead. Loc,
Stanley UD. P NEWCASTLE UPON TYNE.

HOBY Leics
121, 122 SK 6617 5m WSW of Melton
Mowbray. CP(Hby w Rotherby), 585. Mltn
and Belvoir RD. P Mltn Mbry. Ch e, m.
Sch pe. Mltn CC. See also Brooksby,
Ragdale.

HOCKERING Norfolk
125 TG 0713 5m E of E Dereham. CP, 345.
Mitford and Launditch RD. P Drhm.
Ch e, m. Sch pe. SW Nflk CC.

HOCKERTON Notts
112 SK 7156 5m WNW of Newark. CP, 94.
Southwell RD. Ch e. Nwk CC.

HOCKHAM, GREAT Norfolk
136 TL 9592 6m WSW of Attleborough. See
Gt Hckhm.

HOCKLEY Essex
162 TQ 8492 5m NNW of Southend. CP.
Rochford RD. P. Ch e, c, m, v. Sch p2, s.
Malden CC (SE Essx).

HOCKLEY Staffs
120 SK 2200 3m SSE of Tamworth. Loc,
Tmwth MB. P Tmwth. Lichfield and
Tmwth CC (Meriden).

HOCKLEY HEATH Warwicks
131 SP 1572 4m S of Solihull. CP.
Stratford-on-Avon RD. Ch e. Sch p.

Strtfd-on-Avn CC (Slhll). See also
Whitlock's End. To E, Packwood Hse
(NT)*, 16c–17c; 17c yew gdn.

HOCKLIFFE Beds
147 SP 9726 3m E of Leighton Buzzard.
CP, 497. Luton RD. P Lghtn Bzzd. Ch e, v.
Sch pe. S Beds CC. On Roman Watling
Street(A5). H. Hse is Ggn.

HOCKWOLD CUM WILTON Norfolk
135 TL 7388 4m WNW of Brandon.
CP, 848. Downham RD.
P(Hckwld), Thetford. Ch e2, m. Sch p.
SW Nflk CC.

HOCKWORTHY Devon
164 ST 0319 6m W of Wellington.
CP, 192. Tiverton RD. Ch e. Tvtn CC.

HODDESDON Herts
161 TL 3709 4m N of Cheshunt.
UD, 26,071. P. E Herts CC. See also
Broxbourne, Hailey, Wormley. 1m NE,
gatehouse of Rye Hse, famous for plot to
kill Charles II, 1683. Nearby, power stn.

HODDLESDEN Lancs
95 SD 7122 4m SSE of Blackburn. Loc,
Darwen MB. P Dwn.

HODNET Shrops
118, 119 SJ 6128 5m SW of Mkt Drayton.
CP, 1,578. Mkt Drtn RD. P Mkt Drtn.
Ch e, r. Sch p. Oswestry CC. See also
Hopton, Marchamley, Peplow, Wollerton.
Landscape gdns* of Hdnt Hall. Living held
early 19c by Reginald Heber, writer of
well-known hymns; see also Malpas, Ches.

HODSOCK Notts
103 SK 6185 4m NNE of Worksop.
CP, 3,326. Wksp RD. Bassetlaw CC. See also
Langold. Hdsck Priory, moated hse with 16c
gatehouse; gdn*.

HODTHORPE Derbys
103 SK 5476 3m WSW of Worksop. Loc,
Whitwell CP. P Wksp. Sch p.

HOE Norfolk
125 TF 9916 2m N of E Dereham. CP, 253.
Mitford and Launditch RD. Ch e.
SW Nflk CC. See also Worthing.

HOE GATE Hants
180 SU 6213 5m NE of Fareham. Loc,
Soberton CP.

HOFF Westm
83 NY 6717 2m SSW of Appleby. CP, 189. N Westm RD. Ch m. Westm CC. See also Drybeck.

HOGGARD'S GREEN Suffolk (W)
149 TL 8856 5m NNW of Lavenham. Loc, Stanningfield CP.

HOGGESTON Bucks
146 SP 8025 7m W of Linslade. CP, 81. Winslow RD. P Bletchley. Ch e. Buckingham CC.

HOGHTON Lancs
94, 95 SD 6125 4m WSW of Blackburn. CP, 768. Chorley RD. P Preston. Ch e, m. Sch pe. Chly CC. See also Hghtn Bottoms, Riley Grn. On hill to ENE, H. Twr, 16c–17c hse.

HOGHTON BOTTOMS Lancs
94, 95 SD 6227 4m W of Blackburn. Loc, Hghtn CP.

HOGNASTON Derbys
111 SK 2350 4m NE of Ashbourne. CP, 220. Ashbne RD. P Ashbne. Ch e, c, m. Sch pe. W Derbys CC. Ch: unusual carvings on tympanum of Nmn doorway.

HOGSTHORPE Lincs (L)
114 TF 5372 5m ESE of Alford. CP, 494. Spilsby RD. P Skegness. Ch e, m. Sch p. Horncastle CC.

HOLBEACH Lincs (H)
124 TF 3524 7m E of Spalding. CP, 6,620. E Elloe RD. P Spldng. Ch e, b, bc, m, r, v2. Sch ie, j, p, pe, s. Holland w Boston CC.

HOLBEACH BANK Lincs (H)
124 TF 3527 2m N of Holbeach. Loc, Hlbch CP. Ch m. Sch p.

HOLBEACH DROVE Lincs (H)
123 TF 3212 8m SE of Spalding. Loc, Hlbch CP. Ch m.

HOLBEACH HURN Lincs (H)
124 TF 3927 3m ENE of Holbeach. Loc, Hlbch CP. P Spalding. Ch e.

HOLBEACH ST JOHNS Lincs (H)
123 TF 3418 4m S of Holbeach. Loc, Hlbch CP. P Spalding. Ch e, m.

HOLBEACH ST MARKS Lincs (H)
114, 124 TF 3731 4m N of Holbeach. Loc, Hlbch CP. P Spalding. Ch e.

HOLBEACH ST MATTHEW Lincs (H)
114, 124 TF 4132 6m NE of Holbeach. Loc, Hlbch CP. Ch e.

HOLBECK Notts
112 SK 5473 5m SSW of Worksop. CP, 285. Wksp RD. P Wksp. Bassetlaw CC.

HOLBERROW GREEN Worcs
131 SP 0259 4m WNW of Alcester. Loc, Inkberrow CP. P Redditch.

HOLBETON Devon
187, 188 SX 6150 4m SSW of Ivybridge. CP, 598. Plympton St Mary RD. P Plymouth. Ch e, m. Sch p. W Dvn CC (Tavistock). See also Battisborough Cross, Mothecombe.

HOLBORN London
160 TQ 3081 just NNE of Charing Cross. Loc, Camden LB. Hlbn and St Pancras S BC. Lincoln's Inn and Gray's Inn are Inns of Court. Sir John Soane's Museum (High H.).

HOLBROOK Derbys
120, 121 SK 3644 5m N of Derby. CP, 1,386. Belper RD. P DBY. Ch e, m. Sch pe. Blpr CC.

HOLBROOK Suffolk (E)
150 TM 1636 5m S of Ipswich. CP, 1,083. Samford RD. P Ipswch. Ch e, m. Sch p, s. Sudbury and Woodbridge CC. Royal Hsptl Sch for sons of Royal Navy and Royal Marines personnel, moved from Greenwich 1933.

HOLBURN Nthmb
64, 71 NU 0436 4m WNW of Belford. Loc, Lowick CP.

HOLBURY Hants
180 SU 4303 1m W of Fawley. Loc, Fwly CP. P SOUTHAMPTON. Ch r. Sch p.

HOLCOMBE Devon
176, 188 SX 9574 6m ENE of Newton Abbot. Loc, Dawlish UD. P Dlsh.

HOLCOMBE Lancs
95, 101 SD 7816 4m NNW of Bury. Loc, Ramsbottom UD. P Bury.

HOLCOMBE Som
166 ST 6749 3m SSW of Radstock.
CP, 586. Shepton Mallet RD. P Bath.
Ch e2, m, r. Sch im. Wells CC.

HOLCOMBE BURNELL Devon
176 SX 8591 4m W of Exeter. CP, 180.
St Thomas RD. Ch e. Tiverton CC.

HOLCOMBE ROGUS Devon
164 ST 0518 5m WSW of Wellington.
CP, 483. Tiverton RD. P Wllngtn, Som.
Ch e, b. Sch pe. Tvtn CC. At top of hill with
ch, H. Court, 16c mnr hse with gatehouse.

HOLCOT Northants
133 SP 7969 6m NNE of Northampton.
CP, 309. Brixworth RD. P NTHMPTN.
Ch e, m. Daventry CC (Kettering). On shore
of Pitsford Reservoir.

HOLDEN Yorks (W)
95 SD 7749 5m NNE of Clitheroe. Loc,
Bolton by Bowland CP.

HOLDENBY Northants
133 SP 6967 6m NW of Northampton.
CP, 110. Brixworth RD. P NTHMPTN. Ch e.
Daventry CC (Kettering). Gateways dated
1583 remain from former H. Hall. Charles I
imprisoned here, 1647.

HOLDGATE Shrops
129 SO 5689 7m ESE of Ch Stretton. Loc,
Tugford CP. Ch e.

HOLDINGHAM Lincs (K)
113 TF 0547 1m NNW of Sleaford. Loc,
Slfd UD.

HOLE-IN-THE-WALL Herefs
142, 143 SO 6128 3m N of Ross-on-Wye.
Loc, Foy CP.

HOLFORD Som
164 ST 1541 6m ESE of Watchet. CP, 279.
Williton RD. P Bridgwater. Ch e.
Brdgwtr CC. See also Dodington.

HOLKER Lancs
88, 89 SD 3677 3m W of
Grange-over-Sands. Loc, Lr Hlkr CP.
N Lonsdale RD. Morecambe and Lnsdle CC.
To W, H. Hall, mainly Vctrn; on knoll in the
large pk, an ice house.

HOLKHAM Norfolk
125 TF 8943 2m W of Wells. CP, 327.
Walsingham RD. P Wlls-next-the-Sea. Ch e.
NW Nflk CC (N Nflk). H. Hall*, Palladian
hse by Kent, blt 1734, in landscaped grnds
with lake. Seat of Earls of Leicester. Home
of 'Coke of Norfolk', early 19c agricultural
reformer.

HOLLACOMBE Devon
174 SS 3703 2m E of Holsworthy. CP, 63.
Hlswthy RD. Ch e. W Dvn CC (Tavistock).

HOLLAND Surrey
171 TQ 4050 1m SE of Oxted. Loc,
Oxtd CP. P Oxtd.

HOLLAND FEN Lincs (H)
114 TF 2349 7m NW of Boston. Loc,
Bstn RD. P LINCOLN. Ch e, m. Hllnd
w Bstn CC.

HOLLAND, GREAT Essex
150 TM 2119 4m NE of Clacton. See Gt
Hllnd.

HOLLAND-ON-SEA Essex
150 TM 2016 2m ENE of Clacton. Loc,
Clctn UD. P Clctn-on-Sea.

HOLLESLEY Suffolk (E)
150 TM 3544 6m SE of Woodbridge.
CP, 1,319. Deben RD. P Wdbrdge. Ch e, v.
Sch p. Sudbury and Wdbrdge CC. Marshes.
Borstal institution.

HOLLINGBOURNE Kent
172 TQ 8455 5m E of Maidstone. CP, 912.
Hollingbourn RD. P Mdstne. Ch e. Sch p.
Mdstne CC. See also Broad St, Eyhorne St.
On edge of N Downs. Tdr mnr hse. Monmts
in ch to Culpeppers, 17c.

HOLLINGTON Derbys
120 SK 2239 5m SE of Ashbourne.
CP, 164. Ashbne RD. P DERBY. Ch m.
W Derbys CC.

HOLLINGTON Staffs
120 SK 0538 4m NW of Uttoxeter. Loc,
Checkley CP. P Stoke-on-Trent. Ch e.
Sch pe.

HOLLINGWORTH Ches
102 SK 0096 2m NW of Glossop. Loc,
Longdendale UD. P Hyde. Stalybridge and
Hde CC.

HOLLINSCLOUGH Staffs
111 SK 0666 4m S of Buxton. CP, 170.

Hollins Green

Leek RD. Ch e, m. Sch pe. Lk CC. At nearly 1,000ft in Peak Distr National Pk.

HOLLINS GREEN Lancs
101 SJ 6991 6m ENE of Warrington. Loc, Rixton-w-Glazebrook CP. Wrrngtn RD. Ch e. Sch pe. Newton CC.

HOLLINS LANE Lancs
94 SD 4951 7m S of Lancaster. Loc, Forton CP.

HOLLINSWOOD Shrops
119 SJ 6909 1m SSW of Oakengates. Loc, Dawley UD. The Wrekin CC.

HOLLOCOMBE Devon
163, 175 SS 6311 10m ESE of Torrington. Loc, Winkleigh CP. P Chulmleigh. Ch c.

HOLLOWAY Derbys
111 SK 3256 3m SE of Matlock. CP(Dethick Lea and Holloway), 1,077. Belper RD. P Mtlck. Ch e, m. Blpr CC.

HOLLOWAY London
160 TQ 3086 4m N of Charing Cross. Loc, Islington LB. Islngtn N BC (Islngtn N, Islngtn SW). Women's prison, blt mid-19c.

HOLLOWELL Northants
133 SP 6872 8m NNW of Northampton. CP, 348. Brixworth RD. Ch e. Daventry CC (Kettering). See also Teeton.

HOLLYBUSH Worcs
143 SO 7636 3m E of Ledbury. Loc, Castlemorton CP. P Ldbry, Herefordshire. Ch e.

HOLLY END Norfolk
124 TF 4906 3m SE of Wisbech. Loc, Emneth CP.

HOLLYM Yorks (E)
99 TA 3425 2m S of Withernsea. CP, 443. Holderness RD. P Wthnsea. Ch e, m. Bridlington CC.

HOLMACOTT Devon
163 SS 5028 4m NE of Bideford. Loc, Fremington CP. Ch m.

HOLMBRIDGE Yorks (W)
102 SE 1206 6m SSW of Huddersfield. Loc, Holmfirth UD. P Hlmfth, Hddsfld.

HOLMBURY ST MARY Surrey
170, 182 TQ 1144 5m SW of Dorking. Loc, Dkng and Horley RD, Guildford RD. P Dkng. Ch e. Sch pe. Dkng CC. Among wooded hills. Ch blt in memory of his wife, at his own expense, by G.E. Street, 1879.

HOLMBUSH Cornwall
185, 186, 190 SX 0352 2m E of St Austell. Loc, St Astll w Fowey MB. P St Astll. Truro CC.

HOLME Hunts
134 TL 1887 7m · S of Peterborough. CP, 491. Norman Cross RD. P PTRBRGH. Ch e, m. Sch pe. Hunts CC. Fenside vllge.

HOLME Lincs (L)
104 SE 9206 3m SE of Scunthorpe. CP, 153. Glanford Brigg RD. Brgg and Scnthpe CC (Brgg).

HOLME Notts
113 SK 8059 3m N of Newark. CP, 87. Nwk RD. Ch e. Nwk CC. Notable early Tdr ch.

HOLME Westm
89 SD 5278 5m NNE of Carnforth. CP, 627. S Westm RD. P Cnfth, Lancs. Ch e, m, r. Sch p. Westm CC. M6 motorway passes to E of vllge.

HOLME Yorks (N)
91 SE 3582 5m W of Thirsk. CP, 49. Thsk RD. Thsk and Malton CC.

HOLME Yorks (W)
102 SE 1005 7m SSW of Huddersfield. Loc, Homfirth UD. P Hddsfld.

HOLME CHAPEL Lancs
95 SD 8728 3m SE of Burnley. Loc, Cliviger CP. Bnly RD. Ch e. Sch pe. Clitheroe CC.

HOLME HALE Norfolk
125 TF 8807 4m E of Swaffham. CP, 374. Swffhm RD. P Thetford. Ch e, m. Sch pe. SW Nflk CC.

HOLME LACY Herefs
142 SO 5535 4m SE of Hereford. CP, 457. Hrfd RD. P HRFD. Ch e. Sch p. Hrfd CC. Ch full of monmts to Scudamore family, who owned H.L. Hse, 17c mansion enlarged 19c, now mental hsptl.

HOLME MARSH Herefs
142 SO 3454 3m ESE of Kington. Loc,
Lyonshall CP.

HOLME NEXT THE SEA Norfolk
124 TF 7043 3m NE of Hunstanton.
CP, 415. Docking RD. P(Hlme), King's
Lynn. Ch e, m. Sch p. NW Nflk CC (K's
Lnn). Caravans. Hnstntn GC.

HOLME ON THE WOLDS Yorks (E)
98 SE 9646 6m ENE of Mkt Weighton. Loc,
Dalton Hlme CP. Beverley RD.
Haltemprice CC.

HOLME PIERREPONT Notts
112, 121, 122 SK 6239 3m E of
Nottingham. CP, 495. Bingham RD. Ch e.
Sch pe. Rushcliffe CC (Carlton). See also
Bassingfield.

HOLMER Herefs
142 SO 5042 2m N of Hereford. CP, 954.
Hrfd RD. P HRFD. Ch e, m, v. See also
Shelwick. Leominster CC. 12c–13c ch has
detached twr with timber belfry.

HOLMER GREEN Bucks
159 SU 9096 4m W of Amersham. Loc, Lit
Missenden CP. P High Wycombe. Ch e, b.
Sch i, j, s.

HOLME ST CUTHBERT Cumb
82 NY 1047 4m S of Silloth. CP, 446.
Wigton RD. Ch e, m. Sch p. Penrith and the
Border CC. See also Beckfoot, Edderside,
Mawbray, Newtown.

HOLMES CHAPEL Ches
110 SJ 7667 4m E of Middlewich. Loc,
Church Hulme CP. Congleton RD. P Crewe.
Ch e, m2. Sch p. Knutsford CC. Huge rly
viaduct carries Crewe-Manchester line over
R Dane.

HOLMESFIELD Derbys
111 SK 3277 6m NW of Chesterfield.
CP, 1,003. Chstrfld RD. P SHEFFIELD.
Ch e. Sch p. NE Derbys CC.

HOLMESWOOD Lancs
100 SD 4316 6m E of Southport. Loc,
Rufford CP. P Ormskirk. Ch m. Sch pm.

HOLME UPON SPALDING MOOR Yorks
(E)
98 SE 8138 5m WSW of Mkt Weighton.

CP, 1,671. Howden RD. P YORK.
Ch e, m2, r. Sch p. Hdn CC. See also Bursea.
Fine 15c ch with tall twr.

HOLMEWOOD Derbys
112 SK 4365 4m SE of Chesterfield. Loc,
Chstrfld RD. P Chstrfld. Ch m, s2, v.
NE Derbys CC.

HOLMFIRTH Yorks (W)
102 SE 1408 5m S of Huddersfield.
UD, 19,319. P Hddsfld. Colne Valley CC.
See also Brockholes, Hepworth,
Holmbridge, Holme, Honley, Netherthong,
New Mill, Scholes, Thongsbridge,
Upperthong, Wooldale. Wool textile tn.

HOLMPTON Yorks (E)
99 TA 3623 3m SSE of Withernsea.
CP, 209. Holderness RD. P Wthnsea.
Ch e, m. Bridlington CC.

HOLMROOK Cumb
88 SD 0799 3m ESE of Seacale. Loc,
Millom RD. P. Whitehaven CC.

HOLNE Devon
187, 188 SX 7069 3m W of Ashburton.
CP, 348. Totnes RD. P Ntn Abbt. Ch e.
Ttns CC. Moorland vllge above R Dart;
bthplce of Charles Kingsley, 1819.

HOLNEST Dorset
178 ST 6509 4m SSE of Sherborne.
CP, 135. Shbne RD. Ch e. W Dst CC.

HOLSWORTHY Devon
174 SS 3403 8m E of Bude. CP, 1,618.
Hlswthy RD. P. Ch e, m, v2. Sch pe, s.
W Dvn CC (Tavistock).

HOLSWORTHY BEACON Devon
174 SS 3508 3m NNE of Holsworthy. Loc,
Hlswthy RD. P Hlswthy. Ch m. W Dvn CC
(Tavistock).

HOLT Dorset
179 SU 0203 3m NNE of Wimborne.
CP, 1,066. Wmbne and Cranborne RD.
P Wmbne. Ch e, m. Sch pe. N Dst CC. See
also Broom Hill.

HOLT Norfolk
125 TG 0738 9m WSW of Sheringham.
CP, 2,601. Erpingham RD. P. Ch e, f, m, s.
Sch p. N Nflk CC. Mkt tn of Ggn hses blt
after a fire of 1708. Gresham's, grammar sch
founded 1555, now boys' public sch.

HOLT Wilts
166 ST 8561 3m N of Trowbridge.
CP, 1,278. Bradford and Melksham RD.
P Trowbridge. Ch e, v. Sch pe. Westbury CC.
The Courts (NT), early 18c hse; well treed
gdns*.

HOLT Worcs
130 SO 8262 4m W of Droitwich. CP, 396.
Martley RD. Ch e. Kidderminster CC. See
also Hlt Hth. H. Cstle has pele twr, rare in
Midlands.

HOLTBY Yorks (N)
97, 98 SE 6754 5m ENE of York. CP, 111.
Flaxton RD. Ch e. Thirsk and Malton CC.

HOLT END Worcs
131 SP 0769 2m ENE of Redditch. Loc,
Beoley CP.

HOLT HEATH Worcs
130 SO 8163 5m W of Droitwich. Loc,
Hlt CP. P WORCESTER.

HOLTON Lincs (L)
104 TF 1181 5m S of Mkt Rasen. CP(Hltn
cum Beckering), 115. Welton RD. Ch e.
Gainsborough CC. Surprising mosaic reredos
in ch. Disused airfields all round.

HOLTON Oxon
158 SP 6006 6m E of Oxford. CP, 554.
Bullingdon RD. P OXFD. Ch e. Sch s.
Mid-Oxon CC (Henley).

HOLTON Som
166 ST 6826 2m SW of Wincanton.
CP, 224. Wncntn RD. P Wncntn. Ch e.
Wells CC. See also Lattiford.

HOLTON Suffolk (E)
137 TM 4077 1m E of Halesworth. CP, 524.
Wainford RD. P Hlswth. Ch e. Sch p.
Lowestoft CC. White-painted mid-18c
post-mill on bank above rd; large quarry
beyond.

HOLTON HEATH Dorset
179 SY 9490 3m NE of Wareham. Loc,
Wrhm St Martin CP. Wrhm and Purbeck RD.
S Dst CC.

HOLTON LE CLAY Lincs (L)
105 TA 2802 4m S of Grimsby. CP, 869.
Louth RD. P Grmsby. Ch e. Sch p. Lth CC.

HOLTON LE MOOR Lincs (L)
104 TF 0897 3m SW of Caistor. CP, 177.
Cstr RD. P LINCOLN. Ch e. Sch pe.
Gainsborough CC.

HOLTON ST MARY Suffolk (E)
149 TM 0536 4m SSE of Hadleigh. CP, 149.
Samford RD. P Colchester, Essex. Ch e.
Sudbury and Woodbridge CC.

HOLTYE Sussex (E)
171 TQ 4539 4m E of E Grinstead. Loc,
Hartfield CP. Ch e.

HOLWELL Dorset
178 ST 6911 5m SE of Sherborne. CP, 293.
Shbne RD. P Shbne. Ch e, m. Sch pe.
W Dst CC. See also Crouch Hill.

HOLWELL Herts
147 TL 1633 3m NNW of Hitchin. CP, 522.
Htchn RD. P Htchn. Ch e. Sch pe.
Htchn CC.

HOLWELL Leics
122 SK 7323 3m NNW of Melton Mowbray.
Loc, Ab Kettleby CP. P Mltn Mbry. Ch e, m.
Iron stone workings in area.

HOLWELL Oxon
157 SP 2309 8m W of Witney. CP, 42.
Wtny RD. Ch e. Mid-Oxon CC (Banbury).
To SE at Bradwell Grove, Cotswold Wild
Life Pk*.

HOLWICK Yorks (N)
84 NY 9027 3m WNW of Middleton in
Teesdale. CP, 122. Startforth RD.
Richmond CC.

HOLWORTH Dorset
178 SY 7683 7m SE of Dorchester. Loc,
Owermoigne CP.

HOLYBOURNE Hants
169 SU 7341 2m NE of Alton. Loc,
Altn UD. P Altn.

HOLY CROSS Worcs
130, 131 SO 9278 4m SSE of Stourbridge.
Loc, Clent CP.

HOLY ISLAND Nthmb
64 NU 1242 5m NNE of Belford. CP, 190.
Norham and Islandshires RD.
P BERWICK-UPON-TWEED. Ch e, r, v.
Sch pe. Brwck-upn-Twd CC. Sometimes

known as Lindisfarne. At S end, vllge, harbour, ruins of priory, cstle (NT)*. Island can be reached by causeway at low tide only.

HOLYMOORSIDE Derbys
111 SK 3369 3m WSW of Chesterfield. Loc, Walton CP. P Chstrfld. Ch m, v. Sch p.

HOLYPORT Berks
159 SU 8977 2m S of Maidenhead. Loc, Bray CP. P Mdnhd. Sch pe.

HOLYSTONE Nthmb
71 NT 9502 6m W of Rothbury. Loc, Harbottle CP. Ch e. Sch p. Lady's Well (NT)*, where Paulinus reputedly baptized 3,000 people in 627.

HOLYWELL Cornwall
185 SW 7658 3m WSW of Newquay. Loc, Cubert CP. The holy well itself is in cave at far (N) end of H. Bay, accessible only at low tide.

HOLYWELL Hunts
134 Tl 3470 2m E of St Ives. CP(Hlywll-cum-Needingworth), 753. St Ives RD. Ch e. Sch pe. Hunts CC. The holy well, with Vctrn canopy, is in churchyard. Ferry Boat Inn is mdvl.

HOLYWELL Nthmb
78 NZ 3174 3m NW of Whitley Bay. Loc, Seaton Valley UD. Blyth BC.

HOLYWELL GREEN Yorks (W)
96, 102 SE 0819 3m S of Halifax. Loc, Elland UD. P Hlfx.

HOLYWELL LAKE Som
164 ST 1020 2m W of Wellington. Loc, Wllngtn Without CP. Wllngtn RD. P Wllngtn. Ch b. Taunton CC.

HOLYWELL ROW Suffolk (W)
135 TL 7077 8m SW of Brandon. Loc, Mildenhall CP. Ch m.

HOMER Shrops
118, 119 SJ 6101 1m NNW of Much Wenlock. Loc, Mch Wnlck CP.

HOMERSFIELD Suffolk (E)
137 TM 2885 4m SW of Bungay. CP, 168. (Known also as St Mary, S Elmham.) Wainford RD. Ch e. Lowestoft CC.

HOMERTON London
161 TQ 3585 5m NE of Charing Cross. Loc, Hackney LB. Hckny Central BC.

HOM GREEN Herefs
142 SO 5822 2m SW of Ross-on-Wye. Loc, Walford CP. Ch e.

HOMINGTON Wilts
167 SU 1226 3m SSW of Salisbury. Loc, Coombe Bissett CP. Ch e, m.

HONEYCHURCH Devon
175 SS 6202 5m NNE of Okehampton. Loc, Sampford Courtenay CP. Ch e.

HONEY TYE Suffolk (W)
149 TL 9535 6m SE of Sudbury. Loc, Leavenheath CP. Melford RD. Sdbry and Woodbridge CC.

HONILEY Warwicks
131 SP 2472 5m NNW of Warwick. CP, 64. Wrwck RD. Ch e. Wrwck and Leamington CC.

HONING Norfolk
126 TG 3227 3m SE of N Walsham. CP, 305. Smallburgh RD. P: N Wlshm. Ch e, m. Sch pe. N Nflk CC. See also Crostwight.

HONINGHAM Norfolk
125 TG 1011 8m WNW of Norwich. CP, 286. St Faith's and Aylsham RD. P NRWCH, NOR 55X. Ch e. Sch pe. N Nflk CC (Central Nflk).

HONINGTON Lincs (K)
113, 122 SK 9443 5m NNE of Grantham. CP, 125. W Kesteven RD. P Grnthm. Ch e. Grnthm CC. To SE, only major Iron Age fort in Lincs.

HONINGTON Suffolk (W)
136 TL 9174 6m SSE of Thetford. CP, 1,546. Thingoe RD. P Bury St Edmunds. Ch e, m. Sch pe. Bury St Eds CC. H. Airfield to W.

HONINGTON Warwicks
144 SP 2642 1m N of Shipston on Stour. CP, 161. Shpstn on Str RD. P Shpstn on Str. Ch e. Sch pe. Stratford-on-Avon CC (Strtfd). H. Hall, late 17c, beside R Stour.

HONITON Devon
176 ST 1600 16m ENE of Exeter. MB, 5,058. P. Hntn CC. Noted for lace, still made here on a small scale. Consistent Ggn style of High St due to 18c fires.

HONLEY Yorks (W)
102 SE 1311 3m S of Huddersfield. Loc,
Holmfirth UD. P Hddsfld.

HOO Kent
172 TQ 7872 3m NE of Rochester. CP.
Strood RD. P Rchstr. Ch e, m2, r, v2.
Sch p, s. Gravesend CC. Indstrl area N of
Medway. Power stn.

HOO Suffolk (E)
137 TM 2558 3m SSW of Framlingham.
CP, 81. Deben RD. Ch e. Eye CC.

HOOD GREEN Yorks (W)
102 SE 3102 3m SW of Barnsley. Loc,
Stainborough CP. Penistone RD.
P(Stnbrgh), Bnsly. Sch pe. Pnstne CC. To
NE, Wentworth Cstle, grand 18c mansion,
now training college, in large grnds with
temples, statues, and Stnbrgh Cstle,
elaborate Gothic folly.

HOOE Sussex (E)
183 TQ 6809 4m WNW of Bexhill. CP, 401.
Hailsham RD. P Battle. Ch e. Rye CC.

HOOK Hants
169 SU 7253 6m E of Basingstoke.
CP, 1,660. Hartley Wintney RD. P Bsngstke.
Ch e, c, r. Sch p. Bsngstke CC (Aldershot).

HOOK Wilts
157 SU 0784 5m W of Swindon. Loc,
Lydiard Tregoze CP. P Swndn.

HOOK Yorks (W)
97, 98 SE 7625 2m NE of Goole. CP, 1,119.
Gle RD. P Gle. Ch e, m. Sch pe. Gle CC.

HOOKE Dorset
177, 178 ST 5300 6m NE of Bridport.
CP, 119. Beaminster RD. P Bmnstr. Ch e.
W Dst CC.

HOOKGATE Staffs
110, 119 SJ 7435 5m E of Mkt Drayton.
Loc, Ashley CP. Ch m, v.

HOOK GREEN Kent
171, 183 TQ 6535 5m ESE of Tunbridge
Wells. Loc, Lamberhurst CP. P Tnbrdge
Wlls.

HOOK NORTON Oxon
145 SP 3533 5m NE of Chipping Norton.
CP, 1,198. Banbury RD. P Bnbry.

Ch e, b2, m, r. Sch pe, s. Bnbry CC. Ch:
carved Nmn font.

HOOKWAY Devon
176 SX 8598 1m SE of Crediton. Loc,
Crdtn Hmlts CP. Crdtn RD. Tiverton CC
(Torrington).

HOOKWOOD Surrey
170, 182 TQ 2642 1m W of Horley. Loc,
Charlwood CP. P Hly.

HOOLEY Surrey
170 TQ 2856 4m NNE of Reigate. Loc,
Banstead UD. P. Coulsdon.

HOO MEAVY Devon
187 SX 5265 6m SSE of Tavistock. Loc,
Meavy CP.

HOOTON Ches
100, 109 SJ 3678 3m WNW of Ellesmere
Port. Loc, Ellesmre Pt MB. Car factory at H.
Pk to W.

HOOTON LEVITT Yorks (W)
103 SK 5291 6m E of Rotherham. CP, 92.
Rthrhm RD. Rother Valley CC.

HOOTON PAGNELL Yorks (W)
103 SE 4808 6m WNW of Doncaster.
CP, 92. Dncstr RD. P Dncstr. Ch e. Sch pe.
Don Valley CC. Ch mainly Nmn.

HOOTON ROBERTS Yorks (W)
103 SK 4897 4m NE of Rotherham.
CP, 145. Rthrhm RD. P Rthrhm. Ch e.
Rother Valley CC.

HOPE Derbys
111 SK 1783 10m NE of Buxton. CP, 814.
Chapel en le Frith RD. P SHEFFIELD.
Ch e, m. Sch p, s. High Peak CC. Large
cement works to SW; see Bradwell.

HOPE Devon
187, 188 SX 6739 5m SW of Kingsbridge.
Loc, Kngsbrdge RD. P Kngsbrdge. Ch m.
Totnes CC.

HOPE Shrops
118 SJ 3401 8m ESE of Welshpool. Loc,
Worthen CP. Ch e. Sch pe. Hmlt with roadside ch across stream among woods of Hpe
Valley. To S, deserted lead mines.

HOPE BAGOT Shrops
129 SO 5873 5m E of Ludlow. CP, 55.
Ldlw RD. Ch e. Ldlw CC. Beauty spot with
steep wds. Ch has pure Nmn nave and
chancel.

HOPE BOWDLER Shrops
129 SO 4792 2m ESE of Ch Stretton.
CP, 181. Ludlow RD. Ch e. Ldlw CC. Steep
hills.

HOPE MANSELL Herefs
142, 143 SO 6219 3m SE of Ross-on-Wye.
CP, 154. Rss and Whitchurch RD.
P Rss-on-Wye. Ch e. Hereford CC.

HOPESAY Shrops
129 SO 3983 3m W of Craven Arms.
CP, 403. Clun and Bishop's Cstle RD.
P Crvn Arms. Ch e. Sch pe. Ludlow CC. See
also Aston on Clun, Broome.

HOPE UNDER DINMORE Herefs.
142 SO 5052 4m S of Leominster. CP, 428.
Lmnstr and Wigmore RD. P Lmnstr. Ch e.
Sch pe. Lmnstr CC. See also Upr Hill.

HOPPERTON Yorks (W)
97 SE 4256 5m E of Knaresborough.
CP(Allerton Mauleverer w Hpprtn), 102.:
Nidderdale RD. Harrogate CC.

HOPTON Derbys
111 SK 2553 5m SSW of Matlock. CP, 79.
Ashbourne RD. Sch pe. W Derbys CC.

HOPTON Shrops
118 SJ 5926 5m ESE of Wem. Loc,
Hodnet CP. Ch m.

HOPTON Staffs
119 SJ 9426 2m NE of Stafford. CP(Hptn
and Coton), 1,936. Stffd RD. P STFFD.
Stffd and Stone CC. To E, H. Hth, site of
Civil War battle, 1643.

HOPTON Suffolk (E)
137 TG 5200 5m S of Yarmouth.
CP(Hptn-on-Sea), 859. Lothingland RD.
P Gt Ymth, Norfolk. Ch e. Sch pe.
Lowestoft CC. Coastal holiday camp.

HOPTON Suffolk (W)
136 TL 9979 8m W of Diss. CP, 371.
Thingoe RD. P Diss, Norfolk. Ch e, m, v.
Sch pe. Bury St Edmunds CC.

HOPTON CANGEFORD Shrops
129 SO 5480 4m NE of Ludlow. CP, 68.
Ldlw RD. Ch e. Ldlw CC. View to Clee Hill.

HOPTON CASTLE Shrops
129 SO 3678 5m SW of Craven Arms.
CP, 96. Clun and Bishop's Cstle RD. Ch e.
Ludlow CC. Rems of Nmn cstle.
Half-timbered cottages.

HOPTONHEATH Shrops
129 SO 3877 5m SW of Craven Arms. Loc,
Clungunford CP.

HOPTON WAFERS Shrops
129, 130 SO 6376 2m W of Cleobury
Mortimer. CP, 514. Ludlow RD.
P Kidderminster, Worcs. Ch e, m2. Sch pe.
Ldlw CC. See also Catherton, Doddington.

HOPWAS Staffs
120 SK 1704 2m WNW of Tamworth. Loc,
Wigginton CP. P Tmwth. Ch e, m. Sch p.

HOPWOOD Worcs
131 SP 0374 5m N of Redditch. Loc,
Alvechurch CP. P BIRMINHAM.

HORAM Sussex (E)
183 TQ 5717 3m S of Heathfield.
CP, 1,731. Hailsham RD. P Hthfld. Ch e.
Sch p. Rye CC. See also Vine's Cross.

HORBLING Lincs (K)
113, 123 TF 1135 7m SSE of Sleaford.
CP, 469. S Kesteven RD. P Slfd. Ch e.
Sch pe. Rutland and Stamford CC. See also
Br End.

HORBURY Yorks (W)
96, 102 SE 2918 3m SW of Wakefield.
UD, 8,914. P Wkfld. Wkfld BC. Architect
John Carr (Carr of York) born and buried
here. Parish ch blt 1791 at his expense.

HORDEN Co Durham
85 NZ 4441 5m S of Seaham. CP, 12,467.
Easington RD. P Peterlee.
Ch e, m2, r, s2, v4. Sch p, pr, s. Easngtn CC.

HORDLE Hants
179 SZ 2695 3m W of Lymington. Loc,
Lmngtn MB. P Lmngtn.

HORDLEY Shrops
118 SJ 3830 3m SSW of Ellesmere. CP, 283.
N Shrops RD. P Ellesmre. Ch e.
Oswestry CC. See also Bagley.

HORHAM Suffolk (E)
137 TM 2172 4m E of Eye. CP, 233.
Hartismere RD. P Diss, Norfolk. Ch e, b.
Eye CC.

HORKESLEY, GREAT Essex
149 TL 9730 4m NNW of Colchester. See
Gt Hksly.

HORKESLEY HEATH Essex
149 TL 9829 3m NNW of Colchester. Loc,
Gt Hksly CP.

HORKSTOW Lincs (L)
104 SE 9818 4m SW of
Barton-upon-Humber. CP, 158. Glanford
Brigg RD. P Btn-on-Hmbr. Ch e, m. Brgg
and Scunthorpe CC (Brgg).

HORLEY Oxon
145 SP 4143 3m NW of Banbury. CP, 232.
Bnbry RD. P Bnbry. Ch e, m. Sch pe.
Bnbry CC. Ch has wall-painting of
St Christopher.

HORLEY Surrey
170, 182 TQ 2842 5m SSE of Reigate.
CP, 16,052. Dorking and Hly RD. P.
Ch e, b2, m, r, v5. Sch p3, s2. Dkng CC.
See also Meath Grn, Salfords, Sidlow Br.

HORMEAD, GREAT Herts
148 TL 4030 7m NW of Bishop's Stortford.
See Gt Hmd.

HORNBLOTTON GREEN Som
165, 166 ST 5833 7m SE of Glastonbury.
Loc, W Bradley CP. Ch e.

HORNBY Lancs
89 SD 5868 5m ESE of Carnforth.
CP(Hnby-w-Farleton), 483. Lunesdale RD.
P LANCASTER. Ch e, r. Sch pe, s.
Lncstr CC. 19c 'cstle' incorporates parts of
much older one.

HORNBY Yorks (N)
85 NZ 3605 7m SE of Darlington. CP, 176.
Northallerton RD. Ch m. Richmond CC.

HORNBY Yorks (N)
91 SE 2293 4m NW of Bedale. CP, 98.
Leyburn RD. Ch e. Richmond CC.

HORNCASTLE Lincs (L)
114 TF 2669 18m E of Lincoln. UD, 4,096.
P. Hncstle CC, On site of

Roman *Banovallum,* part of whose walls
remain. Bldngs mainly Vctrn. Wharves and
warehouses of old H. Navigation Canal.
Ch has brass of Sir Lionel Dymoke, 1591,
of Scrivelsby Pk, 2m S.

HORNCHURCH London
161 TQ 5487 5m SW of Brentwood. Loc,
Havering LB. P Essex. Hnchch BC. Rsdntl
distr.

HORNCLIFFE Nthmb
64 NT 9249 5m WSW of
Berwick-upon-Tweed. CP, 508. Norham and
Islandshires RD. Ch v. Sch p.
Brwck-upn-Twd CC. On R Tweed by
Scottish border. To N, Union Br over river,
first suspension br blt in Britain (1820).

HORNDEAN Hants
181 SU 7013 4m NNW of Havant.
CP, 5,555. Petersfield RD. P Portsmouth.
Ch m, r. Sch i, je. Ptrsfld CC. See also
Blendworth, Catherington.

HORNDON Devon
175 SX 5280 4m NNE of Tavistock. Loc,
Mary Tavy CP.

HORNDON ON THE HILL Essex
161 TQ 6683 5m NNE of Tilbury. Loc,
Thurrock UD. P Stanford-le-Hope.
Thrrck BC (CC).

HORNE Surrey
170, 182 TQ 3344 4m E of Horley.
CP, 805. Godstone RD. P Hly. Ch e.
E Srry CC (Reigate).

HORN HILL Bucks
159, 160 TQ 0192 3m NNE of Gerrards
Cross. Loc, Chalfont St Peter CP.

HORNING Norfolk
126 TG 3417 3m E of Wroxham. CP, 762.
Smallburgh RD. P NORWICH, NOR 39Z.
Ch e, v. Sch p. N Nflk CC. See also Upr St.
In the heart of the Broads country. Boats
everywhere. Ferry across R Bure.

HORNINGHOLD Leics
133 SP 8097 4m WSW of Uppingham.
CP, 85. Mkt Harborough RD. P Mkt Hbrgh.
Ch e. Hbrgh CC. Early 20c estate vllge.

HORNINGSEA Cambs
135 TL 4962 4m NE of Cambridge.
CP, 355. Chesterton RD. P CMBRDGE.
Ch e. Cambs CC.

HORNINGSHAM Wilts
166 ST 8141 4m WSW of Warminster.
CP, 534. Wmnstr and Westbury RD.
P Wmnstr. Ch e, c. Sch p. Wstbry CC. To N,
Longleat*, Renaissance mansion in large pk;
lion reserve, and other wild animals. Chpl in
vllge may by oldest dissenting place of
worship in England.

HORNINGTOFT Norfolk
125 TF 9323 4m S of Fakenham. CP, 157.
Mitford and Launditch RD. Ch e, m.
SW Nflk CC.

HORNSBY Cumb
76 NY 5150 8m ESE of Carlisle. Loc,
Cumwhitton CP.

HORNS CROSS Devon
174 SS 3823 5m WSW of Bideford. Loc,
Parkham CP. P Bdfd.

HORNSEA Yorks (E)
99 TA 2047 12m ENE of Beverley.
UD, 7,021. P. Bridlington CC. Resort, with
large lake, H. Mere.

HORNSEY London
160 TQ 3088 5m N of Charing Cross. Loc,
Haringey LB. Hnsy BC.

HORNTON Oxon
145 SP 3945 5m NW of Banbury. CP, 318.
Bnbry RD. P Bnbry. Ch e, m. Sch p.
Bnbry CC. 17c mnr hse.

HORRABRIDGE Devon
187 SX 5169 4m SE of Tavistock.
CP, 1,397. Tvstck RD. P Yelverton. Ch e, m.
Sch p. W Dvn CC (Tvstck).

HORRINGER Suffolk (W)
136 TL 8261 2m SW of Bury St Edmunds.
CP, 468. Thingoe RD. P Bury St Eds. Ch e.
Sch pe. Buryy St Eds CC. At entrance to
Ickworth (NT)*, 18c–19c hse in form of
elliptical rotunda; formal gdns.

HORSEBRIDGE Hants
168 SU 3430 6m N of Romsey. Loc, Rmsy
and Stockbridge RD. Winchester CC.

HORSE BRIDGE Staffs
110 SJ 9653 2m SW of Leek. Loc,
Cheadle RD, Lk RD. Lk CC.

HORSEBRIDGE Sussex (E)
183 TQ 5711 1m N of Hailsham. Loc,
Hellingly CP. P Hlshm.

HORSEBROOK Staffs
119 SJ 8810 6m W of Cannock. Loc,
Brewood CP.

HORSEHAY Shrops
118, 119 SJ 6707 just W of Dawley. Loc,
Dly UD. P Telford. The Wrekin CC.

HORSEHEATH Cambs
148 TL 6147 4m WNW of Haverhill.
CP, 359. S Cambs RD. P CAMBRIDGE.
Ch e, m. Sch pe. Cambs CC.

HORSEHOUSE Yorks (N)
90 SE 0481 7m SW of Middleham. Loc,
Carlton Highdale CP. Leyburn RD. P Lbn.
Ch e, m. Richmond CC.

HORSELL Surrey
169, 170 SU 9959 1m NW of Woking. Loc,
Wkng UD. P Wkng.

HORSENDEN Bucks
159 SP 7902 1m W of Princes Risborough.
Loc, Longwick-cum-Ilmer CP. Ch e.

HORSEY Norfolk
126 TG 4622 12m NNW of Yarmouth.
CP, 147. Smallburgh RD. P Gt Ymth.
Ch e, m. N Nflk CC. H. Mere to SW.

HORSFORD Norfolk
126 TG 1915 5m NNW of Norwich. CP.
St Faith's and Aylsham RD.
P NRWCH, NOR 84X. Ch e, m. Sch pe.
N Nflk CC (Central Nflk). See also
St Helena.

HORSFORTH Yorks (W)
96 SE 2337 4m WNW of Leeds.
UD, 19,366. P LDS. Pudsey BC.

HORSHAM Sussex (W)
182 TQ 1730 17m SE of Guildford.
UD, 26,378. P. Hshm and Crawley CC
(Hshm). See also Roffey. Mkt tn and
shopping centre. N-S bypass, but tn still
choked at times.

HORSHAM ST FAITH Norfolk
126 TG 2114 4m N of Norwich. CP(Hshm St Fth and Newton St Fth). St Fth's and Aylsham RD. Ch e, m, r. Sch pe. N Nflk CC (Central Nflk).

HORSINGTON Lincs (L)
113 TF 1968 4m N of Woodhall Spa. CP, 209. Horncastle RD. P LINCOLN. Ch e. Sch pe. Hncstle CC.

HORSINGTON Som
166 ST 7023 3m S of Wincanton. CP, 554. Wncntn RD. P Templecombe. Ch e. Sch p, pe. Wells CC. See also S Cheriton.

HORSLEY Derbys
120, 121 SK 3744 5m NNE of Derby. CP, 677. Belper RD. P DBY. Ch e, m. Sch pe. Blpr CC. See also Coxbench.

HORSLEY Glos
156 ST 8398 5m S of Stroud. CP, 857. Strd RD. P Strd. Ch e. Sch pe. Strd CC.

HORSLEY Nthmb
70 NY 8496 4m NW of Otterburn. Loc, Rochester CP. Ch e.

HORSLEY Nthmb
77, 78 NZ 0966 2m N of Prudhoe. CP, 413. Hexham RD. P NEWCASTLE UPON TYNE. Ch c, m. Hxhm CC.

HORSLEY CROSS Essex
150 TM 1227 3m SSE of Manningtree. Loc, Tendring RD. Harwich CC.

HORSLEYCROSS STREET Essex
150 TM 1228 2m SSE of Manningtree. Loc, Mistley CP.

HORSLEY WOODHOUSE Derbys
120, 121 SK 3944 6m NNE of Derby. CP, 1,277. Belper RD. P DBY. Ch e, m2. Sch p. Blpr CC.

HORSMONDEN Kent
171, 172, 184 TQ 7040 6m WNW of Cranbrook. CP, 1,628. Tonbridge RD. P Tnbrdge. Ch e, b, m2. Sch p. Royal Tunbridge Wells CC (Tnbrdge). Amid orchards. Large grn.

HORSPATH Oxon
158 SP 5704 4m ESE of Oxford. CP, 1,540. Bullingdon RD. P OXFD. Ch e, m. Sch pe. Mid-Oxon CC (Henley).

HORSTEAD Norfolk
126 TG 2619 3m NW of Wroxham. CP(Hstd w Stanninghall), 678. St Faith's and Aylsham RD. Ch e. Sch p. N Nflk CC (Central Nflk). Early 19c weatherboarded water mill.

HORSTED KEYNES Sussex (E)
183 TQ 3828 4m NE of Haywards Hth. CP, 1,256. Cuckfield RD. P Hwds Hth. Ch e, b, c, v. Sch pe. Mid-Sx CC (E Grinstead). N terminus of the revived Bluebell Rly; see also Fletching.

HORTON Bucks
146 SP 9219 4m S of Leighton Buzzard. Loc, Wing RD. Buckingham CC.

HORTON Bucks
159, 160, 170 TQ 0175 4m SE of Slough. CP, 1,024. Eton RD. P Slgh. Ch e. Sch pe. Beaconsfield CC (S Bucks).

HORTON Dorset
179 SU 0307 5m N of Wimborne. CP, 356. Wmbne and Cranborne RD. P Wmbne. Ch e, m2. N Dst CC. Ruined 120ft folly blt in 1700.

HORTON Glos
156 ST 7684 9m SW of Tetbury. CP, 340. Sodbury RD. P BRISTOL. Ch e. Sch pe. S Glos CC. H. Ct (NT)*, partly Nmn hse.

HORTON Northants
146 SP 8154 6m SE of Northampton. Loc, Hackleton CP. Ch e. Among modern housing development scattered survivals (stable block, triumphal arch, 'menagerie') of former hall.

HORTON Nthmb
64, 71 NU 0230 3m NE of Wooler. Loc, Chatton CP.

HORTON Oxon
145, 146 SP 5912 6m NE of Oxford. CP(Htn-cum-Studley), 284. Ploughley RD. P(Htn-cum-Stdly), OXFD. Ch e. Mid-Oxon CC (Henley).

HORTON Som
177 ST 3214 2m W of Ilminster. Loc, Ilmnstr Without CP. Chard RD. P Ilmnstr. Sch p. Yeovil CC.

HORTON Staffs
110 SJ 9457 3m WNW of Leek. CP, 855.
Lk. Ch e, m2. Sch pe. Lk CC. See also
Blackwood Hill, Rudyard.

HORTON Wilts
167 SU 0563 3m ENE of Devizes. Loc,
Bishops Cannings CP. P Dvzs. Ch m. On
Kennet and Avon Canal.

HORTON Yorks (W)
95 SD 8550 7m NNW of Colne. CP, 88.
Bowland RD. Ch v. Skipton CC.

HORTON GREEN Ches
109 SJ 4549 8m E of Wrexham. Loc,
Htn CP. Tarvin RD. Nantwich CC.

HORTON HEATH Hants
180 SU 4917 6m NE of Southampton. Loc,
Fair Oak CP. P Eastleigh. Ch b.

HORTON IN RIBBLESDALE Yorks (W)
90 SD 8172 5m N of Settle. CP, 597.
Sttle RD. P Sttle. Ch e, m. Sch pe.
Skipton CC. See also Helwith Br, New Hses,
Selside. In heart of limestone Craven Distr.
Quarries. 2m E, Pen-y-Ghent, 2,273ft. Many
caves and potholes in vicinity, incl Alum
Pot, 4m NW. 5m N, Long Gill Nature
Reserve.

HORTON KIRBY Kent
171 TQ 5668 5m SE of Dartford.
CP, 2,397. Dtfd RD. P Dtfd. Ch e. Sch pe.
Sevenoaks CC (Dtfd). See also S Darenth.

HORWICH Lancs
101 SD 6311 5m WNW of Bolton.
UD, 16,433. P Bltn. Westhoughton CC. See
also Bottom o' th' Moor. Rly wks.
Coal-mining.

HORWOOD Devon
163 SS 5027 3m ENE of Bideford. CP, 79.
Barnstaple RD. Ch e. Sch p. N Dvn CC.

HORWOOD, GREAT Bucks
146 SP 7731 5m ESE of Buckingham. See
Gt Hwd.

HOSE Leics
122 SK 7329 6m N of Melton Mowbray.
Loc, Clawson and Harby CP. Mltn and
Belvoir RD. P Mltn Mbry. Ch e, b. Sch pe.
Mltn CC.

HOTHAM Yorks (E)
98 SE 8934 5m SSE of Mkt Weighton.
CP, 286. Howden RD. P YORK. Ch e, m.
Hdn CC.

HOTHFIELD Kent
172, 184 TQ 9644 3m NW of Ashford.
CP, 868. W Ashfd RD. P Ashfd. Ch e, m.
Sch p. Ashfd CC. H. Cmmn is nature
reserve.

HOTON Leics
121, 122 SK 5722 3m NE of
Loughborough. CP, 194. Barrow
upon Soar RD. P Lghbrgh. Ch e. Melton CC.
To S, Prestwold Hall*, 18c and earlier hse
with large gdns.

HOUGH Ches
110 SJ 7151 3m S of Crewe. CP, 390.
Nantwich RD. P Crwe. Ch m. Nntwch CC.

HOUGHAM Lincs (K)
113, 122 SK 8844 6m NNW of Grantham.
CP, 201. W Kesteven RD. Ch e. Grnthm CC.

HOUGH GREEN Lancs
100, 109 SJ 4886 2m W of Widnes, Loc,
Wdns MB.

HOUGH-ON-THE-HILL Lincs (K)
113 SK 9246 7m N of Grantham. CP, 409.
W Kesteven RD. P Grnthm. Ch e. Sch pe.
Crnthm CC. See also Brandon, Gelston. Ch
has Saxon twr with outside staircase.

HOUGHTON Cumb
76 NY 4059 2m N of Carlisle. Loc, Stanwix
Rural CP. Border RD. P Clsle. Ch e. Sch pe.
Penrith and the Bdr CC.

HOUGHTON Hants
168 SU 3432 8m S of Andover. CP, 427.
Romsey and Stockbridge RD. P Stckbrdge.
Ch e, m. Winchester CC.

HOUGHTON Hunts
134 TL 2872 3m E of Huntingdon.
CP(Hghtn and Wyton), 2,908. St Ives RD.
P HNTNGDN. Ch e, v. Sch p. Hunts CC.
Beside R Ouse. Boating. Water mill (NT) is
youth hostel.

HOUGHTON Norfolk
125 TF 7928 8m W of Fakenham. See New
Hghtn.

HOUGHTON Sussex (W)
181, 182 TQ 0111 3m N of Arundel.
CP, 117. Worthing RD. P(Hghtn Br), Arndl.
Ch e, r. Shoreham CC (Arndl and Shrhm).
Br over R Arun. Inscription on inn recalls
visit of Charles II, 1651.

HOUGHTON CONQUEST Beds
147 TL 0441 2m NNE of Ampthill.
CP, 875. Ampthll RD. P BEDFORD.
Ch e, m2. Sch p. Mid-Beds CC.

HOUGHTON, GREAT Northants
133 SP 7958 3m ESE of Northampton. See
Gt Htn, Northants.

HOUGHTON, GREAT Yorks (W)
103 SE 4306 5m E of Barnsley. See Gt Htn,
Yorks(W).

HOUGHTON GREEN Lancs
101 SJ 6291 3m NNE of Warrington. Loc,
Winwick CP.

HOUGHTON LE SIDE Co Durham
85 NZ 2221 6m NW of Darlington. CP, 59.
Dlngtn RD. Ch m. Bishop Auckland CC
(Sedgefield).

HOUGHTON-LE-SPRING Co Durham
78/85 NZ 3449 6m SW of Sunderland.
UD, 32,210. P. Hghtn-le-Sprng CC. See also
Colliery Row, Fence Hses, High Dubmire,
Newbottle, New Herrington, Penshaw,
Philadelphia, Shiney Row.

HOUGHTON ON THE HILL Leics
121, 122 SK 6703 6m E of Leicester.
CP, 768. Billesdon RD. P LCSTR. Ch e, m.
Sch pe. Harborough CC (Melton).

HOUGHTON REGIS Beds
147 TL 0123 1m N of Dunstable.
CP, 7,293. Luton RD. P Dnstble.
Ch e, b, m2, r. Sch i, j, p2, pe. S Beds CC.

HOUGHTON ST GILES Norfolk
125 TF 9235 4m N of Fakenham. Loc,
Barsham CP. Walsingham RD. Ch e.
NW Nflk CC (N Nflk). 14c 'Slipper Chpl',
where pilgrims to Wlsnghm left their shoes
(see Lit Wlsnghm). Now RC shrine.

HOULSYKE Yorks (N)
86 NZ 7307 6m S of Loftus. Loc,
Glaisdale CP. Ch m.

HOUND Hants
180 SU 4708 3m SE of Southampton.
CP, 4,992. Winchester RD. Ch e. Sch p.
Eastleigh CC. See also Netley. Largely
unspoilt 12c ch with modern E window.

HOUND GREEN Hants
169 SU 7359 9m S of Reading. Loc,
Mattingley CP.

HOUNSLOW London
160, 170 TQ 1375 11m WSW of Charing
Cross. LB, 206,182. P Middx.
BCs: Brentford and Isleworth; Feltham and
Heston (Brntfd and Chiswick; Flthm; Hstn
and Islwth). See also Brntfd, Chswck,
Flthm, Gunnersbury, Hanworth, Hstn,
Islwth. To W, H. Hth, former haunt of
highwaymen.

HOVE Sussex (E)
182 TQ 2804 1m W of Brighton.
MB, 72,659. P. Hve BC. Rsdntl tn and
resort. Rgncy hses.

HOVERINGHAM Notts
112 SK 6946 8m WSW of Newark. CP, 300.
Southwell RD. P NOTTINGHAM. Ch e.
Sch pe. Nwk CC.

HOVETON Norfolk
126 TG 3018 just N of Wroxham.
CP, 1,466. Smallburgh RD. P Norwich.
Ch e2, r. Sch p, s. N Nflk CC.

HOVINGHAM Yorks (N)
92 SE 6675 8m WNW of Malton. CP, 326.
Mltn RD. P YORK. Ch e, m. Sch pe. Thirsk
and Mltn CC. Medicinal springs. H. Hall,
mid-18c mansion, seat of Worsley family,
with magnificent stables and riding sch in
which annual music festival is held.

HOW Cumb
76 NY 5056 7m E of Carlisle. Loc,
Hayton CP.

HOW CAPLE Herefs
142, 143 SO 6130 4m N of Ross-on-Wye.
CP, 116. Rss and Whitchurch RD. P HERE-
FORD. Ch e. Hrfd CC.

HOWDEN Yorks (E)
97, 98 SE 7428 3m N of Goole. CP, 2,282.
Hdn RD. P Gle. Ch e, m, r, v.
Sch p, pe, pr, s. Hdn CC. Notable 13c–14c
ch with ruined chancel.

HOWDEN-LE-WEAR Co Durham
85 NZ 1633 1m S of Crook. Loc, Crk and
Willington UD. P Crk.

HOWE Norfolk
137 TG 2700 6m SSE of Norwich. CP, 58.
Loddon RD. Ch e. S Nflk CC.

HOWE Westm
89 SD 4588 5m SW of Kendal. Loc,
Crosthwaite and Lyth CP. S Westm RD.
Westm CC.

HOWE GREEN Essex
161, 162 TL 7403 3m SE of Chelmsford.
Loc, Sandon CP.

HOWELL Lincs (K)
113 TF 1346 4m E of Sleaford. CP(Asgarby
and Hwll), 114. E Kesteven RD. Ch e.
Grantham CC.

HOWE STREET Essex
148 TL 6934 6m ENE of Thaxted. Loc,
Finchingfield CP.

HOWE STREET Essex
148, 161 TL 6914 5m N of Chelmsford.
Loc, Gt Waltham CP. P Chlmsfd.

HOWICK Nthmb
71 NU 2517 5m NE of Alnwick. Loc,
Longhoughton CP. P Alnwck. Ch e. Fine
sand and rock coast. Gdn and grnds* of H.
Hall, late 18c.

HOWLE Shrops
119 SJ 6923 4m NW of Newport. Loc,
Chetwynd CP. Wellington RD. Ch m. The
Wrekin CC.

HOWLE HILL Herefs
142, 143 SO 6020 2m S of Ross-on-Wye.
Loc, Walford CP. P Rss-on-Wye.

HOWLETT END Essex
148 TL 5834 3m NNW of Thaxted. Loc,
Wimbish CP.

HOWSHAM Lincs (L)
104 TA 0404 3m SE of Brigg. Loc,
Cadney CP. P LINCOLN. Ch m. Sch p.

HOWSHAM Yorks (E)
92, 97, 98 SE 7362 6m SW of Malton.
CP, 86. Norton RD. Ch e. Howden CC. H.
Hall*, Jcbn with 18c additions.

HOWTON Herefs
142 SO 4129 9m SW of Hereford. Loc,
Kenderchurch CP.

HOXNE Suffolk (E)
137 TM 1877 NE of Eye. CP, 676.
Hartismere RD. P Diss, Norfolk. Ch e, b.
Sch p. Eye CC. See also Heckfield Grn.
Vllge climbs hill; pub at bottom, ch at top.
Questionable legend persists that
St Edmund was martyred here.

HOXTON London
160 TQ 3383 3m NE of Charing Cross. Loc,
Hackney LB. Hckny S and Shoreditch BC
(Shdtch and Finsbury).

HOYLAKE Ches
100 SJ 2189 6m W of Birkenhead.
UD, 32,196. P Wirral. Wrrl CC. See also
Caldy, Frankby, Grange, Greasby, W Kirby.
Resort, well known for golf course beside
mouth of Dee estuary (Royal
Liverpool GC).

HOYLAND NETHER Yorks (W)
102, 103 SE 3600 4m SSE of Barnsley.
UD, 15,812. P(Hlnd), Bnsly. Penistone CC.
See also Elsecar, Platts Cmmn.

HOYLAND SWAINE Yorks (W)
102 SE 2604 1m NE of Penistone. Loc,
Pnstne UD. P SHEFFIELD.

HUBBERHOLME Yorks (W)
90 SD 9278 8m SSE of Hawes. Loc,
Buckden CP. Ch e. Tiny ancient ch with
rood loft, one of the only two in Yorkshire
(see Flamborough).

HUBBERT'S BRIDGE Lincs (H)
114, 123 TF 2643 4m W of Boston. Loc,
Bstn RD. Ch m. Holland w Bstn CC.

HUBY Yorks (N)
92 SE 5665 9m NNW of York. CP, 586.
Easingwold RD. P Sutton-on-the-Forest, YK.
Ch m. Thirsk and Malton CC.

HUBY Yorks (W)
96 SE 2747 5m SSW of Harrogate. Loc,
Weeton CP. P LEEDS. Ch m. Sch pe.

HUCCLECOTE Glos
143 SO 8717 E distr of Gloucester. Loc,
Glcstr CB; CP, Glstr RD. P GLCSTR.
Glcstr BC, W Glos CC. (Glcstr BC.)

HUCKING Kent
172 TQ 8458 6m ENE of Maidstone.
CP, 66. Hollingbourn RD. Ch e. Mdstne CC.

HUCKLOW, GREAT Derbys
111 SK 1777 6m NNW of Bakewell. See Gt
Hcklw.

HUCKNALL Notts
112 SK 5349 6m NNW of Nottingham.
UD, 26,349. P NTTNGHM. Ashfield CC
(Nttnghm N BC). Colliery tn. Ch, in mkt
square, contains tomb of Ld Byron.

HUDDERSFIELD Yorks (W)
96, 102 SE 1416 14m SW of Leeds.
CB, 130,964. P. BCs: Hddsfld E, Hddsfld W.
Textile and engineering tn, largely 19c,
surrounded by steep hills.

HUDDINGTON Worcs
130, 131 SO 9457 6m ENE of Worcester.
CP, 73. Droitwich RD. Ch e. Wcstr BC. H.
Ct, Tdr, black and white, haunted; home of
Wintour family, three of whom were
executed for participation in Gunpowder
Plot.

HUDSWELL Yorks (N)
91 NZ 1400 2m WSW of Richmond.
CP, 303. Rchmnd RD. P Rchmnd. Ch e.
Rchmnd CC.

HUGGATE Yorks (E)
98 SE 8855 6m NE of Pocklington.
CP, 289. Pcklngtn RD. P YORK. Ch e, m.
Howden CC. Blt round grn. N, E, and W, H.
Dykes, extensive prehistoric military
earthworks.

HUGHENDEN VALLEY Bucks
159 SU 8696 2m N of High Wycombe. Loc,
Hghndn CP. Wcmbe RD. P Hgh Wcmbe.
Ch e. Wcmbe CC. To S, H. Mnr (NT)*, once
home of Disraeli. Contains much of his
furniture, books, etc.

HUGHLEY Shrops
129 SO 5697 4m WSW of Much Wenlock.
CP, 68. Atcham RD. P Shrewsbury. Ch e.
Shrsbry CC. Vllge under Wnlck Edge
mentioned in Housman's *Shropshire Lad*.
Ch: scrn; Jcbn plpt.

HUGH TOWN St Mary's, Isles of Scilly
189 SV 9010. Loc, St Mary's CP.

P(St Mary's). Ch e, m. Sch p, s. Sea and air
port for the islands, and the largest town.

HUISH Devon
163, 175 SS 5311 6m SSE of Torrington.
CP, 60. Trrngtn RD. Ch e. W Dvn CC
(Trrngtn).

HUISH Wilts
167 SU 1463 3m NNW of Pewsey. CP, 38.
Psy RD. Ch e. Devizes CC.

HUISH CHAMPFLOWER Som
164 ST 0429 7m NE of Bampton. CP, 228.
Dulverton RD. P Taunton. Ch e. Tntn CC.

HUISH EPISCOPI Som
177 ST 4226 6m WNW of Ilchester.
CP, 945. Langport RD. Ch e, m. Sch p, s.
Yeovil CC. Ch has fine 100ft twr; stained
glass by Burne-Jones.

HULCOTT Bucks
146, 159 SP 8516 3m NE of Aylesbury.
CP, 55. Aylesbury RD. Ch e. Aylesbury CC.

HULL Yorks (E)
99 TA 0928 50m E of Leeds. See Kingston
upon Hull.

HULLAND Derbys
111 SK 2446 4m E of Ashbourne. CP, 170.
Ashbne RD. P(Hllnd Ward), DERBY.
Ch e, m2. Sch pe. W Derbys CC.

HULLAVINTON Wilts
156, 157 ST 8982 4m SW of Malmesbury.
CP, 864. Mlmsbry RD. P Chippenham.
Ch e, b, m. Sch pe. Chppnhm CC. Disused
airfield to S.

HULLBRIDGE Essex
162 TQ 8095 8m NW of Southend. CP.
Rochford RD. P Hockley. Ch v. Sch p.
Maldon CC (SE Essx).

HULME Staffs
110 SJ 9345 3m E of Stoke-on-Trent. Loc,
Caverswall CP.

HULME END Staffs
111 SK 1059 8m ENE of Leek. Loc,
Lk RD. Lk CC. On R Manifold in Peak
District National Pk. Construction of
reservoir in Mnfld valley to N proposed by
Trent River Authority 1970 (see also
Longnor).

HULME WALFIELD Ches
110 SJ 8465 2m NW of Congleton. CP, 124.
Cngltn RD. Ch e. Sch pe. Knutsford CC.

HULVER STREET Suffolk (E)
137 TM 4687 4m SE of Beccles.
CP (Henstead w Hlvr St), 351.
Lothingland RD. P(Hlvr), Bccls. Ch m.
Lowestoft CC.

HUMBERSTON Lincs (L)
105 TA 3105 4m SE of Grimsby. CP.
Grmsby RD. Ch e, m. Sch i, j, pe. Louth CC.

HUMBERSTONE Leics
121, 122 SK 6205 E distr of Leicester. Loc,
Lcstr CB. P LCSTR. Lcstr E BC (NE).

HUMBLETON Nthmb
71 NT 9728 just W of Wooler. Loc,
Akeld CP.

HUMBLETON Yorks (E)
99 TA 2234 8m NW of Withernsea. CP, 213.
Holderness RD. P Hull. Ch e, m.
Bridlington CC. See also Flinton.

HUMBY Lincs (K)
113, 123 TF 0032 6m ESE of Grantham.
CP (Ropsley and Hmby), 571.
W Kesteven RD. Ch e. Rutland and
Stamford CC.

HUMSHAUGH Nthmb
77 NY 9271 5m NNW of Hexham. CP, 531.
Hxhm RD. P Hxhm. Ch e, m. Sch pe.
Hxhm CC. See also Chollerford.

HUNCOAT Lancs
95 SD 7730 2m NE of Accrington. Loc,
Accrngtn MB. P Accrngtn. Power stn.

HUNCOTE Leics
132 SP 5197 6m SW of Leicester. CP, 778.
Blby RD. P LCSTR. Ch e, m. Sch p.
Blby CC (Harborough).

HUNDERTHWAITE Yorks (N)
84 NY 9821 5m NW of Barnard Cstle.
CP, 132. Startforth RD. Ch m.
Richmond CC.

HUNDLEBY Lincs (L)
114 TF 3866 8m ESE of Horncastle.
CP, 46 ♭ Spilsby RD. P Splsby. Ch e, m.
Hncstle CC.

HUNDON Suffolk (W)
148, 149 TL 7348 3m NW of Clare.
CP, 1,081. Clre RD. P Sudbury. Ch e, c.
Sch p. Bury St Edmunds CC. Par incl most
of Stradishall Airfield.

HUNDRED ACRES Hants
180 SU 5911 4m NNE of Fareham. Loc,
Soberton CP.

HUNDRED, THE Herefs
129 SO 5263 4m NNE of Leominster. Loc,
Lmnstr and Wigmore RD. Ch m. Lmnstr CC.

HUNGARTON Leics
122 SK 6907 7m ENE of Leicester.
CP, 297. Billesdon RD. P LCSTR. Ch e, m.
Harborough CC (Melton). Mainly Ggn estate
vllge. To SE, Quenby Hall, Elizn-Jcbn hse
still largely as orig blt.

HUNGERFORD Berks
158 SU 3368 8m W of Newbury. CP, 3,339.
Hngrfd RD. P. Ch e, m2, r, v2. Sch p, s.
Nbry CC. Mainly Ggn tn with Vctrn rly br
over High St. Elaborate and colourful
ceremonies at Hocktide (Tuesday in Easter
week).

HUNGERFORD Hants
179 SU 1612 2m SE of Fordingbridge. Loc,
Fdngbrdge CP. Ch e.

HUNGERFORD Shrops
129 SO 5389 6m ESE of Ch Stretton. Loc,
Munslow CP.

HUNGERFORD NEWTON Berks
158 SU 3571 2m NNE of Hungerford. Loc,
Hngrfd CP.

HUNMANBY Yorks (E)
93 TA 0977 3m SSW of Filey. CP, 1,512.
Bridlington RD. P Filey. Ch e, m2. Sch p.
Brdlngtn CC.

HUNNINGHAM Warwicks
132 SP 3768 4m ENE of Leamington.
CP, 182. Warwick RD. P Lmngtn Spa. Ch e.
Wrwck and Lmngtn CC.

HUNSDON Herts
148, 161 TL 4114 4m E of Ware. CP, 1,095.
Ware RD. P Ware. Ch e. Sch p. E Herts CC.

HUNSINGORE Yorks (W)
97 SE 4253 4m NNE of Wetherby. CP, 108.
Nidderdale RD. P Wthrby. Ch e. Sch p.
Harrogate CC.

HUNSONBY Cumb
83 NY 5835 5m NE of Penrith. CP, 435.
Pnrth RD. Ch m. Sch pe. Pnrth and the
Border CC. See also Lit Salkeld, Winskill.

HUNGSTANTON Norfolk
124 TF 6740 13m NNE of King's Lynn.
UD, 3,901. P. NW Nflk CC (K's Lnn).
Seaside resort, mostly Vctrn. Striped cliffs,
immense sands. Lighthouse of 1830. Ch has
portrait brass of 1506. Golf links to N.

HUNSTANWORTH Co Durham
84 NY 9549 7m NNW of Stanhope.
CP, 151. Weardale RD. Ch e, m. Sch r
NW Drhm CC. Hillside vllge of the 1860s.

HUNSTON Suffolk (W)
136 TL 9768 7m NW of Stowmarket.
CP, 106. Thedwastre RD. Ch e. Bury St
Edmunds CC.

HUNSTON Sussex (W)
181 SU 8601 2m S of Chichester. CP, 623.
Chchstr RD. P Chchstr. Ch e. Chchstr CC.

HUNSTRETE Som
166 ST 6462 6m NNW of Radstock. Loc,
Marksbury CP.

HUNT END Worcs
131 SP 0363 2m S of Redditch. Loc,
Rddtch UD.

HUNTINGDON Hunts
134 TL 2371 17m S of Peterborough.
MB(Hntngdn and Godmanchester), 16,540.
P(HNTNGDN). Hunts CC. See also
Hartford. Tn on R Ouse; formerly
important coach stop on rd to North.
George Inn has galleried yard. Old grammar
sch, where Cromwell and Pepys were pupils,
now museum.

HUNTINGFIELD Suffolk (E)
137 TM 3473 4m SW of Halesworth.
CP, 217. Blyth RD. P Hlswth. Ch e. Eye CC.
Ch roof (interior) brightly painted by vicar's
wife in 19c.

HUNTINGFORD Dorset
166 ST 8130 6m E of Wincanton. Loc,
Gillingham CP.

HUNTINGTON Herefs
141 SO 2453 4m SW of Kington. CP, 144.
Kngtn RD. P Kngtn. Ch e, v.
Leominster CC.

HUNTINGTON Staffs
119 SJ 9712 2m N of Cannock. CP, 1,717.
Cnnck RD. P Cnnck. Ch e, m. Sch p, s.
SW Staffs (Cnnck). Mining distr on S edge
of Cnnck Chase.

HUNTINGTON Yorks (N)
97, 98 SE 6156 3m NNE of York. CP.
Flaxton RD. P YK. Ch e, m. Sch j, p2, s.
Thirsk and Malton CC.

HUNTLEY Glos
143 SO 7219 7m W of Gloucester. CP, 498.
E Dean RD. P GLCSTR. Ch e. Sch pe.
W Glos CC.

HUNTON Kent
171, 172, 184 TQ 7149 5m SSW of
Maidstone. CP. Mdstne RD. P Mdstne. Ch e.
Sch pe. Mdstne CC.

HUNTON Yorks (N)
91 SE 1892 5m ENE of Leyburn. CP, 383.
Lbn RD. P Bedale. Ch e, m, r. Sch p.
Richmond CC.

HUNTON BRIDGE Herts
160 TL 0800 3m NNW of Watford. Loc,
Abbots Langley CP. P King's Langley.

HUNTSHAM Devon
164 ST 0020 3m ESE of Bampton. CP, 132.
Tiverton RD. P Tvtn. Ch e. Tvtn CC.

HUNTSHAW Devon
163 SS 5022 3m NNE of Torrington.
CP, 117. Trrngtn RD. Ch e. W Dvn CC
(Trrngtn).

HUNTSPILL Som
165 ST 3145 3m S of Burnham.
CP(W Hntspll), 1,231. Bridgwater RD.
P Highbridge. Ch e, m. Sch p. Brdgwtr CC.
Gives name to H. River, cut during World
War II to supply water to Puriton explosives
factory. Indstrl and rd development.

HUNTWORTH Som
165 ST 3134 2m SSE of Bridgwater. Loc,
N Petherton CP.

HUNWICK Co Durham
85 NZ 1932 2m SSW of Willington. Loc,
Crook and Wllngtn UD. P Crk.

HUNWORTH Norfolk
125 TG 0635 2m SSW of Holt. Loc,
Stody CP. P Melton Constable. Ch e, m.

HURDSFIELD Ches
110 SJ 9274 just NE of Macclesfield.
CP, 465. Mcclsfld RD. P Mcclsfld.
Ch e, m2, v. Mcclsfld CC.

HURLEY Berks
159 SU 8283 4m WNW of Maidenhead.
CP, 1,931. Cookham RD. P Mdnhd. Ch e.
Windsor and Mdnhd CC (Wndsr). See also
Knowl Hill, Littlewick Grn, Warren Row.
Rems of 11c priory in grnds of Ladye Place.

HURLEY Warwicks
131 SO 2495 4m WSW of Atherstone. Loc,
Kingsbury CP. P Athrstne. Sch p.

HURN Hants
179 SZ 1297 4m NE of Bournemouth.
CP, 381. Ringwood and Fordingbridge RD.
P Christchurch. Ch v. New Forest CC.
Bnmth Airpt to NW.

HURSLEY Hants
168 SU 4225 4m SW of Winchester.
CP, 728. Wnchstr RD. P Wnchstr. Ch e.
Sch pe. Wnchstr CC. See also Standon. 19c
ch blt for Keble, leader of Oxford
Movement. Computer research
establishment at H. Pk.

HURST Berks
159/169 SU 7973 5m E of Reading.
CP (St Nicholas, Hst), 1,248.
Wokingham RD. P Rdng. Ch e, b. Sch pe.
Wknghm CC.

HURST Lancs
101 SD 9400 just NE of Ashton-under-
Lyne. Loc, Ashtn-undr-Lne MB. P (Hst
Brook), Ashtn-undr-Lne.

HURSTBOURNE PRIORS Hants
168 SU 4346 5m E of Andover. CP, 592.
Kingsclere and Whitchurch RD. P Whitchch.
Ch e. Basingstoke CC.

HURSTBOURNE TARRANT Hants
168 SU 3853 5m NNE of Andover. CP, 593.
Andvr RD. P Andvr. Ch e. Sch pe.
Winchester CC (Basingstoke). See also
Ibthorpe. Former Vctrn ch and 17c cottages
converted into Bladon Gallery*, exhibitions
of crafts and pictures.

HURST GREEN Lancs
94, 95 SD 6838 5m SW of Clitheroe. Loc,
Aighton, Bailey and Chaigley CP.
Clthroe RD. P Blackburn. Ch e. Sch pe, pr.
Clthroe CC. 1m NE, Stonyhurst (RC)
College, boys' public sch.

HURST GREEN Surrey
171 TQ 3951 1m S of Oxted. Loc, Oxtd CP.
Ch e, m, v2. Sch p.

HURST GREEN Sussex (E)
183, 184 TQ 7327 3m SW of Hawkhurst.
CP, 767. Battle RD. P Etchingham. Ch e, r.
Sch pe. Rye CC.

HURSTPIERPOINT Sussex (E)
182 TQ 2816 3m SW of Burgess Hill.
CP, 4,802. Cuckfield RD. P Hassocks.
Ch e, b, m, r, v. Sch pe. Mid-Sx CC (Lewes).
See also Sayers Cmmn. 1m NE, St John's
College, Woodard sch for boys. 1m SE,
Danny*, Elizn hse.

HURSTWAY COMMON Herefs
142 SO 2949 6m NE of Hay-on-Wye. Loc,
Eardisley CP

HURSTWOOD Lancs
95 SD 8831 3m ESE of Burnley.
CP(Worsthorne-w-Hstwd), 1,640. Bnly RD.
Ch b. Clitheroe CC.

HURWORTH Co Durham
85 NZ 3010 3m S of Darlington. CP.
Dlngtn RD. P Dlngtn. Ch e, m2, r. Sch p, s.
Bishop Auckland CC (Sedgefield). Teesside
vllge with long grn.

HUSBANDS BOSWORTH Leics
132, 133 SP 6484 6m WSW of Mkt
Harborough. CP, 751. Mkt Hbrgh RD.
P Rugby, Warwickshire. Ch e, b, m, r.
Hbrgh CC.

HUSBORNE CRAWLEY Beds
147 SP 9535 5m WSW of Ampthill.
CP, 382. Ampthll RD. Ch e. Sch p.
Mid-Beds CC.

HUSTHWAITE Yorks (N)
92 SE 5175 3m NNW of Easingwold.
CP, 354. Easngwld RD. P YORK. Ch e, m.
Sch pe. Thirsk and Malton CC.

HUTHWAITE Notts
112 SK 4659 5m W of Mansfield. Loc,
Sutton in Ashfield UD. P Sttn-in-Ashfld.

HUTTOFT Lincs (L)
105 TF 5176 4m E of Alford. CP, 404.
Spilsby RD. P Alfd. Ch e, b, m. Sch p.
Horncastle CC.

HUTTON Cumb
83 NY 4326 6m WSW of Penrith. CP, 296.
Pnrth RD. Sch pe. Pnrth and the Border CC.
See also Penruddock, Troutbeck.

HUTTON Essex
161 TQ 6394 3m ENE of Brentwood. Loc,
Brntwd UD. P Brntwd.

HUTTON Lancs
94 SD 4926 3m WSW of Preston. CP, 1,720.
Prstn RD. P Prstn. S Fylde CC.

HUTTON Som
165 ST 3558 3m SE of Weston. CP, 821.
Axbridge RD. P Wstn-super-Mare. Ch e, v.
Sch pe. W-s-M CC. Wstn-spr-Mre Airpt
to NW.

HUTTON Yorks (E)
99 TA 0253 3m S of Driffield. Loc, Httn
Cranswick CP. P Drffld. Ch m.

HUTTON BONVILLE Yorks (N)
91 NZ 3400 5m NNW of Northallerton.
CP, 70. Nthlltn RD. Ch e. Richmond CC.

HUTTON BUSCEL Yorks (N)
93 SE 9784 5m SW of Scarborough.
CP, 318. Scbrgh RD. P Scbrgh. Ch e, m.
Scbrgh CC (Scbrgh and Whitby).

HUTTON CONYERS Yorks (N)
91 SE 3273 2m NNE of Ripon. CP, 175.
Wath RD. Thirsk and Malton CC.

HUTTON CRANSWICK Yorks (E)
99 TA 0252 3m S of Driffield. CP, 1,063.
Drffld RD. Ch e. Sch p. Howden CC. See
also Crnswck, Httn.

HUTTON HENRY Co Durham
85 NZ 4236 3m S of Peterlee. CP, 2,461.
Easington RD. P Castle Eden. Ch m2, r, s.
Sch pe. Easngtn CC. See also Stn Tn.

HUTTON-LE-HOLE Yorks (N)
86, 92 SE 7090 2m NNE of
Kirkbymoorside. CP, 196. Kbmsde RD.
P YORK. Ch m. Sch pe. Thirsk and
Malton CC. Stream runs through vllge. To
NW, Farndale, wild daffodil reserve. Rydale
Folk Museum.

HUTTON LOWCROSS Yorks (N)
86 NZ 6013 2m SSW of Guisborough. Loc,
Gsbrgh UD.

HUTTON MAGNA Yorks (N)
84 NZ 1212 5m ESE of Barnard Cstle.
CP, 102. Startforth RD. P Richmond. Ch e.
Rchmnd CC.

HUTTON MULGRAVE Yorks (N)
86 NZ 8310 4m W of Whitby. CP, 67.
Whtby RD. Cleveland and Whtby CC
(Scarborough and Whtby).

HUTTON ROOF Cumb
83 NY 3734 9m WNW of Penrith. Loc,
Mungrisdale CP. Sch pe.

HUTTON ROOF Westm
89 SD 5778 3m W of Kirkby Lonsdale.
CP, 161. S Westm RD. P Carnforth, Lancs.
Ch e. Westm CC.

HUTTON RUDBY Yorks (N)
85 NZ 4606 8m S of Teesside (Stockton).
CP, 948. Stokesley RD. P Yarm. Ch e, m.
Richmond CC. Blt round irregular grn with
trees.

HUTTON SESSAY Yorks (N)
91 SE 4776 5m SE of Thirsk. CP, 65.
Thsk RD. Ch m. Thsk and Malton CC.

HUTTON WANDESLEY Yorks (W)
97 SE 5050 6m W of York. CP, 81.
Wetherby RD. Barkston Ash CC.

HUXHAM Devon
176 SX 9497 4m NNE of Exeter. CP, 90.
St Thomas RD. Ch e. Tiverton CC.

HUXLEY Ches
109 SJ 5061 7m ESE of Chester. CP.
Tarvin RD. P Chstr. Ch m. Sch pe.
Northwich CC. To NW is Lr Hall*, moated
17c hse, once home of ancestors of famous
Huxley family.

HUYTON Lancs
100 SJ 4491 6m E of Liverpool.
UD(Htn-w-Roby), 66,629. P LVPL. Htn CC.

HYCEMOOR Cumb
88 SD 0989 8m NW of Millom. Loc,
Bootle CP.

HYDE Ches
101 SJ 9494 5m NE of Stockport.
MB, 37,075. P. Stalybridge and Hyde CC.

See also Gee Cross. Grew as cotton tn; now has divers industries.

HYDE Glos
156, 157 SO 8801 3m SE of Stroud. Loc, Minchinhampton CP. Above Golden Valley; much NT property in area.

HYDE Hants
179 SU 1612 2m SE of Fordingbridge. Loc, Fdngbrdge CP. P Fdngbrdge. Ch e. Sch pe.

HYDE HEATH Bucks
159 SP 9300 2m WSW of Chesham. Loc, Lit Missenden CP. P Amersham. Sch p.

HYDE LEA Staffs
119 SJ 9120 2m SSW of Stafford. Loc, Cstle Ch CP. Stffd RD. P STFFD. Sch pe. Stffd and Stone CC.

HYDESTILE Surrey
169, 170, 182 SU 9640 2m S of Godalming. Loc, Hambledon RD. P Gdlmng. Guildford CC.

HYTHE Hants
180 SU 4207 3m NNW of Fawley. Loc, Dibden CP. P SOUTHAMPTON. Ch e, c, r. Sch i, j, p, s. Ferry to Sthmptn Docks.

HYTHE Kent
173 TR 1634 4m W of Folkestone. MB, 11,949. P. Flkstne and Hthe CC. See also Palmarsh. Resort; old Military Canal and Romney Hthe and Dymchurch light rly run through it. One of orig Cinque Ports.

HYTHE END Bucks
160, 169, 170 TQ 0172 1m NW of Staines. Loc, Wraysbury CP.

I

IBBERTON Dorset
178 ST 7807 6m W of Blandford. CP, 97. Sturminster RD. P Blndfd Forum. Ch e, m. N Dst CC.

IBLE Derbys
111 SK 2457 4m WSW of Matlock. CP, 32. Ashbne RD. Ch m. W Derbys CC.

IBSLEY Hants
179 SU 1509 3m N of Ringwood. CP(Harbridge and Ibsley), 662. Rngwd and Fordingbridge RD. P Rngwd. Ch e, v. New Forest CC.

IBSTOCK Leics
121 SK 4010 3m SSW of Coalville. CP, 4,954. Mkt Bosworth RD. P LCSTR. Ch e, b, m2, v2. Sch ie, j, p, s. Bswth CC. See also Ellistown. Coal-mining and indstrl tn.

IBSTONE Bucks
159 SU 7593 7m W of High Wycombe. CP, 305. Wcmbe RD. Ch e. Sch pe. Aylesbury CC (Wcmbe).

IBTHORPE Hants
168 SU 3753 5m N of Andover. Loc, Hurstbourne Tarrant CP. Ch m.

IBURNDALE Yorks (N)
86, 93 NZ 8707 3m SW of Whitby. Loc, Eskdaleside cum Ugglebarnby CP. Whtby RD. Cleveland and Whtby CC (Scarborough and Whtby).

IBWORTH Hants
168 SU 5654 5m WNW of Basingstoke. Loc, Kingsclere CP.

ICKBURGH Norfolk
136 TL 8194 5m NNE of Brandon. CP, 141. Swaffham RD. Ch e. SW Nflk CC.

ICKENHAM London
160 TQ 0886 2m NE of Uxbridge. Loc, Hillingdon LB. P Uxbrdge, Middx. Uxbrdge BC (CC). Swakeleys*, 17c hse with 22 Dutch gables.

ICKFORD Bucks
158, 159 SP 6407 4m W of Thame. CP, 254. Aylesbury RD. P Aylesbury. Ch e. Sch p. Aylesbury CC.

ICKHAM Kent
173 TR 2258 5m E of Canterbury. CP(Ickhm and Well), 420. Bridge-Blean RD. P Cntrbry. Ch e. Cntrbry CC.

ICKLEFORD Herts
147 TL 1831 2m N of Hitchin. CP, 1,190.
Htchn RD. P Htchn. Ch e, m. Sch pe.
Htchn CC.

ICKLESHAM Sussex (E)
184 TQ 8716 4m SW of Rye. CP, 1,974.
Battle RD. P Winchelsea. Ch e, m. Sch pe.
Rye CC. See also Rye Harbour, Wnchlsea,
Wnchlsea Beach. Ch has good Nmn work.

ICKLETON Cambs
148 TL 4943 4m NNW of Saffron Walden.
CP, 605. S Cambs RD. P Sffrn Wldn, Essex.
Ch e, m, v. Cambs CC. Four of the pillars in
the ch are Roman monoliths taken by the
Nmns from a nearby bldng.

ICKLINGHAM Suffolk (W)
136 TL 7772 7m NW of Bury St Edmunds.
CP, 374. Mildenhall RD. P Bury St Eds.
Ch e2, m. Sch pe. Bury St Eds CC. On
R Lark and edge of Breckland. Roman rd
passes to N; Roman rems found.

ICKWELL GREEN Beds
147 TL 1545 3m W of Biggleswade. Loc,
Northill CP. Revels in May round maypole
on large vllge grn. Thomas Tompion, 17c
clockmaker, worked here.

ICOMB Glos
144 SP 2122 2m SSE of Stow-on-the-Wold.
CP, 133. N Cotswold RD. P Cheltenham.
Ch e. Cirencester and Tewkesbury CC.

IDBURY Oxon
144 SP 2319 5m N of Burford. CP, 105.
Chipping Norton RD. Ch e. Banbury CC.

IDDESLEIGH Devon
175 SS 5608 8m N of Okehampton.
CP, 227. Okhmptn RD. P Winkleigh.
Ch e, m. W Dvn CC (Torrington).

IDE Devon
176 SX 8990 2m SW of Exeter. CP, 598.
St Thomas RD. P Extr. Ch e, c. Sch p.
Tiverton CC.

IDEFORD Devon
176, 188 SX 8977 4m NNE of Newton
Abbot. CP, 274. Ntn Abbt RD. P Ntn Abbt.
Ch e. Sch pe. Totnes CC.

IDE HILL Kent
171 TQ 4851 3m SW of Sevenoaks. Loc,
Sundridge CP. P Svnks. Ch e. Sch pe. Blt

round grn, high on wooded ridge. Much NT
land.

IDEN Sussex (E)
184 TQ 9123 2m N of Rye. CP, 417.
Battle RD. P Rye. Ch e, m. Rye CC. Ch:
priest brass, 15c.

IDEN GREEN Kent
184 TQ 8031 3m SE of Cranbrook. Loc,
Benenden CP. P Crnbrk. Ch c.

IDLESS Cornwall
190 SW 8247 2m N of Truro. Loc,
Kenwyn CP. Truro RD. Ch m. Truro CC.

IDLICOTE Warwicks
145 SP 2844 3m NNE of Shipston on Stour.
CP, 79. Shpstn on Str RD. Ch e.
Stratford-on-Avon CC (Strtfd).

IDMISTON Wilts
167 SU 1937 6m NE of Salisbury.
CP, 1,394. Amesbury RD. Ch e, m. Sch pe.
Slsbry CC. See also Gomeldon, Porton.

IDRIDGEHAY Derbys
111 SK 2848 4m WNW of Belper.
CP(Idrdghy and Alton), 240. Blpr RD.
P DERBY. Ch e. Sch pe. Blpr CC. See also
Ireton Wood.

IDSTONE Berks
157 SU 2584 7m E of Swindon. Loc,
Ashbury CP. Hmlt of brick and chalk below
the ancient Ridgeway, on Wilts border.

IFIELD Sussex (W)
170, 182 TQ 2437 1m WNW of Crawley.
Loc, Crly UD. P Crly.

IFOLD Sussex (W)
169, 181, 182 TQ 0231 5m NW of
Billingshurst. Loc, Plaistow CP.

IFORD Sussex (E)
183 TQ 4007 2m S of Lewes. CP, 240.
Chailey RD. Ch e. Lws CC.

IFTON HEATH Shrops
118 SJ 3237 5m WNW of Ellesmere. Loc,
St Martin's CP. Ch m2. Sch p. Colliery.

IGHTFIELD Shrops
118 SJ 5938 4m ESE of Whitchurch.
CP, 508. Mkt Drayton RD. P Whtchch.
Ch e. Sch pe. Oswestry CC. See also
Calverhall. Ch has 15c canopied brass over
7ft long.

IGHTHAM Kent
171 TQ 5956 4m E of Sevenoaks.
CP, 1,544. Malling RD. P Svnks. Ch e, m.
Sch p. Tonbridge and Mllg CC (Svnks). See
also Ivy Hatch. 1m SW, Oldbury Camp,
largest Iron Age fort in Kent. Monmt in ch
to Cawne family of Ightham Mote (see Ivy
Hatch).

IKEN Suffolk (E)
150 TM 4155 3m W of Aldeburgh. CP, 147.
Deben RD. P Woodbridge. Ch e. Eye CC.
Well sited near head of long Alde estuary.
Ch 'completely surrounded by private
property'.

ILAM Staffs
111 SK 1350 4m NW of Ashbourne.
CP, 175. Leek RD. Ch e. Sch pe. Lk CC. On
R Manifold (here NT, together with other
land in distr). I. Hall now a youth hostel.
Ch: maidens' garlands.

ILCHESTER Som
177 ST 5222 5m NNW of Yeovil. CP, 1,401.
Yvl RD. P Yvl. Ch e, m. Sch p. Yvl CC. See
also Northover. In tn hall is 13c mace,
oldest staff of office in England, perhaps in
Europe.

ILDERTON Nthmb
71 NU 0121 4m SSE of Wooler. CP, 145.
Glendale RD. Ch e. Berwick-upon-Tweed CC.
See also N Middleton, S Mddltn.

ILFORD London
161 TQ 4486 10m ENE of Charing Cross.
Loc, Redbridge LB. P Essex.
Ilfd N BC, Ilfd S BC.

ILFRACOMBE Devon
163 SS 5247 9m NNW of Barnstaple. UD,
9,846. P. N Dvn CC. See also Hele, Lee,
Slade. Resort with several small beaches and
coves.

ILKESTON Derbys
112, 121 SK 4642 8m ENE of Derby. MB,
34,123. P. Ilkstn CC. See also Kirk Hallam.
Mnfg tn.

ILKETSHALL ST ANDREW Suffolk (E)
137 TM 3887 3m SW of Beccles. CP(St
Andrw, Ilktshll), 266. Wainford RD. P Bccls.
Ch e, m. Lowestoft CC. Vast common; a few
cottages scattered round edges. Ch in one
corner; nave walls lean perilously.

ILKETSHALL ST JOHN Suffolk (E)
137 TM 3687 2m SE of Bungay. CP, 33.
Wainford RD. Ch e. Lowestoft CC.

ILKETSHALL ST LAWRENCE Suffolk (E)
137 TM 3784 4m SSE of Bungay. CP, 190.
Wainford RD. P Beccles. Ch e, m. Sch p.
Lowestoft CC.

ILKETSHALL ST MARGARET Suffolk (E)
137 TM 3585 3m SSE of Bungay.
CP(St Mgrt, Ilktshll), 178. Wainford RD.
P Bngy. Ch e. Lowestoft CC. Ch with round
partly Saxon twr stands beside farm near
vllge centre.

ILKLEY Yorks (W)
96 SE 1147 10m NNW of Bradford. UD,
21,828. P. Ripon CC. See also Ben Rhydding,
Burley-in-Wharfedale, Brly Woodhead, Mens-
ton. Roman military stn (Olicana). Medicinal
springs. Rsdntl, resort, 'gateway to Dales'.
16c mnr hse now museum and art gallery.
Just SE, Cow and Calf Rocks, on edge of
I. Moor, which is rich in prehistoric rems.

ILLOGAN Cornwall
189 SW 6744 2m NW of Redruth. Loc,
Camborne-Rdrth UD. P(Illgn
Highway), Rdrth.

ILLSTON ON THE HILL Leics
133 SP 7099 9m ESE of Leicester. CP, 164.
Billesdon RD. P LCSTR. Ch e.
Harborough CC (Melton).

ILMER Bucks
159 SP 7605 3m NW of Princes Risborough.
CP(Longwick-cum-Ilmr), 640.
Wycombe RD. Ch e. Aylesbury CC
(Wcmbe).

ILMINGTON Warwicks
144 SP 2143 5m NE of Chipping Campden.
CP, 537. Shipston on Stour RD. P Shpstn
on Str. Ch e, m, r. Sch pe.
Stratford-on-Avon CC (Strtfd). Handsome
vllge with partly Nmn ch at centre. To SW,
Foxcote, large 18c hse on Glos border.

ILMINSTER Som
177 ST 3614 10m SE of Taunton.
UD, 3,375. P. Yeovil CC. Stone mkt tn,
once with flourishing wool trade. Ch has
lofty twr.

ILSINGTON Devon
175, 187, 188 SX 7876 4m NNE of
Ashburton. CP, 1,384. Newton Abbot RD.
P Ntn Abbt. Ch e, m. Sch pe. Totnes CC.
See also Coldeast, Haytor Vale, Liverton,
Sigford, S Knighton.

ILTON Som
177 ST 3517 2m NNW of Ilminster.
CP, 595. Chard RD. P Ilmnstr. Ch e, m.
Sch . Yeovil CC.

ILTON Yorks (N)
91 SE 1978 3m SW of Masham.
CP(Iltn-cum-Pott), 74. Mshm RD. Ch m.
Richmond CC.

IMBER Wilts
167 ST 9648 6m ESE of Westbury. CP, nil.
Warminster and Wstbry RD. Ch e.
Wstbry CC. Deserted vllge in prohibited
Army battle-training area.

IMMINGHAM Lincs (L)
105 TA 1814 6m NW of Grimsby.
CP, 4,208. Grmsby RD. P Grmsby. Ch e, m.
Sch i, j, p, pe, s. Louth CC. Extensive docks.
Oil refinery, chemical wks.

IMPINGTON Cambs
135 TL 4463 3m N of Cambridge. CP, 1,232.
Chesterton RD. P CMBRDGE. Ch e. Sch j, s.
Cambs CC. Vllge college, blt in 1930s.

INCE Ches
100, 109 SJ 4576 7m NNE of Chester. Loc,
Ellesmere Port MB.

INCE BLUNDELL Lancs
100 SD 3203 3m SSE of Formby. CP, 464.
W Lancs RD. P Hightown, LIVERPOOL.
Ch r. Sch pr. Crosby BC (Ormskirk CC).
I.B. Hall, early 18c hse; domed pantheon of
1802.

INCE-IN-MAKERFIELD Lancs
100 SD 5904 just SE of Wigan. UD, 15,925.
P(Ince), Wgn. Ince BC.

INDIAN QUEENS Cornwall
185 SW 9159 7m ESE of Newquay. Loc,
St Austell RD. Ch m. Sch p. N Cnwll CC.
Origin of name unknown.

INGATESTONE Essex
161 TQ 6599 5m NE of Brentwood.
CP(Ingtstne and Fryerning), 3,549.

Chelmsford RD. P. Ch e, r, v2.
Sch i, je, pe, s. Chlmsfd CC. See also Mill
Grn. Old mkt tn with much modern rsdntl
development. I. Hall*, 16c brick hse, part
let to Essex CC and used for exhibitions.

INGBIRCHWORTH Yorks (W)
102 SE 2205 2m NW of Penistone.
CP(Gunthwaite and Ingbchwth), 298.
Pnstne RD. Ch m. Pnstne CC.

INGESTRE Staffs
119 SJ 9824 4m ENE of Stafford. CP, 116.
Stffd RD. P STFFD. Ch e. Stffd and
Stone CC. Ch prob by Wren. Hall, 17c and
early 19c, now arts centre.

INGHAM Lincs (L)
104 SK 9483 8m N of Lincoln. CP, 594.
Welton RD. P LNCLN. Ch e, m. Sch p.
Gainsborough CC. Derelict airfield with
accompanying ruins.

INGHAM Norfolk
126 TG 3926 7m ESE of N Walsham.
CP, 352. Smallburgh RD.
P NORWICH, NOR 33Z. Ch e. Sch pe.
N Nflk CC.

INGHAM Suffolk (W)
136 TL 8570 4m N of Bury St Edmunds.
CP, 291. Thingoe RD. P Bury St Eds. Ch e.
Sch pe. Bury St Eds CC.

INGLEBY Derbys
120, 121 SK 3526 6m S of Derbys. CP, 56.
Repton RD. Belper CC.

INGLEBY ARNCLIFFE Yorks (N)
91 NZ 4400 7m NE of Northallerton.
CP, 239. Stokesley RD. Ch e, m. Sch pe.
Richmond CC. Arncliffe Hall by Carr of
York.

INGLEBY GREENHOW Yorks (N)
86 NZ 5806 4m ESE of Stokesley. CP, 403.
Stksly RD. P MIDDLESBROUGH, Teesside.
Ch e. Sch pe. Richmond CC. See also
Battersby.

INGLEIGH GREEN Devon
175 SS 6007 7m N of Okehampton. Loc,
Broadwoodkelly CP.

INGLESBATCH Som
166 ST 7061 4m SW of Bath. Loc,
Englishcombe CP.

INGLESHAM Wilts
157 SU 2098 9m NNE of Swindon.
CP, 169. Highworth RD. Ch e. Devizes CC.
See also Upr Inglshm.

INGLETON Co Durham
85 NZ 1720 6m SSW of Bishop Auckland.
CP, 336. Barnard Cstle RD. P Darlington.
Ch e, m. Sch pe. Bshp Aucklnd CC.

INGLETON Yorks (W)
89 SD 6973 6m SE of Kirkby Lonsdale.
CP, 1,887. Settle RD. P Carnforth, Lancs.
Ch e, m. Sch p, s. Skipton CC. See also Chpl
le Dale. In limestone Craven distr. To NE,
Ingleborough, 2,373ft; on lr slopes, many
caves and potholes; most famous are White
Scar Caves* and Gaping Ghyll Pot. Falls
Walk* leads through deep gorge with
numerous waterfalls.

INGLEWHITE Lancs
94 SD 5440 7m N of Preston. Loc,
Goosnargh CP. P Prstn. Ch v.

INGOE Nthmb
77, 78 NZ 0374 7m NNE of Corbridge. Loc,
Matfen CP. Ch m. Sch p. Standing stone;
hut circles.

INGOLDISTHORPE Norfolk
124 TF 6832 5m S of Hunstanton. CP, 488.
Docking RD. P King's Lynn. Ch e. Sch pe.
NW Nflk CC (K's Lnn).

INGOLDMELLS Lincs (L)
114 TF 5668 3m N of Skegness. CP, 790.
Spilsby RD. P Skgnss. Ch e, m. Sch p.
Horncastle CC. Holiday camp. Thousands of
caravans.

INGOLDSBY Lincs (K)
113, 123 TF 0130 7m SE of Grantham.
CP, 212. W Kesteven RD. P Grnthm.
Ch e, m. Sch p. Rutland and Stamford CC.

INGRAM Nthmb
71 NU 0116 8m SSE of Wooler. CP, 172.
Glendale RD. Ch e. Berwick-upon-Tweed
CC. See also Brandon, Branton. 12c–13c
ch by R Breamish. Many prehistoric camps
on hills to W and S, esp Greaves Ash, near
50ft waterfall of Linhope Spout.

INGRAVE Essex
161 TQ 6291 2m SE of Brentwood. Loc,
Brntwd UD. P Brntwd.

INGS Westm
89 SD 4498 2m E of Windermere. Loc,
Hugill CP. S Westm RD. Ch e. Sch pe.
Westm CC.

INGST Glos
155, 156 ST 5887 9m N of Bristol. Loc,
Olveston CP.

INGWORTH Norfolk
126 TG 1929 2m N of Aylsham. CP, 122.
Erpingham RD. P NORWICH, NOR 50Y.
Ch e, v. N Nflk CC.

INKBERROW Worcs
131 SP 0157 5m W of Alcester.
CP, Evesham RD. P WORCESTER. Ch e.
Sch p. S Worcs CC. See also Cladswell,
Cookhill, Holberrow Grn, New End, Stock
Wd. In vicarage, book of maps left by
Charles I on way to Naseby, 1645.

INKPEN Berks
168 SU 3664 3m SSE of Hungerford.
CP, 697. Hngrfd RD. P Newbury. Ch e, m.
Sch p. Nbry CC. See also Upr Grn. Under
Inkpn Hill, with Combe Gibbet on top.
Wansdyke, ancient bank prob thrown up for
defence, runs from here to Bristol Channel.

INNER TEMPLE London
160 TQ 3180 just ENE of Charing Cross.
See Temples, Inner and Middle.

INSKIP Lancs
94 SD 4637 7m NW of Preston.
CP (Inskp-w-Sowerby), 552. Garstand RD.
P Prstn. Ch e, b. Sch pe. N Fylde CC. See
also Crossmoor.

INSTOW Devon
163 SS 4730 3m NNE of Bideford. CP, 782.
Barnstaple RD. P Bdfd. Ch e, m. Sch p.
N Dvn CC. See also Bickleton. At junction
of Taw and Torridge. Yachting,
water-skiing.

INWARDLEIGH Devon
175 SX 5699 3m NNW of Okehampton.
CP, 418. Okhmptn RD. P Okhmptn.
Ch e, b, m. W Dvn CC (Torrington). See also
Folly Gate.

INWORTH Essex
149, 162 TL 8717 1m NW of Tiptree.
CP (Messing-cum-Inwth), 363. Lexden and
Winstree RD. Ch e. Colchester CC.

IPING Sussex (W)
181 SU 8522 2m WNW of Midhurst.
CP, 400. Mdhst RD. Ch e. Chichester CC
(Horsham).

IPPLEPEN Devon
188 SX 8366 3m SSW of Newton Abbot.
CP, 1,128. Ntn Abbt RD. P Ntn Abbt.
Ch e, m. Sch p. Totnes CC.

IPPOLLITTS Herts
147 TL 1927 2m SSE of Hitchin. CP, 1,290.
Htchn RD. Ch e. Sch pe. Htchn CC. See also
Gosmore.

IPSDEN Oxon
158, 159 SU 6385 3m SSE of Wallingford.
CP, 314. Henley RD. P OXFORD. Ch e.
Sch pe. Hnly CC. Wellplace Bird Farm*.

IPSTONES Staffs
111 SK 0250 5m SSE of Leek. CP, 1,470.
Cheadle RD. P Stoke-on-Trent. Ch e, m.
Sch pe. Lk CC. See also Foxt, Froghall.

IPSWICH Suffolk (E)
150 TM 1644 66m NE of London.
CB, 122,814. P. Ipswch BC. See also
Westerfield, Whitton. County tn of E Sfflk.
Indstrl. Port. Large expansion scheduled.
Bthplce of Cardinal Wolsey. Several old
bldngs.

IRBY Ches
100, 108, 109 SJ 2584 5m SW of
Birkenhead. Loc, Wirral UD.
P Heswall, Wrrl. Wrrl CC.

IRBY IN THE MARSH Lincs (L)
114 TF 4663 6m W of Skegness. CP, 131.
Spilsby RD. P(Irby), Skgnss. Ch e, m.
Horncastle CC.

IRBY UPON HUMBER Lincs (L)
105 TA 1904 5m WSW of Grimsby.
CP(Irby), 115. Grmsby RD. Ch e, m.
Louth CC.

IRCHESTER Northants
133 SP 9265 3m SE of Wellingborough.
CP, 2,832. Wllngbrgh RD. P Wllngbrgh.
Ch e, m. Sch i, j. Wllngbrgh CC. See also Lit
Irchstr.

IREBY Cumb
82 NY 2338 6m SSW of Wigton. CP, 479.
Wgtn RD. P Carlisle. Ch e, m. Sch pe.
Penrith and the Border CC. See also Uldale.

IREBY Lancs
89 SD 6575 3m SE of Kirkby Lonsdale.
CP, 73. Lunesdale RD. Lncstr CC.

IRELETH Lancs
88 SD 2277 6m NNE of Barrow. Loc,
Dalton-in-Furness UD. P Askam-on-Fnss.

IRESHOPEBURN Co Durham
84 NY 8638 8m W of Stanhope. Loc,
Stnhpe CP. P Bishop Auckland.

IRETON WOOD Derbys
111 SK 2847 4m W of Belper. Loc,
Idridgehay and Alton CP. Ch m.

IRLAM Lancs
101 SJ 7294 7m WSW of Manchester.
UD, 20,571. P MNCHSTR. Newton CC. See
also Cadishead. Iron and steel wks.
Chemicals.

IRNHAM Lincs (K)
123 TF 0226 6m NW of Bourne. CP, 204.
S Kesteven RD. P Grantham. Ch e. Sch pe.
Rutland and Stamford CC. Ch: 14c
brasses.

IRON ACTON Glos
155, 156 ST 6783 8m ESE of Severn Rd Br.
CP, 1,170. Sodbury RD. P BRISTOL.
Ch e, v. Sch pe. S Glos CC. See also
Latteridge. 15c cross in churchyard.

IRONBRIDGE Shrops
118, 119 SJ 6703 4m NE of Much Wenlock.
Loc, Dawley UD. P Telford. The Wrekin CC
(Ludlow). The br over the Severn gorge cast
in 1778, first cold blast iron br in the world.
Still used by foot passengers.

IRON CROSS Warwicks
144 SP 0652 6m NNE of Evesham. Loc,
Salford Priors CP.

IRONVILLE Derbys
112 SK 4351 3m SE of Alfreton. Loc,
Alfrtn UD. P NOTTINGHAM. Planned as an
indstrl housing estate in mid 19c.

IRSTEAD Norfolk
126 TG 3620 5m ENE of Wroxham. Loc,
Barton Turf CP. Ch e.

IRTHINGTON Cumb
76 NY 4961 2m W of Brampton. CP, 678.
Border RD. P Carlisle. Ch e. Sch p. Penrith
and the Bdr CC. See also Laversdale,
Newby E, Newtown.

IRTHLINGBOROUGH Northants
133 SP 9470 4m ENE of Wellingborough.
UD, 5,145. P Wllngbrgh. Wllngbrgh CC.
Ironworks, footwear factóries.

IRTON Yorks (N)
93 TA 0184 3m SW of Scarborough.
CP, 245. Scbrgh RD. Sch p. Scbrgh CC
(Scbrgh and Whitby).

ISFIELD Sussex (E)
183 TQ 4417 3m SSW of Uckfield. CP, 461.
Uckfld RD. P Uckfld. Ch e. Sch pe.
E Grinstead CC.

ISHAM Northants
133 SP 8873 3m SSE of Kettering. CP, 535.
Wellingborough RD. P Kttrng. Ch e, v.
Sch pe. Wllngbrgh CC.

ISLE ABBOTTS Som
177 ST 3520 4m N of Ilminster. CP, 128.
Langport RD. P Taunton. Ch e, b.
Yeovil CC. Ch: carved twr.

ISLE BREWERS Som
177 ST 3621 4m N of Ilminster. CP, 180.
Langport RD. P Taunton. Ch e. Yeovil CC.

ISLEHAM Cambs
135 TL 6474 7m N of Newmarket.
CP, 1,392. Nmkt RD. P Ely. Ch e, b3, m.
Sch pe. Cambs CC.

ISLE OF DOGS London
161, 171 TQ 3878 2m S of Poplar. Loc,
Twr Hmlts LB. Stepney and Pplr BC (Pplr).
On N bank of Thames; surrounded by river
on three sides and docks on fourth.
Pedestrian subway under river to
Greenwich.

ISLES OF SCILLY
189 (inset) 37m WSW of Penzance. Islands
separately listed: Bryher, St Agnes,
St Martin's, St Mary's, Tresco. Places: Hr Tn,
Lr Tn, Middle Tn: St Mtn's; Hugh Tn:
St Mry's; New Grimsby, Old Grimsby: Trsco.
Reached by boat from Pnznce, by air from
Pnznce and Gatwick. Total pop. 2,428.

ISLEWORTH London
160, 170 TQ 1675 2m E of Hounslow. Loc,
Hnslw LB. P Middx. Brentford and Islwth
BC (Heston and Islwth).

ISLEY WALTON Leics
121 SK 4225 7m SW of Long Eaton. Loc,
Isley cum Langley CP. Cstle Donington RD.
Ch e. Loughborough CC.

ISLINGTON London
160 TQ 3185 3m NNE of Charing Cross.
LB, 199,129. BCs: Islngtn Central,
Islngtn N, Islngtn S and Finsbury
(Islngtn E, N, SW, Shoreditch and Fnsbry).
See also Canonbury, Clerkenwell, Fnsbry,
Highbury, Holloway, Pentonville.

ISLIP Northants
134 SP 9878 just W of Thrapston. CP, 589.
Oundle and Thrpstn RD. P Kettering. Ch e.
Sch pe. Wellingborough CC (Peterborough).

ISLIP Oxon
145 SP 5214 5m N of Oxford. CP, 620.
Ploughley RD. P OXFD. Ch e, m. Sch pe.
Mid-Oxon CC (Henley). Bthplce of Edward
the Confessor, 1004.

ITCHEN ABBAS Hants
168 SU 5332 4m NE of Winchester. Loc,
Itchn Valley CP. Wnchstr RD. P Wnchstr.
Ch e. Sch p. Wnchstr CC.

ITCHEN STOKE Hants
168 SU 5532 5m ENE of Winchester.
CP, 253. Wnchstr RD. Ch e. Wnchstr CC.

ITCHINGFIELD Sussex (W)
182 TQ 1328 3m SW of Horsham. CP, 927.
Hshm RD. Ch e. Sch p. Hshm and
Crawley CC (Hshm). See also Barns Grn. 1m
E, Christ's Hsptl, boys' sch moved from
London in 1902.

ITCHINGTON Glos
155, 156 ST 6586 6m ESE of Severn Rd Br.
Loc, Tytherington.

ITTERINGHAM Norfolk
125 TG 1430 4m NW of Aylsham. CP, 219.
Erpingham RD. P NORWICH, NOR 17Y.
Ch e, m. Sch pe. N Nflk CC. To N,
Mannington Hall, moated 15c hse with
much Vctrn Gothic alteration. Many Vctrn
Gthc edifices in grnds*.

IVEGILL Cumb
83 NY 4143 8m S of Carlisle. Loc,
Penrith RD. P Clsle. Ch e. Sch pe. Pnrth and
the Border CC.

IVER Bucks
160 TQ 0381 2m SSW of Uxbridge.
CP, 10,816. Eton RD. P. Ch e, c, m, r, v.
Sch p, s. Beaconsfield CC (S Bucks). See
also Colnbrook. I. Grove (NT)* at
Shredding Grn is by Vanbrugh.

IVER HEATH Bucks
159, 160 TQ 0283 4m ENE of Slough. Loc,
Ivr CP. P Ivr. Ch e, r. Sch p. Pinewood Film
Studios 1m NW.

IVESTON Co Durham
78 NZ 1350 2m E of Consett. Loc,
Cnstt UD.

IVINGHOE Bucks
146, 159 SP 9416 3m NNE of Tring.
CP, 863. Wing RD. P Leighton
Buzzard, Beds. Ch e, b, v. Buckingham CC.
Considerable area of Chilterns in the vicinity
is NT property, incl I. Beacon, famous
viewpoint.

IVINGHOE ASTON Bucks
147 SP 9518 5m WSW of Dunstable. Loc,
Ivnghoe CP. P Leighton Buzzard, Beds.
Ch m.

IVINGTON Herefs
129 SO 4756 2m SW of Leominster. Loc,
Lmnstr MB.

IVINGTON GREEN Herefs
129 SO 4656 3m SW of Leominster. Loc,
Lmnstr MB.

IVYBRIDGE Devon
187, 188 SX 6356 10m E of Plymouth.
CP, 1,753. Plympton St Mary RD. P.
Ch e, c, m. Sch p, s. W Dvn CC (Tavistock).

IVYCHURCH Kent
184 TR 0227 8m NE of Rye. CP, 211.
Romney Marsh RD. P Rmny Msh. Ch e, m.
Folkestone and Hythe CC. Typical Rmny
Msh vllge. Very large ch.

IVY HATCH Kent
171 TQ 5854 4m E of Sevenoaks. Loc,
Ightham CP. P Svnks. To S, Ightham
Mote*, moated mdvl mnr hse (NT).

IWADE Kent
172 TQ 9067 2m N of Sittingbourne.
CP, 598. Swale RD. P Sttngbne. Ch e. Sch p.
Faversham CC. Mainly indstrl. 1m NE rise
concrete twrs of Kingsferry Br.

IWERNE COURTNEY Dorset
178 ST 8512 4m NNW of Blandford.
Sometimes called Shroton. CP, 311.
Blndfd RD. P Blndfd Forum. Ch e, m.
Sch pe. N Dst CC. See also Farrington.

IWERNE MINSTER Dorset
178 ST 8614 5m N of Blandford. CP, 467.
Shaftesbury RD. Ch e, m. Sch pe. N Dst CC.

IXWORTH Suffolk (W)
136 TL 9370 6m NE of Bury St Edmunds.
CP, 940. Thingoe RD, P Bury St Eds.
Ch e, m. Sch pe, s. Bury St Eds CC. Some
over-sailing hses. Pargetting. I. Abbey,
17c–18c hse with rems of 12c priory.

IXWORTH THORPE Suffolk (W)
136 TL 9173 7m NE of Bury St Edmunds.
CP, 103. Thingoe RD. Ch e. Bury
St Eds CC.

J

JACOBSTOW Cornwall
174 SX 1995 6m S of Bude. CP, 321.
Stratton RD. Ch e, m. Sch p. N Cnwll CC.

JACOBSTOWE Devon
175 SS 5801 4m N of Okehampton.
CP, 171. Okhmptn RD. Ch e. W Dvn CC
(Forrington).

JARROW Co Durham
78 NZ 3265 3m WSW of S Shields.
MB, 28,779. P. Jrrw BC. Tyneside tn.
Shipbuilding. Other industries, esp at Bede
Indstrl Estate. Par ch incorporates rems of
monastery where Venerable Bede lived and
died.

JAYWICK SANDS Essex
150 TM 1513 2m WSW of Clacton. Loc,
Clctn UD. P(Jwck), Clctn-on-Sea. Shacks
behind a sea wall. Martello twrs.

JESMOND Nthmb
78 NZ 2566 N distr of Newcastle. Loc,
Ncstle upon Tyne CB. Ncstle upn Tne N BC.
Contains the pk of J. Dene, romantically
landscaped wooded ravine.

JEVINGTON Sussex (E)
183 TQ 5601 4m NW of Eastbourne.
CP, 188. Hailsham RD. P Polegate. Ch e.
Eastbne CC.

JOCKEY END Herts
147, 160 TL 0313 4m NNW of Hemel
Hempstead. Loc, Gt Gaddesden CP.

JOHNSON'S STREET Norfolk
126 TG 3717 5m E of Wroxham. Loc,
Ludham CP.

JORDANS Bucks
159, 160 SU 9791 2m ENE of Beaconsfield.
Loc, Chalfont St Giles CP. P Bcnsfld. Ch f.
Sch p. Famous Meeting Hse of early
Quakers, some of whom are buried here,
incl William'Penn, founder of Pennsylvania.

JUMP Yorks (W)
102, 103 SE 3801 4m SE of Barnsley. Loc,
Wombwell UD. P Bnsly.

K

KABER Westm
84 NY 7911 2m S of Brough. CP, 107.
N Westm RD. Ch m. Sch p. Westm CC.

KEA Cornwall
190 SW 8142 2m SW of Truro. CP, 1,504.
Truro RD. Ch e, m5. Sch p. Truro CC. See
also Baldhu, Bissoe, Old Kea, Playing Place.

KEADBY Lincs (L)
104 SE 8311 4m E of Crowle. CP(Kdby
w Althorpe), 2,001. Isle of Axholme RD.
P Scunthorpe. Ch m, r. Sch p.
Gainsborough CC. See also Derrythorpe.
Swing br over R Trent. Power stn.

KEAL COTES Lincs (L)
114 TF 3661 8m SE of Horncastle. Loc,
Spilsby RD. P Splsby. Ch m. Hncstle CC.

KEARSLEY Lancs
101 SD 7504 4m SE of Bolton. UD, 11,243.
P Bltn. Farnworth BC (CC).

KEARSTWICK Westm
89 SD 6080 just N of Kirkby Lonsdale. Loc,
Kby Lnsdle CP.

KEASDEN Yorks (W)
90 SD 7266 6m WNW of Settle. Loc,
Clapham cum Newby CP. Ch e, m.

KEDDINGTON Lincs (L)
105 TF 3488 1m NE of Louth. CP, 118.
Lth RD. Ch e. Lth CC. Ch: 15c wooden
eagle lectern, one of six in England.

KEDINGTON Suffolk (W)
148, 149 TL 7046 2m ENE of Haverhill.
CP, 855. Clare RD. P Hvrhll. Ch e, v. Sch pe.
Bury St Edmunds CC. (Sometimes called
Ketton). Many new hses. Ch outstanding;
furnishings from many periods.

KEDLESTON Derbys
120, 121 SK 3041 4m NW of Derby.
CP, 68. Belper RD. Ch e. Blpr CC. K. Hall*,
Ggn hse by Adam and others, in deer pk*
with lake.

KEELBY Lincs (L)
105 TA 1610 3m SSW of Immingham.
CP, 777. Caistor RD. P Grimsby. Ch e, m2.
Sch p. Gainsborough CC.

KEELE Staffs
110 SJ 8045 3m W of Newcastle-under
-Lyme. CP, 1,529. Ncstle-undr-Lme RD.
P Ncstle. Ch e. Sch pe. N-u-L BC. Modern
university in pk of former hall.

KEELEY GREEN Beds
147 TL 0046 3m SW of Bedford. Loc,
Wootton CP.

KEEVIL Wilts
166, 167 ST 9258 4m E of Trowbridge.
CP, 294. Warminster and Westbury RD.
P Trwbrdge. Ch e, m. Sch pe. Wstbry CC.

KEGWORTH Leics
121 SK 4826 4m S of Long Eaton.
CP, 2,645. Cstle Donington RD. P DERBY.
Ch e, b, m2, v. Sch p. Loughborough CC.
Formerly busy mkt and hosiery-mntg tn.
Many old hses. 14c ch almost unchanged.

KEHELLAND Cornwall
189 SW 6241 2m WNW of Camborne. Loc,
Cmbne-Redruth UD.

KEIGHLEY Yorks (W)
96 SE 0641 8m NW of Bradford.
MB, 55,263. P. Kghly BC. See also
E Morton, Haworth, Laycock, Oakworth,
Oxenhope, Riddlesden, Utley. Mnfg tn,
mostly textiles and engineering. To NW,
Cliffe Cstle*, 19c mansion now museum
with formal gdns and aviary.

KEINTON MANDEVILLE Som
165, 166 ST 5430 6m SSE of Glastonbury.
CP, 449. Langport RD. P Somerton.
Ch e, m2. Sch p. Yeovil CC. Bthplce of Sir
Henry Irvine, actor, 1838.

KELBROOK Yorks (W)
95 SD 9044 3m NNE of Colne. Loc,
Earby UD. P Clne, Lancs.

KELBY Lincs (K)
113, 123 TF 0041 5m WSW of Sleaford.
CP (Culverthorpe and Klby), 106.
E Kesteven RD. Ch e. Grantham CC.

KELD Westm
83 NY 5514 just SW of Shap. Loc, Shp CP.
Tiny pre-Reformation chpl (NT) still used
occasionally for services.

KELD Yorks (N)
90 NY 8901 7m N of Hawes. Loc,
Muker CP. P Richmond. Ch m, v. Sch pc.

KELDHOLME Yorks (N)
86, 92 SE 7086 just E of Kirkbymoorside.
Loc, Kbmsde CP.

KELFIELD Yorks (E)
97 SE 5938 4m NNW of Selby. CP, 346.
Derwent RD. P YORK. Ch m. Howden CC.

KELHAM Notts
112 SK 7755 2m NW of Newark. CP, 198.
Southwell RD. P Nwk. Ch e. Nwk CC. K.
Hall, now a monastery, rambling Gothic pile
by George Gilbert Scott.

KELK, GREAT Yorks (E)
99 TA 1058 5m E of Driffield. See Gt Klk.

KELLATON Devon
188 SX 8039 5m SE of Kingsbridge. Loc,
Stokenham CP. P Kingsbrdge. Ch v.

KELLING Norfolk
125 TG 0942 3m NNE of Holt. CP, 556.
Erpingham RD. Ch e. Sch p. N Nflk CC.

KELLINGTON Yorks (W)
97 SE 5524 6m SW of Selby. CP, 606.
Osgoldcross RD. P Goole. Ch e. Gle CC.

KELLOE Co Durham
85 NZ 3436 5m N of Sedgefield. CP, 806.
Drhm RD. P DRHM. Ch e, m2, v. Sch p.
Drhm CC.

KELLY Devon
186 SX 3981 5m SE of Launceston.
CP, 121. Tavistock RD. Ch e. W Dvn CC
(Tvstck).

KELLY BRAY Cornwall
186 SX 3671 1m N of Callington. Loc,
Cllngtn CP. P Cllngtn. Ch m.

KELMARSH Northants
133 SP 7379 5m S of Mkt Harborough.
C P , 1 0 7 . Brixworth RD.
P NORTHAMPTON. Ch e. Daventry CC
(Kettering).

KELMSCOT Oxon
157 SU 2599 11m NE of Swindon.
CP (Kelmscott), 129. Witney RD.
P Lechlade, Glos. Ch e. Mid-Oxon CC
(Banbury). Elizn K. Mnr*, home of William
Morris.

KELSALE Suffolk (E)
137 TM 3865 1m N of Saxmundham.
CP (Klsle cum Carlton), 1,076. Blythe RD.
P Sxmndhm. Ch e, m. Sch pe. Eye CC. Ch
has curious lychgate.

KELSALL Ches
109 SJ 5268 8m E of Chester. CP, 1,119.
Tarvin RD. P Tarporley. Ch e, m. Sch p.
Northwich CC.

KELSHALL Herts
147 TL 3236 3m SSW of Royston. CP, 122.
Hitchin RD. Ch e. Htchn CC.

KELSICK Cumb
75 NY 2050 4m WNW of Wigton. Loc,
Dundraw CP.

KELSTERN Lincs (L)
105 TF 2590 5m WNW of Louth. CP, 68.
Lth RD. P Lth. Ch e, m. Lth CC.

KELSTON Som
156 ST 7067 3m WNW of Bath. CP, 188.
Bathavon RD. Ch e. N Som CC.

KELVEDON Essex
149, 162 TL 8618 4m NE of Witham.
CP. 2,391. Braintree RD. P Colchester.
Ch e, c, r, v. Sch pe. Brntree CC (Maldon).
W. Felix Hall, romantically ruined 17c hse
with classical portico of 1830.

KELVEDON HATCH Essex
161 TQ 5798 4m NNW of Brentwood.
CP, 560. Epping and Ongar RD. P(Klvdn
Cmmn), Brntwd. Ch e. Sch p. Brntwd and
Ongr CC (Chigwell).

KELYNACK Cornwall
189 SW 3729 6m W of Penzance. Loc,
St Just UD.

KEMBERTON Shrops
119 SJ 7304 2m SSW of Shifnal. CP, 220.
Shfnl RD. P Shfnl. Ch e. The Wrekin CC. On
E edge of colliery distr.

KEMBLE Glos
157 ST 9897 4m SW of Cirencester.
CP, 596. Crncstr RD. P Crncstr. Ch e, m.
Sch p. Crncstr and Tewkesbury CC. See also
Ewen. Ch has 13c twr topped by 19c spire.

KEMERTON Worcs
143, 144 SO 9437 4m NE of Tewkesbury.
CP, 426. Evesham RD.   P Tksbry, Glos.
Ch e, r. S Worcs CC.

KEMPLEY Glos
142, 143 SO 6729 6m NE of Ross-on-Wye.
CP, 255. Newent RD. P Dymock. Ch e, b.
W Glos CC. Mdvl wall-paintings in ch.

KEMPSEY Worcs
143 SO 8549 4m S of Worcester. CP, 1,704.
Upton upon Severn RD. P WCSTR. Ch e, b.
Sch p. S Worcs CC. See also Kerswell Grn.

KEMPSFORD Glos
157 SU 1696 8m N of Swindon. CP, 1,577.
Cirencester RD. P Fairford. Ch e. Sch pe.
Crncstr and Tewkesbury CC. See also
Whelford.

KEMPSTON Beds
147 TL 0347 2m SW of Bedford.
UD, 12,790. P BDFD. Bdfd CC.

KEMPSTON HARDWICK Beds
147 TL 0244 3m SSW of Bedford. Loc,
Kmpstn Rural CP. Bdfd RD. Mid-Beds CC.

KEMP TOWN Sussex (E)
182 TQ 3303 E distr of Brighton. Loc,
B r g h t n   C B .   P   B r g h t n
Brghtn CB. P Brghtn. Brghtn, Kemptown BC.
Rgncy squares with fourth side open towards
sea. Large housing estate to N.

KEMSING Kent
171 TQ 5558 3m NE of Sevenoaks.
CP, 3,907. Svnks RD. P Svnks. Ch e, v2.
Sch p. Svnks CC. See also Heaverham.

KENARDINGTON Kent
184 TQ 9732 5m E of Tenterden. CP, 265.
Tntdn RD, P Ashfd. Ch e. Ashfd CC.

KENCHESTER Herefs
142 SO 4343 2m WNW of Hereford. CP, 89.
Hrfd RD. Ch e, v. Sch pe. Leominster CC.
Partially excavated site of Roman tn.

KENCOT Oxon
157 SP 2504 4m NE of Lechlade. CP, 122.
Witney RD. Ch e. Mid-Oxon CC (Banbury).

KENDAL Westm
89 SD 5192 19m N of Lancaster.
MB, 21,572. P. Westm CC. See also
Oxenholme. Largest tn in Westm, with
county council offices; factories producing
footwear, carpets, machinery, tobacco.
Older bldngs incl rems of Nmn cstle,
13c–15c ch, and Abbot Hall, Ggn hse by
Carr of York, now art gallery.

KENDERCHURCH Herefs
142 SO 4028 10m SW of Hereford. CP, 78.
Dore and Bredwardine RD. Ch e. Hrfd CC.
See also Howton.

KENILWORTH Warwicks
132 SP 2872 5m SSW of Coventry.
U D ,   2 0 , 1 2 1 .   P .   W a r w i c k   a n d
Leamington CC. See also Burton Grn. Ruins
of red sandstone cstle (A.M.), Nmn and
later.

KENLEY Shrops
118 SJ 5600 4m W of Much Wenlock.
CP, 104.   Atcham RD.   P Shrewsbury.
Ch e, m. Shrsbry CC. Views of hills to S and
W. Ch has Jcbn plpt and reading desk.

KENN Devon
176 SX 9285 4m S of Exeter. CP, 959.
St Thomas RD. Ch e. Sch pe. Tiverton CC.
See also Kennford.

KENN Som
155, 165 ST 4169 4m NNW of Congresbury.

Kennerleigh

CP, 218. Long Ashton RD. P Clevedon. Ch e. Weston-super-Mare CC.

KENNERLEIGH Devon
176 SS 8207 5m NNW of Crediton. CP, 44. Crdtn RD. P Crdtn. Ch e. Tiverton CC (Torrington).

KENNETT Cambs
135 TL 6968 5m NE of Newmarket. CP, 340. Nmkt RD. P(Kentford), Nmkt, Suffolk. Ch e. Sch p. Cambs CC.

KENNFORD Devon
176 SX 9186 4m S of Exeter. Loc, Kenn CP. P Extr. Ch m.

KENNINGHALL Norfolk
136 TM 0386 6m S of Attleborough. CP, 782. Wayland RD. P NORWICH, NOR 06X. Ch e, b, m. Sch p. S Nflk CC.

KENNINGTON Berks
158 SP 5202 2m S of Oxford. CP, 3,432. Abingdon RD. P OXFD. Ch e, m, r. Sch i, pe. Abngdn CC.

KENNINGTON Kent
172, 173, 184 TR 0244 2m NE of Ashford. Loc, Ashfd UD. P Ashfd.

KENNINGTON London
160, 170 TQ 3077 2m S of Charing Cross. Loc, Lambeth LB. Vauxhall BC. The Oval, Surrey County Cricket Grnd.

KENNYHILL Suffolk (W)
135 TL 6679 8m E of Ely. Loc, Mildenhall CP.

KENNYTHORPE Yorks (E)
92 SE 7865 4m S of Malton. Loc, Burythorpe CP.

KENSAL RISE London
160 TQ 2383 4m WNW of Charing Cross. Loc, Brent LB. Brnt S BC (Willesden E). To SW, K. Grn Cemetery and large gas wks. To SW again, Wormwood Scrubs Prison.

KENSINGTON London
160, 170 TQ 2579 3m WSW of Charing Cross. LB(Knsngtn and Chelsea), 184,392. BCs: Knsngtn, Chlsea (Knsngtn N, Knsngtn S, Chlsea). See also Earl's Court K. Has been royal borough since 1901. Museums: Natural History, Science, Victoria and Albert. K. Palace (part open to public) in K. Palace Gdns.

KENSWORTH Beds
147 TL 0318 2m SSE of Dunstable. CP, 930. Luton RD. Ch e, m. Sch pe. S Beds CC. See also K. Common.

KENSWORTH COMMON Beds
147 TL 0317 3m SSE of Dunstable. Loc, Knswth CP. P Dnstble.

KENTCHURCH Herefs
142 SO 4125 11m SW of Hereford. CP, 290. Dore and Bredwardine RD. P HRFD. Ch e. Hrfd CC. See also Pontrilas. K. Ct*, 14c cstle rebuilt in 18c by Nash for Scudamore family of Holme Lacy, qv.

KENTFORD Suffolk (W)
135 TL 7066 5m ENE of Newmarket. CP, 235. Mildenhall RD. P Nwmkt. Ch e. Bury St Edmunds CC.

KENTISBEARE Devon
176 ST 0608 7m NW of Honiton. CP, 692. Tiverton RD. P Cullompton. Ch e, b. Sch pe. Tvtn CC. See also Blackborough. Ch: Scrn.

KENTISBURY Devon
163 SS 6243 7m ESE of Ilfracombe. CP, 270. Barnstaple RD. Ch e, b, m. Sch p. N Dvn CC. See also Patchole.

KENTISBURY FORD Devon
163 SS 6142 7m ESE of Ilfracombe. Loc, Kentisbury CP. P Barnstaple.

KENTISH TOWN London
160 TQ 2884 3m NNW of Charing Cross. Loc, Camden LB. St Pancras N BC.

KENTMERE Westm
89 NY 4504 5m NE of Windermere. CP, 91. S Westm RD. P Kendal. Ch e. Westm CC.

KENTON Devon
176 SX 9583 6m SSE of Exeter. CP, 2,055. St Thomas RD. P Extr. Ch e, m. Sch p. Tiverton CC, See also Starcross. Ch: scrn ¼m along A379 towards Starcross, entrance to Powderham Cstle*; see Pdrhm.

KENTON Suffolk (E)
137 TM 1965 6m WNW of Framlingham. CP, 148. Hartismere RD. P Stowmarket. Ch e. Eye CC.

KENTON BANKFOOT Nthmb
78 NZ 2068 4m NW of Newcastle. Loc,
Woolsington CP. Cstle Ward RD. P NCSTLE
UPON TYNE. Ch m2. Hexham CC.

KENTS BANK Lancs
88, 89 SD 3975 1m SSW of
Grange-over-Sands. Loc, Grnge UD.
P Grnge-over-Snds.

KENT'S GREEN Glos
143 SO 7423 7m NW of Gloucester. Loc,
Newent RD. W Glos CC.

KENT'S OAK Hants
168 SU 3224 3m NW of Romsey. Loc,
Sherfield English CP.

KENWICK Shrops
118 SJ 4230 3m SSE of Ellesmere. Loc,
Cockshutt CP.

KENWYN Cornwall
190 SW 8145 just NW of Truro. Loc,
Truro MB. Slate-hung 18c room over
lychgate.

KENYON Lancs
101 SJ 6295 5m NNE of Warrington. Loc,
Golborne UD.

KEPWICK Yorks (N)
91 SE 4690 6m NNE of Thirsk. CP, 89.
Thsk RD. P Thsk. Ch e. Thsk and
Malton CC.

KERESLEY Warwicks
132 SP 3184 3m NNW of Coventry. CP.
Meriden RD. P(Krsly End), Cvntry. Ch e, c.
Sch i, j, s. Mrdn CC.

KERNE BRIDGE Herefs
142 SO 5818 3m SSW of Ross-on-Wye. Loc,
Walford CP.

KERRIDGE Ches
101 SJ 9376 2m NNE of Macclesfield. Loc,
Bollington UD. P Mcclsfld.

KERRIS Cornwall
189 SW 4427 3m SW of Penzance. Loc,
Paul CP. W Penwith RD. St Ives CC.

KERRY'S GATE Herefs
142 SO 3933 8m WSW of Hereford. Loc,
Abbey Dore CP.

KERSALL Notts
112 SK 7162 5m SE of Ollerton. CP, 54.
Southwell RD. Ch m. Newark CC.

KERSEY Suffolk (W)
149 TM 0044 2m WNW of Hadleigh.
CP, 373. Cosford RD. P Ipswich. Ch e, v.
Sch pe. Sudbury and Woodbridge CC.
Famous beautiful vllge on hill with
watersplash at bottom, ch at top.

KERSHOPEFOOT Cumb
76 NY, 4782 14m NNW of Brampton. Loc,
Nicholforest CP. Border RD.
P Newcastleton, Roxburghshire. Penrith and
the Bdr CC.

KERSOE Worcs
143, 144 SO 9939 4m SW of Evesham. Loc,
Elmley Cstle CP.

KERSWELL Devon
176 ST 0806 6m NW of Honiton. Loc,
Broadhembury CP. Ch c.

KERSWELL GREEN Worcs
143 SO 8646 5m S of Worcester. Loc,
Kempsey CP.

KESGRAVE Suffolk (E)
150 TM 2245 4m E of Ipswich. CP, 3,382.
Deben RD. P Ipswich. Ch e, b, r. Sch i, p, s.
Sudbury and Woodbridge CC.

KESSINGLAND Suffolk (E)
137 TM 5286 4m SSW of Lowestoft.
CP, 1,883. Lothingland RD. P Lwstft.
Ch e, m. Sch pe. Lwstft CC.

KESSINGLAND BEACH Suffolk (E)
137 TM 5386 4m S of Lowestoft. Loc,
Kssnglnd CP. P Lwstft. Sch pe. Caravans.

KESTLE MILL Cornwall
185 SW 8559 3m ESE of Newquay. Loc,
St Austell RD, Truro RD. P Nquay. Ch m.
N Cnwll CC, Truro CC. To SW, Trerice
(NT)*, mnr hse rebuilt 1571; Elizn
fireplaces and plaster ceilings.

KESTON London
171 TQ 4164 3m S of Bromley. Loc,
Brmly LB. P Kent. Ravensbourne BC
(Brmly).

KESWICK Cumb
82 NY 2623 16m WSW of Penrith.
UD, 5,169. P. Workington CC. Lakes

resort, with some light industry. Coleridge and Southey lived here; the latter buried here.

KESWICK Norfolk
126 TG 2004 3m SW of Norwich. CP, 315. Forehoe and Henstead RD. Ch e. S Nflk CC (Central Nflk).

KESWICK Norfolk
126 TG 3533 5m ENE of N Walsham. Loc, Bacton CP.

KETLEY Shrops
118, 119 SJ 6711 2m E of Wellington. Loc, Wllngtn Rural CP. Wllngtn RD. P Telford. Ch e, m, v. Sch i, j, p. The Wrekin CC. Coal and iron distr.

KETTERING Northants
133 SP 8678 13m NNE of Northampton. MB, 42,628. P. Kttrng CC. See also Barton Seagrave. Footwear mnfg tn of largely late Vctrn development.

KETTERINGHAM Norfolk
126 TG 1503 4m ENE of Wymondham. CP, 157. Forehoe and Henstead RD. P Wndhm. Ch e. Sch pe. S Nflk CC (Central Nflk). Ch: monmts

KETTLEBASTON Suffolk (W)
149 TL 9650 3m ENE of Lavenham. CP, 59. Cosford RD. Ch e. Sudbury and Woodbridge CC.

KETTLEBROOK Staffs
120 SK 2103 just SE of Tamworth. Loc, Tmwth MB. P Tmwth. Lichfield and Tmwth CC.

KETTLEBURGH Suffolk (E)
137 TM 2660 2m SSW of Framlingham. CP, 214. Blyth RD. P Woodbridge. Ch e. Eye CC.

KETTLENESS Yorks (N)
86 NZ 8315 5m NW of Whitby. Loc, Lythe CP. Ch e.

KETTLESHULME Ches
101 SJ 9879 6m NE of Macclesfield. CP, 329. Mcclsfld RD. P Stockport. Ch e, m. Sch pe. Mcclsfld CC.

KETTLESING BOTTOM Yorks (W)
96 SE 2257 5m WNW of Harrogate. Loc,

Felliscliffe CP. Nidderdale RD. P(Kttlsng), Hrrgte. Hrrgte CC.

KETTLESTONE Norfolk
125 TF 9631 3m ENE of Fakenham. CP, 158. Walsingham RD. P Fknhm. Ch e. NW Nflk CC (N Nflk).

KETTLETHORPE Lincs (L)
104 SK 8475 9m WNW of Lincoln. CP, 208. Gainsborough RD. Ch e. Gnsbrgh CC. See also Laughterton.

KETTLEWELL Yorks (W)
90 SD 9772 13m N of Skipton. CP(Kttlwll w Starbotton), 290. Skptn RD. P Skptn. Ch e, m. Sch p. Skptn CC. To NE rises Gt Whernside, 2,310ft. 1½m NE, Park Rash, motor vehicle test hill.

KETTON Rutland
123 SK 9804 4m WSW of Stamford. CP, 1,142. Kttn RD. P Stmfd, Lincs. Ch e, m, v. Rtlnd and Stmfd CC. Famous quarries for Kttn Stone to N. Ch has well known lofty broach spire.

KEW London
160, 170 TQ 1877 2m NNE of Richmond. Loc, Rchmnd upon Thames LB. P Rchmnd, Surrey. Rchmd BC. K. Palace (A.M.), 17c–18c, contains George III relics; Royal Botanic Gdns*, 300 acres.

KEWSTOKE Som
165 ST 3363 2m NE of Weston. CP, 1,050. Axbridge RD. P Wstn-super-Mare. Ch e. Sch p. W-s-M CC. Opposite ch long flight of steps (NT) leads to Worlebury Wds (partly NT) and Iron Age camp.

KEXBROUGH Yorks (W)
102 SE 3009 4m NW of Barnsley. Loc, Darton UD. P Dtn, Bnsly.

KEXBY Lincs (L)
104 SK 8785 4m SE of Gainsborough. CP, 334. Gnsbrgh RD. P Gnsbrgh. Ch m. Sch pe. Gnsbrgh CC.

KEXBY Yorks (E)
97, 98 SE 7051 6m E of York. CP, 210. Derwent RD. P YK. Ch e. Howden CC.

KEY GREEN Ches
110 SJ 8963 2m E of Congleton. Loc, Cngltn MB.

KEYHAM Leics
121, 122 SK 6706 5m E of Leicester.
CP, 105. Billesdon RD. P LCSTR. Ch e.
Harborough CC (Melton).

KEYHAVEN Hants
180 SZ 3091 3m SSW of Lymington. Loc,
Lmngtn MB. P Lmngtn.

KEYINGHAM Yorks (E)
99 TA 2425 6m WSW of Withernsea.
CP, 818. Holderness RD. P Hull. Ch e, m.
Sch p. Bridlington CC.

KEYMER Sussex (E)
182 TQ 3115 3m S of Burgess Hill.
CP, 4,151. Cuckfield RD. P Hassocks.
Ch e, r. Mid-Sx CC (Lewes). Post-mill to N.

KEYNSHAM Som
155, 156 ST 6568 5m SE of Bristol.
UD, 19,007. P BRSTL. N Som CC. See also
Saltford. Ribbon development and factories.

KEYSOE Beds
134 TL 0762 7m WNW of St Neots.
CP(Bolnhurst and Ksoe), 583. Bedford RD.
P BDFD. Ch e, b. Sch p. Bdfd CC. 18c
tablet on ch twr records narrow escape of
William Dickins.

KEYSOE ROW Beds
134 TL 0861 6m W of St Neots. Loc,
Bolnhurst and Ksoe CP. Ch b.

KEY'S TOFT Lincs (L)
114 TF 4957 6m SW of Skegness. Loc,
Wainfleet St Mary CP. Spilsby RD. P(Wnflt
St Mry), Skgnss. Horncastle CC.

KEYSTON Hunts
134 TL 0475 4m SE of Thrapston.
CP(Bythorn and Kstn),244.
Huntingdon RD. P HNTNGDN. Ch e.
Hunts CC. Ch: Perp twr and spire.

KEYWORTH Notts
112, 121, 122 SK 6130 7m SSE of
Nottingham. CP, 2,652. Bingham RD.
P NTTNGHM. Ch e, c, m. Sch p2, s.
Rushcliffe CC (Carlton). Ch: Perp twr and
spire.

KIBBLESWORTH Co Durham
78 NZ 2456 4m S of Gateshead. Loc,
Lamesley CP. Ch m3. Sch p.

KIBWORTH BEAUCHAMP Leics
133 SO 6893 5m NNW of Mkt Harborough.
CP, 1,786. Mkt Hbrgh RD. P LEICESTER.
Ch e, m. Sch pe, s. Hbrgh CC.

KIBWORTH HARCOURT Leics
133 SP 6894 5m NNW of Mkt Harborough.
CP, 592. Mkt Hbrgh RD. Ch e, v. Hbrgh CC.
Post-mill.

KIDBROOKE London
161, 171 TQ 4076 5m ESE of Lndn Br.
Loc, Greenwich LB. Grnwch BC.

KIDDEMORE GREEN Staffs
119 SJ 8508 7m E of Shifnal. Loc,
Brewood CP.

KIDDERMINSTER Worcs
130 SO 8376 16m WSW of Birmingham.
MB, 47,255. P. Kddrmnstr CC. See also
Franche. Carpet-mnfg and other industries.
Largely developed in 19c; modern tn centre
development.

KIDDINGTON Oxon
145 SP 4122 4m NNW of Woodstock.
CP(Kddngtn w Asterleigh), 159. Chipping
Norton RD. P OXFORD. Ch e. Sch p.
Banbury CC. See also Over Kddngtn.

KIDLINGTON Oxon
145 SP 4914 5m N of Oxford. CP, 8,514.
Ploughley RD. P OXFD. Ch e, b, m, r.
Sch i, j, p2, pr. Mid-Oxon CC (Banbury).
2m NW, K. Airfield.

KIDMORE END Oxon
159 SU 6979 4m NNW of Reading.
CP, 1,663. Henley RD. P Rdng, Berks.
Ch e, m. Sch pe. Hnly CC. See also Cane
End, Tokers Green.

KIDSGROVE Staffs
110 SJ 8354 6m NNW of Stoke-on-Trent.
UD, 22,036. P Stke-on-Trnt. Leek CC. See
also Hardings Wood, Harriseahead,
Newchapel, Talke.

KIELDER Nthmb
76 NY 6293 15m WNW of Bellingham.
CP, 462. Bllnghm RD. P Hexham. Ch v.
Sch p. Hxhm CC. In the upper reaches of
the N Tyne near Scottish border. Gives its
name to the vast forest planted by the
Forestry Commission.

KILBURN Derbys
111 SK 3845 2m ESE of Belper. CP, 2,361.
Blpr RD. P DERBY. Ch b, m. Sch p.
Blpr CC.

KILBURN London
160 TQ 2583 4m WNW of Charing Cross.
Loc, Brent LB. Brnt E BC (Willesden E).

KILBURN Yorks (N)
92 SE 5179 6m ESE of Thirsk. CP(Klbn
High and Low), 229. Thsk RD. P YORK.
Ch e, m. Sch pe. Thsk and Malton CC. 1m
N, white horse cut in hillside 1857. In vllge
Robert Thompson's workshop for hand-
carved furniture, mainly ecclesiastical, distin-
guished by mouse trademark.

KILBY Leics
132, 133 SP 6295 6m SSE of Leicester.
CP, 214. Blaby RD. P LCSTR. Ch e, c.
Sch pe. Blby CC (Harborough).

KILCOT Glos
143 SO 6925 6m E of Ross-on-Wye. Loc,
Newent CP. P Nwnt.

KILDALE Yorks (N)
86 NZ 6009 4m S of Guisborough. CP, 159.
Stokesley RD. P Whitby. Ch e, m.
Richmond CC. 1m NW, hut circles where
Iron Age pottery found.

KILDWICK Yorks (W)
96 SE 0146 4m SSE of Skipton. CP, 134.
Skptn RD. P Keighley. Ch e, v. Sch pe.
Skptn CC. Grand 14c–17c ch, 17c hall, 14c
br over R Aire.

KILHAM Nthmb
64, 70 NT 8832 5m SSE of Coldstream.
CP, 185. Glendale RD.
Berwick-upon-Tweed CC. See also Pawston,
Shotton.

KILHAM Yorks (E)
99 TA 0664 5m NNE of Driffield. CP, 737.
Drffld RD. P Drffld. Ch e, m. Sch pe.
Howden CC.

KILKHAMPTON Cornwall
174 SS 2511 4m NE of Bude. CP, 871.
Stratton RD. P Bde. Ch e, m. Sch p.
N Cnwll CC. See also Stibb. Ch: Nmn
doorway; 16c bench-ends; organ, orig in
Westminster Abbey and played by Purcell,
has black and white notes reversed.

KILLAMARSH Derbys
103 SK 4580 8m SE of Sheffield.
CP, 5,425. Chesterfield RD. P SHFFLD.
Ch e, c, m2, v2. Sch p, pe. NE Derbys CC.
See also Norwood.

KILLERBY Co Durham
85 NZ 1919 7m NW of Darlington. CP, 55.
Dlngtn RD. Bishop Auckland CC
(Sedgefield).

KILLINGHALL Yorks (W)
96 SE 2858 3m NNW of Harrogate.
CP, 2,490. Nidderdale RD. P Hrrgte.
Ch e, m. Sch pe. Hrrgte CC.

KILLINGTON Westm
89 SD 6189 3m SW of Sedbergh. CP, 133.
S Westm RD. Ch e. Westm CC.

KILLINGWORTH Nthmb
78 NZ 2870 5m NNE of Newcastle. Loc,
Longbenton UD. P NCSTLE
UPON TYNE 12. New Tn development
round old mining vllge.

KILMERSDON Som
166 ST 6952 2m SSE of Radstock. CP, 453.
Frome RD. P Bath. Ch e, m. Sch pe.
Wells CC. See also Babington. To E,
Ammerdown Pk, Ggn mansion by James
Wyatt; gdns*.

KILMESTON Hants
168 SU 5926 7m ESE of Winchester.
CP, 216. Wnchstr RD. P Alresford. Ch e.
Wnchstr CC.

KILMINGTON Devon
177 SY 2797 2m W of Axminster. CP, 562.
Axmnstr RD. P Axmnstr. Ch e, b. Sch p.
Honiton CC.

KILMINGTON Wilts
166 ST 7736 6m E of Bruton. CP, 320.
Mere and Tisbury RD. P Warminster.
Ch e, m. Sch pe. Westbury CC. See also
Norton Ferris.

KILNDOWN Kent
171, 172, 183, 184 TQ 7035 5m W of
Cranbrook. Loc, Goudhurst CP. P Crnbrk.
Ch e. Sch pe. On edge of Bedgebury Forest
(see Goudhurst). Early Gothic Revival ch
with Munich stained glass.

KILNHURST Yorks (W)
103 SK 4697 4m NE of Rotherham. Loc,
Swinton UD. P Rthrhm.

KILNPIT HILL Nthmb
77, 78 NZ 0355 5m NW of Consett. Loc,
Shotley Low Quarter CP. Hexham RD.
P Cnstt, Co Durham. Hxhm CC.

KILNSEA Yorks (E)
105 TA 4115 9m SSE of Withernsea. Loc,
Easington CP. Ch e.

KILNSEY Yorks (W)
90 SD 9767 10m N of Skipton.
CP(Conistone w Klnsy), 103. Skptn RD.
Skptn CC. Overhung by K. Crag, famous
challenge to rock climbers.

KILNWICK Yorks (E)
98/99 SE 9949 5m SSW of Driffield. Loc,
Beswick CP. P Drffld. Ch e.

KILNWICK PERCY Yorks (E)
98 SE 8250 2m ENE of Pocklington. Loc,
Nunburnholme CP.

KILPECK Herefs
142 SO 4430 7m SSW of Hereford. CP, 164.
Dore and Bredwardine RD. P HRFD. Ch e.
Sch ie. Hrfd CC. Ch mainly late 12c
romanesque with much rich stone carving.

KILPIN Yorks (E)
97, 98 SE 7726 3m NE of Goole. CP, 537.
Howden RD. Hdn CC. See also Balkholme,
Klpn Pike, Skelton.

KILPIN PIKE Yorks (E)
97, 98 SE 7526 2m NNE of Goole. Loc,
Klpn CP. P(Howden Dyke), Gle.

KILSBY Northants
132, 133 SP 5671 4m SE of Rugby.
C P , 6 6 6 . Daventry RD.
P Rgby, Warwickshire. Ch e, v. Sch pe.
Dvntry CC (S Nthnts).

KILTON Som
164 ST 1644 6m E of Watchet. Loc,
Stringston CP. Ch e.

KILTON Yorks (N)
86 NZ 7018 1m W of Loftus. Loc, Skelton
and Brotton UD.

KILTON THORPE Yorks (N)
86 NZ 6917 2m WSW of Loftus. Loc,
Skelton and Brotton UD.

KILVE Som
164 ST 1442 5m E of Watchet. CP, 286.
Williton RD. P Bridgwater. Ch e.
Brdgwtr CC. Rems of 15c chantry near ch.

KILVINGTON Notts
122 SK 8042 7m S of Newark. CP, 37.
Nwk RD. Ch e. Nwk CC.

KIMBERLEY Norfolk
125 TG 0704 3m NW of Wymondham.
CP, 146. Forehoe and Henstead RD. Ch e.
S Nflk CC (Central Nflk). See also Carleton
Forehoe.

KIMBERLEY Notts
112, 121 SK 4944 5m NW of Nottingham.
CP, 4,642. Basford RD. P NTTNGHM.
Ch e, m3. Sch jb, jg & i, s. Beeston CC
(Rushcliffe).

KIMBLE, GREAT Bucks
159 SP 8206 2m NE of Princes Risborough.
See Gt Kmble.

KIMBLESWORTH Co Durham
85 NZ 2647 3m NNW of Durham. CP, 478.
Drhm RD. Ch e, s. Drhm CC.

KIMBLE WICK Bucks
159 SP 8007 3m N of Princes Risborough.
Loc, Gt and Lit Kmble CP.

KIMBOLTON Herefs
129 SO 5261 3m NE of Leominster.
CP, 519. Lmnstr and Wigmore RD.
P Lmnstr. Ch e. Sch pe. Lmnstr CC. See also
Stockton.

KIMBOLTON Hunts
134 TL 0967 7m NW of St Neots. CP, 824.
St Nts RD. P HUNTINGDON. Ch e, bc, v.
Sch p. Hunts CC. See also Stonely. K.
Cstle*, partly 16c and 17c, but mainly 18c
by Vanbrugh; now a sch.

KIMCOTE Leics
132, 133 SP 5886 3m ENE of Lutterworth.
CP(Kmcte and Walton), 389. Lttrwth RD.
Ch e, b. Blaby CC (Harborough).

KIMMERIDGE Dorset
178, 179 SY 9179 5m S of Wareham.
CP, 87. Wrhm and Purbeck RD. P Wrhm.
Ch e. S Dst CC. To SE, K. Bay: dark cliffs
and black jagged boulders. 1m SE,
Smedmore*, 17c–18c hse.

KIMMERSTON Nthmb
64, 71 NT 9535 5m NNW of Wooler. Loc, Ford CP.

KIMPTON Hants
168 SU 2846 5m WNW of Andover. CP, 535. Andvr RD. P Andvr. Ch e. Sch pe. Winchester CC (Basingstoke).

KIMPTON Herts
147 TL 1718 4m NE of Harpenden. CP, 1,551. Hitchin RD. P Htchn. Ch e, m, v. Sch p. Htchn CC. See also Peter's Grn.

KINETON Glos
144 SP 0926 5m ESE of Winchcombe. Loc, Temple Guiting CP.

KINETON Warwicks
145 SP 3351 9m ESE of Stratford. CP, 1,349. Strtfd-on-Avon RD. P WARWICK. Ch e, m, r. Sch pe, s. Strtfd-on-Avn CC (Strtfd). Motte and bailey cstle. Upton Hse(NT)* and gdns. Site of Battle of Edgehill, 1642, to SE.

KINGHAM Oxon
144 SP 2624 4m SW of Chipping Norton. CP, 611. Chppng Ntn RD. P OXFORD. Ch e, m. Sch p. Banbury CC.

KINGSAND Cornwall
187 SX 4350 3m S of Torpoint. Loc, Maker-w-Rame CP. St Germans RD. Bodmin CC. Huddled hses, narrow sts; sand and rock beach.

KINGSBRIDGE Devon
187, 188 SX 7344 11m SSW of Totnes. UD, 3,535. P. Ttns CC. Chief tn of the S Hams. In Fore St, The Shambles, 16c bldng with upper storey protruding over pavement.

KINGSBRIDGE Som
164 SS 9837 6m SSE of Minehead. Loc, Luxborough CP.

KING'S BROMLEY Staffs
120 SK 1216 5m N of Lichfield. CP, 551. Lchfld RD. P Burton-on-Trent. Ch e. Sch pe. Lchfld and Tamworth CC.

KINGSBURY Warwicks
131 SO 2196 5m S of Tamworth. CP. Atherstone RD. P Tmwth, Staffs. Ch e, m2. Sch p, s. Meriden CC. See also Bodymoor Hth, Hurley, Wd End.

KINGSBURY EPISCOPI Som
177 ST 4321 6m NE of Ilminster. CP, 1,067. Langport RD. P Martock. Ch e, m. Sch p. Yeovil CC. See also E Lambrook, Mid Lmbrk, W Lmbrk. Ch: twr.

KING'S CAPLE Herefs
142 SO 5628 4m NW of Ross-on-Wye. CP, 214. Rss and Whitchurch RD. P HEREFORD. Ch e. Sch p. Hrfd CC.

KINGSCLERE Hants
168 SU 5258 6m SE of Newbury. CP, 3,320. Kngsclre and Whitchurch RD. P Nbry, Berks. Ch e, m2. Sch pe. Basingstoke CC. See also Ashford Hill, Hannington, Headley, Ibworth, N Oakley, Plastow Grn. Ch: 17c monmt, 16c brass. Royal Counties showground.

KING'S CLIFFE Northants
134 TL 0097 6m NNW of Oundle. CP, 1,010. Oundle and Thrapston RD. P PETERBOROUGH. Ch e, m, v. Sch pe, s. Wellingborough CC (Ptrbrgh).

KINGSCOTE Glos
156 ST 8196 5m WNW of Tetbury. CP, 252. Ttbry RD. P Ttbry. Ch e. Stroud CC. See also Newington Bagpath.

KINGSCOTT Devon
163 SS 5318 3m ESE of Torrington. Loc, St Giles in the Wd CP. Ch b.

KING'S COUGHTON Warwicks.
131 SP 0858 1m NNW of Alcester. Loc, Alcstr CP.

KINGSDON Som
177 ST 5126 2m N of Ilchester. CP, 312. Langport RD. P Somerton. Ch e, c. Sch pe. Yeovil CC. 1m E, Lytes Cary (NT)*, 15c and later mnr hse with 14c chpl; home of Lyte family for 500 yrs.

KINGSDOWN Kent
173 TR 3748 3m S of Deal. Loc, Ringwould CP. P Dl.

KINGSDOWN Wilts
156 ST 8167 4m ENE of Bath. Loc, Box CP. P Chippenham. Ch v.

KINGSEY Bucks
159 SP 7406 2m E of Thame. CP, 122. Aylesbury RD. Ch e. Aylesbury CC.

KINGSFOLD Sussex (W)
170, 182 TQ 1636 4m N of Horsham. Loc,
Warnham CP.

KINGSFORD Worcs
130 SO 8281 3m N of Kidderminster. Loc,
Wolverley CP.

KINGSHALL STREET Suffolk (W)
136 TL 9161 4m ESE of Bury St Edmunds.
Loc, Rougham CP. Thingoe RD. Bury
St Eds CC.

KINGSHILL, GREAT Bucks
159 SU 8797 3m NNE of High Wycombe.
See Gt Kngshll.

KINGSHURST Warwicks
131 SP 1788 2m W of Coleshill. CP, 10,284.
Meriden RD. P BIRMINGHAM 37.
Ch e, m, r. Sch i3, j2, pr, sb, sg. Mrdn CC.
Outer suburb of Bmnghm.

KINGSKERSWELL Devon
188 SX 8867 3m SSE of Newton Abbot.
Loc, Kerswells CP. Ntn Abbt RD. P Ntn
Abbt. Ch e, m, r, v2. Sch pe. Totnes CC.

KINGSLAND Herefs
129 SO 4461 4m WNW of Leominster.
CP, 848. Lmnstr and Wigmore RD.
P Lmnstr. Ch m. Sch pe. Lmnstr CC. See
also Cobnash, Lawton, Shirl Hth.

KINGS LANGLEY Herts
160 TL 0702 3m SSE of Hemel Hempstead.
CP, 4,255. Hml Hmpstd RD. P.
Ch e, b2, m, v. Sch i, j, s. Hml Hmpstd CC.
See also Rucklers Grn. Fragment of royal
palace on hill to W.

KINGSLEY Ches
109 SJ 5574 6m SSE of Runcorn.
CP, 1,346. Rncn RD. P WARRINGTON.
Ch e, m3. Sch p, pe. Rncn CC. See also
Newton.

KINGSLEY Hants
169 SU 7838 5m E of Alton. CP, 449.
Altn RD. P Bordon. Ch e2, c. Sch pe.
Petersfield CC.

KINGSLEY Staffs
111 SK 0146 2m N of Cheadle. CP, 2,231.
Chdle RD. P Stoke-on-Trent. Ch e, m.
Sch pe. Leek CC. See also Kngsly Holt,
Whiston.

KINGSLEY GREEN Sussex (W)
169, 181 SU 8930 2m S of Halsemere. Loc,
Fernhurst CP. P Hslmre.

KINGSLEY HOLT Staffs
111 SK 0246 2m NNE of Cheadle. Loc,
Kngsly CP. P Stoke-on-Trent.

KING'S LYNN Norfolk
124 TF 6120 39m W of Norwich.
MB, 30,102. P. NW Nflk CC (K's Lnn).
Ancient port, still busy thanks to constant
dredging of Wash. Two notable mdvl chs,
but 18c bldngs predominate esp those round
the Tuesday Mkt and Saturday Mkt. 17c
Custom Hse. Sugar beet refinery. Canning
factory.

KING'S MEABURN Westm
83 NY 6221 4m W of Appleby. CP, 122.
N Westm RD. P Penrith, Cumberland. Ch m.
Sch pe. Westm CC.

KING'S NEWNHAM Warwicks
132 SP 4577 3m WNW of Rugby. CP, 101.
Rgby RD. Ch e. Rgby CC.

KINGSNORTH Kent
172, 184 TR 0039 2m S of Ashford.
CP, 954. W Ashfd RD. P Ashfd. Ch e, m.
Sch pe. Ashfd CC. See also Stubb's Cross.

KING'S NORTON Leics
122 SK 6800 7m ESE of Leicester. CP, 62.
Billesdon RD. Ch e. Harborough CC
(Melton). Large, remarkable 18c ch, in early
Gothic Revival style. 17c mnr hse and
dovecote.

KING'S NYMPTON Devon
163 SS 6819 4m SSW of S Molton. CP, 350.
S Mltn RD. P Umberleigh. Ch e, m. Sch p.
N Dvn CC. Ch: scrn.

KING'S PYON Herefs
142 SO 4350 6m SW of Leominster.
CP, 264. Weobley RD. P HEREFORD. Ch e.
Lmnstr CC. See also Ledgemoor. Ch has 14c
timbered roof. 1m S, Butthouse, timbered
17c hse with gatehouse.

KINGS RIPTON Hunts
134 TL 2676 3m NNE of Huntingdon.
CP, 129. Hntngdn RD. P HNTNGDN. Ch e.
Hunts CC.

KING'S SOMBORNE Hants
168 SU 3631 6m N of Romsey. CP, 1,269.

Rmsy and Stockbridge RD. P Stckbrdge. Ch e, m. Sch pe. Winchester CC. See also Brook, Upr Smbne.

KING'S STANLEY Glos
156 SO 8103 3m WSW of Stroud. CP, 1,530. Strd RD. P Stonehouse. Ch e, b, m2. Strd CC. See also Selsley.

KING'S SUTTON Northants
145 SP 4936 4m SE of Banbury. CP, 1,550. Brackley RD. P Bnbry, Oxon. Ch e, b, m. Sch p. Daventry CC (S Nthnts). See also Astrop, Upr Astrp. Ch: spire.

KINGSTAG Dorset
178 ST 7210 7m SE of Sherborne. Loc, Lydlinch CP. P Sturminster Newton. Ch m. Where Thomas de la Lynde killed a stag of Henry III's.

KINGSTEIGNTON Devon
176, 188 SX 8673 1m NNE of Newton Abbot. CP, 4,833. Ntn Abbt RD. P Ntn Abbt. Ch e, c, r2, v. Sch ie, p, s. Totnes CC. See also Preston. Drain-pipe mnfg tn.

KING STERNDALE Derbys
111 SK 0972 3m E of Buxton. CP, 144. Chapel en le Frith RD. Ch e. High Peak CC.

KINGSTHORNE Herefs
142 SO 4932 5m S of Hereford. Loc, Much Dewchurch CP. P HRFD.

KINGSTON Cambs
134 TL 3455 7m WSW of Cambridge. CP, 151. S Cambs RD. P CMBRDGE. Ch e, c. Cambs CC. Ch has outstanding wall-paintings. Tiny Congregational chpl is thatched.

KINGSTON Devon
187, 188 SX 6347 5m S of Ivybridge. CP, 303. Kingsbridge RD. P Kngsbrdge. Ch e, m. Totnes CC.

KINGSTON Dorset
178 ST 7509 8m ESE of Sherborne. Loc, Hazelbury Bryan CP. P Sturminster Newton.

KINGSTON Dorset
179 SY 9579 4m W of Swanage. Loc, Corfe Cstle CP. P Wareham. Ch e. Twr of ch by G.E. Street (1880) dominates ridge. 1m SW, Encombe*, Ggn hse in picturesque grnds and setting; limited opening.

KINGSTON Hants
179 SU 1402 2m S of Ringwood. Loc, Rngwd CP. Ch v.

KINGSTON IOW
180 SZ 4781 5m SSW of Newport. Loc, Shorwell CP. Ch e.

KINGSTON Kent
173 TR 1951 5m SE of Canterbury. CP, 316. Bridge-Blean RD. P Cntrbry. Ch e. Cntrbry CC.

KINGSTON Sussex (W)
182 TQ 0802 4m W of Worthing. CP, 378. Wthng RD. Arundel CC (Arndl and Shoreham). See also Kngstn Gorse.

KINGSTON BAGPUIZE Berks
158 SU 4098 6m W of Abingdon. CP, 166. Abngdn RD. P Abngdn. Ch e. Sch pe. Abngdn CC. K. Hse is 18c; has newly constructed gdns*. 2m N, 'Newbridge' over R Thames, 14c.

KINGSTON BLOUNT Oxon
159 SU 7399 5m SSE of Thame. Loc, Aston Rowant CP. P OXFORD.

KINGSTON-BY-SEA Sussex (W)
182 TQ 2205 just E of Shoreham. Loc, Shrhm-by-Sea UD.

KINGSTON DEVERILL Wilts
166 ST 8437 5m SSW of Warminster. CP, 211. Wmnstr and Westbury RD. P Wmnstr. Ch e. Wstbry CC. See also Monkton Dvrll.

KINGSTONE Herefs
142 SO 4235 6m WSW of Hereford. CP, 948. Dore and Bredwardine RD. P HRFD. Ch e, m. Sch p, s. Hrfd CC.

KINGSTONE Som
177 ST 3713 1m SE of Ilminster. CP, 99. Chard RD. Ch e. Yeovil CC.

KINGSTONE Staffs
120 SK 0629 3m SW of Uttoxeter. CP, 381. Uttxtr RD. P Uttxtr. Ch e. Sch p. Burton CC. See also Gratwich.

KINGSTON GORSE Sussex (W)
182 TQ 0801 4m W of Worthing. Loc, Kngstn CP.

KINGSTON LISLE Berks
158 SU 3287 5m W of Wantage. CP, 280.
Faringdon RD. P Wntge. Ch e. Sch pe.
Abingdon CC. See also Fawler. In a cottage
gdn is the Blowing Stone, capable of
producing wailing sound if correctly blown.
Reputedly used by King Alfred.

KINGSTON MAURWARD Dorset
178 SY 7191 2m E of Dorchester. Loc,
Stinsford CP. Elizn mnr hse, in grnds of 18c
mansion now Dorset Farm Institute.

KINGSTON NEAR LEWES Sussex (E)
183 TQ 3908 2m SW of Lewes. CP, 435.
Chailey RD. P(Kngstn), Lws. Ch e. Sch pe.
Lws CC. Downland vllge.

KINGSTON ON SOAR Notts
121 SK 5027 6m NNW of Loughborough.
CP, 257. Basford RD. P NOTTINGHAM.
Ch e. Rushcliffe CC. Gypsum mines. Ch:
Babington chantry.

KINGSTON RUSSELL Dorset
177, 178 SY 5891 7m W of Dorchester.
CP, 58. Dchstr RD. W Dst CC. Group of
farms only. 1m S, K.R. Hse, 17c–18c.

KINGSTON ST MARY Som
177 ST 2229 3m N of Taunton. CP, 669.
Tntn RD. P Tntn. Ch e, c. Sch pe. Tntn CC.
Gives name to 'Kngstn Black' apples. Ch:
twr.

KINGSTON SEYMOUR Som
155, 165 ST 4066 3m NW of Congresbury.
CP, 212. Long Ashton RD. P Clevedon.
Ch e. Weston-super-Mare CC.

KINGSTON UPON HULL Yorks (E)
99 TA 0928 50m E of Leeds. CB, 285,472.
P(Hll). BCs: Kngstn upn Hll Central, E, W.
(E, N, W; also part of Haltemprice CC.)
Major seaport; centre of fishing industry.
Bthplce of William Wilberforce, slavery
abolitionist, whose hse is now museum.
Very fine mdvl ch, one of largest parish chs
in England. Museums of outstanding
interest. University.

KINGSTON-UPON-THAMES London
170 TQ 1769 10m SW of Charing Cross.
LB, 140,210. P Surrey. BCs: Kngstn
upn Thms; Surbiton. See also Chessington,
Malden Rushett, Motspur Pk, New Mldn,
Old Mldn, Sbtn. Place where Saxon kings

were crowned – Coronation Stone stands
outside guildhall. Former HQ of Surrey
County Council (County Hall).

KING'S WALDEN Herts
147 TL 1623 4m SSW of Hitchin.
CP, 1,002. Htchn RD. P Htchn. Ch e, m.
Htchn CC. See also Breachwood Grn.

KINGSWEAR Devon
188 SX 8851 4m SW of Brixham. CP.
Totnes RD. P Dartmouth. Ch e, m. Sch p.
Ttns CC. Faces Dtmth across river. Ferries.
Tdr cstle (private), built to guard estuary
with Dtmth Cstle.

KINGSWOOD Bucks
146 SP 6919 7m ESE of Bicester. CP, 107.
Aylesbury RD. P Aylesbury. Ch v.
Aylesbury CC.

KINGSWOOD Glos
155, 156 ST 6573 4m E of Bristol.
UD, 30,269. P BRSTL. Kngswd CC
(Brstl SE BC). See also Hanham, Soundwell.

KINGSWOOD Glos
156 ST 7491 9m W of Tetbury. CP, 881.
Dursley RD. P Wotton-under-Edge. Ch e, v.
Stroud CC. 16c gatehouse (A.M.) survives
from former abbey.

KINGSWOOD Kent
172 TQ 8450 6m ESE of Maidstone. Loc,
Broomfield CP. P Mdstne.

KINGSWOOD Surrey
170 TQ 2455 3m N of Reigate. Loc,
Banstead UD. P Tadworth.

KINGSWOOD Warwicks
131 SP 1871 7m NW of Warwick. Loc,
Lapworth CP. Ch v.

KINGSWOOD COMMON Herefs
142 SO 2954 2m S of Kington. Loc, Kngtn
Rural CP. Kngtn RD. Ch m. Leominster CC.

KINGS WORTHY Hants
168 SU 4932 2m NNE of Winchester.
CP, 2,113. Wnchstr RD. P Wnchstr. Ch e.
Sch p. Wnchstr CC.

KINGTON Herefs
129 SO 2956 12m W of Leominster.
UD, 1,916. P. Lmnstr CC.

KINGTON Worcs
130, 131 SO 9955 9m E of Worcester.
CP, 164. Pershore RD. Ch e. S Worcs CC.

KINGTON LANGLEY Wilts
156, 157 ST 9276 2m N of Chippenham.
CP, 747. Calne and Chppnhm RD.
P Chppnhm. Ch e, bv, m. Sch pe.
Chppnhm CC.

KINGTON MAGNA Dorset
166 ST 7623 5m SE of Wincanton. CP, 307.
Shaftesbury RD. P Gillingham. Ch e, m.
N Dst CC.

KINGTON ST MICHAEL Wilts
156, 157 ST 9077 3m NNW of
Chippenham. CP, 442. Calne and
Chppnhm RD. P Chppnhm. Ch e, c. Sch pe.
Chppnhm CC.

KINGWESTON Som
165 ST 5230 5m SSE of Glastonbury.
CP, 102. Langport RD. P Somerton. Ch e.
Yeovil CC.

KINLET Shrops
130 SO 7180 8m S of Bridgnorth. CP, 501.
Brdgnth RD. P Bewdley, Worcs. Ch e.
Sch pe. Ludlow CC. See also Buttonoak.
Ch, 12c—14c, in grnds of 18c hall;
monmts.

KINNERLEY Shrops
118 SJ 3320 6m SSE of Oswestry. CP, 969.
Oswstry RD. P Oswstry. Ch e, c, m. Sch pe.
Oswstry CC. See also Maesbrook Grn,
Pentre.

KINNERSLEY Herefs
142 SO 3449 8m NE of Hay-on-Wye.
CP, 217. Weobley RD. P HEREFORD. Ch e.
Sch pe. Leominster CC. See also Ailey. Elizn
cstle.

KINNERSLEY Worcs
143 SO 8743 7m S of Worcester. Loc,
Severn Stoke CP.

KINNINVIE Co Durham
84 NZ 0521 3m N of Barnard Cstle. Loc,
Marwood CP. Bnd Cstle RD. Bishop
Auckland CC.

KINOULTON Notts
112, 121, 122 SK 6730 9m SE of
Nottingham. CP, 440. Bingham RD.

P NTTNGHM. Ch e, m. Sch p.
Rushcliffe CC (Carlton).

KINSHAM Herefs
129 SO 3664 3m E of Presteigne. CP, 69.
Kington RD. Ch e. Leominster CC.

KINSHAM Worcs
143, 144 SO 9335 3m ENE of Tewkesbury.
Loc, Bredon CP.

KINSLEY Yorks (W)
103 SE 4114 5m SSW of Pontefract. Loc,
Hemsworth UD. P Pntfrct.

KINTBURY Berks
158 SU 3866 3m ESE of Hungerford.
CP, 1,864. Hngrfd RD. P Newbury.
Ch e, m2. Sch pe. Nbry CC. See also
Avington, Layland's Grn.

KINVER Staffs
130 SO 8483 4m W of Stourbridge.
CP, 5,352. Seisdon RD. P Stbrdge. Ch e, r.
Sch i, j, s. SW Staffs CC (Brierley Hill). See
also Potter's Cross, Stewponey, Stourton,
Whittington. To W, K. Edge (NT), hth and
wds, with Iron Age fort; old rock dwellings.

KINWARTON Warwicks
131 SP 1058 1m ENE of Alcester. CP, 33.
Alcstr RD. Ch e. Stratford-on-Avon CC
(Strtfd). 14c dovecote (NT)*, with over 500
nesting-holes.

KIPPAX Yorks (W)
97 SE 4130 3m NNW of Castleford. Loc,
Garforth UD. P LEEDS. Ch mainly Nmn.

KIRBY BEDON Norfolk
126 TG 2805 4m SE of Norwich. CP, 301.
Forehoe and Henstead RD. Ch e. Sch p.
S Nflk CC (Central Nflk).

KIRBY BELLARS Leics
122 SK 7117 3m WSW of Melton Mowbray.
Loc, Frisby CP. P Mltn Mbry. Ch e, c. Large
handsome ch, mainly 14c. Opening meet of
Quorn hunt traditionally held at K. Gate,
S of vllge.

KIRBY CANE Norfolk
137 TM 3794 4m NE of Bungay. CP, 299.
Loddon RD. P Bngy, Suffolk. Ch e, m.
Sch pe. S Nflk CC.

KIRBY CROSS Essex
150 TM 2120 5m NE of Clacton. Loc,
Frinton and Walton UD. P Frntn-on-Sea.

KIRBY GRINDALYTHE Yorks (E)
93 SE 9067 8m ESE of Malton. CP, 303.
Norton RD. P Mltn. Ch e, m. Howden CC.
See also Duggleby.

KIRBY HILL Yorks (N)
85 NZ 1406 4m NW of Richmond. CP, 54.
Rchmnd RD. Ch e. Rchmnd CC. Neat vllge
set round grn.

KIRBY HILL Yorks (N)
91 SE 3868 1m NNW of Boroughbridge.
CP, 132. Thirsk RD. Ch e. Sch pe. Thsk and
Malton CC. Ch incorporates 8c stonework.

KIRBY KNOWLE Yorks (N)
91 SE 4687 4m NE of Thirsk. CP, 59.
Thsk RD. Ch e. Thsk and Malton CC.

KIRBY-LE-SOKEN Essex
150 TM 2221 5m NE of Clacton. Loc,
Frinton and Walton UD. P Frntn-on-Sea.
Ch e.

KIRBY MILLS Yorks (N)
86, 92 SE 7086 just SE of Kirkbymoorside.
Loc, Kbmsde CP.

KIRBY MISPERTON Yorks (N)
92 SE 7779 3m SSW of Pickering. CP, 171.
Pckrng RD. P Malton. Ch e, m.
Scarborough CC (Thirsk and Mltn). K.M.
Hall*, 18c hse. In grnds: zoo, boating lake,
airfield.

KIRBY MUXLOE Leics
121 SK 5104 4m W of Leicester. CP, 4,931.
Blaby RD. P LCSTR. Ch e, r, v. Sch p2.
Blby CC (Harborough). Moated 15c brick
cstle (A.M.).

KIRBY ROW Norfolk
137 TM 3792 3m NE of Bungay. Loc,
Loddon RD. S Nflk CC.

KIRBY SIGSTON Yorks (N)
91 SE 4194 3m E of Northallerton. CP, 88.
Nthlltn RD. P Nthlltn. Ch e. Richmond CC.

KIRBY UNDERDALE Yorks (E)
98 SE 8058 6m N of Pocklington. CP, 184.
Pcklngtn RD. P YORK. Ch e. Howden CC.
See also Painsthorpe, Uncleby.

KIRBY WISKE Yorks (N)
91 SE 3784 4m NW of Thirsk. CP, 108.
Thsk RD. P Thsk. Ch e, m. Sch pe. Thsk and
Malton CC.

KIRDFORD Sussex (W)
181, 182 TQ 0126 4m NE of Petworth.
CP, 1,143. Ptwth RD. P Billingshurst.
Ch e, c. Sch p. Chichester CC (Horsham).
See also Balls Cross.

KIRKANDREWS UPON EDEN Cumb
76 NY 3558 3m WNW of Carlisle. Loc,
Beaumont CP. P(Kkndrws), Clsle. Ch e.
Sch p.

KIRKBAMPTON Cumb
75 NY 3056 6m W of Carlisle. CP, 348.
Wigton RD. P Clsle. Ch e. Sch pe. Penrith
and the Border CC. See also Lit Bampton.

KIRK BRAMWITH Yorks (W)
103 SE 6211 4m WSW of Thorne. CP, 166.
Doncaster RD. Ch e. Sch p. Don Valley CC.
See also Braithwaite.

KIRKBRIDE Cumb
75 NY 2356 5m NNW of Wigton. CP, 460.
Wgtn RD. P Carlisle. Ch e, m. Sch p. Penrith
and the Border CC.

KIRKBURN Yorks (E)
98 SE 9855 3m SW of Driffield. CP, 1,669.
Drffld RD. P Drffld. Ch e, m. Howden CC.
See also Southburn. Ch almost pure Nmn.

KIRKBURTON Yorks (W)
102 SE 1912 4m SE of Huddersfield.
UD, 19,520. P Hddsfld. Hddsfld E BC. See
also Farnley Tyas, Fenay Br, Flockton,
Grange Moor, Highburton, High Grn,
Kirkheaton, Shelley, Shepley, Thurstonland.

KIRKBY Lancs
100 SJ 4198 7m NE of Liverpool.
UD, 59,759. P LVPL. Ormskirk CC
(Huyton). General industry here and at K.
Indstrl Estate to E.

KIRKBY Lincs (L)
104 TF 0692 3m NW of Mkt Rasen. Loc,
Osgodby CP. Ch e. 12c—14c—18c ch,
restored. To W, Kingerby ch, almost in
ruins.

KIRKBY Yorks (N)
86 NZ 5305 2m SSE of Stokesley. CP, 243.

Stksly RD. P(Kby-in-Cleveland), MIDDLES-BROUGH, Teesside. Ch e. Sch pe. Rich-mond CC.

KIRKBY FLEETHAM Yorks (N)
91 SE 2894 5m W of Northallerton. CP (Kby Flthm W Fencote), 397. Bedale RD. P Nthlltn. Ch e. Sch pe. Thirsk and Malton CC.

KIRKBY GREEN Lincs (K)
113 TF 0857 8m N of Sleaford. Loc, Scopwick CP. Ch e.

KIRKBY IN ASHFIELD Notts
112 SK 4956 4m SW of Mansfield. UD, 23,638. P NOTTINGHAM. Ashfld CC. See also Annesley Woodhouse, New Annsly, Nuncargate. Colliery tn.

KIRKBY LA THORPE Lincs (K)
113 TF 0945 2m E of Sleaford. CP, 278. E Kesteven RD. P Slfd. Ch e. Sch pe. Grantham CC.

KIRKBY LONSDALE Westm
89 SD 6178 11m SE of Kendal. CP, 1,483. S Westm RD. P Carnforth, Lancs. Ch e, m, r2. Sch pe, s. Westm CC. See also Kearstwick. Grey stone tn in Lune valley; the 'Lowtown' of Charlotte Bronte's *Jane Eyre.*

KIRKBY MALHAM Yorks (W)
90 SD 8961 5m ESE of Settle. CP, 65. Sttle RD. Ch e. Sch pe. Skipton CC.

KIRKBY MALLORY Leics
121 SK 4500 5m NNE of Hinckley. Loc, Peckleton CP. P LEICESTER. Ch e. Sch pe.

KIRKBY MALZEARD Yorks (W)
91 SE 2374 5m WNW of Ripon. CP, 529. Rpn and Pateley Br RD. P Rpn. Ch e, m. Sch pe. Rpn CC.

KIRKBYMOORSIDE Yorks (N)
86, 92 SE 6986 7m WNW of Pickering. CP, 1,883. Kbmsde RD. P YORK. Ch e, f, m2, r. Sch p. Thirsk and Malton CC. See also Keldholme, Kirby Mills. Small mkt tn blt round square.

KIRKBY ON BAIN Lincs (L)
114 TF 2462 3m E of Woodhall Spa.

CP, 240. Horncastle RD. P Wdhll Spa. Ch e. Sch pe. Hncstle CC.

KIRKBY OVERBLOW Yorks (W)
96 SE 3249 4m SSE of Harrogate. CP, 296. Wetherby RD. P Hrrgte. Ch e, m. Sch pe. Barkston Ash CC.

KIRKBY STEPHEN Westm
84 NY 7708 9m SE of Appleby. CP, 1,618. N Westm RD. P. Ch e, b, f, m2, r, v. Sch p, s. Westm CC. Small stone-blt mkt tn beside R Eden amid wild moorlands.

KIRKBY THORE Westm
83 NY 6325 4m NW of Appleby. CP, 486. N Westm RD. P Penrith, Cumberland. Ch e, m. Sch p. Westm CC.

KIRKBY UNDERWOOD Lincs (K)
123 TF 0727 5m NNW of Bourne. CP, 177. S Kesteven RD. P Bne. Ch e. Sch p. Rutland and Stamford CC.

KIRKBY WHARFE Yorks (W)
97 SE 5040 2m SE of Tadcaster. CP (Kby Whfe w N Milford), 82. Tdcstr RD. Ch e. Barkston Ash CC.

KIRKCAMBECK Cumb
76 NY 5368 5m N of Brampton. Loc, Askerton CP. Border RD. Ch e. Penrith and the Bdr CC.

KIRKDALE Yorks (N)
86, 92 SE 6785 1m WSW of Kirkbymoorside. Loc, Welburn CP. Ch e. Ch Saxon, with sundial of 1060; Saxon coffin lids and cross. Just SE of ch, cave where stalagmites, fossils, and bones of extinct animals found.

KIRK DEIGHTON Yorks (W)
96 SE 3950 1m N of Wetherby. CP, 481. Wthrby RD. P Wthrby. Ch e, m. Sch pe. Barkston Ash CC.

KIRK ELLA Yorks (E)
99 TA 0229 5m W of Hull. Loc, Haltemprice UD. P Hll. Hltmprce CC.

KIRK HALLAM Derbys
112, 121 SK 4540 1m SW of Ilkeston. Loc, Ilkstn MB. P Ilkstn.

KIRKHAM Lancs
94 SD 4232 7m WNW of Preston. UD, 6,422. P Prstn. S Fylde CC.

KIRKHAM Yorks (E)
92 SE 7365 5m SW of Malton. Loc, Firby CP. K. Priory (A.M.), with rems of 13c gatehouse.

KIRKHAMGATE Yorks (W)
96, 102 SE 2922 2m NW of Wakefield. Loc, Stanley UD. P Wkfld.

KIRK HAMMERTON Yorks (W)
97 SE 4655 6m NE of Wetherby. CP, 384. Nidderdale RD. P YORK. Ch e, m. Sch pe. Harrogate CC. S part of ch almost entirely Saxon.

KIRKHARLE Nthmb
77 NZ 0182 10m SE of Otterburn. Loc, Kirkwhelpington CP. Ch e. Bthplce of Capability Brown, landscape architect, 1715.

KIRKHEATON Nthmb
77 NZ 0177 8m NNE of Corbridge. Loc, Capheaton CP. Ch e.

KIRKHEATON Yorks (W)
96, 102 SE 1818 3m ENE of Huddersfield. Loc, Kirkburton UD. P Hddsfld.

KIRK IRETON Derbys
111 SK 2650 6m ENE of Ashbourne. CP, 314. Ashbne RD. P DERBY. Ch e, m. Sch pe. W Derbys CC.

KIRKLAND Cumb
82 NY 0718 6m E of Whitehaven. Loc, Lamplugh CP. P Frizington. Ch e, m.

KIRKLAND Cumb
83 NY 6432 8m E of Penrith. Loc, Culgaith CP. Ch e.

KIRK LANGLEY Derbys
120, 121 SK 2838 4m WNW of Derby. CP, 550. Belper RD. P DBY. Ch e. Sch pe. Blpr CC.

KIRKLEATHAM Yorks (N)
86 NZ 5921 6m E of Teesside (Middlesborough). Loc, Tssde CB. Tssde, Redcar BC. In ch, grandiose mausoleum by Gibbs, 1740. 17c almshouses, Turner's Hsptl*, with chpl possibly by Wren.

KIRKLEVINGTON Yorks (N)
85 NZ 4309 6m S of Teesside (Stockton).

CP, 257. Stokesley RD. Ch e. Sch pe. Richmond CC.

KIRKLEY Suffolk (E)
137 TM 5391 2m SW of Lowestoft. Loc, Lwstft MB.

KIRKLEYDITCH Ches
101 SJ 8778 2m SE of Wilmslow. Loc, Mottram St Andrew CP. Macclesfield RD. Ch m. Mcclsfld CC.

KIRKLINGTON Notts
112 SK 6757 8m WNW of Newark. CP, 228. Southwell RD. P Nwk. Ch e. Sch p. Nwk CC. Ch has 17c brick twr with staircase turret.

KIRKLINGTON Yorks (N)
91 SE 3181 5m SE of Bedale. CP (Kklngtn-cum-Upsland), 219. Bdle RD. P Bdle. Ch e. Sch pe. Thirsk and Malton CC.

KIRKLINTON Cumb
76 NY 4367 7m NNE of Carlisle. Loc, Border RD. P Clsle. Ch e. Sch p. Penrith and the Bdr CC.

KIRK MERRINGTON Co Durham
85 NZ 2631 1m SSE of Spennymoor. Loc, Spnnmr UD. P Spnnmr.

KIRKNEWTON Nthmb
64, 71 NT 9130 5m WNW of Wooler. CP, 208. Glendale RD. P Wlr. Ch e. Sch pe. Berwick-upon-Tweed CC. See also Hethpool, Westnewton, Yeavering. Small vllge under border hills.

KIRKOSWALD Cumb
83 NY 5541 7m NNE of Penrith. CP, 695. Pnrth RD. P Pnrth. Ch e, c, m. Sch pe. Pnrth and the Border CC. See also Renwick. Belfry of ch stands at top of hill. Rems of mdvl cstle.

KIRK SANDALL Yorks (W)
103 SE 6107 4m NE of Doncaster. CP (Barnby Dun w Kk Sndll), 3,141. Dncstr RD. P Dncstr. Ch e, c, r. Sch i, j. Don Valley CC.

KIRKSANTON Cumb
88 SD 1480 2m W of Millom. Loc, Mllm Whithout CP. Mllm RD. Ch e. Whitehaven CC.

KIRK SMEATON Yorks (W)
103 SE 5116 5m SE of Pontefract. CP, 178.
Hemsworth RD. P Pntfrct. Ch e. Sch pe.
Hmswth CC.

KIRKSTALL Yorks (W)
96 SE 2635 2m NW of Leeds. Loc, Lds CB.
P LDS 5. Lds NW BC. Rems of Cistercian
abbey. Gatehouse now museum.

KIRKSTEAD Lincs (L)
113 TF 1762 1m SW of Woodhall Spa.
CP, 85. Horncastle RD. Ch e. Hncstle CC.
Modern br over R Witham and rly. To E,
very inaccessible, slight rems of 12c abbey
and small chpl.

KIRKWHELPINGTON Nthmb
77 NY 9984 10m E of Bellingham. CP, 302.
Bllnghm RD. P NEWCASTLE UPON TYNE.
Ch e, m. Sch p. Hexham CC. See also
Kirkharle, Newhouses.

KIRMINGTON Lincs (L)
104 TA 1011 5m WSW of Immingham.
CP, 317. Glanford Brigg RD. P Ulceby.
Ch e, m. Sch pe. Brgg and Scunthorpe CC
(Brgg). Disused airfields with attendant
ruins.

KIRMOND LE MIRE Lincs (L)
105 TF 1892 5m ENE of Mkt Rasen.
CP, 55. Caistor RD. Ch e. Sch pe.
Gainsborough CC.

KIRSTEAD GREEN Norfolk
137 TM 2997 5m NW of Bungay. Loc,
Kstd CP. Loddon RD. Ch e. S Nflk CC.

KIRTLING Cambs
135 TL 6857 5m SE of Newmarket.
CP, 357. Nmkt RD. P Nmkt, Suffolk.
Ch e, b, m, r. Sch pe. Cambs CC. See also
Ktlng Grn, Upend. Large brick gatehouse
alone survives from Tdr mnr; can be
glimpsed from just outside entrance to Place
Farm.

KIRTLING GREEN Cambs
135 TL 6856 5m SSE of Newmarket. Loc,
Ktlng CP.

KIRTLINGTON Oxon
145 SP 4919 4m ENE of Woodstock.
CP, 683. Ploughley RD. P OXFORD. Ch e.
Sch pe. Banbury CC (Henley).

KIRTON Lincs (H)
114, 123 TF 3038 4m SSW of Boston.
CP, 3,265. Bstn RD. P Bstn. Ch e, m.
Sch p, s. Holland w Bstn CC. See also Ktn
End, Ktn Holme, Skeldyke.

KIRTON Notts
112 SK 6969 3m ENE of Ollerton. CP, 156.
Southwell RD. P Newark. Ch e. Nwk CC.

KIRTON Suffolk (E)
150 TM 2739 4m NNW of Felixstowe.
CP, 605. Deben RD. P Ipswich. Ch e.
Sudbury and Woodbridge CC.

KIRTON END Lincs (H)
114, 123 TF 2840 3m SW of Boston. Loc,
Ktn CP. P Bstn. Ch m.

KIRTON HOLME Lincs (H)
114, 123 TF 2642 4m WSW of Boston. Loc,
Ktn CP. P Bstn.

KIRTON IN LINDSEY Lincs (L)
104 SK 9398 7m SW of Brigg. CP, 2,553.
Glanford Brgg RD. P(Ktn
Lndsy), Gainsborough. Ch e, b, m. Sch p, s.
Brgg and Scunthorpe CC (Brgg).

KISLINGBURY Northants
133 SP 6959 4m W of Northampton.
CP, 806. Nthmptn RD. P NTHMPTN.
Ch e, b, v. Sch pe. Daventry CC (S Nthnts).

KITES HARDWICK Warwicks
132 SP 4768 5m SSW of Rugby. Loc,
Leamington Hastings CP.

KITTISFORD Som
164 ST 0722 4m WNW of Wellington. Loc,
Stawley CP. Ch e.

KITTWHISTLE Dorset
177 ST 3903 5m SW of Crewkerne. Loc,
Broadwindsor CP. P Beaminster.

KITWOOD Hants
168, 169, 181 SU 6633 5m SW of Alton.
Loc, Four Marks CP.

KIVETON PARK Yorks (W)
103 SK 4983 6m WNW of Worksop. Loc,
Wales CP. P SHEFFIELD. Sch i j.

KNAITH Lincs (L)
104 SK 8284 3m SSE of Gainsborough.
CP, 225. Gnsbrgh RD. Ch e. Gnsbrgh CC.

KNAP CORNER Dorset
166 ST 8023 4m W of Shaftesbury. Loc,
E Stour CP.

KNAPHILL Surrey
169, 170 SU 9658 3m W of Woking. Loc,
Wkng UD. P Wkng.

KNAPP Som
177 ST 3025 5m E of Taunton. Loc,
N Curry CP.

KNAPTON Norfolk
126 TG 3034 3m NE of N Walsham.
CP, 287. Smallburgh RD. P: N Wlshm.
Ch e, m. Sch p. N Nflk CC. Ch has double
hammerbeam roof with 138 angels, c 1500.

KNAPTON Yorks (W)
97 SE 5652 3m W of York. CP, 87.
Nidderdale RD. Barkston Ash CC.

KNAPWELL Cambs
134 TL 3362 8m WNW of Cambridge.
CP, 113. Chesterton RD. Ch e. Cambs CC.

KNARESBOROUGH Yorks (W)
96 SE 3556 3m ENE of Harrogate.
UD, 11,863. P. Hrrgte CC. Set on
escarpment above R Nidd. Rems of 14c
cstle* with museum. Petrifying well*. 15c
chpl cut out of rock face on N side of river,
with figure of St Robert carved alongside.
Small zoo.

KNARSDALE Nthmb
76 NY 6754 5m NNW of Alston. Loc,
Knaresdale and Kirkhaugh CP.
Haltwhistle RD. Ch e. Sch pe. Hexham CC.

KNAYTON Yorks (N)
91 SE 4387 4m N of Thirsk. CP(Kntn
w Brawith), 292. Thsk RD. P Thsk. Ch m.
Sch pe. Thsk and Malton CC.

KNEBWORTH Herts
147 TL 2520 3m S of Stevenage. CP, 3,024.
Hitchin RD. P. Ch e, c2, m, r. Sch p.
Htchn CC. See also Old Knbwth. For K.
Hse* see Old Knbwth.

KNEDLINGTON Yorks (E)
97, 98 SE 7328 3m N of Goole. Loc,
Asselby CP.

KNEESALL Notts
112 SK 7064 4m SE of Ollerton. CP, 178.

Southwell RD. P Newark. Ch e, m. Sch pe.
Nwk CC.

KNEESWORTH Cambs
147 TL 3444 2m NNW of Royston.
CP(Bassingbourn cum Knswth), 2,653.
S Cambs RD. Cambs CC.

KNEETON Notts
112 SK 7146 7m SW of Newark. CP, 101.
Bingham RD. Ch e. Rushcliffe CC (Carlton).

KNETTISHALL Suffolk (W)
136 TL 9780 7m ESE of Thetford. CP, 42.
Thingoe RD. Bury St Edmunds CC. Ch
abandoned.

KNIGHTACOTT Devon
163 SS 6439 7m NE of Barnstaple. Loc,
Bratton Fleming CP.

KNIGHTCOTE Warwicks
145 SP 3954 5m S of Southam. Loc, Burton
Dassett CP. P Leamington Spa. Ch m.

KNIGHTLEY Staffs
119 SJ 8125 7m WNW of Stafford. Loc,
Gnosall CP. Ch e. Sch pe.

KNIGHTON Staffs
110, 119 SJ 7340 5m NE of Mkt Drayton.
Loc, Mucklestone CP. P Mkt Drtn, Salop.
Ch m.

KNIGHTON Staffs
119 SJ 7427 5m N of Newport. Loc,
Adbaston CP. P STAFFORD. Beside Shrops
Union Canal.

KNIGHTON ON TEME Worcs
129, 130 SO 6369 3m ENE of Tenbury
Wells. CP, 423. Tnbry RD. Ch e. Sch pe.
Kidderminster CC. See also Newnham Br.

KNIGHTWICK Worcs
130 SO 7255 7m W of Worcester. CP, 111.
Martley RD. P WCSTR. Ch e.
Kidderminster CC.

KNILL Herefs
129 SO 2960 3m N of Kington. CP, 37.
Kngtn RD. Ch e. Leominster CC.

KNIPTON Leics
113, 122 SK 8231 6m WSW of Grantham.
Loc, Belvoir CP. P Grnthm, Lincs. Ch e.
Sch pe. Estate vllge. To S, K. Reservoir.

KNIVETON Derbys
111 SK 2050 3m NE of Ashbourne.
CP, 276. Ashbne RD. P Ashbne. Ch·e, m.
Sch pe. W Derbys CC.

KNOCK Westm
83 NY 6827 4m N of Appleby. Loc, Long
Marton CP. P Appleby. Ch m.

KNOCKHOLT Kent
171 TQ 4658 3m E of Biggin Hill. CP.
Sevenoaks RD. P Svnks. Ch e. Svnks CC. See
also Knckhlt Pound. Stands very high. To S,
K. Beeches, landmark and viewpoint.

KNOCKHOLT POUND Kent
171 TQ 4859 4m NW of Sevenoaks. Loc,
Knckhlt CP. P(Knckhlt), Svnks.

KNOCKIN Shrops
118 SJ 3322 5m SSE of Oswestry. CP, 251.
Oswstry RD. P Oswstry. Ch e. Sch pe.
Oswstry CC. Only mound remains of former
cstle.

KNODISHALL Suffolk (E)
137 TM 4261 3m ESE of Saxmundham.
CP, 528. Blyth RD. P Sxmndhm. Ch e.
Sch p. Eye CC. See also Coldfair Grn.

KNOLLS GREEN Ches
101 SJ 8079 3m WSW of Wilmslow. Loc,
Mobberley CP. P Knutsford.

KNOOK Wilts
167 ST 9341 5m ESE of Warminster.
CP, 501. Wmnstr and Westbury RD. Ch e.
Wstbry CC.

KNOSSINGTON Leics
122 SK 8008 4m W of Oakham. CP, 339.
Melton and Belvoir RD. P Oakhm, Rutland.
Ch e, m. Sch pe. Mltn CC. See also Cold
Overton.

KNOTT END-ON-SEA Lancs
94 SD 3548 just E across river from
Fleetwood. Loc, Preesall UD. P Blackpool.

KNOTTING Beds
134 TL 0063 4m SE of Rushden.
CP (Knttng; and Souldrop), 258.
Bedford RD. Ch e, m. Bdfd CC.

KNOTTINGLEY Yorks (W)
97 SE 5023 3m ENE of Pontefract.
UD, 16,360. P. Goole CC. See also
Ferrybridge.

KNOTTY CORNER Bucks
159 SU 9392 1m N of Beaconsfield. Loc,
Penn CP.

KNOWBURY Shrops
129 SO 5774 4m E of Ludlow. Loc,
Ldlw RD. P Ldlw. Ch e. Ldlw CC.

KNOWLE Devon
163 SS 4938 1m N of Braunton. Loc,
Brntn CP. P Brntn. Ch m.

KNOWLE Devon
175 SS 7801 3m WNW of Crediton. Loc,
Crdtn Hmlts CP. Crdtn RD. Tiverton CC
(Torrington).

KNOWLE Devon
176 SY 0582 1m NW of Budleigh Salterton.
Loc, Bdlgh Slttn UD. P Bdlgh Slttn.

KNOWLE Warwicks
131 SP 1876 2m SE of Solihull. Loc,
Slhll CB. P Slhll. Large Perp ch; plpt has 17c
hour-glass. To N, Grimshaw Hall, 16c,
half-timbered.

KNOWLE GREEN Lancs
94, 95 SD 6338 7m WSW of Clitheroe. Loc,
Ribchester CP. Ch v.

KNOWLE ST GILES Som
177 ST 3411 2m NE of Chard. CP, 120.
Chd RD. Ch e. Yeovil CC. See also Cricket
Malherbie.

KNOWL HILL Berks
159 SU 8279 4m WSW of Maidenhead. Loc,
Hurley CP. P Reading. Ch e. Sch pe.

KNOWLTON Kent
173 TR 2853 4m SW of Sandwich. Loc,
Goodnestone CP. Ch e.

KNOWSLEY Lancs
100 SJ 4395 5m W of St Helens. CP, 7,131.
Whiston RD. P Prescot. Ch e, r.
Sch p6, pe, pr2, s2. Huyton CC. K. Indstrl
Estate beside E Lancs Rd to N. To SE, K.
Hall, palatial mansion of the Earls of Derby,
in vast pk.

KNOWSTONE Devon
164 SS 8223 7m ESE of S Molton. CP, 212.
S Mltn RD. P: S Mltn. Ch e, m. N Dvn CC.

KNUTSFORD Ches
101 SJ 7578 6m S of Altrincham. UD, 13,765. P. Kntsfd CC. The 'Cranford' of Mrs Gaskell. 2m N, Tatton Pk (NT)*, 18c hse and gdns in pk with large lake.

KYNNERSLEY Shrops
118, 119 SJ 6716 4m NNE of Wellington. CP, 211. Wllngtn RD. Ch e. The Wrekin CC.

KYRE Worcs
129, 130 SO 6264 3m SE of Tenbury Wells. CP, 69. Tnbry RD. P Tnbry Wlls. Ch e. Kidderminster CC.

KYREWOOD Worcs
129, 130 SO 6007 just SE of Tenbury Wells. Loc, Tnbry CP.

INDEX OF BUILDINGS
MENTIONED UNDER PLACES OF A DIFFERENT NAME
Buildings marked with an asterisk are regularly open to the public.
(Museums, although open to the public, are not so marked.)

Building	Mentioned under
* Abbey Hse	Minster, Kent (TR 3064)
Abbot Hall	Kendal
* Abbot's Fish Hse	Meare
Acorn Bank	Temple Sowerby
Acrise Place	Elham
* A La Ronde	Exmouth
Albright Hussey	Albrighton, Shrops (SJ 4918)
* Allington Cstle	Maidstone
Alscot Pk	Preston on Stour
* Althorp Pk	Harlestone
Ammerdown Pk	Kilmersdon
* Angel Corner	Bury St Edmunds
* Anglesey Abbey	Lode
* Anne Hathaway's Cottage	Shottery
* Appuldurcombe Hse	Godshill, IOW
* Arbury	Astley, Warwicks
* Ark, The	Tadcaster
* Ascott	Wing, Bucks
* Ashdown Hse	Ashbury, Berks
Ashdown Hse	Forest Row
Ashridge	Lit Gaddesden
Ashurst Beacon	Dalton, Lancs
Aske Hall	Gilling W
* Astley Hall	Chorley, Lancs
* Attingham	Atcham
* Audley End	Saffron Walden
* Barden Twr	Burnsall
* Bardon Mnr	Washford
* Bateman's	Burwash
* Bayham Abbey	Bells Yew Grn
Bedales	Sheet
* Bede Hse	Lyddington
Bedgebury Pk	Goudhurst
* Beeleigh Abbey	Maldon
* Belchamp Hall	Belchamp Walter
* Belloc's Mill	Shipley, Sussex
* Berrington Hall	Eye, Herefs
Bickham Hse	Roborough, Devon (SX 5062)
* Bladon Gallery	Hurstbourne Tarrant
Blagdon Hall	Stannington, Nthmb
Blake Hall	Bobbingworth
* Bleak Hse	Broadstairs
* Blenheim Palace	Woodstock
* Blithfield Hall	Admaston, Staffs

Building	Mentioned under
* Blue Br Hse	Halstead
Blundell's Sch	Tiverton, Devon
Bollitree Cstle	Weston under Penyard
* Bonner's Cottages	E Dereham
* Boscoble Hse	Tong
* Boughton Monchelsea Place	Boughton Grn
Boughton Pk	Weekley
Bowood Pk	Calne
* Bradley Mnr	Highweek
* Braithwaite Hall	Middleham
* Brantwood	Coniston, Lancs
Brattles Grange	Brenchley
Brewer Street Farm	Bletchingley
* Brickwall	Northiam
Broadlands	Romsey
Broke Hall	Levington
* Broomfield Hse	Southgate, London
Broomholme Priory	Bacton, Norfolk
* Brougham Cstle	Eamont Br
* Browsholme Hall	Bashall Eaves
Bruce Cstle Museum	Tottenham
Burderop Pk	Chiseldon
* Burghley Hse	Stamford, Lincs (K)
* Burton Ct	Eardisland
Butthouse	King's Pyon
* Byland Abbey	Wass
* Cadhay	Fairmile
Caerhays Cstle	St Michael Caerhays
Camoys Ct Farm	Chislehampton
* Capesthorne Hall	Siddington, Ches
Captain Cook Monmt	Easby, Yorks (N) (NZ 5708)
Captain Cook Museum	Gt Ayton
* Carr Hse	Bretherton
Castle Drogo	Drewsteignton
* Castle Hse	Dedham
* Castle Howard	Coneysthorpe
* Cedar Hse	Cobham, Surrey
Chadacre Pk	Shimpling
* Charl(e)ston	Westdean, Sussex (E)
Charterhouse	Farncombe
* Chartwell	Crockham Hill
Chateau Impney	Droitwich
* Chatsworth Hse	Edensor
Chavenage Hse	Beverstone
Chequers	Ellesborough
* Chillington Hall	Brewood
Chipchase Cstle	Wark, Nthmb (NY 8677)
Christ's Hsptl	Itchingfield
* Churche's Mansion	Nantwich
* Claremont	Esher
* Cleeve Abbey	Washford

Building	Mentioned under
* Cliffe Cstle	Keighley
* Clifton Pk	Rotherham
* Clouds Hill	Briantspuddle
Colneford Hse	White Colne
Columbine Hall	Stowupland
Column of British Liberty	Whickham
* Combe Bank	Sundridge
Compton Verney Pk	Combrook
* Compton Wynyates	Winderton
Conygar Twr	Dunster
* Cooke's Hse	W Burton, Sussex (W)
* Coombe Abbey	Brinklow
Cornbury Pk	Charlbury
* Cotehele Hse	Calstock
* Cothay	Greenham, Som
* Courts, The	Holt, Wilts
* Cowdray	Midhurst
Cragside	Rothbury
Cranbury Pk	Otterbourne
Crichel Hse	Moor Crichel
Crittenden Hse	Matfield
Crossways Farm	Abinger Hammer
* Cusworth Hall	Doncaster
* Danny	Hurstpierpoint
* Ditchley Pk	Over Kiddington
* Dorford Hall	Acton, Ches (SJ 6353)
Dorney Wd	Burnham, Bucks
* Dorton Hse	Brill
Douai Abbey	Woolhampton
* Dove Cottage	Grasmere
Downside Abbey	Stratton on the Fosse
Drayton Hse	Lowick, Northants
Duncombe Pk	Helmsley
* Dunstanburgh Cstle	Craster
* Eastbury Mnr Hse	Barking, London
Easton Neston Hse	Towcester
* Egglestone Abbey	Barnard Cstle
	Greta Br
Emmetts	Brasted
* Encombe	Kingston
Fardel	Cornwood
Farringford	Freshwater
* Fenton Hse	Hampstead
Ferne Hse	Berwick St John
Field Place	Broadbridge Hth
Finchcocks	Goudhurst
Flatford Mill	E Bergholt
Flemings Hall	Bedingfield
Flounders' Folly	Culmington
Foley Hse	High Garrett
* Forde Abbey	Thorncombe, Dorset (ST 3703)

Building	Mentioned under
* Forty Hall	Enfield
* Fountains Abbey	Studley Roger
Foxcote	Ilmington
* Foxdenton Hse	Chadderton
* Friars, The	Aylesford
Gadshill	Higham, Kent
* Gainsborough's Hse	Sudbury, Suffolk (W)
Garnons	Mansell Gamage
* Gawthorpe Hall	Padiham
* Gibside Chpl	Rowland's Ghyll
Glassenbury Pk	Cranbrook
Glendurgan Hse	Mawnan Smith
* Godington Pk	Ashford, Kent
* Goodwood Hse	Strettington
* Gorhambury	St Albans
* Grange, The	Rottingdean
Gray's Inn	Holborn
* Great Dixter	Northiam
* Greathead Mnr	Dormans Land
* Great Maytham	Rolvenden
Great Tangley Mnr	Blackheath, Surrey
	Wonersh
Gresham's Sch	Holt, Norfolk
* Greys Ct	Rotherfield Greys
Grimshaw Hall	Knowle, Warwicks
Gryffon Hse	Coddenham
Gulbenkian Museum	Durham
* Gun Hill Place	Dedham
* Haddon Hall	Rowsley
Haileybury College	Hertford Hth
* Hall i' th' Wd	Bolton, Lancs
Hall Place	Leigh, Kent
* Hardwick Hall	Ault Hucknall
* Haremere Hall	Etchingham
* Harvard Hse	Stratford-upon-Avon
* Hatchlands	E Clandon
Haumond Abbey	Uffington, Shrops
* Hayes Barton	E Budleigh
* Heaton Hall	Prestwich
* Hellens	Much Markle
* Heriots	Stanmore, London
Hewell Grange	Tardebrigge
* Hill Top	Near Sawrey
* Hogarth Hse	Chiswick
Holbech Hse	Himley
Hole Pk	Rolvenden
* Holker Hall	Cark
* Holy Cross Priory	Blackboys
Hood Monmt	Butleigh
Horne's Place	Appledore Hth
Horselunges	Hellingly

Building	Mentioned under
* Houghton Hse	Ampthill
* Housesteads	Bardon Mill
Hoy's Monmt	Chale
* Hurst Cstle	Milford-on-Sea
* Ickworth	Horringer
* Ightham Mote	Ivy Hatch
Jenkyn Place	Bentley, Hants
* Jervaulx Abbey	E Witton
Juniper Hall	Mickleham
* Keats Hse and Museum	Hampstead
Kentwell Hall	Long Melford
* Kenwood Hse	Hampstead
Keppel's Column	Thorpe Hesley
Killerton Pk	Broad Clyst
King John's Hse	Tollard Royal
* Kingston Lacy	Pamphill
* Kiplin Hall	Bolton-on-Swale
* Kirby Hall	Gretton, Northants
* Kirkham Hse	Paignton
Knill Monmt	Halse Tn
* Knole	Sevenoaks
Ladham Hse	Goudhurst
Lady's Well	Holystone
* Lamb Hse	Rye
Lambton Cstle	Chester-le-Street
Langley Pk	Gt Waltham
Lanherne	St Mawgan
* Lanhydrock Pk	Bodmin
Larden Hall	Shipton, Shrops
Launde Abbey	Loddington, Leics
Lawrence Cstle (twr)	Dunchideock
Lea Hall	Preston Gubbals
* Leighton Hall	Yealand Conyers
* Leith Hill Twr	Coldharbour
	Dorking
Ley, The	Weobley
Lincoln's Inn	Holborn
Linley Hall	More
Little Clarendon	Dinton, Wilts
* Littlecote	Chilton Foliat
* Little Moreton Hall	Scholar Grn
* Lockleys	Welwyn
* Longford Cstle	Alderbury
* Longleat	Horningsham
* Lord Leycester's Hsptl	Warwick, Warwicks
Lordship Hse	Cottered
Lordship, The	Benington, Herts
* Lotherton Hall	Aberford
* Lower Brockhampton	Brockhampton, Herefs (SO 6855)
* Lower Hall	Huxley
* Lullingstone Cstle	Eynsford

Building	Mentioned under
* Lullingstone Silk Farm	Ayot St Lawrence
Lumley Cstle	Chester-le-Street
* Lyme Hall	Disley
* Lytes Cary	Kingsdon
Magdalen College Sch	Brackley
* Maison Dieu	Ospringe
Mannington Hall	Itteringham
* Marble Hill Hse	Twickenham
* Markenfield Hall	Markington
* Mary Arden's Hse	Wilmcote
* Mary Mitford's Cottage	Threemile Cross
Max Gate	Dorchester, Dorset
Medford Hse	Mickleton, Glos
Mere Hall	Hanbury, Worcs
* Michelham Priory	Upr Dicker
Midway Mnr	Wingfield, Wilts
* Milton's Cottage	Chalfont St Giles
Misarden Pk	Miserden
* Moigne Ct	Owermoigne
Mole Hall	Debden
* Monk Bretton Priory	Barnsley, Yorks (W)
Moot, The	Downton, Wilts
Moreton Hall	Weston Rhyn
* Moseley Old Hall	Featherstone, Staffs
* Mount Edgcumbe	Cremyll
* Mount Grace Priory	Osmotherley
Mount St Bernard Abbey	Whitwick
Moyles Ct	Ellingham, Hants
Moyns Pk	Birdbrook
* Moyse's Hall	Bury St Edmunds
Mulgrave Cstle	Lythe
Murtholme	Gt Harwood
Narford Hall	Narborough
* Naworth Cstle	Brampton, Cumb
Newburgh Priory	Coxwold
* Newby Hall	Skelton, Yorks (W)
New Hse	Whiteparish
* Newtimber Place	Pyecombe
* New Wardour Cstle	Tisbury
Norris Cstle	E Cowes
Norton Place	Bishop Norton
* Nostell Priory	Foulby
Notley Abbey	Long Crendon
* Oakwell Hall	Birstall Smithies
* Odiham Cstle Keep	N Warnborough
Olantigh Twrs	Wye
Old Blundell's Sch	Tiverton, Devon
Old Mnr	Littlehampton
* Old Place, The	Boveney
* Old Soar	Plaxtol
* Old Wardour Cstle	Tisbury

Building	Mentioned under
Orchardleigh	Lullington, Som
Orwell Pk	Nacton
* Osborne Hse	E Cowes
* Osterley Pk	Heston
* Otterden Pk	Charing
* Owletts	Cobham, Kent
Owl Hse	Lamberhurst
* Packwood Hse	Hockley Hth
Palace Hse	Beaulieu
Pannett Pk Museum	Whitby
* Parham Hse	Rackham
* Paycocke's	Coggeshall
* Peckover Hse	Wisbech
* Pelham Mausoleum	Gt Limber
* Pendennis Cstle	Falmouth
Pendon Museum	Long Wittenham
* Penfound	Poundstock
* Penjerrick Gdns	Budock Water
* Pepys Hse	Brampton, Hunts
* Percival Hall	Appletreewick
Peterson's Twr	Sway
* Peveril Cstle	Castleton, Derbys
* Phillipps Hse	Dinton, Wilts
Pigeon Hse	Angmering
Pitt-Rivers Museum	Farnham, Dorset
Place Farm	Kirtling
Place Farm	Tisbury
* Polesden Lacy	Gt Bookham
* Porch Hse	Potterne
Portledge	Alwington
* Prestwold	Hoton
Prior Pk	Combe Down
* Puttendon Mnr	Lingfield
Pynsent Monmt	Curry Rivel
* Pyte Hse	Newtown, Wilts
Quarr Abbey	Binstead
Quarters Hse	Alresford, Essex
* Quebec Hse	Westerham
* Queen Elizabeth's Hunting Lodge	Chingford
Quenby Hall	Hungarton
* Quex Pk	Birchington
* Raby Cstle	Staindrop
* Ragley Hall	Arrow
* Redheath	Croxley Grn
* Restormel Cstle	Lostwithiel
Revolution Hse	Whittington, Derbys
* Richborough Cstle	Ash, Kent (TR 2858)
	Sandwich
* Roche Abbey	Maltby, Yorks (W)
Rokeby Hall	Greta Br
Roos Hall	Beccles

Building	Mentioned under
* Rose Cstle	Raughton Head
* Rudding Pk	Harrogate
Ruskin Museum	Coniston, Lancs
* Rycote Chpl	Gt Haseley
Rydale Folk Museum	Hutton-le-Hole
Rymans	Apuldram
St Audries	W Quantoxhead
* St Cross Hsptl	Winchester
St David's Ruin	Harden
* St Giles Hse	Wimborne St Giles
St John's College	Hurstpierpoint
* St John's Jerusalem	Sutton-at-Hone
St Leonard's Hsptl	Tickhill
* St Leonard's Twr	W Malling
* St Mary's	Bramber
Salford Hall	Abbot's Salford
* Salisbury Hall	Shenley
* Salmestone Grange	Margate
* Saltram	Plympton
* Sandham Memorial Chpl	Burghclere
* Scotney Cstle	Lamberhurst
Serby Hall	Scrooby
* Sewerby Hall	Bridlington
Sezincote	Bourton-on-the-Hill
* Shallowford	Norton Br
Shardeloes Pk	Amersham
Sharpham Hse	Ashrpington
Sheffield Pk	Fletching
Shrubland	Coddenham
* Shugborough	Gt Haywood
Sir John Soane's Museum	Holborn
Sir Tatton Sykes Monmt	Garton-on-the-Wolds
* Sizergh Cstle	Sedgwick
* Smedmore	Kimmeridge
* Smithills Hall	Bolton, Lancs
* Spade Hse	Sandgate
* Sqerrys Ct	Westerham
* Steeton Hall Gatehouse	S Milford
* Stoneacre	Otham
Stone Gappe	Glusburn
Stonemason's Museum	Gt Bedwyn
Stonyhurst College	Hurst Grn, Lancs
Storr's Twr	Hilton
* Stourhead	Stourton, Wilts
Stowe	Chackmore
Studley Royal	Studley Roger
* Sudeley Cstle	Winchcombe
Sundorne Cstle	Uffington, Shrops
* Swakeleys	Ickenham
* Swarthmoor Hall	Ulverston
Swinsty Hall	Fewston

Buildings	Mentioned under
* Syon Hse	Brentford
* Tatton Pk	Knutsford
* Temple Mnr	Strood
* Temple Newsam Hse	Leeds, Yorks (W)
* Tewes	Lit Sampford
Thoresby	Perlethorpe
Tiptofts Farm	Wimbish
* Tower of London	Wapping
Treago	St Weonards
Trecarrel	Trebullett
Tregothnan	St Michael Penkevil
Trelissick Hse	Feock
Trelowarren	Mawgan
Tremeer	St Tudy
* Trerice	Kestle Mill
* Turner's Hsptl	Kirkleatham
Turner's Twr	Hemington
* Turton Twr	Chapeltown, Lancs
* Uppark	S Harting
* Upton Hse	Kineton, Warwicks
Vestry Hse Museum	Walthamstow
* Vyne, The	Sherborne St John
Wakehurst Place	Ardingly
* Wakeman's Hse	Ripon
Walburn Hall	Downholme
Walcot	Lydbury N
* Wallington Hall	Cambo
Washington Hse	Lit Brington
* Waterston Mnr	Puddletown
* Watt's Picture Gallery	Compton, Surrey
Weir, The	Swainshill
Wellbrook Mnr	Peterchurch
Wellington College	Crowthorne
Wellington Monmt	Heckfield
Wentworth Cstle	Hood Grn
Westwood Hse	Droitwich
Wharley Hall	Eastcote, Warwicks
* Whatton Hse	Hathern
* White House, The	Munslow
* White Ladies' Priory	Tong
White Lodge	Richmond, London
* Wightwick Mnr	Tettenhall
* Wilderhope	Longville in the Dale
Willetts Twr	Brompton Ralph
	Elworthy
Willy Lott's Cottage	E Bergholt
Wimpole Hall	Arrington
* Wolterton Hall	Wickmere
Woodcroft Cstle	Etton, Hunts
* Woodend	Scarborough
* Woolaton Hall	Nottingham

Buildings	Mentioned under
Woolbridge Mnr	Wool
Wool Hse	Loose
Woollas Hall	Eckington, Worcs
Wordsworth Museum	Grasmere
Wrest Pk	Silsoe
* Yardhurst	Gt Chart

ACKNOWLEDGEMENTS

The following works of reference have been consulted:-

Index of Place Names (Census 1961)	HMSO
Census 1971 Preliminary Report	HMSO
Postal Addresses	Issued by the Post Office
Official List Part III, 1965 Annual Addenda 1966–9	HMSO
Boundary Commission for England, Second Periodical Report	HMSO
Crockford's Clerical Directory	OUP

Of the many works consulted for the descriptive matter, in addition to my own notes, I specially acknowledge the debt I owe to Sir Nikolaus Pevsner's *Buildings of England* series, and to various *Shell County Guides* and *Travellers Guides*. For general background I have found Professor W.G. Hoskins' *The Making of the English Landscape* particularly helpful.

I am happy to acknowledge the assistance I have received from officials of the Ministry of Education & Science and the Department of the Environment, and from county education officers.

Finally, I gratefully acknowledge the invaluable help given by my wife in the compilation of this gazetteer.